'*The Global Business Environment* encourages students to draw on complex and critical ways of interpreting the world economy. The text shows how it is essential to consider the multiple and interacting stakeholders that make the decisions that influence global business, by taking a multi-level perspective on the processes shaping, and being shaped by globalisation. Globalisation is a sophisticated phenomenon and this text succinctly captures the diverse challenges and opportunities accompanying it.' **—Dr Alexander Kriz,** *The University of Queensland Business School, Australia*

'This textbook is ideal for all levels of ability – both students who are new to the business discipline and those who wish to deepen their existing knowledge, as it manages to be both straightforward in approach and sophisticated in the extent of its coverage. There is a clear learning path through the book, with helpful cases and insightful questions to stimulate your thinking and guide you through the issues. I highly recommend it.' **—Dr Maxine Clarke,** *Loughborough University School of Business and Economics, UK*

'Clear, informative and theoretically developmental. This is the best global business environment textbook with a focus on sustainability.' **—Dr W. Guillaume Zhao,** *Lakehead University, Canada*

'*The Global Business Environment* by Janet Morrison is a magnificent guide full of global best practices and outstanding business cases that truly help prepare students for a globalised market.' **—David Keighron,** *University Canada West, Canada*

'Once again, Morrison has produced a fresh edition that keeps pace with the development of concepts and cases for studying the international business environment. I am particularly impressed with the coverage of the ecological environment, ethics and social responsibility—subjects which have gained interest from students and become more central in the global business environment.' **—Dr Daniel Tisch,** *The University of Auckland, New Zealand*

'This book fills a unique niche in the crowded international business textbook market. By focusing on the global environment of business, Morrison provides a rich contextual investigation of the factors shaping and constraining the global marketplace. This new edition is augmented with up-to-date cases and a broader focus on sustainability... The book has rich business vocabulary, explains concepts well, and has a comprehensive glossary.' **—Laura D'Antonio,** *George Washington University, USA*

'This is an excellent and very comprehensive textbook for all who want to get a better understanding of doing business on an international scale. The book offers a complete overview of the concepts students require to get a better understanding of the international business environment and has been enriched with many useful case studies. I highly recommend this book for use on any course of international business.' **—Rik S. F. van Zutphen LL.M,** *Nyenrode New Business School, Netherlands*

'*The Global Business Environment* is an essential book for any undergraduate, particularly those in the first year of their studies. The book provides a clear and coherent overview of business economics in the current climate.' **—Dr Sophie Bennett-Gillison,** *Aberystwyth University, UK*

'As a teacher it is very rewarding when you notice students becoming interested in all kinds of global business issues, especially through the interactive use of an excellent textbook, such as *The Global Business Environment*. This new edition offers really engaging pedagogy, international scope and up-to-date case studies.' **—Jos Bakermans,** *Hogeschool Utrecht, Netherlands*

Also by Janet Morrison and published by Red Globe Press:

The International Business Environment
International Business
Business Ethics

Janet Morrison

This edition published 2020 by

RED GLOBE PRESS

Previous editions published under the imprint PALGRAVE

Red Globe Press in the UK is an imprint of Macmillan Education Limited, registered in England, company number 01755588, of 4 Crinan Street, London, N1 9XW.

Red Globe Press® is a registered trademark in the United States, the United Kingdom, Europe and other countries.

ISBN 978-1-352-00897-5 paperback

This book is printed on paper suitable for recycling and made from fully managed and sustained forest sources. Logging, pulping and manufacturing processes are expected to conform to the environmental regulations of the country of origin.

A catalogue record for this book is available from the British Library.

A catalog record for this book is available from the Library of Congress.

CONTENTS IN BRIEF

CONTENTS

LIST OF FIGURES

LIST OF TABLES

CASE STUDY GRID

Note: All these case studies have an international dimension. Countries shown in this grid are either the main focus of the discussion or the home country of the company.

Chapter short title	Short title of case study	Geographic focus (see note above)	Main topics	Page
1 The business in focus	Levi Strauss	US	Branding; global markets; company stock market listing	3
	Taking a company private	US	Entrepreneurship; public v. private companies; example of Tesla	13
	Samarco mining disaster and BHP Billiton	Brazil Australia	Company liability for disaster; regulation; environmental concerns; sustainability	25
	Ikea	Sweden	Business model; changing consumer lifestyles; country differences; corporate governance; sustainability	31
2 Globalization	SoftBank	Japan	Innovation; globalization; international investment strategy	35
	Harley-Davidson	US	Manufacturing; location advantages; changing markets; international trade	45
	US Midwest car industry	US	Car manufacturing; loss of competitive advantage; social impacts from the loss of jobs	59
	Zara	Spain	Fashion industry; business model; retailing supply chains; expansion of online retailing; sustainability	68
3 Cultural environment	Qatar	Qatar	Economic development and resource wealth; migrant labour; human rights	75
	Women allowed to drive in Saudi Arabia	Saudi Arabia	Society and religion; culture change; human rights	86
	Russia raising the pension age	Russia	Ageing population; social protections for pensioners; changing society	106
	South Africa	Republic of South Africa	Social and racial divides; political reform; poverty and inequality; sustainable development	111

Chapter short title	Short title of case study	Geographic focus (see note above)	Main topics	Page
4 Economic environment	Chinese economy slows	China	China's economic model of state direction and market reforms; negative impacts of China's rapid growth	116
	Mexico's shift towards socialism	Mexico	Socialist policies of the new government; social and economic reforms	135
	India's super-rich	India	Indian conglomerates; business and political ties; risks of corruption; inequality	144
	Jaguar Land Rover	UK India	Car industry in the UK; uncertainty over Brexit; shift to greener motoring	153
5 Political environment	A populist president in Brazil	Brazil	Nationalist populism; economic development and agribusiness; risks of deforestation	158
	Political risks in Mali	Mali	Fragile democratic state; risks of Islamic terrorism; climate change; sustainable development	173
	Setbacks to the rule of law in Poland	Poland EU	EU concerns over weakening rule of law in a member state; independence of the judiciary	182
	Authoritarianism in Turkey	Turkey	Authoritarian rule; weakening of democratic institutions; political divide between Muslim population and westernized urban population	200
6 Legal environment	Uber and other ride-hailing companies	US China UK	New technology business models; regulatory issues in different locations; driver status	205
	The Costa Concordia sinks	Italy	Legal issues of liability in the sinking of the ship; civil and criminal law	210
	AT&T and antitrust	US	Competition law; government interventions against monopolies; the role of regulation; the risks of break-up for monopolists	223
	Facebook	US EU	Data protection; political advertising; corporate governance; ethics; regulation of social media	235

Chapter short title	Short title of case study	Geographic focus (see note above)	Main topics	Page
7 Trade	Huawei	China	Telecoms industry; Chinese business; global expansion strategy opposed by the US	241
7 Trade	Soya beans and US-China trade	US China	Tariffs on imports spark trade friction; US farming interests; Chinese market for soya bean imports	260
7 Trade	Canada's motor industry	Canada	Interdependence in cross-border supply chains; impacts on communities; the new NAFTA agreement	268
7 Trade	Glencore	Democratic Republic of Congo (DRC)	Global business of trade and mining giant; mining in a conflict zone of the DRC; legal risk	274
8 Finance	Carillion	UK	Financial collapse of a large employer; outsourcing of public services; corporate governance	279
8 Finance	Funding Circle	UK	Entrepreneurship; peer-to-peer lending; debt financing; stock exchange listing	291
8 Finance	Bayer Monsanto takeover	Germany US	Cross-border takeover; legal and ethical issues on GM crops	304
8 Finance	Argentina's financial crisis	Argentina	Fallout from sovereign debt crisis; reforming government finances; role of the IMF; impacts of financial crisis on society	308
9 Technology	Automation	UK Global business	Technological innovation and economic development; automation displacing jobs and causing impacts in societies	313
9 Technology	Lego	Denmark	Innovation towards sustainable plastic substitutes; competitive strategies in differing markets	317
9 Technology	AbbVie pharmaceutical	US	Patent protection and public interest; costs of medicine; the role of generic medicine	329
9 Technology	Apple	US	iPhone markets and competition in innovations; diversification at Apple; outsourcing business model and ethical issues	338

Chapter short title	Short title of case study	Geographic focus (see note above)	Main topics	Page
10 Ecology	Death of diesel	EU	Dangerous emissions from diesel engines; VW scandal over diesel engines; carmakers changing to cleaner alternatives; role of government regulation	345
	Oil companies and reforestation	The Netherlands Norway	Carbon offsetting; pressures to respond to climate change; investors' influence on oil companies' sustainability strategies	363
	Saving the Taj Mahal	India	Pollution; historic sites and surrounding communities; sustainable development	370
	Plastic waste	US China UN	Growth of plastic waste in consumer society; disposal of waste; UN convention on plastic waste	373
11 Ethics and CSR	UK textile industry	UK	Fast fashion industry; 'sweatshop' conditions; factory safety and workers' protections	378
	Gambling and football	UK	Online betting companies; role of gambling companies in sponsoring football; ethics of promoting gambling; role of self-regulation	389
	Status of workers in the gig economy	UK	Status of self-employed workers; issues of workers classified as self-employed when facts suggest they are not; employment protection rights	393
	Sackler and Purdue Pharma	US	Marketing of opioids and ethical issues; lawsuits against Purdue Pharma; unease among recipients of Sackler cultural donations	413
12 Sustainable business: the prospects	10 years on from the global financial crisis	US UK	Assessment of recovery after the crisis; regulatory reform of banking; economic concentration in the global economy	418
	Burberry destroys stock	UK	Brand reputation; overproduction and waste; social responsibility	424
	Bangladesh textile industry	Bangladesh	Sustainable development; fire and safety accords by foreign brands	440
	Tech billionaires turn philanthropists	US	Microsoft, Facebook and Amazon; market economies' evolution into market societies; tech billionaires' market-oriented approach to philanthropy	455

AUTHOR'S ACKNOWLEDGEMENTS

Writing a wide-ranging textbook is a daunting task, even with the experience of four previous editions. Again, I have done all the research and writing myself. But the finished book owes much to those who have helped in the process of seeing this project through to the finish. I am greatly indebted to the staff of my publishers, Red Globe Press. They include my editor, Ursula Gavin, and assistant editor, Milly Weaver. For the book's cover design, I owe thanks to Toby Way, whose inspiring design has admirably captured the conceptual theme of the book. And I am grateful to the copy-editor, Ann Edmondson.

Numerous anonymous reviewers have contributed to the final shape and content of this book. They include those who gave advice on how the fourth edition could be improved, much of it based on their experience of using the book and listening to the feedback from their students. I also appreciate the feedback I received from the reviewers who read this new edition at the manuscript stage and offered many valuable suggestions. I am grateful for all their remarks and suggestions. I have made adjustments to the content based on their feedback, and I am confident that their contributions have strengthened the final version of the text. I hope they will be happy with this new edition.

Writing long books is rather a solitary endeavour for a sole author, and one that greatly impacts on family and friends. I owe special thanks to my husband, Ian Morrison, for his patience and moral support throughout the ups and downs of this project.

As with previous editions, I have turned to a host of distinguished scholars and theorists – past and present. In a world where the new is so often deemed to be better than the old, the profound insights we can glean from thinkers of earlier eras tend to be overlooked. The student might well miss out on rich resources that are easily accessible. In the course of writing this book, I have drawn on the insights and observations of respected scholars and thinkers who have been an inspiration, and who I hope will equally inspire readers. Many of their works are cited in these pages, and their discourses feature in video links included in the chapters. To all of these scholars, I owe utmost gratitude.

ABOUT THE AUTHOR

Janet Morrison, now retired, was a senior lecturer in strategic and international management at Sunderland University Business School in the UK, where she enjoyed a long career in teaching, research, curriculum development and course administration. She taught international business modules at undergraduate and postgraduate levels, including International Business Environment, Management in a Global Environment, Japanese Business and the Social and Cultural Environment of International Business. She was programme leader for undergraduate international business degrees and the MBA in International Management.

Janet's academic background goes back to her first degree (in political science and history) at Mary Washington College of the University of Virginia in the US (now the University of Mary Washington), followed by a master's degree from the University of Toronto in Canada and, later, a law degree from the University of Newcastle-upon-Tyne in the UK. She also studied in Chicago, Oxford and Nagoya in Japan.

Her published research includes articles in a range of areas, including corporate governance, Japanese business and corporate social responsibility. She is the author of *International Business* (2009) and *Business Ethics* (2015), both published by Red Globe Press.

PREFACE TO THE FIFTH EDITION

The fifth edition of this book has presented both challenges and opportunities. Changes are reshaping nearly every dimension of the global business environment. Providing the reader with coherent explanations has been a challenge, but it has also presented an opportunity to delve deeper into the transformations taking place. As always in writing a new edition, I seek not just to highlight changes, but to advance new analysis to help readers make sense of it all. This time, the changes have been momentous and far-reaching – demanding considerably more research, rewriting and new content. I have tried to maintain a systematic approach to these tasks, incorporating new content in ways that highlight continuity as well as breaks with the past. Changes can often seem sudden, when in fact they have been building up over time. The global financial crisis was an example, seemingly taking the world by surprise, but, with hindsight, it became apparent that warning signs had been overlooked. In our digitalized world, we are bombarded by the media describing this week's headline event or issue. Useful though this is, it is akin to a snapshot: it offers only sketchy contextual explanation, and leaves unanswered questions from the student's point of view. Why is this story making the headlines, and what does it mean for the future? I have sought to provide wider explanations and insights on events and topics of current relevance, with implications for the future.

Momentous changes have taken place since the last edition of this book. Capturing these changes in both businesses and societies has been a major challenge. New content covers many areas of the environment, from ecology and the economic environment to the political environment and societal issues. Topics include the climate emergency, changes in work, the power of tech giants, ongoing trade wars and the changing political environment that has seen the rise of populists and nationalists. These are some of the areas of change that are now shaping the global economy and impacting on business decision-making. I have aimed not just to 'update' chapters in a superficial sense, but to impart some sense-making overview of current trends in the many dimensions of the business environment.

Much of the strength of earlier editions has been in lucid explanations of foundation material, which remain the best basis on which to understand the environmental shifts taking place, along with their impacts on organizations. Hence, foundation concepts are still core to the book, and in some respects have been expanded. These are interpreted in new contexts and explored in new case studies which focus on the current changing environment.

The main challenges for today's businesses are encapsulated in the theme of sustainability, as reflected in the book's subtitle, 'towards sustainability?'. This brings together six related themes: individual and societal wellbeing; climate change and ecology; technological change; economic prosperity for societies; governance that promotes social goods; and financial stability. To what extent are goals of sustainability inching forward in each of these dimensions, and what should businesses, individuals and governments be doing to advance them? Probing for answers to these questions is a primary focus of the book, with a section on sustainability in every chapter.

Foremost in my thinking has been the need for meaningful engagement with the needs of a student readership, wherever in the world this book is accessed. As in previous editions, I have borne in mind the needs of students at both undergraduate and postgraduate levels, including those with little background in business studies and those for whom English is a second language. This book's clear expression and easy-to-read writing style have been highly valued by students since the book's first publication. The book's relevance to students from a variety of educational backgrounds and studying on a variety of business courses have been among its enduring strengths, which I have kept at the forefront of my approach to this new edition.

I am pleased that students and lecturers in a wide range of countries have found this book helpful, and that international students have found the text easy to read. This fifth edition has been written with this wide readership in mind. I hope that it will again prove stimulating, relevant and enjoyable for readers. New case studies on topics of broad interest should help to bring the text alive. I hope readers will be encouraged to find out more from my many recommendations for further reading. For readers familiar with previous editions, I hope the finished book will measure up to your expectations, and for those new to this book, I hope especially that student readers will find it enjoyable as well as illuminating.

Janet Morrison

INTRODUCTION

Since the last edition of this book, profound changes have taken place in the global business environment, impacting on long-held ways of thinking and patterns of doing business. They include escalating trade wars, damaging climate change impacts, the deepening power of dominant corporations, and, at the level of society, widening inequalities that threaten societal wellbeing. A result has been rising global insecurity that affects all areas of the business environment. Adding to the uncertainties, there has been a resurgence of nationalist populist leaders around the world, whose extreme nationalist agendas pose threats to constitutional governance frameworks and, more broadly, to international peace and co-operation. The image on the cover of this edition features Dalian, a port in Northeast China. A major centre for commodity trading, Dalian takes pride in its role in China's economic success. But it is now caught up in trade wars between China and the US (featured in a case study in Chapter 7). Moreover, these trade disputes are not confined to the two superpowers, but radiate out to other trading countries and their societies. Will sustainable solutions emerge to resolve these disputes and, more broadly, to alleviate the threats to global security?

A priority for the student of business and management is a sound understanding of the multiple dimensions of the business environment. This is a first step towards gaining insight into the changes now reshaping the global economy. When this book was originally conceived, the aim was to offer international perspectives that ventured far beyond those of existing business environment textbooks, which reflected limited managerial outlooks. The first edition, back in 2002, aimed to broaden that focus, geographically and culturally, adopting an approach that set it apart from competitors. Throughout later editions, it has sought to shine a light on the changes that shape international business. They have included the processes of globalization, the rise of emerging markets, and the reconfiguring of global politics, reflecting China's challenges to the US on the world stage. The fifth edition continues in this vein, probing the issues that are emerging as critical for businesses in finding sustainable ways forward.

What makes this book stand out?

Since its first edition, this book has taken a dynamic approach, blending foundation knowledge with critical discussion of the issues that relate to international business. All textbooks on this subject now take in international content, but most of this is a patchwork of chunks of knowledge, often because the books are written by a number of different people. This book is different. This text takes a systematic approach, presenting foundation theory and knowledge, from which to explore the interactions and tensions between the players in the business environment. Companies are skilled at presenting themselves and their activities in ways that show them in a good light. But that is only a partial picture. This book presents a fuller picture, shining a light on the negative as well as the positive. The reader thus gains an insight that neither texts on formal systems nor media content on particular companies can provide. Moreover, the book conveys the ways in which changes evolve, shaping business strategies and, importantly, government policies, which are now more important than ever in business contexts. The chapters present the academic

background, the current issues, the business implications and the crucial interactions with other parties, including governments, stakeholders and international bodies. No other textbook covers this ground as thoroughly. Here are four examples of how this approach unfolds:

- Who are the key players? This new edition spans business on all continents, at differing stages of development and in diverse cultural contexts – not simply as market opportunities for western businesses, but as players on the global scene in their own right. Governments increasingly come into this picture, active in global investment and seeking to attract foreign investors. Case studies reflect these trends. They feature decision-making dilemmas of executives in a wide spectrum of companies from Lego, the toymaker, to Facebook. Case studies on governance range from the dramatic changes taking place in South Africa to the populist president of Brazil.
- Why are law and politics important? It is sometimes said that law is just for specialists, to be consulted when needed. Despite their importance in shaping strategies, the legal and political environments have received only cursory attention in rival textbooks, sketching out formal systems, but not probing these influences in depth. This book offers substantive analysis of how legal and political considerations impact on business. These are considerations that arise in the formative stage of policy. Important trends in today's world include the growth in populist ideologies, the rise in authoritarian leaders around the world, and the legal challenges to businesses in numerous sectors, from the gig economy to the tech giants. Legal issues are key to much business strategy, as is the highly charged political atmosphere in many countries. This text confronts them through explanations of background in the text, accompanied by case studies.
- Many companies, large and small, feature in these pages. Who owns and controls the company in question? Why does it matter? From the first edition onwards, corporate ownership and control have featured in both the text and case studies. While other textbooks have settled for bland statements about companies taking decisions, this book has looked behind the corporate façade to ask, 'who in the company is taking the decisions, and in whose interests?' Insightful answers to these questions have never been as vital, or as revealing, as they are now. Members of the Sackler family, owners of the pharmaceutical company, Purdue Pharma, are an example, featured in a case study. Corporate governance and stakeholder issues remain prominent in this edition, reflecting the rise in critical awareness of issues of corporate accountability around the world.
- Since the first edition, a strength of this book has been a focus on human rights in business contexts. Foundation principles and human rights law are explained, and many business-related examples are presented, to demonstrate the relevance of human rights in practice for businesses in the global economy. Over the years, the relevance of human rights has expanded: the body of law has grown and there is more litigation in this area. There is now a wider variety of cases that involve human rights breaches, from forced labour to the right to join a trade union. While this gives hope for those who have suffered, the rising incidence of breaches suggests that businesses have a long way to go in applying legal and ethical principles.

Successive editions of this book have continued to stress its underlying international approach, aiming to acquaint readers with the issues and trends now shaping the global environment, and also those that are likely to feature prominently in the future. Key to this aim is attention to the academic background underpinning discussion of current

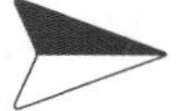

issues in each chapter, and, it is hoped, helping readers to form their own critical perspectives. As globalization has enveloped an increasing number of countries and every type of business – from agriculture to taxis – international interactions have multiplied beyond what most people would have thought possible. New players come on the international scene virtually every day, including companies, business groupings, international organizations and individual people – each of whom is capable of making a difference in the way business is conceived and carried on. New complexities can be exciting, but can also be daunting to take on board, without the appropriate background in the business environment.

How does a start-up become a multi-billion-dollar global business in just a few years? This – and many other – intriguing aspects of the current international environment are explained and explored in this new edition. This edition contains a total of 48 case studies, four in every chapter. Each chapter has an opening case study, a closing one, and two mini case studies. Six of the case studies focus on companies featured in a previous edition, with new analysis and updates. This edition, like earlier ones, takes a critical approach, reflected in the book's subtitle: *towards sustainability?*. The subtitle poses a question and elicits a range of answers. A simple yes or no is not possible, but a more achievable goal is to conceive a framework in which answers can emerge over time. The relevant evidence will be presented coherently, highlighting the strides that are being made towards sustainability, along with the setbacks. Identifying the setbacks and suggesting ways to go forward will help in answering the question posed in the title.

The global business environment: towards sustainability?

Previous editions have focused on critical themes: globalization; emerging economies; changing societies; corporate social responsibility (CSR) and sustainability. These themes remain relevant, and, indeed, all have acquired higher profiles, along with greater critical awareness, since the last edition. In this edition, they are reframed and interwoven within the overall perspective of sustainability, shown in the figure below. Throughout the chapters that follow, we will shine a light on the many diverse players in the global environment, assessing them in terms of the criteria of sustainability.

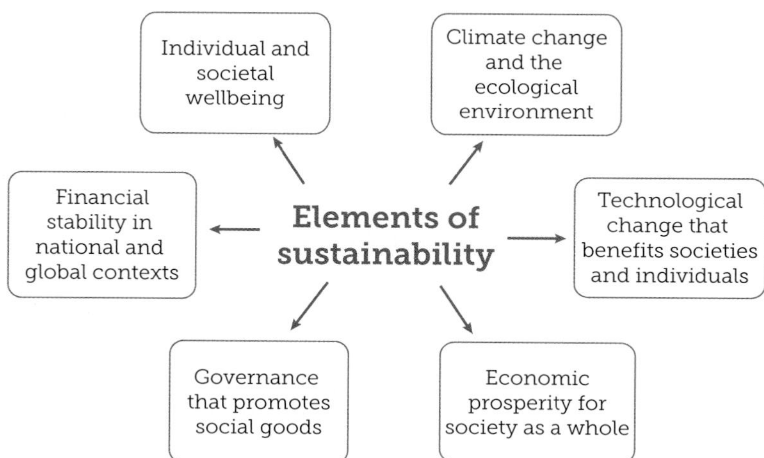

Figure Elements of sustainability

Sustainability rests on the principle that people of today's generation should lead their lives, organize their businesses, and set in place systems of governance that do not jeopardize the ability of future generations to fulfil their needs. Sustainability is

sometimes taken to be simply about the natural environment, but it is much broader than that, taking in all aspects of the business environment. The principle of sustainability encourages a business to think of stakeholders in the future, not just the present. Six aspects of sustainability can be highlighted, as shown in the figure. These are not just issues, but ways of going about business activities in contexts where legal and moral responsibilities arise, and where societies and values matter. The elements in the figure are as follows:

- **Individual and societal wellbeing**
  Every human being should be able to access basic needs, such as adequate nutrition and housing, and everyone also aspires to a fulfilling life, enjoying good health, education and a decent job. Wellbeing is both individual and societal. Cultural and social dimensions are critical to everyone's sense of dignity and belonging. They are recognized as core ethical principles and human rights in international law. They are the subject of safeguards and institutions in most societies, and are essential to the legacy of institutions that will be passed on to future generations. It is up to both governments and businesses to ensure that these values are upheld through sustainable policies and strategies.
- **Climate change and the ecological environment**
  Climate change is one of the biggest – and most urgent – of the challenges facing the planet. Measures to reduce emissions, reduce the use of plastic and clean up the air, are priorities for global leaders. In today's world, businesses play an active role in governance at the national and international levels, working with governments and non-governmental bodies, and influencing policies. Much of that interaction is positive, helping to adapt business aims to societal needs. However, many businesses view these interactions as self-serving, for example, in efforts to persuade governments and lawmakers to bend laws and policies towards their interests. Such an approach might satisfy shareholders in the short term, but an alignment of business aims with societal goals will support the legitimacy of both governments and business players in the long term.
- **Technological change that benefits societies and individuals**
  Technological change has been the driver of economic development, bringing innovations that transform industries – and also societies. While these changes have been responsible for rising living standards, improved health, advanced communications and a host of other benefits, they have also had negative impacts, often in terms of loss of jobs. Ideally, changes should be sustainable, helping all to enjoy the benefits. But new technology tends to benefit, above all, the innovating companies that gain monopolistic control, and the workers who have the relevant skills and education to carve out new careers for themselves. When technological advances are captured by the few, they are unsustainable. It requires governments and socially responsible businesses to focus on how new technologies can be utilized to benefit all, with appropriate regulation and accountability.
- **Economic prosperity for society as a whole**
  Businesses play vital roles in shaping how societies function and change. Much of the discussion in this book focuses on globalization and how it transforms not just production, but whole societies. The spread of global supply chains has been key to the economic development of today's emerging economies. China is the leading example, and is featured on the cover of this book. But how sustainable is this development? Negative impacts have included the rise of workplace environments that infringe human rights, environmental degradation associated

with industrialization, and unsustainable agriculture. While emerging economies have seen rises in living standards generally, they still face high levels of inequality and weak social protection systems. Moreover, as economic growth has slowed, governments' aims to reduce national debt and rein in public spending are under pressure. For businesses that have focused on short-term profit-seeking, sustainability requires rethinking business models in terms of stakeholder interests.

- **Governance that promotes social goods**
  Governance concerns the interaction of both political and business actors. These relations, ideally, are co-operative, transparent and focused on public goods. Legitimate institutions and the rule of law should underpin governance structures, leading to public confidence that the government is working for everyone, not just the business and political elite. In many countries, this ideal of sustainable democratic institutions is under threat, even in countries that have been considered to have stable democratic systems, such as the US and UK. The rise of extreme nationalist populism is one of the factors, but so, too, is the rise of corporate power, such as the tech giants, Facebook, Apple, Microsoft and Amazon. Refocusing governance on societal goals is vital to achieving sustainable institutions that govern in the public interest.
- **Financial stability in national and global contexts**
  The global financial crisis of 2008 was blamed on the excessively risky strategies of global banks, and also on regulatory failures. In the recession that followed, unemployment and economic hardship left a trail of despair for millions of workers. The capitalist assumptions of self-regulating markets were criticized as unsustainable and in need of reform. Reforms have followed, but not the structural root-and-branch reforms many had envisaged. Financial markets have experienced booming years, and corporate profits have soared, while wages and jobs have had a much less robust recovery. How sustainable is this situation? Rethinking how financial markets can become more stable and sustainable would entail more of a stakeholder focus and a reform of corporate governance. It would also entail a shift in corporate culture away from a short-term view of financial performance to one of long-term value.

In each chapter, an assessment of sustainability challenges is set out in a section just before the conclusions. The issues raised in these discussions are revisited in the book's final chapter, Chapter 12.

Plan of the book

The book retains the same organization as the last edition. This takes the reader in a logical progression of chapters from the foundation material to the more focused business contexts. It also reflects the organization of this subject that is adopted in many course syllabuses. There follows an outline of the chapters, with a brief description of each.

Part 1: Business in the global environment

Chapter 1 – The business enterprise in focus

Basic concepts and terms that describe business organizations and processes are introduced. They include business formation, ownership and corporate governance. Outline guides to the dimensions of the business environment and the spheres of the environment – local, national and international – are presented. Terms used in the critical discussion of business issues are introduced here, laying the groundwork

for the critical analysis that follows in the later chapters. Many readers will already be acquainted with some of the basic concepts defined here, but I would urge that it is helpful to take time to become re-acquainted with them. Companies differ. What exactly does owning a share involve? Possibly not what many people might assume.

Chapter 2 – Globalization and the business environment

Theories of globalization from the perspective of the firm are the foundation of this chapter, which examines critically processes and impacts of globalization. The chapter looks at developments in global supply chains and markets, asking what economic benefits have flowed, and to whom. Globalization has become contentious for a number of reasons that draw in wider considerations for business strategists. These include weak world trade growth and trade tensions, human rights questions over sourcing products in low-cost locations, and the rise of nationalist trade policies.

Part 2: Dimensions of the business environment

Chapter 3 – Culture and societies

Values and norms of behaviour lay the foundations for understanding other dimensions of the environment. Despite globalization, differences between national cultures remain powerful, highlighting the importance of cross-cultural understanding in business contexts. Theories of culture are examined critically, highlighting the need to look behind categories such as 'individualist' and 'collectivist', which have tended to cloud more complex cultural realities. We look critically at today's factory environments in terms of human rights. Expanded sections on migration, urbanization and ageing societies are included, reflecting the growing challenges facing businesses and governments.

Chapter 4 – The global economic environment

Basic concepts used to describe economic systems are introduced. Economic indicators shed light on national economic systems, but, looking behind the statistics, their limitations are evident. Human development criteria are defined, giving a more complex picture of societies, and also revealing the effects of inequality, which is discussed in greater depth in this edition. National economic systems are described and critically assessed. Have market economies in today's world been exemplars of a sustainable capitalism? Or have other models, such as social democratic systems, proved to be better at achieving inclusive growth? China's economic model has seen growth falter, questioning its claim to sustainable development.

Chapter 5 – The political environment: politics and business intertwined

Basic concepts of politics are introduced. Internal and external political risks are discussed. Democratic and authoritarian systems are described and compared, noting in particular the role of business in governance. There is a new section on ideologies, including nationalist populism. There is also an expanded discussion of the risks to democratic institutions posed by authoritarian and populist leaders. There is a section on the European Union, and a new section on Brexit, with explanation of the relevant background. Politics at the global level is witnessing shifts in the balance of power among countries, notably with the rise of China. The rise of nationalist leaders is also a source of instability in global politics, with impacts on business.

Chapter 6 – The legal environment

We start by explaining the basics of a legal system, looking at differing national legal systems. The areas of law that particularly concern international business are explained, as is the legal harmonization that has taken place, facilitating international transactions. Competition law, which seeks to maintain competitive markets, is highlighted as an area in which governments and regulators can play a role in reining in monopolies and anti-competitive behaviour. We also look at how companies have broadened their approach to legal risk, bypassing laws as well as actively seeking to overturn legal obstacles through litigation, lobbying, and using procedures such as international arbitration. The growing influence of international law is now evident in the business environment, alerting companies to obligations that extend beyond national legal systems.

Part 3: Drivers of international business

Chapter 7 – International trade and globalization

Trade theories provide the foundational concepts for this chapter. International trade is closely linked to the supply chains. Globalization has reached many new markets, creating opportunities, but also encountering risks. While open markets should benefit all, relations between trading nations are highly unequal: richer countries benefit and poorer countries are at a disadvantage. The World Trade Organization (WTO) has long attempted to achieve multilateral trade agreements designed to benefit all, but national interests still take precedence. Trade tensions have risen in recent years, with a rise in protectionist policies of national governments, notably the US. The US has sought to curtail the activities of the WTO and other inter-governmental bodies, raising questions over the future of multilateralism in trade relations.

Chapter 8 – Global finance

Cross-border finance benefits companies and whole economies. However, globalization of financial markets has also led to increasing risks, as shown in the financial crisis of 2008. This chapter looks at the finance function for businesses and for economies, including recent developments that have sought to restore global financial stability. The roles of the IMF and World Bank are assessed, especially in respect of handling national financial crises. Excessive borrowing has affected companies, householders, and whole economies. Merger and acquisition activities, often involving huge 'mega mergers' are discussed in the context of the public interest and competitive markets. Rethinking finance in terms of sustainability requires a return to the fundamentals: should finance be devoted to serving productive activities and consumers, or does moneymaking as an end in itself have a role to play? The sustainability of financial markets is not assured.

Chapter 9 – Technology and innovation

Innovation lies at the heart of economic development and improvements in wellbeing. Creative destruction has been at the heart of much technological innovation, and its implications are discussed. Disruptive technology can have negative impacts, such as the rise of automation and the monopolist control exerted by the giant tech companies. Both are topics of case studies. Technology transfer offers prospects for developing countries to benefit technologically from foreign investment, global supply chains and trade. But advances in technology are not easily diffused, and the owners of much technology, such as patented inventions, take steps to retain control over their use. Technology offers the prospect of improvements in many areas of human wellbeing, including medicine, agriculture and clean energy. These are key to sustainable solutions, yet their development, regulation and accessibility remain in doubt.

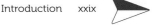

Part 4: Global challenges and sustainability

Chapter 10 – Ecology and climate change

Climate change and environmental degradation are global issues that must be addressed by governments and businesses. Rising emissions, notably from the extensive use of fossil fuels, have given impetus to international efforts to avert the worst impacts of climate change, especially the risks to low-lying countries from rising sea levels. Goals set out in the landmark Paris accord of 2015, which was unique in reaching a consensus between developed and developing countries, now look in jeopardy. Businesses are vital in translating government targets into real progress in the necessary technology and infrastructure. Yet, in practice, many businesses are ambivalent towards climate change measures. In addition, some governments have prioritized economic goals over climate and agriculture concerns.

Chapter 11 – Ethics and social responsibility

This chapter begins with the philosophical foundation of ethical theories, taking into account cultural diversity and differing perspectives of morality. For a business, ethical dilemmas are posed constantly. Many managers might think pragmatically that, if they are able to get away with unethical or illegal behaviour, then they are in the clear. Ethical obligations are one of the dimensions of corporate social responsibility (CSR), which takes in the interests of all stakeholders. CSR also focuses on legal obligations, which are increasingly framed in terms of international standards. Human rights receives more coverage in this edition. There are sections on decent work, the living wage, the gig economy, forced labour, and workers' rights to organize. The human rights of vulnerable workers are often poorly protected in national law, and also weakly enforced, both in developing and developed countries.

Chapter 12 – Sustainable business: the prospects

This chapter begins by revisiting the six elements of sustainability, explaining how each has been illuminated by the various business and government players that have been highlighted throughout the book. The next section assesses the risks in the global environment from a number of perspectives: economic and financial; social and cultural; rising nationalism and geopolitical tensions; and risks in the natural environment. There follows a section on government and business responsibilities in the areas where sustainable progress is at risk. They include democratic institutions and stakeholder concerns. Finally, there is a discussion of the prospects for a sustainable future.

Chapter features

This book is designed to present the content in a logical and easily accessible manner. Although ideally a reader would begin with Chapter 1 and read each successive chapter in order, the book has been designed so that any chapter can be read independently. The reader is guided to earlier relevant material. In some cases, key words that are introduced in earlier chapters are highlighted again in later chapters, along with a brief explanation. For readers who have read all the previous chapters, please consider the repetitions just a helpful reminder.

Chapter features are outlined below, divided between those at the beginning of the chapter, those in the body of the text, and those at the end of each chapter.

At the beginning of each chapter...

- An **Outline** of the sections in the chapter.
- The **Learning Objectives** of the chapter clarify particular outcomes which the reader can expect.
- An **Opening case study** sets the scene for the chapter, raising issues which will arise in the text. This case study usually features a company's responses to the changing environment in national and international contexts. There are four questions for discussion. References within the case study are given at the end of the chapter. As an additional feature in this edition, recommendations for further reading are given at the end of the case study.

In the body of the chapter...

- **Key words** appear in bold, and are defined in the text as they appear. They also appear in the margin of the page, roughly next to where they appear in the text. Key words include concepts, principles and major international institutions. They also feature in a Glossary at the end of the book.
- **References** are given in parentheses in the text, for example, (Tellis, 2009). There is a references section at the end of each chapter. It includes references from all the case studies in the chapter.
- **Web references** appear after the name of the relevant organization in the text. Most refer to companies or organizations that relate to the point being discussed. Beware – while every effort has been made to provide up-to-date online references, websites are subject to change and content moves about. However, organizations often provide a link to the new web address.
- **Mini case studies** – This is a new feature. There are two in each chapter. They offer a variety of subjects, some on a country, some on a company and some on an event of relevance. Questions for discussion and suggestions for where to 'find out more' are given at the end.
- **The way I see it...** – This is a feature from the last edition. There is one of these in each chapter. Each except the one in the last chapter is an updated version of one that appeared in the last edition. The quote is revisited in light of what has happened since then, and there is a question for analysis and discussion, coupled with a recommendation for further reading. The quotes are chosen for their timeliness and the insight they offer.
- **Shining a light on business decisions** – These boxes appear throughout the chapter. They raise questions and issues which invite the reader to examine the topic critically in a business context.
- **Video link: Enhance your understanding** – This is a new feature that appears in all chapters. The video link is designed to provide additional insight and understanding of a relevant topic. It appears in an appropriate position in the text. Many of the videos are lectures or interviews by distinguished academics who are recognized specialists in the specific area being discussed. Some are documentaries on particular relevant topics. All are interesting, informative and provocative.

At the end of the chapter...

- **Closing case study** – This case study features a company or national environment, raising relevant issues in national and international contexts. All raise issues of sustainability, governance and social responsibility, reflecting the book's conceptual framework. Questions for discussion and a recommendation for further reading appear at the end.

- **Multiple choice questions** – This is a quick self-test quiz on what you have read in the chapter.
- **Review questions** are designed to cover all the topics in the chapter. There are 15 questions. They are an aid to learning for self-study, or they can be the basis of group discussion. They are also a helpful revision aid.
- Two **assignments** are given after the review questions. These are broader in scope than the review questions. They require some independent research and offer an opportunity to present a considered analysis in a structured way.
- **Further reading** gives an indication of other sources to read that provide both further information and differing critical perspectives on the topics in the chapter.
- **References** – All the references in the chapter are listed at the end of the chapter.

At the end of the book...

- **Glossary** of key words. This contains all the key words highlighted in bold in the text (and also in the margins).
- **Index** – There is a comprehensive index at the end of the book.
- **Atlas** – There is a section of **maps** at the end of the book. Identifying and understanding the geographical location of countries and regions might seem incidental, but is immensely useful in understanding the substantive issues discussed in the text.

This book is intended to provide the reader with as up-to-date a picture of the business environment as can be expected in a book that covers a huge range of topics. Information becomes out-of-date overnight, simply because of the many changes taking place on a daily basis. The figures contain data as up-to-date as was possible from publicly available sources. Inevitably, there is a time lag in data becoming available to the public. For each figure in this book, the relevant international source is given, and the reader can find more up-to-date data when they are available. It is hoped that the trends that are apparent from the figures should provide an indication that will be helpful to readers, even if not all the data are up-to-date.

Many of the chapters, notably Chapters 4, 5, 11 and 12, are rather long and dense in content. These chapters contain new sections, for example those on Brexit, the rise of populism, human rights in the workplace and the rise of corporate power in the technology and media sectors. The reader can be selective, concentrating on those sections of particular interest. Rather than reducing the length of these chapters, it seemed preferable to allow the reader to decide which sections to focus on, in the knowledge that the others can be read at a later time.

This new edition is intended to build on the strengths and distinctiveness of earlier editions, while raising the important issues facing businesses in the global environment. It is hoped that, in addition to its academic value, it will be interesting and stimulating to read.

TOUR OF THE BOOK

The two chapters in this part form a foundation for the book as a whole. In any study of business, there is a distinction between matters relating to the enterprise itself, often termed the 'internal' environment of the business, and matters relating to the external environment, such as markets where it aims to sell its products. Although this division is oversimplified, as we will find in later chapters, it helps to use these

Introduction to each of the four parts of the book
The introduction appears at the beginning of each part. It provides a summary of what will be discussed in each chapter in that part.

Outline of chapter and learning objectives
The opening page of each chapter provides a quick guide to what is covered in the outline of the chapter. The learning objectives will help you organize your study and track your progress.

Outline of chapter

Introduction

What does the business enterprise exist to do?
Purpose and goals
The company in society: Stakeholders and corporate social responsibility (CSR)

How does the enterprise carry out its goals?
It all starts with entrepreneurs
Companies: the engines of business activities
Functional areas within the enterprise
The multinational enterprise (MNE)
Corporate governance: shareholders and other stakeholders

This chapter will enable you to

- Identify a variety of purposes pursued by business enterprises in the changing environment
- Evaluate the differing types of ownership and decision-making structures through which enterprises pursue their goals
- Appreciate the roles played by stakeholders in diverse enterprises
- Gain an overview of dimensions and layers of the international business environment, together with an ability to see how their interactions impact on firms
- Gain an overview of ways in which principles and practices of sustainability are integrated

OPENING CASE STUDY

The iconic brand of Levi Strauss
Nowadays, when we think of an iconic brand, we tend to think of a brand such as Apple's iPhone, but there is an iconic brand that has been around much longer, and is popular with many more people from different walks of life worldwide. The original blue jeans made famous by Levi Strauss are universally popular, whether the wearer is richer or poorer, younger or older, keen on

'Chip' Bergh, who took over as Chief Executive Officer (CEO) in 2011. He had come from the consumer products company, Procter & Gamble, and set about renewing the Levi Strauss brand, refashioning its appeal to today's consumers. He felt that when consumer brands persist in producing the same products for the same markets, without an eye to innovation, they soon

Opening and closing case studies
Case studies at the beginning and end of each chapter feature businesses of all sizes, from every corner of the globe. Questions at the end of each case study give you a chance to reflect further. There are also recommendations for further reading.

CLOSING CASE STUDY

Ikea at the crossroads
India might seem an unlikely market for Ikea, the Swedish furniture retailer, to open new stores, but these are changing times in global consumer markets, and the rising middle classes in

Ikea's executives have responded to the challenges of changing shopping habits by opening smaller stores in city centres. For example, it operates pop-up shops for kitchens in a number of

Mini case studies
Two shorter case studies in each chapter focus on a business, a country or a particular issue. There are questions that invite you to think more about the issues, and a recommendation for reading to find out more.

MINI CASE STUDY

Taking a company private
Elon Musk, the flamboyant CEO (chief executive officer) of Tesla, the electric car company, announced in 2018 that he had 'funding secured' to take his company back into private ownership (Campbell and Pooley, 2018). Tesla had been listed on the Nasdaq exchange in 2010, and was worth over $70 billion. Taking it private would involve a mammoth undertaking to buy out the investors,

ments. Wh
because of
they have
sometimes
Most e
ings of frus
sures on t
publicly li

Glossary
Key terms are highlighted in bold colour and defined in the text where they appear, and collated in an alphabetical glossary at the back of the book for reference.

functional areas
activities of a business which form part of the overall process of producing and delivering a product for a customer

Shining a light on business decisions

These boxes pose specific situations and issues that confront businesses, and invite you to consider the ways in which relevant business decisions are taken in a wide range of circumstances.

How can the board of directors better perform its res monitoring management decisions?

Boards of directors have been the targets of criticism in recen acquiescent when managers were pursuing risky strategies. In directors who are themselves CEOs are not likely to 'rock the independent director contribute to more effective monitoring

The way I see it ...

On the competitive environment, 'The lesson to me is differentiate yourself...Move up the value chain. Being cheaper isn't enough. Being the low-cost provider is temporal.'

Sam Palmisano, former CEO of IBM, in an interview with CRN technology news, 23 February, 2011, at www.crn.com

Sam Palmisano guided IBM through a period (2003–2011) when it was making the transition from hardware to services, and also towards social goals, for example, in local supply chains that take into account community needs. He is now the head of the Center for Global Enterprise (www.thecge.net), which focuses on sustainability in the global environment. See 'IBM's Sam Palmisano: Always put the enterprise ahead of the individual', article and podcast, 18 January 2012, Knowledge@Wharton, at http://knowledge.wharton.upenn.edu

What advice would Palmisano offer to today's high-tech giants on the sustainable business?

The way I see it...

Quotes from a range of people and organizations raise different perspectives or pose dilemmas for you to consider, either on your own or in discussion with others. Rival viewpoints are sure to emerge.

Video links: enhance your understanding

The video links feature leading authorities on relevant dimensions of the business environment. They are an ideal way to enhance your learning.

Startups

Startups fail for many reasons. See what these experts on entrepreneurship say about success – and failure. 'Why do so many startups fail?', The Big Question from Chicago Booth, 30 November 2015.

Video link: Startups
https://youtu.be/l_9OGlnAT58

✓ Assignments

1 Offer advice to the following CEO: Ralph
EU country. The business has been highly
built up the business from its early days a
business model. Ralph has recently had ar
that values his company at €1 billion. He is
business. What should he do? Set out yo
offer.

2 The PESTLE analysis was designed to illu
environment. How can it be adapted to
broader scope, bringing in regional and gl

Review questions

1 How does a business decide what its goals will
2 Define stakeholders and explain the stakeholde
3 What is CSR, and why is it becoming more imp
goals?
4 What are the advantages and disadvantages of
5 What are the aspects of the limited company wl
business ownership?

Further reading

Bartlett, C., and Ghoshal, S. (2002) *Managing Across Borders: The transnational solution*, 2nd edition (Boston: Harvard Business School Press).
Brooks, I. (2018) *Organisational Behaviour: Individuals, groups and organisation*, 5th edition (Pearson).
Hickson, D., and Pugh, D.S. (2007) *Writers on Organizations* (London: Penguin).
Kay, J. (2007) *Foundations of Corporate Success* (Oxford: Oxford University Press).
Maon, F., Lingreen, A., and V. Swaen (2009) 'Designing and implementing corporate social responsibility: An

integrati
practice
Prahalad, C.
Pyramid
Pugh, D.S. (
readings
Tricker, R.I. (
policies
Press).
Wheelen, T.,
(2017) *S*
edition (

References

Campbell, P., and Pooley, C., 'Tesla tumbles as SEC accuses Musk of fraud', *The Guardian*, 29 September 2018.
Carroll, A.B. and Shabana, K.M. (2010) 'The business case for corporate social responsibility: A review of concepts, research and practice', *International Journal*

Milne, R. (20
3 Febru
Murman, J.
entrepre
Manage

Review and revise

The end of each chapter has a number of features to help you review and master what you have studied. There are review questions, assignments and suggestions for further reading.

For references and mastering the key terms and concepts

A Glossary of all key terms is at the end of the book. References are at the end of each chapter.

Visit the companion website at www.macmillanihe.com/morrison-gbe-5e for further learning and teaching resources.

DIGITAL RESOURCES

Companion website

There is a **companion website** for this book (**www.macmillanihe.com/morrison-gbe-5e**) where there is a range of teaching and learning materials.

Teaching resources

Instructors who adopt this book on their course gain access to a selection of password protected resources to help plan and deliver their teaching:

- Chapter-by-chapter sets of Microsoft PowerPoint slides
- Suggested answers to case study questions, along with guidelines for group discussions
- Guideline answers to questions in the 'Shining a light on business decisions' boxes, and questions on the quotes that occur in boxes on 'The way I see it...'
- Outline answers to the review questions at the end of each chapter, and outline answers for the assignments
- A testbank of multiple choice questions for structured tests
- Updated case studies from previous editions of the book

Learning resources

- Updated case studies from previous editions of this book
- Flashcards of useful key terms in the book

LIST OF ABBREVIATIONS

AGM	Annual General Meeting
AI	artificial intelligence
BRIC	Brazil, Russia, India and China
CEE	Central and Eastern Europe
CEO	Chief Executive Officer
CMA	Competition and Markets Authority (UK)
CSR	corporate social responsibility
ECJ	European Court of Justice
EU	European Union
FDI	foreign direct investment
FTA	free trade agreement
GATT	General Agreement on Tariffs and Trade
GDP	gross domestic product
GHGs	greenhouse gases
GMOs	genetically-modified organisms
GNI	gross national income
HDI	Human Development Index
ICC	International Criminal Court
ICJ	International Court of Justice
ICCPR	International Covenant on Civil and Political Rights
ICESCR	International Covenant on Economic, Social and Cultural Rights
IMF	International Monetary Fund
IPCC	Intergovernmental Panel on Climate Change (UN)
ISDS	investor-state dispute settlement
IT	information technology
ILO	International Labour Organization
IP	intellectual property
IPO	initial public offering
M&A	merger and acquisition (activity)
MNE	multinational enterprise
NAFTA	North American Free Trade Agreement
NGO	non-governmental organization
OECD	Organisation for Economic Co-operation and Development
PLC	public limited company (UK)
PPP	purchasing power parity
RTA	regional trade agreement
R&D	research and development
SDGs	Sustainable Development Goals
SEC	Securities and Exchange Commission (US)
SME	small-to-medium-size enterprise
TPP	Trans-Pacific Partnership
TRIPS	Trade-related Aspects of Intellectual Property (agreement)
UK	United Kingdom
UN	United Nations
UNESCO	UN Educational, Scientific and Cultural Organization
US	United States of America
USMCA	United States-Mexico-Canada free trade agreement (successor to NAFTA)
WHO	World Health Organization
WTO	World Trade Organization

BUSINESS IN THE GLOBAL ENVIRONMENT

The two chapters in this part form a foundation for the book as a whole. In any study of business, there is a distinction between matters relating to the enterprise itself, often termed the 'internal' environment of the business, and matters relating to the external environment, such as markets where it aims to sell its products. Although this division is oversimplified, as we will find in later chapters, it helps to use these contexts for the initial formulation of concepts and identification of issues, which will become nuanced in later chapters.

Chapter 1, *The business enterprise in focus*, examines the business itself, its goals and how it goes about achieving them. The chapter begins by looking at the most basic question of all: what does the business exist for? Many issues come into play, including what the enterprise exists to do, what it is offering the public and how it should be run. Basic concepts are introduced, including those relating to company formation and those relating to the analysis of business strategies. Issues of sustainability and corporate social responsibility are introduced. Businesses are part of the societies in which they operate. They are expected to address impacts on stakeholders and on society generally. The last two sections in Chapter 1 introduce the business in its external environment, setting out the dimensions which will form the basis of separate chapters.

In Chapter 2, *Globalization and the business environment*, we change focus to the external environment, with rapidly changing markets and production based on global supply chains. The many processes which are grouped together under the broad heading of 'globalization' are examined critically, assessing impacts on business organizations, governments and societies. Globalization represents a range of different processes, from high-speed communications to converging consumer tastes. These processes have led to economic benefits flowing to companies and to national economies. However, negative impacts on societies and the environment are a continuing concern, casting doubts on sustainability. In recent years, national trade policies of leading trading countries have shifted focus to domestic economic goals, causing trade tensions that have impacted on global supply chains.

© Hero Images

THE BUSINESS ENTERPRISE IN FOCUS

Outline of chapter

This chapter will enable you to

- Identify a variety of purposes pursued by business enterprises in the changing environment
- Evaluate the differing types of ownership and decision-making structures through which enterprises pursue their goals
- Appreciate the roles played by stakeholders in diverse enterprises
- Gain an overview of dimensions and layers of the international business environment, together with an ability to see how their interactions impact on firms
- Gain an overview of ways in which principles and practices of sustainability are integrated into the business environment

OPENING CASE STUDY

The iconic brand of Levi Strauss

Nowadays, when we think of an iconic brand, we tend to think of a brand such as Apple's iPhone, but there is an iconic brand that has been around much longer, and is popular with many more people from different walks of life worldwide. The original blue jeans made famous by Levi Strauss are universally popular, whether the wearer is richer or poorer, younger or older, keen on fashion or not. And although Levi Strauss conjures up an image of the American west, their jeans are popular all over the world, in both rural and urban settings.

The company was founded in 1853 by a wholesale dry goods merchant who emigrated to the US from Germany. Levi Strauss made his way to California in the era of the great Gold Rush. Working with a partner who was a tailor, they had the idea of riveted jeans for workwear that, according to company legend, would be sold to gold miners. Levi Strauss jeans were patented in 1873, and the business grew steadily. Denim jeans became popular well beyond people engaged in tough, outdoor work. The market for denim jeans was becoming very competitive, and other companies, such as Wrangler, were also attracting loyal customers. The US was their main market, and sales at Levi Strauss reached a peak of $7.1bn in 1997. In the years that followed, denim jeans were facing competition from a range of other brands and products. Gap was offering a wide range of casual wear, and the advent of new fabrics such as lycra offered a more comfortable fit for users, especially those looking for a combination of fashion and comfortable apparel for leisure activities of all sorts. Were denim jeans losing their appeal? Levi jeans has remained a private, family-owned company for most of its existence. It was listed as a public company in 1971, but was de-listed in 1985, reverting to private ownership. In that period, the manufacturing of its clothing shifted from mainly US factories to overseas factories. By the 2000s, its US factories had almost all disappeared. This was a trend that affected the entire clothing industry in the US, as jobs in clothing and textiles shifted to lower cost locations, mainly in Asia.

Competitive pressures signalled that the company needed to rethink its product offering and its brand in order to survive in a changing environment. Coming to the rescue was Charles 'Chip' Bergh, who took over as Chief Executive Officer (CEO) in 2011. He had come from the consumer products company, Procter & Gamble, and set about renewing the Levi Strauss brand, refashioning its appeal to today's consumers. He felt that when consumer brands persist in producing the same products for the same markets, without an eye to innovation, they soon become jaded. The company, he felt, should look to new designs and new, improved fabrics. Stretch fabrics were introduced, and more design appeal was sought. While Levi Strauss's products had always been more popular with men, he set about developing ranges that would be popular with women. He also had an eye on expansion in other markets. It was not long before sales were growing in Europe and Asia, although the US still accounts for 59% of its sales. The venerable old brand faced stiff competition from fast fashion companies such as H&M, which had lower prices and sleek designs. There was also strong competition from the value stores that appealed to highly price-sensitive shoppers. Moreover, retailing was fast becoming transformed by the growth in online sales. Levi Strauss thus had to move with the times. Has it succeeded?

Sales rose to nearly $5 billion in 2017. As a sign of its new-found confidence, Levi Strauss opened its own flagship store in Times Square in New York in 2018. Here it offers bespoke tailoring services for customers and a nostalgic step back in time in its on-site Levi Strauss museum. For most older customers, denim jeans bring back pleasant memories of their own lives. Levi Strauss has worked to depict itself as an authentic brand in a world in which people have become used to

Wall Street traders mark the debut of Levi Strauss on the New York Stock Exchange.

throwaway fashion. The idea of spending on something that is authentic and lasting seems especially to have struck the right note with millennial-generation customers. In 2018, the ownership of the company was still mainly in the hands of the descendants of Levi Strauss. But its renewed success has encouraged the family to take the company public again. The company was listed on the New York Stock Exchange in March 2019, and enjoyed a rise in value of 30% on the first day's trading. The new stock was oversubscribed, in a sign that many investors wanted to own a slice of this iconic company and its history. The Wall Street traders on the floor of the exchange set the tone by wearing Levi jeans for the occasion.

Questions

- What are the competitive pressures facing Levi Strauss?
- What makes Levi Strauss an iconic brand?
- In your opinion, why have the descendants kept the company under their own control all these years?
- What are the challenges now facing Levi Strauss?

Further reading

See the article by Dominic Rushe, 'Levi's shakes off the troubles by embracing the past', 17 November 2018, in *The Guardian*, at www.theguardian.com

Also see 'Levi Strauss shares surge on first day of trading', BBC news, 21 March 2019, at www.bbc.co.uk

Introduction

Business activities shape the daily lives and aspirations of people all over the world, from the farmer in rural Africa to the executive of a large American bank. Business enterprises present a kaleidoscope of different organizations and goals, catering for customers ranging from the shopper purchasing a loaf of bread to the giant oil company agreeing to carry out exploration for a government. Business enterprises and their environments have become more complex and interconnected in recent years, with expanding and deepening ties in diverse locations. Expansion has brought increased risks and greater challenges for managers. They must adapt to differing environments and rapidly changing circumstances. They also serve a more informed public than that of only a few decades ago. The international public is more aware than ever of corporate activities, largely due to the pervasiveness of the internet and social media. Challenges for managers are heightened by a growing perception that companies bear responsibilities for their actions in societies. All business organizations, whatever their size and geographical scope, are faced with key questions to which they must respond.

We begin this chapter by identifying these key questions behind the business enterprise, which are, 'What do we exist to do?' and 'How should we be carrying out our goals?'. We then look at how enterprises come into existence, how decision-making takes place and, importantly, the responsibilities of decision-makers for their actions. A number of basic terms relating to companies and their governance are introduced. Business discourse often refers to 'shareholder value', but what exactly is a 'share' in a company, and why does it matter? These basic concepts are crucial in describing the organizational aspects of the company, which reflect its values and influence its behaviour. As will be seen, the company's ownership, organization and behaviour are shaped by aspects of the business environment.

As the global economy has expanded, there is a wider range of companies and countries engaged in global business. Moreover, states and state-related organizations are playing increasingly active roles. We highlight two cross-cutting views of

the international environment. The first is the differing dimensions of the environment, including economic, cultural, political, legal, financial, ecological and technological. The second is that of spheres, from the local through to the national, regional and global. We thus provide a practical framework for understanding how enterprises interact through each dimension in multiple geographical environments. The last section of the chapter focuses on the challenges and responsibilities that have been highlighted, in particular, building sustainable business and the regulatory environment.

What does the business enterprise exist to do?

The street trader in India and the Silicon Valley executive might not seem to have much in common: they are worlds apart in geography, culture and technology. But they have more in common than meets the eye. Both seek to offer products that will please customers, and both must respond to changing tastes and lifestyles in order to make money to keep the enterprise afloat. This is the essence of business everywhere. **Business** refers to any type of economic activity in which goods or services (or a combination of the two) are supplied in exchange for some payment, usually money. This definition describes the basic exchange transaction. The types of activity covered include trading goods, manufacturing products, extracting natural resources and farming. **International business** refers to business activities that straddle two or more countries. Businesses nowadays routinely look beyond the bounds of their home country for new opportunities. Moreover, although it used to be mainly firms in the more advanced regions of the world (such as North America, Europe and Japan) which aspired to expand into other countries, we now see businesses from a much wider range of countries 'going global'. These include Chinese, Indian, African and Latin American firms. Consequently, in most countries, there are likely to be both domestic and foreign companies competing alongside each other. Today's international businesses come from a variety of backgrounds and represent a diverse range of organizations – from family firms to state-owned companies. There is thus a wide spectrum of purposes and goals lying behind international businesses.

business any type of economic activity in which goods or services (or a combination of the two) are supplied in exchange for some payment, usually money

international business business activities that straddle two or more countries

for-profit organizations businesses that aim to make money

not-for-profit organizations organizations such as charities, which exist for specific good causes in societies

social enterprise an enterprise that lies between the for-profit and not-for-profit organization, aiming to make money but using it for a social cause

Purpose and goals

A business enterprise does not simply come into existence of its own accord. It is created by people with ideas about products or services, who may emerge in any society or geographic location, and who bring their own values and experience to bear on it. Particular national environments, with their distinctive values and social frameworks, are formative influences on founders of businesses. Entrepreneurs might simply seek personal gain for themselves and their families, but many will envisage an overarching purpose or mission of contributing to society through employment and wealth creation. They will have some idea of what type of entity they wish to create in terms of organization. They must also focus on the specific goods or services they wish to offer, and to whom. These objectives might change frequently, while broader goals are more enduring. Both the decision-makers and the circumstances will change, but the underlying question confronting them is 'what purpose are we fulfilling or should we be fulfilling?'. Most of the world's businesses aim to make money, and are sometimes referred to as **for-profit organizations**, to distinguish them from **not-for-profit organizations**, such as charities, which are established to serve specific good causes in societies. A third category is the **social enterprise**, which lies somewhere between the two: it aims to make money for a social cause rather than as profit for the owners. These are broad categories, and these types of enterprise vary considerably from country to country.

business model a broad term covering an organization's reasons for existing, its goals and the means it adopts to achieve them

innovation activities that lead to new and improved products and services

supply chain series of stages involved in producing a product or service, from sourcing through to production, distribution and delivery to the customer, where each stage is co-ordinated to link with other stages in the process

Although for-profit enterprises aim to make a financial gain, most founders would say that their goal is not simply to make money, but to offer products which will satisfy customers. It need not be a wholly new product, but one that is more innovative technologically or a better design than rivals' products. It could be a 'greener' product than those of rivals, such as a more fuel-efficient car, reflecting goals of a sustainable business. Alternatively, a firm might simply focus on delivering a standard product or service more cheaply than its competitors. These are all aspects of the firm's **business model**, which is a broad term covering the organization's goals and means of achieving them. The business model is about *why* the company exists, as well as about *how* it aims to serve customers. A business model is not set once and for all by founders, but can be changed over time to reflect innovation and changing markets (see Ovans, 2015). **Innovation** brings to mind the creation of new products that displace the older ones, but it also encompasses improvements and new ways of doing things (discussed fully in Chapter 9). Innovation lies at the heart of many business models, especially those in high-tech sectors, where it is key to maintaining competitiveness.

Apple of the US has acquired an enviable reputation for its iconic iPhone, sold at premium prices, but the company has come under fire over the working conditions in the factories in which the phones are made, mainly in China. The basis of Apple's business model has been its innovative products, but also crucial has been its strategy of having products manufactured in low-cost locations within a supply chain that is designed to serve markets globally. The **supply chain** visualizes the production process as a succession of stages, from sourcing and manufacture through to delivery. Supply chains have become global, as firms seek the most advantageous location for each stage. The supply chain is also referred to as a 'value chain', whereby value is added at each stage, as discussed in the next chapter. While this is applauded as a global strategy from the business perspective, it can be criticized on ethical grounds in a number of contexts. Consumer products, from basic essentials to expensive goods, are routinely made by exploited workers in poor countries – an uncomfortable reality for companies and their brands. The huge profits Apple accumulates from iPhone sales are deposited in foreign locations, in order to avoid the tax bills that would arise in the US. These arrangements, too, can be criticized as unethical. Apple is not alone. Many companies arrange their businesses to reduce tax burdens. They would argue that the pursuit of economic goals is, after all, what they are founded to do. This approach, however, sits uneasily with mission statements which typically depict the company as enhancing the quality of life. Consumers and investors have increasingly criticized an aggressive profit-seeking approach, pointing out that companies are part of the societies in which they operate: their economic power entails social responsibilities. Governments, too, have introduced legal reforms that seek to compel companies to pay tax in the countries where they operate, rather than utilize tax-avoidance structures. The for-profit company is just that, but there is a growing awareness that a pursuit of both economic and social goals is, in the long term, a more sustainable way in which to frame business goals (Carroll and Shabana, 2010). This point recurs throughout this book.

The company in society: Stakeholders and corporate social responsibility (CSR)

As the last section highlighted, answering the question, 'what do we exist to do?' is more complex than might appear. A business seeks to enrich its owners, but it will not succeed unless it satisfies customers who purchase its products and services. Its activities involve employing people, acquiring productive assets, using resources and interacting with official authorities and other organizations in communities.

stakeholder broad category including individuals, groups and even society generally, that exerts influence on the company or who the company is in a position to influence

These relationships all involve the business in society. These interests are referred to broadly as stakeholders. A **stakeholder** may be anyone, including individuals, groups and even society generally, that exerts influence on the company or who the company is in a position to influence (Freeman, 1984). The impacts may be direct or indirect, identifiable people or a more general notion of the community as something distinct from its current members. As Figure 1.1 shows, stakeholders who have direct relations with the company include owners, employees, customers and suppliers. These might be located in any country where the firm does business. A government authority can be a direct stakeholder if it has an ownership stake, but it is more likely to be an indirect stakeholder, framing the legal environment in which the firm operates. Indirect stakeholders, while they affect and are affected by the company's operations, cover a range of broader societal interests, which enjoy fewer direct channels of communication with managers. They include the local community, society generally and the ecological environment affected by the company's operations. Employees in a company's supply chains are also stakeholders, but commonly do not directly interact with the lead company.

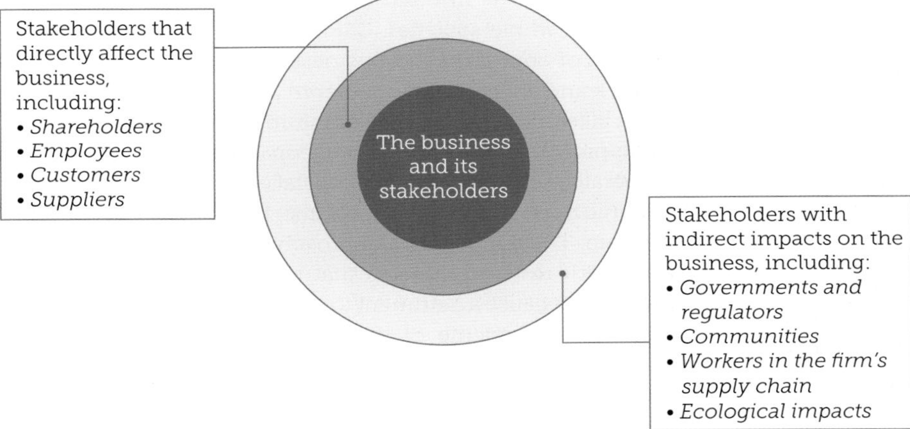

Figure 1.1 The business and its stakeholders

In a company which operates mainly in its own domestic market, managers have a fairly clear idea of their main stakeholders. Their employees and customers are readily identifiable. In a company which operates internationally, identifying stakeholders is far more difficult – and more challenging. The company's branded products could be made by workers in other locations, who are employed by a different company and have little contact with the company whose brand appears on the products. This strategy is typical of companies that operate through global supply chains. A term often used in the context of seeking cost-saving solutions is **outsourcing**, which covers any activity which an organization considers can be more advantageously carried out by another firm, often in another country. The activity is usually one formerly carried out 'in-house', which the firm decides to contract out to another firm, with the aim of reducing costs. Outsourced manufacturing is one of the more prominent of these. It is exemplified by Nike, Gap and other familiar brands such as Levi Strauss, featured in the opening case study. Numerous business functions can be outsourced. Among them are IT and call centres. This is often referred to as 'business process outsourcing' (BPO). Closely associated with this approach is '**offshoring**', a term used specifically to refer to outsourced activities that take place in advantageous jurisdictions such as those with lax regulation and low taxation. Financial arrangements are often the subject of offshoring strategies. The policy of seeking the most advantageous location for each aspect of the business is one of the

outsourcing term covering any activity which an organization considers can be more advantageously carried out by another firm, often in another country

offshoring term covering an outsourced activity that can be carried out in a jurisdiction where weak regulation and tax advantages offer attractions

major trends associated with globalization, which we discuss in the next chapter. But it also exemplifies an aggressively profit-maximizing approach to the business which arguably jeopardizes stakeholder interests.

For the company with activities and supply links in different countries, identifying and responding to stakeholder interests can be complex and involve taking decisions which have profound impacts in societies. A decision to close a factory can be made for purely internal economic reasons, but its impacts on employment and communities can be far-reaching. Stakeholders are important interests that impact on the firm's business performance, but stakeholder management also has a normative dimension, as an aspect of business ethics (Carroll and Shabana, 2010). For example, managers introduce measures to foster the health and wellbeing of employees not simply because people will work harder if they have healthier lives, but because it is the right thing to do. This ethical principle is rooted in the concept of **human rights**, which are basic, universal rights of all individuals, wherever they are. Upholding human rights is central to the firm's broader role in society. The approach to business activities which accords with these values is **corporate social responsibility (CSR)**. CSR as an approach recognizes that, in addition to economic responsibilities, the firm has legal, moral and social roles. These refer to both individuals and whole societies. CSR has become rather an umbrella term, covering a spectrum of approaches to business objectives, which are highlighted throughout this book and are brought together in a critical assessment in Chapter 11.

human rights basic, universal rights of all individuals, wherever they are, which transcend social and cultural differences

corporate social responsibility (CSR) an approach to business which recognizes that the organization has responsibilities in society beyond the economic role, extending to legal, ethical, environmental and social roles

sustainability the principle that business should be carried out in ways which do not cause a detriment to the ability of future generations to fulfil their needs

CSR takes a long-term view of the company's goals. Pure profit-seeking is a short-term approach that, in reality, can jeopardize the ability of the company to continue to generate profits. In what is often called the 'business case' for CSR, the firm places economic goals in a longer timeframe, maintaining its capacity to generate profits in the future. This longer term approach involves the **sustainability** of the firm's business, which rests on the idea that today's business should be carried out in ways which do not cause a detriment to the ability of future generations to fulfil their needs. An overarching theme of this book, sustainability takes into account the firm's impacts on communities and the natural environment. The principle of sustainability encourages a business to think of stakeholders in the future, not just the present. Most firms would probably say they uphold goals of stakeholder involvement, CSR and sustainability, but firms differ markedly in their commitment of resources to these goals. Many see these as costs which jeopardize the company's profit-making activities. Possible conflicts between social goals and economic goals underlie much of the discussion of challenges and responsibilities which occurs throughout the book.

SHINING A LIGHT ON BUSINESS DECISIONS

What does the business exist to do?

Think of a company whose products you regularly purchase. How would you describe its business model? Think about why you are buying its products and whether you feel loyalty to the brand. For example, it might be because the product is good quality, cheap or convenient. But it could also be because the brand stands for values that you support.

How does the enterprise carry out its goals?

Although we speak of a *firm* forming goals and carrying them out, it is actually the *people* running the firm who take key decisions. In this section, we look at the players and processes which make it function. We focus here initially on the forms, structures and processes which constitute a legal framework; this is a necessary consideration before the firm can get on with what it is 'really' about, such as manufacturing. Most businesses start in a small way, with founders who become the first owners. They bear considerable responsibility, especially in the early stages of the business. Having a great idea for a business is only the beginning. They must create a legal and organizational structure to carry it out, and decide on how it will be

financed and managed. Each of these aspects of the business has an international dimension for many enterprises, adding to the possible complications, but also offering tantalizing opportunities.

It all starts with entrepreneurs

entrepreneur person who starts up a business and imbues it with the energy and drive necessary to compete in markets

A person who starts up a business, usually with his or her own money, is known as an **entrepreneur**. This is a broad category. Entrepreneurs exist in every society, but they differ markedly in their goals and outlooks. In developing countries, most entrepreneurs are highly localized in their activities and market. In villages throughout developing countries, the 'subsistence entrepreneur' serves the local community, managing to make a living but harbouring no intentions to expand (Schoar, 2010). The majority of entrepreneurs in developing countries are subsistence entrepreneurs. It is often observed that what is needed to propel economic development in poor countries is the more ambitious and innovative entrepreneur, who aspires to grow from a start-up to a bigger business (Schoar, 2010). The 'transformational entrepreneur' is that kind of person, reflecting the predominant image of the entrepreneur as a person with a sense of mission, a great deal of energy and a willingness to take risks. When governments speak of the need to encourage entrepreneurs, it is this type of highly motivated businessperson they have in mind. The business environment plays an important role in encouraging – or discouraging – the entrepreneur, as shown in Figure 1.2.

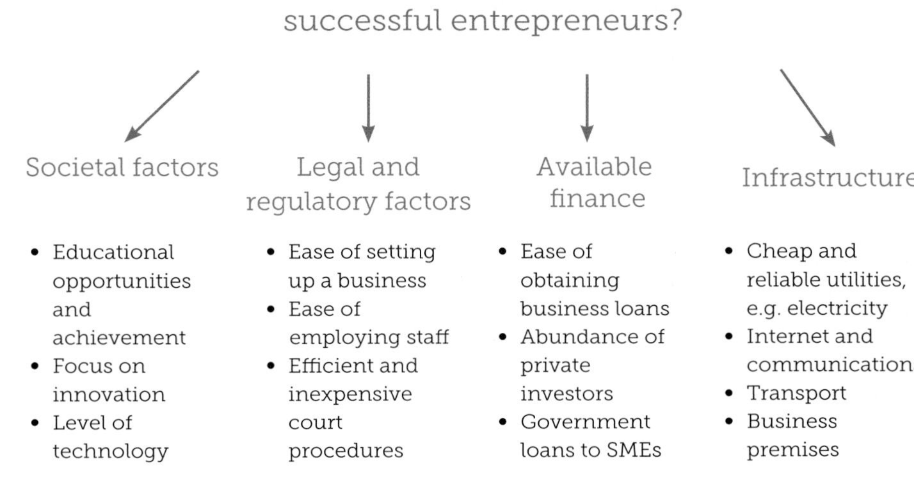

Figure 1.2 Country factors contributing to entrepreneurship

While all of the factors highlighted in Figure 1.2 are influential, some are more immediate in their impacts, and others are broad aspects of a country's environment. Availability of finance and business regulation have immediate impacts on start-up businesses. **Regulation** refers to the laws and rules relating to a particular type of activity or sector. The term covers both formal legal requirements and less formal guidance such as codes of practice. When formalities of forming a business are streamlined or access to finance is facilitated, a rise in new businesses is likely to result. The effects of improvements in education are slower in their impacts, as are improvements in infrastructure. On the other hand, the relaxation of strict labour laws can have more immediate effect, as a change in the law encourages businesses to hire more staff. It could also be observed that where labour laws are very restrictive, for example, limiting an employer's ability to dismiss an unsatisfactory employee, informal employment is common and workers are vulnerable to

regulation broad term covering laws and rules relating to a particular type of activity or sector

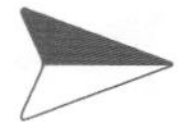

exploitation. India is an example of this restrictive environment. Facilitating entrepreneurs by encouraging them to employ people formally should lead to more secure livelihoods for workers.

A new business is usually referred to as a 'start-up'. The founder of an enterprise is traditionally known as a **sole trader**, but now more commonly referred to as a **self-employed** person. The self-employed person is an independent contractor, and can be contrasted with the **employee**, who works for another person (the employer), usually for wages, and whose work is controlled by the employer. The employer is obliged to comply with laws that protect employees, which typically include sick pay, paid holidays and social charges. While there might seem to be a clear distinction between an employee and a self-employed person, in fact, the distinction is blurred. Much work is casual, such as work paid by the hour, with no commitment to a set number of hours per week. The worker on a **zero-hours contract** is obliged to be available for work, but is not guaranteed a minimum number of hours of work. With the rise of digital platforms such as Uber, the ride-hailing company, the **gig economy** has become more prevalent in the modern work environment. Traditionally, the gig economy is associated with musicians and actors, who, as freelance workers, move from one job to the next. Now, the gig-economy worker is more often the person whose work derives from a digital platform. In some businesses, such as delivery services, workers are classified as self-employed although their work is to a large extent controlled by the company that takes them on (discussed in Chapter 11). The company is thus able to avoid the costs and obligations that fall on an employer. The worker in this situation can experience the worst of both worlds: compelled to follow orders from the company, but not enjoying benefits of employment status such as paid holidays. This practice has been reviewed by courts in a number of countries, including the UK, where judges tend to look at the reality of the relationship, rather than the labels used by the parties (see the discussion in Chapter 11). Uber, the ride-hailing company, is an example, featured in a case study in Chapter 6.

sole trader/ self-employed person person who is in business on his or her own account

employee person who works for another (the employer), usually for wages, and whose work is controlled by the employer

zero-hours contract employment arrangement whereby the worker is available for work but paid only for the hours worked, and the employer has no commitment to provide work

gig economy category of work in which the person's working life consists of moving from one job to another, typically working as a self-employed person

The business of the sole trader has no independent existence separate from its owner. In practice, this means that if the business fails, the personal wealth of its owner can be used to cover the business's debts. In the worst scenario, the owner's resources could be wiped out in order to pay business debts. This risk is known as 'unlimited liability', and is one of the major drawbacks of being self-employed. Securing finance is one of the major challenges of the start-up business. The business at this stage might have only one or two employees, or even none, although it is common for family members to help out. It is a **small-to-medium size enterprise (SME)**. This category covers the vast majority of the world's business enterprises. The classification of SMEs is given below:

small-to-medium size enterprise (SME) business ranging from micro-enterprises of just one person to firms with up to 249 employees

- Micro: 0–9 employees
- Small: 10–49 employees
- Medium: 50–249 employees
- Large: 250 or more employees

SMEs range from informal micro-enterprises to firms with up to 249 employees, making this a highly diverse category. These firms provide an important source of employment and economic activity in all countries. SMEs employ more people worldwide than large firms, in both developed and developing countries (de Kok et al., 2013). In developing countries, where levels of poverty are high, SMEs can be significant in job creation (de Kok et al., 2013). SMEs are a vital source of innovation, from agriculture to pharmaceuticals. SMEs in the high-technology sector are actively sought by large enterprises, keen to exploit their innovative ideas. High-tech

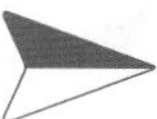

SMEs set their sights on global markets from the outset. These are often referred to as 'born-global' firms (Tanev, 2012). Whereas a firm traditionally expands gradually from its local and national environment, the born-global firm's owners think from the outset in terms of international markets. Most are not the flamboyant risk takers that are sometimes depicted in the media. The successful entrepreneur is more likely to pursue a prudent strategy based on assessing each risk and keeping it within reasonable bounds (Murman and Sardana, 2012).

Many well-known firms have grown from start-ups into global organizations. McDonald's, founded as a single hamburger outlet in the 1950s, is an example, as is Microsoft (founded in 1975) and Google (founded in 1998). Of the three, it is striking that Google, the most recent, has grown the quickest, becoming the world's dominant internet search engine in just a few years. The fact that these firms are all American is indicative that the cultural environment, as well as the legal and financial institutions, was favourable to entrepreneurs. Even so, the failure rate among start-ups is high, and any entrepreneur will admit that luck played a part in getting the business established.

Startups

Startups fail for many reasons. See what these experts on entrepreneurship say about success – and failure. 'Why do so many startups fail?', The Big Question from Chicago Booth, 30 November 2015.

Video link: Startups
https://youtu.be/l_9OGlnAT58

franchise business agreement by which a business (the franchisee) uses the brand, products and business format of another firm (the franchisor) under licence

For individual entrepreneurs, the franchise business provides an attractive route to starting a business. The **franchise** agreement allows a businessperson to trade under the name of an established brand, backed by an established organization (the 'franchisor'), while retaining ownership of the business. Under the agreement, the business owner ('franchisee') pays fees to the franchisor organization for the right to sell its products or services. The franchisee does not have the freedom over the business that an independent owner would have, but stands a greater chance of success due to the strength of the established business 'formula' of the brand. Besides McDonald's, Burger King and other fast-food chains, there are numerous other goods and service providers, such as car rental companies, which have grown through the use of franchising.

Companies: the engines of business activity

company legal form of organization that has a separate legal identity from its owner(s)

A business can carry on indefinitely as an unincorporated association or enterprise, that is, without formal corporate status. However, when it grows beyond a size that can be managed personally by the owner, it is usual for the owner to register it as a company, to give the business a separate legal identity and separate financial footing. The **company**, also called a 'corporation', is a legal entity separate from its owners. Registration with the correct authorities in each country (or individual state in the US) constitutes its formal creation, drawing a line between the company's obligations and those of the owner(s). This means that its finances and legal obligations, such as tax, are separate from its owners. It is also possible to register as a European company within the EU, although for purposes such as taxation, the company is still considered a national entity. The company takes on a separate existence from its owners at the point when it is registered, by filing documents of its purpose and constitution with national authorities.

Companies vary widely in their formation, legal status, ownership and goals. Most of the companies featured in this book are registered companies that are commercial enterprises whose founders go through the process of registration in a particular location. The person who invests money in the company, either at its formation or later, acquires shares in it. The **share** represents ownership of the company to the extent of the amount invested. The whole of a company's shares are its share capital, also known as its **equity**. The **shareholder** is liable up to the amount invested, and therefore enjoys **limited liability**. The founders are likely to be the first and largest shareholders (also known as stockholders). The introduction of limited liability made owning shares more attractive as an investment, and paved the way for widespread share ownership by the investing public. The shareholder who buys the company's shares is providing capital to enable it to function. The larger the stake (that is, holding of shares), the more influence the shareholder will expect to exert, although, in practice, controlling interests may make this difficult. A share in a company carries certain rights, including the right to receive dividends and (normally) vote in annual general meetings (AGMs). Importantly, the shareholder is a 'member' of the company, whereas the creditor of the company is not.

share in a company, represents ownership of the company to the extent of the amount invested

shareholders legal owners of a company

equity in corporate finance, the share capital of a company

limited liability principle that the shareholder is liable up to the amount that person or entity has invested in the company

private limited company company whose shares are not publicly traded on a stock exchange

Registered companies may be private or public companies. The main distinction between the two is that shares in the public company (or a portion of them) are traded on a stock exchange, whereas shares in the private company cannot be traded on exchanges. The **private limited company** tends to resemble the family business in which the owner retains control. It has few shareholders, and these are 'insiders', often related. It is not allowed to sell its shares to the public. Private companies often face problems over raising capital, but some, such as Silicon Valley start-ups, have been successful in finding financial backers known as 'venture capitalists', who are willing to invest large sums in their businesses. Uber is an example, discussed in the opening case study in Chapter 6. So long as financial backers continue to invest in a new company, owners are likely to keep the company private, thereby ensuring their continuing control of the business.

The private company faces fewer requirements for disclosure of its financial position than the public company. Although most are SMEs, many large international businesses choose to remain private companies. An example is Bosch, the German engineering company. Private companies are key economic players in Germany and many other countries. Private companies are thus significant players in the global economy.

public limited company (PLC) company which lists on a stock exchange and offers shares to the public

initial public offering (IPO) first offering by a company of its shares to the public on a stock exchange; also known as 'flotation'

The **public limited company (PLC)** is a registered company that offers shares to the public, and is usually referred to simply as a public company. It invites the public to subscribe for its shares in an **initial public offering (IPO)**, also known simply as a 'listing' or 'flotation' on a stock exchange. Stock exchanges are regulated under national legal frameworks, and also governed by their own listing rules (see Chapter 8). Typically, they specify that only a portion of a company's shares need be floated publicly, that is, offered to the general public, in order to be listed. This portion can be only 20%, or even lower. The remaining shares are generally owned by a few insiders, or, in some cases, government bodies. For example, Gazprom, the Russian gas giant, is listed on the London Stock Exchange, but the company is majority owned by the Russian government. This arrangement is not uncommon, and can seem confusing. A public limited company listed on a stock exchange is considered legally to be in the *private sector*, whereas a *public-sector* entity is owned and controlled by the state. When a government decides to 'privatize' a state-owned organization, it begins by registering the company as a PLC. Gazprom, for example, was formerly the gas ministry of the USSR. Conversely, when a PLC is taken over by the state, it is said to be 'nationalized'.

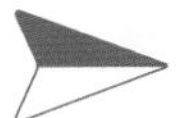

Should we take the plunge and go public?

If an entrepreneur has a successful business as a private company, it used to be thought a logical progression to go public, but this is no longer considered to be necessarily the best way forward. Why would the entrepreneur be tempted to go public? Think of the potential benefits and also the risks.

The public company faces scrutiny of its accounts by national regulators in the country in which it is registered, and in countries where its shares are listed on exchanges. It should be noted, however, that global scanning for the most advantageous location affects these decisions, just as it affects the location of production facilities. The company might register in an offshore location such as a Caribbean state, where oversight is minimal, and it could well decide to list on a stock exchange where the regulatory requirements are weak, and where the dominance of insiders is not an obstacle. In the US, nearly half of all public companies are registered in the tiny state of Delaware. While not strictly offshore, it offers many attractions that offshore registration offers, and appeals to business founders who wish to maintain control of their companies. Among companies that have registered in Delaware are the familiar ones such as Facebook, but also thousands of companies that are little more than shell entities that are linked in opaque corporate ownership structures. Delaware's advantages include the ease with which company registration is facilitated and the business-friendly stance of its courts, but the darker side is facilitating non-disclosure of company ownership and activities.

In 2012, the number of registered corporate entities in Delaware exceeded the number of human beings in the state: there are just over 900,000 registered companies and under 900,000 people (Wayne, 2012). It is thus worthy of note at this early juncture that founders of companies which 'go public' often wish to 'have their cake and eat it': they wish to attract the public to buy shares, but they also wish to retain control of the company and take the major decisions themselves. Google, for example, has a dual share structure whereby founders' shares carry more voting rights than ordinary shares (they are weighted 10 to 1). Some public companies decide to take the reverse route and go back to being private companies. Some entrepreneurs wish to re-assert control over their business, as shown in the mini case study that follows.

MINI CASE STUDY

Taking a company private

Elon Musk, the flamboyant CEO (chief executive officer) of Tesla, the electric car company, announced in 2018 that he had 'funding secured' to take his company back into private ownership (Campbell and Pooley, 2018). Tesla had been listed on the Nasdaq exchange in 2010, and was worth over $70 billion. Taking it private would involve a mammoth undertaking to buy out the investors, and it soon emerged that he did not have the means to accomplish this feat. He faced legal action from the US regulator, the Securities and Exchange Commission, for making false statements. While Musk attracted investors in Tesla because of his appeal as a technological visionary, they have reason to be concerned about his sometimes erratic behaviour and statements.

Most entrepreneurs can appreciate the feelings of frustration arising from the external pressures on their companies when they become publicly listed. Market analysts are constantly focused on the latest share price, with little long-term view of the health of the company. Financial results are typically reported four times a year, leading to tensions surrounding expectations each quarter. There are numerous other regulatory obligations that pertain to public companies. For example, whereas a private company can appoint any directors it wishes, the public company is obliged to appoint some independent directors, who can represent the wider interests of all the investors. This is a protection for the investing public, but can be seen by founders as an obstacle to realizing their vision. Because a range of investors and their interests are involved, the public company is in the glare of publicity. A larger-than-life entrepreneur, such as Richard Branson, has been keen on media attention when marketing his products, but has objected to media attention when it focuses on how his companies are run. His company, Virgin, was floated in 1986, but taken private again two years later.

The traditional CEO is careful in all media communications, aware that any statements could be misinterpreted and have a negative impact on the company's share price. Many entrepreneurs in today's high-flying tech companies are the opposite of this traditional CEO. They have grown their companies rapidly, often attracting outside investors who have seen the potential of their innovative ideas in the process. This attraction helps to explain the popularity of Tesla's shares, which translated into rising share prices, despite weak financial performance in the company's carmaking business. The modern entrepreneur's drive and vision can seem incompatible with the constraints of the listed company.

Questions

- What were the factors in Tesla's success?
- Would you advise investing in Tesla, or would you consider it too risky an investment?

Find out more

See the article focusing on Elon Musk, 'Colliding with reality', by Richard Waters and Peter Campbell, 16 June 2018, in the *Financial Times*.

Functional areas within the enterprise

functional areas activities of a business which form part of the overall process of producing and delivering a product for a customer

Every enterprise, whether large or small, involves a number of different types of activity, or **functional areas**, which form part of the overall process of providing products for customers, often in numerous markets around the world. Physical resources, including plant, machinery and offices must be organized, and functions such as finance, production and marketing must be co-ordinated, to enable the entire enterprise to function smoothly as a unit. Every business carries out basic functions, such as finance, even though in a small business, it is unlikely to hire specialists in each area. By contrast, a large organization has separate departments. The importance of particular functional areas depends in part on the type of business. Product design and production, along with research and development (R&D), feature mainly in manufacturing firms, whereas all firms have need of finance, human resource management (HRM) and marketing functions. These functions cover the entire life of a product, from the design stage to the delivery of a final product to the customer. They even extend beyond the sale, to include after-sales service and recycling.

Core functional areas are set out in Figure 1.3. At the centre of the figure is the company's central management, which is responsible for overall strategy. These senior managers determine what the company's goals are, and how best to achieve them. They are responsible for co-ordinating the activities of each functional area. We look at the part played by each of these functions in turn.

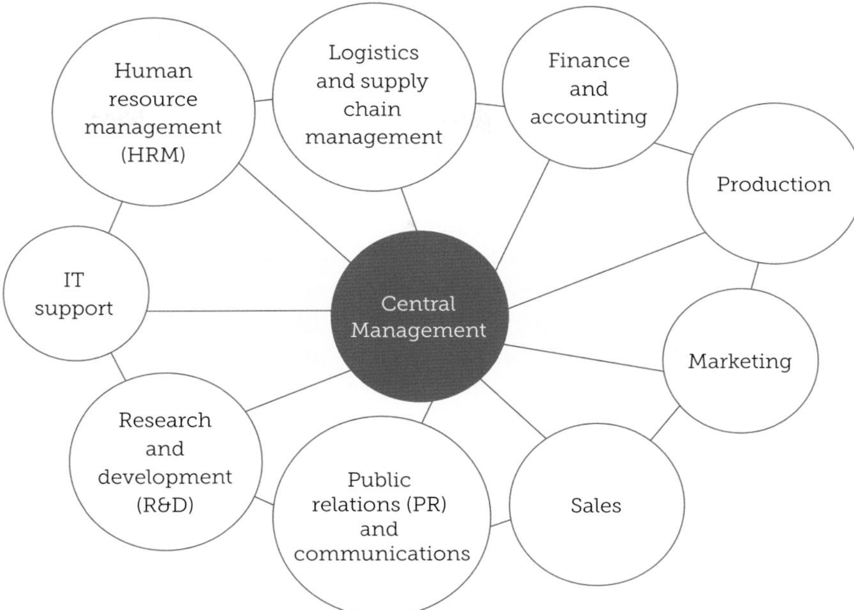

Figure 1.3 Functional areas of a business organization

- Finance and accounting – This function concerns control over the revenues and outgoings of the business, aiming to balance the books and to generate sufficient profits for the future health of the firm. This function is far more complex in large public companies than in SMEs. Trends towards more innovative finance and international operations have called for considerable professional expertise. At the same time, as discussed earlier, legal duties of financial reporting and disclosure are now increasingly under the spotlight. The company's chief financial officer (CFO) is a board member, and bears responsibilities for compliance with legal requirements.
- Production – Production spans the entire process of producing a product for sale in markets. This function covers tangible goods and services, and often a combination of both. Production focuses on the operational processes by which products are manufactured. Quality, safety and efficiency are major concerns of production engineers and managers. Quality and safety have become more challenging as manufacturing has shifted to diverse locations, and in some instances, companies have brought back to the home country operations that had been carried out by low-cost workers in outsourced factories. This is likely to occur in operations where computerized systems and robotics reduces the need for workers.
- Logistics and supply chain management – This functional area is closely linked to production, as supply chains are crucial to the production process. This is especially true for the manufacture of products that involve numerous components sourced externally. It is crucial for logistics solutions, involving transport and warehousing of products, to be as efficient and reliable as possible, to keep costs under control and to deliver orders to customers on time and according to their contractual terms.
- Human resource management (HRM) – Formerly known as 'personnel management', HRM focuses on all aspects of the management of people in the organization, including recruitment, training, and rewarding the workforce. In the large, hierarchical organization, these activities are formally structured,

whereas in the small organization, they tend to be carried out informally, with less paperwork and less reliance on formal procedures. Organizations have become sensitive to the need to take into account the individual employee's own goals and development, as well as the needs of the company. International HR strategy is challenging. Each country has its own set of employment laws, and in each country, social and cultural factors play important roles in work values and practices. International HR managers increasingly realize the fact that motivating staff in different locations requires differing approaches and reward systems.

- Marketing – Marketing covers a range of related activities, including product offering, branding, advertising and pricing. Marketing aims to satisfy the needs and expectations of customers with products that offer a winning combination of value and attractive price. While global companies aim to create a strong brand image across their product range, they adapt products and marketing communications to differing country markets. They rely on market research to understand customer preferences in each market, both in terms of products and customer relations. Marketing is an area in which regulation is an important consideration, national authorities playing an active role in regulating, for example, product safety and advertising.
- Sales – Sales are central to any business, and sales specialists work closely with marketing specialists to establish the company's products in particular markets and to launch new products. Sales specialists must focus on how best to sell particular products in each market, including how best to price it to generate sales. The company's competitive position in each market depends heavily on the expertise of those in its sales department.
- Research and Development (R&D) – R&D is the function of seeking new knowledge and applications which can lead to new and improved products or processes. R&D activities are part of the larger focus on innovation in the company, and can take place within any of the functions listed in this section. R&D can focus on scientific and technical research, which is key to new product development. Pharmaceutical companies typically spend huge sums on R&D, as new medicines are their chief source of profits. For a media or internet company, innovation relies on creating new content (often adapted to new markets) and new ways of delivering content to the consumer.
- IT and support services – It has become all too common for IT problems to upset production schedules, cause customers to be disappointed and cost substantial sums of money to put right. The security of the organization's data and systems can be threatened, posing long-term risks to the business. Having reliable and secure IT systems able to cope with the changing needs of the business, along with the ability to respond quickly to glitches in the system, is crucial to a business. This support function is central to the firm's activities in all the functional areas, as an IT malfunctioning in one can have knock-on effects in others. The IT system must support the gathering and storage of the firm's data, facilitate internet networking with other firms, and offer security against threats such as leakage of data and cybercrime.
- Public relations (PR) and communications – The traditional function of PR, which suggests a focus on publicity, has given way to a greater emphasis on quality communications involving the range of a company's stakeholders. While ongoing communication is essential to stakeholder relations, it is also vital in relation to regulatory authorities, consumers and the general public. The rise in social media has transformed communication channels, enabling companies to reach a wider

public, and also enabling consumers to acquire information about the company – often information that the company might prefer not to be disclosed through the social media. Managing communications is thus an important function for meeting consumer and investor expectations and also answering their concerns. Documents such as an annual CSR or sustainability report have become an important aspect of the large company's approach to communication.

An organization's central management has the ultimate control over the ways in which these functional areas carry out the company's goals. While each area is distinctive, all must be co-ordinated with each other, as Figure 1.3 shows. Finance and IT are crucial to each of the functional areas – and there is likely to be tension regarding the allocation of funds. For example, should the marketing budget be reduced in order to focus more on R&D? In today's company, where costs are a paramount concern, the possibility of outsourcing business processes is relevant to most of these functional areas. We have seen that production is often outsourced, and many 'back-office' activities, such as accounting, finance, administration and customer relations can be outsourced to specialist service providers, often in low-cost locations.

Each of the business functions adapts and changes as a business expands internationally, as the following examples show:

- Financial reporting will involve different regulatory environments and accounting standards.
- Operations will be linked in global production networks.
- HRM will adapt to different cultures and laws.
- Marketing strategy will be designed for differing markets.
- R&D will be configured in different locations according to specialist skills in each.

For the international manager, an understanding of the differing cultural environments where the company operates, and the various functional activities which take place in each unit, are crucial to the overall achievement of the company's goals. A company's approach to these challenges depends heavily on its own background and its relations with stakeholder organizations.

The multinational enterprise (MNE)

Both private and public companies abound in the international environment. As they extend their operations outwards from their home countries, their organizations become more complex. A company can grow 'organically' by increasing its capacity and going into new markets without making major structural changes to the organization. When company executives become more ambitious internationally, they contemplate changes with deeper structural implication. A result has been a thriving global market in corporate ownership and control. As its strategy evolves, a company might buy other companies and sell those it no longer wishes to own. It might also buy stakes in other companies, often as a means of participating in a network of firms, rather than for purely ownership motives. This constant re-configuration of companies and businesses has become a prominent feature of the global business environment. In these ways, companies can grow relatively quickly internationally and adapt their businesses organizationally as changes in the competitive environment occur. The main organizational arrangement through which these changes take place is the multinational enterprise.

multinational enterprise (MNE) an organization which acquires ownership (whole or partial) or other contractual ties in other organizations (including companies and unincorporated businesses) outside its home country

The **multinational enterprise (MNE)** is a broad term signifying a lead company (the parent company) which has acquired ownership (whole or partial) and other contractual ties in other organizations (including companies and unincorporated businesses) outside its home country. The parent company co-ordinates the business activities carried out by all the organizations within the MNE's broad control.

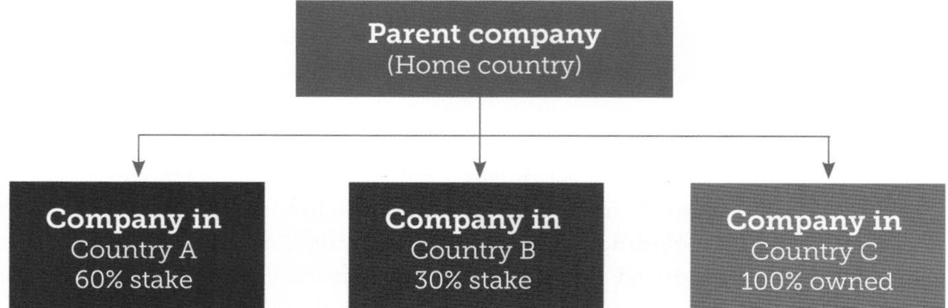

Figure 1.4 The multinational enterprise (MNE)

The MNE as an organizational form is not a strictly legal category, but it is recognized as central in international business organization and has been a key driver of globalization, discussed in the next chapter. The term covers businesses of all sizes, from SMEs to global companies with hundreds of thousands of employees. It covers private companies as well as public ones. Typically, the parent company located in the home country co-ordinates the activities of other companies in the group. If the parent company owns a majority stake in another company, that other company is a **subsidiary**. Where the ownership stake is less than half, the other company is considered an **affiliate** company. The MNE thus operates through a range of subsidiaries and affiliates, usually connected in supply chains. The parent company can exert strong control over a subsidiary, or it can operate on a loosely co-ordinated basis, delegating much decision-making to local managers. A simple MNE is shown in Figure 1.4. In the figure, only the company in Country C is wholly owned and controlled. It is thus a subsidiary company. The parent has a 60% equity stake in the company in Country A, making it also a subsidiary, as this gives the parent a controlling stake. The 30% stake in the company in Country B makes this company an affiliate. MNEs can have quite complex webs of affiliates, and in some countries, especially in Japan and South Korea, affiliates own shares in each other, known as 'cross-shareholding', thereby giving the parent company effective control over an affiliate even though it might own only a small stake itself.

subsidiary company a company owned wholly or substantially by another company, which is in a position to exert control

affiliate company organization connected through ownership stake or other strategic ties to an MNE, often in supply chains

holding company an umbrella company that owns the multiple companies or divisions that make up the business

The MNE parent company can be a **holding company**, that is, simply an umbrella company that owns the multiple companies or divisions that make up the business. An example is Google's parent company, Alphabet. The parent company is likely to be registered in its home country, and its subsidiaries registered in the countries where they carry out their activities. Hence, the subsidiary can be viewed as a 'local' company, even if controlled by a foreign parent. In some countries, foreign investors are not permitted by law to own 100% of a local company, but a sizeable stake can bring considerable power. In another twist, a private parent company can control subsidiaries which are publicly listed in their countries of operation (an example is the steel company, ArcelorMittal). Managing subsidiaries in different country environments is one of the major challenges for today's international managers, heightened by the expansion of competitive MNEs from developing and emerging economies.

Corporate governance: Shareholders and other stakeholders

The sole trader or sole owner of a company may well take all the major decisions for the business, unfettered by the wishes of other owners and not accountable to anyone else within the business. Still, even a micro-enterprise has stakeholders, in

that it exists in a community, has customers, makes an environmental impact and must comply with regulatory authorities. A company's highest decision-making processes constitute its corporate governance.

corporate governance the highest decision-making structures and processes in the company

Organisation for Economic Co-operation and Development (OECD) organization of the world's main developed economies, which supports market economies and democratic institutions

Corporate governance refers to the highest decision-making structures and processes in the company. It differs from business to business, and is influenced by national economic, social, cultural and legal environments. It reflects broad perspectives on the company's role in society, which have come under the spotlight in the wider debate on corporate governance and CSR in recent years. A company's own heritage and corporate culture influence its corporate governance, both formally and informally. National governments have oversight of corporate governance, but most are reluctant to intervene actively in what is considered the internal governance of private-sector companies. Many would prefer the law to lay down broad principles rather than prescriptive frameworks, on the grounds that a one-size-fits-all approach is not appropriate.

The **Organisation for Economic Co-operation and Development (OECD)** (at www.oecd.org), which was established by representatives of the world's main developed economies in 1961, has been active in giving guidance on corporate governance (see Chapter 2 for details of the OECD). The OECD's overarching principles support market economies and democratic institutions. Since 1999, it has published a set of Principles of Corporate Governance, which are intended to guide companies generally on best practice. These have become recognized as benchmark principles globally. While they are addressed mainly to large public companies, they are relevant to both public and private companies, and apply to companies with differing board structures (discussed below). Moreover, they are now addressed to the G20 group of countries, which include developing and emerging economies.

OECD and G20 representatives took part in discussions that culminated in the publication of the most recent version, which was issued in 2015, replacing the 2004

Table 1.1 Corporate governance principles recommended by the OECD and G20

Principle	The corporate governance framework should:
1	• Promote transparent and fair markets • Be consistent with the rule of law • Support effective supervision and enforcement
2	• Protect and facilitate the exercise of shareholder rights • Ensure the equitable treatment of all shareholders, including minority and foreign shareholders
3	• Provide sound incentives throughout the investment chain and provide for stock markets to function in a way that contributes to good corporate governance
4	• Recognize the rights of stakeholders established by law or through mutual agreements • Encourage active co-operation between corporations and stakeholders in creating wealth, jobs, and the sustainability of financially sound enterprises
5	• Ensure that timely and accurate disclosure is made on all material matters regarding the corporation, including the financial situation, performance, ownership and governance
6	Board responsibilities: • Ensure strategic guidance of the company, effective monitoring of management by the board and the board's accountability to the company and the shareholders • Apply high ethical standards and take into account the interests of stakeholders • Align key executive and board remuneration with the longer term interests of the company and shareholders • Exercise effective independent judgment on corporate affairs • Consider a sufficient number of non-executive board members capable of exercising independent judgment

Source: OECD (2015) *G20/OECD Principles of Corporate Governance*, OECD Publishing, at www.oecd-ilibrary.org

directors individuals appointed by the company to bear ultimate responsibility for the company's activities; collectively referred to as the board of directors

board of directors body comprising all the directors of a company, including executive and non-executive, which is accountable to the company's shareholders; can be a single board or a two-tier board

co-determination principle of stakeholder participation in corporate governance, usually involving a two-tier board, with employee representation on the supervisory board

executive directors directors who actively manage the company

chief executive officer (CEO) the company's senior executive, who oversees its management and is accountable to the board of directors

management all the processes of planning, organizing and controlling the firm's business

version (OECD, 2015). Participants were keenly aware that corporate governance had come under the spotlight following the financial crisis. Key principles in the new version appear in Table 1.1, above. They largely replicate those in the previous version, including the recognition of the role of stakeholders, the protection of the status of minority shareholders and the assertion of the need for non-executive directors to be independent. However, it is notable that the first principle now asserts the need for 'fair' markets, rather than 'efficient' markets, as had appeared in the 2004 version.

Although the senior executives are probably the most influential people in the company, the highest legal authority is its board of directors. **Directors** bear ultimate responsibility for the company's activities. Collectively, they constitute the **board of directors**, accountable to the company's shareholders. Structures differ from country to country. In Germany and other European countries, a two-tier board of directors is the norm. A supervisory board holds the ultimate authority for major decisions, while a management board is responsible for day-to-day management. The single board is the norm in the Anglo-American type of structure, shown in Figure 1.5. It is based on the belief that shareholders' interests are paramount. Board members have oversight over major decisions and owe duties to act in the best interests of the company as a whole, which, in practice, is equated with the interests of the shareholders. Where the state controls a company, there is a potential conflict between the government's political goals and the best interests of the company as an enterprise. For example, executives might wish to slim down the workforce, but political leaders wish to retain as many jobs as possible. The supervisory board in the two-tier system includes employee representation, reflecting the principle of **co-determination**. The two-tier model is often said to represent a stakeholder approach to governance, in contrast to the focus on shareholder value that characterizes the single-tier model. However, the supervisory board in the German two-tier structure has also been criticized as being under the control of dominant shareholders (Enriques and Volpin, 2007).

The directors who actively manage the company are its **executive directors**, headed by a **chief executive officer (CEO)**. The CEO occupies a pivotal role in decision-making and management of the company. The CEO is at the pinnacle of the company's **management**, which consists of all the processes of planning, organizing and controlling the firm's business. The firm's managerial staff are all responsible to the CEO. In turn, the CEO must answer to the board, maintain the

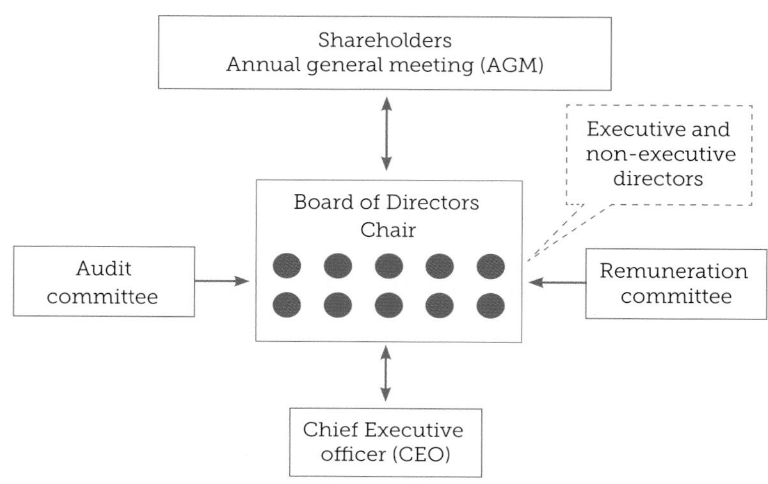

Figure 1.5 The single-tier board of directors

 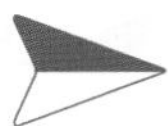

confidence of shareholders, inspire the company's workforce and deal with an array of stakeholders. Whenever the company's fortunes take a turn for the worse, the CEO is in the firing line.

non-executive directors part-time company directors who are independent of the firm's management and owners

Non-executive directors are considered independent of the firm's management and owners, although independence is questionable in some cases: in many countries personal ties and ownership stakes are considered not to impact on independent status. The non-executive director carries out board duties on a part-time basis, and, in theory, exerts more objective judgment on the company's activities than working managers do. The onus is on non-executives to take their responsibilities seriously, and actively query the CEO over strategy. Non-executives are equally liable legally for corporate wrongdoing which they ought to have been aware of. There has been a tendency to appoint other CEOs and retired CEOs as non-executive directors. Having a managerial viewpoint themselves, these appointees are hardly likely to offer an outsider's perspective. This approach is now changing, as uncritical boards have been implicated in a number of situations where misguided strategies and excessive executive rewards were allowed to go unchecked. An example is Enron, the energy trading company which collapsed in 2001. Enron had a corporate governance system which looked admirable on paper. However, its senior executives were able to steer the company towards their own goals, and the bodies which should have provided a check on their actions (such as the board and its committees) failed to do so.

More recently, excessive risk-taking was blamed in a series of bank failures which led to the global financial crisis of 2008, including Lehman Brothers of the US, once the country's fourth-largest investment bank, which collapsed under a mountain of $60 billion in bad debts. Other banks, deemed to be too big to fail, such as Citigroup, were rescued by US government bailouts. The UK government came to the rescue of major banks, RBS and Lloyds. These banks had become highly globalized and indebted, and had also become imbued with a corporate culture that rewarded short-term gains which involved excessive risk-taking (see Chapter 8). Executives of failed banks seemed to escape unscathed following the crisis, even continuing to receive bonus payments. It was acknowledged that regulatory failures, as well as misguided strategies by managers, had been to blame. Could better regulation have prevented the crisis? This is discussed in Chapter 8 and revisited in Chapter 12, in the context of managing a sustainable business.

Company law is a part of the national law in most countries. These laws generally relate to company formation, the formal obligations of directors and financial reporting requirements. In areas where there are formal laws, compliance is mandatory. However, there are many areas of corporate governance, such as the issues listed in the OECD Principles in Table 1.1, that are not usually covered by company law. Some are covered by guidance set out in codes of practice that are non-binding. This is sometimes called 'self-regulation': companies are urged, but not compelled, to adopt best practices. The UK first adopted such a code in 1992. The code has undergone several revisions, the current version of which is the UK Corporate Governance Code of 2018 (Financial Reporting Council, 2018). This latest code relies on the 'comply or explain' approach, placing the onus on the company to either comply or explain why it is not complying with each principle in the code. This means that executives cannot simply ignore principles such as the appointment of non-executive directors: they have an obligation to provide meaningful explanations if they choose not to do so. Although the code has been recently revised, consultation began almost immediately between the UK government, businesses and regulatory bodies, with a view to further reforms of the regulatory framework on corporate governance. Among the issues that were addressed were executive remuneration, the role of the non-executive directors and the duty to strike a balance between shareholder value and the interests of other stakeholders, notably employees. This new review thus reflects the public disquiet that has continued to fester following corporate failures and controversial practices, including excessive executive remuneration and tax avoidance arrangements. Will a change of corporate culture be possible, or will a more heavy-handed regulatory approach be adopted? We will return to the ongoing issues surrounding corporate governance in Chapter 11.

How can the board of directors better perform its responsibilities of monitoring management decisions?

Boards of directors have been the targets of criticism in recent years, for having been acquiescent when managers were pursuing risky strategies. In particular, non-executive directors who are themselves CEOs are not likely to 'rock the boat'. What benefits can the independent director contribute to more effective monitoring of the company?

An overview of the global environment

The dimensions of the business environment stem largely from the characteristics which go to make up societies: every society has a cultural heritage, a social makeup, distinctive economic activities, political arrangements, one or more legal frameworks and technological capacities. A description of each of these aspects of a society gives a picture of the society as a whole. These dimensions do not stop at national borders. For each dimension, there is an array of interactions ranging from the local community to national and international influences. In fact these interactions have multiplied with deepening globalization. We look first at the distinctive characteristics of each dimension.

Multiple dimensions and the PESTLE analysis

PESTLE analysis of a national environment which stands for political, economic, socio-cultural, technological, legal and environmental dimensions

A common tool of analysis of the business environment is the **PESTLE** analysis, as shown in Figure 1.6. Next to each of the six dimensions there is a short list of three aspects of the dimension that make it distinctive. Many more items could be listed, but these lists highlight some of the main features. These aspects are described briefly in the text that follows.

The PESTLE analysis provides a tool for analyzing six key dimensions of the environment. This book devotes a chapter to each of these, and includes a separate chapter on the financial environment. The financial environment is closely related to the economic dimension, but nonetheless merits a separate chapter. National economic systems remain the backbone of the global economy: how they work for businesses and societies is a major focus of this chapter. The chapter on the financial environment provides an explanation of global financial markets and their interactions with national factors. The dimensions of the environment are interrelated. Insofar as the PESTLE analysis takes the dimensions separately, it is a blunt tool for analysis. It also tends to take a rather static view, not capturing changes over time. In this book, we aim to do both: to look at background forces and changes taking place. In many instances, there is tension between established norms and institutions, on the one hand, and newer forces seeking to bring about changes – often changes emanating from outside the country. Bearing these dynamics in mind, we describe each of these dimensions below, in the order that they appear in the PESTLE analysis, with the addition of the financial environment at the end.

Figure 1.6 PESTLE analysis in the international business environment

Political
• Political stability • Form of government, e.g. democratic, authoritarian • Level of freedoms, e.g. freedom of expression and association • Incentives to foreign investors • Level of transparency in political decision making • Level of corruption in business and political ties
Economic
• Level of economic development • Trends in GDP • Rate of inflation • Wage levels and level of unemployment • Strength of currency and convertibility • Rates of taxation
Socio-cultural
• Growth rate of population, and age distribution of population • Language(s) • Main religious and cultural groupings • Educational attainment levels • Level of social cohesion • Role of women
Technological
• Government spending on R&D • Legal regime for patent protection • Energy availability and costs • Transport infrastructure and costs • Innovation system, including availability of skilled workforce • Level of technology transfer
Legal
• Rule of law • Independent judicial system • Fair, impartial implementation of the law • Contract law and procedural clarity • Recognition of international law • Adherence to human rights law
Environmental
• Environmental protection measures • Climate change impacts • Biodiversity • Pollution, such as reductions in urban air pollution • Clean technology • Recycling technology

The dimensions in detail are as follows:

- Political (Chapter 5) – This dimension focuses on the formal system of government and on the groups that vie for political power in the country. Political systems vary from those with democratic institutions to those where authoritarian structures rule out most meaningful democratic participation. All businesses, domestic and foreign, seek a stable political environment, but whether democracy is more stable is not self-evident. Political risks arise in any system, and businesses take these into account in making investment decisions.

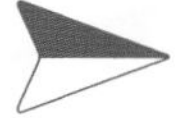

- Economic (Chapter 4) – What kind of economic activities make up the livelihoods of the country's population? What are the country's sources of wealth and how industrialized is it? Historically, industrialization contributes to growth and economic development. But growth should lead to **sustainable development**. Sustainable development looks beyond current needs to those of future generations, covering all in society as well as environmental concerns. Globalization, and especially the role of foreign direct investment (discussed in the next chapter), have been major trends, promoting economic growth in many developing economies.

sustainable development view of economic development involving continuing investment for future generations, taking into account the long-term viability of industries, both in terms of human values and environmental protection

- Socio-cultural (Chapter 3) – This dimension looks at the values, attitudes and identities of the groups that make up a society, including minority groups. Social cohesion is an aspect of the environment that concerns businesses, especially in any context of possible social tension. The education system of the country, from primary education to university level, is an indicator of the country's commitment to the individual betterment of all its inhabitants. While the spread of western consumer lifestyles associated with economic development are a global phenomenon, national cultures remain a potent force.
- Technological (Chapter 9) – To what extent does the country encourage the use of applied scientific knowledge for practical purposes? The depth of a country's scientific education and training, as well as the extent of government funding for R&D, are indicators of the country's technological environment. It is important for businesses that new products and inventions which are the creative outputs of their researchers are protected in law. These are assets that can be protected by laws relating to **intellectual property (IP)**. They include patents for the firm's inventions; copyright for written works, music, film and software; and trademarks, such as company logos. As countries climb the technological ladder, the protection and enforcement of IP rights are demanded by businesses.

intellectual property (IP) property in intangible assets, such as patents, copyrights and trademarks, which can be legally protected

- Legal (Chapter 6) – Every country has one or more systems of laws, backed up by the authority of the state. This area covers how laws are made and how they are enforced in practice. In any country, businesses look for clarity and predictability in the laws which pertain to them, with fair, impartial implementation and enforcement. These characteristics indicate the existence of the rule of law in a country. Where a country is fragmented, with differing lawmaking authorities in separate regions, instability can result, making it more difficult to do business in the country, especially for foreign firms unfamiliar with the differing authorities. Cross-border legal actions, involving both national and international law, have become more significant for companies in the era of deepening international ties.
- Environmental (Chapter 10) – This dimension focuses on sustainability and environmental protection. Environmental degradation in today's world has been caused largely by human activity, especially through industrialization, urbanization and modern large-scale agriculture. Businesses are gaining greater knowledge and awareness of the environmental impacts of their operations in differing locations, as well as their impacts on global phenomena such as climate change. Resource scarcity and climate change are increasingly becoming imperatives for corporate strategists to take into account.
- Financial (Chapter 8) – Finance, including banking and other financial services, is essential for governments, businesses and individuals. National financial systems differ in their openness to outsiders, their transparency and their levels of regulation. Most countries' financial systems have become more open in

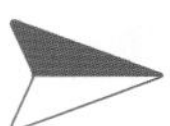

recent years, but the trend towards global financial markets has led to raised levels of risk and volatility. These risks can have devastating impacts in societies, as the global financial crisis of 2008 has shown. Regulation at both national and international levels has become a crucial element in maintaining financial stability.

MINI CASE STUDY

The Brazilian mining disaster and BHP Billiton

BHP Billiton is one of the world's leading mining companies. It is one of the world's largest iron ore exporters, the other large competitors being Vale of Brazil and Rio Tinto of Australia. BHP Billiton and Vale came together to form a joint venture, Samarco, to operate an iron ore mine in Brazil. A catastrophic accident at the Samarco mine occurred in 2015, when an earthwork dam that contained mining waste burst and set off a mudslide of iron ore waste into the river, the Rio Doce. The collapse of the dam killed 19 people. It destroyed several small communities and became Brazil's worst environmental disaster to date. The water supply of hundreds of thousands of people was contaminated. The owners of the joint venture had experienced difficulties with the drainage, and changed the design of the dam between 2011 and 2012. However, the drainage became less efficient, leading to a dangerous build-up and ultimately to the collapse of the dam. The mine could not re-open for the foreseeable future, and BHP Billiton was compelled to write off its investment.

Samarco was legally a separate company, and both civil and criminal proceedings were launched against it. Its president, five other executives and one contractor were charged with homicide over the disaster. While Samarco and its staff were more directly involved, the design failing would have been a matter for the owners of the joint venture. Compensation for the social and environmental damage, along with remedial actions, would amount to huge sums, for which the owners of Samarco were liable. An agreement between the two owners and Brazil's federal authorities set the claim at a sum of nearly $47 bn, with initial payments to be made to help the victims.

In Australia, shareholders in BHP Billiton commenced legal action against the company, arguing that they had suffered losses as a result of the disaster. Three thousand investors joined the lawsuit against the company. The company's value had declined some $14 billion in the months following the disaster, the share price falling 22%. BHP Billiton was thus embroiled in legal actions from the accident itself and from the consequent economic losses suffered by its investors.

Mining is a perilous business in any environment. The risks in this particularly sensitive region in Brazil meant that design issues had to be beyond doubt, and extra precautions and monitoring should have been constant preoccupations. These high standards were not observed, and the result was Brazil's worst mining disaster up until

A tragic mining disaster at Samarco in Brazil, pictured here, shone the spotlight on the role of global mining companies.

then. Unfortunately, a similar dam collapse followed four years later in the same region, with a far higher death toll. The tragedy in 2019 took place near the town of Brumandinho. The mine was operated by Vale, and the death toll was estimated to be in the region of 280 people. The tragedy was again linked to the accumulation of mining waste which caused a mudslide. Brazil's mining regulator has now recognized that this type of system is not safe, ordering existing operations to be phased out and no new projects to be licensed. However, Vale faces legal liability for the failure of its safety procedures. Several executives were arrested shortly after the disaster.

Questions

- Where does the greater part of the blame lie for the collapse of the dam?
- Which dimensions of the business environment are involved in this case study? Explain the relevance of each of these.

Find out more

See the article by Dom Phillips, 'Brazil dam disaster: Firm knew of potential impact months in advance', 1 March, 2018, in *The Guardian*.

The multi-layered environment

Any dimension will have a layered perspective in terms of geography, as shown in Figure 1.7. For example, the political environment is made up of the local community, national government and international relations. For enterprises, it is necessary to see both the small picture, such as local politics, as well as the big picture, which might be the country's position in relation to trading partners. In fact, understanding the big picture sometimes helps in understanding local currents, and vice versa. Thus, local political leaders could well wish to attract a foreign investor from a country with which there is a trade and investment agreement.

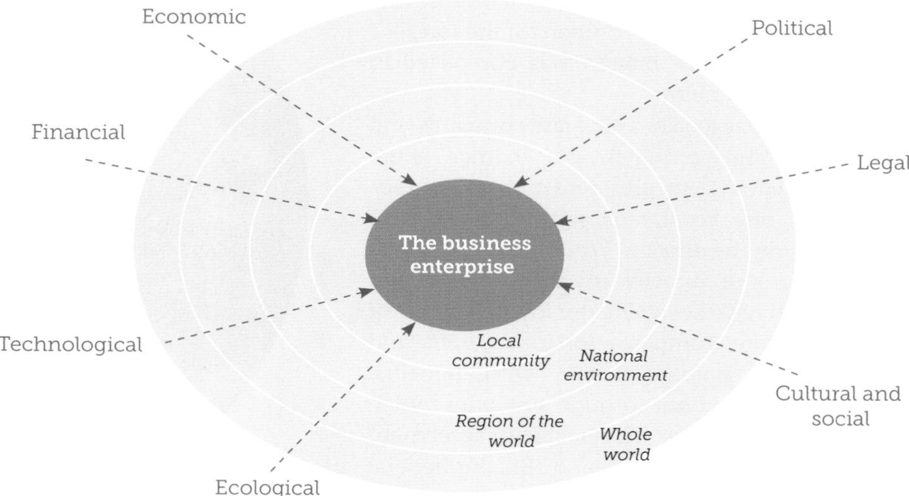

Figure 1.7 The dimensions and layers of the international environment

It is common to speak of *global* firms facing competition in the *global* environment, but in fact, global competition is frequently played out in local environments. Local companies, with their intimate knowledge of local markets, can be some of the toughest competitors which global companies encounter. An example is the stiff competition faced by McDonald's in China from local fast-food chains.

The international environment can be conceived as layered spatial areas, visualized as concentric circles, beginning with the smallest unit, the local community. Local communities exist in the larger unit of the country, which is itself part of a geographic region, and beyond that, the world. These layers are shown in Table 1.2. The table gives examples of key phenomena as well as relevant institutions and organizations in each sphere. There is considerable interaction and interdependence among these different spheres as countries and regions become more interconnected. Growing connectedness among people and organizations is a quintessential aspect of globalization, discussed in the next chapter. It is tempting to fall for the view that all aspects of the business environment are inevitably moving towards the global, but this would be a mistake. Some aspects of the international environment have seen greater international co-operation, such as the Paris climate change agreement of 2015, but each layer of the environment has its own characteristics and players. Although they are becoming interconnected, they are not melding together into a whole, but retain distinctiveness, which business strategists ignore at their peril.

Table 1.2 Dimensions and layers of the international environment

Layers & Dimensions	Local community	National environment	Region of the world	Whole world
Socio-cultural	Families; local customs; schools; urban or rural	National culture; language; sense of shared history	Cultural affinity across the region; movement of people between countries	Human rights; world religions; consumer culture
Economic	Local businesses; predominant industries	National industries; industrial structure; national income and economic growth	Degree of economic integration; regional trade relations	Global economic integration; WTO and multilateral trade agreements; global companies and industries
Political	Local government and politics	Political system; degree of civil and political freedoms	Degree of political co-operation; shared institutions (e.g. the EU)	International governmental co-operation (e.g. the UN)
Legal	Delegated lawmaking; planning; health & safety	Rule of law; independent judiciary and court system; national legislation	Legal harmonization; mutual recognition of court judgments	International law and the International Court of Justice (ICJ)
Technological	Schools and colleges; research centres	National school system; universities; government funding for R&D	Cross-border research ties; co-operation among universities	Global spread of breakthrough technology; global R&D networks
Financial	Penetration of banks and financial services	National financial system; regulatory system	Cross-border financial flows; regional regulation (e.g. the European Central Bank)	Global financial flows; international institutions (e.g. the IMF & World Bank)
Environmental	Ecosystems; pollution levels; air quality	Areas of environmental stress; environmental protection laws	Regional institutions; co-operation over regional resources (e.g. rivers)	Climate change; international co-operation on emissions reduction

We look at each of these layers from the perspective of the business.

- Local community – Wherever the MNE operates or where its products are made, there will be a local community in which its impacts are immediate. A factory or other industrial process affects local people and the natural environment in the area. Production can bring jobs and wealth, but impacts on the environment can potentially be damaging. These are stakeholder issues which involve dialogue within local communities.

- National environment – The national environment is probably the most influential for a business. National laws cover company regulation, employment conditions and the environment. A country's national culture is influential in strategic decisions about potential markets and location of operations. A country's political system and leadership decide the policies which influence how stable it will be for foreign business investors.
- Region of the world – Every country is located in a region and is drawn into relations with neighbouring countries. These relations can give rise to conflicts – regional wars are sadly not uncommon. But, more often, relations between neighbours are beneficial. Regional trade agreements have flourished in recent years, allowing for free movement of goods between countries in the region. The European Union (EU) is the most highly developed regional grouping (discussed in Chapters 4 and 5). Regions can pool resources to deal with common threats such as climate change.
- World – There is increasing awareness of global phenomena, such as climate change, which require co-operation among all players, both businesses and governments, at all levels. Global regulatory frameworks have been established to co-ordinate these efforts. This is happening in respect of climate change. It is also happening in the area of human rights and financial regulation. Although national structures have been dominant in these areas, international frameworks are gaining authority. The international organizations highlighted in Table 1.2 are introduced in the next chapter. Business strategists are now looking beyond national regulation to rule-making at international level.

The way I see it ...

On the competitive environment, 'The lesson to me is differentiate yourself...Move up the value chain. Being cheaper isn't enough. Being the low-cost provider is temporal.'

Sam Palmisano, former CEO of IBM, in an interview with CRN technology news, 23 February, 2011, at www.crn.com

Sam Palmisano guided IBM through a period (2003–2011) when it was making the transition from hardware to services, and also towards social goals, for example, in local supply chains that take into account community needs. He is now the head of the Center for Global Enterprise (www.thecge.net), which focuses on sustainability in the global environment. See 'IBM's Sam Palmisano: Always put the enterprise ahead of the individual', article and podcast, 18 January 2012, Knowledge@Wharton, at http://knowledge.wharton.upenn.edu

What advice would Palmisano offer to today's high-tech giants on the sustainable business?

The enterprise in a dynamic environment: Building sustainability

What is the best long-term strategy for the firm? What should it be doing, and where? These questions involve sustainability, looking beyond questions such as how successful the firm's products are in today's consumer markets. The challenges become more complex as the business becomes extended globally, through supply chains, diverse investors and evolving markets. An issue raised early on in this chapter was that of how the firm sees its business in the future. Apart from the subsistence entrepreneur, who has few aspirations except making a living, businesses seek more than simply to

carry on in existence in the future. Most businesses have goals that reflect values and a mission of a higher order, such as innovating to produce better products or products that use fewer scarce resources. Indeed, the firm that adopts a 'business as usual' approach in today's international markets could face a harsh awakening when rivals' innovations win over its customers. The aspects of sustainability are shown in Figure 1.8, which was featured in the Introduction to this book. Here, we look at how they apply to a range of direct stakeholders as well as broader considerations of societal wellbeing.

It has become customary to say that the company exists to enhance shareholder value, as we have noted. But while this is often equated with rising share price and rising profits, these goals, too, look rather limited in today's world. Economic prosperity, to be sustainable, must encompass society as a whole. But economic prosperity is only one aspect of human wellbeing. The notion of individual and societal wellbeing encompasses human rights and social justice as essential elements. Similarly, action on climate change and the natural environment promote a sustainable future for individuals, families and whole communities. These challenges confront governments as well as businesses. The figure highlights governance that promotes social goods. Crucially, governance includes both business actors and government actors, as well as international actors such as inter-governmental organizations.

The global financial crisis of 2008 brought home to all the need for prudent regulation to ensure financial stability. Yet, as we will find throughout this book, risks continue to abound in global financial markets, and corporate leaders are under the spotlight for the ethics of their business models and strategies. All stakeholders, including shareholders, look for innovative products, but also products which reflect high ethical standards, including attentiveness to issues such as human rights, the environment and social goals. These are among the challenges of the sustainable business. Just looking to the next set of profit figures is short term. The sustainable business thus embraces responsibilities that reflect its participation in society.

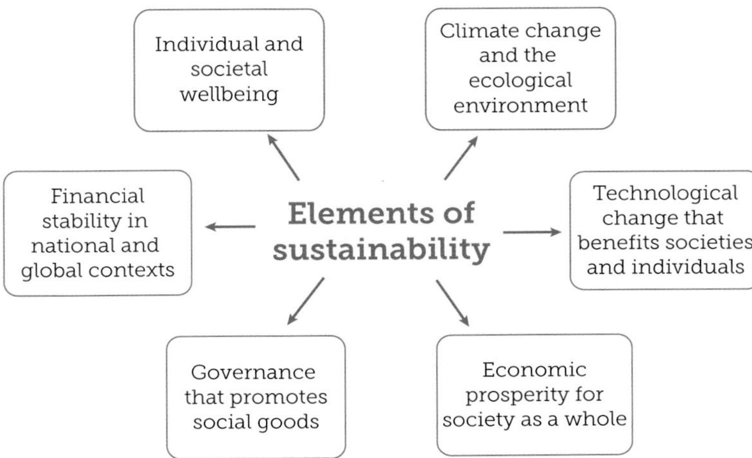

Figure 1.8 Elements of sustainability

Technological change is usually viewed as bringing improvements and efficiencies in processes, bringing economic benefits to the innovative firms at the forefront of technological advances, and to the societies in which the new technology is adopted. Entrepreneurial businesses are often highly innovative. Much technological innovation is now focused on sustainable goals, such as green technology, but technological change inherently disrupts existing ways of doing things, often leading to the demise of old industries, along with the livelihoods of people who had depended on them. MNEs are now able to achieve maximum efficiencies from global supply chains, benefiting from the use of low-cost manufacturing environments. This trend, discussed further in the next chapter, has had significant impacts in both home and host countries. Consumers in developed countries have benefited from a huge range of products at lower prices than those manufactured in their own countries. Host economies have benefited from the investment of foreign companies, the employment created, and the opportunities to gain valuable technological expertise. That, at least, is the theory. In practice, questions arise as to how sustainable this outsourcing model is over time. The MNE is likely to move to an even cheaper manufacturing location when the opportunity arises, leaving behind a range of economic, financial and social challenges for the governmental authorities of the former host country.

When a firm fails or chooses to close down operations in a given location, the impacts can be far-reaching, extending well beyond the loss of jobs in that firm. Other businesses in the community, such as retailers and caterers, will become precarious. Unemployment inevitably rises, and so does public spending on unemployment and other benefits. People who had no direct connections with the company could well find themselves out of work and struggling financially. It is no wonder that governments come under political pressure to tighten the regulation of foreign investors. Most regulation occurs at the national level, but global companies can – and do – choose countries on the basis of their 'light-touch' regulation, avoiding those that are more stringently regulated. We have highlighted national regulatory failures in the finance sector. Competition among countries to attract foreign investors has become a familiar feature of the global environment. Countries where taxes and social charges levied on companies are high tend to attract fewer foreign investors than countries without these provisions. This situation creates an apparent 'race to the bottom' which is anathema to building sustainability from a country's perspective. It is arguable that co-operation among governments to co-ordinate regulations would be a way of responding to the aggressive profit-seeking strategies of some MNEs. While this might seem unlikely in a competitive economic environment, political leaders, as well as corporate decision-makers, are now recognizing the need for encouraging sustainability in wealth-generating activities.

Conclusions

This chapter has highlighted internal aspects of a variety of business enterprises, including goals, organization and governance, which influence how they go about their activities and how decisions are taken. The relevant terminology, from IPOs to stakeholders, will recur throughout the book. The values and interests of the individual people behind corporate logos are key to shaping how the business behaves. The backgrounds of these actors on the business landscape have become increasingly diverse. Understanding diverse business environments has thus risen as a priority for managers. As this chapter has shown, the context provides much valuable information about firm behaviour in the past, and the ways in which changes might take place in the future. The chapter has provided an overview of the multiple dimensions of the environment which will be explored in future chapters. It has also set out the differing geographic layers of the environment, from local to international, which impact on the business enterprise. An awareness of these layers helps to understand why firms behave as they do. A local issue, such as emissions from a factory, is a matter for the inhabitants of the community most affected. It is an issue that should be addressed by their government (both local and national). But it is now also a global concern in that emissions contribute to rising temperatures globally.

The geographical scanning of MNEs has had consequences in the ways companies perceive the international environment. Developing countries which host outsourced manufacturing are no longer perceived as remote by brand owners and consumers. Workers in outsourced factories are stakeholders of the MNE, even though not employed by it. The host country's government, too, is a stakeholder, whose law and policies are influential for the MNE. In addition, growing concern at

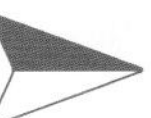

international level regarding human rights has heightened awareness of this issue among the company's most valued stakeholders – its shareholders. For the student of international business, the coming together of global and local forces is one of the aspects of the business environment which is becoming most challenging.

CLOSING CASE STUDY

Ikea at the crossroads

India might seem an unlikely market for Ikea, the Swedish furniture retailer, to open new stores, but these are changing times in global consumer markets, and the rising middle classes in emerging economies are attracting some of the world's most established retailers. Hardly any could be considered more established in western developed economies than Ikea, famous for its self-assembly furniture and lifestyle furnishings. Ikea's business, originating as a small shop in rural Sweden in 1943, was the creation of its legendary founder, Ingvar Kamprad. By all accounts, Kamprad had an extraordinary entrepreneurial flair, and his vision drove the business throughout his long career, until his death in 2018 at the age of 91. By then, he had ceased to take an active role in running the company, but his departure symbolically marked a crossroads in Ikea's history. How would it cope with the changing environment, especially without the visionary flair of the founder?

Ikea has been highly successful in developing a business model that taps into the needs of consumers for affordable furniture and furnishings. It has expanded to 411 stores in 49 countries. These are huge out-of-town warehouse-type stores. Customers usually drive a considerable distance to the store, and take away the flat-pack furniture to assemble at home. Ikea's expansion coincided with a combination of surging car ownership and home ownership, often in rapidly-growing suburban areas on the outskirts of cities. Customers were often young families looking to furnish their new homes on a relatively tight budget, undeterred by the challenges of assembling the furniture themselves. Contrast this scenario with today's environment. Younger customers are still looking for affordability, but are likely to be living in rented apartments in city centres, far away from a traditional Ikea store, and they are less likely to be car owners. They tend to make many of their purchases online, where they can compare prices among competing sellers.

Ikea's executives have responded to the challenges of changing shopping habits by opening smaller stores in city centres. For example, it operates pop-up shops for kitchens in a number of European cities. It is also working to develop its online catalogue that will function independently of its stores. More radically, it is planning other digital advances, allowing its goods to be sold on third-party websites such as Amazon and Alibaba. And, of course, it is expanding in emerging markets such as China and India. Ikea has long expanded into new markets, and has adapted to national preferences in each. For example, its restaurant menus that feature Swedish meatballs are adapted to tastes in differing countries. Offering chicken and vegetarian meatballs in its restaurants in India is relatively straightforward. But furniture

Flat-pack furniture appeals to budget-conscious consumers, but assembling it can be a challenge.

retailing is more challenging in India. Indians are not accustomed to DIY furniture assembly. Lower middle-class customers are looking mainly for low prices, whereas more affluent customers seek high-quality wood items, which they tend to buy from Indian firms. Ikea could find itself occupying the uncomfortable middle ground. Still, in a country of 1.25 billion people, that middle ground would still consist of a lot of potential consumers.

Although the Swedish flags were waving proudly at the inauguration of the Indian store, Ikea, in fact, is hardly a Swedish company. The many companies that make up its complex structure are organized under two parent companies, both owned by foundations which are located in Liechtenstein and the Netherlands. These corporate structures were designed to minimize tax and to cast a veil over the two companies' governance. It is clear that the family has maintained overall control over the companies. The founder was said to be worth €58 billion in the years before his death, making him among the world's richest men. Ethical question marks continue to cast a shadow over the companies' tax arrangements, and there are challenges, too, for Ikea's sustainability profile. The company is one of the world's biggest users of timber. Much of its furniture is of lower quality compressed wood, which is not very durable. The company has been criticized for this approach of producing vast quantities of low-cost, disposable furniture which is environmentally unsustainable. It has taken this criticism seriously, and has explored recycling solutions. But it is difficult to escape the fact that the quintessential Ikea product, such as the Billy bookcase, is at the heart of its business model. Ikea is at the crossroads of a new era without its visionary founder, and is confronting both competitive and ethical challenges. In a strategic innovation, Ikea has launched a subsidiary company that specializes in purpose-built, low-cost housing. Beginning in Scandinavian countries, the new company has now launched in the UK. This new venture recognizes the growing need for sustainable housing that is affordable and relatively simple to construct.

Questions

- What are the strengths of Ikea's business model?
- In what respects has retailing changed since Ikea conceived its large-format stores in out-of-town locations?
- Have you been to an Ikea store? If so, how would you rate it as a shopping experience?
- What are the challenges facing Ikea, and what are its prospects of meeting them?

Further reading

See the article by Richard Milne, 'What will Ikea build next?', 3 February 2018, in the *Financial Times*, at www.ft.com

Multiple choice questions

Visit www.macmillanihe.com/morrison-gbe-5e to take a quick self-test quiz on what you have read in this chapter.

Review questions

1. How does a business decide what its goals will be?
2. Define stakeholders and explain the stakeholder approach to corporate strategy.
3. What is CSR, and why is it becoming more important in the formation of corporate goals?
4. What are the advantages and disadvantages of being a sole trader?
5. What are the aspects of the limited company which distinguish it from other types of business ownership?
6. What is distinctive about the entrepreneurial enterprise?
7. What is a franchise arrangement? Give some examples.
8. How does a private company differ from a public limited company (PLC)?
9. What is distinctive about the MNE as a type of organization?
10. How does corporate governance differ from the day-to-day management of a company?

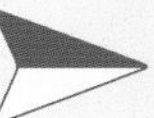

11 Why are independent (non-executive) directors considered essential in corporate governance?
12 Explain the shareholder and stakeholder perspectives on corporate governance.
13 What is the role of stakeholders in the two-tier board of directors?
14 Describe each of the main functions within the business enterprise.
15 What are the advantages and limitations of a PESTLE analysis?

✓ Assignments

1 Offer advice to the following CEO: Ralph is the CEO of a high-tech company in an EU country. The business has been highly innovative in computing expertise. He has built up the business from its early days as a start-up, and now has an established business model. Ralph has recently had an offer for the business from a large MNE, that values his company at €1 billion. He is tempted, but he would lose control of the business. What should he do? Set out your advice on whether he should take the offer.

2 The PESTLE analysis was designed to illuminate specific dimensions of a national environment. How can it be adapted to take into account other dimensions and broader scope, bringing in regional and global impacts?

Further reading

Bartlett, C., and Ghoshal, S. (2002) *Managing Across Borders: The transnational solution*, 2nd edition (Boston: Harvard Business School Press).

Brooks, I. (2018) *Organisational Behaviour: Individuals, groups and organisation*, 5th edition (Pearson).

Hickson, D., and Pugh, D.S. (2007) *Writers on Organizations* (London: Penguin).

Kay, J. (2007) *Foundations of Corporate Success* (Oxford: Oxford University Press).

Maon, F., Lingreen, A., and V. Swaen (2009) 'Designing and implementing corporate social responsibility: An integrative framework grounded in theory and practice', *Journal of Business Ethics*, 87(1): 71–89.

Prahalad, C.K. (2009) *The Fortune at the Bottom of the Pyramid* (Philadelphia: Wharton School Publishing).

Pugh, D.S. (ed) (2008) *Organization Theory: Selected readings*, 5th edition (London: Penguin Books).

Tricker, R.I. (2015) *Corporate Governance: Principles, policies and practices*, 3rd edition (Oxford University Press).

Wheelen, T., and Hunger, J., A. Hoffman, and C. Bamford (2017) *Strategic Management and Business Policy*, 15th edition (Pearson).

References

Campbell, P., and Pooley, C., 'Tesla tumbles as SEC accuses Musk of fraud', *The Guardian*, 29 September 2018.

Carroll, A.B. and Shabana, K.M. (2010) 'The business case for corporate social responsibility: A review of concepts, research and practice', *International Journal of Management Reviews*, 85–105.

De Kok, J., Deijl, C. and Veldhuis-Van Essen, C. (2013) *Is Small Still Beautiful? Literature review of recent empirical evidence on the contribution of SMEs to employment creation* (Geneva, ILO).

Enriques, L., and Volpin, P. (2007) 'Corporate governance reforms in continental Europe', *The Journal of Economic Perspectives*, 21(1): 117–140.

Financial Reporting Council (2018) UK Corporate Governance Code, at www.frc.org.uk

Freeman, R.E. (1984) *Strategic Management: A stakeholder approach* (Boston, MA: Pitman).

Milne, R. (2018) 'What will Ikea build next?', *Financial Times*, 3 February.

Murman, J. and Sandana, D. (2012) 'Successful entrepreneurs minimize risk', *Australian Journal of Management*, 38(1): 191–215.

OECD (2015) *G20/OECD Principles of Corporate Governance*, OECD Publishing, at https://oecd-ilibrary.org

Ovans, A. (2015) 'What is a business model?', *Harvard Business Review*, 23 January, at www.hbr.org

Schoar, A. (2010) 'The divide between subsistence and transformational entrepreneurship', *Innovation Policy and the Economy*, 10(1): 57–81.

Tanev, S. (2012) 'Global from the start: the characteristics of born-global firms in the technology sector', *Technology Innovation Management Review*, March, 5–8.

Wayne, L. (2012) 'How Delaware thrives as a corporate tax haven', *New York Times*, 30 June, at *www.nytimes.com*

Visit the companion website at www.macmillanihe.com/morrison-gbe-5e for further learning and teaching resources.

GLOBALIZATION AND THE BUSINESS ENVIRONMENT

Outline of chapter

This chapter will enable you to

- Gain an overview of globalization
- Identify and interpret differing impacts of globalization in differing national environments, including developed and developing countries
- Distinguish the main modes of internationalization, together with their underlying rationales
- Understand globalization's impacts on societies
- Critically assess sustainability in the global environment

OPENING CASE STUDY

SoftBank, the Japanese technology giant

Technological innovation has a long history in Japan, but many of its famous companies, such as Sony and Toshiba, have been rather eclipsed in recent years by other Asian companies, especially younger companies from China. SoftBank, however, is a company that has taken a rather different route from its compatriots, largely thanks to the guidance of its founder, Masayoshi Son. Son started the company as a telecommunications business in 1981. Since then, he has guided the business towards a greater emphasis on technology and innovation. He has overseen a strategy of acquiring companies that offer prospects for future growth through innovation. And he has also started an investment fund that focuses on exciting innovations. This two-pronged strategy marks him out as more adventurous and willing to take risks than the more conservative image of most Japanese business leaders. As a result, SoftBank has become a technological conglomerate with prospects of development in a number of research areas.

In keeping with Son's knack for spotting transformative new technologies, SoftBank invested in both Didi, the Chinese ride-hailing company, as well as Uber, its major rival. SoftBank has also formed a partnership with Toyota, to research self-driving vehicles. SoftBank introduced its robot, Pepper, to the world in 2014, creating a media stir with the claim it could sense human emotions. The company drew attention in the UK when it acquired the technology company, ARM, in 2016 (see the case study on ARM in the 4th edition of this book, which can be found in the web materials). This acquisition took place after the referendum on Brexit, indicating that SoftBank's confidence in ARM weighed more heavily in its decision than the possibility of Britain leaving the EU.

SoftBank's most recent headline-grabbing event has been the IPO of its Japanese mobile phone business. This was billed as one of Japan's largest ever IPOs, and it raised a sum equivalent to $23 billion, which is nearly as much as that of Alibaba's listing in New York in 2014. SoftBank's IPO, however, was very different in conception. Jack Ma of Alibaba structured his company to retain tight control within his circle of partners. Son was offering 87% of the shares to individual retail investors in Japan, hoping to deliver an attractive dividend payout to these small investors. The shares were priced at a single price of 1,500 yen a share, and he was confident that the IPO would be a huge success. The flotation was even advertised on television – a first in Japan for an IPO. In the event, the shares sold well, 90% selling to ordinary domestic investors, but the IPO proved disappointing, with the shares falling 15% on the first day's trading in late December, 2018. IPOs are always unpredictable to some extent, but, on this occasion, political uncertainties and trade tensions had unsettled global markets.

Son aimed to use much of the money raised in the IPO to fund investments in new technologies through SoftBank's Vision Fund. This is a private equity fund founded in 2017, which has raised over $90 billion from big investors. Saudi Arabia is the major investor, and Apple is also an investor. The role of Saudi Arabia came into question, however, when the Saudi journalist, Jamal Khashoggi, was killed in October 2018, and people close to Saudi Arabia's government were implicated in the crime. A number of business leaders stayed away from a Saudi investment forum due to take place shortly after Khashoggi's disappearance. Son was among those that withdrew from the forum, along with the CEOs of Google and Uber. Son had been thinking of a second Vision Fund, but put that idea on hold, following the doubts over Saudi investments. However, the Saudi government has become a significant investor in new technology companies, and it seemed likely in early 2019 that those investments would continue.

In concept, the Vision Fund represents the SoftBank founder's vision of encouraging the transformative technology

Passengers seek information from Pepper, the robot

that will shape the future. His business acumen and entrepreneurial zeal have been key to turning SoftBank into the technology giant it is today. Along the way, many ideas have faltered, but many have succeeded, and his un-Japanese propensity to take risks has proved to be key to SoftBank's success to date.

Questions

- What were the key features of SoftBank's IPO?
- How does uncertainty in the global environment impact on Softbank's strategy?
- What are the benefits Son hoped to achieve through the Vision Fund?
- Why has Son felt the need to rethink the strategy of the Vision Fund?

Further reading

See the article by Wataru Suzuki, 'SoftBank's Vision Fund 2: more firepower, bigger questions', *Nikkei Asian Review*, 28 August 2019, at https://asia.nikkei.com

Introduction

Since about the second half of the twentieth century, the world has experienced changes in all dimensions of the environment, which have come to be grouped together under the heading 'globalization'. These changes have by now touched nearly everyone, from city dwellers in the rich economies to farmers in rural Africa. Every type of business activity and all sizes of organization have been affected. Industries such as oil stand out as global in nature, but so too do industries like textiles and clothing, which have traditionally been local and national. MNEs have been the main drivers of these changes, but SMEs, too, have benefited from opportunities to broaden their horizons in numerous sectors. Hallmarks of globalization are interconnectedness and interdependence between people, organizations and governments. These ties have been facilitated by improvements in technology, especially in telecommunications, the internet and transport. Yet, while all would agree that the global economy is a reality, the extent and depth of its reach, along with its impacts, are continually debated. Globalization is often praised for its role in economic development, but criticized for social and environmental impacts. There have been winners and losers, in terms of countries, industries and employment, as this chapter will highlight. It will also join the debate on the future of globalization and its impacts in differing contexts. If economic development is to be sustainable, then social and environmental impacts of globalization should be taken into consideration.

The chapter begins by defining globalization, highlighting differing perspectives. The expansion of global production has contributed to economic development, but we find that for many developing countries the good news comes laced with bad, and development's benefits often do not reach the whole of society. Who is to blame? MNEs as key players are a focus of the chapter. Their internationalization strategies are discussed, highlighting the leading theories. While FDI has been transformative, its growth has taken place alongside the broad trend towards global supply chains and outsourcing. These trends have had unequal impacts in the global economy. We identify winners and losers, but we find that the task is more fraught than it seems. A country can be a winner today, attracting significant FDI, but if investors turn away or fail to live up to expectations, FDI can look more like a detriment than a blessing. Such are the contradictions of globalization. These are highlighted in a section on the depth of globalization across the different dimensions of the global environment.

We find that negative impacts on societies have multiple causes, including both corporate behaviour and government policies. The challenges for globalization to be tamed by sustainability are discussed in the final section of the chapter.

The many faces of globalization

We are constantly being reminded that we live in a globalized world. People in the world's richer countries have become accustomed to low-cost consumer goods, internet access from just about anywhere, and worldwide travel as a routine occurrence. Global companies have made this new consumer lifestyle a reality. But in the process, corporate leaders have acquired vast economic power to control outcomes in societies and to bend governments to their corporate agendas. While many people and groups have gained in terms of economic prosperity – at least in the short term – people in both richer and poorer countries are fearful for their livelihoods, living conditions and natural environment. They are also fearful that global companies that are essentially geared to profit-seeking will put at risk core moral values that are central to human dignity, including fulfilling careers, self-expression, political voice and other human rights.

globalization processes by which products, people, companies, money and information are able to move quickly around the world

market mechanisms for exchange of something of value, usually goods or services, for a price, usually money

Globalization can be defined as processes by which products, people, companies, money and information are able to move quickly around the world as decision makers desire, with few cross-border impediments in their way. It is facilitated by an opening of markets in each of these respects. The dismantling of barriers to trade and investment has opened the way for companies to internationalize their businesses. This essentially capitalist notion of the market is a crucial assumption. The **market** refers to mechanisms for exchange of something of value, usually goods or services, for a price, usually money. While in the narrow sense, the market is a place where transactions take place, in the broader sense, the market can refer to the aggregate of transactions in a sector or a geographic area, even globally. Hence, marketing specialists speak of the 'European market'. Markets thrive where there is freedom for individuals and organizations to pursue transactions as they desire: the fewer impediments, the greater the scope for free markets. While these assumptions can be queried (as discussed later in this chapter), it is helpful to be reminded of the closeness between free-market assumptions and globalization (Friedman, 2000). Where barriers to trade proliferate and governments protect their national economies, globalization cannot thrive. The era of the Great Depression leading up to the Second World War was such a period. The dismantling of trade barriers in the post-war period led to more open markets and growth in cross-border flows of goods and services, in processes we now group together as globalization. These processes are linked to the spread of capitalism globally. They highlight the ascendancy of large (mainly American) capitalist companies into global economic forces, challenging the power of states. The tension between powerful companies and states, whose governments wield political power within their borders, has created uncertainty for businesses. A recent increase in barriers to trade has been associated with a renewed nationalism in government trade policy, which can adversely affect cross-border business. Trade tensions between the US and China, in particular, have caused concern within large companies whose businesses are globally integrated.

Businesses thrive on an ability to enter foreign markets easily, and MNEs have had the organizational ability to make the most of the opportunities of global markets. These opportunities have driven globalization in both production and in markets. MNEs have developed supply-chain strategies to co-ordinate different stages of production in the most advantageous location. Subsidiaries, affiliates and contractual partners all play roles in the different stages, from sourcing of materials through to production, distribution and delivery to the end consumers. This approach to production can be referred to as a **value chain**, as each stage in the chain adds value to the final product. Globalized production has become highly developed, with MNEs now able to co-ordinate complex supply chains.

value chain concept which identifies the value created at each stage in the production process

MNEs are able to serve consumers across the world with their products. A product line, such as a new range of clothing from Burberry, might be launched globally, allowing customers to purchase online wherever they are in the world. Burberry shops, however, will differ somewhat in the product lines they offer in different national markets. Burberry is marketed as a global brand that is distinctively British (see www.burberryplc.com). Globalization in many sectors has taken the form of global strategies to deliver specific products to local markets. Food is a sector in which local tastes matter. McDonald's has been famous for its ability to adapt to local tastes, while focusing on the brand's core products, although this formula has come under strain with the rise of innovative competitors.

Although international trading links and colonialism in the eighteenth and nineteenth centuries connected nations around the globe, these earlier eras did not see the depth of interaction which characterize globalization as we experience it today. The use of the term began only in the 1960s and gained common currency only in the 1980s (Waters, 2001: 2). A divergence of views has emerged on the nature and extent of these trends. An extreme view, known as 'hyperglobalization', views globalization in a positive light, bringing about a 'borderless' world in which local differences melt away and a global civil society emerges. This rather idealistic view gathered momentum in the late 1990s. Its proponents thought that all countries and communities would become connected through the spread of free-market capitalism, and that the autonomy of individual nation-states would gradually shrink (Ohmae, 2000). Friedman viewed technology, especially the internet, as a key force in this process, bringing about the integration of markets and empowering individuals and investors. As these processes unfolded, the division of the world into nation-states would become less significant (Friedman, 2000).

The depiction of globalization by the hyperglobalizers is optimistic, stressing empowerment facilitated in the globalized environment. But this view has aroused both sceptics and critics. Sceptics point to the continuing differences between developed and developing countries, as well as the assertiveness of governments keen to preserve national interests. Critics voice fears that the rise of global capitalism has had detrimental consequences in societies, their cultures and the natural environment. Friedman can point to the fact that the citizen who is empowered by the internet can be a potent force in these respects, helping to bring decision makers to account (Friedman, 2016). However, global companies and governments also have the tools of the internet to reinforce their power, sometimes in repressive ways. This has been apparent in the rise of the social media giants such as Facebook, which are now being subjected to scrutiny by national regulators. Such moves reflect signs of a backlash against globalization.

The post-war economic power of the US has been closely identified with globalization, evidenced in the might of its multinationals and the influence of the US in international relations. The concentration of economic power in the hands of large corporate forces, able to bend states to their will, sent alarm bells ringing in many quarters. The debate moved to the streets, as anti-globalization protests became a regular occurrence at international governmental conferences, beginning with that of the WTO in 1999 in Seattle, Washington.

In the ensuing decade, the integration of numerous countries into the global economy provided a more finely grained picture of how globalization was actually affecting differing countries' economies and societies. Globalization has not been a

single, all-encompassing process sweeping the globe, but processes which reflect the independent actions of many different players in different places.

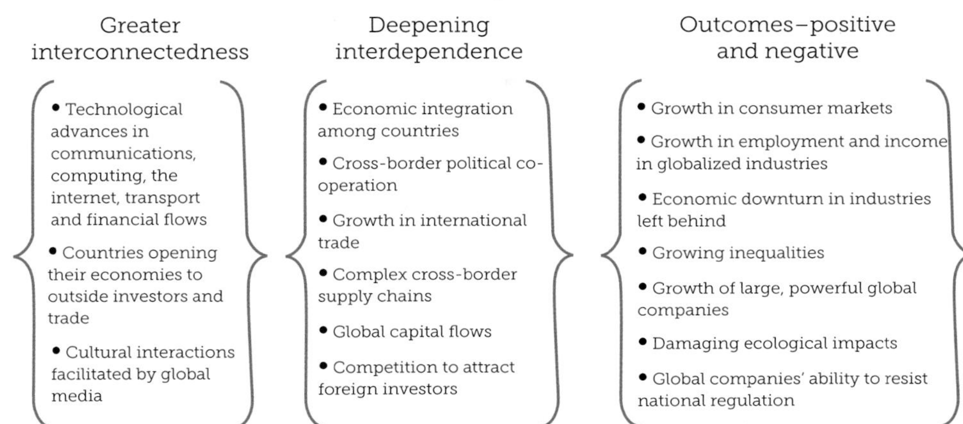

Figure 2.1 Globalization processes and their outcomes

interconnectedness improved communications across national borders, facilitated by advances in technology, computing and the internet

interdependence links based on complementarities and co-operation between two or more countries or organizations

Globalization processes are set out in Figure 2.1. The two overarching themes are interconnectedness and interdependence. The first, **interconnectedness** is facilitated by advances in technology, computing and the internet, which allow networking to take place routinely between people in different geographical locations. Moreover, business interactions increasingly overlap with social networking sites. Advances in transport, such as container shipping, have facilitated trading ties. MNEs have become the drivers of globalized production, evolving supply chains to deliver products to consumers in an ever-increasing range of markets. Financial flows have also benefited from the internet and IT, allowing cross-border investments and transactions to be made quickly and easily. These have thrived in an environment in which governments have opened their economies to market forces from overseas.

Turning to the second theme in Figure 2.1, growing **interdependence** among countries has taken place. It might appear that countries would thereby lose their autonomy, but more subtle processes are taking place. Rather than the withering away of national autonomy, we are seeing countries asserting a sovereign right to act. In many cases, they willingly co-operate with other countries for common goals. In processes not unlike those transforming companies, countries are seeing themselves as linked together in their pursuit of prosperity and wellbeing. As economic integration deepens, so does interdependence, between countries and between business enterprises. A gradual opening up of national economic and financial systems to outside investors has been accompanied by the liberalization of trade. These trends towards market liberalization have been seized on by some as indicators of the spread of global capitalism, a central tenet of the hyperglobalizers.

However, market reforms have varied in both their substance and pace among countries. Countries with authoritarian systems, such as China, have used market tools to achieve national aims, rather than to transform themselves into free-market systems. Governments see foreign investment as leading to economic growth, especially in the form of domestic jobs, but fear allowing the loss of control over these economic forces. Countries that have seen impressive economic growth from globalization, including China, South Korea, and India, have not wholeheartedly embraced free markets, but retained governmental controls and policies such as subsidizing key industries (Rodrik, 2012). Government policies have also evolved in the US, where trade and investment policies reflect national interest above all. US governments are alert to the fact that China subsidizes its industries, providing it a competitive boost in global markets. Of course, the US also subsidizes industries such as farming, which is a source of exports, many of them to China. This is a good indication of the tension inherent in interdependence (see the mini case study in this chapter and a mini case study on trade in Chapter 7).

Turning to the outcomes in the third column of Figure 2.1, globalization processes have taken place unevenly, affecting different dimensions of the environment in different ways. The globalization of consumer markets has seen the rise of an urban middle-class consumer culture, based on American lifestyle images, that pervades countries on all continents. This does not imply that culture in a deeper sense is becoming globalized, but it does suggest that people everywhere can buy smartphones and eat McDonald's meals. Rodrik (2012) points out that globalization processes are essentially disruptive. For example, shifts in manufacturing to new locations in developing countries are disruptive in both the new environment and the one left behind. These processes have affected countries in differing ways, leading to inequality emerging both within and between countries, between those who have benefited and those who have not. Beneficiaries have included the favoured locations for low-cost production, while low-skilled jobs in advanced economies have been rapidly disappearing.

Globalization

This is a wide-ranging interview on the many facets of globalization by Joseph Stiglitz, former Senior Vice President and chief economist of the World Bank. The subject is 'Globalization and its discontents revisited'. The interview is with *New York Times* reporter, Peter S. Goodman, and took place 22 November, 2017.

Video link: Globalization
https://youtu.be/_z0D4F064Hc

Economic development: country differences

primary production agriculture, mining and fishing

secondary production industrial production, concentrated in factories

tertiary sector economic activity that consists of services

industrialization transformation of an economy from mainly agricultural production for domestic consumption to an economy based on factory production, with potential for export

Every country has distinctive characteristics which influence the nature of the economic activities which make up its national economy. Economic activity can be divided into three broad sectors: **primary production**, which includes agriculture, mining and fishing; **secondary production**, which is industrial production; and the **tertiary sector**, which consists of services, such as tourism and financial services. All three types of activity are carried out in every economy, but there are big differences in their proportions. It is usual for countries to progress economically in stages, from primary industries to manufacturing and then to services, which are considered more advanced. There are exceptions to this pattern. Some countries rich in natural resources rely mainly on these activities to generate wealth, but this can be a short-sighted policy as the day will come when the resources run out. Seeking to diversify to maintain steady growth is more advisable, although not always easy to achieve in practice. We will look at national economic systems closely in the next chapter, but here we look at how countries are broadly classified in terms of economic activities, noting especially the effects of globalization.

Globalization is closely linked to industrialization, which normally drives economic development. **Industrialization** is the process of transformation of an economy from mainly agricultural production for domestic consumption to an economy based on factory production, with potential for export. Industrialization enhances a country's capacity for wealth creation and economic growth, especially if its companies grow into successful MNEs. Industrialization is therefore linked to economic development.

economic development can refer to any change in a country's overall balance of economic activities, but usually refers to industrialization and resultant changes in society

Although **economic development** can refer to any change in a country's overall balance of economic activities, it usually refers to the industrialization and resultant changes in society whereby jobs are increasingly located in industrial sectors. Britain was the earliest country to industrialize, from the early nineteenth century onwards, followed by other European countries and the US. Many inventions, such as the steam engine, electric turbine and railway locomotive, originating in Britain, spread to Europe and the US. Following the Second World War, when many European countries and Japan faced the task of rebuilding infrastructure and industrial capacity, the US was well placed to forge ahead with large-scale manufacturing, meeting growing demand for consumer goods. By the late 1960s, however, Japan's industrial development was gaining momentum, turning it into a global industrial power in sectors such as car manufacturing. By the 1980s, Japanese manufacturers threatened American industrial domination. By then, South Korea was gaining ground in some of the same sectors as Japan, such as electronics and cars. Samsung and LG have become global forces in electronics, and Hyundai has become a global carmaker. More recently, China and, to a lesser extent, India have enjoyed the rapid growth associated with economic development driven by industrialization.

It is customary to classify countries according to economic indicators. Broadly, the countries with greater income are the most developed; the poorest are the least developed. Of course, economic criteria alone do not tell the whole story: 'development' encompasses criteria other than economic indicators. The UN Development Programme (www.undp.org) uses the broader notion of 'human development' for its **Human Development Index (HDI)** (www.hdr.undp.org) which ranks countries according to three sets of criteria: economic, health (including life expectancy) and education (UNDP, 2014). The HDI provides a fuller picture of wellbeing in societies than economic criteria alone. Nonetheless, economic criteria are widely used indicators, and are helpful for country comparisons, but their limitations should be borne in mind.

Human Development Index (HDI) UN ranking of countries according to three sets of criteria: economic, health (including life expectancy) and education

The UN and World Bank are the chief international organizations that classify all the world's economies. The World Bank (www.worldbank.org) focuses on gross national income (GNI) per capita, that is per head of population. Its categories are as follows (World Bank, 2018):

- Low income: $995 or less
- Low middle income: $996 to $3,895
- Upper middle income: $3,896 to $12,055
- High income: $12,056 or more

The World Bank designates all low- and middle-income countries as developing countries. Only those in the high-income category are developed. The UN uses three broad categories: developed, developing and transition economies. These overlap with those used by the World Bank. The world's **developed countries** are mostly industrialized economies, highly integrated in the global economy (see Table 2.2). They include North America, EU countries and Japan, which are known as the 'Triad countries'. Australia and New Zealand are also in this category. The more recently admitted EU member states in Central and Eastern Europe have now joined the group of developed countries. Thirty-four of the world's economies are members of the **Organisation for Economic Co-operation and Development (OECD)** (www.oecd.org). From its creation in 1961, the OECD has had a membership of mainly advanced, high-income countries. With increasing globalization, its membership is has become more mixed, to include a number of emerging economies. Colombia is the most recent of these to have joined. Besides member countries, the OECD works closely with partner countries. OECD members and partners are shown in Table 2.1.

developed countries countries whose economies have become industrialized and have reached high income levels

Organisation for Economic Co-operation and Development (OECD) (www.oecd.org) organization of the world's mainly developed, high-income economies

Table 2.1 OECD member and partner countries

Member countries	Partner countries
Australia, Austria, Belgium, Canada, Chile, Colombia, Czech Republic, Denmark, Estonia, Finland, France, Germany, Greece, Hungary, Iceland, Ireland, Israel, Italy, Japan, Korea, Latvia, Lithuania, Luxembourg, Mexico, Netherlands, New Zealand, Norway, Poland, Portugal, Slovakia, Slovenia, Spain, Sweden, Switzerland, Turkey, UK and US	Brazil, China, India, Indonesia, South Africa

Source: OECD, Global reach, at www.oecd.org, accessed 26 June 2019.

developing countries countries in the process of industrialization and building technological capacity

transition economies economies of Eastern Europe and the CIS (Commonwealth of Independent States, including Russia) that are making the transition from planned economies to market-based economies

Countries changing from agricultural to industrial production fall within the broad category of **developing countries**. These countries have often been referred to as the 'third world', but this term is now seldom used as it reflects the polarized thinking of the post-war period known as the 'cold-war' era, which was dominated by tension between the western capitalist countries, the 'first world', and the communist bloc countries, the 'second world'. These cold-war categories have been rather superseded by events, mainly the fall of the Soviet Union and the rise of market economic reforms around the world.

The vast majority of the world's countries are within the category of developing countries. There are huge variations in levels of development and extent of industrialization among these countries. Some base industrial development on abundant low-cost labour, as China has done. Some are resource-rich exporters, such as Nigeria, which is an oil producer. Many of the more globalized of these economies are referred to as 'emerging' economies, discussed below. Developing countries are mainly in South America, Africa and Asia. The UN has a separate category for the **transition economies** of South-Eastern Europe and the Commonwealth of Independent States (CIS), with the addition of Georgia. Although Georgia officially left the CIS in 2009, its economy is included in this category due to its geographic proximity and economic similarities.

Table 2.2 Economic development: UN classification of countries

Category	Countries
Developed	Australia, Austria, Belgium, Bulgaria, Canada, Croatia, Cyprus, Czech Republic, Denmark, Estonia, Finland, France, Germany, Greece, Hungary, Iceland, Ireland, Italy, Japan, Latvia, Lithuania, Luxembourg, Malta, Netherlands, New Zealand, Norway, Poland, Portugal, Romania, Slovakia, Slovenia, Spain, Sweden, Switzerland, UK, US
Transition economies	Albania, Armenia, Azerbaijan, Belarus, Bosnia and Herzegovina, Georgia, Kazakhstan, Kyrgyzstan, Republic of North Macedonia, Moldova, Montenegro, Russian Federation, Serbia, Tajikistan, Turkmenistan, Ukraine, Uzbekistan
Developing	*(selected)* Algeria, Angola, Argentina, Bolivia, Botswana, Brazil, Chile, China, Colombia, Costa Rica, Cuba, Cyprus, Ecuador, Egypt, Guatemala, India, Indonesia, Iraq, Kenya, Kuwait, Lesotho, Malaysia, Mexico, Mongolia, Morocco, Nicaragua, Nigeria, Pakistan, Peru, Philippines, Saudi Arabia, Singapore, Somalia, South Africa, Thailand, Tunisia, Turkey, United Arab Emirates, Uruguay, Venezuela, Viet Nam.
Least developed	*(selected)* Afghanistan, Angola, Bangladesh, Benin, Burkina Faso, Cambodia, Chad, Comoros, Democratic Republic of Congo, Equatorial Guinea, Ethiopia, Gambia, Guinea-Bissau, Haiti, Malawi, Mali, Mozambique, Myanmar (Burma), Nepal, Niger, Rwanda, Sierra Leone, Somalia, South Sudan, Sudan, Tanzania, Timor Leste, Togo, Uganda, Yemen, Zambia.

Source: UN (2018) *World Economic Situation and Prospects 2018, Country classifications*, pp. 141–5, at www.un.org/development/desa, accessed 27 June 2018.

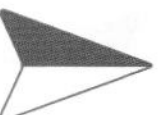

least-developed countries the world's poorest developing countries

The UN's last category is the **least-developed countries**. Mainly in sub-Saharan Africa and South Asia, they are the poorest countries among the developing countries. These countries, which have the world's fastest-growing populations, are mainly primary agricultural producers, with little industrialization. Most have been adversely affected by globalization, suffering from volatility in global commodities markets, weak transport infrastructure and poor communications networks. These societies have fallen behind other developing countries, experiencing extreme poverty, poor health conditions and limited educational systems. Moreover, these countries, which are most at risk from the effects of climate change and extreme weather, are those with the least resources to meet the challenges.

emerging economy fast-growing developing country, typically becoming increasingly globalized

BRIC countries collective reference to Brazil, Russia, India and China, as a grouping of emerging economies

A final category of country is the **emerging economy**, or emerging market. This is a fluid category of developing countries – mostly large in area and population – that have enjoyed rapid economic growth and have gained in importance in the global economy. The grouping of the **BRIC** countries – Brazil, Russia, India and China – was coined in 2001. They have come together in summit meetings, and, in 2010, were joined by South Africa, adding the 'S' to make them the BRICS. These five countries are home to about 40% of the world's population, making them large potential markets. However, as noted, the category is a fluid one: Indonesia and Mexico both have larger populations than South Africa (South Africa's population is about 55 million, whereas Indonesia's is 261 million). At the other end of the spectrum, the resource-rich states of the Middle East, although small in area and in population, have become important global players. The notion of the BRICS as a group has thus become less relevant as the diversity among these economies has become more pronounced.

The emerging economies represent a diverse picture in terms of globalization. In Asia, China has led the world in manufacturing mass-produced goods, and based its development on exports. Russia and Brazil have seen growth derived from natural resources: Russia's wealth is based mainly on gas, and Brazil is a large exporter of iron ore and agricultural commodities. India has benefited from a growth in manufacturing, although its progress has been slow. The Middle Eastern states have been dependent on oil and gas, which, like other resources, are subject to price volatility in global markets. Emerging markets have seen benefits from globalization, but have had to contend with the risks. Countries relying on exports, such as China, have been adversely affected by slowdowns in spending in the advanced economies, while the resource-rich countries, such as Russia and Brazil, have seen slowing demand for energy and commodities. In this respect, the interdependence associated with globalization has meant that economies are tending to move in sync. Slowdown in developed countries that are large importers impacts on economies in the developing countries that rely on exports.

Developing countries, such as those in Africa, have sought to attract foreign investors to drive economic growth. Many are rich in natural resources, but lack the capital and expertise to exploit their potential. However, channelling the wealth towards sustainable development is a formidable challenge in these countries. Also of global concern is the huge gap that remains between the world's rich countries and the poorest – those classified as the least developed. Globalization is now reaching many of these countries, such as Ethiopia and Bangladesh, raising questions over the human aspects of development.

National economies and globalization

Weigh up the benefits and risks associated with globalization from the perspectives of:

(a) a poor developing country that has oil reserves

(b) an emerging country that has abundant low-cost labour

MNEs and internationalization

In this section, we shift perspective to the MNE. The company which seeks to expand internationally eyes the potential gains from production and markets outside its home country. The internationalization of its activities offers opportunities which greatly exceed those offered at home, even if its home is a large country such as the US or China. Most MNEs do not simply go on a shopping spree, acquiring ownership of foreign assets, but build strategic ties with foreign organizations, such as suppliers, which enhance their ability to create value.

Companies from a wide range of countries have now become players in global supply chains and markets, challenging the established MNEs in both mature consumer markets and newer emerging markets. SMEs, once seen as essentially local, can now become part of worldwide supply chains, raise capital from foreign investors and recruit talented people globally. In this section, we look at why and how companies internationalize.

Why do companies internationalize?

A company does not decide to branch out internationally on the basis of rather abstract observations that we now live in a global economy, but because the firm itself sees business opportunities such as efficiencies in production and new markets. For companies, as for people, the grass might seem greener on the other side, but there is much at stake. For a business, a failed foreign venture can lead not just to financial loss, but can bring down the entire company. Companies therefore need good reasons to venture abroad, and reasonable confidence that the potential benefits outweigh the risks. There are both **'pull' factors** which attract the company to a foreign location and **'push' factors** which influence the company to branch out from its home country or other countries where it currently does business. The following motives come into play:

'pull' factors factors in a country which attract the company to a foreign location

'push' factors factors in a company's home country which persuade it to seek growth potential overseas

- New markets – A new market is a strong 'pull' factor for a company, especially if growth in its home market begins to slow. However, the new market needs to be one where the firm's products are likely to be popular and lead to growth in market share.
- More efficient production – Companies are constantly seeking ways of producing products and delivering services more efficiently. They seek to benefit from scale economies, that is, savings which come with large-scale production. The country with relevant skills and low labour costs is thus attractive, although transport costs and long delivery times must be taken into account.
- Proximity to key resources – A company that requires abundant supplies of a key raw material is likely to choose a location close to supply. For this reason, food processing plants are often located in agricultural areas.
- Access to technology and skills – A company which relies on specialist technology tends to seek out locations where these activities are flourishing, and where skilled researchers are available. For this reason, SMEs in life sciences often locate in the proximity of large pharmaceutical companies.
- Proximity to customers – A company that has traditionally exported its products might find that it can deliver a better, more customized, service if it establishes a presence near its customers. It thus learns more about the market firsthand.
- Deterioration in the home business environment – There are many possible 'push' factors which influence companies to look beyond their home country or

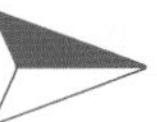

to shift from a foreign country where they have become established. Market saturation is one. For the large retailer, market saturation could be reached if availability of large sites becomes limited or planning regulations become stricter. Changes in taxation and regulation in a country can contribute to an exodus of companies to more advantageous locations.

Push and pull factors can combine to encourage companies to globalize. For example, a company that sees limited scope to grow in established markets in advanced economies is likely to look to emerging markets for better prospects of market growth.

MINI CASE STUDY

Harley-Davidson rides global markets

Harley-Davidson, the quintessentially American motorcycle manufacturer, has embarked on a strategy of internationalization, shifting some of its production to overseas locations and expanding into global markets. It has been driven by weakening sales in America for several years, a sliding share price, and, more recently, trade policies of the US government that could be damaging in the long term.

The company is based in Milwaukee, Wisconsin, where it was founded in 1903. It is strongly rooted in the city, where it holds anniversary events every five years, attracting enthusiastic bikers for a celebration of the gleaming motorbikes and biking lifestyle that have made it the American icon it is today. While these large machines attract devoted fans, most of these are older customers. Younger people nowadays are likely to favour lighter bikes, including electric bikes. And they are often looking for cheaper, simpler bikes than a Harley. The average age of the Harley owner is now 47, whereas it was 32 in 1990. Older fans are unlikely to buy another bike, and many are selling their bikes secondhand, creating competition for Harley in selling new bikes. The company would ideally be attracting younger enthusiasts, but only 6% of Harley owners are between 16 and 24. Attracting international buyers has become one of its priorities. Its bikes are popular in much of Asia, and it is building smaller-engine bikes for markets such as India.

Traditionally, Harley-Davidsons have been made in the US, as befits an iconic American brand. Indeed, President Trump has been photographed with Harley's CEO in front of the White House, publicizing his America First policy. However, for manufacturing companies, global supply chains are now the norm, and cost considerations are central to decision-making. Harley-Davidson is no exception. In addition to its factories in the US, it has assembly plants in Australia, Brazil, India and Thailand. In 2018, Mr Trump announced new tariffs on imported aluminium and steel, to protect American jobs. This would adversely affect Harley-Davidson, which uses these imported inputs. In retaliation, the EU announced a rise in tariffs on selected products, which included motorcycles imported into the EU. Tariffs on Harley's bikes would rise from 6% to 31%. This would add $2,200 to the price of each motorbike sold in Europe. There were 40,000 sold in the EU in 2017. The company announced that it would absorb this additional cost, in order to maintain its EU sales. But it is now planning to build up production at its facility in Thailand, for shipping to EU member states. This news did not go down well with Mr Trump, who immediately criticized Harley for the decision. In fact, many of the company's employees and customers would agree, believing that moves that 'paint them as un-American would worry them' (*Financial Times*, 2018, cited below).

The culture of motorcycling revolves around passionate enthusiasts.

Questions

- What are the challenges facing Harley-Davidson?
- Is it un-American for the company to manufacture abroad? Explain the reasons.

Find out more

See the article on Matt Levatich, Harley-Davidson's President and CEO, 'Overseas ride by Harley boss sends Trump into a spin', in the *Financial Times*, 30 June 2018.

Modes of internationalization

modes of internationalization methods by which companies expand internationally

export selling products in a country other than the one in which they are made

MNEs choose from a variety of methods to internationalize, known as **modes of internationalization**, shown in Figure 2.2. A firm might choose different modes in different locations, and at different stages in its internationalization experience. The firm embarking on international activities for the first time tends to choose a low-risk strategy, such as **exporting** its products from its home country. If foreign demand is promising, it might establish a sales office in selected foreign markets, giving it a presence in the market and allowing it to control activities such as customer service.

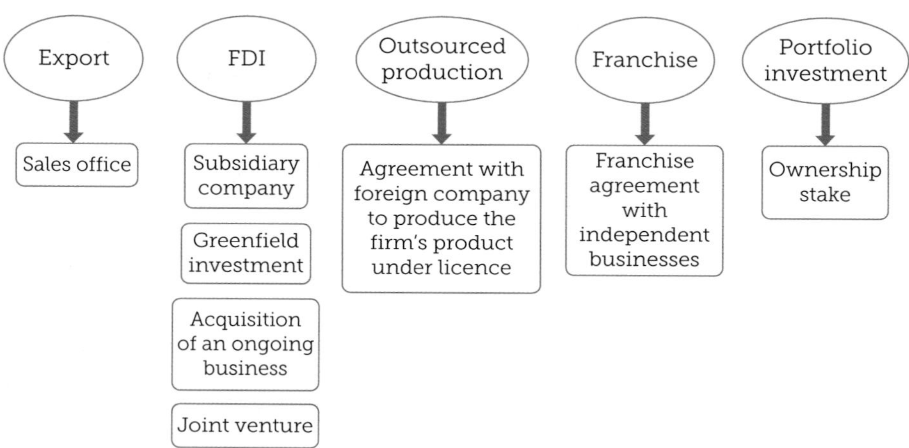

Figure 2.2 Modes of internationalization

foreign direct investment (FDI) investment in productive assets in a foreign country, with a view to exerting control over operations

greenfield investment FDI which focuses on a new building project, such as a factory, in a foreign location

By means of **foreign direct investment (FDI)**, the company invests in productive assets in a foreign country, acquiring them wholly or partly and using this ownership stake to exert control over operations. The investing company thereby acquires deeper involvement in the host country than the company which simply relies on exporting its products to foreign countries, without a physical presence in them. FDI is generally considered to be the main driver of globalization (Dunning, 1993), as it is characterized by this deeper level of integration in global production networks.

As Figure 2.2 shows, the MNE contemplating FDI has a number of options. As we found in Chapter 1, a parent company might set up a foreign subsidiary which it wholly owns, or it might take a lower stake, still aiming to control operations. The subsidiary gives it a legal footing in the country, from which it can grow. If the MNE is a manufacturing company, it might decide to invest in building a plant on a **greenfield** site. This type of project is typically carried out by a subsidiary set up for the purpose. The greenfield investment represents a significant commitment to the country as it involves a large capital outlay, with probably little prospect of immediate

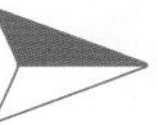

profits. This is a long-term strategy which MNEs might consider for a variety of reasons. They include the attraction of lower costs than in its home country and the availability of skilled labour in the host country (see Figure 2.3). Another consideration is the imposition of trade barriers such as tariffs in the foreign market, which deter exporters. The foreign company wishing to enter the market must therefore consider FDI, enabling it to manufacture locally.

acquisition type of FDI in which an investor purchases an existing company in a foreign location

The MNE in a hurry to gain a foothold in a foreign market often chooses to purchase an existing business. **Acquisition** allows the MNE to start operations in the country almost immediately, and is common in sectors such as retailing and mining. In manufacturing, there might be a time lag, while the plant is adapted to make the new owner's products, but this is shorter than would be possible on a greenfield site, where the plant is built from scratch. Some acquirers purchase the whole business, including the brand, and carry on production under the new management. An acquisition in a new market can also be advantageous in that the MNE can gain local knowledge and expertise from the acquired firm. In emerging economies, many of the companies that are sold are through government privatizations of old, inefficient businesses. In this situation, the MNE takes on an ambitious project, needing to inject capital and retrain staff.

joint venture an agreement between companies to form a new entity to carry out a business purpose, often an FDI project

A company that is reluctant to enter a foreign market on its own, or is barred from doing so by state controls, can form a **joint venture**, whereby it works with a partner firm to carry out FDI. The MNE's partner in the joint venture tends to be a local firm, whose local knowledge will enhance their chances of success. The joint-venture partner can be a state-owned company. The partners form a new company, each taking an equity stake. In many emerging economies, foreign companies are required to go down the joint-venture route, as foreigners are legally barred from wholly owning a locally-registered company. The need to enter a country via a joint venture can be a means for the host country to acquire technology. In China, for example, the joint venture has been seen as a means of acquiring western technology from joint-venture partners.

outsourced production as a mode of internationalization, contractual arrangement whereby a company has its branded products produced by another company in a foreign location

The middle range of options presented in Figure 2.2 is **outsourced production**, a route favoured by brand owners. Outsourcing (introduced in Chapter 1) rests on agreement by the MNE with a local company that the latter will produce the goods or deliver the service within the terms of a contract between the local company and the MNE. The local company is sometimes a foreign investor itself. The manufacturing of Apple's iPhones and iPads in China, for example, is carried out by firms such as Foxconn, a Taiwanese company, which also manufactures for other brand owners, both in China and other countries. For MNEs in clothing and other consumer products, the outsourcer manufactures under licence from the MNE brand owner, being required to produce the products as needed to the specifications laid down in the licence agreement. The aim of outsourced production tends to be to reduce costs by locating production in a low-cost country, from where products are exported to consumers in other markets. This strategy has been key to MNE investment in China and other Asian economies.

franchising business agreement whereby a business uses the brand, products and business format of another firm under a licence

In some sectors, such as fast food and hotels, companies have opted for **franchising**, which involves a licence agreed with a business (the franchisee) to make and deliver the product in accordance with the requirements of the brand owner (the franchisor) (see the discussion in Chapter 1). While franchising has long been popular within national markets, international franchising has offered greater international opportunities with the rise of global brands. The local businessperson makes a considerable capital investment, but probably feels this is money well invested, as the brand attracts customers. The brand owner, in turn, is able to expand internationally through a network of franchises, without the burden of significant capital outlay in each country. On the other hand, the franchisor must be alert to the different regulatory environment and in each country, as well as differences in local tastes. McDonald's has famously adapted its offerings to cultural preferences in different countries. It acquires direct ownership of outlets in some foreign markets, whereas its outlets in the US are generally franchise operations.

The MNE that desires to internationalize, but is reluctant to invest in physical assets, might choose **portfolio investment**, which consists of buying shares or other securities in a foreign company, with a view to making financial gains on the investment. These gains are often viewed as short-term. The portfolio investor usually acquires small stakes in companies, and is sometimes restricted legally or politically from big purchases through capital controls in the country. **Sovereign wealth funds**, which are entities owned by a sovereign state, are familiar portfolio investors in many sectors. Usually keeping investments below 10% in any one company, sovereign wealth fund managers maintain a focus on the public purposes for which they are responsible. Where an investor is able and willing to acquire a large stake, usually 30% or more, it gains a strong position from which it can exert considerable control in both corporate governance and management. In this case, its role would shift closer to that of the foreign direct investor, who combines ownership and control.

portfolio investment buying shares of other securities of a company with a view to making a financial gain

sovereign wealth fund entity controlled by a government which invests state funds and pursues an investment strategy, often active in global financial markets

Companies design internationalization strategies to derive the greatest potential from each market, using different entry modes in different countries, influenced by the local conditions and government policies in each. Their choice also depends on the strengths of the firm itself and the degree of risk the company is willing to undertake. In some markets, such as the large emerging markets, companies see so much growth potential that they are often willing to take greater risks. For this reason, FDI in emerging markets has become a major trend.

Choosing a mode of internationalization

What mode of entry would you recommend for each of the following, and why?

(a) A Japanese car manufacturer who wishes to sell cars in European markets

(b) A large food retailer from a European country, who wishes to enter the Chinese market

(c) A Chinese manufacturer of appliances such as refrigerators and washing machines who wishes to enter the American market

FDI and the global economy

FDI has been a major contributor to globalization. As we have just seen, it is by no means the only mode of internationalization, but it is the one which represents the deepest commitment in a host country, whereby the investor and host society develop the deepest interactions. In this section, we analyze these cross-border activities and their impacts.

Why does the firm choose to invest in a foreign location?

Why would a firm choose to take the risks of investing in assets overseas when trading relationships would be a feasible alternative? The answers lie largely in the greater scope for penetration of foreign markets through FDI.

International trade goes back to ancient times, while FDI is a relatively new phenomenon. Foreign investment by companies flourished in the nineteenth and early twentieth century. Although transnational manufacturing took place in the Victorian era, the big overseas investors were in primary sectors such as mineral extraction and agricultural products. In the period before 1914, the UK was the largest holder of foreign capital assets, the majority in developing countries where British colonial rule provided

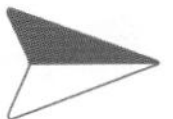

an institutional umbrella (Dunning, 1993). The inter-war period saw the rise of protectionist barriers between countries, which discouraged trade and encouraged companies to focus on home markets. However, the political leaders who met to devise a framework for new co-operative agreements after the Second World War paved the way for more open markets, which we now link to globalization.

location advantages inherent advantages of a country or region, such as access to transport, access to raw materials and low labour costs

Until about the 1960s, firms tended to carry out manufacturing activities in their home countries. But FDI was beginning to take off. One of the main drivers was **location advantages** that were offered in foreign environments. These could be advantages of a country as a whole, or they could be found in a region or city within a country. 'Country-specific advantages' refer to a country as a whole, while location advantages often refer to regions or cities. For example, Silicon Valley in California would offer location advantages for a high-technology firm, while China offers country-specific advantages for manufacturers of consumer products. Key location advantages are shown in Figure 2.3.

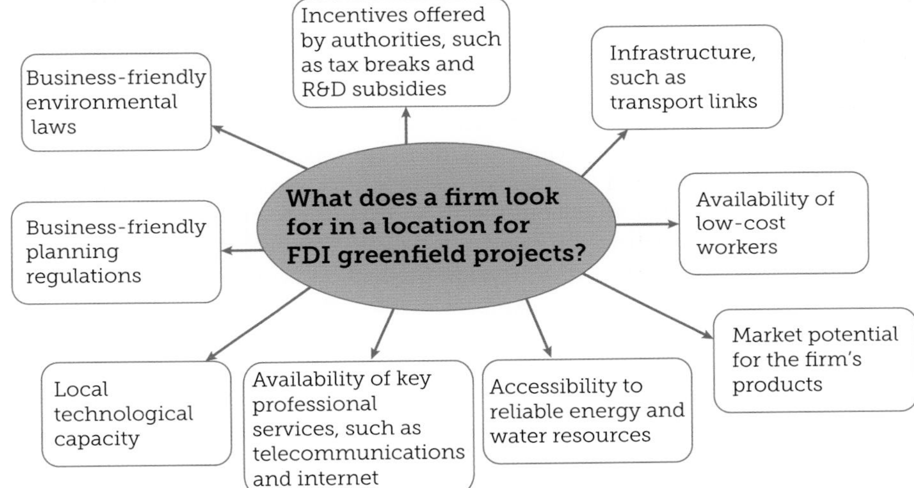

Figure 2.3
Location advantages for firms contemplating greenfield FDI

Choosing the right location is a major concern for the firm contemplating FDI. It is especially critical for any firm looking to invest in a greenfield project, as it involves a long-term commitment and considerable capital outlay. Figure 2.3 shows some of the major issues the prospective investor must research. The greenfield site is typically preferred for manufacturing companies wishing to build a factory from scratch. As the figure shows, the firm must consider a host of factors. Inevitably, some answers will be positive and some will be negative: a balance must always be struck, which will involve taking risks that the negative factors will be manageable. For example, a location in a developing country such as India might offer a pool of local workers, but weak infrastructure and unreliable electricity and water supplies. Wishing to attract investors, Indian authorities now offer incentives and also help to smooth the way in planning processes that are notoriously bureaucratic. India also offers a large market for many consumer goods, which will tempt foreign investors. India's location advantages are those of a developing country, but what about a developed country like the US? Foxconn, the Taiwanese company that manufactures for Apple, announced in 2017 that it would build a factory on a greenfield site in Wisconsin in the US. Foxconn chose Wisconsin for the $10 billion factory largely because of the $3 billion in state subsidies it was offered. From Foxconn's perspective, the investment looked particularly advantageous financially, but from the perspective of the host economy, the picture was less clear, as Foxconn has had a patchy record of keeping its promises in terms of job creation.

Theorizing FDI

Theorists of FDI have highlighted the importance of location in the decision-making process, but their theories take in a number of other factors. One of the earliest of these theorists was Stephen Hymer, who sought to explain what advantages would be gained from the firm's perspective (Hymer, 1975). Hymer spoke of location advantages of some countries over others, such as access to transport and lower costs than in the firm's home country. Such advantages are not an unqualified benefit, though, as the firm would be entering a foreign environment where it had little local knowledge. Why would a firm undertake the risk, rather than simply investing in shares? The answer lay in the ability of the foreign firm to make the most of its **ownership advantages** in the host country. The foreign firm would have resources such as technology, production skills and organizational skills which local firms lacked. These ownership advantages were firm specific, giving the foreign firm a competitive advantage.

ownership advantages resources specific to a firm, such as patents, which can be exploited for competitive advantage

A second relevant theory is the **product life cycle theory** of Raymond Vernon (Wells, 1972). Writing in the 1960s, when American companies were in the ascendant, Vernon envisaged all new products as originating in the US. He wrote particularly about the growing American appetite for mass-produced consumer goods such as televisions and washing machines. He traced the life cycle of the new product from its launch in the US, to export to other markets, and, finally, to being manufactured in cheaper locations for export to US consumers. In the early phase, demand at home leads to expansion, and demand overseas, which is limited to high-income groups, is satisfied by exports. As the market matures and overseas demand grows, foreign production begins to take off, and these products supplant US imports in overseas markets. At the same time, cost factors come into play, the product becomes more standardized and production is increased. US producers are likely to shift production overseas, first to the higher-income markets (such as Europe). These production facilities are able to export to other countries, and even back to the US, but as costs rise in Europe, companies shift production again, this time to low-cost locations, such as Asian developing countries.

product life cycle theory theory of the evolution of a product in states, from innovation in its home market to dissemination and production in overseas markets

Vernon combined concepts of location advantages and ownership advantages. In his rather US-centric view of the world, innovation capacity was an ownership advantage enjoyed by US companies, and other countries were not as competitive. Nonetheless, the core idea that companies will locate production in the most advantageous place was to be influential in later theories. Most notable among these has been Dunning's **eclectic paradigm**, also known as the 'OLI paradigm', based on three sets of advantages: ownership (O), location (L) and internalization (I) (Dunning, 1993). The OLI paradigm was designed to explain FDI from the firm's perspective, mainly focusing on foreign production. It was called 'eclectic' because the three variables derived from diverse theories and disciplines. The ownership and location variables were to be found in trade theories, and internalization derived from transaction cost economics. The three variables are summarized below:

eclectic paradigm theory of FDI devised by Dunning, based on three sets of advantages: ownership (O), location (L) and internalization (I); also known as the 'OLI' paradigm

- Ownership-specific advantages – These include property rights over assets, broadly defined to include both tangible resources (such as manufacturing plants) and intangible resources (such as intellectual property rights). Ownership of capital and natural resources strengthen the firm's competitive position. The firm's technology in the form of patents reflects its innovative capacity which generates future innovations. Crucial to the exploitation of these resources are the firm's organizational and entrepreneurial skills.
- Location-specific advantages – These focus on country-specific advantages. They include the economic, cultural and political environments of a country, in comparison with the firm's home country. Low-cost labour as a location advan-

tage was highlighted by earlier theorists, but Dunning expanded the notion in the FDI context. In addition to low-cost labour, access to raw materials, transport and infrastructure, he highlighted political policies such as government incentives to foreign investors. Dunning's highlighting of incentives for foreign investors has turned out to be more important than he perhaps envisaged when writing over two decades ago.

The size of the potential market for the firm's products in the country (and region) is another location advantage, although one which might involve a longer-term horizon in the case of developing countries. More recently, technological capacity in a country such as India is a location advantage, as R&D activities there are less costly than in developed countries. Most foreign investors nowadays look to negotiate advantageous packages of terms with the host government, including benefits such as tax holidays. Without them, a greenfield FDI project is unlikely to go ahead.

- Internalization advantages – These look to the reduction in transaction costs through hierarchical organization as an alternative to reliance on markets. A firm might find it advantageous to gain control of the supply of raw materials or components by buying the supplier outright. The firm thus avoids the transaction costs associated with obtaining supplies on an exchange basis in markets. Taking over the supplier leads to **vertical integration**, which gives the firm greater control over supplies. This can be advantageous from several viewpoints. It allows the firm to monitor quality more closely than would be possible dealing with an independent supplier. The firm can also keep tighter control of intellectual property, which can be a risk in countries where legal protections are weak. In this respect, there is overlap between ownership and internalization advantages. On the other hand, the advantages of vertical integration must be weighed against the costs and risks associated with outright ownership, which involves a long-term commitment (Buckley and Hashai, 2009). If the firm relies on exchange deals for supply, it is in a position to change suppliers relatively easily if a better deal presents itself, using global scanning to seek out the best deal. The flexibility offered by supply chains has thus persuaded many MNEs of their benefits over internalization, due to the liabilities arising from organizational arrangements.

vertical integration strategy of the MNE that consists of acquiring firms in its supply chain

The OLI paradigm aids firms contemplating FDI by highlighting the different variables and their interactions. It can thus help in weighing up the likely benefits against the risks and costs. Dunning's theory coincided with rapid growth in FDI, as firms were seeking greater efficiencies of globalized production, often to be found in developing countries. These MNEs were mainly from the developed countries, where technological capacity and protection of intellectual property were concentrated. In today's world, these concerns have become increasingly important to MNEs in extended supply chains. Again, Dunning's analysis of two decades ago has remained highly relevant. Many firms are adopting strategies to reduce the risks lurking in global supply chains and to safeguard their intellectual property. Foreign investors are still predominantly based in the developed countries, but these investors are being challenged by the rise of companies from emerging economies that are ambitiously pursuing their own global strategies.

Which businesses have been the big winners from globalization?

Globalization has opened up opportunities for businesses in new markets and new locations of production. But it has also posed threats. The firm that was once a national company is now operating and competing in numerous markets – which present new risks.

Which businesses have benefited the most from globalization?

Leaders and challengers: which countries are gaining from FDI?

FDI inflows aggregate value of investments that flow into a country

FDI outflows aggregate value of investments from a country's organizations to overseas destinations

FDI inward stock the total value of foreign investments that a country has attracted

FDI outward stock the total value of foreign investments made by a country's nationals

The movements of FDI around the world can be measured in terms of types of investments, their origins and destinations. This information provides valuable insights into globalization processes. **FDI inflows** are the aggregate value of investments which flow into a country, and **FDI outflows** are the aggregate value of investments from a country's organizations to overseas destinations. These are calculated on an annual basis. The total value of foreign investments that a country has attracted is its **FDI inward stock**, and the total value of investments made by its nationals is its **FDI outward stock**. The extent of a country's firms' involvement in FDI is a good indicator of its economic integration and interdependence with other countries. The country that is a major host for foreign investment in manufacturing, such as China, is likely to see economic growth and healthy trade statistics. If a country's outflows and inflows are unbalanced, say, by strong outflows and weak inward investment, this might be an indication of a weak domestic business climate. Japan is an example. Where the balance is tipped towards inward investment, this might be an indication that the country enjoys location advantages, but its domestic firms are not globally competitive – yet. In the case of China, domestic companies are catching up rapidly, in building local capacity and in outward expansion.

How do inflows and outflows of investment reconfigure the global economy? Outward movements of capital are dominated by developed economies, as shown in Figure 2.4. Developed countries' share of outward FDI stood at 71% in 2017 (UNCTAD, 2018). All these economies except China and Hong Kong (a special administrative region of China) are developed economies. Developing countries attract inflows largely because of their location advantages. The predominant trend in FDI has been the shift of production of a huge range of products from high-cost countries to low-cost countries. Although it had embarked on market reforms from 1979, it was only from about the late 1990s, that China pursued a concerted strategy of attracting export-oriented manufacturing, largely based on inward FDI. In the years that followed, many more emerging economies have been integrated into global supply chains, bringing rising prosperity and economic growth to host countries. Companies from key emerging economies have also become active outward investors. Again, China has been at the forefront, and is the only economy in the top ten of outward investors. Russia lies just outside this list, in eleventh place.

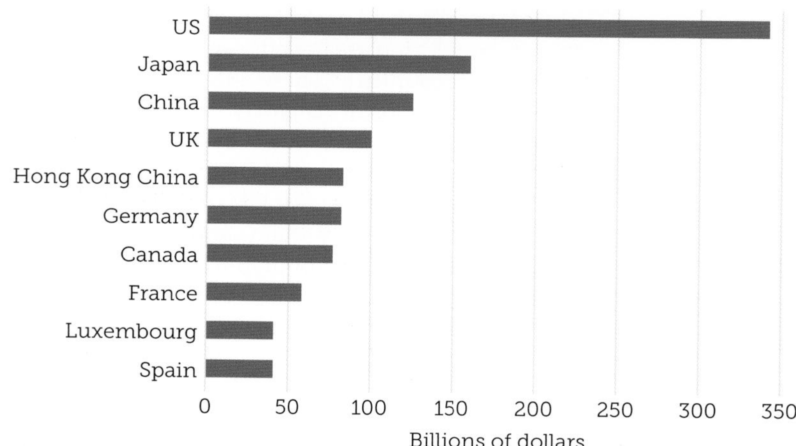

Figure 2.4 **The world's top ten outward-investing economies in 2017**

Source of data: UNCTAD (United Nations Conference on Trade and Development), *World Investment Report 2018*, 6 June 2018, p. 4, at http://unctad.org, accessed 23 September 2019.

The decades from 1990 onwards were remarkable in terms of FDI. Inward flows of FDI increased at a rate of 13% a year from 1990 to 1997. Two boom years of 1998 and 1999 enjoyed FDI increases averaging 50% annually. These rises coincided

with the years of the 'dotcom' bubble in internet and high technology companies. The bubble burst in 2001, and recovery was gradual in the immediate aftermath. Thereafter, FDI regained momentum in 2004, but this growth, too, came to an abrupt end, as shown in Figure 2.5. The global financial crisis of 2008 sent shockwaves around the world, weakening financial systems and discouraging investors. Since the crisis, FDI has slowly resumed, but growth has been uneven. As Figure 2.5 shows, FDI inflows to developed countries have stuttered. The value of large cross-border corporate acquisitions in 2015 and 2016 boosted these figures. They included the takeover of Syngenta, the Swiss pesticide and seed company, by state-owned ChemChina, and the purchase of American tobacco company Reynolds American by the UK company, BAT (British American Tobacco), to create the world's largest tobacco company. The dearth of large takeovers in 2017 is the main reason for a fall of 37% in FDI to developed economies. Flows to developing countries have been more stable, but declined in 2016. While Asian FDI inflows remained strong, flows to Africa declined in 2017, as investors were possibly deterred by economic and political uncertainties.

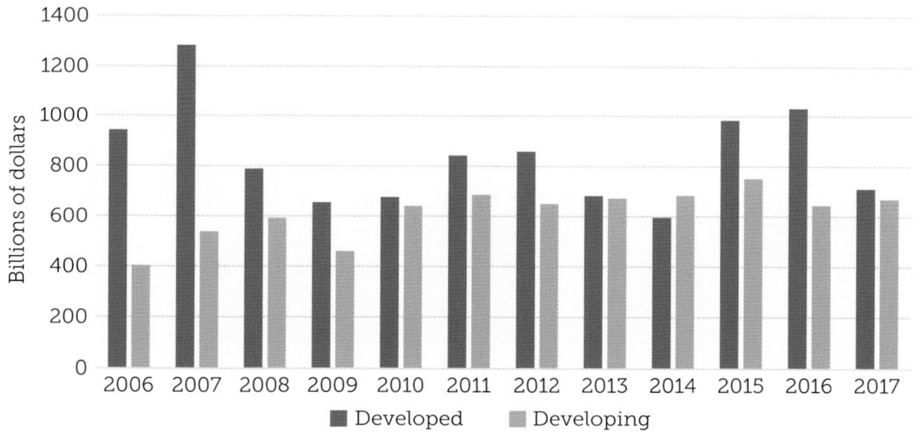

Figure 2.5 Inflows of FDI in developed and developing economies

Source of data: UNCTAD (United Nations Conference on Trade and Development), *Foreign Direct Investment: Inward and outward flows of stock*, UNCTADstat data centre, at http://unctadstat.unctad.org, accessed 21 June 2019.

Emerging MNEs, often owned or controlled by a state, have gained confidence and expertise in global markets, and have become active outward investors. Many of these companies have enjoyed success through FDI in developing countries, benefiting from their familiarity with issues common to other developing countries, such as a weak institutional environment. As they have gained confidence, they have also set their sights on developed countries, asserting their global competitiveness.

China has enjoyed strong growth in both inward and outward flows of FDI. As Figure 2.6 indicates, Chinese inward investment enjoyed steady growth from 2000 onwards, but the momentum slowed from 2014 onwards. This is partly attributable to the fact that, although China had been a favoured low-cost location, wages and other costs have long been on the rise, and other countries, such as India and Bangladesh, have become cheaper and more attractive to investors in sectors such as clothing. China's leaders have also sought to shift focus to more sustainable industries and high-technology sectors. These policies are designed to promote economic growth in sectors that offer greater added value than low-technology manufacturing. Chinese MNEs, many of them state-owned, have become active globally, as shown by the rise in outward FDI. As Figure 2.6 shows, in 2000, Chinese companies spent just under one billion dollars in outward investment on acquisitions and greenfield projects. This had increased to a staggering $196.1 billion in 2016, but declined in 2017. In part, this decline was due to slowing economic growth – from rates of growth over 10% annually in the preceding decade to rates closer to 7%. The decrease in China's outward FDI was also a sign of slowing expansion in global value chains and slowing growth in new greenfield projects (UNCTAD, 2018). China is now focusing on FDI projects that look to future sustainable growth. In 2018, the Chinese lithium-ion battery maker, Contemporary Amperex Technology, agreed a deal with BMW of Germany, with a view to building a factory to make its batteries in Europe. This billion-euro deal signalled the Chinese company's hope to benefit from growing demand for its batteries in Europe.

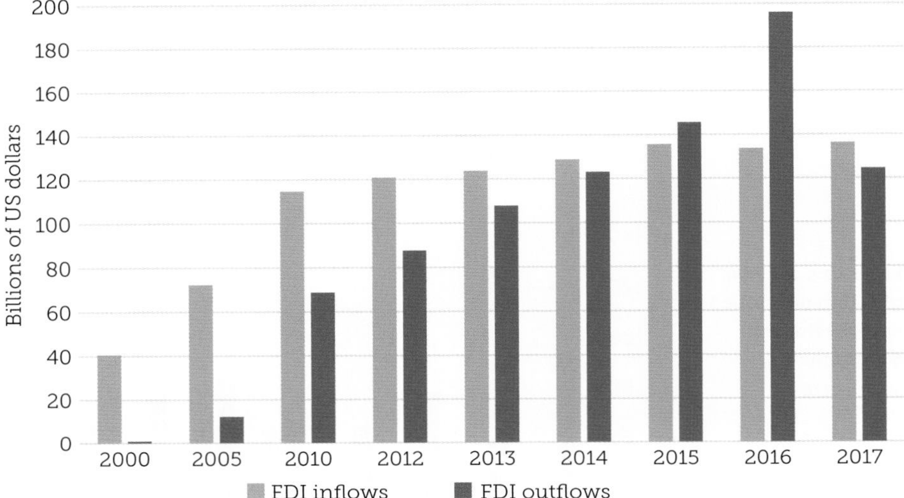

Figure 2.6 China's FDI: inflows and outflows

Source of data: UNCTAD (United Nations Conference on Trade and Development), *World Investment Report 2018*, 6 June 2018, Annex Tables 1 and 2, at http://unctad.org

China has become a significant investor in the US. China's growing need for imported food – and especially meat – prompted the Chinese company, Shuanghui, China's largest pork producer, to take over Smithfield, the US's largest pig-farming company, in 2013. This acquisition created one of the world's largest pig-farming companies, and also represented a significant consolidation in global factory-farming methods. Many Chinese acquisitions in the US have had government backing and, most recently, have targeted technology companies in the US. However, these acquisitions have met with some resistance in recent years. The proposed takeover of a US manufacturer of semiconductors was rejected by US authorities in 2017, on national security grounds. Even though this is a low-technology sector, it was felt to be significant because of its significance in supply chains related to national security.

In its World Investment Report of 2018, the United Nations Conference on Trade and Development (UNCTAD) highlighted the factors affecting a slowing down of FDI in the global economy. They noted an increase in the number of countries that are now more critical of foreign investors. There has been a marked increase in the number of trade disputes under treaty-related dispute-settlement procedures (see the discussion in Chapter 6). This is an indicator of growing conflicts in relations between investors and host countries. They also note rising tensions in trade relations. US President Trump has taken an America-first stance, raising tariffs with major trading partners, including China, Japan and the EU. Predictably, these countries have responded with retaliatory measures. Tit-for-tat rises in tariff barriers tend to be damaging for all parties. Although the president has expressly aimed to foster US interests, the barriers could damage US exporters and deter would-be foreign investors.

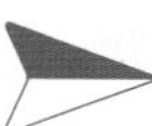

The way I see it...

On Tata's goals to 'go global', '...not just to increase our turnover, but also to go to places...where we would participate in the development of the country. We have endeavoured to play that role in Bangladesh, South Africa, Sri Lanka, Dubai and Singapore.'

Ratan Tata, Chairman of India's Tata Group, in an interview in August, 2006, 'Vision of the future', at www.tata.com

Tata's expansive vision showed the extent of the company's global ambitions. But those ambitions drove a range of investments that ultimately seemed to cause strains within the structure and with stretched finances. The purchase of Jaguar Land Rover (JLR) in the UK in 2008 was one of the many high-profile investments. The change of CEO in 2016 coincided with a need to simplify the structure and the goals in the light of a changing world of financial risks and political uncertainties. That year, Tata sold its UK steelmaking operations.

See the article, Tovey, A. (2018) 'Tata's £1.5bn swoop on Jaguar Land Rover, a decade on: the sale of the century?', *The Telegraph*, 4 June. Disappointed with falling sales and concerns over supply chains, Tata was doubtful about the future prospects of JLR. (See the case study on JLR in Chapter 4.)

In what respects would Tata be advised to adjust its focus to emerging economies, especially its home economy, India, for future growth?

Impacts of FDI in societies

FDI can be highly beneficial to national economies, whether as a destination for foreign investors or an economic boost for the country's own companies. But impacts differ widely. Investments typically combine both positive and negative aspects. FDI inflows can be highly beneficial to host economies, both developed and developing. They bring jobs, wealth creation and economic growth in the host country. A country's outward FDI generates wealth for its companies and revenues for the government. Its consumers also benefit, as they will pay less for imported goods and services. However, FDI's benefits are unevenly spread, and negative impacts can outweigh the benefits in societies. This is particularly relevant in the case of inward investment, as investments such as new mines, greenfield factories and foreign takeovers of existing factories have direct impacts in the country, especially a developing country. We look at the outcomes in developing and developed economies in turn.

Developing countries

For developing countries, the benefits of inward FDI can be transformational, promoting industrialization and formal employment with salaried work. FDI can boost economic development and bring **technology transfer**, whereby skilled workers in the host country are able to learn from the technology of the foreign investor. These **spillover effects** from FDI are also possible where the foreign investor, for example, in a greenfield project, uses local suppliers and service providers. The latter companies can gain both technological and managerial skills which can be valuable in building domestic innovative capacity (see Figure 2.7). However, FDI inflows do not always deliver hoped-for benefits. MNEs derive value from the ownership of technology embodied in intellectual property. They often seek to limit technology transfer in host economies, for fear of nurturing local competitors (see Chapter 9). Much manufacturing FDI is of a low-skilled nature. A concern for governments is that attracting low-technology FDI can lead to the country struggling to rise up the technological ladder to higher-value manufacturing and high-tech industries.

technology transfer process of acquiring technology from another country

spillover effects benefits to local firms in host countries from FDI

Inward FDI: the developing economy's perspectives

What are the possible positive impacts?

- Jobs and rising incomes
- Technology transfer
- Spillover benefits in the local economy
- Revenue flows to host governments
- CSR commitments, e.g. education and healthcare
- Improvements in societal wellbeing

What are the possible negative impacts?

- Poor conditions for many workers, with weak employment protection
- Possible negative impacts on the environment
- Financial gains flow to business and political elites, rather than all in society
- CSR commitments of investors do not materialize

Figure 2.7 **Inward FDI flows: how do they affect developing economies?**

MNEs target developing countries largely for their location advantages. Low-cost labour is an overwhelming attraction, and jobs are a major benefit from the host country's perspective, as shown in Figure 2.7. Manufacturing operations can be carried out either by local companies on an outsourcing basis or by foreign investors from a third country. These investors build factory complexes in the host country, often to manufacture products under global brand names. For example, Apple's iPhones are assembled in Taiwanese-owned Foxconn factories in China. Foxconn specializes in this type of FDI, and is astute in doing advantageous deals with host governments.

However, much FDI, especially in poor countries, is adversely affected by weak governance and weak accountability, which can lead to gains being concentrated in the hands of government and business leaders, rather than societal wellbeing. Workers in these factories are stakeholders, but they are not employees of the MNE whose brand name appears on the products. The MNE can take the position that legally it has no responsibility for them. However, when reports of mistreatment are publicized, public opinion tends to the view that the global brand owner shoulders some of the blame.

There is justifiable concern over the sustainability of the low-cost manufacturing model. The model relies heavily on cheap labour, especially migrant workers coming from rural areas to the industrial complexes run by the manufacturers. In China's period of rapid growth, this development model became widespread. Workers are housed in the factory complex, where a highly regimented way of life is maintained, dominated by long hours of repetitive work. Separated from their families, these workers often endure poor living and working conditions. Migrant workers, in particular, are vulnerable to exploitation. A growth in migrant labour has been an aspect of globalization, raising issues of human rights and responsibility for the wellbeing of workers. Factory owners who have outsourcing agreements with MNEs are responsible as employers, but the situation becomes complicated when the factory owner contracts work out to subcontractors, as is commonly the case. MNE brand owners could be said to be morally responsible, if not directly legally responsible. Often, they are not aware that manufacturing is being carried out by subcontractors. MNEs are attracted to countries where workers' legal protections are weak. Worker discontent has led to social unrest and strikes in China, where the authorities have responded with higher wages. Improving wages, reducing hours, enforcing rest days and allowing workers to organize leads to better working conditions, but these developments are not viewed so positively by the companies involved, who tend to focus on rising costs. Where costs rise, foreign investors seek other locations where costs are lower and regulation weaker. This poses dilemmas for the government and for the foreign investor.

For resource-rich developing countries, FDI offers the possibility of wealth generation on a big scale. But exploiting resources can be fraught with difficulties, including technical challenges, infrastructure deficiencies and corruption. For this reason, many poor developing countries suffer from a 'resource curse', which has been a source of disappointment in so many, especially in Africa (UNECA, 2013). Major oil companies, such as Royal Dutch Shell and BP are long established in developing countries, and have built up expertise in oil and gas exploration and extraction. These skills are vital to unlock resource potential, especially if reserves are located in difficult environments, both geologically and politically. Resource-rich countries, including Nigeria, Russia, Iraq, Sudan and Venezuela, are some examples of countries that have suffered from poor governance and political instability. Their governments wish to realize gains from ownership and control over energy assets, but they are compelled to rely on foreign investors, who are awarded exploitation rights and production contracts. Although energy-rich countries have turned to western expertise in the past, they are now attracting the BRIC countries.

For the developing country, the prospect of a deep-pocketed foreign investor is a mixed blessing. Host-country governments focus on the benefits of FDI to their economies as portrayed by the foreign investor. However, in reality, the investing firm is more focused on returns to its investors than on the benefits to the host country. For the MNE, location advantages are constantly shifting, and inward investors migrate as the balance of advantage shifts to new locations. For development to be sustainable, governments in developing countries would ideally look more to nurturing domestic industries than to relying on foreign investors. But this is easier said than done. In most developing countries, the injection of foreign capital remains essential to economic development.

Developed countries

Foreign investors are attracted to developed economies largely because of their market potential, but costs are a major consideration that might give them pause for thought. The investor might seek to manufacture or assemble products near large markets. Thus, export-oriented manufacturing in Mexico is clustered in the region near the US border. However, this option runs the risk of trade barriers, should trade relations with the US sour. Manufacturing within the country can bypass tariff barriers which would apply to imports. Thus, both foreign and domestic companies will arguably improve their products in competing to grab the consumer's attention. The benefit for consumers is thus a positive impact of inward FDI, as shown in Figure 2.8. Overall, however, the impacts of FDI in a developed country can be mixed, especially in terms of jobs and societal wellbeing.

Inward FDI: the developed economy's perspectives

What are the possible positive impacts?

- Jobs and career prospects for local workers
- Economic prosperity in local community
- Rise in tax revenues (depending on incentives to investor)
- Greater choice in consumer markets
- Improvements in societal wellbeing

What are the possible negative impacts?

- Many workers (e.g. those with inappropriate skills) lose out
- Uncompetitive domestic industries lose out
- Possible negative impacts on the environment
- Possible rise in inequality and social divisions

Figure 2.8 Impacts of inward FDI in developed economies

America's large car companies enjoyed a boom period in the post-war golden age of manufacturing, satisfying demand from eager American consumers. Detroit, Michigan, was the capital of the motor industry and the quintessential symbol of its industrial might, but its glory days were numbered. Failure to innovate and poor industrial relations between managers and powerful trade unions were among carmakers' gnawing problems. From the 1970s, competition started to bite, especially from Japanese carmakers with innovative lean manufacturing methods (see Chapter 3). Japanese car manufacturers built greenfield factories to sidestep trade barriers and also operate outside the grip of the trade unions. German carmakers soon followed suit, with new factories springing up in southern states – areas with little manufacturing legacy. So competitive were the newcomers that they oversaw a gradual decline in the fortunes of the American carmakers. Consumers took to the Japanese brands, which offered a winning combination of quality and low prices. Detroit's factories declined from a peak of 200,000 workers in 1950 to just 20,000 in 2012 (see the mini case study that follows). Vast areas became industrial wastelands, and the population decreased from 1.86 million in 1950 to 700,000 in 2012. Two of the three large American car companies, General Motors and Chrysler, collapsed financially, requiring bailouts by the US government following the financial crisis of 2008. Ford was the only one of the three not to have needed a bailout.

Japanese companies and American consumers benefited from the new greenfield manufacturing. But other impacts were more ambivalent. New factories create jobs and offer career prospects for local workers with the appropriate skills. But many unemployed people lack the skills to take up jobs in new factories, and new factories typically employ fewer people than their predecessors. Automation in manufacturing has seen robots take over many tasks. Research in the area of **artificial intelligence (AI)** has proceeded rapidly. AI is the area of computer science which researches ways in which machines can be developed to work and solve problems like humans. An example is the self-driving car. An implication is that in many industries, operations do not absorb the same number of workers that older industries required. Automation is thus disruptive in its impacts (see the case study in Chapter 9). Its impacts are separate from globalization processes, but have similar consequences: fears associated with job insecurity in many types of employment, from factory jobs to call centres.

artificial intelligence area of computer science which researches ways in which machines can be developed to work and solve problems like humans

In favoured locations where new jobs bring optimism and better employment prospects, the community will see greater economic activity flowing to other businesses that set up in the area. The increase in tax revenues ideally can help to fund public services such as education and health. However, where incentives have been offered to attract the investor, these revenues might be limited, at least for an initial period. Incentives to investors can be controversial. Waiving taxes for the foreign investor meets with objections from local businesses that pay taxes at the full rates. Foreign investors might also enjoy relaxation in regulations. This incentive might also encounter objections from the community. If the investor is receiving obvious preferential treatment from local political leaders, there can be an upsurge in tensions within the community.

The locations in developed countries which attract foreign investors are often those where de-industrialization has taken its toll and unemployment levels are high. Japanese car manufacturers have been attracted to parts of the UK where old industries such as steel, coal mining and shipbuilding have declined. These areas have also benefited from European structural funds targeted at poorer regions. An example of Japanese investment is the carmaker, Nissan, which built a factory in Sunderland in the North East of England. Significantly, the Japanese managers in Sunderland encouraged a constellation of related businesses, bringing spillover effects to the

region. Toyota has invested in an engine factory in Deeside in Wales. Similarly, Ford has built an engine factory in Bridgend in Wales. These, and other, foreign carmakers manufacture largely for export to the EU, benefiting from the EU's internal single market, where there are no customs barriers. These factories have become integrated in global supply chains. There are thus combined gains from FDI and globalization itself. Although these regions are among those that would suffer most economically from Britain's exit from the EU (Brexit), a significant majority of voters in all three areas voted 'leave' in the 2016 referendum on exiting the EU (61% in Sunderland, 54.6% in Bridgend and 56% in Flintshire, where the Deeside factory is located).

How could this result be explained? Although there are benefits flowing to those directly and indirectly involved in the new industries, the benefits do not automatically trickle down to all in society. Despite the fall in unemployment, these areas remain among the poorest in the UK. People who see little opportunity for a better life tend to feel left behind. To these citizens, the leave campaign's simple idea of 'taking back control' sounded appealing. Of course, it would never be as simple as portrayed by campaigners, but the emotional appeal contained in the slogan won over many voters. In the years following the referendum, voters were to discover that withdrawal towards a more country-centric approach would jeopardize the investments that had brought increasing prosperity. In 2019, Ford decided to close the engine factory in Bridgend. Uncertainties surrounding Brexit would have been a factor (discussed further in Chapter 5).

MINI CASE STUDY

Vanishing car jobs in the US Midwest

The CEO of General Motors (GM), Mary Barra, faced some difficult decisions in 2018, assessing the reality of the changing car market in the US. The Lordstown plant, near Youngstown, Ohio, which makes the Chevy Cruze compact sedan (saloon), was planned to close in March, 2019. Sedans and traditional passenger cars, once the mainstay of car sales, have fallen out of favour in recent years, with the growing preference among consumers for SUVs, crossovers and light trucks. These utility vehicles now make up 40% of the market. Other important trends to take into account have been the rise of electric and self-driving cars. Sales of the Chevy Cruze fell 21% in 2018, leaving Ms Barra in little doubt that drastic restructuring would have to take place. Altogether, four factories, employing 11,000 people, would be closed. Some of these workers could be transferred to other factories, but, for family reasons, many workers would not be able to shift location easily. Lordstown had suffered when the steel works closed in the late 1970s, and the jobs offered by GM provided a lifeline. But manufacturing jobs in Ohio continued their decline. GM collapsed in 2008, and was bailed out with taxpayer funding.

Other models under the Buick, Chevrolet and Cadillac brands would be cut, leading to a shrinking of GM's workforce of about 15%. The Chevy Cruze would continue to be made in Mexico, for non-US markets. On the news of the radical restructuring in November 2018, GM's shares rose 7.9%, but the overall share price for the year was about 7% down from that of a year earlier. Shareholders would have been assured that the restructuring would re-align the company towards the market changes that are rapidly occurring. Still, doubts remain over GM's strength in China, where it has been successful in boosting sales. The slowdown

Car manufacturing has played a vital role in American industrialization, but globalization has brought about painful adjustments for American carmakers.

in China is likely to have a dampening effect on overall performance.

Many workers in the Midwest, in areas such as Youngstown, had voted for Trump in 2016, persuaded that he would bring back jobs and factories. But this was a tall order in a world in which globalization had already progressed seemingly unrelentingly. Disappointment with the job losses would possibly dent Mr Trump's support in the area. This area of post-industrial adjustment has suffered as a result of globalization. While GM can change its manufacturing strategy to regain competitiveness, areas such as these in Ohio have suffered from the negative impacts of globalization.

Questions

- Why is GM's restructuring so drastic?
- What are the challenges lying ahead for GM, in adapting to changing markets in the US and in global markets?

Find out more

See the article by Patti Waldmeir, 'GM job losses fail to dent Trump support in Ohio stronghold', in the *Financial Times*, 22 December 2018.

Globalization across key dimensions of the environment

This section takes an overview of globalization across the dimensions of the international environment, highlighted in Chapter 1. These dimensions will be discussed in detail in the chapters that follow. Here, we highlight the varied impacts of globalization in each, identifying the players involved. We place both positive and negative impacts in contexts, revealing inherent tensions in globalization processes. These are shown in Figure 2.9.

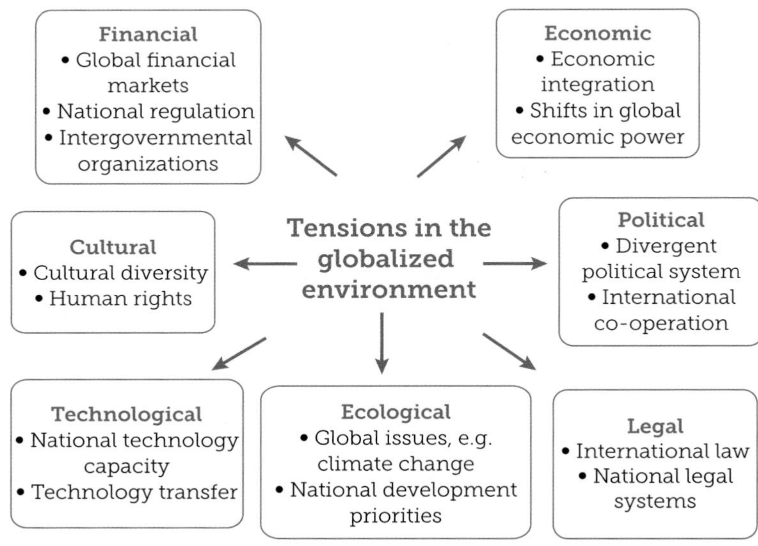

Figure 2.9 Unfolding tensions stemming from globalization

As the figure shows, within each dimension there are counterpoised forces at work, often revolving around conflicts between local or national pressures and global concerns. In each of the boxes, the local or national factor is listed first, followed by the wider global factors. We now look at these in more detail.

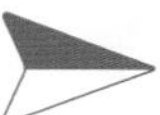

- Economic environment – Countries have their own distinctive economic systems which have evolved over long periods, some more market oriented and others more state controlled. Globalization has brought greater integration among national economies. They have become interdependent, but this does not mean that they have converged. Some countries have benefited greatly from globalization: the emerging economies are examples, as their manufacturing prowess (in the case of China) and abundant natural resources (in the case of Brazil) serve global markets. These countries have grown in economic power globally. Whereas the US as the world's largest economy was considered the dominant economic power in the decades following the Second World War, there are now multiple powerful players in the global economy, notably the emerging economies. None has yet taken over from the US as the world's dominant economic power. Globalization has led to greater interdependence among all players, but there remain huge divergences in economic power globally.

  Economic conditions in one country impact on the economies of other countries with which it has ties, including its neighbours, home countries of inward investors and its trading partners. But poor countries risk missing out on the potential benefits of FDI, while having to rely on global markets for energy and commodities. In what might seem a paradox, economic inequality between countries can thus be exacerbated by globalization.

  Moreover, inequalities have arisen within countries favoured by internationalizing firms. In these countries, globalized companies and appropriately skilled workers have benefited. China, for example, has a growing affluent middle class, but it has seen growing inequality (Wildau and Mitchell, 2016). The top 1% in China own one-third of the country's wealth – a percentage that, although high, is not as high as the wealth of the top 1% in the US, which is 42%. However, China is theoretically a communist state. Chinese researchers highlight two factors in particular: large variations from region to region in China and the large gap between urban and rural inhabitants (Xie and Zhou, 2014). Both are aspects of globalization. Export-oriented industrialization has favoured urbanized areas and **export processing zones (EPZ)** specifically set up to attract foreign investors wishing to export.

export processing zones geographic areas where goods can be imported and exported duty-free

- Political environment – National political systems around the world remain diverse, reflecting the fact that each country's politics is rooted in its own heritage and values. On the other hand, political co-operation across borders has taken place, largely as a result of the increase in economic and other ties between countries. Deeper political integration across borders has been fostered within the European Union (EU), which has EU-wide political structures, but this example is exceptional and is under strain from nationalist forces within member countries, as discussed in Chapter 5. Political integration, in general, has not followed from economic integration. But greater co-operation among sovereign states has progressed, largely through the **United Nations (UN)** and its agencies. The UN (www.un.org) was formed in the aftermath of the Second World War, chiefly to prevent future threats to global security and to promote peaceful co-operation among member states. It does not operate as a government, but seeks to achieve agreement among sovereign players. Some might lament that the UN cannot coerce members to come into line with resolutions which represent the majority of its members, but this limitation reflects a widespread wariness among national governments to cede powers to supranational organizations. International public opinion, as well as long-term self-interest, can be effective in persuading governments to co-operate with others to solve global problems. However, the nationalist perspective of the US

United Nations (UN) the world's largest and most authoritative inter-governmental organization

government since the election of President Trump has set back the role of the US in international institutions, as discussed in Chapter 5.

Also dating from the post-war period, the **General Agreement on Tariffs and Trade (GATT)** has sought, through successive rounds of negotiations, to promote agreements among countries to dismantle trade barriers. The **World Trade Organization (WTO)** (www.wto.org), created in 1995, became a successor to the GATT, re-enforcing the belief that freer trade benefits all countries, both large and small. The WTO's banner of freer and fairer trade has become somewhat tattered, however, as many governments have tended to pay only lip service to its goals, putting national economic and political concerns first. The US has become a prominent voice in criticizing the WTO, indicating its shift towards a more national view of its trade interests.

General Agreement on Tariffs and Trade (GATT) series of multilateral agreements on reducing trade barriers

World Trade Organization (WTO) successor to the GATT, set up to regulate world trade and settle trade disputes among member countries

- Legal environment – National legal systems are closely connected to sovereign national political systems. In countries where there is a strong sense that the law should operate independently of political influences, an independent judicial system open to all is considered an important institution in the safeguarding of civil and political rights. In countries where the legal system is controlled by political elites, the legal system lacks independence. This is considered a significant risk factor for firms doing business in these locations. Firms doing business in China, where legal institutions are weak and politicized, are well aware of the risks. However, there is a growing body of international law, to which countries willingly commit themselves, in a process which is inching towards global legal standards. Central to this process is the **International Court of Justice (ICJ)** (www.icj-cij.org), founded in 1920, which is headquartered in The Hague, in the Netherlands. In the area of human rights, in particular, international law is the benchmark, and is now incorporated in the national law of many countries, as well as the EU. Regional lawmaking in many areas, most developed in the EU, is also influential for cross-border businesses, affecting numerous areas of law, including employment, competition and consumer rights. Microsoft and Intel, two giant American companies, have both been fined by the EU court for breaches of competition law. More recently, Google has been found to be in breach of EU competition law and privacy law. A global company would be unwise to believe that because it is large and dominates its sector worldwide, it is somehow above national and EU law.

International Court of Justice (ICJ) UN-sponsored international court which hears legal cases relating to disputes between member states

- Ecological environment – Globalization is often blamed for environmental degradation, but the processes taking place are complex. Industrialization, which got under way long before the current era of globalization, is a direct cause of pollution, the depletion of natural resources and destruction of natural ecosystems. Industrialization is itself associated with urbanization, industrialized agriculture, the growth in transport and growing need for energy, all of which contribute to environmental degradation. Where globalization comes into play is in the mounting speed of these destructive processes in the post-war era. China's rapid industrialization, driven by an insatiable appetite for energy and natural resources, has resulted in a particularly woeful toll on the environment, with record levels of air pollution and dangerous depletion of water supplies. China is now the world's largest emitter of greenhouse gases, which are largely responsible for climate change (see Chapter 10). Climate change is a global issue, and the **UN's Climate Change Panel** (www.ipcc.ch) has been active in urging all countries to sign up to emissions reductions through global agreement, first in the Kyoto Protocol of 1998, and now in the 2015 Paris accord. However, as in other dimensions highlighted in this section, governments are slow to commit their countries to emissions reductions and other measures which they perceive

UN Climate Change Panel UN body which brings together research on climate change and makes recommendations for action by member states

could damage national interests. Again, we find that global problems have local impacts, and governments tend to see global issues through national lenses. The expressed intention of President Trump of the US to withdraw from the Paris accord is indicative of the country-centric approach to global issues.

- Technological environment – It was once assumed that technological advances, especially in high-tech industries, would come from America and be diffused through the rest of the world. Much innovation *has* emanated from America, and American entrepreneurs have stood out in exploiting new ideas. However, as other countries have improved scientific education and technology infrastructure, technological excellence has become more widespread. A factor has been the diffusion of technology through FDI, whereby local workers gain skills through technology transfer, which can boost domestic firms. Technology transfer has been a major positive aspect of globalization, benefiting developing countries. Internet technology has facilitated the operation of extended supply chains. Technological innovations have transformed much manufacturing, often leading to greater automation. But while the disruptive effects of technology are beneficial in terms of production, they raise issues for societies and governments, who must adapt to rapid technological change, and, if need be, devise regulatory frameworks that take account of new technology. The worker who has suffered from redundancy and the town whose obsolete factory has closed are likely to view globalization in a negative light. So, too, is the traditional taxi driver who has lost business to the driver utilizing Uber's digital platform, even leaving aside the self-driving taxi (also developed by Uber).
- Financial environment – Globalization of financial markets has progressed swiftly, due to advances in communications technology and liberalization of national financial systems. Banks and other financial services companies became global players, prospering from innovative financial instruments, a liberalized financial sector in many countries, and light regulation in key financial centres (discussed further in Chapter 8). While governments welcome capital flows, many have become susceptible to the risks of liberalization, highlighted in recurring financial crises of the last two decades. The Asian financial crisis of 1998 showed the risks of opening up fragile domestic financial systems to volatile capital flows from foreign investors. A mismatch emerged between huge globalized financial markets and the predominantly national structures which regulate finance in each country. Excessive risk-taking, especially in investment banking, led to a global financial crisis in 2008, which saw some large banks fail and others, deemed to be too big to fail, bailed out by the governments of their home countries, even though the banks had larger operations abroad than they did at home.

  The **International Monetary Fund (IMF)** (www.imf.org) and **World Bank** (www.worldbank.org), both established in the aftermath of the Second World War, aid countries in financial distress and maintain international financial stability (see Chapter 8 for a further discussion). Their roles could be enhanced, but, as with international bodies generally, this would require agreement by sovereign member states to give oversight roles to supranational bodies – a step many are reluctant to take.

International Monetary Fund (IMF) agency of the UN which oversees the international monetary and financial systems

World Bank organization established in the aftermath of the Second World War to fund development projects and broader development programmes

- Cultural and social environments – Distinctive cultural identities, especially national cultures, seem incompatible with globalization. A growing 'global middle class' which shares similar tastes and lifestyles, might seem to be oblivious of national borders. These new, mostly urbanized, consumers are changing from traditional cultures, based on rural and family ties, towards a culture based more on material consumption and individualist values. A fear is that people are becoming 'rootless', disconnected from traditional attitudes and values which have ensured stability and observance of norms of social behaviour within societies over the centuries. An undercurrent is disquiet that the new consumer society is essentially shaped by American culture. The growing middle class in emerging economies is taking on characteristics of an American lifestyle, notably greater consumption of meat and processed foods. The international expansion of companies such as Coca-Cola and McDonald's can be perceived as Americanization, which is a more culture-laden concept than globalization. Giant American companies are criticized by those who fear the disruptive impacts of globalization in undermining social and cultural values.

Traditional cultural values and national identities can persist even though overlaid with the material trappings of consumer society. Certainly, global companies aim to satisfy differing consumer needs and tastes in different countries, implying that localization is an adjunct of globalization. This, if anything, reinforces their global economic reach, giving rise to anti-globalization arguments that take in both anti-capitalist and nationalist narratives.

Many societies in today's world have become multi-cultural, largely through immigration. And many people travel to other countries for temporary work. Cultural minorities, whether residents or visiting workers, are at risk of discrimination and exploitation. A rise in intolerant nationalism, which is now perceptible in a number of countries, including the US and a number of European countries, can result in anti-immigration policies and in greater tensions in multi-cultural communities. Nationalism and globalization are an uneasy combination. As noted above, anti-globalization voices often take aim at the dominance of giant American companies. The 'America first' stance of the US has been one of economic nationalism, but the US under President Trump has also vigorously pursued anti-immigration policies.

The enjoyment of cultural rights is recognized as a human right, and is reinforced by the UN's cultural conventions under the authority of **UNESCO** (the UN Educational, Scientific and Cultural Organization, at www.unesco.org). Migrant labour is often organized along lines of ethnic or cultural groupings. Such workers, typically working in factories, mines, agriculture and construction sites far from their homes, are vulnerable groups. These workers are vulnerable to breaches of their human rights, including excessive working hours and poor safety conditions. They highlight an aspect of globalization that places human rights at risk. There is a sad irony here, as the idea of human rights is inherently global, pertaining to human beings wherever they are and whatever their culture.

UNESCO (the UN Educational, Scientific and Cultural Organization) UN agency that promotes peace and security through collaboration in these areas, notably in respect of upholding human rights

The tensions between global and national or local forces are evident in each of these dimensions. But these are not simple 'either-or' choices in many cases. A government might open its borders to global companies, encouraged to think that foreign investment is in the country's best long-term interest. Growing integration into the global economy, it hopes, will bring growth and prosperity. But these decisions involve risks that sometimes harm local interests, including domestic industries, local workforces and the natural environment. The global company might be expected to think in terms of higher international labour standards, as befits the idea that it is 'above' national jurisdictions. But the opposite is more likely: the global company seeks out particular countries for location advantages, including lower costs, weak employee protection laws and weak regulation.

Globalization and sustainability: how compatible are they?

Sustainability challenges arise in connection with globalization, particularly in contexts of FDI and outsourcing that have damaging impacts on societies and individuals. Globalized production, aided by accommodating governments, has led to

wealth creation and economic growth. But, as we have seen, income growth in a national economy does not automatically translate into improved wellbeing in society. A major challenge is therefore harnessing globalization processes to improve wellbeing for all while protecting the ecological environment. These aspects of sustainability are shown in Figure 2.10.

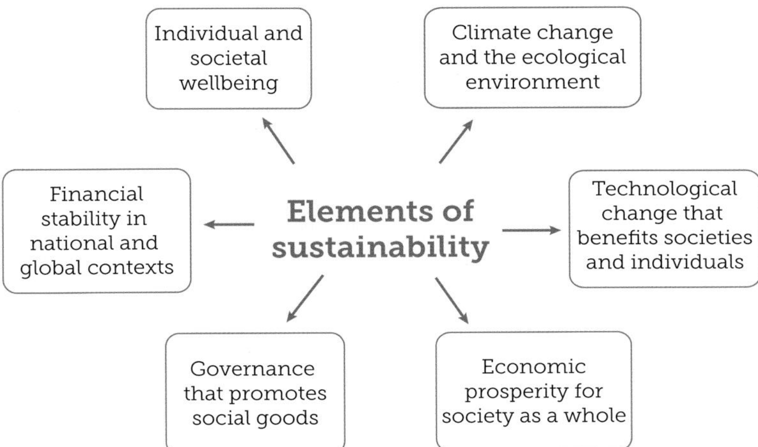

Figure 2.10 Elements of sustainability

Issues of sustainability have become more urgent as industrialization and markets have encompassed more countries. These processes have been driven by MNEs through FDI and global supply chains – both at the heart of globalization. Internationalization processes have rested on the strategies of MNEs, designed to gain scale efficiencies and to expand into markets globally. These goals are inherent in capitalist outlooks. Opening of markets and industrialization have helped to deliver economic prosperity in numerous economies, notably in China and other Asian countries which have prioritized export-oriented manufacturing. As shown in Figure 2.1, location advantages always revolve around potential gains for corporate owners. Among the most influential of these is cheap labour. Cheap labour is associated particularly with developing economies, but does not stop there. Poor regions in some developed economies offer comparable location advantages, including relatively low wages, weak employment protection laws, and incentives such as low taxes. This has been particularly evident since the global financial crisis of 2008, which had more damaging economic impacts in developed countries than in developing ones. Weakly regulated global financial markets prior to the crisis reminded the world of the toxic risks that can destabilize global capitalism.

The OECD has found that, although post-crisis economic recovery has strengthened in most of its member states, wage stagnation and widening inequality in labour markets has been a disquieting trend, threatening sustainability. It found that public belief in the recovery is being eroded, with widening gaps between winners and losers (OECD, 2018). People with high-level skills have found quality employment in well-paid jobs in the companies that are prospering the most, many in areas such as computing and information systems. But these are the few. Most of the jobs available to ordinary workers with limited skills are in low-paid manual work. These jobs offer little in the way of security or quality employment, and wages have stagnated: wage rises are at half the rate they were before the crisis. What is more, the situation for these workers – and would-be workers – is deteriorating. There has been a decline in collective bargaining and trade union membership, which are known to contribute to better conditions of work. While training could help to raise the prospects of low-paid workers, these workers are three times less likely to receive training than high-paid workers. Their jobs, moreover, are less secure, often short term and part-time. Many are in sectors where automation is a threat. Insecurity is particularly evident in work in the gig economy. The out-of-work find that protection systems have been scaled back since the crisis: fewer than one in three jobseekers now has entitlement to unemployment benefit. The rate of poverty among low-paid workers has actually risen during the post-crisis recovery. In 2015, on average 10.6% of working-age people lived in poverty in the OECD, a rise from 9.6% in 2005 (OECD, 2018). The OECD presents a picture of economic trends that are ultimately unsustainable. The lion's share of income and benefits go to earners at the top of the ladder, while those further down see their situation deteriorating.

Can the direction of these trends be changed to promoting sustainable and inclusive prosperity? Technological change is another factor that is opening new opportunities for businesses and suitably skilled workers, but posing threats to those without appropriate skills. Business leaders would argue that it is for businesses to pursue corporate goals that benefit shareholders, and that this constitutes the limit of their responsibility. For example, a reduction in the number of workers needed is a clear cost benefit, and the social consequences are not a concern for the company. Companies taking a purely economic view of their responsibilities are now finding this stance evokes increasing criticism among stakeholders and in international public opinion generally. But they are disinclined to change their business models unless compelled to do so, say, by new laws.

Sustainability is an urgent issue for governments, especially in the context of sustainable development. But for many, especially in emerging economies, development equates to economic development measured by growth figures. In China, rapid economic growth brought employment and better wages, but in a context of poor working conditions and the extensive use of migrant labour, carrying risks of violations of human rights. Such workers are crucial to many industries globally, including construction and mining, in addition to the manufacturing of consumer goods. These workers have little security and little scope to voice grievances. As noted above, they are not alone. In developed economies, economic growth can exist alongside a deterioration in pay and conditions for workers and a weakening of social protections generally.

Corporate leaders think of obligations to shareholders first and foremost. These involve maximizing profits from a short-term perspective. Responsibilities to workers as stakeholders do not weigh so heavily, although they are vital to business success over the long term. Social and environmental responsibilities contribute to building sustainability into a business model. Can changes in governance bring about the necessary changes in behaviour?

While we might think that 'governance' refers only to matters of government policy, this is not the case in today's world. Governance responsibilities fall on both governments and businesses. Businesses seek political and regulatory arrangements that favour their activities, and they are often involved in formulating policies. Abiding by national law is one of the primary obligations of any business, as CSR principles highlight. However, CSR involves going beyond legal obligations, to abide by ethical principles and stakeholder interests. In practice, many businesses seek ways of sidestepping national laws as well as social responsibilities. Globalization has facilitated these manoeuvres. The globalized company has become astute at setting up legal entities in advantageous locations to avoid tax in countries where it operates. These arrangements are facilitated by governments of accommodating countries who act as financial centres, but effectively deny many governments of tax revenues that could fund public spending on social goals. Such arrangements adversely affected both developed and developing countries. Although this suggests that globalization has had detrimental impacts on building sustainability, these

 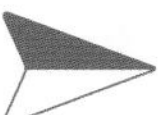

outcomes are not inevitable. Regulation of businesses at national level has been the norm, and global companies have feasted on playing one country off against another. By contrast, co-operation of regulators and lawmakers at the intergovernmental level has lagged behind, but is gathering pace within national governments and companies that are placing sustainability before profits.

Conclusions

Companies have been drivers of globalization through their global strategies, but other factors, including the role of governments, have also been influential. Seeing the economic potential of opening their economies to foreign investors, governments have played crucial roles, interacting with MNEs to facilitate the deepening ties and interconnections that we witness in today's world. The post-war boom in FDI was initially dominated by developed countries, where western consumer societies, especially the US, became the aspirational example for others to follow.

As the focus of FDI strategies shifted to developing countries, impacts have been dramatic. Location advantages such as low-cost labour and natural resources have attracted MNEs. The large emerging economies have been at the forefront of this shift. As these economies have grown, emerging MNEs have themselves become FDI investors, in both developing and developed countries. The globalization of production has seen supply chains reaching a growing range of countries. The impacts in societies have been uneven. Developing countries have seen dramatic changes, enjoying rising incomes and economic growth. In many poor countries, large numbers of people have been lifted out of poverty. The growing middle classes in many countries are testimony to the benefits of globalization, but the persistence of rural poverty and poor quality of life, including poor health provision and education, are indicators of the negative side of globalization. So too are the poor working conditions for low-skilled, low-paid workers. Moreover, many millions of people that are now part of the growing lower middle class in emerging economies are still teetering on the edge of poverty, as expectations of further upward mobility recede. Also adding to globalization's negative impacts are the detrimental effects to the environment of rapid industrialization.

For developed economies, globalized production has brought a flood of imported consumer products from low-cost manufacturing centres. But, while this is good news, it is clouded by the effects of de-industrialization in former manufacturing strongholds. For many people in developed countries, disappearing jobs are what they think of when the word 'globalization' is mentioned. At the same time, the poor working and living conditions of many low-paid workers in both developed and developing countries are increasingly being blamed on corporate behaviour. Corporate profits have grown for successful globalized MNEs, able to offshore operations and reduce tax exposure by choosing advantageous locations.

Companies are now in the spotlight for social responsibilities. Governments in host countries that have welcomed FDI are now seeing the risks of social unrest from poor labour conditions. A country's inhabitants expect their government to regulate fairly the activities of globalized companies within their territories. Equally importantly, governments are expected to ensure that the benefits of globalization are translated into wellbeing for all. However, the reality is often growing inequality and instability. There are growing pressures from consumers bearing down on both companies and governments to become more socially responsible in their behaviour. In addition, international pressures can be influential. The mismatch between powerful globalized businesses and relatively weak global governance is often observed (UNDP, 2014: 120). Moves towards greater international co-operation among companies and governments are the roles of international bodies that focus on raising labour standards and achieving societal goals. However, in today's business environment, there are multiple centres of economic power. Global tech giants, oil companies and financial firms have become highly globalized power centres, but, counter-weights are emerging in national contexts, including political, social and environmental pressures to rein in globalization processes.

CLOSING CASE STUDY

Zara: the challenges of staying on top in global fashion

Zara is a fashion brand that has excelled in winning over consumers to shop at its retail premises around the globe. But retailing is changing rapidly, moving towards online shopping and leaving the bricks-and-mortar shops behind. At least, that has been the experience of many retailers battling against the 'Amazon effect'. Zara has been a success story so far, but its growth in the past has been driven largely by opening more stores. That is now changing, as it grapples with the challenges of online innovations and issues of sustainability.

Zara is the creation of Inditex, the fashion empire based in Spain. Since its formation in Galicia in northern Spain in 1975, Zara's founder, Amancio Ortega, has revolutionized the business of retail fashion, from design through to production and distribution to its shops. In the process, Zara has shaped consumer expectations about fashion retailing in the world's shopping centres. Where once fashion retailers would offer a new range each autumn and spring, Zara continually renews the offering, at intervals as short as two weeks. When a line is successful, follow-up orders can also be delivered at very short notice, supplanting lines that are not. This constant renewal and responsiveness is at the heart of Zara's business model. While Zara shares this approach with 'fast fashion' retailers, it emphasizes sustainability, in contrast to the approach of retailers who sell clothing very cheaply and encourage a throwaway attitude among consumers.

Zara aims to create an enjoyable shopping experience at its city-centre stores like this one in Kolkata in India.

The expertise that has gone into developing Zara's production and distribution is now being directed towards applying new digital technology to its logistics operations. Its strategy has shifted towards slowing the pace of new store openings, focusing on the larger, high-profile stores and investing more in its online sales. There are now over 2,000 Zara stores worldwide, and if the other Inditex brands, such as Massimo Dutti and Bershka, are taken into account, the company as a whole has over 7,000 stores in 96 markets. It is aiming to sell online in all of its markets.

Far from being part of a declining retail scene in so many town and city centres, Zara has taken pride in its elegant stores, many located in some of the most prestigious shopping streets. The aspirational shopping experience has long been a focus of the company's management, and such an approach was never more important than it is now. The enjoyable experience is, after all, the one area in which the online retailer cannot compete. Neither, of course, can the functional low-cost store that sells on price alone. Primark, for example, is a low-cost retailer with no online

presence. Zara, by contrast, seeks to attract the consumer at an aesthetic level, with attractively displayed stock in a pleasant environment. The opening of its new flagship store in Milan in 2018 was indicative of this approach, inviting the shopper to take part in the celebration. Digital innovations in the shops themselves add a new dimension to the experience. One of these is augmented reality (AR), which are interactive experiences that add a whole new dimension for the customer.

Zara store managers see firsthand what lines are popular and which are not. They are given considerable scope to take decisions on orders, and they are in frequent contact with the company's headquarters in Spain, where the commercial managers and designers can respond immediately. The responsiveness of the manufacturing process owes much of its efficiency to the fact that Inditex relies heavily on factories in relatively close proximity to its HQ. Over 50% of its products are made in Spain, Portugal, Morocco and Turkey. Morocco and Turkey offer relatively low-cost labour. Labour in these countries is not as cheap as in Asia, but the lower transport costs and speed of fulfilling orders make these closer manufacturing locations advantageous. On the other hand, much manufacturing for the Zara brand does take place in Asia, where much of the world's garment manufacturing is now concentrated. These are low-wage economies where poor working conditions, and safety doubts have come to taint any company involved in fast fashion. Inditex has been involved in Bangladesh, where the collapse of the Rana Plaza factory, in which over a thousand people died, brought to the world's attention the dangerous conditions suffered by garment workers. Inditex has been part of the Accord on fire and building safety, along with other western companies (see the case study in Chapter 12).

The Inditex approach to global fashion retailing has been highly profitable. Surging sales in emerging markets are now helping to ensure future growth, as its online platform is launching in countries such as India and Turkey. Inditex saw a rise of 41% in online sales in 2017, and online sales now account for 10% of the total (BBC, 2018). Profits were up 7% and revenues reached over €25 billion for the year. Inditex has taken pride in its investment in technology and logistics, and also its sustainability initiatives. It announced in 2019 that all Zara clothes would be made from sustainable fabrics by 2025, with other Inditex brands to follow. Since 2015, it has operated schemes to collect used stock for recycling. Consumers are increasingly concerned over issues of ethics in the entire supply chain, including production, human rights issues and recycling of used clothing. Zara has been among the leaders in its approaches to sustainability.

Questions

- What are the aspects of the Inditex business model that have proved crucial to its success?
- In what ways has digitalization affected Zara's business?
- In what ways has the business model been able to adjust to the challenges of online retailers?
- How would you assess Zara from a sustainability perspective?

Further reading

See the article by Scarlett Conlon, 'Zara clothes to be made from 100% sustainable fabrics by 2025', in *The Guardian*, 17 July 2019.

Multiple choice questions

Visit www.macmillanihe.com/morrison-gbe-5e to take a quick self-test quiz on what you have read in this chapter.

? Review questions

1 What are the defining characteristics of globalization?
2 In what ways are there anti-globalization trends that are affecting businesses?
3 What is the Human Development Index, and why is it an important indicator in international business?
4 What is distinctive about emerging economies, as compared to those that are simply designated 'developing' economies?
5 What are the main motives behind MNE internationalization strategies?
6 Compare modes of internationalization in terms of degrees of involvement in the host country.
7 What are the advantages of FDI as an entry mode?
8 What is greenfield investment as a mode of FDI, and what are the benefits to the foreign investor?
9 Explain the position of the brand owner who opts for outsourced production?
10 How have the post-war shifts in international power led to (a) growing FDI; and (b) changing patterns of FDI?
11 What does the product life cycle theory contribute to our understanding of FDI?
12 What are the elements of Dunning's eclectic paradigm of FDI?
13 Looking at the impacts of globalization in differing dimensions of the international environment, which are the most globalized, and why?
14 To what extent has the legal environment become globalized?
15 How are MNEs rethinking supply chains in terms of sustainability?

✓ Assignments

1 Examine the major globalization processes at work in today's world economy, and assess to what extent globalization is becoming more fragmented, with gains in some respects and national resurgence in others.

2 Assess the extent to which MNEs' FDI strategies have generated re-thinking of global and local factors in terms of sustainability.

Further reading

Bourguignon, F. (2015) *The Globalization of Inequality* (Princeton University Press).

Dicken, P. (2014) *Global Shift*, 7th edition (London: Sage).

Eriksen, T. (2014) *Globalization: The key concepts*, 2nd edition (Bloomsbury).

Hirst, P., Thompson, G. and Bromley, S. (2009) *Globalization in Question*, 3rd edition (Cambridge: Polity Press).

Keane, J. (2010) *Global Civil Society?* (Cambridge: Cambridge University Press).

Lechner, F. and Boli, J. (2019) *The Globalization Reader*, 6th edition (Oxford: Wiley-Blackwell).

Roberts, J., Hite, A. and Chorey, N. (eds) (2014) *The Globalization and Development Reader: Perspectives on development and global change*, 2nd edition (Oxford: Wiley-Blackwell).

Rodrik, D. (2012) *The Globalization Paradox: Democracy and the future of the world economy* (Oxford University Press).

❐ References

BBC (2018) 'Online sales surge boost Zara owner Inditex', 14 March, at www.bbc.co.uk

Buckley, P. and Hashai, N. (2009) 'Formalizing internationalization in the eclectic paradigm', *Journal of International Business Studies*, 40: 58–70.

Dunning, J. (1993) *Multinational Enterprises and the Global Economy* (Wokingham: Addison Wesley).

Friedman, T. (2000) *The Lexus and the Olive Tree* (Anchor Books).

Friedman, T. (2016) 'The age of protest', *New York Times*, 13 January, at www.nyt.com

Hymer, S. (1975) 'The multinational corporation and the law of uneven development', in Radice, H. (ed.) *International Firms and Modern Imperialism* (Harmondsworth: Penguin).

OECD (2018) OECD Employment Outlook 2018, OECD Publishing, Paris, at http://dx.doi.org/10.1787/empl_outlook-2018-en

Ohmae, K. (2000) *The Invisible Continent: Four strategic imperatives of the new economy* (London: Nicholas Brealey Publishing).

Rodrik, D. (2012) *The Globalization Paradox: Democracy and the future of the world economy* (Oxford: Oxford University Press).

UN (2014) *World Investment Report* (Geneva: UN).

UNCTAD (United Nations Conference on Trade and Development) (2018) World Investment Report 2018, 6 June 2018, at http://unctad.org

UNDP (2014) *Human Development Report 2014* (New York: UNDP).

UNECA (United Nations Economic Commission for Africa) (2013) *Africa-BRICS Cooperation: Implications for growth, employment and structural transformation in Africa* (Addis Ababa: UNECA).

Waters, M. (2001) *Globalization*, 2nd edition (London: Routledge).

Wells, L.T. (ed.) (1972) *The Product Life Cycle and International Trade* (Boston, MA: Harvard Business School Press).

Wildau, G. and Mitchell, T. (2016) 'China income inequality among the world's worst', *Financial Times*, 14 January 2016, at www.ft.com

World Bank (2018) 'Classifying countries by income', at https://datatopics.worldbank.org/world-development-indicators/classifying-countries-by-income (accessed 23 September 2019).

Yu Xie and Xiang Zhou (2014) 'Income inequality in today's China', *Proceedings of the National Academy of Science of the USA*, 111(19): 6928–6933.

 **Visit the companion website at www.macmillanihe.com/morrison-gbe-5e for further learning and teaching resources.**

PART 2 DIMENSIONS OF THE BUSINESS ENVIRONMENT

In this Part, we shift from the enterprise in a globalized world to dimensions of the international environment relating to societies – their cultures, how they are governed and how their legal systems impact on people. The first is Chapter 3, *Culture and societies*. An overview of national cultures, languages and religions forms an introduction to the chapter. Culture theories are presented in relation to business environments. The chapter looks at corporate cultures in different contexts, including stakeholder considerations. Aspects of changing societies that are posing particular challenges include migration, human rights and ageing populations. These are issues of sustainability, not just for governments, but also for businesses.

Chapter 4, *The global economic environment*, introduces national economies and economic systems. Understanding global forces depends crucially on grasping how national economies function, along with the ways in which decision-makers form policies. Emerging economies have been at the forefront of economic growth and globalization. Global economic integration is proceeding apace, but there remains huge diversity among national economic systems, reflecting differing cultural and historical influences. Market reforms have transformed China, but the Chinese economy remains guided by its communist government and its state-centred system. Slow recovery and pressures on public spending have caused governments to rethink social policies and sustainable growth. In particular, widening inequality and the need for inclusive growth have been key themes of the economic environment.

In Chapter 5, *The political environment: politics and business intertwined*, we look both at formal institutions and the changing roles of businesses in governance. Political institutions change over time. The adoption of democratic institutions has been a trend in the post-war period, notably in the post-colonial and post-communist countries. But democratic setbacks and the strengthening of authoritarian governments has led to a rethink of democratic values and institutions. In many countries, powerful economic interests are jeopardizing public institutions that should serve all in society. Populism and nationalism have become more widespread in many countries, including the US and European countries. Nationalist policies have impacted on domestic politics and also international relations, creating a more adversarial environment. The UK's Brexit process is discussed in detail, highlighting the adversarial tone of the policy debate.

The role of institutions is taken up again in the following chapter, Chapter 6, *The legal environment*. Here we focus on both national and international law. First, we examine national legal systems, and their differing approaches to civil and criminal law. For international businesses, legal risk varies between national systems. The business is concerned particularly about contracts with suppliers and customers, contracts for services, dealing with governments and dealing with affiliate companies in differing environments. Stakeholders increasingly expect corporate leaders to abide by both the letter and the spirit of the law. As in the political environment, legal considerations are increasingly taking on an international dimension. MNEs must now adapt to the obligations recognized in international law, notably in areas of human rights and the environment. In the EU, businesses must also comply with EU law, including the jurisdiction of the European Court of Justice. The chapter highlights the risks to the rule of law that are increasing in a number of states, causing uncertainty in the business environment.

© Getty, Westend61

CULTURE AND SOCIETIES

Outline of chapter

This chapter will enable you to

- Understand the nature and origins of cultural diversity in societies
- Identify cultural dimensions as an aid to comparing national cultures
- Assess the role and impacts of different organizational cultures in the business environment
- Gain an overview of the ways in which societies change over time, including processes of industrialization and urbanization
- Understand how businesses and governments can contribute to sustainable development in the context of societal wellbeing

OPENING CASE STUDY

Spotlight on Qatar

The Arab states of the Middle East have captured global attention, largely because of their abundance of energy resources. These desert societies have long historical roots, their traditional social structures and cultures being dominated by Islam. As states in this region have flourished economically, their conservative religious values have shown a marked contrast with modern western values that predominate in the global economic environment. Qatar, has been one of the more prominent of these states, notably due to its rise to prominence through extracting and producing liquified natural gas (LNG). From the 2000s onwards, the growth of this sector helped to drive its rapidly developing economy, bringing rising wealth and aspirations to take its place on the global stage. Qatar's capital, Doha, came to world notice with the Doha round of multilateral trade negotiations organized by the WTO in 2001. The state investment authority of Qatar has been active around the world, investing in many different sectors. The investments include banks (Barclays, Santander), prestige real estate (the Shard in London and the Empire State Building in New York) and shops (Harrods and J. Sainsbury). Qatar was in the news in 2010, when it was chosen as the location for the 2022 World Cup competition by the international football federation (FIFA). As a desert country that is transforming itself into a modern state, Qatar faces numerous challenges at the levels of institutions and infrastructure, but also crucial is the cultural shift that is entailed in changing social values.

Resource wealth has made Qatar one of the world's richest nations, but one marked by an extreme divide between rich and poor within its borders. Qatar has a population of about 2.69 million people, but its wealth is concentrated in the hands of its permanent population of Qataris, who number about 500,000 people, making up about 10% of its population. The remaining 90% are expatriates, who are temporary residents. About half of these are migrant labourers or workers who work in unskilled, poorly paid jobs. They are mainly from South East Asia; Indians are the largest group. These workers are classified as temporary residents only: even if they have lived in the country a number of years and see it as their home, they cannot acquire the right to live there permanently, participate in civic life or enjoy any benefits or social protections offered by the state. In recent years, migrant workers have been working on the sites of the eight new stadiums and other facilities for the World Cup. This has brought the conditions of their work and living arrangements into the limelight.

Human rights concerns have led to pressure on Qatar's leadership to bring in reforms of its laws on the rights of migrant workers. Under the Kafala labour system, workers are, in effect, owned by their employer, who has control over their movements. Exploitation and poor living conditions of construction workers have been major concerns on the sites of the World Cup venues. Reports of forced labour, appalling conditions and deaths of workers have led to calls for changes (Ratcliffe, 2018). Qatar's authorities have responded to criticisms of these conditions, and a change in the law in 2018 allows most workers to leave their employers and return to their home countries without first having to get their permission. This is a step forward, but it remains the fact that many employers confiscate workers' passports. There have also been changes in the law on domestic workers, mainly women, of whom there are many thousands. These workers are particularly vulnerable to exploitation, mistreatment and restrictions on their freedom of movement. They are now entitled to a contract of employment, but still fall outside the reform of the Kafala system.

Qatar has embarked on immense building projects to construct World Cup venues.

The spotlight on workers in Qatar has served to alert its leaders that in this rapidly-changing country, human rights of all workers are a matter of concern. How-ever, these changes take time to become implemented in practice, and they depend on effective enforcement. Minimum wage laws and laws on hours of work are examples. In addition to the new stadiums, the rapid expansion of hotel capacity has received attention. Between 2014 and 2018, the number of hotel rooms grew by 81%. Much of this new building is in the five-star luxury category, where the atmosphere is one of glitz and glamour. But for the migrant workers in these hotels, including security staff, cleaners and gardeners, life can be a constant struggle. While their pay is meant to be a few hundred dollars a month, many have had to pay recruitment agents, often through loans which leave them indebted for years. These workers are often employed by subcontractors. Hotel companies that have used subcontractors have been criticized for turning a blind eye to the mistreatment of workers, including non-payment of wages and excessively long hours. Unlike workers on construction sites, workers in hotels are highly visible to the hotel's guests, who might well be dismayed by the demeaning situation of workers in an ultra-luxurious setting.

Qatar's society is becoming more in tune with the influx of western values, through visitors and businesses. And Qataris themselves are increasingly expanding their horizons. Many young Qataris seek educational opportunities in the world's international universities. These changes are bound to have impacts on this conservative society and culture in the country over the long term. Qatar as host to the World Cup was an idea that seemed highly unlikely back in 2010. The country is rapidly turning the vision into reality, while its values and cultural outlook are changing more gradually.

Questions

- What are the social and economic divisions that exist in Qatar's society?
- What are the human rights issues that exist in Qatar, and to what extent are businesses to blame?
- Why was the World Cup so important to Qatar?
- In your view, are the human rights issues gradually being resolved, or are they impossible to resolve, given the society's structure? Explain your reasoning.

Further reading

For a picture of Qatar at the time it was designated as host for the World Cup, see Robert Yates' article, 'The desert blooms: culture in Qatar', 23 January, 2011, in *The Guardian*. In what ways have perceptions about Qatar changed since then?

Introduction

Globalization has brought people from different parts of the world and from different cultural backgrounds into routine contact with each other, and with each other's cultures. Greater interaction suggests increasing understanding across cultures, but for international business, cultural differences remain significant. Despite globalization, products are designed for the cultural preferences of particular markets. And managers involved in cross-border business activities must be sensitive to differences in languages, value systems and norms of behaviour. In short, being attuned to cultural differences is a vital aspect of doing business in a globalized world.

This chapter has two broad aims. The first is to gain an understanding of how culture influences business activities and organizations across the globe. While globalization is seen as giving rise to a global culture, local cultural identities are not withering away, but are adapting and persisting in the new global environment. The second aim is to understand how societies are changing and what factors are in evidence. These include impacts of globalization, industrialization, urbanization and climate change. Globalization is now increasingly affecting developing countries,

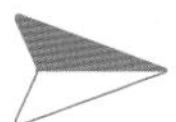

where economic development is taking wing. But globalization's societal impacts in developing regions are uneven, raising concerns for wellbeing among weaker groups in societies. We begin by defining culture, looking at the dimensions of culture in society, and the makeup of specific cultural identities among the world's peoples.

What is culture and how is it relevant to business?

culture a shared way of life of a group of socially interacting people

ethnocentrism unquestioning belief that one's own culture and ways of doing things are the best

polycentrism openness to other cultures and ways of doing things

Culture has been defined in many different ways, reflecting the variety of cultural phenomena that can be observed. Language, religious ritual, and art are just a few examples of cultural symbols whose shared meanings form the unique fingerprint of a particular society. **Culture** can be broadly defined as, 'a shared way of life of a group of socially interacting people, transmitted from one generation to the next, via acculturation and socialization processes, that distinguish one group's members from others' (Ronen and Shenkar, 2013: 868). Culture denotes a cohesive social group, which could be a whole society or a smaller group such as a tribe or ethnic group. Inevitably, we all view and interpret the world around us through a cultural 'filter' to some degree. **Ethnocentrism** denotes the inflexible approach of relating to the world only in terms of our own culture, while **polycentrism** is the approach of attempting to overcome our own cultural assumptions and to develop an openness and understanding of other cultures. Successful international business relationships depend in large measure on developing a polycentric approach in situations where cross-cultural issues arise, such as joint ventures.

Culture can spring from a variety of sources that commonly overlap, as shown in Figure 3.1. An individual person is likely to identify with a national culture, a peer group of people the same age, and possibly an organized religion. Culture includes values and beliefs shared by a group, and also norms of behaviour expected of group members. Values relate primarily to notions of good and evil, right and wrong. Notions of the individual in relation to the group are core to any culture. Ideas about the value and role of the individual in society are paramount in national culture, as the figure shows. They include the value of the individual person, a sense of identity and a sense of homeland. Norms relate to patterns and standards of behaviour. They shape what is considered normal and abnormal behaviour within the group. Manner of dress, food and the etiquette associated with eating and drinking are also obvious distinguishing features of a culture. Norms often reflect values, and, like values, can derive from religious beliefs and take on religious significance in many societies. Norms may also reflect customs that distinguish societies one from another. For businesspeople, an understanding of differing local cultures is needed

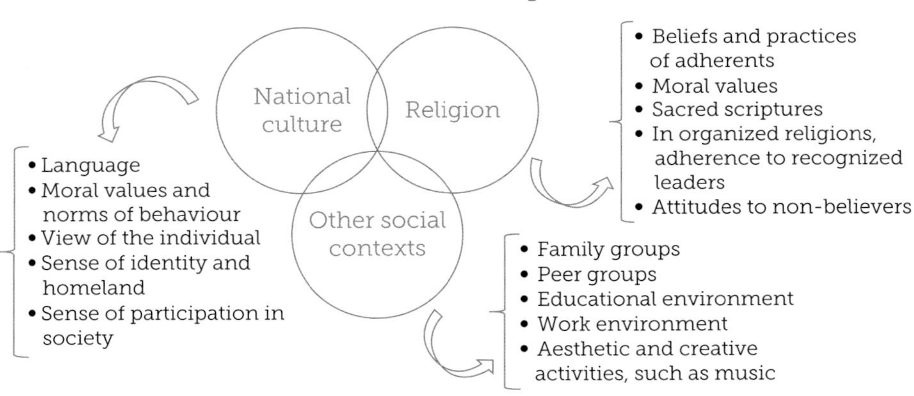

Figure 3.1 **Aspects of culture**

in the context of doing business and in broader social relations in different countries. For companies which operate in differing locations, understanding local culture is an aspect of a CSR strategy: local communities are key stakeholders.

Values and norms of behaviour are learned in a social context – we are not born with them. For this reason they are not fixed and static, but are capable of change. Societies evolve over time, and individuals may change when they move to a new environment. Organizations, too, change over time, and they are likely to change as they expand internationally. One of the themes of this chapter is the extent to which growing interactions between cultures are leading to **cultural convergence**. The growth of international markets and global brands such as McDonald's and Nike seem to indicate convergence towards a global or 'cosmopolitan' culture. Certainly, this is the view of the more ardent advocates of globalization (Bird and Stevens, 2003). At the other extreme, some commentators, pointing to the persistence of differing national cultures, assert that **cultural divergence** remains a reality, despite globalization processes (Berger, 2002). A more moderate view is that 'cultural learning' through interaction is leading to cultures being 'globally interwoven', acknowledging the potential of culture change from globalization (Bird and Fang, 2009: 141). In this vein, Ralston proposes the idea of 'crossvergence' as a continuum in between the polar opposites of convergence and divergence, reflecting gradual processes of cultural integration (Ralston et al., 2008).

cultural convergence diverse cultures gradually becoming more alike through increasing interactions

cultural divergence differences among cultures, especially those that persist despite globalization

The fact that companies design products and communications for particular cultural preferences in different markets is an indication of persisting cultural diversity. The Big Mac and Coca-Cola epitomize the uniform standard product for all markets that is commonly used as an example of globalization. But in fact, the companies behind both these products have offerings for different markets, and also products that aim to reflect culture change. McDonald's has long been sensitive to differing local tastes, offering the teriyaki burger in Japan, for example, although relying on their core brands as the mainstay of the business. Coca-Cola, too, has revised its global strategy, offering different products to suit consumers in different markets, under a variety of brand names. However, in a trend that reflects globalization, both companies are responding to concerns about healthy eating and sustainable sourcing being voiced by consumers everywhere, in emerging and developed countries alike. Kraft Heinz, a maker of many processed food products, saw mediocre sales in 2018, causing its shares to fall 27%. The maker of Velveeta and Kool-Aid, among many other familiar brands, has found that consumers are turning to healthier foods and also to cheaper products from discounters.

National cultures and states: the dynamics of identity

A nation or people is a distinctive social group with its own culture and identity. Nations have numerous defining characteristics, including language, ethnic identity, shared values and often a sense of geographic homeland. However, above all, belonging to a nation imparts a sense of cultural identity that carries an emotional attachment and 'psychological bond' with others in the same grouping (Connor, 1978). Together, these elements come together in the concept of a **national culture**, representing a blend of a nation's distinctive characteristics. Despite the imprecision surrounding the concept, national culture gained in prominence as an analytical tool in the hands of Geert Hofstede (1994). He was largely responsible for highlighting national culture as a key concept in explaining cultural dimensions, and his framework remains influential (Stahl and Tung, 2014). Hofstede's research has shown that people have acquired their basic value systems by the age of ten (Hofstede, 1994). It is during these formative years that national culture exerts its strongest influence, through family and early schooling. National culture influences

national culture distinctive values, behavioural norms and shared history which distinguish one nation from another

family life, education, organizational culture, and economic and political structures. The sense of belonging to a nation is one of the most important focal points of cultural identity. In the course of time, myth mixes with historical events in the collective memory, and the associated symbols serve as powerful emotive links between present and past, and even future.

nation-state social, administrative and territorial unit into which the world's peoples are divided

The world's peoples are divided into nation-states. The **nation-state** as a concept combines national culture with the territorial and political structures of the state. In this chapter we focus on national cultures, and in Chapter 5, we focus on the political environment of the state. There is a notable misfit between nations and states: there are many more nations than states in the world. Only a few states are home to a single homogeneous nation – Japan is one of the few. Most states are home to more than one national culture. American culture, identified with the US, is probably the most well-known national culture, although the US hardly represents a national culture that is homogeneous. Due to immigration, there remains a diversity of cultural identities existing alongside the sense of being American.

In Israel, a law passed in 2018 recognizes Israel as the 'nation state of the Jewish people' (BBC, 2018). The implications of the law were unsettling for Israel's Arab minority of 1.8 million people, or about 20% of the population. The law was controversial, passing Israel's Parliament with a vote of 62 to 55. The close vote reflected political divisions on the nature of the state and also gave rise to concerns about the strength of the country's democratic institutions.

The state as a territorial unit, rather than the nation, has become the dominant unit globally. Most of the world's states are in fact home to multiple national cultures, usually a predominant one and a number of minority groups. There are two main reasons. First, through immigration, people move to other countries, usually in search of betterment and security. Secondly, in many countries there are indigenous peoples whose communities pre-date the arrival of colonizing outsiders who later founded the state. Historically, nations have sought self-determination for their own people. New nation-states thus represent the culmination of national aspirations. Largely as a result of the break-up of colonial empires, the number of nation-states has grown dramatically since the end of the Second World War. However, many of these states have proved to be ill-fitting administrative containers for the multiple social and ethnic groups within their borders.

Internal social tensions characterize many of the world's states, especially where there are minority ethnic groups and racial divisions. Rights not to be discriminated against on grounds of race, ethnicity, religion or gender are among the human rights set out in one of the UN's foundation documents, the Universal Declaration of Human Rights of 1948 (www.un.org). All UN member states are committed to implementing it, and many global companies recognize it as a guiding principle in their sustainability policies. Nonetheless, in practice, there is considerable discrimination in national environments and in business practices. Minority groups in society are usually poorer and less well educated than fellow citizens in mainstream groups. Members of ethnic minorities are typically employed in low-skill, poorly paid jobs in manufacturing, mining and agriculture. As these industries have become globalized, the use of migrant workers, including indigenous peoples, has become a trend, especially in developing countries. They are vulnerable to exploitation and risks to health. The UN has long focused attention on the rights of minorities, including indigenous peoples, who are at risk of forced labour and other breaches of human rights (UNIASG, 2014). The UN highlights that the discrimination and harsh treatment endured by indigenous peoples in these industries are not only harmful to the people involved, but jeopardizes 'social cohesion and inclusive development' in the countries where they take place (UNIASG, 2014: 1).

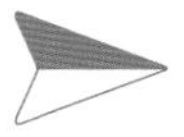

cultural distance in cross-border business relations, cultural gap between those involved, especially where the parties are from very different cultural environments

When a MNE invests in a country that is culturally very different from its own, it is sometimes said that **cultural distance** can be a negative factor (Stahl and Tung, 2014). Similarly, cultural distance can come into play where there is a cultural gap between the MNE and a joint-venture partner or affiliate. Globalized production and supply chains lead to cultural learning through interactions and a growing appreciation of the cultural environment in different countries. At the same time, MNEs face challenges over human rights. Discrimination on grounds of race, ethnicity, gender or religion exists in many cultures. Companies are challenged to take an ethical stance, upholding human rights in these situations where they are at risk.

There are thus tensions between global and local influences. Moreover, just as individuals experience culture change in their lives, national cultures, too, change over time. It could be said that, although cultural changes take place within societies, national cultures remain foundation stones (Inglehart and Baker, 2000). A national culture in which a sense of history permeates identity, can evoke a sense of deep meaning in life that is remarkably durable. This is evident even in countries which have gone through processes of industrialization. Traditional rural ways of life give way to urban living and salaried work, but national cultures persist.

Identifying with the nation-state or with a separate cultural identity?

Think of a nation-state which you are familiar with. Does it tend towards a strong national culture, or are there diverse cultural identities within its borders? If the latter, explain what they are and in what ways they might potentially create disunity within the state.

Where there are separate cultural identities within the state, how does this environment impact on foreign businesses that wish to invest in the country?

Languages in a globalized world

low-context culture culture in which communication is clear and direct, rather than relying on patterns of behaviour

high-context culture culture in which communication relies heavily on the behavioural dimension, such as 'body language'

Language is the basic means of communication between people, which facilitates social interaction and fosters a system of shared values and norms. Language is much more than the vocabulary and grammar that make up written and spoken expression. E.T. Hall distinguishes between 'low-context' and 'high-context' cultures (Hall, 1976). In a **low-context culture**, communication is clear and direct; speakers come straight to the point and say exactly what they mean. America is a good example of a low-context culture. In the **high-context culture**, much goes unsaid; depending on the relationship between the speakers, each is able to interpret body language and 'read between the lines'. In this type of culture, ambiguity is the norm, and directness is avoided. Asian cultures fall into this type. For Americans, meeting with people from high-context cultures can seem frustrating, as they are unsure where they stand, while their Asian counterparts are unsettled by their directness of approach, which may come across as insincerity.

Languages are not as clear-cut to identify and quantify in terms of numbers of speakers as might be thought. Some languages, such as Chinese and Arabic, are best viewed as a family of languages, rather than a single language. Table 3.1 shows the languages spoken by the largest numbers of people as first languages. Mandarin Chinese is the main Chinese language group. It is notable that seven of the ten most widely spoken first languages are from the BRIC countries. The large numbers of Spanish and Portuguese speakers are due mainly to the prevalence of Spanish in Latin America and Portuguese in Brazil. Hindi, Bengali and Punjabi are Indian languages. It is now common for people to acquire a second language, often in the context of education and business. The number of people who speak English as a second language could well exceed a billion

Table 3.1 The world's ten most widely spoken languages, 2019
(first-language speakers)

Language	Number of first-language speakers (millions)
Chinese	1,311
Spanish	460
English	379
Hindi	341
Arabic	319
Bengali	228
Portuguese	221
Russian	154
Japanese	128
Lahnda/Punjabi	119

Source: Eberhard, David M., Simons, Gary F. and Charles D. Fennig (eds) (2019) *Ethnologue: Languages of the World*, 22nd edition (Dallas, Texas: SIL International).

globally. However, estimating the number of second-language speakers involves an element of guesswork. There are probably millions of people in the world who speak English to some extent but lack the fluency that would generally be expected of a second-language speaker.

In most countries, one or more dominant languages exist alongside minority languages, which may be concentrated in specific geographical regions. Canada has two official languages, English and French, and the minority French speakers have a history of separatist activism. Switzerland, by contrast, has four official languages (German, French, Italian and Romansh) which co-exist in harmony. Linguistic diversity within a state may arise in several different ways:

- A minority language may represent a native culture, such as the Indian nations which inhabited North and South America before the arrival of European settlers. The US, Australia and South Africa are all settler societies, where conflicts erupted between the new arrivals and existing native cultures. These tensions are still observable today, as evidenced by the second-class citizen status of which native Americans complain.
- Colonizing states introduced their own language into their colonies. The western imperial powers of the sixteenth to the nineteenth centuries included the British, French, Dutch, Belgians, Spanish and Portuguese. All left their national languages in their colonies, where the colonial language became that of the elites, as well as that of government and administration. The many indigenous peoples spoke native languages, but struggled to maintain their cultures in the tide of colonialism. Brazil has a large indigenous population. These indigenous peoples face issues of discrimination, land rights and environmental degradation in the Amazon areas which they inhabit.
- Immigration can create linguistic diversity. Immigrants are faced with the difficulties of **assimilation** in a new culture, or maintaining a separate identity. Where immigrants are concentrated geographically, they may form a **subculture** in which they speak their home language.

assimilation of cultures process by which minority cultures become integrated into the mainstream culture of a nation

subculture minority culture in a society, often associated with immigrant communities

Governments' education policies regarding minority languages are often contentious. They can be directed towards protecting minority cultures or, alternatively, compelling schools to teach the dominant language in order to facilitate assimilation of minority cultures into the mainstream culture. In countries that have

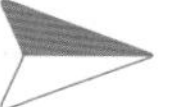

decentralized authority in regions or provinces, the regional authorities may wish to maintain the local language in the school system as a means of maintaining the local culture. In Spain, there are several 'autonomous regions', where regional languages, such as Catalan, predominate. Catalonia has seen a rise in separatist nationalist sentiment in recent years, encouraged by separatist politicians who point to the economic prosperity of Catalonia, which contrasts markedly with the recession that has deeply affected other Spanish regions.

English has gained an importance as a global language that extends far beyond the number of native speakers. It is the commonest second language in the global media and the dominant language in international business. However, its dominance is now challenged by the rise in Chinese, due to the rapid increase in Chinese internet use. The top ten languages among internet users are shown in Figure 3.2. Internet use has grown rapidly in China, where internet users now represent over half the population. This percentage compares with internet use in English-speaking countries, where internet penetration is about two-thirds of the total population. The Arab world has seen the most rapid growth in internet use. Here, there are now 226 million internet users, representing 51% of Arabic speakers.

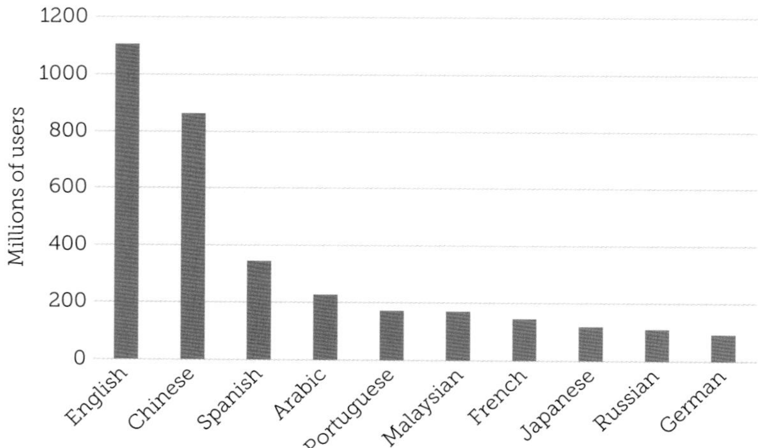

Figure 3.2 **The top ten languages on the internet, 2019**

Source: Internet World Stats, 30 April 2019, at www.internetworldstats.com, accessed 26 June 2019.

For the many people who travel internationally, English is a recognized means of communication, often when neither of the parties speaks English as a first language. These globetrotters include not only businesspeople and diplomats, but tourists, sportspeople, academics, and students. The English language in these contexts is an intercultural means of communicating. Businesspeople are likely to use English in their international business activities, but speak their own first language at home. By the same token, while Hindi is the official language of India, English as an associate national language facilitates communication between the many non-Hindi-speaking groups. India is one of the world's most multi-lingual countries, with fourteen major languages, and many more minor ones. English is spoken by about 50% of India's population. Moreover, in the country's booming IT sector, the use of the English language is proving a location advantage. India's executives are highly travelled. As of 2019, CEOs born in India headed two American technology giants, Google and Microsoft.

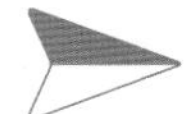

English, the global language?

English-speaking businesspeople sometimes say that there is little point in learning a foreign language, as everyone nowadays speaks English. Do you agree or disagree, and why?

What advantages can be had by the foreign firm that has a policy of using the local language with business partners and customers in overseas markets?

Religions: cornerstones of beliefs and cultural identities

religion set of beliefs and moral precepts which guide people in their lives

In many cultures, values and beliefs are determined by religion. Even people who do not consider their values derived from religion often have some religious connection. It is estimated that 84% of the world's people identify with a religious group (Sherwood, 2018). And most of these are younger people than those with no religious affiliation. This suggests that the lure of religion is thriving in today's world. There are many thousands of distinct religions and religious movements among the world's population. They range from simple folk religions to highly refined systems of beliefs, with set rituals, organized worship, sacred texts and a hierarchy of religious leaders. A **religion** calls on its followers to believe in supernatural forces which affect their lives, and to follow prescribed moral rules. Religion may exercise considerable secular and political influence, and can form a major unifying force in society. Religious divides, both within states and between states, can also be a source of friction. According to research published in 2014, hostilities involving religion increased globally between 2007 and 2012, encompassing 33% of countries in 2012. The regions which saw the largest increases were the Middle East and North Africa, and Asia-Pacific (Pew Research Center, 2014). Because of the large populations in these regions, the chances are that most people in the world live in countries that are affected in some way by religious hostility.

Religious freedom is a human right, and is reinforced by UN conventions, notably the International Covenant on Civil and Political Rights (ICCPR) which most countries have ratified. Even those that have not ratified, such as China, often recognize freedom of religion. In practice, hostilities against religious groups, consisting of intimidation and violence, can arise in societies where there are religious tensions, often where government restrictions are in place, but also in countries where freedom of religion is recognized in law. Government restrictions on religion exist in about one-third of the world's countries, among them some of the world's most populous. These are countries where social hostilities involving religion are also prevalent. They include Egypt, Indonesia, Pakistan, Russia, Burma, China and India. Overall, 76% of the world's population live in places where social hostilities involving religion and government restrictions on religion are high (Pew Research Center, 2014). Also of concern is the rise in incidents of abuse against religious minorities in society, which occur in 47% of the world's countries.

Religions with the largest following globally are shown in Figure 3.3. The two major religions are Christianity and Islam (whose adherents are called Muslims). Both are 'monotheistic', i.e. believing in one God, in contrast to 'polytheistic' religions such as Hinduism, in which there is a panoply of gods. Christianity and Islam are both 'proselytizing religions', which means that they deliberately aim to expand numbers and convert new followers. Both are organized religions. Folk religions, including indigenous religions and traditional African religions, comprise numerous types of religious groupings, often tribal and highly local, lacking the organizational structures of the major religions. They are widespread, their followers numbering 405 million globally, mainly in the Asia-Pacific region, India and Brazil.

Over a billion people worldwide, or 16% of the global population, are considered unaffiliated to any particular religion. Nonetheless, many of those in this category believe in a supreme being or spiritual dimension, and many engage in some religious practice, such as occasional religious services. We look at the major organized religions in this section.

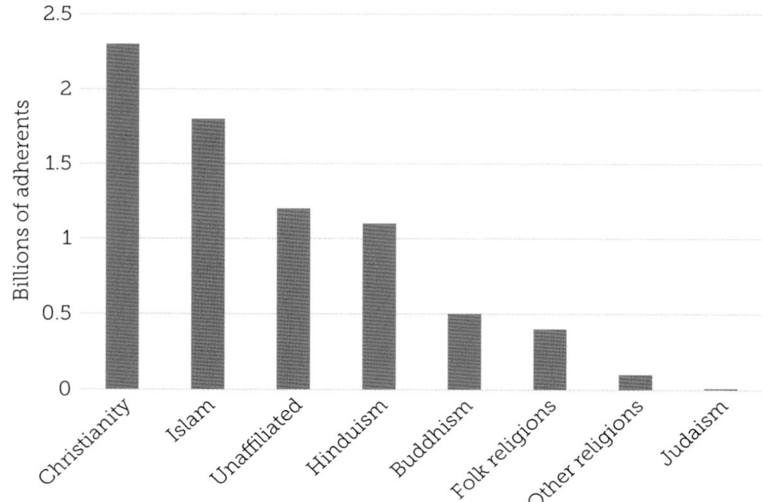

Figure 3.3 Religious affiliation in the world

Source: Pew Research Center (2017) 'The changing global religious landscape', 5 April, at www.pewforum.org, accessed 23 September 2019.

Christianity

Christianity monotheistic religion based on belief in Jesus Christ, whose teachings are in the Bible

About 2.3 billion people, or 31% of the world's population, identify with Christianity in some way. Through missionary activity, **Christianity** has spread from Europe and America to all parts of the globe. While all Christians believe in the divinity of Jesus Christ and regard the Bible as authoritative, differences of interpretation have led to a great deal of fragmentation among Christians. The first of Christianity's major splits occurred in the eleventh century, between the Orthodox Church and the Roman Catholic Church.

The second major split in the Christian world occurred in the sixteenth century, when the Protestant churches separated from Rome. Protestantism is associated with the principle that individual salvation is achievable independently of the institutional church. Protestants went on to establish themselves throughout Europe and America, through different denominations, such as Methodists and Baptists. The Roman Catholics are now by far the more numerous, numbering about 1.3 billion people. Followers of the Orthodox rites, numbering some 300 million, are still very influential in many countries, such as Greece and Russia.

The rise of an 'evangelical' tendency within Christianity has been a recent trend globally, including mainly Protestants and, to a lesser extent, Catholics. Central to the evangelical Christian are strict adherence to Biblical scriptures and a belief in personal conversion, as in the notion of the 'born-again' Christian. An emphasis on missionary activity is linked to the primacy of personal salvation. Evangelical Christians are among the more fundamentalist of Christians – conservative theologically and socially. Numbers of Catholics and Protestants have risen substantially in Latin America and Africa, much of this growth within the more evangelical tendency. By contrast, in the more ageing populations of Europe, Christians have

declined in number. Perhaps surprisingly, Christianity is also on the rise in China, despite government restrictions. There are estimated to be 115 million Protestants and 10–12 million Catholics in China (Sherwood, 2018).

Islam

Muslims number about 1.8 billion globally, representing 24% of the world's population. They are spread among many different countries, mainly in the Middle East, Africa and Asia. The country with the largest Muslim population is Indonesia, where Muslims number over 200 million. They make up a majority of the population in over thirty countries, and large minorities in others. Through immigration, Muslims now form significant minorities in most European countries. The number of Muslims in Europe is on the rise, mainly due to natural increase, there having been an estimated 2 million more births than deaths between 2010 and 2015 (Pew Research Center, 2017). The world's Muslims have a median age of 23, while the world's Christians have a median age of 30. Muslims are the fastest-growing major religious group in the world, and it is likely that they will overtake the number of Christians globally by 2050.

Islam monotheistic religion based on the teaching of the prophet Mohammed, as revealed in the Koran; followers are referred to as Muslims

Founded by the prophet Mohammed in the seventh century, **Islam** unites its followers through shared faith, shared ritual in everyday life, and belief in the words of the Koran, the sacred book. Of the two major branches of Islam, Sunni and Shi-ite, the Sunnis are far more numerous. For the Muslim, religious ritual is part of everyday life, not confined to worship on a particular day of the week. While codes of conduct form part of the values of all religions, Islam is particularly endowed with formal prescriptive guidance in all aspects of life, including social relations, social behaviour, rules for the consumption of food and drink, and the role and appearance of women in society. Religious leaders play an important guiding role, and are influential, particularly in education.

An enterprise culture is fostered in Muslim societies, and economic development is promoted. However, it is forbidden to earn a profit based on the exploitation of others. Interest payments are forbidden, and as a result, banking has developed systems complying with Islamic law. Islamic banking and finance show the adaptability of religious institutions to modern business conditions. Similarly, state courts have grown up in Muslim countries, where traditionally there were only religious courts. State courts can apply both religious law and western-style commercial law, signifying an accommodation with western legal forms.

The issue of westernization divides Muslims. 'Westernization' refers to a society's adoption of western culture and values, and is associated with processes of modernization, while 'Islamic fundamentalism' refers to maintenance of the supremacy of Islam in all aspects of society. Some militant Islamic fundamentalist groups, mainly Sunnis, have become major destabilizing forces in Middle Eastern countries. They are considered jihadists because of their fundamentalist view of a duty to fight for the supremacy of their version of Islam. Among them is Al Qaeda, a loose grouping that is associated with terrorist activities, notably the attack on the World Trade Center in New York in 2001. More recently, the rise of the Islamic State of Iraq and Syria (or ISIS), also referred to as ISIL (the Islamic State of Iraq and the Levant), has become prominent. The Islamic State, as its name suggests, aspires to territorial control, and made inroads in Syria and Iraq, seeking to overthrow existing social and political structures. It built up significant military force. Its brutal tactics have led to condemnation internationally. ISIS views not just western sympathizers and Christians as enemies, but also other Sunni fundamentalist groups, including local Sunni tribes in the regions they target. The growth in extremist religious groups such as ISIS highlights that religious hostilities often come mixed with other social and cultural dimensions, including ethnic divisions. A worrying aspect of the rise of extremists has been its adept use of social media to spread its influence and recruit new followers.

MINI CASE STUDY

Lifting the ban on women drivers in Saudi Arabia

In Saudi Arabia, only men have been allowed to have driving licences. Women who drove illegally risked being arrested and even imprisoned. But this changed in June 2018, when a decree from King Salman came into effect, allowing Saudi women to drive for the first time. Henceforth, women could drive their own cars. This was a huge step forward for women's rights in the country, and was marked by celebrations on the evening of 23rd June. At the stroke of midnight on the 24th, they would no longer be banned from driving.

For families, the new law would potentially make a big difference in lifestyle – and family spending. For many, paying a chauffeur had become an essential expense of family life, taking women family members to work, shopping, medical appointments, educational establishments and social events. There has been plenty of business for the 800,000 foreign chauffeurs working in Saudi Arabia, mainly in Riyadh. Apart from the expense of paying for chauffeurs, the inflexibility of the rigid rules was a major disappointment for Saudi women, many of whom have become highly educated and employed in a range of professional jobs.

The freedom to drive a car has been a turning point for Saudi women.

© Getty, Jasmin Merdan

The change in the law has come about largely because of the changed vision of the country being projected by the Crown Prince Mohammed bin Salman. He has sought to propel the country into modernity. Bans on girls participating in sport in public schools and the ban on watching football in stadiums have also been lifted. A factor weighing with the government in lifting the ban on women driving has also been the country's economic situation. Its dependence on oil has meant that declining oil prices place strain on the country's finances, and also on family finances. The government has hoped to encourage more women to contribute to economic activity (Michaelson, 2019). The percentage of women working remains relatively low, at 16.8% of the country's workforce. The government is hoping to raise this percentage, with a Women in the Workplace initiative. The idea of equal pay for equal work is recognized, but has not as yet become a reality. Women earn roughly half of what men earn.

Reforms in the law towards removing discrimination against women have been urged strongly by the UN, in accordance with human rights conventions, but have encountered considerable resistance from the religious establishment, who resist any changes. The male guardianship system is an example, compelling women to have permission from a male relative for many decisions and activities. For Saudi women, the lifting of the ban on having a driving licence has been an important step forward, but only a step along the way towards equality.

Questions

- What is the significance of lifting the ban on driving for Saudi women?
- In your view, can changes in the law bring about changes in culture in Saudi Arabia?

Find out more

See the article, 'Saudi Arabia's enduring male guardianship system', published 8 January 2019, on the BBC's news, at www.bbc.co.uk. An article on the participation of women in the workforce is by Ruth Michaelson in *The Guardian*, entitled 'An "oasis" for women? Inside Saudi Arabia's vast new female-only workspaces', 20 July 2019.

Asian religions

Asia has been a rich source of some of the world's oldest religions. Hinduism, Buddhism, Confucianism, among many others, originated in Asia and still have millions of followers.

Hinduism

Hinduism polytheistic religion whose followers are concentrated in India

caste system social stratification system based on birth, associated with Hinduism

Unlike either Christianity or Islam, **Hinduism** is polytheistic, its believers worshipping many different gods through many different rituals. The sheer diversity of Hinduism is a major feature, despite the fact that geographically Hindus are mostly concentrated in the Indian subcontinent. Hindus make up 80% of the population of India. Hinduism is an ancient religion, older than all other major world religions. In keeping with its ancient origins, Hinduism resembles a folk religion, associated with rural communities and accessible to illiterate as well as literate followers. An important social and economic aspect of Hinduism is the **caste system** of rigid social stratification. It holds that a person is born into a particular station in society's hierarchy, which is fixed for life. For example, those at the bottom, the 'untouchables' have no prospect of rising out of this group into a higher caste. Numbering an estimated 160 million people, India's untouchables often suffer discrimination. This system, while officially abolished in the modern state, is still a force in Indian society, as is Hinduism itself. The Hindu nationalist party, the Bharatiya Janata Party (BJP), won a decisive victory in 2014, and again in 2019. However, the grip of the BJP on government raised concerns among India's Muslims, who number 172 million people and constitute 14% of the population. The ascendency of Hindu nationalism has also led to fears that media freedom and freedom of expression generally could be curtailed, undermining India's democratic values.

Buddhism

Buddhism Asian religion based on the teachings of Buddha

Like Hinduism, **Buddhism** originated in India, where it has some five million followers. Buddhism has also been an important religious influence in China and Japan. A feature of the Buddhist heritage in all these countries has been its assimilation with other religions: in Indian temples Buddhism and Hinduism mingle; in Japan, Buddhist temples and Shinto shrines rub shoulders. Buddhism does not recognize the many gods of Hinduism; nor does it subscribe to the caste system. The Buddha's teachings form the basis of the religion. They centre on the 'eight-fold-path' whereby the individual goes through a series of rebirths before reaching *nirvana*. As the Buddha's teachings were never written down, Buddhism split into a number of different schools. The two major ones are the Hinayana, which subscribes to a more ascetic lifestyle, and is followed mainly in Sri Lanka, Thailand, and Burma; and the Mahayana, which is less austere, and is followed in China and Japan. From this latter school arose Ch'an Buddhism, or Zen Buddhism, which became a quite distinctive sect, highly influential in the cultures of both China and Japan. Zen's attraction has been its simplicity and directness, with its emphasis on meditation and rejection of dogmatic teaching.

Most Buddhists live in countries where Buddhism is a minority religion. An exception is Myanmar (Burma), where Buddhism, the established religion, has a record of suppression of minority groups, including Muslims. Although the country is outwardly making the transition from military to civilian rule, violations of human rights by the country's military against Muslims, notably the Rohingya people, have set off criticism internationally. In 2017, the UN Human Rights Office, whose investigators were barred from Myanmar, reported continued serious human rights violations, gathered from interviews with fleeing Rohingyas in neighbouring Bangladesh (UN Human Rights Office, 2017). By May 2018, the exodus of Rohingyas had become the world's fastest growing refugee crisis, with over 900,000 Rohingyas being given humanitarian aid in a refugee camp in Bangladesh – mostly women and children (UNOCHA, 2018).

Confucianism

Confucianism ancient Chinese ethical and philosophical system based on the teachings of Confucius

Confucianism is often considered the cornerstone of Asian values. Founded in the fifth century BC by the Chinese philosopher, Confucius, Confucianism is more a set of moral precepts than a religion. Simon Leys, the modern translator of the *Analects of Confucius*, describes it as 'an affirmation of humanist ethics...the spiritual cornerstone of the most populous and oldest living civilization on earth' (Leys, 1997: xvii). At the heart of Confucianism is the family and 'filial piety', the paramount value of family loyalty. The countries with a strong Confucian heritage – China, Korea and Japan – have in common the prevalence of family-based social organization. In China, Confucianism was rejected by the communist revolution of 1949, but nationalists fleeing to Taiwan maintained Confucian beliefs, evidenced in temples and religious practices. Confucian heritage links many Asian economies, including Japan, South Korea, Taiwan and Hong Kong, where Confucian values have been adapted to the needs of modernization.

Many religions, including the Asian religions, Christianity and Islam, can be found in China and India, the two largest emerging economies. In both, cultural identity and religion are closely linked. In China, relations between Tibet, with its own distinctive culture and Buddhist religion, and central government authorities, have long been tense.

Culture theories: what do they tell us about people and businesses?

Differences in national cultures and attitudes have been the subject of considerable research. Here, we delve into two of the main theories that relate to the international business environment. They are the theories of Geert Hofstede and Fons Trompenaars.

Hofstede's cultural dimensions

Hofstede developed a theory of culture which holds that cultural and sociological differences between nations can be categorized and quantified, allowing us to compare national cultures. Hofstede's research was carried out in fifty countries, among IBM employees in each country. An obvious weakness of the research is its reliance solely on IBM employees, who are a special group in themselves, and need not be representative of the countries in which they live. However, his research does yield interesting comparisons between national cultures, and has served as a benchmark for cultural research.

Hofstede distinguishes four cultural dimensions in his initial research. He later added a fifth, although this additional dimension has been queried, as noted below. He uses these dimensions to compare value systems at various levels: in the family, at school, in the workplace, in the state, and in ways of thinking generally. The cultural dimensions are:

1 Power distance, or the extent to which members of a society accept a hierarchical or unequal power structure. In large power distance countries,

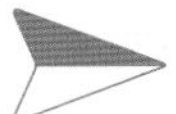

people consider themselves to be inherently unequal, and there is more dependence by subordinates on bosses. The boss is likely to be autocratic or paternalistic in these countries – a situation which subordinates may respond to positively, or negatively. In small power distance countries, people tend to see themselves more as equals. When they occupy subordinate and superior roles in organizations, these situations are just that – roles, not reflecting inherent differences. Organizations in these countries tend to be flatter, with a more consultative style of management. Asian, Latin American and African countries tend to have large power distance, while Northern Europe has relatively small power distance.

2 Uncertainty avoidance, or how members of a society cope with the uncertainties of everyday life. High levels of stress and anxiety denote high uncertainty avoidance countries. These cultures tend to be more expressive and emotional than those of low uncertainty avoidance countries. The latter have lower anxiety levels, but their easy-going exterior may indicate simply greater control of anxiety, not its non-existence. High uncertainty avoidance countries are Latin American, Latin European and Mediterranean countries, along with Japan and South Korea. Ranking relatively low are other Asian countries and other European countries.

3 Individualism, or the extent to which individuals perceive themselves as independent and autonomous beings. At the opposite extreme to individualism is collectivism, in which people see themselves as integrated into 'ingroups'. High individualism scores occur mainly in the English-speaking countries, while low individualism is prevalent in Latin American and Asian countries. Hofstede remarks that management techniques and training packages, which almost all originate in the individualist countries, are based on cultural assumptions which are out of tune with the more collectivist cultures (Hofstede, 1994).

4 Masculinity, or the extent to which a society is inclined towards aggressive and materialistic behaviour. This dimension tends to present stereotyped gender roles. Hofstede associates masculinity with assertiveness, toughness, and an emphasis on money and material things. At the opposite extreme is femininity, which denotes sensitivity, caring, and an emphasis on quality of life. Conflict and competition predominate in more masculine environments, whereas negotiation and compromise predominate in more feminine environments. According to Hofstede's results, the most masculine countries are Japan and Austria, while the most feminine are Sweden, Norway, the Netherlands and Denmark.

5 Long-term vs. short-term orientation, or people's time perspectives in their daily lives. Hofstede added this dimension as a result of work by another researcher, Michael Harris Bond, who found different time orientations between western and eastern ways of thinking. Short-term orientation stresses satisfying needs 'here-and-now', and is more characteristic of western cultures, whereas long-term orientation stresses virtuous living through thrift and persistence, and is prevalent in eastern cultures (Hofstede, 1996). Later scholarship suggests that this dimension is problematic, as these two orientations are not polar opposites. Research indicates that both are present in Asian cultures (Fang, 2003). The different methodology underpinning the fifth dimension is also questionable. Unlike the original research based on IBM employees, the fifth dimension was based on surveys of students. For these reasons, the original four dimensions are treated as the key variables in Hofstede's theory.

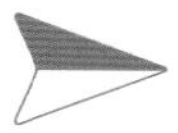

Table 3.2 Ranks of selected countries on four dimensions of national culture, based on research by Hofstede
Rank: 1 = highest; 53 = lowest

	Power distance rank	Individualism rank	Masculinity rank	Uncertainty avoidance rank
Group 1 (high PD + low Individualism)				
Brazil	14	26–27	27	21–22
Indonesia	8–9	47–48	30–31	41–42
Malaysia	1	36	25–26	46
Mexico	5–6	32	6	18
Group 2 (low PD + high individualism)				
Finland	46	17	47	31–32
Germany	42–44	15	9–10	29
Netherlands	40	4–5	51	35
Sweden	47–48	10–11	53	49–50
UK	42–44	3	9–10	47–48
USA	38	1	15	43
Group 3 (varying patterns)				
France	15–16	10–11	35–36	10–15
Greece	27–28	30	18–19	1
Japan	33	22–23	1	7

Source of data: Hofstede, G. (1994) *Cultures and Organizations* (London: HarperCollins), various tables.

Hofstede was able to make correlations and group countries together in clusters, as shown in Table 3.2. For countries in Group 1, high power distance combines with low individualism, suggesting that where people depend on ingroups, they also depend on power figures. Conversely, in cultures where people are less dependent on ingroups, shown in Group 2, they are also less dependent on powerful leaders. There are some anomalies, however. France seems to have high individualism, but also medium power distance. Japan seems to be roughly in the middle in both power distance and individualism. Japanese companies are usually depicted as collectivist ingroups, akin to family relationships. This apparent contradiction in the research could reflect the nature of his survey sample, which focused on employees of a large American multinational company. However, the anomalies could also reveal a shortcoming of the methodology, which is that the dimensions are all set out along bipolar lines, each dimension expressed in terms of polar opposites. This type of analysis tends to classify cultures in an 'either-or' way: a culture is individualist, or it is collectivist. This rather oversimplifies how people behave. People might behave as individualists in some respects, but as collectivists in others (Williamson, 2002). In other words, in many cultures 'both' is more accurate than 'either-or'. This might help to explain why France and Japan seem to show what look like contradictory results.

Hofstede explains his ideas on culture

This is an interview, 'Geert Hofstede on Culture', that took place on 10 October 2011. The interviewer is Gert Jan Hofstede.

Video link: Hofstede explains his ideas on culture
https://youtu.be/wdh40kgyYOY

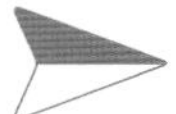

Trompenaars' theory of relationships

More recent research by Fons Trompenaars also used the individualism/collectivism continuum as a key dimension. Trompenaars' research involved giving questionnaires to over 15,000 managers in 28 countries (Trompenaars, 1994). He identified five relationship orientations. These are:

1. Universalism vs. Particularism. In cultures with high universalism, people expect to be valued in accordance with the same criteria and rules that apply to all. The more particularistic cultures value relationships more than formal rules. Western countries such as the UK, Australia and USA, Trompenaars found, tend to rate highly in universalism, whereas China rated highly in particularist relationships. Equality of opportunity is associated with a universalist society, in which each person feels more encouraged to pursue personal goals than would be the case in a particularist society (Cullen et al., 2004). Universalism is thus linked to individualism.
2. Individualism vs. Collectivism. This relationship mirrors one of Hofstede's four dimensions, but the findings were somewhat different. Trompenaars found Japan to be much further towards the collectivist extreme. On the other hand, Mexico and the Czech Republic, which Hofstede had found to be more collectivist, now tend to individualism. This finding could be explained by the later date of the research data, reflecting the progress of market economies in both regions: the impact of the NAFTA free trade agreement in the case of Mexico, and the post-communist transition to a market economy in the case of the Czech Republic.
3. Neutral vs. Emotional. In a neutral culture, people are less inclined to show their feelings, whereas in an emotional culture, people are more open in showing emotion and expressing their views. In the findings, Japan has the most neutral culture, and Mexico the most emotional.
4. Specific vs. Diffuse. In a specific culture there is a clear separation between work and private life. The notion of 'work-life balance' reflects this thinking. In diffuse cultures, 'the whole person is involved in a business relationship' (Trompenaars, 1994: 9). Doing business in these cultures, therefore, involves building relationships, not simply focusing on the business deal in isolation. The US, Australia and the UK are examples of specific cultures, while China is an example of a diffuse culture.
5. Achievement vs. Ascription. In an achievement culture, people derive status from their accomplishments and record. In an ascription culture, status is what matters, which could relate to birth, family, gender or age. The US and UK are achievement cultures, whereas China and other Asian cultures are ascription cultures. In business dealings in an Asian context, therefore, the key individual is invariably the person of the highest status.

The research of Trompenaars showed correlations similar to those found by Hofstede. Individualist cultures are associated with high universalism and also high achievement orientation. We find these characteristics in western countries where the individual pursuit of self-interested goals is strong. This view of the individual is at the heart of capitalist economic theory, and also democratic political systems (as discussed in the next two chapters). The tendencies of Asian cultures are towards collectivism and high power distance. But it would be an oversimplification to view east–west divergence solely along bipolar lines. The relationship between the individual and society is complex. In Asian societies, there is a nuanced view of the individual in society, rather than as a polarized view of the individualist–collectivist dichotomy (Fang, 2003).

Theories regarding clusters of countries with similar cultures contribute to the convergence/divergence debate. While geographic proximity tends to suggest cultural similarities, other aspects of culture, such as language and religion, are also influential. Ronen and Shenkar, who carried out research on cultural clusters in the 1980s, carried out research again two decades later. They found that, despite the march of globalization, cultural divergence remains a reality, as do clusters of cultures identified in their original research (Ronen and Shenkar, 2013). The research of Hofstede and Trompenaars shed new light on the diversity among national cultures, dispelling the assumption that there is 'one best way' of managing and organizing people. International companies had assumed the universal application of management theories, but theories of organization and management have evolved in the era of globalization. Just as standardized products do not suit all markets, organizations cannot be standardized, but must adapt to local social and cultural profiles.

Organizations in the global environment: what are their cultural guideposts?

Organizations have the attributes of culture, but not necessarily those of a single national culture. Organizations evolve as entities in their own right, interacting with differing cultural environments that influence how they are managed and the roles they play in society.

Organizations through cultural lenses

organizational culture an organization's values, behavioural norms and management style; also known as corporate culture

Organizational culture or 'corporate culture', like national culture, focuses on values, norms and behavioural patterns shared by the group, in this case, the organization. Elements of organizational culture include the following:

- Common language and shared terminology
- Norms of behaviour, such as relations between management and employees
- Preferences for formal or informal means of communication within the company and with associated companies
- Dominant values of the organization, such as high product quality and customer orientation
- Degree of empowerment of employees throughout the organization
- Systems of rules that specify dos and don'ts of employee behaviour.

The organization, however, unlike the nation, is an artificial creation. Corporate culture is one that is deliberately fostered among employees, who may have come to the company from a variety of different cultural backgrounds. Companies tend to reflect the national culture of their home country, despite globalization of their operations (Ronen and Shenkar, 2013). However, MNEs take different approaches to organizing and managing activities that span different continents.

Some multinational corporations see a strong corporate culture as a way of unifying the diverse national cultures represented by employees. Others evolve different organizational cultures in different locations, in effect incorporating a multi-culturalism within the company. The need to manage cultural diversity may arise through a number of routes: the acquisition of a foreign subsidiary, a merger with another company, or a joint venture. In joint ventures, in particular, the need for co-operation and trust between partners is the key to long-term success.

Bartlett and Ghoshal devised a typology of international companies that highlights the extent of localization and the importance of the firm's own corporate culture. Their four models are as follows (Bartlett and Ghoshal, 1989):

- **The multinational model**, or 'multidomestic' model – This is a highly decentralized model. Subsidiaries are managed as autonomous units, with strategy-making powers for their areas.

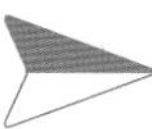

- **The international model** – In this model, operations are decentralized and local managers have considerable latitude, but the firm's headquarters formulates overall strategy.
- **The global model** – This model features global strategy and centralized management. This system is a one-size-fits-all approach to both strategy and management. It has proved inflexible in changing markets and ill-suited to adapting to diverse consumer tastes.
- **The transnational model** – This model represents a balance between central control and local responsiveness. This is achieved through networks based on supply-chain configurations, which can be continually reconfigured to adapt to changing consumer demand.

While globalization might seem to point to the global model, in fact, the transnational has gained ground in recent decades. This is largely because of the balance between globalization and localization that has evolved in supply chains. But with the evolution of supply chains, organization and management have also evolved. We have noted in Chapter 2 that MNEs select locations for their comparative advantages, leading to uneven development both within and between countries.

Managerial culture: how it has evolved in the global economy

Fordism approach to an industrial organization based on large factories producing standardized products for mass consumption, named after the automobile magnate, Henry Ford

The global company is typified by a system known as '**Fordism**', derived from the system implemented in the factories of the Ford Motor Company. Its founder, Henry Ford pioneered the use of the moving assembly line to produce standardized products in large volumes. Formerly, cars were craftsmen-made vehicles: a single craftsman might spend a long time building just one engine. Prices were high, and volumes low. Fordism revolutionized car production, meeting growing consumer demand in America from the early twentieth century onwards. On the moving assembly line, the production process was broken down into small tasks, each timed down to the second and each performed by a different worker. The worker had no control over the process: the job had become simply one of repeating the same task over and over. This was the key to mass production. It was welcomed by consumers, but was monotonous for workers.

The employer
• Belief that there is one best method for every task
• Methodical breakdown of each task
• Achieve maximum output and efficiency
• Close control of workers
Taylorist scientific management in theory
The employee
• Trained to perform a task in the most efficient way, timed by management
• Viewed as a pair of hands – absence of individual involvement
• Monetary compensation deemed to be sufficient motivation
The firm
• Maximum prosperity
• Cooperative relations between employers and employees

Figure 3.4 **Taylorist scientific management in theory**

Source of concepts: Taylor, F. ([1911] 2004) *The Principles of Scientific Management* (New York: Harper and Brothers); ebook published by Project Gutenberg eBooks, 2004.

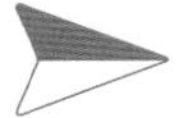

scientific management theory of management in which each worker's task is strictly defined and is part of a production process that is controlled in minute detail; devised by Frederick Taylor

Ford adopted principles derived from theories of '**scientific management**', devised by Frederick Taylor in the early 1900s, and usually referred to as 'Taylorism' (Taylor, 2004). The main aspects of the theory are shown in Figure 3.4. In a Taylorist system, the worker's task is strictly defined and is part of a production process that is controlled in minute detail (Pruijt, 2000). While there seems to have been no explicit aim on the part of Ford to adopt Taylor's principles, there were clear similarities in practice. Workers had become 'replaceable cogs' in a production machine (Krafcik, 1988: 43). This resulted in greater efficiency, higher production and lower prices for consumers. But for workers on assembly lines, repetitive monotonous work offered little personal satisfaction. All control rested with the management, and workers' tasks were equivalent to tasks done by machine. Paying workers higher wages was seen as a way of compensating them for the absence of any sense of personal involvement in the job.

Taylor believed that money was the worker's sole motivation: greater output would lead to greater monetary reward, and this would be sufficient to satisfy workers. Taylor criticized 'sweat-shops', and stressed the importance of workers' health, but mainly in the context of productivity gains (Taylor, 2004). Although the Taylorist vision was one of mutual self-interest between employer and employee, confrontational relations between trade unions and management became associated with Fordist operations. Fordism's inflexibility and lack of innovation also proved to be shortcomings.

Innovations for which Japanese companies, notably Toyota, can take credit, brought about a rethinking of mass manufacturing, taking into account the human element. Toyota looked back to the 'minds + hands philosophy of the craftsman era' (Krafcik, 1988: 43). If workers are given responsibilities and a variety of tasks, their working lives would be improved – as would operational quality. Workers were organized into teams, where ideas could be exchanged, and continuous improvement would be facilitated. We would now refer to such innovations as '**empowerment**', bringing individual responsibility into the frame. Toyota pioneered systems of **lean production** and **just-in-time (JIT)** supply of components, enabling companies to reduce the huge inventories of stock that had characterized mass manufacturing in the past. Toyota's production system did not totally reject either Fordism or Taylorist principles. It adapted them to more flexible production. The firm was able to reduce the time taken to complete each product, while maintaining continuous flow. The system achieved these efficiencies by adopting a co-operative approach to employee relations. The Toyota system was also better adapted to satisfying consumer tastes and fostering innovation. While the Toyota system was applied in a Japanese environment, it has been adopted by car companies around the world, indicating that the core concepts of empowerment and continuous improvement engaging managers and workers are adaptable to other cultural environments.

empowerment approach to management that focuses on individual responsibility

lean production approach to mass production that aims to reduce waste and maintain continuous flow; associated with Japanese car company, Toyota

just-in-time (JIT) system which relies on a continuous flow of materials, governed by split-second timing

Principles associated with Taylorism retained an attraction in environments of low trust between managers and workers, where tight control is perceived to be needed. The Soviet Union was attracted to Taylorism in its drive to industrialize. This was in a brutal, authoritarian police state with a planned economy, where there was no recognition of workers' rights as individuals. This cultural model is one of high power distance and collectivism. The Soviet system proved to be cumbersome and inefficient, failing to modernize and innovate. We might have assumed that its collapse would have demonstrated conclusively the weaknesses of such a system – on both ethical grounds and grounds of sustainability. Nonetheless, there has been a resurgence in Taylorist management in today's globalized economy.

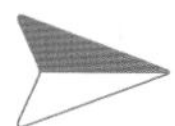

Contemporary scientific management

In mass-market manufacturing of products such as electronic gadgets and apparel, the highly regimented work environment recalls Taylorist principles. Manufacturing of these products has gravitated to developing countries, where labour costs are low, as are the skill levels of available workers. Factory owners such as Foxconn run rigidly controlled factories, demanding long hours and strict discipline. Owners of these factories would say that such regimes are necessary in order to fill huge orders at short notice, as demanded by the global companies they supply. But the work is unpleasant and stressful. The workers in these complexes are in some ways more exploited than those who worked in America's large car factories of the Fordist era. Today's electronics and apparel workers, mainly in Asia, tend to be migrants, often from rural regions. They have little voice in the workplace and little access to representation of their interests, unlike the powerful trade unions that existed in Fordism's heyday.

Taylorism is not confined to outsourced manufacturing. Nor is it confined to developing countries. Other types of workers in the global economy work in similarly harsh and dehumanizing conditions. Among them are workers in the warehouses of Amazon, the internet retailing giant, who complain of excessive pressures to achieve continuous flow in fulfilling orders.

The way I see it ...

'...to work in – and I find it hard to type these words without irony seizure – a "fulfilment" centre, is to be a tiny cog in a massive global distribution machine. It's an industrialised process on a truly massive scale, made possible by new technology'

Carole Cadwalladr, on work in Amazon's warehouse in Swansea, Wales, in *The Observer*, 1 December 2013.

In 2018, another diary of a worker in an Amazon fulfilment centre was published. See Anonymous, 'Our new column from inside Amazon: "they treat us as disposable"', *The Guardian*, 21 November. The worker, who wished to remain anonymous for fear of reprisal, highlights that workers are essentially 'extensions of the machine'. Amazon has raised the minimum wage to $15 per hour, but the worker in question still finds it hard to make ends meet. By 2018, Jeff Bezos, Amazon's founder and the world's richest man, was contemplating the building of new headquarters. He met a hostile reception by some local people in New York, and dropped the company's plans for the New York location (see the closing case study in Chapter 12).

In addition to the inhumane conditions, widening inequality has become an issue with the recent Amazon worker. Why has the higher minimum wage received only lukewarm response?

We might think that all firms now recognize more humane values than Henry Ford saw in workers, but Amazon is closer to some of the harsher aspects of scientific management. These warehouses are spreading in market economies such as the US and European countries, where one might not expect to see the dehumanizing treatment of workers to be considered acceptable. New technologies used by Amazon in its warehouses, or fulfilment centres, allow the management to give orders to the 'picker' through a device worn on the picker's wrist. The device instructs the picker which product to pick next, all the while monitoring every action.

Although Foxconn factories are associated with China, the company now has factories in numerous developed and emerging countries with 'free' labour markets and, in theory, a recognition of workers' rights. These operations share a management emphasis on extracting the maximum of output for a minimum of cost from compliant workers who are treated simply as production operatives. This approach is essentially market oriented and capitalist: for the company, profits are what matters and workers are not seen as human beings, but as means to achieving higher corporate profits. Taylor himself took what now seems a more moderate view that humane treatment of workers was a good idea, as a happier workforce would perform their tasks better. Modern proponents of scientific management take a shorter-term view, seeing the worker as a cog in the machine – a cog which can always be replaced. Moreover, unlike the inflexible Fordist factories of the past, today's global company is mobile. It can scan the world for the locations that offer the maximum potential for cost-cutting and profit generation.

Franchising, which has also flourished in the era of globalization, lends itself to scientific management principles, sometimes referred to as 'McDonaldization'. Production of menu items is controlled in minute detail, much of it governed by machines. Workers are, in effect, an extension of the machine. McDonald's is an example of the global model in Bartlett and Ghoshal's typography. McDonald's traditionally delivers a standardized product that is the same in all of its outlets, no matter where in the world (Pruijt, 2000: 3). McDonald's has been criticized as an employer, on numerous grounds, including low pay, sex discrimination, penalizing workers who voice grievances and banning trade union activities. McDonald's business model is built on this approach to workers. It is perhaps not surprising that strikes and protest events have been used by workers to draw public attention to the company's practices.

The strategy of the globalized company overseeing operations in numerous countries has rested on playing off different locations in terms of profit maximization. Environmental, societal and ethical concerns are seen as risks that can impair profitability, not as positive values that are imbedded in strategic goals. This global scanning approach need not be a worrying development. After all, the global company could well adopt a global perspective featuring international standards in human rights, labour relations and measures to reduce climate change impacts, many of which are weak in national cultural environments. The worrying side of today's corporate elites is that aggressive profit-seeking takes over the conversation at decision-making level. That approach equates to the 'law of the jungle', in which the powerful win and the weak lose out.

In this scenario, the weak are the workers at the bottom. The world of work for low-skilled, low-paid workers is precarious, as well as stressful, no matter where in the world they are. Moreover, many of today's work arrangements, including agency work and the digital platforms that drive the gig economy, reinforce the precariousness of work. The general decline in trade unions and other types of dialogue between management and workers helps to explain this situation, tipping the balance even more in favour of corporate owners. This also explains why there is little hope for better conditions of employment and little prospect of betterment in living standards for those at the bottom.

Culture of the workplace: Have we moved on?

The Fordist factory was not a very pleasant place for workers. But scientific management principles, now more highly refined and utilizing technology, are still a reality. What are the implications for management culture and improving workplace conditions?

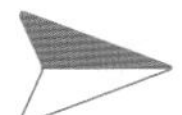

Changing societies present challenges for decision-makers

In this section, we look at how societies change, and whether human wellbeing is changing for the better – or worse. Societies are constantly changing, some in dramatic ways and others in ways that are scarcely perceptible. Industrialization, which has taken place rapidly in some countries, brings changes in people's livelihoods and style of life, which becomes urbanized as people move from the countryside to cities. Mobility also encompasses movements of people to other countries, usually for the hope of a better life. Economic development generally brings growing prosperity, improvements in health and longer life expectancy. However, rapid urbanization in the absence of supportive infrastructure and services can result in poorer healthcare and wellbeing. Moreover, changes such as urbanization and industrialization often have detrimental impacts on social and cultural aspects of people's lives. People wish to make a good living for themselves and their family, but money alone does not lead to wellbeing. Figure 3.5 sets out the elements that make up the wellbeing of the person in society.

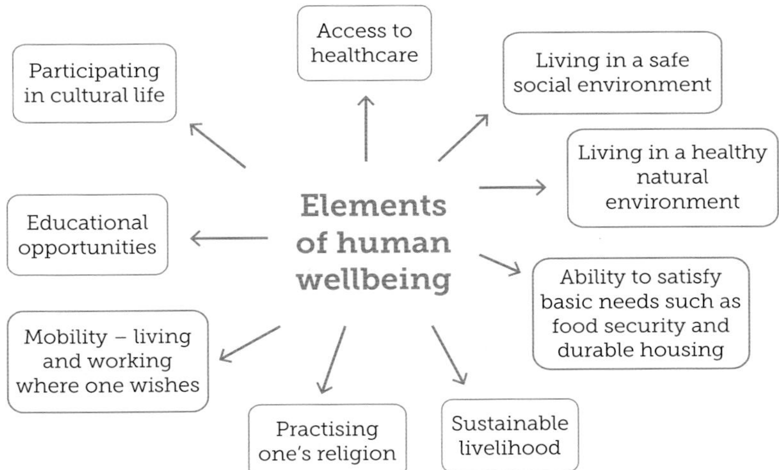

Figure 3.5 **Elements of human wellbeing**

As Figure 3.5 shows, wellbeing is multi-faceted. Each of us wishes to make a living, but a livelihood is something more: it encompasses the capacity – involving both assets and social relations – to achieve a viable living into the future (de Haas, 2010: 18). While these elements centre on the individual person, they also entail responsibilities which rest with the governments and the organizations that interact with governments. For example, the practice of religion and participation in cultural life require an environment where there is freedom for multiple cultures and religions to exist, without fear of suppression or harassment. Education, healthcare and a healthy natural environment are desired by everyone, but these are often more aspirations than reality. Governments bear much responsibility for policies and programmes, through legislation and public spending. Businesses also bear responsibilities. They are creators of economic activity that hold out the potential for the prosperity of whole societies. They offer employment and provide services communities need. However, these activities can be instrumental in negative ways too. Negative impacts are environmental degradation, pollution, utilization of water and displacement of people and wildlife. In this section, we look at key trends in changing societies, highlighting their impacts.

Migration: more people on the move in fragile environments

migration movement of people from one place to another, which can be within a country or between countries, with a view to making a new life in the new location

The urge to move to 'greener pastures' is not a recent phenomenon. People have been on the move throughout history. These movements are broadly referred to as **migration**. Migration can be internal, from one place to another within the same country, or it can be international, from one country to another. Many people simply set out on their own, but many, especially people in poor countries, are more likely to turn to agents who organize groups of migrant workers for particular locations. In these instances, migration is voluntary. However, much migration is not. People are sometimes compelled to leave their homes because of circumstances, or find themselves in a grey area between moving voluntarily and being forced to move. People can be driven out of their homes by fear for their security, such as religious persecution or the eruption of violent conflict. Forced migration can occur following natural disasters, when people move en masse away from the disaster zone. In general, 'immigrants' refers to people coming into a country, and 'emigrants' refers to people leaving a country. These terms suggest a straightforward permanent move, but migration in today's world is more complex than these terms imply.

remittances money sent by migrant workers back to their families in their home location

Much migration is temporary, or intended to be temporary. If people are forced to leave their homes due to conflict or disaster, they probably wish to return if it is feasible. Although globalization has brought greater mobility for many, people seeking work abroad find there can be steep administrative hurdles in cross-border movements. Many people on the move lack the official documents required to work in another country. For those who are lucky and find work in the new country, the move can be fruitful. Migrants typically send money in the form of **remittances** back to relatives in their home country, where they retain family ties. New and old 'homes' can be seen as complementary to each other, as part of a whole family's 'household livelihood strategy' (de Haas, 2010: 17). 'Push' and 'pull' factors are involved, and tend to operate in tandem. Economic opportunities are among the main pull factors (IOM, 2013: 33). Moving from a low-income country to a high-income one is the traditional route taken by migrants, looking for employment and a better life. However, many migrants fall outside this pattern, sometimes moving from one high-income country to another, in hope of better economic opportunities, or from one low-income country to another, for similar reasons. 'Push' factors include poor or precarious livelihoods, poor healthcare and low levels of wellbeing. Climate change is now a major push factor in regions prone to drought or flooding. These factors all pertain in developing countries, such as those in Asia and Africa. A household in a poor country might well decide that if a member can secure work elsewhere, it will add another source of valuable income.

For migrants, life can be a struggle, both to get to the new country and to carve out a life there. The wellbeing of migrants comes well down the list of priorities in the political perspectives of many of the world's governments, even though migrants fill vital roles in their societies. Those who flee their home countries out of desperation often suffer the most. The deaths that occur among desperate people who attempt precarious journeys, across militarized borders or in small boats, remind us of the human suffering that drives people to leave intolerable situations in their home countries. As the last section noted, companies seek migrant labour in many countries, mostly in unskilled work. The oil-rich economies of the Middle East rely almost entirely on migrants in their construction industries. These workers are mainly from India, Nepal, Pakistan and Bangladesh. Organizations of middlemen play a significant role in the migrant labour market, which is now globalized. While legal in theory, there is a fine line between legitimate employment agencies and people traffickers. An inhabitant of Nepal, for example, will turn to agency middlemen for work abroad, such as building work in the Middle East. He will probably demand large payments, often taking the form of long-term debts that become a

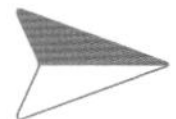

burden on the worker and his family. These workers are in a vulnerable position from both the viewpoint of the poor conditions they endure, and their subservient status in relation to the firms that control their movements. As globalization has reached deeper into developing economies, human rights and the wellbeing of migrants have become global issues.

Also of major concern is forced migration, which occurs when people are displaced in large numbers due to conflict or disaster. Natural disasters include floods, hurricanes, tsunamis, and earthquakes. Other types of disaster bear the stamp of human intervention, and can be equally devastating. They include environmental disasters, famine and chemical spills, that can involve the displacement of whole communities. Roots of conflict can be political, religious, ethnic, communal or simply criminal activity. Violent conflict is most likely to flare in countries where there are tensions between ethnic and religious groups, political insurgency, terrorist activity and organized crime. Some of these causes overlap, such as terrorism by extremist religious groups. People in the affected areas often move to other areas of their own country to seek safety, becoming internally displaced people.

refugee person forced to move to another country for safety reasons

asylum right of a person to live in another country, granted on application to authorities in that country, and based on showing a well-founded fear of persecution in the person's home country

The UN makes a distinction between displaced people and **refugees**, who are people forced to move to other countries because of persecution, war or other violent conflict, in order to seek safety (UNHCR, 2017). In 2018, there were 68.5 million displaced people in the world. Of these, 40 million were internally displaced and 24.5 million were refugees (UNHCR, 2018). Half of the refugees were under the age of 18. Unlike internally displaced people, refugees have rights to be protected in international law, including the right to humanitarian aid. The refugee can apply for **asylum** in the new country, applying through that country's relevant procedure, which includes showing a well-founded fear of persecution in his or her home country. Of the 68.5 million displaced people in 2018, 3.1 million were asylum seekers.

The number of refugees in EU countries reached 6 million in 2016, an increase of 273,000 during the period mid-2015 to mid-2016. During the same period, the number worldwide grew to 16.5 million. Looking at overall international migration, the OECD's 2018 International Migration Outlook reported that 5 million people permanently migrated to OECD countries in 2017, representing the first decline in numbers observable since 2011 (OECD, 2018). In 2017, 1.23 million people applied for asylum in OECD countries. This number, too, is fewer than in 2016 (which was 1.5 million), but still high compared to years before the surge in 2015. The main countries from which refugees came were Afghanistan, Syria and Iraq.

A welcome for Syrian refugees in Madrid, Spain.

Whereas in the 1980s, most refugees were located in developed countries, by 2018, 85% of the world's refugees were seeking haven in developing countries (UNHCR, 2018). Afghanistan and Syria are among the main countries from which people flee conflicts. Conflict, drought and famine have driven people from South Sudan and Somalia. Since 2015, there has been an exodus of 2.7 million refugees from Venezuela to other South American countries, due to the country's collapsing economy and services. Basic humanitarian needs are a priority for refugees, but in host countries that are already struggling to provide adequate infrastructure and health services, the tasks are all the more challenging, placing strains on the receiving countries. UN agencies help to provide humanitarian aid, as do non-governmental organizations (NGOs). But these bodies cannot resolve the underlying conflicts that lead to forced migration. There are about 3 million Afghan refugees living in Pakistan, some of these having been there since the Russian invasion of their country in 1979.

Historically, many countries have welcomed immigrant workers, particularly during periods of rapid growth. Post-war economic development in France and Germany depended in large measure on immigrant labour. In Germany, many of these immigrants came as 'guest-workers', on short-term contracts. Millions of these workers, a large proportion of whom were Turkish, stayed on and have become settled. Indeed, during Turkey's recent economic development, its government has sought to encourage Turks who had settled in Germany to return to Turkey, to impart valuable know-how they had gained from their years in Germany. The resource-rich countries of the Persian Gulf region, including Kuwait, Dubai, Qatar and Saudi Arabia, depend on migrant workers, as shown in the opening case study. At the higher levels, many are skilled and professional people offering vital services in these economies. These 'ex-patriots' see this work as temporary, and, in any case, they are not legally entitled to remain indefinitely in these countries. At the opposite end of the spectrum are the migrant labourers on construction sites, mentioned above. These workers are also crucial to these countries' development plans. The many global companies who drive investment in these countries also benefit, but for workers and their families back in their home countries, concerns over health risks and working conditions are a constant reminder of their vulnerable status.

Migration impacts on both the sending and receiving countries. Professional people from developing countries, such as scientists, doctors and engineers, have long travelled to industrialized regions for self-betterment. Their departures can be seen as a 'brain drain' which deprives their home countries of their skills, but their presence is welcomed in host countries. Unskilled migrants are a different story. They tend to take jobs that citizens of developed countries are disinclined to do. Agricultural work, construction work and domestic service are typical jobs filled by migrants. These people pose a number of issues for both government and society in recipient countries. Employment, housing, healthcare and education are some of the main areas where they have particular needs, often because of language difficulties. However, governments can be reluctant to provide them the services that local people are entitled to. Indeed, in many countries, immigration is a political issue: local people view immigrants as taking their jobs and using services such as the health services.

Remittances sent by workers back to their home countries contribute to the economies of many developing countries, as shown in Figure 3.6. The money sent by each might seem to be too small to matter, but, cumulatively, these sums add up to improving life in villages, larger communities and ultimately the whole society. Remittances worldwide fell in 2009, in the aftermath of the 2008 financial crisis, but

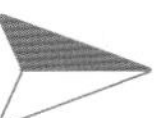

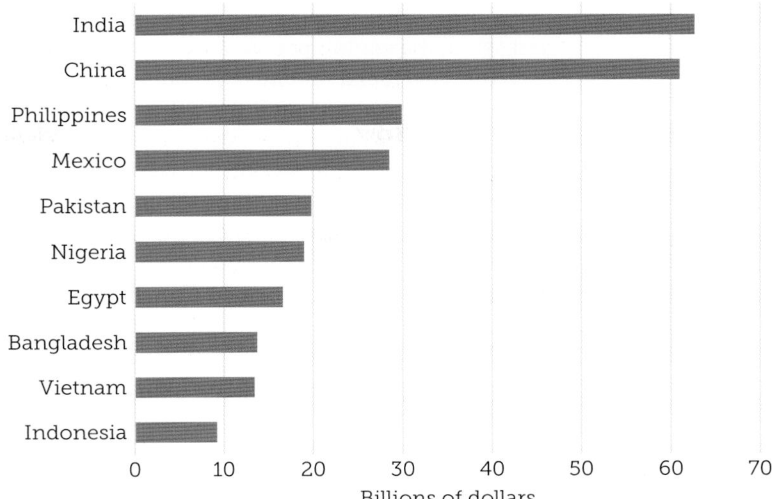

Figure 3.6 **Countries in receipt of the largest remittances from international migrant workers**

Source of data: World Bank (2019) *Migration and Development Brief 31*, April 2018, at www.worldbank.org, accessed 23 September 2019.

resumed growing soon afterwards. In 2018, total remittances grew by 9.6% on 2017, to $529 billion. As the figure shows, India and China are the leaders in the amount remitted by their citizens from working abroad.

There are estimated to be 14 million Indians born in India but living abroad. Among the most illustrious are the CEOs noted earlier in this chapter, but Indians work abroad in a huge variety of jobs. The $78.6 billion in remittances flowing into India is still only 2.9% of India's GDP, while the much lower remittances sent back to small countries such as Nepal are more important in the overall economy, amounting to 28% of Nepal's GDP. A worrying aspect of remittances is the very high level of costs incurred in transferring money back to home countries: on average, 7% of a sum of $200 transferred goes to one of the few dominant companies that handle the bulk of remittance transfers. The UN has argued that this should be reduced to 3%, by highlighting the extortionate costs in its Sustainable Development Goals (see the later discussion in this chapter). Remittances are vital for developing countries. While these flows are a help, there are inherent limitations in the contribution of remittances to achieving development goals. Ultimately, government direction and funding programmes are required to build the infrastructure, provide health services and promote universal education that is needed to achieve sustainable development.

Globalization's impacts: migrant workers

Migrant workers in low-skilled jobs abroad are part of the globalized labour market. They are employed by local companies, under local regulations, but have minimal legal rights in the country where they work. Who should bear responsibilities for the wellbeing of foreign migrant workers in low-skilled employment, such as construction?

Rush to the city: where is urbanization creating the biggest challenges?

urbanization process of large-scale shift of population from rural areas to cities

Migration from rural areas to cities was commonplace long before industrialization. People were 'on the move' not just for economic motives, but for social and cultural reasons as well. The process by which a growing proportion of the population shifts to the cities is termed **urbanization**. In 1950, the world's population was predominantly rural, only 30% living in urban areas. The year 2008 was a turning point, when the world's urban population passed 50%. By 2018, the balance had shifted further, and 55% of the world's people were urban dwellers. However, there are stark contrasts between developed and developing regions. As Figure 3.7 shows, developed countries in North America and the EU are now over 75% urban. Urbanization in these countries has taken place over a long period of industrialization and economic growth following the Second World War. This process contrasts sharply with the urbanization taking place in developing and emerging economies. In developing countries, urbanization is taking place more rapidly and leading to rapid transformation in societies that present challenges for governments.

China has been transformed from a predominantly rural country with a population only 16% urban in 1960 to an industrialized economy that was 58% urban in 2017. Urbanization and economic development have contributed to poverty reduction and improved wellbeing, including better healthcare. However, the example of China demonstrates that rapid urbanization can be detrimental to sustainable development. China's urban residents suffer from poor air quality, which impacts on long-term health. Sustainable development should include economic development, social development and environmental protection. However, China's development model has focused mainly on economic development, driven by industrialization. India, by contrast, has not experienced similar rapid industrialization, and remains predominantly rural, although there has been a significant rise in the percentage of urban residents, from 18% in 1960 to 34% in 2017.

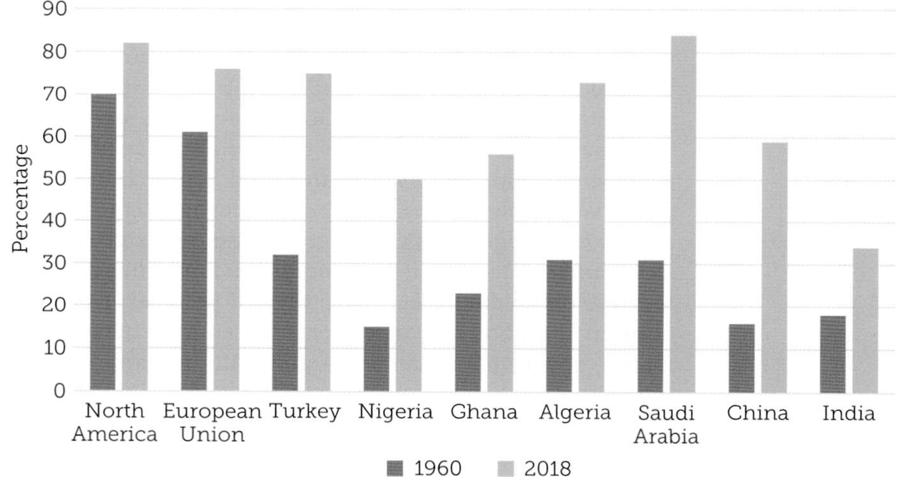

Figure 3.7 Urban population as a percentage of total population

Source of data: World Bank data, Urban population, at data.worldbank.org, accessed 29 June 2019.

Turning to other developing countries shown in Figure 3.7, Turkey stands out as an example of rapid urbanization, industrialization and economic growth. However, Turkey's growth has been driven by the strong leadership of its president, who has become increasingly authoritarian, raising questions about its long-term political stability. Political tensions, in turn, represent deep divisions in Turkish society, again suggesting that the economy is faltering in promoting sustainable development (see the case study in Chapter 5). The urbanization taking place in poorer developing countries also gives rise to concern in terms of sustainable development. Africa has seen widespread urbanization, but there are variations. Northern Africa is far more urbanized than sub-Saharan Africa. Algeria, in Northern Africa, is now predominantly urban. Nigeria has seen rapid urbanization, and the country is now roughly half urbanized, but urban growth has brought growing social and economic challenges.

African economic growth has been impressive in recent years, but the prevalence of urban poverty has led to a questioning of the assumption that growing cities would lead to economic growth and human development going hand in hand (UN Habitat, 2016). In Africa, people tend to move to the cities from poor regions because rural livelihoods cease to be viable. This can be because of drought, environmental degradation or simply because precarious agriculture can no longer support their families. The movement of rural inhabitants to cities in the least-developed countries creates huge challenges. These cities struggle to provide infrastructure, safe water, electricity and other services. The effects of climate change, rising inequality and resource scarcity are issues in these fast-growing urban areas. Newcomers often concentrate in informal settlements. Housing shortages, health risks and unemployment create urban insecurity. In particular, the levels of youth unemployment in the slums raise concerns over security. At the opposite end of the housing spectrum, recent urbanization has seen new urban areas springing up outside the main cities, many designed as residential areas for the growing number of affluent people, benefiting from Africa's globalized economic and financial activities. However, these serve to highlight the inequality associated with urbanization: the affluent improve their lifestyles and the slums suffer from high unemployment. Whereas forward-looking policies could be directed towards urban job creation and sustainable development, African cities tend to suffer from weak governance, allowing situations to worsen. Sprawling urban areas have come under even greater strain with the rise in forced migration and the need of migrants for humanitarian aid (UN Habitat, 2016).

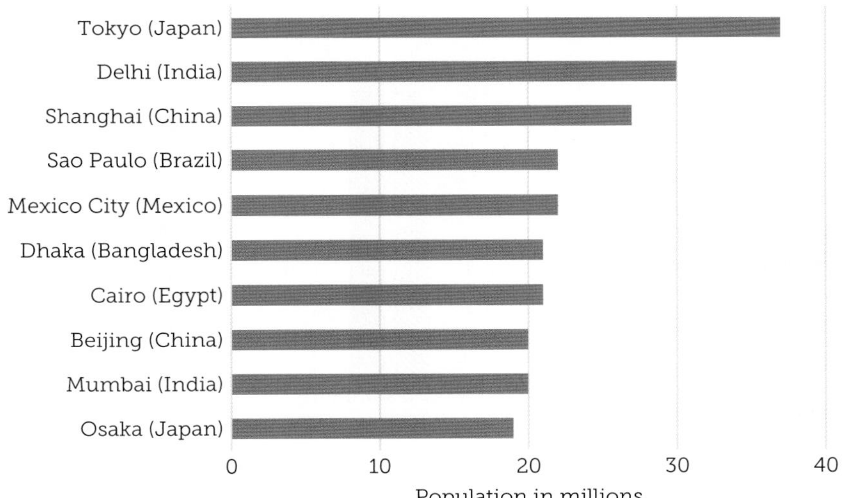

Figure 3.8 **The world's top ten most populous cities: UN forecasts for 2020**

Note: These are the UN's estimates of the world's largest urban agglomerations in 2020.

Source of data: UN, Department of Economic and Social Affairs, Population Division (2018) World Urbanization Prospects: the 2018 Revision, online edition, at https://esa.un.org/unpd/wup, accessed 29 June 2019.

The world's largest cities were once concentrated in the developed world, but now eight of the ten largest cities in the world are in emerging economies, as shown in Figure 3.8. Only two of the top ten, Tokyo and Osaka, are in a developed country. Tokyo and Osaka have long been among the world's largest cities, and Japan is 94% urban. Most of the world's urban population lives in Asian cities, accounting for seven of the top ten. But many of Asia's fastest-growing cities are in economies that are still predominantly rural: India is 34% urban and Bangladesh is 36% urban. Both countries still have high levels of poverty, including both urban and rural poverty. Rapidly growing cities in emerging economies struggle to create sufficient employment and economic activity to underpin sustainable development.

Urbanization in the developing world

In urban areas, it should be easier than in the countryside to deliver health services, organize education and build durable housing. But urbanization in developing countries often turns into slums. What role can businesses play in improving living conditions?

Changing populations and ageing societies

The world's population in 2019 stood at 7.7 billion, a number that had risen by about a billion over the previous twelve years. The global population is likely to be 8.5 billion in 2030 and 9.7 billion in 2050. Population growth globally is uneven: some populations are growing more rapidly than others, and some are hardly growing at all. About 5.8 billion people – 60% of the total – live in either Asia or Africa. Two countries, China and India, are home to 37% of the world's people. India is in the region of Central and Southern Asia, shown in Figure 3.9. The most rapid population growth is occurring in sub-Saharan Africa. This region comprises some of the world's least-developed economies. As the figure shows, their populations are expected to nearly double by 2050 (UN Population Division, 2019). These countries are already struggling with rising poverty and inequality, inadequate nutrition, poor housing, inadequate health services and educational systems that do not reach all in society. Rapid population growth in these poor developing countries will create further challenges for their governments. Moreover, as we have seen, international migration has impacted on these societies, adding to these challenges.

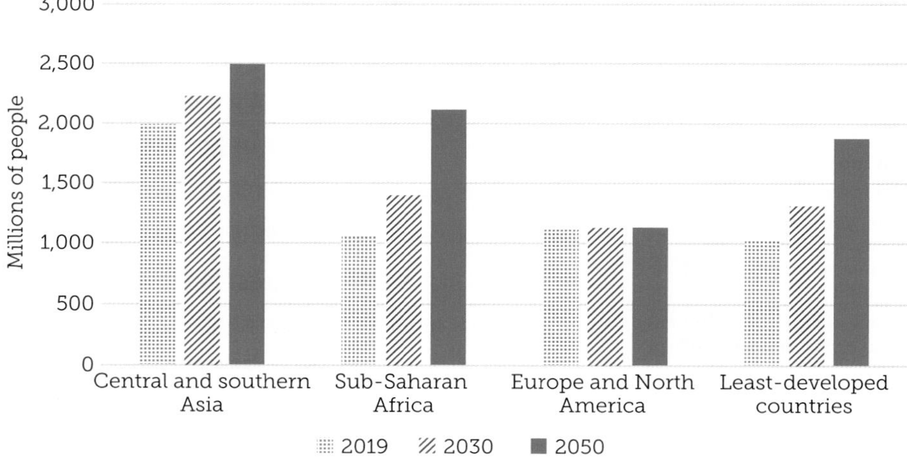

Figure 3.9 Key UN projections of population growth
Source of data: UN Population Division (of the UN Department of Economic and Social Affairs), *World Population Prospects 2019 Revision*, Table 1, p. 6 (New York: UN).

demographic change changes in whole populations brought about by rises and falls in the birth rate and death rate, as well as migration

ageing demographic trend characterized by a rising proportion of older people in a population

The most common way in which populations grow is increase in the number of births over deaths. Populations change constantly. They change naturally over time and across space. **Demographic change** refers to these population changes. They include births, deaths and migration. Demographic changes, while they take place at a slow pace, can have profound long-term effects on societies. **Ageing** is the rising proportion of older people in the total population. Improved health and living conditions result in lower mortality rates and greater life expectancy than earlier generations. Other important factors are declining fertility rates and improvements in the treatment of diseases. Life expectancy is rising in all regions of the world. Globally, life expectancy at birth is expected to rise from 71 years in 2015 to 77 by 2050. Africa is expected to see the sharpest rise, a gain of 11 years in life expectancy from 60 years in 2015 to 71 by 2050. However, improving life expec-

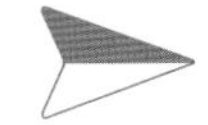

tancy in Africa depends on continued progress against HIV/AIDS and other life-threatening conditions.

About 26% of the world's people are under the age of 15. Developing countries have younger populations than those in the developed countries. In Africa, children under the age of 15 formed 41% of the population in 2017, and young people aged 15 to 24 accounted for a further 19% (UN Population Division, 2017). To put these percentages in perspective, the equivalent figures for Europe are 16% under 15 and 11% aged 15 to 24. For the developing countries of Africa, there are challenges in providing the education and investment in jobs which allow people to enjoy fulfilling lives. These countries are becoming rapidly urbanized, but those drifting into urban areas from precarious livelihoods in the countryside often find poor living conditions and few jobs. High unemployment and lack of educational opportunities are a distressing feature of much urban sprawl.

Ageing populations have been a trend in developed countries for many years. In 2017, people over the age of 60 numbered 962 million globally, and this number is expected to more than double by 2050, reaching 2.1 billion (UN Population Division, 2017). Globally, people over 60 comprise 13% of the population. But this percentage is much higher in the developed regions: 25% of the population in Europe and 22% of the population in North America are over 60. In Italy, 29% of people are over 60. Two-thirds of the world's people over 60 live in developing regions (see Figure 3.10). By 2050, nearly 8 out of 10 of the world's over-60s will be in developing regions. Most of these older people will be living in Asia, where the proportion of older people will double, from 12% in 2017 to 24% in 2050. By then, in Europe, 35% of the population will be over 60, amounting to 250 million people, up from 185 million in 2017. In Africa, the percentage will have risen from 5% in 2017 to 9% of the total population, which represents 227 million, a figure similar to the total in Europe.

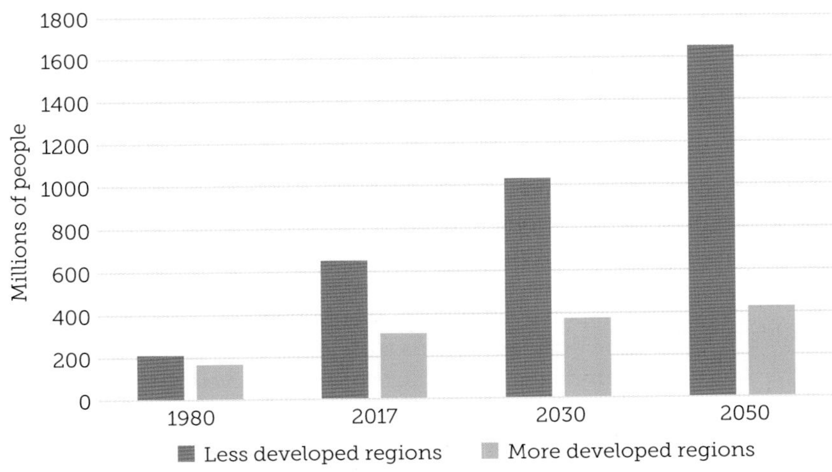

Figure 3.10 Expected growth in the number of people aged 60 or older

Source of data: UN (2017) Department of Economic and Social Affairs, Population Division, *World Population Ageing 2017* (ST/ESA/SER.A/408), Table II.1, p. 10.

Governments in developed countries have long been aware of the challenges posed by ageing populations. One is a dwindling labour force. In 2018, Japan embarked on a policy of admitting foreign workers from poorer Asian countries, such as the Philippines and Vietnam, to make up for gaps in the Japanese labour force. These jobs fall in a number of sectors, including skilled and unskilled. Developing countries are also facing the challenges of ageing populations, only it is happening more quickly, and the numbers of older people are higher. Worldwide, 68% of people of retirement age receive a pension, either contributory or non-contributory (ILO, 2017). The percentage is highest in the advanced economies of North America and western Europe, where nearly everyone is entitled to a pension. However, state-supported pension schemes are often limited. Most governments aim to fund pensions through contributions by earners and investments made by pension funds. However, there are risks that pension funds will be inadequate to maintain the wellbeing of pensioners as the number rises. This is despite the fact that developed countries have tended to raise the statutory retirement age. Developing countries have far less established pension schemes. In eastern Asia, nearly 70% of people are covered by pension schemes, but in southern Asia, the proportion drops to only 23.6%. Eastern Asia includes China, Japan and South Korea, while southern Asia includes the poorer and more rural economies of India and Bangladesh. Since the mid-2000s, China has made significant strides in achieving universal pension coverage for both urban and rural populations.

In general, in developing countries, the proportion of people who can expect a pension is low. In sub-Saharan Africa, only 22.7% of people can expect to receive a pension. In these countries, where a large proportion of employment is in the informal economy, only 9% of people are employed in jobs that have contributory pension schemes. It therefore falls to families to provide for older relatives. Poor families in these situations, often living hardly above subsistence level themselves, do not have the resources to look after older relatives.

Many older people continue to work, either out of financial necessity or simply to keep active. While it is good news that people are increasingly fit and able to work for longer, it is a concern if the numbers of older people living in poverty are rising. Old-age poverty has become a growing concern in both developed and developing countries. Despite the existence of established pension systems in developed countries, there are increasing pressures on public spending and growing pressures on healthcare systems. Coverage provided by state pension schemes is highly variable, and many pensions are inadequate to prevent pensioners falling into poverty. Pensioner poverty has become an issue in Europe, North America and Australia, where pensioner income has not kept pace with wages earned by the working population.

Gender inequalities in old-age income are common in both developed and developing economies. In general, women have less financial security in old age than men, and are therefore more at risk of falling into poverty. Women who have cared for children have often had interrupted careers. Many have worked informally in a variety of jobs. These are all factors that contribute to the risk of poverty among older women. Women who are divorced or single are more likely to experience poverty. In many countries, widowed older women have no source of income other than the survivor's benefits from the husband's pension. Wellbeing in old age is an important part of the overall picture of human development that an economy should be directed towards sustaining, but ageing societies are posing challenges for governments in both developed and developing economies.

MINI CASE STUDY

Raising the pension age in Russia causes controversy

As in many countries around the world, Russia has found that the rising numbers of pensioners and longer life expectancy are placing state finances under pressure. People in work contribute to the state's coffers, but where the workforce is not increasing, a rising pension burden creates a problem for the government. In Russia, the pension age has been 55 for women and 60 for men. Vladimir Putin has been in power for nearly two decades, in successive offices of prime minister and president. He has consolidated his power as president following his most recent election in 2012. He has no doubt considered raising the pension ages, but has held back

on this sensitive issue, largely because of the criticism that would be unleashed, leading to a fall in his popularity. This is a crucial consideration in a country where his authoritarian leadership rests largely on the nationalist sentiment that he sees as his main source of political strength. However, in 2018, he felt compelled to raise the pension ages from 60 to 65 for men, and from 55 to 60 for women. He initially raised the pension age for women to 63, but softened his stance, and raised it by only five years. The changes are due to come into force gradually, over a number of years.

Russia stands out as a country with a large discrepancy in life expectancy between men and women: just over 66 for men and 77 for women. In most countries, the difference would be about five years, whereas in Russia it is twice that. Life expectancy has risen since the fall of the Soviet Union, but even so, life expectancy for men is disappointingly low, and is not rising as much as might be expected in a country with relatively high human development. Russia is ranked 49 in the UN's Human Development Index. Under the new system, the average man would have little expectation of enjoying his retirement. A large number would not live long enough to collect their pensions at all.

The announcement of the changes led to widespread protests up and down the country. As street protests spread, Mr Putin's approval ratings fell, but he felt that the financial situation demanded that he would have to go through with the changes. He spoke out to the public, putting the reform in terms of national security: the pension system could collapse without the reform, he said. But for pensioners, this was a bitter pill. Some of the protesters argued that the crisis in state finances is caused not by pensions but by the spending on military activities in Crimea, in pursuit of Mr Putin's aggressive foreign policy. Protesters have encompassed a broad political spectrum, from communists to nationalists and opposition parties.

Russia's ageing population, dwindling workforce and pressure on finances are recognized as genuine causes for the government to take action. But widespread disquiet has been an unsettling consequence for Mr Putin's leadership.

Questions

- Why is raising the pension age a very sensitive issue in Russia?
- The protests that occurred were not so focused on political as on social issues. What was their significance?

Find out more

See the article, 'Grey power: Could Russia's pensioners be the downfall of Vladimir Putin?', in the *International Business Times*, 7 September 2018.

Building sustainability in the socio-cultural environment: where does responsibility lie?

Whereas international businesses have long focused their attention on the more developed regions of the world, they now set their strategic sights more and more towards developing countries, extending globalization's reach. These emerging countries are not simply less industrialized versions of the developed countries most are familiar with. They present whole new sets of challenges: weak governmental institutions; widespread poverty; low levels of human development; social unease among diverse ethnic, cultural and religious groups; and vulnerabilities to adverse social and economic impacts of climate change. Businesses can offer much in terms of investment, jobs, improved technology and improved infrastructure. But they also bear much responsibility for the more problematic impacts their activities have in society. A new factory, for example, can contribute jobs and skills, but if it displaces a whole community or pollutes a river that a community relies on, its social impacts can outweigh the benefits, and its activities will not contribute to sustainability. Migrant labour is widespread: it is prevalent in Chinese manufacturing, and it is used extensively in sectors such as construction in developing economies. Livelihoods, the ecological environment and societal wellbeing are at risk from corporate investment that is framed mainly in terms of corporate goals rather than societal goods. It might be argued that the latter are matters for governments, but the governance of FDI projects involves a range of stakeholders: governments, communities and companies. For economic development to be directed more broadly towards human development, sustainability must be a core goal.

UN Sustainable Development Goals (SDGs)

1 End extreme poverty (less than $1.90 a day)

2 End hunger; achieve food security and sustainable agriculture

3 Ensure good health and wellbeing

4 Ensure inclusive and quality education

5 Achieve gender equality

6 Ensure safe drinking water and sanitation for all

7 Ensure affordable, clean energy for all

8 Promote decent work and inclusive, sustainable economic growth

9 Promote inclusive and sustainable industrialization, including infrastructure and innovation

10 Reduce inequality within and between countries

11 Make cities safe, inclusive and sustainable

12 Ensure sustainable consumption and production

13 Combat climate change

14 Conserve the oceans and seas

15 Promote sustainable use of land

16 Promote peace, justice and inclusive institutions

17 Strengthen global partnership for SDGs

Figure 3.11 UN Sustainable Development Goals (SDGs)
Source: UN General Assembly (2015) 'Transforming our world: the 2030 agenda for sustainable development', Resolution A/RES/70/1, 21 October, at www.un.org/ga, accessed 23 September 2019.

In 2015, the UN launched the Sustainable Development Goals (SDGs), a set of 17 broadly conceived and ambitious goals for the following 15 years. The SDGs are shown in Figure 3.11. As the figure shows, all the SDGs relate to aspects of human wellbeing in the context of a sustainable environment, including industrial, urban and ecological dimensions. There is a notable emphasis on how governance, including both government and businesses, can bring about progress in achieving these outcomes. These goals will be referred to in relevant sections throughout this book. We begin with those particularly relevant to the social and cultural environment. The first five address specific aspects of human wellbeing. The first of these is ending poverty, which involves providing the necessary social protections for the poorest and most vulnerable in society. Social protections are shown in detail in Figure 3.12. SDGs 2–5 focus on food security, health, education and gender equality. Also relevant to this chapter are SDG 8, on decent work, and SDG 11 on sustainable cities – a highly important goal in the context of rapid urbanization, especially in developing countries.

social protection the set of policies and programmes designed to reduce and prevent poverty and vulnerability through the life cycle

Social protection, also known as social security, is an essential area of policy for achieving sustainable development. It is defined as 'the set of policies and programmes designed to reduce and prevent poverty and vulnerability through the life cycle' (ILO, 2017: 1). Social protection can be funded in a variety of ways, including contributory schemes and non-contributory schemes financed from tax revenues. Governments are in a position to provide social protection through programmes supported by public funding. Comprehensive programmes can promote human

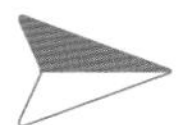

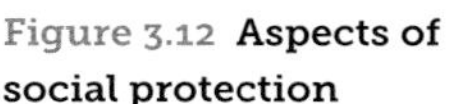

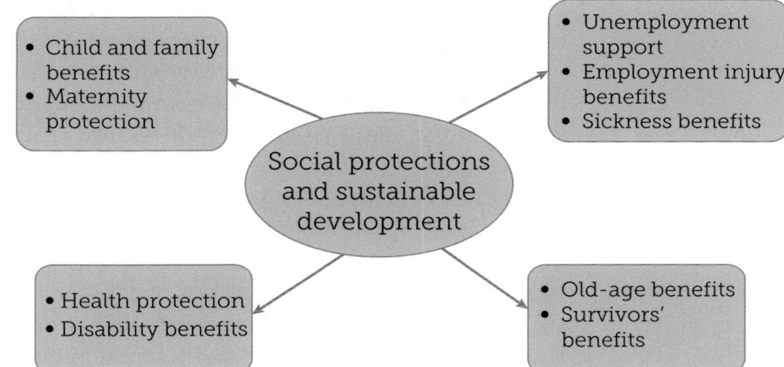

Figure 3.12 Aspects of social protection

Source: ILO (International Labour Organization) (2017) *World Social Protection Report 2017–19: Universal social protection to achieve the Sustainable Development Goals*, pp. 3–5, at www.ilo.org, accessed 23 September 2019.

development, political stability and inclusive economic growth. Human development, introduced in Chapter 2 (p. 41), comprises three sets of indicators, economic prosperity, health and educational attainment. Where governments either choose not to fund social protection programmes or feel unable to do so because of lack of resources, the results for society are likely to be low levels of human development, political instability and growing inequality. The ILO reports on progress in a range of social protections that span the entire life cycle, shown in Figure 3.12. They fall into broad groupings: family benefits, including a focus on mothers and children; protections of working people; protections for people in old age; and protections of the disabled and most vulnerable in society. Although social protection is a human right and an essential aspect of human development, most of the world's people can only hope for the benefits shown in the figure. A majority of the world's population (55%) cannot claim even one of these benefits; 45% are protected by at least one, but even for these more fortunate people, most elements of social protection are beyond reach. Only 29% of the world's people enjoy comprehensive social security, leaving 71% covered partially or not at all.

This chapter has highlighted the changes taking place in the socio-cultural environment of businesses globally. In developed economies, they include the changing nature of employment, a decline in traditional industrial jobs, a deterioration in low-paid workers' conditions of employment, and the challenges of ageing societies. Key changes in the work environment have been driven by technological innovations introduced by businesses. While they have brought beneficial technological advances and new skills, other consequences have been more problematic. There has been widespread upheaval in jobs markets, as old skills give way to new ones, leaving many workers behind. New technologies associated with artificial intelligence have created new jobs for those with appropriate skills, but many low-skilled workers have seen their jobs replaced by automation. It is commonly thought that a company bears no responsibility for workers it lets go because their work ceases to exist, but socially responsible companies will take steps to find alternative work for these workers. In many countries, companies are legally compelled to do so, or, alternatively, to offer them financial compensation. Education and training are concerns that involve both governments and businesses. A sustainable approach would include co-operative programmes to re-train workers and offer continuous opportunities for re-training throughout a person's career. In practice, most of the world's workers can only dream of these opportunities for self-development.

Companies have been at the forefront of investing in the developing economies, where social impacts have also been dramatic. Key issues include rapid industrialization, rapid urbanization, impacts of migration and ageing populations. These changes offer opportunities to improve human wellbeing in many ways. New industries bring employment; urban environments are generally able to provide better services; and migrant workers are grateful for jobs.

However, much of the employment associated with globalized industries has brought exploitation to workers, many of them migrants. Unregulated urban sprawl, as happens in many of the least-developed countries, is detrimental to health and wellbeing. Rapid urbanization, with its potential for unrest, has become one of the major challenges faced by governments in developing regions. These challenges are not insoluble. Governments engaging with companies can plan business activities that provide employment, build social cohesion and serve human needs. Education, training and healthcare provisions can be built into investment projects. However, such a vision requires businesses to focus on social responsibilities rather than short-term profits. The good news for such businesses is that socially responsible projects are more sustainable, and generate greater value in the long term.

Conclusions

The cultural environment presents a paradox for international business. While globalization has extended supply chains that knit businesses ever closer together, differing cultural outlooks among companies and societies remain potent. Research on cross-cultural management is not likely to become redundant anytime soon. On the other hand, cultural dimensions highlighted by Hofstede now seem to be more blurred than his research suggested. The individualism–collectivism dichotomy, which is appealingly simple, no longer seems to reflect the way cultures evolve and people behave. All of us, whatever our cultural background, have individualist leanings to some extent, while at the same time desiring to be part of something bigger – and also more meaningful – in our lives. All of us also wish for improved wellbeing in our lives. But in the many diverse societies that make up the global economy, cultural differences remain potent, as do variations in human wellbeing.

The internationalized business seeks to satisfy the needs and wants of consumers in all its markets. Its managers dream of a global product that appeals universally, but they know that sales depend on attracting and pleasing consumers in different markets. The goal of success in all markets is brought closer by globalization. The global company has become adept at maximizing location advantages at every stage in a supply chain. Efficiency gains are maximized, and costs are minimized, typically through manufacturing in developing countries and choosing other locations for their specific advantages in other respects. It is in the supply chain that the negative impacts of globalized production on societies come into focus, and are increasingly scrutinized in a context of sustainability. Poor working conditions, exploited labour, poor living conditions for migrant workers and displacement of families are commonplace in global production. Governments have been slow to react to these conditions, largely because they are keen to attract global companies. Companies have long recognized the importance of consumers as stakeholders, but have tended to see workers in terms of costs of production, rather than as stakeholders whose wellbeing matters in terms of achieving corporate goals.

Governments in both developed and developing countries now view the changes taking place in society as posing challenges for policies and public funding. Migration has risen up the agenda, as has the issue of providing for human wellbeing in rapidly urbanizing areas. Governments are now confronting urgent needs to address the extent of social protections, especially in the context of ageing populations. These social issues are now aspects of stakeholder responsibilities that businesses must address.

CLOSING CASE STUDY

Better prospects in South Africa for all in society?

When South Africa's era of apartheid ended in 1994, there began a journey of democratic transition. Apartheid enshrined white minority rule over the country's black majority, supported by institutional segregation. When that regime was toppled, there were hopes that the new democracy would see the emergence of a rainbow nation. Two main aspects were the hopes of economic participation for all people regardless of race, and the ushering in of a more unified society where racial divides would fade away. In both respects, the new democracy has disappointed. The country was hailed as one of the new emerging economies on the global stage, but it has failed to live up to expectations. Racial divides remain a reality, and problems of poverty and lack of economic opportunity are particularly poignant for the poor black population, who had pinned their hopes on the changes to take place in the new era. These black South Africans have become disillusioned because of the continuing deprivation they endure. In recent years, social divisions have been further exacerbated by the influx of refugees from other African countries, many fleeing poverty and instability in countries such as Somalia, Angola, the Democratic Republic of Congo and Zimbabwe. The presence of these refugees has given rise to social tensions.

South Africa's economy should be in a strong position. It is rich in natural resources, generating income from exports of mining and agricultural commodities. While the end of apartheid offered an opportunity to introduce economic reforms that would move the country towards more sustainable development, the reforms that were made were limited. The reform agenda has been determined by the dominant political party, the African National Congress (ANC), which led the overthrow of apartheid. Large businesses still tend to dominate the landscape, many now with black African owners. Business models remain focused on profits rather than social goals. And there are also numerous state-owned businesses. While these should ideally serve the public interests, they have become vehicles for enriching those who manage them, thus breeding corruption. The business environment under the ANC became entangled in wide-scale corruption, draining the state of resources. In 2018, the ANC took drastic action to remove the country's president for the last nine years, Jacob Zuma. It removed Mr Zuma from the presidency of the party, which had the effect of removing him from the office of president of the country. A new president, Cyril Ramaphosa, took over, facing a mammoth task of reining in corruption, restoring the public finances and alleviating the many social problems that had festered under the previous government.

Among the most difficult challenges is the plight of the poor and unemployed, suffering in inadequate housing and coping with a weak educational system. Unemployment is officially 26.7%, but is closer to 30% in reality. Youth unemployment is higher still, in the region of 50%. These people at the bottom of the pyramid are the predominantly black majority. The challenge for the government is to foster economic growth that encompasses all people. South Africa is one of the world's most unequal countries (see the section on inequality in Chapter 4), with a concentration of wealth in the big cities, such as Johannesburg and Cape Town, contrasting markedly with the deprivation outside the cities, mostly affecting the black population. Diversifying the economy and attracting investors are priorities for Mr Ramaphosa.

Dependence on mining exports has left the economy vulnerable when global markets take a downturn, as is currently the case in sectors affected by trade tensions. Investment in manufacturing, as has occurred in China through FDI, would help to create jobs. But South Africa's task is made difficult because of the entrenched position of its ruling business elites and its endemic corruption. Attracting investors is an uphill task in countries such as South Africa, which have poor governance and political instability. The plight of

South African townships like this one suffer from poverty and the lack of durable housing.

the black majority has not been alleviated as hoped for in 1994. Instead, the economy has been directed towards enriching the few at the top, which, in effect, has led to a worsening of the racial divides that still persist. Democracy brought the hope of the rule of law, equality before the law and equal opportunity. In elections in 2019, Mr Ramaphosa faced the voters and was elected president, but with a majority of only 57.5%. This was the smallest winning margin for the ANC since 1994. He promised a new era, to tackle corruption and to build the social cohesion and economic participation that the overthrow of apartheid had promised.

Questions

- Why is racial tension still a reality in South Africa?
- What steps could be taken to restore economic opportunity for all?
- What aspects of the social and cultural environment would deter foreign investors in South Africa?
- In what ways is South Africa moving towards sustainable development?

Further reading

See the article, 'Zuma exit gives ANC final chance', by David Pilkington and Joseph Cotterill, 17 February 2018, in the *Financial Times*.

Multiple choice questions

Visit www.macmillanihe.com/morrison-gbe-5e to take a quick self-test quiz on what you have read in this chapter.

Review questions

1. What are the main elements of culture?
2. Explain the essential aspects of national culture. How can they change over time?
3. What is 'cultural distance', and how does it affect the MNE?
4. What are the differences between a 'high-context' and 'low-context' language? Why do these differences matter in business negotiations?
5. What are the divergent currents in predominantly Muslim societies?
6. What has been the impact of Confucianism on firms in Asia, including their organizations and ways of doing business?
7. What are the essential cultural dimensions described by Hofstede in his research?
8. How do the rankings of national culture produced by Hofstede shed light on international management practices in different locations?
9. List the main elements of organizational culture. Why is 'culture clash' a common problem in mergers between large companies?
10. What is Taylorist scientific management? In what ways is it continuing to be influential?
11. What are the challenges posed by ageing populations in developed and developing countries, from government and business perspectives?
12. Why has international migration become an increasingly important social issue?
13. What ethical issues arise for migrant workers who travel to other countries for work?
14. What are the problems associated with urbanization, and why have they become most acute in developing countries?
15. Why are social protection provisions necessary in achieving sustainable development goals (SDGs)?

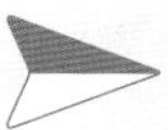

✓ Assignments

1 Assess the use of migrant labour for manufacturing companies involved in global supply chains, in terms of human wellbeing and sustainable development.

2 Assess the impact of demographic changes on the business environment in (a) advanced economies, and (b) developing economies.

Further reading

Baker, S. (2015) *Sustainable Development*, 2nd edition (Routledge).

Bartlett, C., Ghoshal, S. and Beamish, P. (2007) *Transnational Management: Text, cases and readings in cross-border management*, 5th edition (McGraw-Hill).

Berger, P. and Huntington, S. (eds) (2002) *Many Globalizations: Cultural diversity in the contemporary world* (Oxford: Oxford University Press).

Hofstede, G. (1994) *Cultures and Organizations: Software of the mind* (London: HarperCollins).

Pugh, D. and Hickson, D. (2007) *Writers on Organizations*, 6th edition (London: Penguin).

Schein, E.J. (2016) *Organizational Culture and Leadership*, 5th edition (London: John Wiley & Sons).

Schneider, S., Stahl, G. and Barsoux, J.L. (2014) *Managing Across Cultures*, 3rd edition (Harlow: Pearson Education).

Thomas, D. and Peterson, M. (2017) *Cross-cultural Management: Essential concepts*, 4th edition (Sage).

Trompenaars, F. (1994) *Riding the Waves of Culture* (New York: Irwin).

Usunier, J.-C. and Lee, J. (2009) *Marketing Across Cultures*, 5th edition (London: Financial Times Prentice Hall).

References

Bartlett, C.A. and Ghoshal, S. (1989) *Managing across Borders: The transnational solution* (Cambridge, MA: Harvard Business School Press).

BBC (2018) 'Jewish nation state: Israel approves controversial bill', BBC news, 19 July 2018, at www.bbc.com/news

Berger, P. (2002) 'The cultural dynamics of globalization', in Berger, P. and Huntington, S. (eds) *Many Globalizations* (New York: Oxford University Press), pp. 1–16.

Bird, A. and Fang, T. (2009) 'Cross cultural management in an age of globalization', *International Journal of Cross Cultural Management*, 92(2): 139–143.

Bird, A. and Stevens, M. (2003) 'Toward an emergent global culture and the effects of globalization on obsolescing national cultures', *Journal of International Management*, 9: 395–407.

Connor, W. (1978) 'A nation is a nation, is a state...', cited in Hutchinson, J. and Smith, A. (1994) *Nationalism* (Oxford: Oxford University Press), p. 36.

Cullen, J., Parboteeah, K.P. and Hoegl, M. (2004) 'Cross-national differences in managers' willingness to justify ethically suspect behaviors: A test of institutional anomie theory', *Academy of Management Journal*, 47(3): 411–21.

de Haas, H. (2010) 'Migration and development: a theoretical perspective', *International Migration Review*, 44(1): 227–64.

Fang, T. (2003) 'A critique of Hofstede's fifth national culture dimension', *International Journal of Cross Cultural Management*, 33(3): 347–368.

Hall, E.T. (1976) *Beyond Culture* (New York: Doubleday).

Hofstede, G. (1994) *Cultures and Organizations: Software of the Mind* (London: HarperCollins).

Hofstede, G. (1996) 'Images of Europe, past, present and future', in Joynt, P. and Warner, M. (eds) *Managing Across Cultures: Issues and perspectives* (London: International Thomson Business Press), pp. 147–65.

Inglehart, R. and Baker, W. (2000) 'Modernization, culture change and the persistence of national values', *American Sociological Review*, 65: 19–51.

ILO (International Labour Organization) (2017) *World Social Protection Report 2017–19: Universal social protection to achieve the Sustainable Development Goals*, at www.ilo.org

IOM (International Organization for Migration) (2013) *World Migration Report 2013*, at www.iom.int

Krafcik, J. (1988) 'Triumph of the lean production system', *Sloan Management Review*, 30(1): 41–52.

Leys, S. (1997) (trans. and ed.) *Analects of Confucius* (New York: W.W. Norton & Co.).

Michaelson, R. (2019) 'An "oasis" for women: Inside Saudi Arabia's vast new female-only workspaces', *The Guardian*, 20 July.

OECD (2018) *International Migration Outlook 2018* (Paris: OECD Publishing).

Pew Research Center (2014) 'Religious hostilities reach six-year high: Report', 14 January, at www.pewresearch.org

Pew Research Center (2017) 'The changing global religious landscape', 5 April, at www.pewforum.org

Pruijt, H. (2000) 'Repainting, modifying, smashing Taylorism', *Journal of Organizational Change Management*, 13(5): 1–11.

Ratcliffe, R. (2018) 'Qatar law change hailed as milestone for migrant workers in World Cup run-up', *The Guardian*, 6 September.

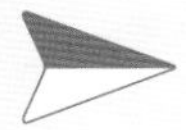

Ralston, D., Holt, D., Terpstra, R. and Yu Kai-Cheng (2008) 'The impact of national culture and economic ideology on managerial work values: a study of the United States, Russia, Japan and China', *Journal of International Business Studies*, 39: 8–26.

Ronen, S. and Shenkar, O. (2013) 'Mapping world cultures: Cluster formation, sources and implications', *Journal of International Business Studies*, 44: 867–97.

Sherwood, H. (2018) 'Religion: Why faith is becoming more and more popular', *The Guardian*, 27 August.

Stahl, G. and Tung, R. (2014) 'Towards a more balanced treatment of culture in international business studies: The need for positive cross-cultural scholarship', *Journal of International Business Studies*, 1–24.

Taylor, F. ([1911] 2004) *The Principles of Scientific Management* (New York: Harper & Brothers).

Trompenaars, F. (1994) *Riding the Waves of Culture* (New York: Irwin).

UN Habitat (2016) *World Cities Report, Urbanization and Development: Emerging futures*, at www.unhabitat.org

UNHCR (UN High Commissioner for Refugees) (2017) 'What is a refugee?' at www.unrefugees.org/what-is-a-refugee/, accessed 11 Aug 2017.

UNHCR (UN High Commissioner for Refugees) (2018) *Global Trends Report* 2018, at www.unhcr.org

UN Human Rights Office (2017) *Interviews with Rohingyas fleeing Myanmar since 9 October 2016*, at www.ohchr.org/Documents/Countries/MM/FlashReport3Feb2017.pdf

UN Population Division (2017) *World Population Ageing 2017* (ST/ESA/SER.A/397) (New York: UN).

UN Population Division (2018) *World Urbanization Prospects: the 2018 Revision*, online edition, at https://esa.un.org/unpd/wup

UN Population Division (2019) *World Population Prospects: the 2019 Revision*, at https://population.un.org/wpp

UNIASG (Inter-Agency Support Group on indigenous peoples' issues) (2014) *Thematic Paper on Indigenous Peoples' Access to Decent Work and Social Protection*, June, at www.un.org

UNOCHA (United Nations Office for the Coordination of Humanitarian Affairs) *Rohingya refugee crisis*, at www.unocha.org/rohingya-refugee-crisis, accessed 20 July 2018.

Williamson, D. (2002) 'Forward from a critique of Hofstede's model of national culture', *Human Relations*, 55(11): 1373–95.

Visit the companion website at www.macmillanihe.com/morrison-gbe-5e for further learning and teaching resources.

© Getty Images/Juice Images RF

THE GLOBAL ECONOMIC ENVIRONMENT

Outline of chapter

Introduction

National economies: income and growth
- Gross national income and gross domestic product
- Economic growth
- Inequality and why it matters

Unemployment

Other key economic indicators: inflation and balance of payments

Balancing the national economy

Classifying national economic systems

Market economies
- The liberal market model
- Social market models
- Asian capitalist systems

Mixed economies: China and India

The economies of Central and Eastern Europe

Regionalization: focus on the EU
- The economies of the EU and eurozone
- Enlargement and the future of the EU

The economic environment: towards sustainability?

Conclusions

This chapter will enable you to

- Define and apply the major concepts used to analyze the economic environment
- Identify divergent economic systems in their social and political contexts
- Assess impacts of globalization on economic systems and in societies
- Appreciate economic issues that affect regional integration
- Critically question the extent to which countries are making progress towards sustainability in their national economies

OPENING CASE STUDY

Economic slowdown in China

China became a successful example of economic development based on manufacturing for global markets. People throughout the world have felt the effects. Exports from its manufacturing centres, such as Guangdong, have supplied consumer goods from clothes to televisions. Its fast-growing economy created seemingly insatiable demand for raw materials, energy and commodities supplied from producing countries around the globe. The growing prosperity of Chinese consumers has created markets for an array of goods from western companies – from iPhones to motor vehicles. But China's boom years could not last forever. Much of the economic growth was fuelled by borrowing, leading to a build-up of debt, which became a concern for China's leadership, especially when the effects of the financial crisis of 2008 dampened demand in global markets. More recently there have been tensions with its largest trading partner, the US, which have seen rising trade barriers that have affected China's exports and made its imports more costly.

China's growth has been slowing for a number of years. Its leaders have recognized that its 10% growth rate over the last two decades could not be maintained, but they fear a steep decline in growth, as this would jeopardize job creation. They take the view that the country is making a transition from a focus on rapid growth to a focus on sustainable growth, which relies less on exports and more on domestic consumption. This change of policy is consistent with a new policy tilted towards quality of life for China's population. The pollutant industries and energy consumption of the country's period of rapid growth have left environmental scars and risks to health. Shifting to the more high-tech sectors is part of a new phase of development, and will also lead to a better quality of life. However, this shift is gradual, and, for the time being, mass manufacturing remains central to economic growth. We can see the current trends in China's consumer behaviour.

The once-exuberant consumers in Shanghai have become more cautious in their spending in the city's upmarket shopping streets.

China is the largest manufacturing country and the largest market for cars. But following two decades of growth, sales of cars fell by 6% in 2018, to 22.6 million. Geely, China's largest carmaker, saw flat sales, and major foreign companies reported falling sales. Volkswagen and General Motors, both reliant on China for about 40% of their global sales, saw falls in sales of over 10%. While sales of electric vehicles are rising, these are only a tiny proportion of total sales. Tax concessions and easy credit had been boosting car sales, and both were wound down in 2018, helping to dampen sales. A factor has been the slowdown in the property market, also affected by greater restrictions on borrowing which had been introduced to tame the rise in household debt. Adding to the woes of car dealers has been the rise in tariffs on imported cars. For Chinese people who are now more closely examining their finances, concerns such as paying for health and education are weighing heavily. It is indicative that sales of iPhones have fallen in China, as consumers opt for less expensive Chinese brands. A response by some of retail outlets has been to lower the price of iPhones – a move criticized by Apple. Apple is also concerned that the trade friction between the US and China could well affect their business, as their phones are almost all made in China, for export to US customers.

China's economic development model was based on the introduction of free-market forces from the early 1980s onwards. The government is still ultimately controlled by the Communist Party. State-owned enterprises are an important part of the economy, but they are inefficient and debt-laden, and in need of reform. The downside of any reform, however, is that they are large employers, and reluctant to downsize in the way that private-sector companies would do. Private-sector companies have been a bright prospect for China's focus on more sustainable development. The Chinese government changed the definition of

small-to-medium size company in 2018, to allow a larger number of these firms to borrow at advantageous rates, in the hope that this stimulus would give the economy impetus. Job creation remains a primary concern for the country's leadership, crucial to averting social and political unrest.

Questions

- Why has China's growth rate slowed in recent years?
- In what ways is China's economic development model changing?
- Why is China's economy a concern for global markets?
- What are the risks of social and political unrest if the Chinese economy continues to decline?

Further reading

For an insight into changing consumer behaviour, see Lily Kuo's article, 'Cautious consumers feel the pinch as Chinese economy slows', 18 January 2019, in *The Guardian*.

Introduction

The global economic environment reflects increasing and deepening globalization, and at the same time, diversity among national economies. The world's nearly 200 countries differ widely in their size, geography, population, climate and natural resources. These differences have direct effects on the types and intensity of economic activity that are viable. For example, trade is traditionally more likely to prosper in a coastal state than in a land-locked one. States rich in natural resources, such as minerals and oil, have developed national economies built around these natural endowments. In addition, each national economy exists in a cultural and political environment which influences policymakers' decisions on resources and public spending. Increasingly, the economic environment is seen in terms of impacts on societies.

This chapter will begin by looking at the tools with which economists measure and compare national economies. The data generated in these ways allow policymakers to assess economic performance and design national policies. We will examine the major types of national economic system which characterize most of the world's economies. They range from market capitalist models to those in which state controls predominate. These are not simply economic systems in isolation, but represent divergent pictures of society. A trend observable across all continents in recent years has been the expansion of global supply chains, bringing greater opportunities for business enterprises – and also greater impacts in societies, both positive and negative. In an economic environment which has become highly interconnected, the role of national governments has evolved, retaining a pivotal role domestically, and also taking on regional and international perspectives.

National economies: income and growth

national economy the aggregate of economic activities of governments, businesses and individuals within the national framework of a nation-state

The global economic environment is made up of economic activities conducted by individuals, businesses and governments within national frameworks. The aggregate of these activities form a **national economy**. In each of the world's countries, a range of **economic indicators** can be used to measure these activities, revealing the nature and vibrancy of the national economy. Is the economy growing? Are there enough jobs for those who want them? How is public money being spent? These are some of the many issues that affect the economy. Responding to these questions

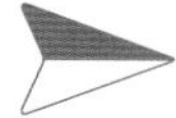

involves more than simply assessing available data in a vacuum. Economic data speak volumes about the nature of a society, its values and the way it is governed. This chapter will highlight these interactions between economic and social environments.

economic indicators statistical measures used to analyze a national economy; notable indicators are economic growth and GDP per capita

macroeconomics the study of national economies

microeconomics the study of economic activity at the level of individuals and firms

Economists study both the overall activity in the national economy and the lower-level economic activity which takes place between businesses and consumers. **Macroeconomics** is the study of national economies, while **microeconomics** refers to the study of economic activity at the level of individuals and firms. The two areas of economic study are related. Data compiled for each of the economic indicators at the microeconomic level are fed into macroeconomic analysis.

Flows of economic resources in the economy can be depicted as a model based on circular flows. While this type of model is greatly over-simplified, it does serve to show the interaction between the main groups, businesses and consumers, as can be seen in Figure 4.1. Businesses provide employment and wages to households, while consumers spend earned income on goods and services. At the same time, both businesses and individuals pay taxes to government, which are used to fund public spending and social security. By increasing or decreasing public spending or by altering the tax regime, it is possible for government to influence spending by firms and consumers. For example, public spending on government projects will provide firms with more orders and greater need for workers. These workers, in turn, will purchase consumer goods. Therefore, the 'injection' of government funds will have had a general effect on the economy, referred to by economists as a 'multiplier' effect, because of its ripple effects across the economy. It should also be noticed that effects of international flows are taken into account in Figure 4.1. Consumers buy imported products, which is depicted as a 'leakage' from the circular flow. Similarly, when firms export products, the income that arises is an injection, as is overseas investment.

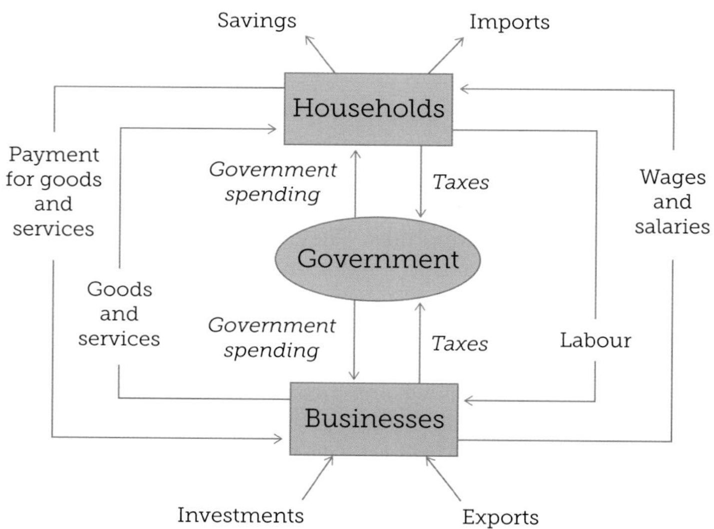

Figure 4.1 **Circular flows of income in an economy**

gross national income (GNI) the total income from all the final products and services produced by a national economy within a single year

Gross national income and gross domestic product

The economy of a country is capable of being measured in a number of ways. One of these is **Gross National Income (GNI)**. GNI represents the total income from all the final products and services produced by a national economy, including income that national residents earn from overseas investments, in a given year. It is the broadest measure of a nation's economic activity.

gross domestic product (GDP) the value of the total economic activity produced within a country in a single year, including both domestic and foreign producers

purchasing power parity (PPP) means estimating the number of units of the foreign currency that would be needed to buy goods or services equivalent to those that the US dollar would buy in the US

Gross Domestic Product (GDP) represents the value of the total economic activity produced within a country in a single year, including both domestic and foreign producers. GDP and GNI vary enormously from one country to another. Figure 4.2 shows GNI for some of the world's largest economies. These calculations are based on **Purchasing Power Parity (PPP)**. PPP estimates the number of units of the foreign currency which would be needed to buy goods or services equivalent to those which the US dollar would buy in the US. The advantage of using PPP estimates is that they more accurately reflect relative living standards in different countries. The US has long been the world's largest economy, but, on PPP calculations, China has now overtaken the US, with a GNI of over $23 trillion, compared to US GNI of $19.6 trillion. India's impressive recent growth has seen it rise to third place.

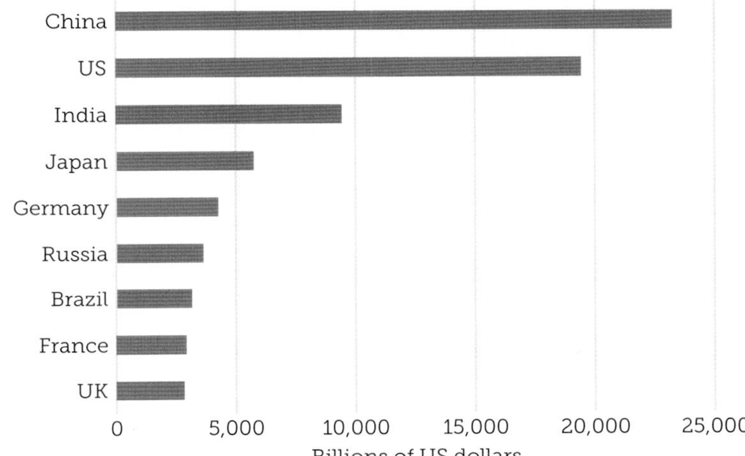

Figure 4.2 GNI (PPP) of selected large economies, 2017

Source of data: World Bank, International Comparison Programme Database, GNI (PPP), at https://data.worldbank.org, accessed 19 June 2019.

For comparisons between countries, GDP or GNI per capita (per head) gives a better idea of a society's prosperity, as it takes the population into account. There are huge differences in per capita GNI across the world. US GNI per capita was $60,200 in 2017. The countries featured in Figure 4.3 are the same as those in Figure 4.2, but the order is very different. The advanced economies had GNI per capita of between $43,000 and $60,000. There is a wide gap between these countries and the developing and emerging countries. There is also considerable variation among the emerging countries. China's GNI per capita was $11,850 in 2013, having more than tripled since 2000. By 2017, it had reached $16,760, marking a continuing rise in living standards. But the average income still lags behind that of the advanced economies. India is by far the poorest of these emerging economies, with a GNI per capita of about $7,060, less than half that of the Chinese citizen. African countries, especially those in sub-Saharan Africa, are among the world's poorest in terms of GNI per capita, in the range of just several hundred dollars.

GNI or GDP per capita represents an average figure. It does not take account of the distribution of wealth within the country. Some countries have extremes of wealth between the rich and poor, while others are more egalitarian, although their GNI per capita could be similar. India has a low GNI per head, but is nonetheless seen as a huge potential market because of its large – and rapidly growing – middle class of an estimated 600 million consumers, eager to buy products such as televisions and mobile phones. This information is valuable for

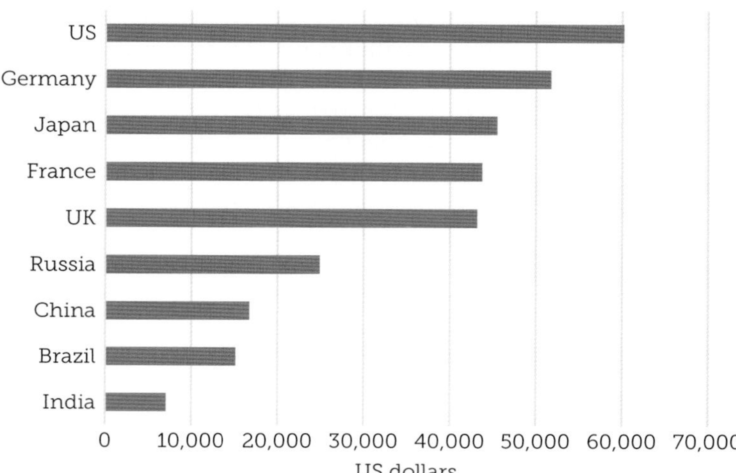

Figure 4.3 GNI per capita (PPP) in selected large economies, 2017

Source of data: World Bank, International Comparison Programme Database, GNI per capita (PPP), at https://data.worldbank.org, accessed 19 June 2019.

companies whose marketing strategy is targeted at emerging markets, as well as for foreign investors. When India's growing middle-class prosperity is placed in the context of Indian society overall, however, the picture is rather different. India has seen growing inequality and persisting high levels of poverty, indicating that economic growth is uneven.

Economic growth

economic growth a country's increase in national income over time; negative growth occurs where the economy is contracting

Economic growth refers to a country's increase in national income over time, indicating expansion in the production of goods and services. The growth in GDP per capita is a measure often used by economists. A growing economy signifies improvement in material wellbeing, but this does not necessarily lead to overall improvement in wellbeing in a society. Societal wellbeing is broader than income and includes improvements in health and education, as recognized in the UN's concept of human development (discussed in Chapter 2).

There is abundant evidence that economic growth leads to poverty reduction and is crucial to achieving development goals (Rodrik, 2012). Indeed, most of the dimensions of wellbeing depend to some extent on economic growth. Despite its acknowledged limitations, it remains a key indicator (Aghion and Howitt, 2009).

Economic development depends on growth. Theories of economic growth have traditionally focused on external, or exogenous, factors, which were seen as given. Theorists now focus more on endogenous factors, which are internal to the economy. These include levels of technology, educational attainment and investment activities. They involve choices made by private individuals and also government policies. For example, government policies could encourage an entrepreneur to invest in technological innovation. A range of institutions, both formal (such as legal protections) and informal (such as a bureaucracy based on meritocracy) come into play (Rodrik, 2009). The level of technological innovation reflects a country's education policies and spending decisions (see Chapter 9). While government spending on primary and secondary education provides the groundwork, spending on higher education is seen as crucial to making the transition to a more technologically advanced economy (Aghion and Howitt, 2009: 312).

National economies need to grow in order to create jobs and sustain livelihoods for growing populations. China's economy grew at annual rates of over 9% over the two decades from 1994 to 2014 (Giles, 2014). Historically, such growth rates are rare, and usually occur during phases of 'catch-up', when countries are aiming to catch

up with richer, more technologically advanced countries (Piketty, 2014: 97). China's growth has now slowed, as shown in Figure 4.4. Following the end of the Second World War, European economies grew strongly in the 1950s and 60s. In the 1970s and 80s, Japan underwent rapid industrialization in its efforts to catch up with the advanced western economies. As these economies became mature, growth slowed. In general, the advanced economies have relatively slower growth than emerging economies, as Figure 4.4 shows. Although world per capita GDP grew at a rate of 3% from 1950 to 1973, a normal rate of growth is closer to 1% (Maddison, 2007: 72). But expectations rise during periods of prosperity, and many policymakers would now view a growth rate of 1% as disappointingly low.

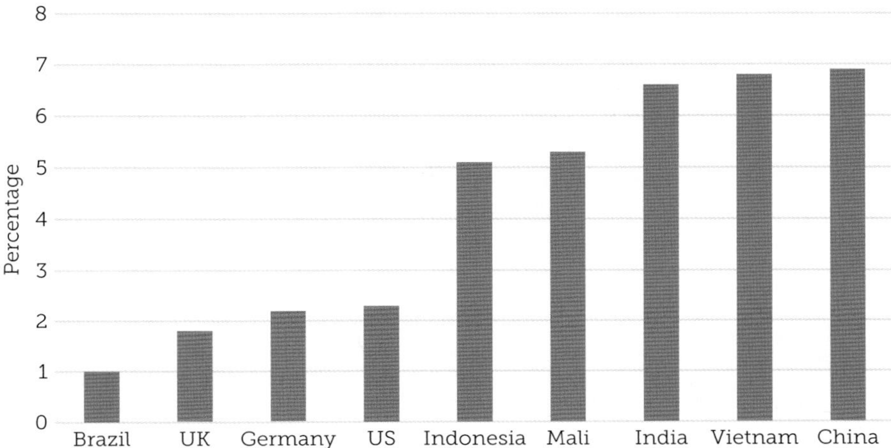

Figure 4.4
GDP growth in selected economies, 2017

Source of data: World Bank, Data, GDP Growth (annual %), at https://data.worldbank.org, accessed 19 June 2019.

What propels economic growth? The classic picture of economic development is one of industrialization leading to economic growth. Apart from China, most of the countries with the highest growth over the last two decades do not fit this picture. Economic growth in African countries has largely depended on exploitation of natural resources and trade in agricultural commodities. Mali (with 5.3% growth) exports gold and other minerals, along with agricultural produce. However, it is exposed to the volatility of global markets. The economy of Equatorial Guinea, which is almost entirely dependent on oil and gas, saw negative growth (−3.2%) in 2017, which, although disappointing, represents a modest recovery from −6% in 2016. It has been affected by declining global oil prices and diminishing reserves. The government is attempting to diversify its economy into other sectors such as manufacturing, but high inequality, widespread poverty and poor human development are challenges. The country's GNI per capita (PPP) was nearly $20,000 in 2017, still placing it among the high-income countries, despite its period of economic downturn. However, its human development ranking was a lowly 135 out of 188 countries (UNDP, 2016), indicating a very low level of societal wellbeing. This huge discrepancy places it among the societies with the largest gap between wealth of the richest and the low level of wellbeing of the poorest.

inclusive growth economic growth that brings improved living standards and greater economic security for all in society

Equatorial Guinea is a stark reminder that headline economic growth can mask the realities of hardship for large portions of a society. Development should be inclusive, that is, bringing wellbeing to all in society. In their assessments of development, international organizations look increasingly at the bigger picture of who benefits from growth (OECD, 2014). **Inclusive growth** involves improved living standards and greater economic security for all in society, along with social

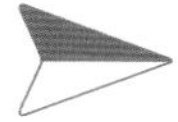

programmes to improve quality of life. In a highly unequal economy dependent almost exclusively on oil wealth, growth is unlikely to bring the benefits of development to all. These economies are in need of diversification to provide sustainable employment in non-oil activities.

prosperity in an economy, healthy economic growth and rising standards of living

recession two consecutive quarters of negative economic growth in an economy

depression situation in which an economy deteriorates significantly, diminishing by one-tenth in size

Fluctuations from periods of prosperity to downturn are part of what economists refer to as the business cycle. Longer cycles can be distinguished from shorter-term fluctuations, which are more closely identified with the business cycle. Although economists differ in their explanations of causes and indicators, four phases can be identified: prosperity, recession, depression and recovery. **Prosperity** is signified by healthy economic growth and rising standards of living. There are high levels of employment and wages, which lead to growing consumption. A **recession** can be narrowly defined as two consecutive quarters of negative economic growth, although economists prefer to look at the broader picture of the economy. Declining output in a recession is usually accompanied by rising unemployment and weak demand in the economy, as both consumers and businesses spend less. If these indicators continue to deteriorate, and the recession is prolonged, it can become a **depression**, which occurs when the economy has diminished by one tenth in size. The Great Depression of 1929 provided a warning for later generations. Since then, financial crises, especially the financial crisis of 2008, continue to demonstrate that market instabilities can have damaging impacts on societies.

A growing economy: what does it mean for businesses?

Businesses seek locations where economic growth will help them to prosper as enterprises. One attraction is rising incomes leading to rising consumer sales. List three other aspects of a sound, growing economy that will influence a business to invest. In what way is each of these likely to encourage new investors?

Inequality and why it matters

inequality the difference in wealth or income between the richest and poorest in society

Inequality can be viewed from a global or a national perspective. Here, we look at inequality within national economies, while the global perspective will be discussed later in this chapter. Defining and measuring equality are difficult, involving a range of methodologies, but, nonetheless, there is a consensus among scholars that national economies of both developed and developing countries have seen rising inequality. **Inequality** refers to the difference in wealth or income between the richest and poorest in society. If this gap is widening in an economy, it means that people at the top are seeing increasing gains, pulling away from those further down the economic ladder. The consequences of widening inequality are significant for the long-term health of economy as a whole and also for the individual inhabitants, with negative impacts on families' standard of living and, over the long term, risks to the stability of society (Bourguignon, 2015). Economists distinguish between income inequality and wealth inequality. Wealth is much more concentrated than income. There are significant variations among countries, even among countries that fall within the category of relatively rich market economies. The wealthiest 10% in the US own 80% of the country's wealth and receive about 40% of total income. In France, the top 10% own 50% of the country's wealth and receive about 30% of total income. Divergences such as this reflect differing government policies on inequality – and also different visions of society. We look first at wealth inequality.

Wealth can be defined as the 'current market value of all the assets owned by households, net of all their debts' (Stanford Center on Poverty and Inequality, 2016: 39). It includes financial assets such as company shares, and non-financial assets such as property in land and personal property like fine art, private jets and yachts. A country's top 10% (or 'decile') is likely to have considerable financial assets and also

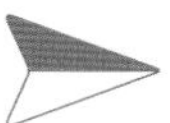

great wealth in real estate, which can be passed on to future generations within families. These assets are capable of generating income as well as appreciating in value. For example, company shares yield dividends and land generates rent, much of which is typically reinvested in similar classes of assets. The rich tend to get richer. In the US, the total wealth of just three people – Jeff Bezos (founder of Amazon), Bill Gates (founder of Microsoft) and Warren Buffet (a major investor) – is equal to that of half the entire nation. By contrast, while ordinary citizens are likely to have some savings, their main wealth lies in the value of the home they live in. When there is a property-market crash, as in the years 2007–8 in the US, they are in a precarious position, whereas the rich are better able to weather financial crises due to the diversity of their assets. Inheritance tax and wealth tax are means that can be used by governments to prevent widening inequality. Most countries impose some form of inheritance tax. Direct wealth taxes are much less common, but they are imposed by France, Norway and the Netherlands.

Income inequality can be measured as the net income of a household or individual, after taxes and after transfers that have been received, such as food subsidies and housing allowance. This constitutes the disposable income of the household, and represents 'net inequality'. In contrast, 'market inequality' is based on income before tax. Net inequality is lower than market inequality in any given country. The traditional tool used to measure income inequality is the **Gini index**, which ranges from 0, where income is shared equally among all, to 1, where all income goes to one household or person. The UN presents the Gini index as ranging from 0 to 100. European countries, such as Norway and Germany, have relatively low net inequality. However, inequality is on the rise in both these countries. Norway (25.9) has seen only a slight rise since 2013, but Germany has seen a rise from 28.3 to 30.1 between 2013 and 2015 (UNDP, 2016). The US (41.1, up from 40.8 in 2013) has higher and widening inequality. The world's most unequal countries tend to be in Latin America, Asia and Africa. Mexico (48.2), Brazil (51.5) and Colombia (53.6) stand out. Many African countries are also in this category, most notably South Africa (63.4). China's Gini index rose from 30 in the 1980s to over 50 in 2010 (OECD, 2014). This rise was to be expected following market reforms which led to rapid economic growth (Bourguignon, 2015). In 2013, it had fallen to 42.1, but rose slightly to 42.2 in 2015 (UNDP, 2016). At the same time, levels of poverty in China have been dramatically reduced, due to the growth in globalized manufacturing, employing millions of workers. In the decade to 2017, manufacturing wages tripled. However, for those left behind, there are few provisions in terms of a 'safety net' to help the poorest in society. This is true of most emerging and developing countries.

Gini index tool used by economists to measure income inequality

The richer economies tend to provide more safety-net programmes to meet the basic needs of the disadvantaged in society, such as the unemployed and those on very low incomes, but the US is a major exception. Here, the prevailing free-market assumptions (discussed later in this chapter) are averse to government spending to meet basic needs such as healthcare and housing (Stanford Center on Poverty and Inequality, 2016). Average wages in the US have been stagnant for decades in real terms. The incomes of many Americans in work are so low as to push them below the official poverty threshold. In an investigation of poverty in the US by the UN's special rapporteur in 2017, attention was drawn to the rise in extreme poverty (Alston, 2017). Mr Alston highlighted that one out of every eight people in the US, 40 million in all, fell beneath the official poverty threshold set by the Census Bureau each year. Almost half of these 40 million people live in extreme poverty, with incomes less than one-half the poverty threshold (Alston, 2017). This UN-sponsored report was viewed as a stark warning by a number of US politicians who have prioritized issues of poverty and human rights.

It is illuminating to look at the share of income going to those at the top: the top 10%, top 1% or top 0.1%. A global trend has been the increase in the share of income of those at the top. Figure 4.4 shows this trend in the US from 1970 onwards, where the share of the top 10% grew from 34% in 1970 to 47% in 2014. During that period, the share of the bottom 50% decreased from 21% in 1970 to 12.5% in 2014. The top-income data give an indication of the power, real and potential, of the people with the largest incomes. The increasing share of the richest in the US has been reflected in a growth in lobby activity aimed at influencing government policies (discussed in the next chapter). Researchers behind the data in Figure 4.5 have said in their *World Inequality Report* that, while income inequality has increased in most countries, the rate of increase has varied considerably. In Western European countries and the US, the top 1% had a share of about 10% of their country's income in 1980. By 2016, this share had risen to 12% in Western Europe, but was up to 20% in the US, representing a startling rise in inequality (Alvaredo et al., 2018). The authors attributed this rise to educational inequalities in the US, combined with tax policies that benefited the rich. During these decades, Western European countries pursued educational and wage-setting policies that were more favourable to the middle classes and lower-income.

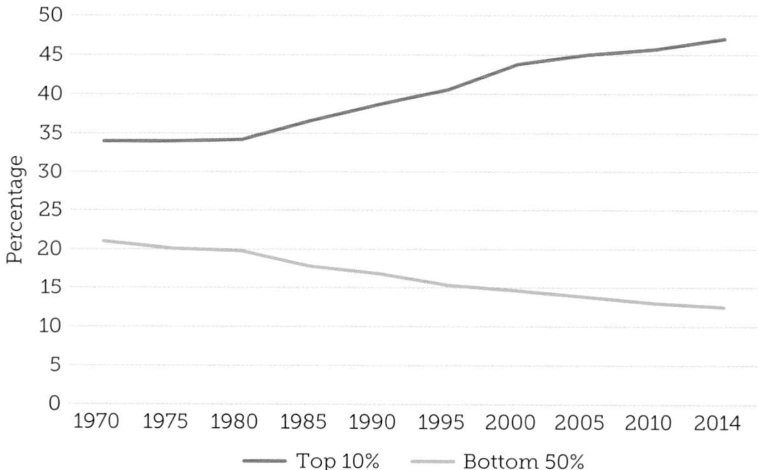

Figure 4.5 **Pre-tax income shares of the top 10% and bottom 50% in the US, 1970–2014**

Source: World Inequality Database, maintained by the Paris School of Economics, at http://wid.world/, accessed 18 June 2019.

The ethical aspects of inequality are capable of divergent viewpoints. Many economists would say that the inequalities associated with capitalism are part of its inherent dynamic, which, in general, has brought huge economic benefits to societies. Critics would argue that where there is extreme inequality in society, the lack of opportunity for self-fulfillment suffered by those at the bottom constitutes injustice (Rawls, 1996: 79; Sen, 2010: 231). To the extent that access to opportunities to pursue a good education and fulfilling job depends heavily on being born into a high-earning family, then equality of opportunity is diminished. This inequality of opportunity at the outset of a person's life is a precursor of inequality in standard of living that follows (Bourguignon, 2015: 61). Sen refers to equality of opportunity in terms of 'capabilities': 'a person's capability to do the things he or she has reason to value' (Sen, 2010: 231). The authors of the Stanford Center's *Poverty and Equality Report* (cited above) found that, although the US is thought of as the 'land of opportunity', being born into a high-earning family matters much more in the US than it does in most well-off countries.

Inequality: explanation and analysis

This is a lecture by Emmanuel Saez, Professor of Economics, at the University of California at Berkeley. He is speaking at the Canadian Centre of Policy Alternatives and University of British Columbia's Vancouver School of Economics. The lecture is on wealth and income inequality: evidence and policy implications, 28 November, 2014.

Video link: Inequality: explanation and analysis
https://youtu.be/ueHJzaDD_Mw

Inequality can undermine social cohesion and lead to political instability. But does it adversely affect a country's economic growth? Bourguignon argues that excessive inequality negatively impacts on economic efficiency. This view is supported by research that shows widening inequality is increasingly associated with risks of crisis and threats to sustainable growth (Ostry et al., 2014). Underlying causes of the financial crisis of 2008 were the financial excesses of the very rich that had spiralled out of control. The crisis highlighted that the growing wealth of the rich is not solely an indication of economic power. It also signifies their growing ability to control political outcomes, including light-touch regulation, low taxes and other policies that help to maintain their wealth – and power. However, social and political stability can be a consequence, which can in turn dampen growth.

High inequality adversely affects the sustainability of growth (Ostry et al., 2014). Expressed positively, lower net inequality leads to more sustainable growth. Redistribution is a way of compensating for high inequality. Redistributive policies include investing in education and healthcare, even though these benefit everyone, not just the poor. More targeted redistributive policies would be higher taxes for high earners and social spending aimed at the poorest. A 'progressive' taxation policy would impose a higher rate of tax on those with the higher incomes, thus aiming to mitigate inequality. Some economists would argue that such measures adversely affect growth, as they can constitute disincentives. But others would advise a more nuanced approach, saying that investing in education and social insurance both aids growth and reduces inequality. The US has high market inequality and also high inequality of net income, combined with low levels of redistribution. Ethical arguments against inequality have met with little resonance in the US in the past. But redistribution policies might find more favour in the US, if policymakers were persuaded that moderating inequality would contribute to sustainable growth.

Why should businesses be concerned about rising inequality?

Inequality is inherent in capitalism. Still, economists now see inequality as posing a danger to capitalism's long-term viability. Why is this?

Would you consider rising inequality to be a risk in the business environment, that would impact on business decision-making. Why?

Unemployment

unemployment the percentage of people in a country's labour force who are willing to work but are without jobs

'Full employment', contrary to what it implies, is used by economists to refer to a country's natural rate of unemployment which exists in all societies. What we commonly refer to as **unemployment** reflects the percentage of people in the country's labour force who are willing to work but are without jobs. National governments use differing definitions of unemployment. There is a generally accepted definition which dates from the 1982 International Conference of Labour Statisticians and is recognized by the International Labour Organization (ILO). This 'ILO definition' (ILO, 2014: 70) includes people who are:

a. without work in either paid employment or self-employment;
b. currently available for work, that is, available for paid employment or self-employment during a specific reference period; and
c. seeking work (by taking specific steps, such as applications to employers or registering with an employment exchange) within a specific reference period.

Specific rules about who is included and excluded from national statistics differ from country to country, making comparisons hazardous. Moreover, in every country, there are probably significant numbers of people who are 'hidden' from the statistics, such as 'discouraged workers', who have ceased to look for a job, and casual workers who were not registered employees in the first place.

Unemployment may be 'structural', meaning that there are not enough available jobs in the economy to provide work for the people seeking employment. Often this occurs because of changing technology, which leaves behind workers with outdated skills. It can also occur where industries relocate to other regions or other countries. The shift of much manufacturing from developed to developing countries, especially in Asia, represented a loss of jobs for manufacturing workers in western economies. A second type of unemployment is 'frictional', referring to the usual turnover in the labour force that happens, for example, when people are out of work and looking for new jobs. When demand in an economy falters and economic growth slows, unemployment tends to rise, as firms lay off workers and cease hiring. Unemployment rose during the financial crisis of 2008–9, reaching levels of 9% or more in the advanced economies. Despite a resumption in growth following the crisis, unemployment seemed to remain stubbornly high, reminding governments that economic growth does not necessarily lead to significant job creation. In the years following the crisis, the countries affected have seen modest reductions in unemployment, but at the same time a growing number of workers in precarious types of jobs in the gig economy. These are jobs in which the worker is described as a self-employed contractor, even in contexts where the work is controlled by managers in a larger organization. These jobs lack security of employment and social protections (such as sickness pay and paid holidays) that traditional types of employment confer.

Government policies are influential in promoting job creation. Policies which promote innovation and training can help to mitigate the impacts of unemployment in particular sectors. Governments can also make it easier for new businesses to start up. If their businesses are successful, these entrepreneurs are likely to take on employees, but it can take years for start-up businesses to increase appreciably in size. Many start-ups, such as those in the high-tech sectors, commonly employ few full-time staff directly. They are likely to contract for specific services, and these activities generate work for suitably skilled people. Developing economies often encounter a dilemma. They need to create jobs to satisfy the needs of their growing populations, but at the same time, they wish to move up the technology ladder, which implies encouraging innovative companies that employ fewer people than the low-technology sectors.

Youth unemployment is a particular concern for governments, as young people aspire to embark on careers that will blossom over a lifetime. Young people who have never had a job find it increasingly difficult to obtain fulfilling work. The growth in youth unemployment is shown in Figure 4.6. Countries in

The despair of unemployment has been devastating for young people.

© Getty, xijian

North America, Western Europe and Eastern Europe experienced rises in youth unemployment from 2008 to 2012. These were the years during which these economies were coming to terms with the effects of the financial crisis, and by 2017, the situation had improved. On the other hand, due to weak growth, Latin American countries, whose economies are highly sensitive to any weakness in global commodities markets, have seen rising youth unemployment. The most worrying statistics shown by the ILO data are those of North Africa and Arab states, where youth unemployment is particularly high. The large numbers of unemployed young people are a cause of concern for governments. They are, in effect, existing on the fringes of society at a period in their lives when they would expect to be setting out to realize personal goals and build careers. Moreover, those in work are mostly in insecure jobs in the informal sector, with no contract of employment and no job security.

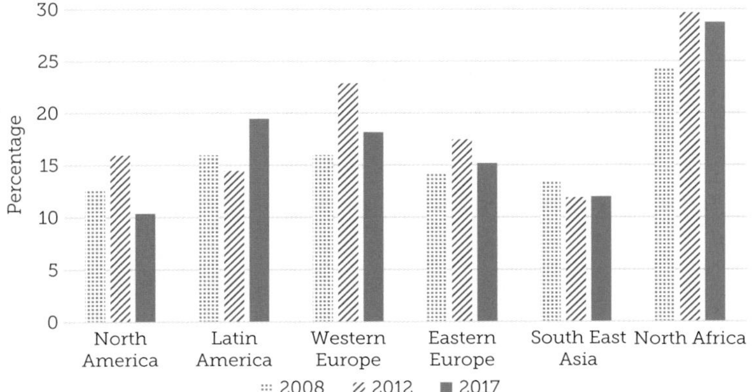

Figure 4.6 Youth unemployment around the world

Source: ILO (2017) *Global Employment Trends for Youth 2017*, Table C2, p. 101, at www.ilo.org, accessed 23 September 2019.

High unemployment is a cause of social instability which can lead to social and political unrest. Extremist groups, including religious sects, are active in these uncertain environments. Along with inequality, unemployment has been highlighted as a source of risk in the global economy (WEF, 2015). Much of the tension in the rapidly growing urban areas across the developing world stems from the presence in the streets of young people without work. These people, many of whom have educational qualifications, represent huge potential contributions to their societies, which could be turned into reality with appropriate responses from government and businesses.

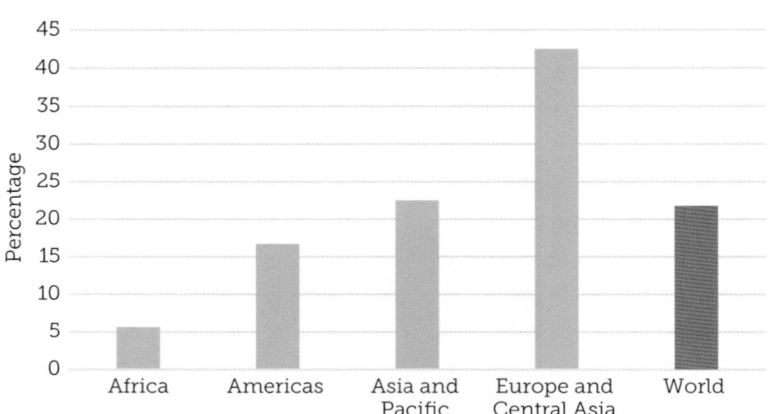

Figure 4.7 Social protection coverage for the unemployed, by region

Note: 'Unemployed' is the ratio of unemployed people receiving cash benefits to the total of unemployed people.

Source of data: ILO (2017) *World Social Protection Report 2017–2019* (Geneva, ILO), p. xxx.

Unemployment benefits, including state-funded cash payments, are among the key aspects of social protection that provide security and alleviate poverty. Even though social security policies are recognized human rights, the ILO estimates that only 21.8% of the world's unemployed workers are entitled to unemployment benefits (ILO, 2017). Moreover, in the countries where these programmes exist, the coverage provided can be very limited, leaving these people and their families in vulnerable circumstances. There are big variations globally, as shown in Figure 4.7. Unemployment benefits are generally highest in European countries, where nearly half of unemployed people are eligible, but in most of the world's regions, the percentage is much lower. In the Americas, 16.7% are covered. In Africa, only 5.6% are covered.

In China, where social programmes and employment protection are gradually being rolled out, migrant workers are excluded from these protections, leaving them without any income safety net if they lose their jobs. These workers are also excluded from the other elements of social protection. The growth in the use of migrant workers in supply chains is linked to globalization. Globalization has driven China's economic growth, and the workers employed in the country's manufacturing hubs have seen rising wages, but the social protection that these workers now expect has lagged behind.

Other key economic indicators: inflation and balance of payments

In this section, we look at two further economic indicators: inflation and balance of payments. The indicators discussed so far are interlinked. In a healthy economy, we would expect to see low inflation, low unemployment and a positive balance of payments. In today's world, we find a rather more mixed picture among national economies.

inflation the continuing general rise in prices in an economy

Inflation can be defined as the continuing general rise in prices in the economy. Its effect is to make the country's currency worth less. The opposite phenomenon is

deflation general decline in prices in an economy, associated with recession and falling demand

'**deflation**', or a general fall in prices. Deflation is likely to occur in periods of recession, reflecting falling demand.

The rate of inflation is expressed as a percentage rise or fall in prices with reference to a specific starting point in time. Economists point to a number of causes of inflation. 'Demand-pull' and 'cost-push' arguments are two of the most commonly advanced causes. The demand-pull explanation holds that demand in the economy is the key factor, which may be the result of cheap borrowing or tax cuts. It encourages producers to raise prices, and these then lead to rises in wage demands as workers strive to maintain their standard of living. The cost-push argument holds that rising costs drive up prices. As a significant element of costs is accounted for by wages, this theory becomes linked with the demand-pull argument. Rising wage costs tend to be passed on to consumers in the form of higher prices, thus creating what is known as the 'wage-price inflationary spiral'.

consumer price index index which tracks the percentage rise or fall in prices, with reference to a particular starting point in time

These rises and falls in inflation are tracked in the **consumer price index** for every country, usually making allowances for seasonal adjustments, such as seasonal variations in food prices. Each country has its own consumer price index, including a diversity of components in its calculations. For this reason, making comparisons between countries is imprecise and can give only an approximate picture of inflation. There is a single, harmonized Consumer Price Index (CPI) used within the eurozone, which enables more accurate comparisons between member states. The European Central Bank (ECB) set 2% as its target rate of inflation in 2004, when inflation was generally higher, but many EU states experienced inflation rates at near zero in the recession of 2008–9. In the following years, inflation remained low, in line with weak recovery and falling fuel prices. In Britain, following the referendum vote in 2016, which led to the decision to leave the EU, inflation rose, mainly due to the fall in the value of the currency. Here, inflation had reached 3.1% by winter, 2017.

balance of payments total credit and debit transactions between a country's residents (including companies) and those of other countries over a specified period of time

current account in connection with a country's balance of payments, account based on trade in goods, services and profits and interest earned from overseas assets

capital account in connection with an economy's balance of payments, account based on transactions involving the sale and purchase of assets, such as investment in shares

Rising inflation is a concern for governments. A country's domestic producers will find their goods less competitive in global markets, and foreign investors may turn to countries where inflation is lower. High inflation tends to force up interest rates, to enable investors to achieve a real return on their investments. However, high interest rates may adversely affect growth rates, by reducing domestic demand. Rising prices of food and other essentials are particularly worrying, and can lead to social instability in low-income countries, where spending on food constitutes a large proportion of a family's income. For this reason, many governments subsidize food and other essentials such as fuel.

The importance of energy costs as a driver of inflation was highlighted in the oil price shocks of the 1970s, which quadrupled the price of oil. Resultant increases in energy and transport costs affected all industrial sectors and sent inflation soaring in developed economies. To bring down inflation, governments can resort to imposing controls on prices or wages, but these measures can be damaging. In particular, they can lead to rising unemployment, as employers cut back on costs. In an environment of relatively low inflation, monetary policy seeks to prevent inflationary pressures arising.

The **balance of payments** refers to credit and debit transactions between a country's residents (including companies) and those of other countries. Transactions are divided into the current account and capital account. The **current account** is made up of trade in goods (the merchandise trade account), services (the services account), and profits and interest earned from overseas assets. The **capital account** includes transactions involving the sale and purchase of assets, such as investment in shares. If a country has a current account deficit, this means it imports more goods and services than it exports. If it has a current account surplus, it exports more than it imports. The current account balance is often calculated as a percentage of GDP. In Figure 4.8, we see that Germany has the largest trade surplus. China has also had a trade surplus, but this has shrunk as imports have grown. The US and UK have current account deficits, more pronounced in the case of the UK. Both countries import far more goods and services than they export. The UK has experienced trade deficits for over three decades, largely due to falls in manufacturing exports and the fall in North Sea oil exports. In 2017, the value of services exports from the UK was in surplus, but this could not compensate for weakness in manufacturing exports.

Percentage
10
8
6
4
2
0
-2
-4
-6
-8
2013 2014 2015 2016 2017 2018
Germany China UK US

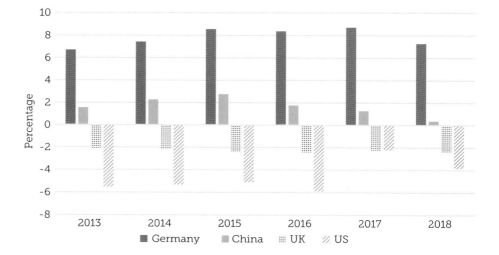

Figure 4.8
Current account balance as a percentage of GDP in selected economies

Source of data: OECD Statistics: International trade and balance of payments, at https://data.oecd.org, accessed 1 July 2019.

The balance of payments reflects demand both at home and abroad. It reflects the relative costs of production, indicating to what extent a country's industries are globally competitive. Exchange rates (which will be discussed in Chapter 8) are an important factor. Governments can exert influence by varying the exchange rate or by imposing tariff barriers such as import duties and quotas. China has sometimes been accused of keeping its currency low in order to aid exporters. The world's main trading countries are now linked in regional and multilateral trade groupings which, as will be discussed later, have brought down trade barriers. When the US under President Trump imposed new tariffs on imported goods in 2018, the action raised the risk of retaliation by trading partners. On the other hand, WTO rules, discussed in Chapter 7, allow a number of exceptions, permitting countries to restrict imports for reasons of national security.

Balancing the national economy

Governments seek policies which ensure economic growth, low inflation, and low unemployment, but there is considerable divergence of opinion on the extent to which they should intervene, or, alternatively, allow market forces to prevail. The role of government varies considerably between different types of economic system, which will be discussed in greater detail in sections to follow. For present purposes, we broadly define the ways in which governments act in the national economy. Governments may act directly as economic players, or indirectly in regulating the environment in which businesses operate. Governments in many countries play a direct role in state-owned and state-controlled companies. Governments are also ultimately responsible for the legislative and regulatory systems with which businesses in the country must comply.

fiscal policy budgetary policies for balancing public spending with taxation and other income in a national economy

monetary policy economic policies for determining the amount of money in supply, rates of interest and exchange rates

Policy-making falls under two headings. **Fiscal policy** refers to the budgetary policies for balancing public spending with taxation and other income, whereas **monetary policy** refers to policies for determining the amount of money in supply, rates of interest, and exchange rates. In many economies, a major role in monetary policy lies with the country's central bank, which is at the pinnacle of the country's financial system. It is responsible for issuing the country's notes and coins, and sets basic interest rates. It is also the banker to the government and the lender-of-last-resort. Most central banks, including the European Central Bank (ECB), are institutionally independent of government, to help to ensure that policy will not be based on short-term political considerations.

At international level, the International Monetary Fund (IMF), which will be discussed further in Chapter 8, has oversight of international exchange rate stability, and has also considerably expanded its role into areas of economic policy, once thought to be purely 'domestic' national policy. The institutional framework has thus become more complex as globalization has impacted on national economies. This intervention receives mixed responses in differing environments. IMF intervention in the Asian financial crisis of 1998 was widely perceived as misjudged (Stiglitz, 2002), whereas in the global financial crisis of 2008, several economies received emergency IMF loans. They included Iceland, Ireland and Hungary – all countries which had enjoyed impressive growth due to globalization, but whose exposure to global capital flows put them at risk from sudden financial shocks.

Governments raise and spend huge sums of money. Their priorities and means differ according to the country's political system. Especially relevant is the concentration or dispersal of political power. In countries where economic and political power is concentrated in an elite, the priority is to retain the existing system while maintaining stability among a citizenry that has no effective voice over policies. This often entails public spending on social programmes. In countries where leaders are accountable to the electorate, governments would be expected to be more responsive to public interest and societal wellbeing. In reality, many countries fall between these extremes: elected leaders in democratic societies are under pressure to reduce public spending, not simply as a matter of keeping a balanced budget, but to placate large businesses, especially the wealthy businesspeople who fund political parties. At the other end of the spectrum, politicians concerned about social justice and inequality press for progressive tax policies and safety-net programmes.

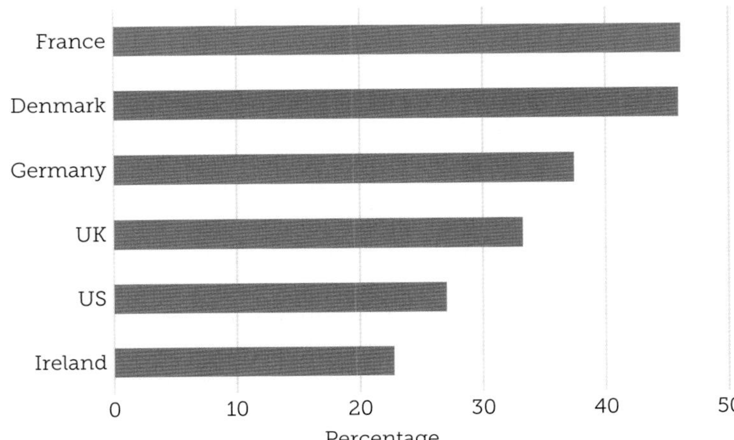

Figure 4.9 Tax revenues as a percentage of GDP, 2017

Source of data: OECD Statistics, *Tax Revenue as a Percentage of GDP*, at www.oecd.org, accessed 16 June 2019.

In democratic systems, governments must present annual budgets to elected legislators, who scrutinize how the money is being raised and how the government proposes to spend it. Public spending is funded, in the main, from direct and indirect taxation, social security contributions, and borrowing. Income tax is a direct tax, while taxes on goods and services, such as consumption tax and value-added tax (VAT), are indirect taxes. The balance between direct and indirect taxation is a sensitive issue. Income tax falls on both individuals and companies, and most countries derive more income from individual income tax than from corporation tax. Money taken in by governments in taxation is often expressed as a percentage of GDP. This percentage can be high, and there are big discrepancies between countries, as shown in Figure 4.9. France and Denmark have the largest tax receipts of the countries featured, and, in general, developed countries have higher levels of taxation and public spending than developing ones. An exception is the US, where tax revenues are relatively low, due to the policies dating from the 1980s that favour lightening tax burdens on the wealthy. While these tax cuts were initiated by a president from the Republican Party, President Reagan, Democratic presidents who followed him did not reverse these cuts to any great extent (see a discussion of these political parties in Chapter 5). A dramatic reduction in tax burdens on businesses and wealthy individuals was introduced in 2017, under Republican president Donald Trump, reaffirming his government's commitment to the agenda of favouring large businesses. Ireland, which comes near the bottom of the figure, has pursued a policy of attracting global companies through its very low corporation tax.

Governments enjoy a budget surplus when they receive more in revenue than they spend. 'Good housekeeping' principles would suggest that governments, like households, should not spend more than they take in. It is common, however, for governments to be in deficit, spending more than they receive in revenue. The debt that accumulates over the years is known as the **national debt**. National debt, expressed as a percentage of GDP, can grow to large proportions, causing considerable problems for government finances, and, in extreme cases, even the payment of interest becomes problematic. The **national budget balance** is the extent to which public spending exceeds receipts from taxes and other sources. Governments are more likely in today's world to have budget deficits rather than surpluses. Most economies saw marked deterioration in government finances from the fallout of the financial crisis which started to bite in 2008–9.

national debt the total debt accumulated by a central government's borrowings over the years

national budget balance the extent to which public spending exceeds receipts from taxes and other sources

Several factors can be highlighted. Tax revenues and revenues from other sources rise during prosperity, but diminish when incomes fall. In periods of recession, there are pressures on public spending, as the numbers claiming social benefits, such as unemployment and housing benefits, are rising. Tax revenues are falling due to weak productivity. The countries affected by the financial crisis were concerned about their high levels of government debt, and, adding to their worries, a number were called on to bail out failed banks and other failing companies from public funds. Faced with the continuing need to make interest payments on government debt, some governments, including Spain and Italy, reduced social entitlements such as unemployment benefits and pensions in the years following the crisis. Ireland funded the bailout of its banks with money drawn from its state pension reserve fund.

The economic indicators discussed here are intertwined, both in times of prosperity and times of downturn. Economic growth depends heavily on rising consumer demand, which helps to provide employment. When demand is low, businesses struggle and unemployment rises. In the economic upheavals of recession, governments reach for 'stimulus' measures to bring about recovery. Injecting public money into the economy, in the form of subsidies to particular

industries or groups, is one. Maintaining low interest rates is another, in the hope of encouraging investment.

Government support for banks has just been mentioned, and extends to other measures such as guaranteeing bank lending. Confidence in the banks is essential for any economy, and a banking collapse, as numerous financial crises have shown, can lead to economic recession in the wider economy. The need for government regulation in the financial sector rose to the top of the agenda following the global crisis of 2008. It also fuelled debate about the deeper issue of the role of government in the economy generally. Do differing political cultures and systems influence economic growth positively or negatively? Differing economic systems are associated with differing political institutions, which, as we find in the next section, have profound impacts on prosperity and wellbeing in societies as a whole.

Classifying national economic systems

In the period following the Second World War, the major economic systems were classified as polar opposites, with capitalism at one end and socialism at the other. This view reflected political as well as economic views in the cold-war period, when economic systems were seen in the context of dominant ideologies – complete world pictures of societal structures and human values. **Capitalism** rests on the idea of the market as the basis of an economy, with a maximum of economic freedom for individuals to pursue private enterprise. In any market, there is an exchange of something of value, such as labour, for a price, which in this case is wages. The capitalist sees this arrangement as an essentially valid exchange, although, as we will see below, the rise in inequality has led to a rethinking of how capitalism works in practice.

capitalism economic system based on market principles, entailing an exchange of something of value, such as labour, for something else, typically a 'price' in the form of wages

socialism economic model which rests on the belief that societal goals rather than private profit should be the basis of the economy

planned economy economic system based on total state ownership of the means of production, in which the state controls prices and output

By contrast, **socialism** rests on the belief that society as a whole rather than the private profit of individuals should be the basis of the economy. The socialist takes the view that capitalism is exploitative, leading over time to a class system in which there are extremes of wealth and power. Those at the top become richer, while the poor become poorer. And this is not simply about lack of income. The many at the bottom are denied the means to realize their own goals in life, suffering a denial of their essential human dignity. In practice, the states established along the lines of a socialist economic model did not fulfill these aspirations. The socialist states were the state-planned, collectivist economies, ruled by communist party dictatorships. The Soviet Union and China were dominant among the main **planned economies**. With the downfall of the Soviet Union and market reforms taking place in the other major socialist power, China, this polarized view has given way to a much more fragmented spectrum of contrasting economic systems.

Post-communist countries have introduced market reforms designed to promote the transition from socialism to capitalism. Cuba, whose communist revolution dates from 1959, has been one of the few avowedly communist states left. It has been subject to a US embargo, and has struggled to cope with deficiencies in its state-run agricultural sector. Cuba is now starting to open its economy. Cuba voted in February 2019, to approve its newly revised socialist constitution, which includes pro-market reforms and the right to private property, alongside recognizing the Communist Party as the single legitimate political party. Although relations between Cuba and the US had started to thaw during Mr Obama's presidency, which ended in 2016, these moves have not been continued under his successor, Mr Trump, who is strongly anti-communist.

Type of economy	Main characteristics	National examples
Planned economy	• State control • Collectivist ideology	North Korea–highly authoritarian Cuba–some liberalization
Liberal market economy	• Capitalist free market • Individualist • Democratic values • Minimal government intervention	US–free-market model, with limited government welfare role UK–stronger government role than the US in social protection
Social market economy	• Market tempered by social values • Democratic values • Government role in promoting social justice	Scandinavian countries, France, Germany – emphasis on social protection and strong role of the state
Mixed economy	• Capitalist elements • Elements of state control	China–authoritarian political system combined with economic liberalization India–market liberalization under state guidance; democratic political system

Figure 4.10 **Overview of different economic systems**

A national economic system is not just about a country's economic activities, but about its society and its political institutions, as the second column of Figure 4.10 reveals. In any society, cultural values and social structures are linked to economic activities. The main characteristics highlight the role of the state and also the cultural values that support economic life. The historian, David Landes, says, 'If we learn anything from the history of economic development, it is that culture makes all the difference' (Landes, 1998: 516). In classifying economic systems, we are reaching into the social and cultural aspects of the country. We are also focusing on the country's political institutions, which feature in the second column of the figure. Indeed, some economists argue that political institutions are powerful determinants of the economic system:

> 'Economic institutions shape economic incentives: the incentives to become educated, to save and invest, to innovate and adopt new technologies, and so on. It is the political process that determines what economic institutions people live under, and it is the political institutions that determine how the process works' (Acemoglu and Robinson, 2012: 42).

Acemoglu and Robinson go on to distinguish between 'inclusive' and 'extractive' economic and political institutions. Inclusive institutions rest on opportunities for all in society to achieve prosperity and a better life. Extractive institutions concentrate power in the hands of an elite few, with little or no accountability to the wider population. Their wealth and economic power enable them to forge economic and political institutions that perpetuate their own dominance.

Figure 4.10 provides an overview of the main types of economic system, along with the chief characteristics and examples of countries within each. National economic systems do not fall into neat categories, but they do rest on a mixture of the above principles, depending largely on the values of a country's culture and political climate. Economies also change over time, moving towards greater liberalization in some periods and shifting towards stronger government control in others. Nevertheless, there are conceptual differences underpinning the different types of economic system.

The planned economy is probably the only distinctively 'pure' model, and even these closed economies are now opening up somewhat to outside influences. The two types of market economy have varying degrees of open markets and varying

views of the role of government. The liberal market economies view state intervention as a necessary evil, while the social market economies take a positive view of the state's promotion of social cohesion. All the market economies emphasize democratic values, although their political systems differ. It is common to define the mixed economy in the broad sense as one in which both state ownership and markets exist side by side. This definition is so broad that it would encompass just about every economy in the world, and is therefore not very helpful. Here, we take the view that the mixed economy is one in which capitalist elements, including free enterprise, competition and private property, are weaker than in the market economies. The mixed economy, while recognizing private enterprise, lays less stress on individual freedoms and democratic values. Some, such as China, retain the legacy of communist planned economies. India has a democratic political system and a vibrant market economy, but its roots in socialism have left a legacy of the strong state. Many countries, such as transitional economies and Latin American countries, fall into the same broad category, which can lead to some tension between the state's vested interests and newer market forces.

MINI CASE STUDY

Mexico turns towards socialism

In Mexico's presidential election in 2018, the landslide victory of Andres Manuel López Obrador ('Amlo' for short), the former mayor of Mexico City, marked a political shift towards socialism. His party, Moreno (the National Regeneration Movement), was founded only in 2014. Labelled a populist and a socialist, his appeal to voters was that he aimed to clean up Mexico's notoriously corrupt business and political system, and to restore hope to all Mexicans that they can enjoy a better life. He has set his sights against what he sees as the destructive power of large business interests that have been dominant in Mexico's economy and have been too close to the two main political parties, both of which suffered electoral losses in 2018. The two main parties were perceived as exploiting 'crony capitalism', mutually re-enforcing favours between government officials and business leaders. In his campaign, Mr Obrador appealed to all who wish to see social justice and an end to corruption. He has also prioritized stamping out the organized crime and violence that have blighted much of Mexico. Under Mexico's traditional parties, the economy has seen little of the economic growth, improvements in standards of living and reduction in poverty that voters would have hoped for, as wealth has been concentrated within the business and political elite.

Shoppers and street traders go about their activities in a busy town in the southern state of Chiapas, Mexico.

In his first year in office, López Obrador focused on economic development, such as infrastructure projects, and on social priorities, such as help for the young, the old and the disabled. He has said he respects businesses and will not nationalize them. His goal is to improve the wellbeing of ordinary

people – people like his own modest family, who ran a village store in southern Mexico. He has been supported by rich and poor, and people of all ages. As an indicator of his approach to serving the people, he held a referendum on what to do about the building of a new airport for Mexico City. López Obrador's predecessor had enthused over a new airport. However, it is on a lake site that is linked to an aquifer that is vital to Mexico City. Mexico City is prone to drought, and this is an important consideration. The airport site is also home to 150 species of migratory birds. The public voted to stop the building, which was one-third completed. There are now plans to extend the existing airport instead.

The new president has had to contend with the hostility emanating from Mexico's powerful neighbour, the US, where President Trump has threatened new tariffs, in retaliation over the flow of migrants across the border. López Obrador has placed hope in the new trade agreement that is replacing NAFTA (see Chapter 7). He wishes to co-operate with the US while pursuing policies on migration that respect human rights. He is aiming to build up a fund of $15 billion that would promote jobs and development in the Central American countries that are now sending the largest flows of refugees towards the US border.

Questions

- Describe the socialism of López Obrador.
- In the presidential election, he gained as much support from the rich and educated as he did from the poor. Why is this, in your view?

Find out more

See the background article by Tom Phillips, '"We're in the abyss": How despair in Mexico set Amlo on the verge of presidency', 30 June 2018, in *The Guardian*.

Market economies

Market economies encompass a wide range of systems, with diverse cultural backgrounds. While they would all subscribe to capitalism in some form, they differ in the extent they would make market forces subordinate to other values, mainly through governmental regulation. Capitalism was the force behind nineteenth-century industrialization in Europe and the US, but their paths have diverged, reflecting differing cultural backgrounds.

The liberal market model

liberal market economy capitalist economic system in which supply and demand, as well as prices, are determined by free markets; also known as the free market economy

The **liberal market economy** refers to capitalism in what is considered to be its purest form, or *laissez-faire* capitalism. It is also referred to as the 'free market economy'. Commentators often refer to this model misleadingly as the 'Anglo-Saxon' model, but 'Anglo-American' is more accurate, in view of the fact that the US is the pre-eminent exponent. Capitalism rests on principles of private enterprise and freedom of individuals to pursue business activities as they wish. The underlying assumption of capitalism is that, through each individual's pursuit of self-interested economic activity, society as a whole benefits. The main examples of the *laissez-faire* model are Britain and the US. These economies are characterized by high individualism, as described by Hofstede in his cultural dimensions (discussed in Chapter 3). Other examples are Australia and Canada, which suggests that the spread of this model in the English-speaking world was linked to shared historical roots. As Figure 4.10 indicates, democratic values go along with the individualist culture of these countries. In these societies, civil and political freedoms are commonly thought to be linked to economic freedom. This assumption has been questioned, however, in economies such as China, where market liberalization has proceeded independently of political liberalization.

The economist, Adam Smith, envisaged an 'invisible hand' guiding the market system in his *Wealth of Nations* (Smith [1776] 1950), implying that markets are

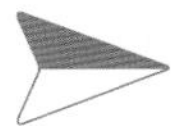

self-regulating. The principle that governments should refrain from intervention came to be enshrined in much economic thinking, but in practice, governments have frequently felt compelled to intervene on a number of public-interest grounds. Markets are deemed to be inherently competitive. Businesses compete on the basis of supply and demand: producers supply goods and services to satisfy consumer demand. It is well known, however, that if one supplier becomes dominant in a market, squeezing out smaller rivals, that firm, known as a **monopoly**, is able to dictate prices. Similarly, control by two or more firms, known as **oligopoly**, allows these firms to co-ordinate pricing. In these cases, most countries accept that regulation is needed to control market abuse and restore competition. In other words, governments intervene to *maintain* markets (Rodrik, 2009). Competition law (discussed in Chapter 6) has become integral to the smooth functioning of market economies.

monopoly domination by one firm over the market for particular goods or services, enabling the firm to determine price and supply

oligopoly domination of an industry by a few very large firms

Contrary to the image of stability implied by the invisible hand, markets can be volatile and unpredictable. Stock markets and individual companies are susceptible to swings in levels of confidence which can seem to verge on the irrational. Stock market crashes bring down the well-managed companies along with the reckless ones.

Capitalist systems have long acknowledged the need for government regulation. Indeed, Adam Smith himself recognized that markets cannot stand alone (Sen, 2010). Regulation is essential to ensure openness, fairness and stability in markets, helping to retain public confidence and long-term viability. Where regulation is non-existent or fails, crises can result, as in the financial crisis of 2008, which began in the US, where weak regulation prevailed. As was discussed earlier, widening inequality and weak social protections in the US can also undermine the stability of the economy and threaten its long-term viability. Extreme inequality, however, is not an inevitable feature of the capitalist economy. Redistributive policies and progressive taxation can be effective ways to tame market forces in ways that support the wellbeing of all in society. This is not an alien concept in America. Social welfare programmes have been part of government spending policies for many years, but they tend to be seen as contrary to free-market principles.

The way I see it...

'I went to the doctor once. He just made me lie down. He never gave me pills. But when I got the bill, I just freaked out because it was a lot of money [a week's wages for farm labour, her main source of income]. I was thinking, what did the doctor do for this money? Did he dress me in gold? So now I don't go to the doctor, even if I get sick. I just wait it out.'

Theresa Azuara, a 64-year-old Mexican who has lived and worked in Hidalgo County in Texas for 22 years, but has no right to legal residence or citizenship and therefore no entitlement to health insurance under Obamacare. Interviewed for *The Guardian*, 19 November 2015.

Theresa is convinced that despite the hardship, poverty and insecurity, living in the US is better than life in Mexico.

Three years on, and following the promises of President Trump to have a wall constructed on the Mexican border, the US is very divided on migration. Migrants are fleeing from desperate conditions south of the border. Those from Mexico are declining in number, while migrants from Central American countries are increasing. See Borger, J. (2018) 'Fleeing a hell the US helped create: why Central Americans journey north', *The Guardian*, 19 December. In this article, the author discusses the relevant background in Guatemala, El Salvador and Honduras – and America's role.

What political issues are involved in US migration? What policy solutions could be adopted to deal with migration – without building a wall?

Social market models

The concept of the welfare state dates from the aftermath of the Great Depression of 1929, when the US and other western governments introduced systems of social security, unemployment benefit and other welfare programmes. In the US, these programmes were part of a New Deal for rebuilding and reform, including regulatory reform of the financial system. Welfare programmes such as help for the unemployed and healthcare for the elderly date back to this era. These measures could be seen as an essential social safety net in the market economy, but for many, promoting social justice is seen as a goal in itself. In the US, the social priorities that underpinned the New Deal have given way to the ascendency of powerful business interests both in the economy and the political system (see the opening case study in Chapter 12). In many European countries, there has been more of a consensus on the need to balance social values and market freedoms. These countries have adopted the **social market** model, which gives a social-justice dimension to the capitalist model. Its main features are state ownership or control in key sectors and extensive social welfare programmes which reduce the inequalities inherent in the pure capitalist model. State ownership and private ownership exist side by side. Major enterprises such as heavy industry, banks, oil companies and airlines are likely to be state-owned. Seen as national champions, they are naturally protected from takeover bids, making them less prone to the volatilities which private-sector companies experience. On the other hand, state-owned enterprises are a drain on the public purse, and have gained reputations as being less efficient than private-sector firms. A hybrid solution has been to 'privatize' public-sector enterprises by listing them as public companies in which the state retains a large shareholding and private investors are invited to take up a minority of 'floating' shares.

social market economy capitalist market economy with a strong social justice dimension, including substantial welfare state provisions

The social market model has evolved differently in the diverse societies which have adopted it. The Scandinavian countries have been grouped together broadly in what is often termed the 'Nordic' or just 'Scandinavian' social model. High taxes and high levels of public spending have characterized their extensive social support systems, and state ownership is part of this picture of social priorities. This social model has shifted in recent years, however, towards more market involvement, for example, in limited privatization of healthcare. These governments have reined in public spending and reduced budget deficits. They have also stressed transparency and accountability among providers of public services, for both public and private providers.

Healthcare is a key element of wellbeing. For an individual or family, poor health and lack of means to pay for healthcare are closely associated with high levels of poverty, weak educational prospects and poor prospects of obtaining fulfilling employment. In countries that have established a national health service, public funding is the main means of providing close to universal health coverage. As noted above, however, many services are privatized in these systems, ideally with public scrutiny of the process. Many countries, especially emerging and developing countries, lack the resources to run a comprehensive national health service. The consequence is that out-of-pocket payments for healthcare are necessary, leaving many poor people unable to access the healthcare they need. Healthcare is often financed through insurance companies. The individual or the employer pays a subscription to the insurance company, that covers medical expenses when they arise – or at least a portion of them. In the US, which has no national health service, insurance schemes are important. Here, the large insurance companies behind them are powerful players in the nation's healthcare landscape. Legislation in 2010, the Patient Protection and Affordable Care Act (known as 'Obamacare' as it was a priority for President Obama) introduced a system of insurance intended to have universal coverage.

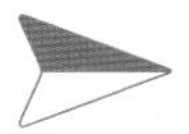

Not everyone was covered, but many more people (especially those with pre-existing medical conditions) had access to insurance under the scheme than would have had without federal government backing. President Obama's successor, Mr Trump, a Republican, aimed to abolish Obamacare, but the programme had considerable support at the grassroots level that influenced elected legislators.

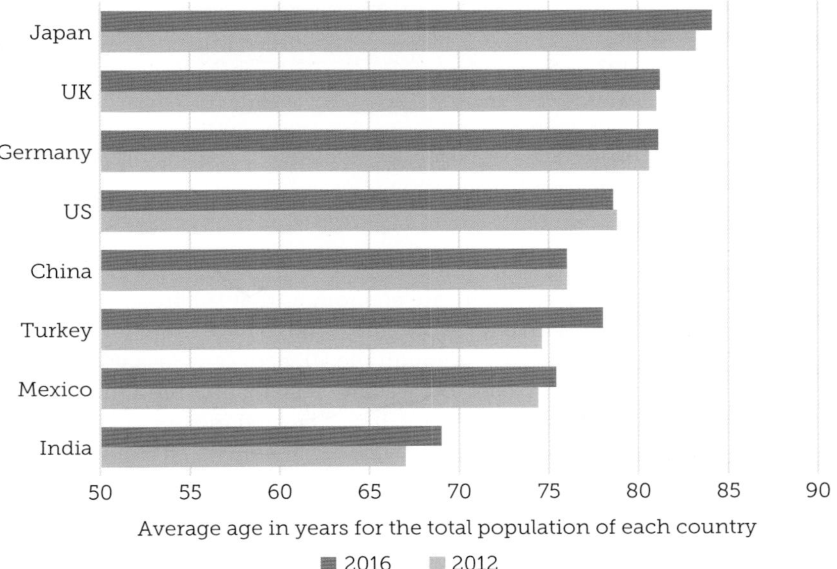

Figure 4.11 Life expectancy in selected countries, 2012 and 2016

Source of data: *OECD Health Statistics 2018*, at www.oecd.org/health/health-statistics, accessed 20 June 2019.

A key health indicator, life expectancy, can be used to compare the effectiveness of health in different societies. Life expectancy tends to be much higher in the advanced economies, where nutrition, housing, and medical treatment are better and more widely available than in developing and emerging economies. However, there are differences among countries that reflect differing economic systems and varying approaches to spending on health. Looking at Figure 4.11, we see that Turkey, India, Mexico and China have poorer life expectancy than the advanced economies in the top half of the figure. Three of these countries have seen improvement in the four years highlighted, but China has not. Despite its intention to improve health outcomes, average life expectancy did not rise in the four years, remaining at 76 years. Of the four advanced economies at the top of the list, the US has the lowest life expectancy. The three top economies all saw an increase in life expectancy, while average life expectancy in the US *fell* over the four years, from 78.8 years to 78.6 years. In the UK, the increase was very modest, from 81 to 81.2. Experts in the UK expressed surprise and concern that improvements in life expectancy seemed to have stalled (Triggle, 2017). Relevant factors include education, employment conditions, poverty and lifestyle. They have also been critical of the National Health Service (NHS), as spending on social care has not kept up with the numbers of people in need.

Spending on healthcare varies dramatically among countries, as Figure 4.12 shows. These figures include both government-funded and privately-funded healthcare. As the figure shows, spending in the US, which amounts to 17% of GDP, far outstrips any other country. Nonetheless, Americans cannot expect to live as long as inhabitants of other developed countries. It is not surprising that politicians are concerned that massive expenditure is producing poorer health outcomes than in other comparable countries. Germany and Denmark, where health spending is

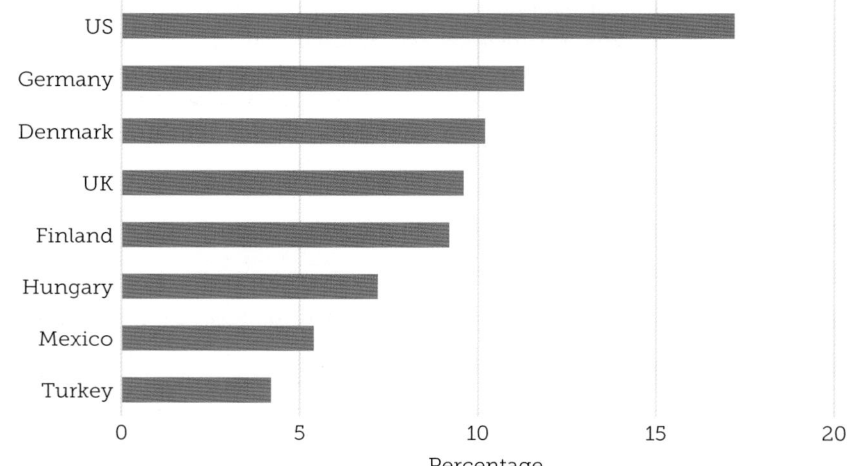

Figure 4.12 **Health expenditure as a percentage of GDP in selected countries, 2017**

Note: includes both public and private expenditure

Source of data: *OECD Health Statistics 2018*, at www.oecd.org/health/health-statistics, accessed 20 June 2019.

relatively high, are economies that fall broadly within the social market model. The social market economies tend to have lower levels of inequality than the liberal market models. Although the UK economy falls within the liberal economic model, the NHS is closer to a welfare-state institution, although with many services outsourced to private providers. It was created in 1948 by the post-war Labour government and was designed to provide healthcare for all that was free at the point of delivery.

The social market economy prioritizes social welfare as valuable in itself, while the economies that tend more towards the free market see social welfare as necessary to moderate the impacts of market forces in society. Countries that espouse the social market model also tend to be more attuned to issues of environmental protection and depletion of natural resources than the pure market economy. These issues are encompassed in the model's recognition of ethical principles as an adjunct to market considerations.

Why would an investor choose to invest in a social market economy?

The investor famously looks for a low-tax environment with maximum enterprise freedom and little in the way of employment protections. The social market economy is the opposite: high social contributions and social accountability. What is in it for the investor?

Asian capitalist systems

The East and South East Asian market economies are often grouped together as representing variations on the free-market model. Japan and South Korea can be highlighted as offering distinctive economic systems. Though different, they share key characteristics. Both were later to industrialize than the economies of Europe and America, and in both, economic development has been guided by the state. They also share a democratic political system, with civil, political and economic freedoms. For these reasons, we place these countries in the broad category of market economies. Although they share with the social-market economies a strong state perspective, theirs is not the western welfare-state model of the European countries. Both have far less developed welfare systems than would be the norm in western economies. These countries are more in the collectivist than individualist cultural tradition. Their Asian cultural heritage emphasizes the role of the family and

that of the company as a kind of family, looking after the whole person, rather than taking the narrow view of the worker as an employee.

Japan, like Germany, faced the task of rebuilding its industries after the Second World War. The state provided economic guidance, and hence Japan is looked on as exemplifying the 'developmental state' model (Johnson, 1982). The use of 'industrial policy', rather than outright state ownership, has been a chief feature of its economic development, relying on co-operation between the three centres of power – the bureaucracy, politicians and big businesses. Business in Japan has traditionally been organized around groups of companies, or *keiretsu*, linked by cross-shareholdings and informal networks with suppliers and customers. The *keiretsu* remain active in supply-chain relations in globalized environments. Where one major player exits a country, for example, the decision of Honda to stop manufacturing in Britain in 2021, partner companies are likely to follow. From a position of economic powerhouse in the 1980s the Japanese economy descended into stagnation in the 1990s. This followed a collapse in the banking and financial system brought on by a sharp fall in asset values and imprudent lending. Recovery came belatedly, in about 2004, but has been hesitant. Japan's leading companies, including Toyota and Sony, have remained globally competitive, despite newer competitors from South Korea, Taiwan, and, of course, China.

keiretsu grouping of Japanese companies characterized by inter-firm ties and cross-shareholdings

South Korea, too, has taken its own distinctive development path. Here, economic development owes its impetus to the large family-owned conglomerates, or *chaebol*, which expanded aggressively overseas during the 1980s. These groups include Hyundai, Samsung and LG. South Korean companies were severely affected by the Asian financial crisis of 1997–8, its companies having accumulated excessive debt, in a business environment where family considerations mattered more than objectively sound business practices. Restructuring these companies along more transparent lines of governance was one of the reforms that later governments have undertaken, although the strong cultural heritage has worked against radical reforms. A strong cultural heritage can be viewed as an 'anchor' against the more flamboyant characteristics of free markets (Mahbubani, 2009). Samsung's domination by its founding family is an example, its smartphones posing competitive challenges for Apple's iPhones. Samsung suffered a setback with a major recall of a defective model in 2016, from which it rebounded with increased overall profits. However, investor confidence was shaken by the jailing of a family leader for corruption. The company responded in 2017 with a restructuring of its executive, replacing its two joint CEOs with three new co-CEOs, in a move aimed at restoring confidence in its corporate governance.

chaebol family-dominated industrial conglomerate characteristic of business organization in South Korea

Lastly, China, the largest Asian country, has also undertaken market reforms, but still within the framework of the one-party state bequeathed by the communist revolution. We therefore classify China as a mixed economy, discussed in the next section.

Mixed economies: China and India

The **mixed economy** is the last category in Figure 4.10, combining market elements with institutional structures controlled by the state. China is the main example, with its embrace of two systems: capitalism as an economic system and an authoritarian political system controlled by the communist party. China's political leadership retains ultimate control of the economic levers that shape market reforms. By contrast, India has a democratically elected government, but in a context of strong state guidance. Their development paths have been different, but both provide examples of state-led development which other emerging economies have emulated.

mixed economy economic system which combines market elements with state controls

China

China covers a huge territory, and is home to diverse peoples, the largest being the Han Chinese, tracing their roots to the ancient Han dynasty. China's long history revolves around successive empires that have subsumed regional minority groups and led to conflicts. These tensions, along with unity imposed from central authorities, give some indication of the social currents in China today. Although later than other Asian countries in economic development, China is now asserting itself as a regional and global power – economically, militarily and politically. The current state of China (its full name is the People's Republic of China) dates only from the Communist revolution of 1949 led by Mao Zedong. The ruling party structures were roughly modelled on the Soviet system, and these remain the formal framework. However, the underpinning ideology has seen numerous shifts. The Maoism of the early years (based on the teachings of Mao Zedong), loosely based on Marxism-Leninism, has given way to a more nationalist perspective. It was only in 1979 that the shift towards an open economy began, under the leadership of Deng Xiaoping.

Thereafter, China's economy grew dramatically, achieving 10% average growth rates for the next two decades. The prosperity of its people has also grown, although there are wide variations between the rural standard of living and that enjoyed by the new urban dwellers. China's economic development has rested on globalization, but only in limited ways. As we found in Chapter 2, globalization implies an opening up to cross-border flows of capital and goods. China has been slow to open its economy in both these respects. China's development has rested on industrialization and improved infrastructure. Its leadership sought to benefit from its abundance of low-cost labour by aiding investment in export-oriented manufacturing. It welcomed foreign investors to Special Economic Zones, where they could import inputs duty-free, avoiding the usual import duties in place to protect state enterprises (Rodrik, 2012: 152). The economic model relied on migrant workers travelling from rural areas to the urban manufacturing complexes. Liberalizing reforms, including the introduction of private property, reducing quantitative restrictions on imports and allowing foreign financial institutions to operate in the country, have come about only slowly, and after the country's period of rapid growth. As Figure 4.13 shows, China's growth has now slowed, and the leadership is focusing on more sustainable growth.

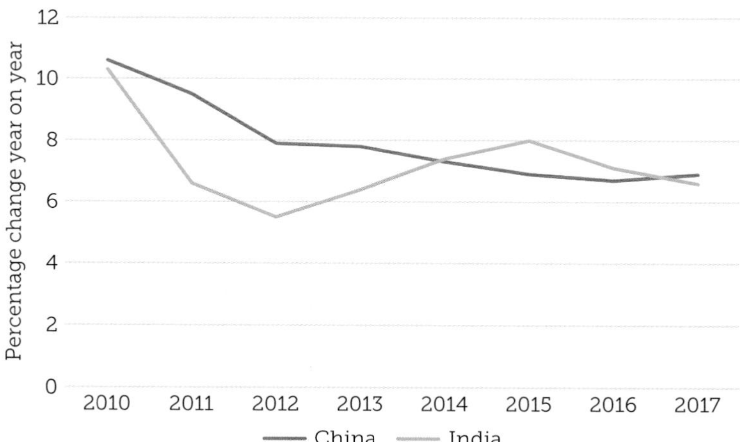

Figure 4.13
Economic growth in China and India

Source of data: World Bank databank, World Development Indicators, at https://data.worldbank.org, accessed 20 June 2019.

China's state-directed economic development has been successful in transforming it into a manufacturing superpower. In the process, nearly half a billion people have been lifted out of absolute poverty (Rodrik, 2012: 149). China ranked 86 out of 189 countries in the Human Development Index in 2018 (UNDP, 2018). But development remains

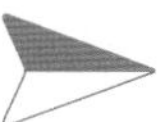

uneven, and has been accompanied by rising inequality. Rapid development, including massive investment in fossil-fuel power generation, has resulted in detrimental impacts on the environment and societal wellbeing. Air pollution has become an urgent issue, leading to social tensions, which could boil over into political instability. Chinese people, while they have greater economic freedom, still enjoy little in the way of civil and political freedoms that are recognized as human rights and core social values. China's dependence on millions of migrant workers from rural areas has also cast doubt on the sustainability of its economic model.

In its most ambitious expansion project, China launched the Belt and Road Initiative in 2017, aiming to develop trade links by land and sea, taking in Central Asia and reaching out to Europe, Africa and the Middle East. Large infrastructure projects involving vast capital investment by China are promoting economic links, and also helping to cement Chinese influence in the many countries along these economic corridors. They involve some 28 different countries, but there are numerous investment projects that extend further afield and are only tenuously linked with the Belt and Road Initiative itself. These projects have had a strategic theme, helping China to establish itself as a global player to rival the US – which has not played a part in these initiatives. The initiatives have attracted criticism for their expansionist aims and also for their environmental impacts. While rail links are applauded, many of the projects involve Chinese companies building coal-fired power stations in other countries.

India

Like China, India has long historical roots and diverse ethnic groups. However, far from being an imperial power itself, India was subsumed into the British Empire, becoming an independent state in 1948. Partly because of its colonial legacy, India would seem to be closer to a market economy than China. There is considerable economic freedom, and its government is accountable through democratic elections. It has a legal tradition resting on the rule of law, also part of the colonial heritage. However, India was founded as a socialist state in 1948, and retains a legacy of the strong state prone to heavy-handed regulation. Its market reforms have been guided by government, which, for many years was reluctant to welcome FDI. India has become more open to foreign investors, but the western investor must enter the market through a joint venture with an Indian partner, and the foreign investor is likely to face numerous regulatory hurdles.

India's economy benefited from growth in computing and high-tech service sectors from the 1990s onwards, but its manufacturing industries have been slow to expand, largely because of poor infrastructure and very restrictive employment protection laws that deterred companies from hiring workers. India's economic growth, shown in Figure 4.13, slowed following the global financial crisis, and then resumed its growth trajectory.

In comparison with China, India invariably looks the weaker in terms of development. The ruling Congress Party lost elections in 2014, and was replaced by the Hindu Nationalist party, led by Narendra Modi. In 2019, he won again by a large majority, campaigning on a nationalist and populist message to voters. Modi has sought to introduce business-friendly reforms, including eliminating many of the bureaucratic impediments to businesses and also investing in infrastructure. While welcomed by large companies, these reforms are met with more scepticism by many in India's society, fearful that profits will come before local concerns and social welfare. India remains a much poorer and less developed country than China. And inequality is growing. In 2000, the top 10% accounted for 39.8% of income, and by 2010, this percentage had risen to 55.4% (World Inequality Database). The bottom 50% accounted for 20% of the country's income in 2000, and this percentage had declined to 16% by 2010. India's HDI ranking is 130 out of 189 countries (UNDP, 2018). In terms of gender equality, India is classified by the UN in the lowest of five groups of countries, placing it among the countries with the widest gender inequality. The UN's Multidimensional

Poverty Index, which covers health, education and living standards, finds that 43.9% of the Indian population live in poverty (UNDP, 2018). In terms of social wellbeing, India's economic development has been disappointingly uneven.

MINI CASE STUDY

The rise of India's super-rich

During its first 30 years of independence, India's economy was based on a conservative socialist model, in which the state was in charge of major businesses and private enterprise was frowned on. Economic growth was held back by inefficient businesses, and many in key industries were loss-making. In 1991, just as globalization was getting under way, India's government set about liberalizing the economy and encouraging private enterprise. By 1998, the fruits of these changes were beginning to show through, and the economy enjoyed strong growth from 1998 to 2008. This period saw the dramatic rise of India's new super-rich, feasting on the new opportunities to acquire wealth – and power. Their rise has given India the doubtful distinction of presiding over record growth in the number of billionaires. In the mid-1990s, there were only two Indians among Forbes' billionaires' list; by 2016, there were 84. By then, India had the same level of GDP ($2.3 trillion) that China had in 2006. At that point, China had just 10 billionaires, whereas India had eight times that number. By 2018, their number had climbed to 104 (Elkins, 2018). Their rise is exemplified by Mukesh Ambani, the head of the business empire, Reliance Industries. His home, Antilia, is a 27-floor palatial skyscraper, complete with a gilded ballroom, hanging gardens, an indoor football pitch and six floors that house the family's cars. Antilia catches the observer's attention as it towers over Mumbai's extensive slum areas. Also catching headlines was the lavish wedding of his daughter in 2018, which involved flying in guests to the wedding in dozens of chartered planes.

The rapid gains amassed by India's new super-rich have relied on ties between businesses and politicians, in which each was able to garner rewards: politicians received funds from businesses and tycoons were rewarded with favouritism, cheap loans and other concessions. The system thrived on so-called 'crony capitalism'. Industrialists like Ambani were able to obtain loans cheaply, often from state-owned banks, and spend freely, acquiring businesses from oil refineries to telecoms. Meanwhile, the poor of Mumbai became increasingly bitter at the sight of Antilia. India remains a poor country, despite its class of super-rich individuals. Scandals involving allegations of fraud and money-laundering among India's tycoons have become common in the media. When Narendra Modi took over as president in 2014, he saw vividly the risks to India's development model in the rampant growth of corporate debt, the risks to the banking sector and the extent of corruption. He promised to clean up corruption, but it has

India's inequality is highlighted by the high-rise skyline of Mumbai, alongside the slums where much of the city's population live.

become endemic. Rising inequality poses threats to India's democratic system and threatens sustainable development, while the lavish lifestyles of the super-rich make uncomfortable headlines.

Questions

- What has caused the boom in billionaires in India?
- What are the risks to India's ability to promote sustainable economic development?

Find out more

See a review by Meghnad Desai, entitled 'The rich and the raj', in the *Financial Times*, 3 July 2018. He is reviewing the book, *The Billionaire Raj: A journey through India's new gilded age*, by James Crabtree (published by Oneworld, 2018).

The economies of Central and Eastern Europe

privatization process of transforming a state-owned enterprise into a public company and selling off a proportion of the shares to the public, usually involving the government retaining a controlling stake

The economies of Central and Eastern Europe (CEE) are grouped together as mixed economies largely for historical reasons. These were transition economies, making the transition from planned economies to market-oriented economies. Politically, they embarked on the transition from authoritarian regimes to democratic structures. **Privatization**, involving the conversion of state enterprises to privately owned and operated companies, was central to this process. Former state-owned firms were sold and new start-up enterprises were encouraged. These processes were put in motion when the Soviet bloc started to break up in 1989. East Germany was united with West Germany in 1990. States in Central and Eastern Europe were reborn and launched strategies of economic development. They include Hungary, Poland, Croatia, the Czech Republic, Slovakia, Slovenia, Estonia, Lithuania, Latvia, Romania and Bulgaria. These countries have been classified as developed economies, and all are now EU members (see Table 4.1). Economic development in other republics formed from the break-up of the Soviet Union has been less successful. These countries, listed in Table 2.2, include Ukraine, which is discussed below.

To varying degrees, the CEE economies that have become EU members have sought foreign investors to drive economic development. While this might indicate their embrace of globalization through expanding global supply chains, the reality is that these economies have mainly turned their sights towards Western European economies, notably Germany, which is the destination of 59% of their exports. About 80% of the FDI flowing to the CEE countries has been from Western Europe. FDI has helped to promote investment and growth in sectors such as car manufacturing and business services, but the bulk of the FDI has targeted financial services. Between 2004 and 2008, one-fifth of the net FDI into these countries was in the financial sector (McKinsey Global Institute, 2013). In 2013, foreign owners held 85% of the equity of the top ten banks in the region. Car manufacturing also took off in the 2000s. Volkswagen took over the ailing Skoda company in the Czech Republic, and Renault transformed Dacia in Romania, the Dacia brand now contributing strongly to Renault's overall performance.

The CEE countries enjoyed economic growth averaging over 5% annually between 2004 and 2008. Workforces were skilled and well educated. The business environment was market-friendly and institutionally stable. Wages were about 75% lower than in Western European countries, and lower still in Romania and Bulgaria. Corporation tax was low. But there were risks lurking in the growth model of these countries. Investment and consumption were both heavily dependent on debt funding, and much of this debt was foreign, involving risky exposure to volatile financial markets. Domestic consumption was rising, and, although this contributed to growth, the low levels of domestic saving and rising consumer debt made these economies vulnerable to financial shocks. Rising property prices led to housing bubbles in several countries. When the financial crisis struck, immediate impacts were a dramatic drop in FDI inflows and in domestic consumption.

Economic growth in these countries has gradually recovered from the effects of the financial crisis, and their growth now outpaces their EU neighbours to the west. The Czech Republic, Poland and Hungary enjoyed growth of 4% or over in 2017, but the star performer has been Romania, where annual growth was 6.9% in 2017. More robust financial regulation has placed their financial systems in a stronger position since the crisis, and these countries have low unemployment as well as low inflation. On the other hand, they face a number of challenges. They have received a considerable boost from EU structural funds, but, in some, anti-EU sentiment and the rise of authoritarian political leaders have caused tensions. The ascendency of extreme nationalist political parties across the region poses threats to political stability and challenges to EU institutions.

Russia has been the exception to the steady recovery enjoyed by other transition economies. Russia's economy is dependent on resource wealth in oil and gas. In recent years, it has suffered from falling oil prices and also from international sanctions imposed following its annexation of part of Ukraine (discussed in the next chapter). Having been the largest of the Soviet republics, Russia privatized its large industries rapidly, unleashing a new powerful capitalist class, but without the regulatory institutions which are common in mature market economies. The gas ministry was transformed into Gazprom. A result was the growth of a class of powerful oligarchs in major industries, creating political tensions. Russia adopted a new constitution in 1993, but its democratic aspirations have only been partially fulfilled.

The rise of Vladimir Putin was responsible for reining in the oligarchs and restoring stability following a financial crash in 1998, but this process resulted in a consolidation of leadership in the all-powerful ruling party. Gazprom's ownership reverted to the state in this process. Russia under Putin has continued to exert economic and political pressure in the former Soviet territories, despite their formal independence. Ukraine has been an example.

Ukraine has suffered divisive tensions between the more western-oriented region in the west of the country and the more Russia-leaning population of the east. Ukraine's government had aspired to EU membership, but these hopes became jeopardized when violent clashes led to Russia's annexation of the strategically important Crimean peninsula in 2014. This territorial incursion into a sovereign neighbour's territory met with international condemnation, prompting trade sanctions on Russia. Russia's economy, weakened from the fall in the price of oil in global markets, became further weakened by the imposition of sanctions. The Russian economy suffered from a slight contraction of −0.2% in 2016, but as the price of oil stabilized, growth of 1.5% was achieved in 2017. Nonetheless, Russia continues to be vulnerable to oil price fluctuations. The Ukrainian instability affected the economic environment, in that both domestic and foreign investors were discouraged. Other post-Soviet states suffer similar tensions, between continuing Russian influence and the desire to nurture closer ties with western countries. Under Putin's leadership, political and economic power have become more highly concentrated in state entities dominated by his circle of associates. Although post-Soviet Russia introduced market structures at the outset, it has become more state-dominated. Similarly, the fledgling democratic transition has suffered reversals as a more authoritarian political system has tightened its grip.

Regionalization: focus on the EU

regionalization growing economic links and co-operation within a geographic region, both on the part of businesses and governments

Regionalization has been taking place throughout the world, despite the forces of globalization. By **regionalization**, we mean growing economic links and co-operation within a geographic region, both on the part of businesses and governments. Economic ties, such as trade, can lead to what is termed 'shallow' integration, in that there need be little physical presence of the foreign company in its destination market. FDI, which entails establishing operations in the foreign location, represents a deeper involvement in local economies as stakeholders, although foreign investors, too, can withdraw from markets as their strategies change. Regionalization at a deeper level involves not just liberalized trade and investment, but deepening institutional ties and political co-operation. The extent of regionalization differs among the world's regions. In many, diverse economies and disparate cultural and political backgrounds tend to limit the deepening of ties. Regional trade agreements, discussed in the next chapter, have sprung up in every continent. Examples include the North American Free Trade Agreement (NAFTA) and the Asean agreement of South East Asia. These agreements have focused mainly on reducing trade barriers between member economies.

European Union regional grouping of European countries which evolved from trade agreements to deeper economic integration

The **European Union (EU)** (www.europa.eu), by contrast, has progressed beyond trade deals to take on regional governmental functions, becoming a supra-national structure, potentially challenging the sovereignty of member states. However, the vision of the EU from its foundation in the 1950s, when memories of the Second World War were still fresh, included creating a closer political union as a force for peace, co-operation and security. This was an ambitious project, as, even among the original members (shown in Table 4.1), there was economic diversity. Diversity became much greater as more states joined, including poorer states and former communist states. Despite economic integration, the enlarged EU and eurozone have not brought economic convergence.

The economies of the EU and eurozone

The EU encompasses a population of over half a billion people, and, taken as a whole, it was the world's second-largest economy in 2017, with a GDP of nearly $17 trillion. The world's largest economy in 2017 was the US, with a GDP of $19 trillion. The EU in 2017 comprised 28 member states; of these, 19 were members of the single-currency eurozone (see Table 4.1). The year 2004 was a turning-point, when the union absorbed 10 new states, often referred to as the 'accession 10', distinguishing them from the pre-2004 states, which make up the 'EU 15'. As we have seen, most of these new states are transition economies.

Table 4.1 Membership of the EU and eurozone

Members of the eurozone are shown by an asterisk (*)

Date of EU entry	State
1957	Belgium*, France*, Germany*, Luxembourg*, the Netherlands*, Italy*
1973	Denmark, Ireland*, the UK
1981	Greece*
1986	Portugal*, Spain*
1995	Austria*, Finland*, Sweden
2004	Cyprus*, Malta*, Czech Republic, Hungary, Poland, the Slovak Republic*, Slovenia*, Latvia*, Lithuania*, Estonia*
2007	Bulgaria, Romania
2013	Croatia

The EU project aimed to create a single market, in which goods, people, information and capital can move freely. The process has been mapped out in a series of treaties, beginning with the Treaty of Rome in 1956. The opening up of trade in goods and FDI among member states has been a success story, but other aspects of integration, such as services and transport across national borders have not yet been liberalized. The free movement of people within the EU was tested in 2015, with the influx of refugees from war-torn countries such as Syria. Hungary, a transit state for refugees making their way to Germany and other states, sealed its borders with Serbia and Croatia to prevent their movement. This measure was criticized on human rights grounds. The EU Commission set quotas of migrants for each member state, but Hungary and Poland opposed the scheme. Hungary held a referendum in 2016 on whether to accept the EU plan on quotas. While 98% of those voting rejected EU quotas, the vote was invalid due to low turnout, failing to reach the required 50% threshold.

The EU is committed to liberal goals of free markets and rolling back the state. Any liberalization or harmonization of rules involves the co-operation of national governments, willingly ceding powers to EU structures. National governments are highly sensitive to the political power of groups and interests within their own countries. The rise of nationalist populist political parties in most EU member states threatened to create obstacles to greater cohesion of values within the EU. Wide divergence in income among member states, as shown in Figure 4.14, is indicative of the tensions that translate into political divisions within EU institutions. The EU's history to date has been one of member governments pursuing domestic policy objectives within EU structures, rather than taking an EU-wide perspective.

Economic and Monetary Union (EMU) EU programme centred on the single currency and an independent central bank that sets monetary policy for eurozone member states

euro the single currency of the EU

eurozone member states of the EU which have satisfied the Maastricht criteria and joined the EMU

In theory, governments remain responsible for the prudent management of their own economies, where national economic systems retain their distinctive characteristics. They retain control of fiscal policies such as spending and taxation, but in matters of monetary policy, the EU plays an important role. All member states are members of the **Economic and Monetary Union (EMU)**, which, although its name implies genuine economic union, is in practice well beneath this level of uniformity. The highest level of co-ordination is among the member states who have adopted the single currency, the **euro**. There are now 19 members of the **eurozone**, whose monetary policy is governed by the European Central Bank.

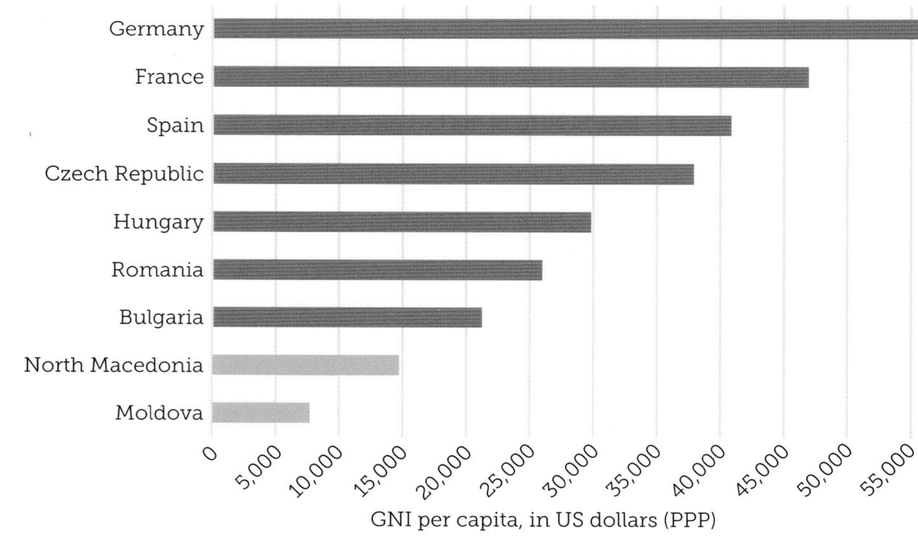

Figure 4.14 Income variations among a selection of existing and aspiring EU member states, 2018

Note: Aspiring member states, the Republic of Northern Macedonia and Moldova are shown in a lighter shade.

Source: World Bank database, GNI per capita, at https://data.worldbank.org, accessed 3 July 2019.

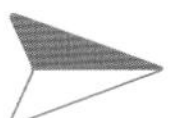

Central to the process of economic integration was the introduction of the single currency. The elimination of exchange rate risk and reduction in transaction costs, have contributed greatly to growth in trade and FDI. The euro as a currency came into existence in 1999, and went into use as a cash currency in 2002. Membership of the eurozone involves relinquishing power over exchange rates and interest rates to the European Central Bank. For eurozone member states, monetary policy is thus governed by the ECB, while fiscal policy continues to be controlled by national authorities. This apparent inconsistency has been highlighted as a weakness which contributed to the eurozone debt crisis that unfolded in the aftermath of the financial crisis (Lane, 2012).

Any EU member state wishing to join the eurozone must first fulfill a number of criteria, known as the Maastricht convergence criteria, set out in the Maastricht Treaty, which came into effect in 1993. A cornerstone of the Maastricht Treaty is the stability and growth pact, which commits all EU governments, whether in the eurozone or not, to keep budget deficits in check. As budget deficits have mounted in most European countries, this is one of the important hurdles for prospective eurozone members. An applicant country must become part of the EMU, and comply with the Exchange Rate Mechanism (ERM) system, by which its currency is loosely pegged to the euro. This means that its currency fluctuation against the euro must remain within relatively tight bands. The EMU dates from 1979, and the ERM was updated in 2004, to become ERMII, with which current applicants must comply. The full convergence criteria are listed below:

- Price stability – The rate of inflation must be no more than 1.5% higher than the three member states with the lowest inflation rates.
- Sound public finances – The government's budget deficit must be below 3% of GDP.
- Sustainable public finances – National debt should not exceed 60% of GDP.
- Exchange rate stability – The country should have been in the ERM for two years, without having devalued its currency within that time.
- Long-term interest rates – The country's interest rate must not be more than 2% higher than that of the three countries with the best performance in terms of price stability in the EU.

These criteria have been somewhat overtaken by events in recent years. A number of existing eurozone member states built up huge debt burdens in the 2000s. These burdens included corporate and household debt, in addition to sovereign debt. Greece and Italy both had national debt in excess of the 60% fiscal limit when admitted to the eurozone in the first place. Greece saw this debt burden swell to 175% in the following years. Ireland was weighed down by out-of-control household debt, which, together with government and corporate debt, amounted to 400% of GDP. Radical cuts in public spending were introduced in these ailing eurozone countries, and bailout aid was organized by the IMF and EU. Greece has long teetered on the edge of sovereign default and forced withdrawal from the eurozone. By 2014, both Spain and Ireland were on the road to economic recovery, posting economic growth. However, these economies remain fragile. Ireland is heavily dependent on a few large multinationals that benefit from its low tax regime. Greece remains heavily indebted and has high unemployment. Spain has fared better. Unemployment is falling, but still high at 17%. Wages are stagnant and inequality is rising. Spain's centre-right governing party of six years fell in 2018, and was replaced by the socialist party, which is committed to an inclusive economic recovery.

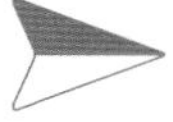

Enlargement and the future of the EU

The process of enlargement has been at the heart of the EU since its inception, bringing the prospect of greater prosperity and stability to the wider region. However, the debate over the EU has gone on almost as long. Applicant countries face a long process of assessment, during which they must persuade the EU that their country is a market economy, a functioning democracy and an upholder of the rule of law. Questions over these issues have been raised in relation to some of the 'accession 10' countries. For example, the governments of Hungary and Poland have veered away from the rule of law and democratic values. Following the admission of Romania and Bulgaria in 2007 – both of which raised issues regarding corruption and the rule of law – there was a gap in new admissions. Croatia, formed from the former Yugoslavia, joined in 2013. Other states in the region have applied, including Kosovo, Serbia, North Macedonia and Albania. In these countries, issues of corruption, organized crime and weakness of the rule of law are impediments. The largest of the applicant countries is Turkey, a Muslim country traditionally seen as straddling Europe and Asia, but whose secular and democratic constitution would seem to shift it closer into the European sphere. However, the increasingly authoritarian leadership of its former prime minister, now president, Recep Erdogan suggests a shift away from EU criteria.

Tension over future enlargement was one of the factors that delayed the Lisbon Treaty, which took effect in 2009. The treaty represents an amended version of a constitutional treaty that failed ratification hurdles in several member states. The difficulties encountered in securing ratification of the Lisbon Treaty reflect member states' scepticism about the benefits of the EU in terms of national interests. The spectre of national economic protectionism is one which has long haunted the EU, especially in the context of countries in which nationalist politicians have criticized the EU's liberal reform policies as threats to national sovereignty. EU enlargement has been about the prospects of economic gains winning out over these inward-looking forces. These gains have been real enough in new member states: businesses have flourished from greater cross-border activity, and governments have welcomed the structural funds which have flowed into poorer economies. The 'cohesion' funds (at nearly €59 billion), along with subsidies for agriculture (included in 'sustainable growth' at €60 billion), are the largest shares of the EU's budget, as Figure 4.15 shows.

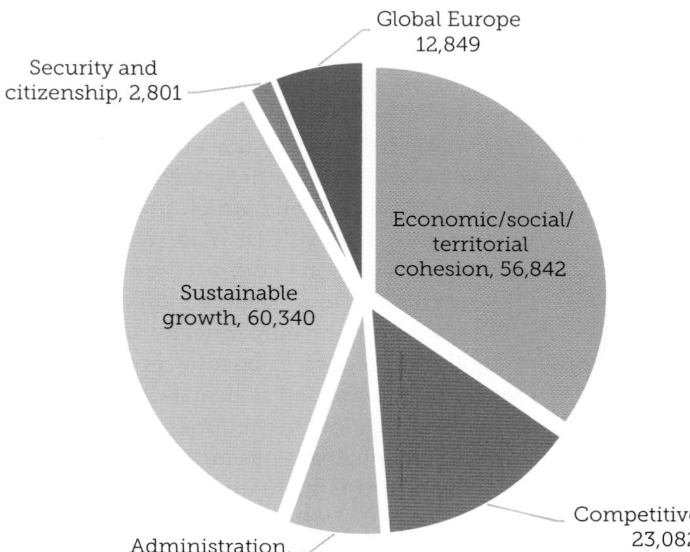

Figure 4.15 Breakdown of the EU's 2019 budget

Notes:

Total budget is €166.7 billion.
Chart indicates expenditure in billions of euros under each budget heading.

Source: EU Commission, Annual Budget 2019, Figures and documents, at www.ec.europa.eu/budget/annual, accessed 4 July 2019.

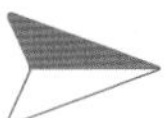

The EU Commission has remained committed to market reforms, but these have taken place only very gradually, and governments have tended to retain a mindset which ranks countries as winners or losers in terms of EU funding. Poorer countries have been winners in this respect, as the lion's share of the EU budget is devoted to aiding poorer regions and vital sectors. The extent to which there is the basis of a definable regional capitalism is much debated. A model of European capitalism closer to the free-market model has been a beacon for many within the EU, but national governments have retained a strong grip on institutional direction within its structures. The fact that the financial crisis struck Ireland, a leader in market reforms, has clouded prospects of further market liberalization. Iceland, which in 2009 applied to join the EU, was also a casualty of the financial crisis, its banks having become vastly overstretched in global financial markets. Another possible applicant is the former Soviet republic of Moldova, one of Europe's least-developed economies, with per capita GNI of just $7,680 (see Figure 4.14). The country is now an independent republic, but, like neighbouring Ukraine, is heavily influenced by Russia.

The EU is unlikely to repeat the ambitious enlargement exercise that took place in the mid-2000s. Both the Netherlands and France voted 'no' in referendums on the constitutional treaty which preceded the Lisbon Treaty, largely for fear of paving the way for further enlargement. Inhabitants of the richer member states shoulder the financial burdens of the EU, which have grown to huge proportions. They question why they should be burdened with propping up member states which they feel have failed to act responsibly in managing their internal economies. They point to weak governance, out-of-control public spending, corruption and lack of transparency in some member states, which, they fear, could threaten the whole edifice.

Brexit name given to the process whereby the UK would exit the EU

In June 2016, the UK voted in a referendum to leave the EU, by a majority of 52% for 'leave' to 48% for 'remain'. The protracted process known as **Brexit** was officially launched in March 2017, with departure from the EU projected to be in 2019 (see discussion in Chapter 5). This is the first occasion in the EU's history that a member state has notified the Commission of its wish to leave, and the process inevitably ventures into uncharted territory. Resolving the many issues, such as citizens' rights, future trading relations and the status of EU law, has proved to be extremely difficult for negotiators on both the EU and UK sides. The process has impacted on other member states, whose businesses are integrated in supply chains with the UK, and whose citizens have been living and working in the UK through the freedom of movement allowed under the EU's single market.

The EU at the crossroads

Divergent national perspectives and goals have clouded the EU's future, causing many to predict its ultimate breakup. What impacts would a break-up of the EU have on the thinking of European business leaders who are planning their strategies for the next decade?

The economic environment: towards sustainability?

Businesses, governments and stakeholders, such as consumers and ecological concerns, desire a business environment that delivers economic prosperity over the long term. For business leaders accustomed to taking a short-term view of maximizing profits, building sustainability entails a longer and broader perspective, taking into account societal and environmental concerns, both at the national and global level. More than ever, businesses are now likely to take a global view of their strategies, singling out countries for location advantages. A country's economic environment is a key aspect of the PESTLE analysis (introduced in Chapter 1), which aids corporate strategists. A national economy will be targeted for advantages such as availability of

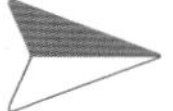

low-cost labour, resource wealth or a crucial stage in a global supply chain. Similarly, a large emerging economy, such as India, is favoured for its large potential market. But market potential must be tempered by a broader view of the social context. As we have seen, there are significant questions hanging over India's development model. Inequality is rising, gender inequality is a particular concern, and human development indicators are low. Rising average incomes point to improving standards of living, but form only part of the story. If growth is not sustainable, then there is a question mark over the direction in which the development model is heading. This chapter has argued that to be sustainable, growth needs to be inclusive. Growth that benefits the few and leaves the many behind is not sustainable.

China has been more successful than India in raising incomes, but in other respects still faces many challenges. Healthcare, education and a healthy natural environment are essentials of social wellbeing, but do not flow automatically from economic growth. The Chinese government has introduced strong pollution control rules, but it is paying a price in reduced factory output and contracting employment, which lead to lowered economic growth. China's period of rapid growth produced economic prosperity, with impressively rising GDP per capita. But inequality has grown, and the government faces challenges of improving societal wellbeing and environmental standards.

Every economic system – whether planned or market-driven – must be judged in terms of sustainability. Sustainability as a concept includes not merely economic factors, but also issues such as whether the environment and non-renewable resources are being managed sustainably. It also concerns issues of social wellbeing. Is the economy creating enough jobs, and are there welfare safety nets for those stuck at the bottom? It is now recognized that the ecological environment is another priority. Governments in these countries prefer market mechanisms in principle over direct intervention.

As we have seen, the liberal market model in its pure form lacks a defined social-conscience dimension. Still, British and American companies have taken a lead in corporate social responsibility (CSR), even when their governments have shown only reluctant support for measures such as controlling greenhouse gas emissions. A company could well choose to invest in production in a developing country with weak environmental standards, over a costlier location with higher standards. Many would take this decision on economic grounds, but this could be rather short-sighted. Technological improvements could bring down costs, making the costlier country a more competitive location over time, whereas the operations in many developing countries might not be sustainable in the long term. Similarly, investing in a developing country where wages are low and social welfare is minimal might seem a viable cost-saving strategy, but is unsustainable as well as unethical. The investing firm is wise to look to the broader economic and social picture when surveying comparative economic environments. Companies play key roles in all national economies, their activities providing the jobs and income that generate prosperity in society as a whole. This role brings responsibilities to look beyond the interests of corporate owners to the broader interests of stakeholders, paramount among whom are employees and communities.

Strategy choices for MNEs in emerging markets

Emerging markets are now the focus of many MNE strategies, but they pose challenges in terms of sustainability. On what principles should today's MNEs design emerging-market strategies?

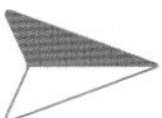

Conclusions

Expanding markets and deepening interconnectedness are hallmarks of globalization. Businesses have been drivers of globalization, pushing into new locations in terms of production as well as markets. Their activities bring societies and organizations closer together, facilitated by advances in communications technology. Markets in goods and services, notably including financial services, have expanded from national to global proportions, as countries have opened their economies to the potential benefits of globalization. Both business and state players have been active in this process. Companies see business opportunities, and states see opportunities for economic growth through investment and job creation. Thus, the interests of market players and states seem to coincide: companies and governments eye potential gains. But, with hindsight, governments and businesses alike have probably underestimated the risks in globalized markets and their impacts on national economies. Economists tend to view a market as inherently stable and self-adjusting, reflecting fluctuations in supply and demand. A national economy, however, can be destabilized by external shocks, often revealing underlying internal weaknesses, as happened when the global financial crisis struck in 2008. A national economy requires governmental watchdogs and regulators to ensure that markets function effectively. But this still leaves many unanswered questions. How much government is too much; who is being served by markets; and if markets are now global, what can a national government do anyway?

Answering these three questions has been at the heart of this chapter. The liberal market model resists government intervention in principle, but this model took a knock in the financial crisis. The countries that have opted for more state-centred economic models were less affected by the global economic crisis and recession that ensued. States that advocate a social market model have long been sceptical of the impacts of markets in society, as profit-seeking firms naturally aim to generate wealth for private owners. Growing inequality, weak social welfare and resulting weak social cohesion can ultimately undermine stability in society. Advocates of the social market model demand that businesses operate in a regulatory framework that focuses on social goals. But in a globalized world, why would a foreign investor opt to invest in a country that has high corporate taxes and social charges, high levels of government regulation and requirements, for example, to provide social benefits for employees? All of these are costs that would deter any investor. The investor would surely prefer a country with low taxation, low wages, little regulation and no social agenda. Of course, the choice is not likely to be as crude as this. Most governments at least nod towards the need to pursue societal goals. However, the globalized economic environment has highlighted divergent national economic systems. It has become clear that some economic models, especially those focused on rapid development, are unsustainable and could undermine the very growth on which they are predicated. Inclusive growth, incorporating social goals, is thus the more trustworthy route to sustainable development, benefiting both societies and businesses.

CLOSING CASE STUDY

Uncertainty weighing on Jaguar Land Rover in the UK

Jaguar Land Rover (JLR), owned by the Indian conglomerate, Tata, is the UK's largest car company, employing 40,000 people in 2018. When Tata took over the company in 2008, there was optimism over the company's prospects. Sales surged, and prospects for jobs growth were good. By then, Britain's car industry was mostly in foreign ownership, many of the plants owned by Japanese carmakers, Toyota, Honda and Nissan. These companies had extensive supply-chain ties with EU countries, and exported cars to EU markets. The Brexit referendum in 2016, which resulted in a vote to leave the EU, cast a shadow over these car manufacturers' strategies. In addition to Brexit uncertainty, JLR was faced by challenges over the future of diesel engines. Government environmental policy was turning against diesel by raising fuel duty, thus discouraging the purchase of new diesel vehicles. Declining sales of diesel cars was inevitable. By 2018, JLR was becoming concerned that sales in China were declining amidst China's economic slowdown. Meanwhile, Brexit uncertainty was continuing to be an uncertainty hanging over future investment decisions.

In late 2018, JLR announced it needed to cut costs by some £2.5 billion. It would cut 4,500 jobs globally, most of the cuts in its UK workforce of 40,000. By the time of this announcement, it had already cut 1,000 temporary workers at its Solihull plant that makes Range Rovers and Land Rover Discovery SUVs. Reducing working hours and having longer Christmas holidays were also planned. Whereas annual investment of £4.5 billion had been anticipated, it would be reducing this to £4 billion. Sales of Land Rovers had slumped in China and in Europe in 2018. In China, where Jaguar is seen as an iconic brand, consumers are spending less on big-ticket purchases as the economy slows. In Europe, the shift away from diesel has been a factor. In the Volkswagen scandal of 2015, it emerged that the company had been using defeat devices to understate emissions – a practice that was more widespread in the industry than had appeared. Government policy and consumer sentiment turned against diesel. Britain is JLR's largest market, and 90% of its sales in 2018 were diesel vehicles, making it particularly vulnerable to the shift to other fuels. The company has been planning to invest in electric cars, but, with hindsight, these plans should probably have been advancing more quickly.

Uncertainty looms over the future of this Land Rover assembly line in the UK.

© Getty, Bloomberg / Contributor

Since the Brexit referendum of 2016, JLR had been warning that uncertainty over the terms of Brexit was affecting its forward planning. The free movement of goods under the EU's single market was crucial to its supply chains. Based on just-in-time movements of parts, the supply chains rely on free movement, unhindered by border checks, which would be time-consuming. During the following years, prolonged uncertainty for businesses such as JLR was damaging. In the event of no deal, or 'hard' Brexit, severe blockages at the borders would be unavoidable, as official cross-border customs checks would be required. For Jaguar Land Rover, a no-deal Brexit would be the worst possible scenario.

Large German carmakers, Mercedes and BMW, are rivals of JLR in the luxury car market globally. They are affected by some of the issues discussed above: the flight from diesel and the slowing market in China. They are larger companies with much larger volumes of sales than JLR. JLR enjoyed sales of over 600,000 cars globally in 2017, a 7% increase on 2016. But compare this to the total of more than two million sold by BMW. BMW has 8,000 workers in the UK, making Mini and Rolls Royce cars. It has said that these workers would be at risk if there is a hard Brexit. Carmakers everywhere are having to adjust to new realities, but Jaguar Land Rover faces a rather more complicated set of challenges in the UK.

Questions

- What are the challenges facing Jaguar Land Rover?
- In what ways would supply chains of carmakers be affected by a hard Brexit?
- How should Jaguar Land Rover change its strategy?
- Should Jaguar Land Rover simply close down operations in Britain and shift to other locations? Explain your reasons.

Further reading

See Kevin Rawlinson's article, 'Jaguar Land Rover's £80 bn UK investment plan at risk after hard Brexit', 4 July 2018, in *The Guardian*.

Multiple choice questions

Visit www.macmillanihe.com/morrison-gbe-5e to take a quick self-test quiz on what you have read in this chapter.

Review questions

1. In what ways is the circular flow diagram useful to show overall economic activity in the national economy?
2. How are GDP and GNI per capita used to compare countries, and what are their limitations?
3. Define inflation, and explain what its damaging effects can be on a national economy.
4. Why is the balance of payments important to policymakers, and why are governments concerned if there is a current account deficit?
5. Why is economic growth an important indicator, and what are its limitations?
6. What is 'inclusive growth', and why has it become a concern of governments?
7. Why is rising inequality a concern for governments?
8. In what ways do governments control monetary policy, and how has their room for manoeuvre become more limited with economic integration?
9. What are the distinguishing characteristics of capitalism?
10. What are the weaknesses of the liberal market economy?
11. Which countries are considered strongholds of the social market model of capitalism, and how are their economies evolving?
12. What are the elements of the transition process towards a market economy in (a) China; and (b) the transition economies of Central and Eastern Europe?
13. What are the sources of friction within the EU?
14. Which of the economic models described in this chapter is most aligned with sustainability, and why?
15. What are the challenges in terms of sustainability that fall on foreign companies investing in developing economies?

Assignments:

1. For a national government that seeks to promote growth, investment and employment, assess which are the best economic policies and why?
2. To what extent is China's state capitalism a valid economic model which can be emulated by other developing economies, and to what extent can it be criticized as not promoting sustainable development?

Further reading

Acemoglu, D. and Robinson, J. (2012) *Why Nations Fail: The origins of power, prosperity and poverty* (London: Profile Books).

Begg, I. (2012) *Economics for Business*, 4th edition (New York: McGraw-Hill).

Bootle, R. (2010) *The Trouble with Markets: Saving capitalism from itself* (London: Nicholas Brealey Publishing).

Collier, P. (2018) *The Future of Capitalism: Facing the new anxieties* (Allen Lane).

De Grauwe, P. (2018) *Economics of Monetary Union*, 12th edition (Oxford: Oxford University Press).

Deaton, A. (2013) *The Great Escape: Health, wealth and the origins of inequality* (Princeton: Princeton University Press).

Dunning, J. (ed) (1997) *Governments, Globalization and International Business* (Oxford: Oxford University Press).
Gros, D. (2009) *Economic Transition in Central and Eastern Europe: Planting the seeds* (Cambridge: Cambridge University Press).
Landes, D. (1998) *The Wealth and Poverty of Nations* (London: W.W. Norton & Co.).
Maddison, A. (1991) *Dynamic Forces in Capitalist Development* (Oxford: Oxford University Press).
Morgan, M. and Whitley, R. (2014) *Capitalisms and Capitalism in the Twenty-first Century* (Oxford: Oxford University Press).
Parkin, M., Powell, M. and Matthews, K. (2007) *Economics*, 7th edition (New Jersey: Addison Wesley).
Piketty, T. (2014) *Capital in the Twenty-first Century* (Cambridge, MA: Harvard University Press).
Piggott, J. and Cook, M. (2006) *International Business Economics* (Red Globe Press).
Walter, A. and Zhang, X. (eds) (2014) *East Asian Capitalism: Diversity, continuity and change* (Oxford: Oxford University Press).
Yasheng Huang (2010) *Capitalism with Chinese Characteristics: Entrepreneurship and the state* (Cambridge: Cambridge University Press).

❒ References

Acemoglu, D. and Robinson, J. (2012) *Why Nations Fail: The origins of power, prosperity and poverty* (London: Profile Books Ltd).
Aghion, P. and Howitt, P. (2009) *The Economics of Growth* (Cambridge, MA: MIT Press).
Alston, P. (2017) Report following visit to the US by the UN Special Rapporteur on extreme poverty and human rights, 15 December, at www.ohchr.org
Alvaredo, F., Chancel, L., Piketty, T., Saez, E. and Zucman, G. (2018) *World Inequality Report*, at www.wid.world
Bourguignon, F. (2015) *The Globalization of Inequality* (Princeton: Princeton University Press).
Elkins, K. (2018) 'There are more billionaires in the US than in China, Germany and India combined', 15 May, CNBC, at www.cnbc.com
Giles, C. (2014) 'Productivity crisis haunts power league', *Financial Times*, 16 October, at www.ft.com
ILO (2014) 'KILM9: Total unemployment', in *Key Indicators of the Labour Market* (KILM), at www.ilo.org
ILO (2017) World Social Protection Report 2017–2019 (Geneva, ILO).
Johnson, C. (1982) *MITI and the Japanese Miracle* (Stanford: Stanford University Press).
Landes, D. (1998) *The Wealth and Poverty of Nations* (London: Little, Brown & Company).
Lane, P. (2012) 'The European sovereign debt crisis', *Journal of Economic Perspectives*, 26(3): 49–68.
Maddison, A. (2007) *Contours of the World Economy, 1–2030AD* (Oxford: Oxford University Press).
Mahbubani, K. (2009) 'Lessons for the west from Asian capitalism', in The Future of Capitalism, *Financial Times*, 12 May, at www.ft.com
McKinsey Global Institute (2013) *A New Dawn: Reigniting growth in Central and Eastern Europe*, December, at www.mckinsey.com/mgi
OECD (2014) *China: Structural Reforms for Inclusive Growth*, March, at www.oecd.org
Ostry, J., Berg, J., Charalambos, G. and Tsangarides, G. (2014) *Redistribution, Inequality and Growth*, IMF discussion note, April, at www.imf.org
Piketty, T. (2014) *Capital in the Twenty-first Century* (Cambridge, MA: Harvard University Press).
Rawls, J. (1996) *Political Liberalism* (New York: Columbia University Press).
Rodrik, D. (2009) *One Economics: Many recipes* (Princeton: Princeton University Press).
Rodrik, D. (2012) *The Globalization Paradox* (Oxford: Oxford University Press).
Sen, A. (2010) *The Idea of Justice* (London: Penguin Books).
Smith, A. ([1776]1950) *An inquiry into the Nature and Causes of the Wealth of Nations* (London: Methuen).
Stanford Center on Poverty and Inequality (2016) *The Poverty and Inequality Report 2016, Pathways*, Special Issue, at www.inequality.com
Stiglitz, J. (2002) *Globalization and its Discontents* (London: Allen Lane).
Triggle, N. (2017) 'Life expectancy rises grinding to a halt in England', BBC news, 18 July, at www.bbc.co.uk
UNDP (United Nations Development Programme) (2016) *Human Development Report 2016: Human development for everyone* (New York: United Nations).
UNDP (United Nations Development Programme) (2018) *Human Development Report 2018, Statistical Update*, at www.hdr.undp.org
WEF (World Economic Forum) (2015) Global Risks 2015, 10th edition (Geneva: World Economic Forum).
World Inequality Database, maintained by the Paris School of Economics, at http://wid.world/

 **Visit the companion website at www.macmillanihe.com/morrison-gbe-5e for further learning and teaching resources.**

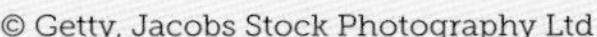
© Getty, Jacobs Stock Photography Ltd

THE POLITICAL ENVIRONMENT: POLITICS AND BUSINESS INTERTWINED

Outline of chapter

Introduction

The political sphere

How does political authority arise and subsist?
- Defining characteristics of the state
- Authority to govern: changing political environments
  - *Constitutions and the rule of law*
  - *Political beliefs and ideologies*
  - *The rise of extremist ideologies*

Political risk: threats and uncertainties
- Internal risks in state and society contexts
- External threats to the state

Democracy and authoritarianism
- Authoritarianism
- Democracy: in theory and practice

Governmental institutions in national contexts
- Overview of the functions of government
- Systems of government
- Elections as participation

Political life in practice
- Political parties and related groups
- Business engagement in political processes

Focus on the European Union
- EU institutions: democratic reforms
- Britain's path towards exiting the EU

Global politics
- International institutions
- The shifting balance of power in global politics

The changing political environment: reaching for sustainability?

Conclusions

This chapter will enable you to

- Appreciate the characteristics of nation-states and how they are evolving in the global environment
- Gain an understanding of sources of political legitimacy and authority
- Identify the dimensions of political risk in business decision-making globally
- Assess the extent to which democracy and authoritarian governments are evolving in the current global environment
- Evaluate the changing roles of business globally in political contexts, in light of ethical and societal responsibilities.

OPENING CASE STUDY

A populist president in Brazil

Following thirteen years of government by the left-wing Workers' Party (PT), the elections in October 2018 ushered in a new era of nationalist populism in Brazil, with the victory of Jair Bolsonaro as president. Mr Bolsonaro had a strong law-and-order agenda and conservative Christian outlook. Brazil's economy had endured years of damaging recession and corruption. Rule by the Workers' Party ended with the impeachment of the president, Dilma Rousseff, in 2016. Her impeachment marked the end of the era of socialist rule. An interim government was in place between 2016 and 2018.

Jair Bolsonaro is a veteran politician and former army captain, who has pledged to wipe out corruption and crime. His fiery rhetoric played well at rallies and on social media. He blames Brazil's economic troubles on the years of socialist rule. That era commenced with President Lula da Silva in 2003, who was admired by his supporters as the president who brought many millions of Brazilians out of poverty, and transformed the economy to the powerhouse that guaranteed its place among the stellar emerging economies. Lula oversaw the growth of the large state-owned companies, such as Petrobas, the oil company, and he greatly increased social spending. He was brought down dramatically, mired in corruption scandals over wrongful payments from large companies both to the party and to himself. As a result, he was sentenced to 12 years in jail, but his loyal supporters have always maintained that his prosecution was unjust and politically motivated.

Deforestation in the Amazon rainforests has speeded up under the presidency of Jair Bolsonaro.

Mr Bolsonaro's political leanings are towards nationalism and economic strength through strong government. His authoritarian tendencies are evident from his approval of the military dictatorship that ran Brazil from 1964 to 1985. He has pledged to rid the country of corruption and crime, which in his campaign rhetoric he linked to the 'communism' of the Lula era. He favours strong-arm tactics of police repression to deal with crime. He takes a strong pro-gun stance, and is likened in this respect to President Trump in the US. In January 2019, Mr Bolsonaro introduced legislation to relax gun laws, making it easier for Brazilians to acquire guns. President Trump would find Mr Bolsonaro's views similar to his own in this and other respects, such as business-friendly policies, conservative Christian values and climate change scepticism.

Mr Bolsonaro has inherited an economy dependent on large businesses, including the large state-owned companies. He would probably not privatize the latter, but he spoke of privatization when appearing at the World Economic Forum in Davos in 2019, stating that privatization would be part of his programme to promote entrepreneurialism and economic development. He favours the large agribusiness companies that are the backbone of Brazil's commodity exports. This policy stance brings him into direct conflict with those who fear for the Amazon's rainforests and for the human rights of indigenous peoples. He is relaxing regulations that protect the Amazon rainforests, 60% of which are within Brazil's borders. There are now growing fears for the protection of biodiversity and the Amazon's fragile ecosystem. Deforestation has been on the increase in recent years, and it has accelerated under Mr Bolsonaro. By July 2019, it was estimated that monthly deforestation was taking place at a rate 88% above the preceding year (Reuters, 2019). Satellite images reveal the scale of the destruction. An area the size of a football pitch is cleared every minute, mostly to make way for cattle

grazing, to satisfy the world's increasing demand for meat. The president has decided that authority over the Amazon's indigenous people – who number over a million – will be within the Ministry of Agriculture, which is dominated by the agribusiness lobby. This decision was considered an ominous sign of risks to their human rights, along with his plan to create indigenous reserves.

Mr Bolsonaro's attitude towards the Amazon has sent alarm bells ringing well beyond Brazil's borders, as deforestation is a major contributor to climate change. He has been a critic of the Paris agreement on climate change, and has threatened to withdraw from it. As of the end of 2018, he had not done so, but at the annual UN climate change conference, held in Poland in 2018, he announced that Brazil would withdraw its offer to host the next climate change conference. While he cited budget reasons for not wishing to host the conference, it is likely that the underlying reason is his antipathy towards measures to deal with climate change.

Questions

- What are the main elements of Bolsonaro's populism? How does he differ from Lula da Silva?
- How are the poor likely to fare under the Bolsonaro government?
- Bolsonaro is prioritizing economic development over environmental concerns. Who is likely to gain?
- In your view, will foreign investors be attracted to Brazil under its new president, or shy away?

Further reading

See the article from the BBC, 'Jair Bolsonaro beyond the soundbites: What are his policies?', 28 October 2018, at www.bbc.co.uk

Introduction

From global corporations down to family-run enterprises, businesses desire a stable and reasonably predictable environment in which to carry on their activities. As interaction between government and business has grown, the importance of political stability has become more apparent. In the political dynamics of every society both internal and external factors come into play. Internal governmental structures and processes form a political system, responsible for containing and channelling conflict, and promoting the collective good of society. Just as no two societies are identical, no two political systems are identical.

People everywhere wish to see public order maintained, public services function efficiently, and government officers carry out their duties. But they want more besides. A police state can offer security, but it hardly offers a conducive environment for a happy life. People wish to have a good education, a good job and the prosperity it brings, not simply for material wellbeing but for a better quality of life in a society which values the dignity of every individual. Democracy has long been a beacon to peoples all over the world as a system in which governments are held accountable to the people, and every person's voice counts. But, although democracy as a system has spread across the globe, many nominally democratic systems fall short of the stability and legitimacy hoped of them. With large swathes of the globe under non-democratic systems, basic issues such as the merits of democracy are coming into question. Democracies, both established and fledgling, are undergoing changes that seem to undermine democratic values, such as the dignity of the individual and political equality. Businesses are affected by the actions of all types of government, many of which fall beneath standards of the rule of law. The focus of much future business strategy is in emerging markets with authoritarian and semi-authoritarian leadership. Relations with governments raise ethical challenges in every country, but the challenges are greater in countries where political and legal institutions are weak and possibilities of corruption are high. This chapter will focus on political systems in a variety of states, and their implications for global business.

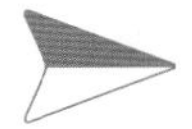

The political sphere

politics processes by which a social group allocates the exercise of power and authority for the group as a whole

Politics has been defined in numerous different ways, but all highlight the function of conflict resolution in society. Broadly, **politics** refers to processes by which a social group allocates the exercise of power and authority for the group as a whole. Breaking down the definition into three elements, *first* there is the existence of a social group – the word 'politics' derives from the Greek word *polis*, meaning city-state, a political community. Conflict is inevitable within societies, and politics provides the means of resolving conflict in structured ways. *Secondly*, politics concerns power relations. The contesting of power in society arises from groups and individuals with a wide range of viewpoints – ideological, economic, religious, ethnic or simply self-interested opportunistic. In democratic societies political parties are the most high-profile players on the political scene, but political authorities interact with a range of interests in society, including businesses and numerous interest groups, in arriving at policy decisions.

The *third* element is the terrain of politics – the social group as a whole. While politics occurs in every organization, we are concerned here with agenda-setting for a society as a whole. Its scope is thus public life, rather than particular organizations. For the citizen of ancient Athens, this distinction did not exist: participation in the city-state was both civic and moral in nature, the polis providing the means to the good life. Later developments, especially the growth of secular states in Europe and increasing emphasis on the worth of the individual, led to a separation between public and private spheres. The sphere of politics is public life, institutions of the state, governmental structures and the process by which individuals come to occupy offices of state.

civil society sphere of activities in society in which citizens are free to pursue personal interests and form associations freely

pluralism existence in society of a multiplicity of groups and interests independent of the state

The private sphere is often referred to as **civil society**, a term which covers the sphere in which citizens have space to pursue their own personal goals. Private individuals and businesses, trade unions, religious groups and the many sub-national associations which exist in pluralist societies are all part of civil society (Laine, 2014). We noted in Chapter 3 that most countries are home to people of diverse national cultural backgrounds. Historically, civil society is a western concept, and is associated with states where national cultures value liberal principles, including **pluralism**, that is, the presence of many different groups and interests in society. However, in recent years, the notion of civil society has broadened beyond the idea of groups within a state, to become a more globally focused concept. It has thus broken out of ideas of national societies, and has gravitated more towards ideas and values that cross national borders (Laine, 2014: 66). For example, volunteer groups such as non-governmental organizations (NGOs) are cross-border in their approaches to global issues. In some countries where civil society groups are perceived as threats to stability, NGOs and other groups face restrictions and even suppression.

From a business perspective, the political sphere in any country is likely to be perceived as an obstacle to achieving its goals. Politics is often pictured as officials imposing bureaucratic requirements, rule changes that increase costs and growing statutory regulation in areas such as employment and consumer protection. All of these add to the burdens of doing business, which a businessperson is inclined to feel hampers the firm's ability to achieve its goals.

Figure 5.1 shows a number of public policy areas where political decisions and government frameworks have impacts on businesses within the state's borders. In all these areas, governments aim to uphold public interest in some way, whether by promoting public goods or curtailing potential harm. Without laws in areas such as employment protection, businesses are unlikely to go very far in introducing employee rights. Indeed, a trend has been for businesses to categorize workers as

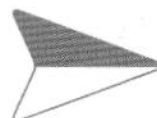

Figure 5.1 **Impacts of political policies on business**

self-employed, in order to avoid obligations owed to employees (discussed in Chapter 11). Similarly, business activities that are environmentally damaging are likely to persist until legislation is enacted to curtail them. Most people would say that the curtailing of activities such as unfair trade practices, exploitative employment practices or unsafe workplaces is justified. It has also become increasingly accepted that financial regulation and maintaining fairness in markets are in the public interest. Recall the markets-versus-state issues discussed in the last chapter. While businesses dislike government constraints on their activities, they welcome policies – and public spending – on research and innovation, education and helpful trade and investment policies.

Although liberal thinking distinguishes between public and private spheres, they are not easy to separate. Businesses regularly interact with governments, taking part in policy formation and in regulatory frameworks. Privatization of public services is now occurring in many different economies, even those that espouse the social market model. In the UK, public/private partnerships have been formed as means of financing investment in public services, such as hospitals. At the same time, services such as healthcare and social care are being outsourced to private-sector companies. The simple dichotomy of public and private domains, therefore, is being replaced by a more reciprocal relationship between the state and business enterprises. This offers businesses opportunities, but, as these activities involve public-sector services, it might be expected that the company will shift its corporate outlook towards social responsibilities. This shift is not always forthcoming: businesses that take on delivery of public services remain private-sector companies, and their directors take the view that shareholders must come first. The public/private dichotomy is blurred in the delivery of services, but the business decision-making is focused ultimately on how to deliver returns to owners. Governments should thus be wary of business involvement in services such as running schools or transport (see the opening case study in Chapter 8 on this subject). The result could be that investment for the long term is sacrificed to generating profits. Tension between business outlooks and the needs of society thus continue to exist.

How do political considerations influence business?

Businesses tend to have a negative view of politicians, as interfering in their activities and preventing them from achieving their business goals. On the other hand, businesspeople are keen to engage with politicians, looking to promote more business-friendly policies, such as laws that reduce regulation or offer financial benefits to firms.

In your view, should governments take a more friendly approach to business, or should they take a harder approach, on the assumption that businesses will always seek ways around regulation, presuming that they can probably get away with it?

How does political authority arise and subsist?

In geographical and organizational terms, the world is divided into nation-states. The nation-state combines the idea of national culture with the concrete, territorially-defined unit of the state. Nation-states have come to be referred to simply as 'states', reflecting the dominant unit. As we saw in Chapter 3, there is a misfit between states and nations: many people identify with national cultures different from the predominant one in the state where they live. Historically, people belonging to a nation have asserted rights to self-determination with the achievement of a territorial state ruled by its own government and subordinate to no higher authority. Indeed, self-determination is the foundation stone of the UN's human rights conventions (see Chapter 11, p. 383). New nation-states are often born of separatist movements within existing states. They can be labelled 'nationalist', denoting national identity, and also 'liberationist', denoting the desire to be free from state rule regarded as illegitimate. The dismantling of colonial empires in the years following the Second World War gave rise to newly independent states. Some 17 new states were born out of the break-up of the Soviet Union in 1990–91. Numerous new states, however, seem to bring together social and cultural groupings that do not necessarily form a cohesive society. To many, the state is an embodiment of national aspirations. To others, it gets in the way of people's aspirations. And to some, it is a tool of oppression, preventing people realizing their rights of self-determination.

Defining characteristics of the state

The nation-state was defined in Chapter 3 as the social, administrative and territorial unit into which people everywhere are divided. Here, we focus on the state as a set of authoritative institutions that are responsible for lawmaking and governance over its defined territory, backed up by authorized powers of coercion. This definition highlights three defining principles of statehood: territoriality, sovereignty and the authorized use of coercive power. The state occupies a geographically-defined territory, within whose boundaries it has jurisdiction. Disputes over territory can be particularly bitter, and have led to innumerable wars. Maintaining border controls, all would agree, has become more problematic, as territorial boundaries generally have become more permeable with the processes of globalization. These developments are welcomed by firms, facilitating growth in cross-border business, but permeable borders are also seen by governments as a source of insecurity.

Although the state is still the legal gatekeeper controlling what crosses its borders, this role has become more daunting with the growing international flows of goods, people, information and money. Importantly from a national economic standpoint, the state also controls access to natural resources such as mineral reserves and oil in its territory. It is not surprising that countries such as Venezuela and Mexico, on

gaining independence, nationalized their oil industries, but both later took steps towards liberalization and privatization. However, residual authority remains in state hands in the case of resource rights, giving governments the upper hand: a licence to mine granted to a private-sector firm is always at risk of being withdrawn at a later date.

The post-colonial states of Africa have generally followed inherited borders from the colonial period, which were artificially drawn and did not reflect ethnic groupings. Except for Rwanda and Burundi, none of the 34 modern African states corresponds to pre-colonial boundaries. Two consequences have followed: historic groupings are divided between states, and a state's population may comprise groups which are historic enemies (Hawthorn, 1993). Ethnic conflict has been an inevitable result. In these situations states struggle to maintain control and a sense of legitimacy over all their inhabitants. The pictures of flows of refugees from conflict into neighbouring countries have become a saddening feature of modern politics, highlighting the vulnerability and interdependence of states.

sovereignty the supreme legal authority of the state

unitary system system of authority within a state in which all authority radiates out from the centre

federal system system of government in which authority is divided between the centre and regional units

A second defining feature of statehood is **sovereignty**, which denotes the supreme legal authority of the state. Sovereignty has an internal and external aspect. A state has 'internal' sovereignty, in that it possesses ultimate authority to rule within its borders; all other associations within society are subordinate. In a **unitary system**, all authority radiates out from the centre. There may well be local and regional governments, but they lack autonomous authority. States where there are strong regional identities often choose constitutions based on a **federal system**, whereby authority is shared between a central government and regional governments. The US is an example, where the 50 individual 'states' have considerable legal and political authority, but the federal government remains paramount. In federal systems, the central government of the state as a whole is the ultimate authority. A weaker central government characterizes the system known as a 'confederacy', in which the component states have ultimate authority. This principle might seem to have been settled by the US Constitution in 1787, but the principle of 'states' rights' has long been an issue, even though the supporters of federalism were the victors in the Civil War of 1861–65. Nigeria is another example of federalism, where religious and cultural divides are recognized by the federal constitution.

The state's legal authority is supported by a monopoly of the legitimate use of coercive force, in the form of military and police forces. This is the third of the defining characteristics of states. There are many states where these institutions are imperfect or even failed. If an armed militia seizes power and ousts an established government, the new government has *de facto* power, but is not the legitimate sovereign.

'External' sovereignty refers to the position of states in the international context, where all states recognize each other as supreme within their own borders. The principle of mutual recognition, known as the 'sovereign equality of states' governs the conduct of international relations between states. This notion of sovereignty lies at the heart of the UN, forming the basis of international law. However, in practice, economic and political power are crucially interrelated. The era of globalization has seen a questioning of the continuing autonomy of states in economic terms, and it is sometimes said that state sovereignty is an outmoded concept (Jackson, 2003). Economic globalization has proceeded rapidly, expanding the role of large global companies, which can seem to dwarf state authorities. In addition, companies have acquired deepening ties with governments, bringing their activities into the sphere of politics and giving them a quasi-political role. Global politics remains dominated by state players, but corporate representatives are highly visible and active in national policy-making and at international governmental gatherings on global issues. The principle of sovereign authority still underlies lawmaking authority within the state, as well as the authority to create international law, but the inputs of business leaders are now commonplace in these processes.

Authority to govern: changing political environments

Authority in any organization concerns the recognized right to exercise power over others. The organization could be a company, a religious group, a political party or a whole state. Authority in each of the world's sovereign states rests on some foundation recognized as giving legitimacy to rulers and their system of governance. At least, that is the starting assumption for legitimate governance. But in many states authority is contested, and sometimes the divisions threaten the existence of the state. Where a country is divided by extreme social or religious divisions, there is no generally accepted source of authority and the outcome could be civil war among the main groups or simply a break-up of the state into separate regions. Where this happens, the country is referred to as a 'failed' state. Here we examine the most common sources of legitimacy in states, and we also look at how changes in society and the economy impact on issues of authority to govern.

Constitutions and the rule of law

constitutionalism set of rules, grounded in a society's shared beliefs, about the source of authority in the state and its institutional forms

rule of law principle of supremacy of the law over both governments and citizens, entailing equality before the law and an independent judiciary

In most modern states, legitimacy, in theory, is founded on constitutionalism. **Constitutionalism** implies a set of rules, grounded in a society's shared beliefs, about the source of authority and its institutional forms. Constitutionalism stands for the **rule of law**, above both ruler and ruled. Its underlying principle is that the institutions of government derive their power from these pre-existing rules. Actual officeholders will change from time to time, and, indeed, a vital function of a constitution is to provide for smooth change in the transfer of power. But the constitution, setting out the ground rules, provides continuity and legitimacy. Inherent in constitutionalism are the control by the civilian authority over the military and the existence of an independent judiciary (court system).

Most of the world's constitutions are written. The major exception is the British constitution. However, while the UK has no separate constitutional document, much legislation, which is contained in Acts of Parliament, is constitutional in nature. However, the mere existence of a constitutional document is no guarantee of accountable government. There are some states where, despite a written constitution, the rule of law is weakly established. In these countries, authoritarian rulers sometimes cloak themselves in the legitimacy of a constitution, although this device is simply a façade for autocratic rule. Some of the former Soviet republics are among the countries with constitutional institutions that are subordinated to autocratic rule, usually bolstered by elections in which only the leadership's choice of candidates can run for office.

In a traditional monarchy, such as the Arab state of Saudi Arabia, heredity in the royal lineage is the legitimating principle. The ruling family dynasty asserts absolute authority. In practice, absolute monarchy is rare. Absolutism implies that the monarch is able to rule as a pure tyrant, totally unaccountable, but traditional monarchies have tended to be more limited than this image suggests (Henshall, 1992). In practice, traditional monarchies have engaged in consultation and co-operative relations with representatives of different interests in society. Decentralization and localized decision-making are also aspects of monarchies in practice. Over time, monarchy often gives way to a constitutional monarchy, in which the monarch remains the formal head of state under a constitution that enshrines democratic institutions in government. Some examples are Britain, Japan and Spain. Other constitutional

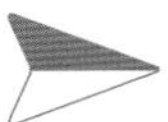

states are republics, where sovereignty rests in principle and in practice with representative institutions, usually headed by a president.

Constitutionalism and the rule of law are notably at risk in countries where society is ethnically divided, religiously divided or highly unequal economically. In these countries, governments struggle to assert their authority. Each of these types of tension can give rise to political conflict within the state.

Political beliefs and ideologies

ideology all-encompassing system of beliefs and values, or world-view

Most people hold beliefs in how political authority should be exercised. They might believe, for example, in universal suffrage and freedom of speech. These are important pillars of democracy, but do not themselves amount to an **ideology**, which is a more comprehensive and systematic set of beliefs. Ideology as a source of legitimacy is a coherent system of beliefs about cultural identity, the nature of community and the role of individuals within it. A political ideology focuses on the identity of the community and its claims to exercise legitimate authority over people. It involves moral rules and social norms that bind the community together. Liberal democratic values underpin democratic states. They include individual rights, political pluralism and accountability of governments to the electorate through regular meaningful elections. Thus, liberal democracy, taken as an amalgam of all these principles, has the characteristics of an ideology. The right to participate in representative government offers the hope of a better tomorrow: if the current government is not listening to my voice, I can vote for an alternative in the next election.

The belief system linked to a political ideology is often grounded in an economic system. Capitalism as an economic model rests on the primacy of economic freedom, along with the right to own private property and to accumulate wealth. These capitalist assumptions underpin many of the 'liberal' aspects of the term 'liberal democracy'. Democratic reforms came long after market economies were thriving in European countries. Socialism as an ideology is often seen as the ideological opposite of capitalist ideology, as we saw in Chapter 4. However, it should be remembered that socialist thinking covers a wide political spectrum. In much political discourse, social justice underpins social democratic thinking and social market economies. Political parties that uphold these values are active in most liberal democratic systems. By contrast, socialism as an ideology has driven revolutionary movements globally, morally justifying the overthrow of oppressive regimes, and paving the way for self-determination of peoples under an egalitarian system based on a planned economy. Examples are the communist revolutions that have overturned existing regimes in both traditional monarchies, as in Russia, and capitalist systems, as in Cuba. Communist revolutions take over the state, replacing existing governments with communist party dictatorships, as in China. This type of system claims authority from the people, but there is generally only limited accountability to citizens and little in the way of individual freedoms. China has introduced market reforms, but retained communist party rule at the pinnacle of the political system. Cuba has limited democratic elections within the single-party system. After a referendum on its new constitution in 2019, it has introduced political and economic reforms, such as limiting the president's term of office and introducing labour rights for those who work in the private sector.

After the Second World War, the assertion of power by the Soviet Union (USSR) under the dictatorship of Stalin sent alarm bells ringing in the US, leading to the so-called 'cold war', dominated by a clash of ideologies between communism and the American model of liberal democracy. The contrast between these two world-views greatly influenced international politics between 1945 and 1991. Since the collapse of the Soviet Union, China has been the leading communist country, followed by a dwindling number of smaller states, such as Cuba and North Korea. Since its communist revolution in 1959, Cuba has consistently maintained its communist system, but has gradually introduced reforms, as noted above. One might conclude that with the fall of the Soviet model of communism, the liberal democratic model had clearly emerged dominant globally. However, ideologies can endure after governments that adopted them have fallen. China's communist system has changed over time, becoming more liberal in respect to capitalist enterprises and private property, but not in respect of political reform. It has been officially described as 'socialism with Chinese characteristics', implying that its state-guided economy upholds the egalitarian principles that underpin socialism, its ideological foundation (Westcott, 2018). Russia embarked on both liberal reforms and democratic elections, but under Vladimir Putin, it has shifted towards a more state-dominated economy and authoritarian political system. Both reflect an aggressively nationalist ideology.

The rise of extremist ideologies

An ideology can be a set of beliefs based on a group's assertion of moral supremacy over others, making its believers see themselves on a mission to vanquish opposing world-views. We have noted that independent states can be born out of the nationalist aspirations of peoples wishing to break away from existing states. Nationalism as an ideology can also be a powerful political force within the state itself, spurring expansionist policies, including territorial expansion and economic outreach.

nationalism belief system that is based on the cultural identity, interests and right of self-determination of a nation or people

Nationalism in an extreme sense extols the moral supremacy of a particular nation over others, and denies that rival ideologies have any legitimate right to exist. Fascism, an extreme nationalist ideology, reached its zenith in fascist Germany and Italy. In these countries, the state became the embodiment of fascist ideology. While these fascist states were defeated in the Second World War, fascist groups still exist in many states which have adopted democratic institutions. Such groups can attract considerable electoral support, often as a protest vote against the existing government, but also as a show of support for extreme nationalist policies, such as suppression of minorities and rejection of immigrants. When their leaders are elected, they can become a threat to existing democratic institutions. The extremism of these groups fits uneasily into a liberal democratic state.

populism political ideology or movement based on restoring power to 'the people', as opposed to existing political elites; often based on nationalist values and anti-immigrant rhetoric

Nationalism is often associated with **populism**, a broad term that can apply to a distinctive ideology or a movement with a vaguer set of beliefs that bring followers together. Whether an ideology or a looser belief system, it is based on the idea of the good of the people, as opposed to elites. When used broadly, it can refer to a belief that the rich are too powerful and that the government should do more for those lower down in society. The use of 'populism' in America has historically referred to this set of beliefs, and has been associated with progressive Democrats. The US president, Franklin D. Roosevelt was an example of this view. Populism in this broad sense is rooted in democratic principles. By contrast, populism as an ideology rests on an idealized view of 'the people' as morally pure and homogeneous, set against corrupted political and economic elites (Mudde, 2017). This view is more nationalist in its foundations. Often, the 'people' as a concept is conceived in ethnic terms, as the native population, in contrast to immigrants who are viewed as outsiders. For this reason, 'nativism' and intolerance are among its characteristics. In this book, the term 'populism' refers to this ideological definition.

The populist believes there is an irreconcilable antagonism between the people and the established elites, in which the people are urged to rise up and claim back their rightful sovereignty (Mudde, 2004). This is essentially a winner-takes-all mentality. Recently, Hungary and Poland have both seen the rise of extreme nationalist political leaders, who, when elected, seek to dismantle liberal democratic institutions, including the independent judiciary and independent media. Their tendency

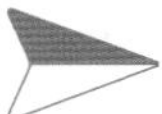

is thus more authoritarian than democratic. In Turkey, the president, Recep Erdogan, exemplifies populism, as shown in the case study in this chapter. Through executive actions, he has greatly enhanced the personal power of the presidency, whittling away the checks and balances built into the constitution. He has brought the judiciary under his control, suppressed political dissent and restricted the operations of rival political parties. He has clamped down on media freedom and on freedom of speech generally. His autocratic rule has thus brought Turkey closer towards a police state, as the closing case study shows.

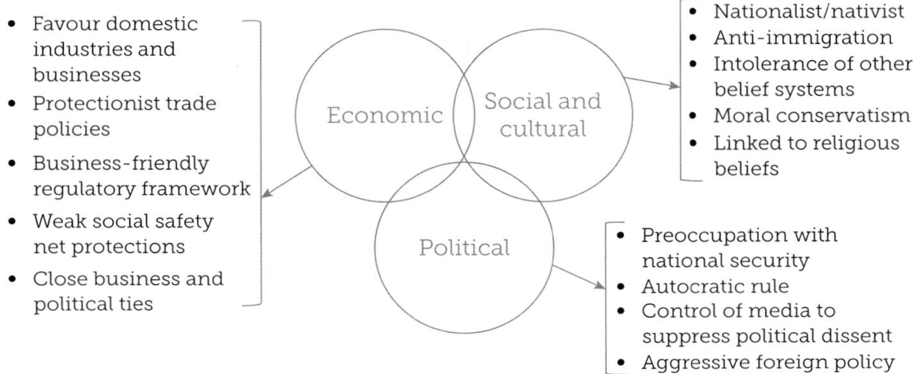

Figure 5.2 **Facets of populism**

Figure 5.2 shows a breakdown of populism along lines that reflect key dimensions of the business environment. Every populist movement is shaped by the conditions in the country where it takes hold. In some, religious and ethnic tensions are paramount, while in others extreme inequality is the major source of tension. In the US, the rise of Donald Trump from property magnate to US president, in the general election of 2016, exemplifies a number of these facets. Mr Trump campaigned on a nationalist agenda of 'make America great again'. He promised a better tomorrow for poor and disheartened citizens who felt that the traditional political parties had ignored them, and who felt their voices were not being heard in government. This is in the American populist tradition. Behind their disenchantment there were the following economic grievances:

- In many industrial regions, globalization had taken its toll. New technology was either replacing workers or requiring fewer workers, while older skills had become redundant. The loss of manufacturing and mining jobs especially affected the states known as the 'rustbelt' states (recall the mini case study in Chapter 2). Here, those left behind dreamt of a return to the America of the 1960s, when the country was the world's industrial powerhouse, and workers could aspire to continuing economic prosperity.
- In areas where the financial crisis of 2008 had been the harshest in terms of employment and housing, many inhabitants still remained mired in economic woes, eight years after the crisis. Making matters worse, the government had bailed out failed companies, and executives responsible for the financial crisis had escaped unscathed.
- In many sectors, such as the service industries, where jobs were still available, wage levels for ordinary workers had remained stagnant for many years, and large numbers of working people remained below the poverty line, relying on uncertain welfare benefits. On the other hand, corporate leaders and the richest 10% had seen their share of the country's wealth continue to rise.

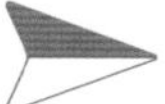

Mr Trump's nationalism was reflected in a strong anti-immigrant policy and a strong national security emphasis, based on a fear of terrorism, which he associated with Islamic terrorists. Once he had taken office, his executive orders to ban entry to the US from predominantly Muslim countries reflected this view. Another element of Mr Trump's campaign rhetoric included the extolling of conservative Christian values (as indicated in Figure 5.2). Evangelical protestants (described in Chapter 3) were numerous in much of rural America. In poor states such as West Virginia, which had seen the demise of its mining industry, Mr Trump won 68.7% of the vote in 2016. On the other hand, West Virginia also has a history of leftwing activism against the oppression of mining companies (Catte, 2019). Hence, there is an overlap in the support for rightwing populists and leftwing Democrats (for a further discussion of these categories, see the section on political parties in this chapter).

Populists typically attain power through elections conducted according to constitutional frameworks. This was the case in Turkey, the US, Poland and Hungary. However, populists tend to be inherently against liberal democracy (Mudde, 2017). When in office they seek to circumvent constitutional law and feel able to take the law into their own hands. Executive orders can often be within the letter of the law, but not within the spirit of the law. This is a gradual process, accomplished piecemeal, but individual measures can have a cumulative effect of threatening the rule of law. Democratic systems are not usually overthrown overnight, but can deteriorate gradually, as the autocratic leader chips away at democracy's foundations (Sunstein, 2018). It is not the document itself that will protect a society against authoritarian rule. After all, many authoritarian states have written constitutions. It is the depth of democratic values within a society that will sustain democracy and the rule of law.

Resurgence in ideological politics: What does it mean for businesses?

Nationalist and populist leaders are gaining ground in many countries, exerting a strong, charismatic leadership approach. In countries where they have taken over the reins of government, they are likely to be active in shaping business policies that reflect their strong views. In what ways is this likely to be good news for businesses – or bad news?

Political risk: threats and uncertainties

In the aftermath of the Second World War, political leaders were anxious to put in place an institutional framework at the global level which would ensure peace and security. This was the impetus behind the setting up of the UN, as well as other international bodies such as the IMF and World Bank. The unfolding post-war period saw growing economic prosperity – a good indicator of the benefits of peaceful co-existence among nation-states. But in the decades that followed, has the world become a safer place in which to live and do business?

political risk uncertainties associated with the exercise of governmental power within a country, and from external sources

Political risk for businesses is the extent to which they are affected by uncertainties associated with the exercise of governmental power within a country, or from external forces. We look first at internal aspects of political risk, and then turn to external threats.

Internal risks in state and society contexts

Changes in national law and policy that might adversely affect businesses, such as nationalization within a particular sector, are risks that have direct effects on a business.

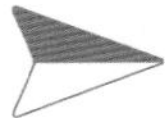

Venezuela's socialist government nationalized numerous assets in the 2000s, including oil assets, gas assets and a rice mill. All had been owned by foreign companies. Traditional views of political risk focus on four types of government action: confiscation, expropriation, nationalization and deprivation, known as CEND for short (Toksoz, 2014). In the broader context of the business environment, there are numerous sources of tension that can contribute to political risk. Social unrest, industrial unrest and dissatisfaction with the government are sources of political risk. Of course, these types of instability can occur anywhere. And government responses are crucial. The tensions are often resolved, but they can spill over into deeper instability. Generally, developed countries with more established political institutions, usually democratic, are more able to contain tensions than developing countries where political institutions are in the formative stages. We have seen in the last section that populist political parties and their leaders can represent internal risks of destabilizing democratic institutions. They also act to exacerbate divisions in society by polarizing political debate.

Globalization has seen economic integration among a wide variety of states, both developed and developing. Rising growth rates and economic development have placed many developing economies in the spotlight as new drivers of the global economy (see Chapter 4). We might assume that political risk is low where economic prosperity is high. If incomes and standards of living are rising, this contentment is good news for the government. In democratic systems, if the economy is suffering a downturn or recession, the electorate is inclined to vote out the governing party. A change of government in a stable, developed country should not be particularly destabilizing in terms of political risk, but, as we have seen, even seemingly stable democracies can backslide. For developing and emerging countries, political risk is a major factor for investors.

Globalization's star performers have been the BRIC economies, first highlighted in 2001, mainly for their impressive growth rates, which outshone those in the developed regions and suggested a shift in global economic power (O'Neill, 2001). This assessment, however, was one based mainly on economic indicators. As we discovered in the last chapter, economic data give only a partial picture of a country's wellbeing. They give few clues about governance, political stability and sustainable growth policies. The BRICs all presented elements of political risk in the form of social and ethnic tensions, high levels of inequality and weak governmental accountability. These risks have largely been contained, but remain concerns. Two of the original BRICs, India and Brazil, are democracies, while China and Russia are not. China's leaders are concerned over potential unrest that could spill over into political unrest. They have improved wages and employment conditions on the one hand, and have stamped out signs of public dissent on the other.

Meanwhile, other large emerging economies have come to the fore, including Indonesia, South Africa, Nigeria, Turkey and Indonesia. Are these other emerging economies becoming more stable politically? Economic dependence on natural resources is an issue for many of the emerging economies. Brazil and Russia derive their prosperity mainly from natural resources. The same is true of Indonesia, South Africa, Nigeria and Mexico. Of the original BRICs, all have seen stuttering growth, giving rise to political tension. Brazil has had serious corruption scandals involving government and state-owned companies. Brazil's president Dilma Rousseff was impeached in 2016, and her successor faced calls for impeachment in 2017, while former president, Lula, has been convicted of corruption. Russia's economy has suffered from falling oil prices and an embargo imposed for incursions into Ukraine. China has seen slowing export sales, and has faced rising trade tensions with the US.

Countries that are mainly dependent on resource wealth or commodities are inherently vulnerable to falling demand. With large populations and large numbers of poor people, these countries face challenges of creating jobs and improving wellbeing for all in society. But, while democratic institutions exist in all the newer emerging economies noted above, social and political tensions run high and can spill over into civil disorder and even violent clashes. This constitutes political risk. Nonetheless, companies seize opportunities for expansion that these countries present. But foreigners face high levels of political risk in entering these markets. The apparent flowering of liberal reforms might suggest that these countries are becoming more like western political environments, where democratization and constitutional governments took hold in the context of economic reforms. However, these large emerging economies have taken different development paths. Although they have democratic institutions, most are ruled by closed leadership groups. They are acutely conscious of threats to stability from within their countries, and they are also sensitive to regional instabilities that can boil over into hostilities. Spending on defence and national security has increased markedly in unstable regions of the world.

External threats to the state

Although, in theory, sovereign states recognize the sovereignty of each other, in practice, wars and violent conflicts short of war have historically played a large part in politics at the global level. Following the Second World War, this was the impetus behind the setting up of the UN and the putting in place of negotiating processes to build a body of international law that would deter violations of sovereignty. The UN Charter states that members should neither threaten nor use force against the 'territorial integrity or political independence' of any state, or act in ways that are 'inconsistent with the purposes of the UN' (UN Charter, Article 2.4). There are two exceptions. The first is use of force authorized by the UN Security Council (Article 42) and the second is acting in response to 'armed attack' (UN Charter, Article 51). Nonetheless, the prohibition on the use of force has appeared to be weakening. The post-war period saw a build-up in military establishments by the chief players of the cold-war period, the US and Soviet Union (now Russia). In 1999, NATO (the North Atlantic Treaty Organization) intervened in Kosovo.

Iraq's invasion of Kuwait in 1991 was against UN principles, and the Security Council immediately condemned the invasion (Sands, 2005). By contrast, the US led an invasion of Iraq in 2003 on the grounds that the country was a threat to global peace and security and that it sponsored terrorism (Sands, 2005: 181). The government of President Bush was convinced that 'regime change' was needed. There was no UN authorization and little evidence to support the invasion, which toppled the country's government. In 2014, Russia invaded Crimea, seizing territory. This annexation was met with economic sanctions by the US, under then-president Obama, and European governments. In 2017, President Trump authorized attacks against Syria as a response to Syria's chemical weapons attacks. He also authorized intensified bombing attacks in Yemen as part of his anti-terrorist offensive. The protagonists in these cases could all argue that they had strong moral grounds for their actions, but none were sanctioned by the Security Council. They were all breaches of the UN Charter, and, importantly, the US and Russia are members of the Security Council that have powers of veto. These issues are further discussed in the section on global politics later in this chapter.

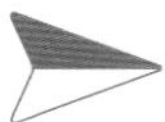

The US accounts for 36% of global military expenditure, a percentage that is down from 46% in 2009. In 2018, the US spent nearly $649 billion on defence, which is 2.6 times the money spent by the country in second place, China (SIPRI, 2019). The extent of the American military presence around the world is difficult to assess. In 2012, the US Department of Defense reported that it managed over 5,000 sites worldwide (US Department of Defense, 2012). By 2015, this number had been reduced to just over 4,800, reflecting a policy of reducing the government's footprint (US Department of Defense, 2016). These sites contain a total of 562,000 facilities, including buildings and linear structures such as runways and roads. Most of these are in the US and in US overseas territories, but 587 US military sites are in other countries. Many additional installations, sites and assets come under its control, or the control of subcontracted companies. The US relies heavily on the services of people working for private-sector contractors, in both combat activities and back-up services. Although little information is made available, it is estimated that as many as half the American forces in the Iraq war were employed by private-sector companies (Isenberg, 2009).

Globally, military spending reached a total of $1.8 trillion in 2018, which was 2.6% higher than in 2017 (SIPRI, 2019). This is 2.3% of global GDP. Military expenditure is a broad category, covering money spent on both hardware and services, including salaries and pensions of military personnel. As Figure 5.3 indicates, the US stands out from other countries in military expenditure. The figure shows the amount spent by each of the selected countries, and also the percentage of that country's GDP that is devoted to military spending. China has increased its military spending in recent years, as its global power has grown, but its military spending is still well behind that of the US. China is fearful of the threat posed by the extensive American military presence in Asian countries, including Japan, South Korea and the Philippines. Other countries with large military budgets include those in the Middle East, where regional tensions are a major factor. Of the countries in this figure, Saudi Arabia spends the highest percentage of GDP on military expenditure, a reflection of regional tensions.

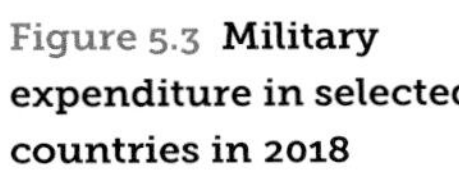

Figure 5.3 Military expenditure in selected countries in 2018

Note: Percentage of GDP appears alongside the name of each country

Source: Stockholm International Peace Research Institute (SIPRI), SIPRI Military Expenditure Database, at www.sipri.org, accessed 4 July 2019.

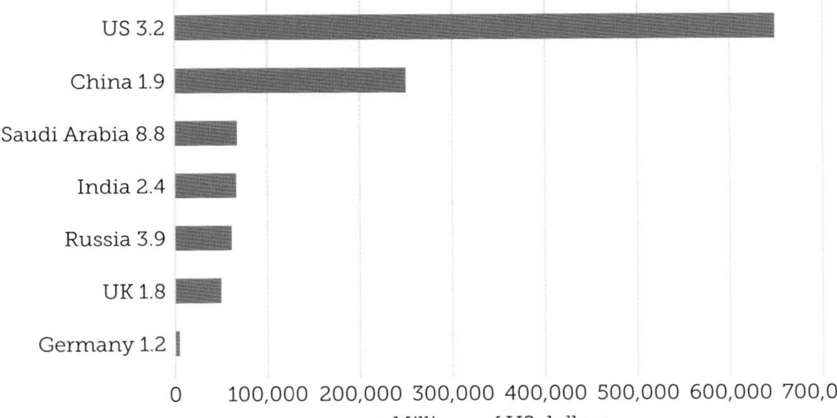

Increased military spending is a worrying trend which can be linked to internal instabilities, regional tensions or threats from terrorism. The Middle East has seen all these factors. Traditional autocratic rule in many Middle Eastern Arab states

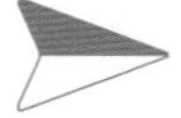

started to crumble in 2011, in what was known as the 'Arab spring'. Uprisings in Egypt, Tunisia and Libya led to periods of political uncertainty and instability, the effects of which have lingered. Indeed, Libya has become a failed state. Some of those protesting were calling for democracy, but many were groups associated with Islamist terrorism. There have been civil wars in Syria, Afghanistan, Iraq, Yemen and Libya. In all these countries, terrorists associated with the Islamic State have been active.

terrorism action by an individual or group intended to inflict dramatic and deadly injury on civilians and create an atmosphere of fear, generally for a political or ideological purpose

Terrorism is a threat that raises concerns for all governments. Terrorist threats may emanate from numerous sources, including disenchanted groups within a society or from outside the state. Sometimes these two sources overlap. **Terrorism** has been defined broadly as action meant 'to inflict dramatic and deadly injury on civilians and to create an atmosphere of fear, generally for a political or ideological (whether secular or religious) purpose' (UN Policy Working Group, 2002). Terrorists have access to funding from sources such as illicit trading, and they can lay hands on abundant weaponry. They have become adept at striking targets that achieve maximum impact. Terrorists are highly mobile, and they have become skilled at using the internet and social media for propaganda purposes. They have developed abilities to target states and organizations with cyber attacks. Businesses and governments face considerable risks, not just in physical locations which have a history of terrorist attack.

Following the attacks on the World Trade Center and the Pentagon in 2001, the US set its sights against the threats of Islamic terrorists, notably, the Islamist group, al-Qaida. The then-US president, George W. Bush, initiated a global 'war on terror' which attempted to legitimize pre-emptive strikes in other countries on the grounds that terrorism had become global and that any country could therefore be the target of a US strike for 'harbouring' terrorists (Wolin, 2008). In the years following 2004, the US has operated a programme whereby unmanned 'drones' fire at targets associated with al-Qaida in the areas where it is active. Although alleged terrorists have been targeted in these attacks, the US military has acknowledged that in some cases they target an area, rather than particular individuals (Timm, 2015). These attacks have aroused criticism for violations of human rights. The US has maintained that the drone strike programmes are in keeping with international law, stressing that the strikes take place in war zones. However, the justification put forward is a 'global war doctrine', which would allow it to target al-Qaida anywhere in the world (Boone, 2013). Such a sweeping doctrine on the part of the US flouts principles of state sovereignty and human rights, potentially sowing seeds of greater insecurity and mounting human rights violations. The US has asserted its global role in moral terms as grounded in values of democracy and due process. But the right it asserts to intervene militarily anywhere in the world suggests behaviour more associated with autocratic regimes, undermining its claims of moral leadership globally.

Worrying militarization of conflicts has seen links between internal instabilities and external threats. Military solutions tend to bring temporary peace only, and then hostilities are likely to flare up again. The reasons behind invasions and wars in today's world have tended to focus on upholding principles of morality and justice. But the country that feels the need to take the law into its own hands undermines the system of international law backed by institutions established by the UN to maintain peace and security (Hathaway and Shapiro, 2017). It is in the interests of all countries – and all businesses – that international law and UN institutions are the recognized legal means by which peace and security can be sustained. Without them, the 'might-is-right' approach thrives, bringing with it the very insecurity that the UN sought to consign to history.

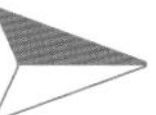

MINI CASE STUDY

Political risks in Mali

For many in the West, Mali is known mainly as the homeland of its legendary singer-songwriter, Salif Keita, who has eloquently portrayed to the world the fragilities of life in Mali. Mali is a large country in West Africa, where the semi-arid Sahel desert covers a large area, in which farming is the predominant means of livelihood. The country is now living on the edge in terms of climate change, and also living in the cauldron of insurgencies organized by Islamist terrorists. These threats have destabilized the country, challenging its fragile political system and economy. Malians had reasons to be optimistic in 1992, when democracy replaced a military dictatorship. The country has a long history and is famous for its rich cultural heritage of Timbuktu, but much of this has been destroyed by Islamist terrorists. Islamic insurgency and a military coup in 2012 in the north and central regions resulted in the Islamist separatists gaining territorial control over parts of the country. They were repelled with the aid of the French military. In 2013, democratic elections were held, in which Ibrahim Boubacar Keita won the presidency. There followed a peace agreement with the Islamic separatists. This was a fragile arrangement, however, and violent attacks continued. UN peacekeeping forces attempt to keep down the violent attacks. In the presidential election of 2018, Keita won a second term, but only after a runoff election, and amidst violence that marred polling day. He faced a difficult task of restoring some semblance of stability.

Mali's Great Mosque of Djenné, a famous mud mosque, has a history going back to the thirteenth century, although the current building dates from 1907.

Despite the challenges of maintaining security, Mali has had economic growth of 5.5%, largely because of its natural resources, including gold. It remains a poor country, however, ranking 182 out of 189 countries in the UN Human Development Index published in 2018 (UNDP, 2018). The task of promoting sustainable development in Mali has taken on new challenges with the 'gathering storm' of climate change, referred to in the recommended article below. Increases in temperatures in the Sahel are higher than the global average, threatening the country's precarious subsistence agriculture, through drought and soil degradation. Violence has broken out between communities under strain from the risk of hunger. This instability is exacerbated by the violent attacks of the Islamist groups. Although the situation can seem hopeless, local mediators are seeking peaceful reconciliation between communities to alleviate the hardship.

Questions

- What are the causes of political risk in Mali?
- What are the challenges currently facing Mali? How can they be resolved, if at all?

Find out more

See the article by Lyse Doucet, 'The battle on the frontline of climate change in Mali', from the BBC, 22 January 2019.

Business assessment of political risk

For the company doing business in an overseas location, political risk comes in many guises. Assess the political risk for a foreign company in each of the following: (a) a military dictatorship; (b) a state in which a majority cultural grouping systematically suppresses a minority subculture; and (c) a monarchy where the ruling family asserts absolute authority.

Democracy and authoritarianism

democracy system of elected government based on free and fair elections and universal suffrage

authoritarianism rule by a single leader or group of individuals, often sustained by an ideology associated with a one-party state

Political systems are often classified along a continuum, with democracy at one end and authoritarianism at the other. Democracy broadly covers a range of political systems falling under the phrase, 'rule by the people', but popular sovereignty in theory can issue in a great diversity of institutional forms. In basic terms, **democracy** is rule by the people, through elected governments. **Authoritarianism** is rule by a single leader or small group of individuals, with unlimited power, usually dependent on military support to maintain stability.

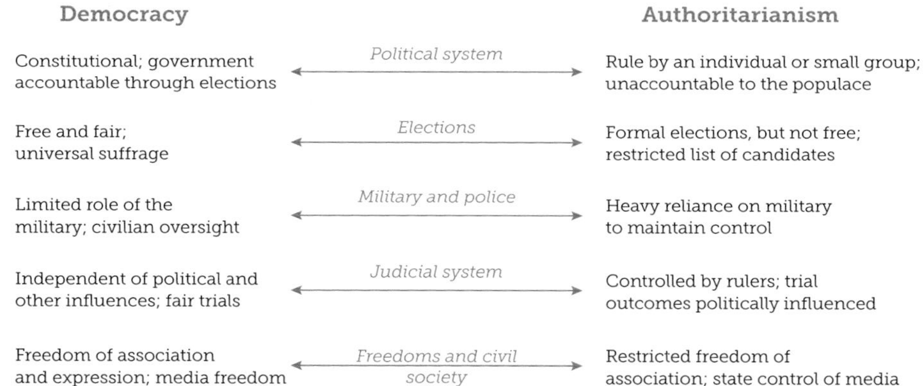

Democracy
Authoritarianism
Constitutional; government accountable through elections
Political system
Rule by an individual or small group; unaccountable to the populace
Free and fair; universal suffrage
Elections
Formal elections, but not free; restricted list of candidates
Limited role of the military; civilian oversight
Military and police
Heavy reliance on military to maintain control
Independent of political and other influences; fair trials
Judicial system
Controlled by rulers; trial outcomes politically influenced
Freedom of association and expression; media freedom
Freedoms and civil society
Restricted freedom of association; state control of media

Figure 5.4 Democracy vs. authoritarianism

Figure 5.4 contrasts democracy and authoritarianism. Aspects of democracy and authoritarianism are presented on a continuum, showing the key institutions that are influential in assessing whether a system inclines more towards democracy or more towards the authoritarian. The political system in a democracy is based on representative institutions which endure beyond the life of a particular government. The system promotes pluralism and individual freedoms, safeguarded by representative institutions. Authoritarian rule is based on personal power which does not tolerate political dissent or freedom of expression. Military and police establishments are essential in all countries, but they loom larger in an authoritarian regime. In a country with democratic institutions, we would expect there to be less reliance on

force, as the justice system and political accountability of governments are of greater significance. Elements of civil society are a crucial indicator of democratic rights. Whereas there is freedom of association and expression in a democracy, these rights are suppressed in the authoritarian regime, often with force.

Authoritarianism

In an authoritarian government, power is concentrated in the hands of the few, and this elite is largely unaccountable to the citizens for its actions. Authoritarian regimes vary from repressive military regimes to systems which have some democratic forms, such as elections, to choose among state-approved candidates. In all these cases, personal rule by a single leader or small group of individuals is the norm. These leaders have usually come up through the ranks of the military or the party in a one-party state. All independent political forces are banned, and any opposition to the regime is seen as a threat, typically suppressed by military force. Freedom of expression, a free press and freedom of association are all restricted. The judicial system is not independent, but run as an administrative arm of the state. The populist leader tends to fall into the authoritarian category, intolerant of either political dissent or the interests of any group outside the nationalist vision of the people. When the populist wins elections, the victor feels mandated to impose this nationalist ideology. Hugo Chavez in Venezuela and Victor Orban in Hungary both engineered the re-writing of their countries' constitutions, imposing executive authority on democratic institutions and the judiciary (Mudde, 2017).

Populism

A lecture by Cas Mudde, entitled, 'The rise of populism: from Le Pen to Trump', dated 29 May 2017. Professor Mudde is at the University of Georgia's School of Public and International Affairs, Athens, Georgia, USA.

Video link: Populism

https://youtu.be/wPt__1iALJo

Does the authoritarian government play a more positive role in countries focused on economic development? The economic success of China has led to a reappraisal of authoritarian governments. It might be thought that the authoritarian regime is inherently rigid, and that sooner or later it will topple. However, China's leadership has proved to be resilient, adapting to changing internal and external conditions, and using market reforms to boost economic growth. The Chinese leadership engages in a balancing act between freedom and control: balancing freedom of enterprise and state regulation, and balancing internet freedom and state censorship. It has been called an 'authoritarian capitalist' alternative to democracy (Plattner, 2010). While it had been assumed that authoritarian regimes inherently lack the moral credentials of legitimacy to govern that democratic systems offer, there is now a good deal of admiration for China's accomplishments, leading to a view that authoritarian governments are not as bad for societies as western political views have depicted them. It has been noteworthy that Donald Trump, reflecting his own belief in a strong executive, has shown deference towards authoritarian and militarist leaders, including the Russian and Chinese leaderships.

The 'economy first' view of development prioritizes economic development, implying that democratic reforms can be left until a later stage. This view is most notably exemplified by China, where the authoritarian regime has used oppressive means to retain its tight grip on power. Many developing countries now see this model as a legitimate alternative to received western views about liberal democracy, apparently unperturbed by the current lack of individual freedoms and weak human rights record. This view arguably rests on a mistaken conception of democracy as simply a set of formal mechanisms such as elections.

Businesspeople desire a stable environment, and some would argue that a stable authoritarian country is better for business than a turbulent democratic one. Many states under autocratic leadership maintain stability of a kind, through suppression of dissent and the use of coercive force. However, these tendencies indicate that the authoritarian government is inherently unsustainable. It naturally favours those in power, to the detriment of the wellbeing of all in society, creating the risk of political upheaval. Tensions beneath the surface can give rise to uprisings, as happened in the Arab spring. Political risks arise in both autocratic and democratic states. In the former, a foreign company can conclude a contract with the current leaders, only to find it altered unilaterally by new leadership at a later date. In a democracy, a change of government usually takes place at regular intervals along constitutional lines, but policy changes can still happen at any time. Furthermore, ethical concerns weigh with many companies. Does the firm wish to be seen doing business in a country with a record of human rights abuses? A firm could well decide that its apparent acquiescence risks damaging stakeholder relations both within the company and in other markets.

Democracy: in theory and in practice

Democracy is a system of government that is based on the principle of sovereignty of the people. This is rather an abstract idea, famously elucidated by Abraham Lincoln, who spoke of government 'of the people by the people and for the people' in his Gettysburg Address (Lincoln, 1863). Most definitions of democracy focus on the formal institutional aspects of representational institutions, including elections and the right to vote. These institutions are grounded in principles that emphasize the equality of all under the law. Thus, where citizens are seen as equal before the law, all should have the right to vote. The following is a list of identifying characteristics of democracy:

1. **Rule of law**, based on a constitution which establishes representative institutions, accountability of governments, and an independent judiciary. Thus, executive power is kept in check.
2. **Free and fair elections**, at relatively frequent intervals. These must provide for a free choice of candidates and the peaceful removal of representatives from office when they fail to secure enough votes, in accordance with the constitution. Reports of independent monitors are usually seen as a guarantee that the election has not been tainted by fraud.
3. **Universal right to vote for all adults**. Voting alone is the most minimal form of participation.
4. **Freedoms of expression, speech and association**. These political rights are essential to ensure competitive elections, in which all interests and groups may put forward their candidates. There should be independent media providing alternative sources of information to which citizens have access.
5. **Majority rule and minority rights**. Most countries have minority groups, who are often fearful that they will be oppressed by the majority. There must be safeguards to protect minorities as an essential element of civil society.

Most of the rights and freedoms listed above make 'liberal democracy', focusing on the role of the individual citizen, in a way analogous to the notion that economic liberalism is rooted in individualism. Citizens have diverse interests and values. They have ideas about what policies they wish to see adopted by government, and they feel they have a right to make these preferences weigh with elected governments (Gilens and Page, 2014). This, after all, is what gives a democracy its legitimacy. Many countries that have emerged from a colonial past have become fledgling democracies, but it is often difficult to graft democracy onto the cultural

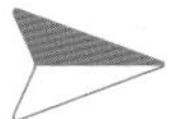

roots of authoritarianism. The former Soviet republics fall into this category, many still under autocratic leadership, despite the formalities of voting.

In the more established pluralist environments that characterize liberal democracies, numerous groups and interests, including business organizations, vie for political influence, raising the risk that the views of the average citizen are drowned out. It is not uncommon for citizens to feel disillusioned with politicians, who can often appear to serve their own interests rather than those of the electorate. Americans' trust in their government has fallen substantially in the last 50 years. Surveys of Americans by Pew Research Center show that in 1958, 73% of citizens expressed trust in the government. By 2017, the percentage of those surveyed who trusted government to do the right thing all or most of the time was down to just 20% (Pew Research Center, 2017). Is this just a sign that the political system cannot please everyone all the time, or deeper concerns about democracy?

Empirical academic research has concluded that in the US, economic elites and organized groups based on business interests have greater impacts on government policies than the wishes of ordinary citizens (Gilens and Page, 2014). The research found that on 1,779 public policy issues, where there is a proposed change, what matters is the support of the economic elites and organized business interests. These scholars concluded that, while Americans enjoy many of the features of democracy, such as regular elections and freedom of speech, 'America's claims to being a democratic *society* are seriously threatened' [my italics] (Gilens and Page, 2014: 577).

A political system that is outwardly democratic can mask a society in which inequalities effectively deny a voice to ordinary citizens. Formal institutions are therefore necessary, but not sufficient, to construct a democracy. Minimal 'electoral democracy' can be distinguished from liberal democracy, which stipulates pluralism and political freedoms for individuals and groups. Beyond liberal democracy, lies 'social democracy', which focuses on the broader social and economic spheres in society. Social democracy is concerned with the underlying social and economic conditions in a society, which contribute towards deeper participation than just voting. A sharply divided or unequal society, in which power is concentrated in an entrenched ruling elite, is not a democracy in this substantive sense, even though it may have a constitution and regular elections. As the research by Gilens and Page suggests, however, liberal democracy, which enshrines political freedoms and equality, can itself deviate from its participatory roots if the economic elite wield decisive power over political institutions. Liberal democracy therefore risks slipping backwards towards a system more akin to a minimal electoral democracy. Political scientists, Hacker and Pierson, point to the 'economic hyperconcentration' of entrenched elites as the force behind the decline of broad participation by ordinary people in democratic processes (Hacker and Pierson, 2010: 302). It can be argued that in these circumstances, there are likely to be growing numbers of disillusioned voters who feel their voices do not count and who feel that expectations of economic prosperity for themselves and their children are shrinking. These are voters that would naturally gravitate towards progressive leftwing politicians, but they are also drawn to populist politicians of both the left and the right.

Does business favour democracy?

Businesses everywhere favour a stable and predictable political environment. Does this necessarily mean a democracy? What aspects of democracy are businesses likely to see as conducive to their goals, and what aspects are not?

Democracy cannot always withstand shocks to the system, and can become destabilized. In what ways have the ideals of democracy been set back globally? Look at both established democracies and countries with limited democratic institutions.

Governmental institutions in national contexts

government structures and processes of the state by which laws are made and administered; also refers to the particular officeholders at any given time

A state encompasses people, territory and institutions, while **government** refers to the particular institutions by which laws are made and implemented. It can also refer to the particular individuals in office at a given time, as in 'the government of the day'. The institutions are enduring, but the occupants of office change over time, either by succession built into the system, or by irregular means, such as usurpation of authority. Where constitutions are respected by all, governments, in theory, should function smoothly and transparently. But in many places, the formal institutions are in place, while the occupants of office and their political roles are linked more to power and factional favours than the rule of law. We look first at the functions of government and then at the types of government that aim to maintain the legitimate exercise of political authority.

Overview of the functions of government

separation of powers the division between legislative, executive and judicial functions, or branches

legislative the lawmaking function within government

executive the function of government that administers laws and policies

judicial the function of government that interprets the law and provides checks on the other two branches

checks and balances principle by which the three branches of government share constitutional authority and accountability

It is customary to think of government as comprising three functions or branches: legislative, executive and judicial. The division of functions between the three is known as **separation of powers**. The **legislative** is the lawmaking branch. The legislature is central in a democracy, as it represents the electorate. The **executive** is at the head of government, responsible for administration and policy. The **judicial** function, located in the court system, interprets the law and thereby keeps a check on the other two branches. The system thus functions through the principle of **checks and balances**. Figure 5.5 shows the way the US Constitution envisaged checks and balances working. No branch has complete authority to act on its own. The president has important functions, such as the appointment of cabinet ministers and Supreme Court justices, but these appointments must be approved by the Senate. The president can negotiate treaties such as trade agreements, but these must be ratified by the Senate. However, where there is legislation in place, the law often delegates authority to the president to issue 'executive orders' under that authority. In this way, a president can issue executive orders on important issues, such as the raising of tariffs against other countries. The president's order of 2017 restricting immigration from predominantly Muslim countries was ostensibly issued under authority of a federal law, but the order was soon tested in the courts, indicating a concern that the president could be overstepping his constitutional authority (Strauss, 2018). The president is the commander-in-chief of the armed forces, but cannot declare war on another country: this can only be done by Congress.

Of the three branches, the US Congress as the lawmaking branch holds considerable legal authority. It controls the purse strings over federal tax and spending, and it must pass all laws. While the president can veto a bill, this veto can be overridden by a two-thirds vote in Congress. Congress alone – not the Supreme Court – has the power to impeach a president. It lies with the judiciary to see that the constitution is upheld. The Supreme Court is the ultimate court that decides on issues of constitutionality.

In general, law and policy therefore emanate mainly from legislative and executive branches, and more specifically from political interplay between the two, depending on the balance of power within the system. In practice, most systems have considerable overlap between these functions. We look at each branch in turn, beginning with the legislative.

Most countries have a national assembly of representatives, whether elected or not. In authoritarian systems, the assembly is merely advisory, rubberstamping the decisions made by the ruling elite. This type of assembly has no actual lawmaking

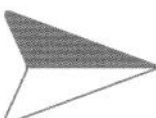

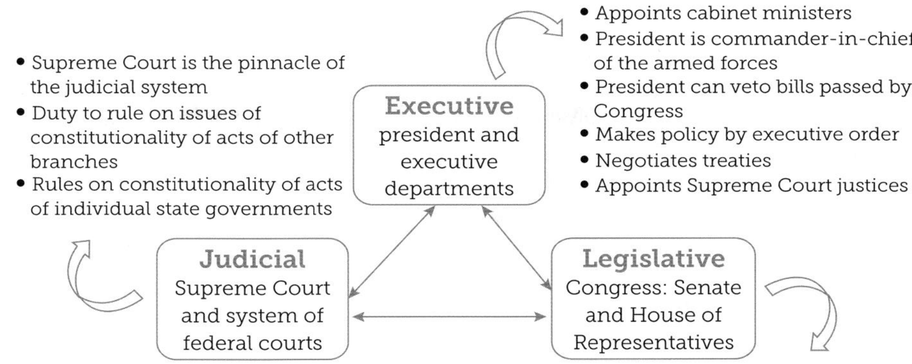
Executive
president and executive departments
• Appoints cabinet ministers
• President is commander-in-chief of the armed forces
• President can veto bills passed by Congress
• Makes policy by executive order
• Negotiates treaties
• Appoints Supreme Court justices
Judicial
Supreme Court and system of federal courts
• Supreme Court is the pinnacle of the judicial system
• Duty to rule on issues of constitutionality of acts of other branches
• Rules on constitutionality of acts of individual state governments
Legislative
Congress: Senate and House of Representatives
• Lawmaking authority–Bills must pass both houses
• Must pass tax and spending legislation
• Congress can override an executive veto with a 2/3 vote
• Right to declare war
• Right to impeach the president and other federal officers
• Senate: approves appointments of cabinet ministers and justices of the Supreme Court; ratifies treaties

Figure 5.5 **Constitutional checks and balances: the US model**

legislative assembly body of elected representatives within a state, which has lawmaking responsibilities

powers. In a democracy, the **legislative assembly** lies at the heart of the political system, representing the sovereignty of the people. It carries the main lawmaking function, but this function operates differently in different systems of government, all of which have legislative powers expressly provided in their constitutions. Many countries have legislatures consisting of two houses (bicameral), where the lower house is the main lawmaking body. In the US, both houses, the House of Representatives (the lower house) and the Senate (the upper house) are directly elected. In the UK only the House of Commons (the lower house) is elected. The unelected upper house, the House of Lords, is often seen as anomalous, and has been a subject of much debate concerning its future composition and powers. Its role has been gradually reduced to one of a revising chamber. But this is not necessarily to belittle its role: on occasion the scrutiny paid by its members to particular pieces of legislation plays a vital critical role in the overall process of lawmaking. It is likely to undergo further reform, but not to be abolished.

The third branch of government, the judicial, acts as a check on the legislative and executive. The legal environment in general will be discussed in the next chapter. Here we focus on the judicial function as a branch of government. The judicial function is carried out by the state's system of courts. In a constitutional system, the judges are tasked with ensuring that the country's laws passed by the legislature are consistent with the constitution. For firms and individuals, the way that the laws are applied in practice in the country's courts is of utmost importance. The rule of law and an independent judiciary are core to any constitutional system, and are crucial to a functioning democracy. These principles imply that the law is above any individual, whether an officeholder or a rich and powerful private person. To be independent, the members of the judiciary should be seen to be impartial: a judge who is in the pay of an interest group is not suitable for office. In order for the judicial function to act as an effective check on the other two branches of government, procedures must be devised to call officeholders to account if they have acted unlawfully. The member of the legislature who takes money from a firm for helping to secure a government contract is acting unlawfully, although many firms seek such advantages through payment of politicians.

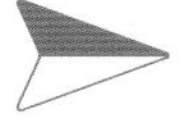

Systems of government

The second branch, the executive, provides strong leadership in some systems, and only a co-ordinating role in others. We look at three types of system: presidential, parliamentary and 'hybrid'. A summary of their characteristics is shown in Table 5.1. These will now be discussed.

Table 5.1 Systems of government

	Presidential	Parliamentary	Hybrid system
Advantages	Strong executive based on popular mandate; fixed term of office	Executive reflects electoral support in parliament	Strong executive imparts unity; prime minister co-ordinates parliamentary programme
Disadvantages	Possible disaffection among electorate	Thin majority may lead to breakdown of government	Conflict between president and prime minister
Stability	Stable executive, but legislature may be dominated by the opposing party, stifling lawmaking agenda	Stable if prime minister has a large majority; coalition and minority governments can be unstable	Fixed-term president imparts stability; but successive coalition governments can be unstable in multi-party systems

presidential system system of government in which the head of the executive branch, the president, is elected by the voters, either directly or through an electoral college (as in the US)

A **presidential system** is thought of as producing a strong chief executive, as presidents are normally directly elected and thus have a personal mandate. The US is the leading example of a presidential system, but here – largely due to the founding fathers' inherent fear of a purely democratic vote – the president is not directly elected. The US Constitution provides that an electoral college is assembled after a general election, to which each state sends delegates representing its voters' choice. Typically, where a candidate wins, say 51% of the vote, all the state's delegates are allocated to that candidate. Although it rarely happens, the winning candidate in the electoral college may not be the one that received the most votes in the country as a whole. In 2016, Mrs Clinton, the Democratic candidate, won by 3 million votes in the country as a whole, but lost to Mr Trump in the electoral college. In light of the thinking of the constitution's authors, it is perhaps paradoxical that the electoral college system delivered a non-mainstream, populist winner, while a direct democratic vote would have produced a more mainstream victor.

Checks on executive power are provided by a country's constitution and also by a vigorous two-party system that is reflected in the legislature. Latin American countries have been proponents of the presidential system, and in these countries a strong presidency is often grounded in political culture, in which nationalism and populism are prominent features. Inherent drawbacks of the 'winner-takes-all' nature of presidential elections are that supporters of the losing candidates may feel alienated, while the winner may overestimate the popular mandate, 'conflating his supporters with the people as a whole' (Linz, 1993: 118). Supporters of minority parties are thus inclined to feel that their interests are not being served by the system. The president should focus on the public interest, but in practice, often focuses on promoting the interests of the majority party, including business interests. The closing case study on Turkey highlights these risks.

Although the US presidential system exemplifies a strong executive, the US president's position is more complicated than might appear. As commander of the armed forces, the US president has enormous authority over military deployment, and presidents have expanded national security powers, such as mass surveillance. However, in many important areas, such as health, trade and justice, legislators in Congress are in a strong position to challenge the executive. The

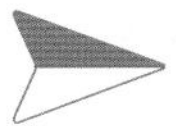

president's policies often face an uphill battle in Congress, especially as Congress must approve the necessary funding.

parliamentary system system of government in which voters directly elect members of parliament, from whom a prime minister is chosen

In a **parliamentary system**, the voters directly elect members of parliament, from whom a prime minister and cabinet are selected, usually from the political party with a majority of seats. This is often called the 'Westminster model', as the leading example is the UK. The efficient running of a parliamentary system depends greatly on the nature and number of a country's political parties. It is usually felt that it works best in a stable two-party system of 'government' and 'opposition' parties, in which the opposition is, in effect, an alternative government. A coalition government of Conservatives (with 306 seats) and Liberal Democrats (with 57 seats) was the outcome of the UK general election in 2010. This partnership proved difficult to manage because of policy differences. The outright victory of the Conservatives in 2015 gave them the mandate that had eluded them in 2010. However, the 2017 general election again plunged the country into an unstable situation. The Conservatives were the largest party, but lacked a majority, negotiating an agreement with a Northern Irish party, the Democratic Unionist Party (DUP) to support it in critical votes.

Turnout in democratic elections is indicative of belief in the democratic process. Turnout in UK general elections was in the 70–80% region throughout most of the post-war period, and dived to a low of 59.6% only in 2001 (see Figure 5.6). It then climbed in successive elections, reaching 68.7% in 2017. The turnout among the 18–24 age group reached a low of 38% in 2005, but had climbed to 58% in 2015, largely as a result of efforts to encourage people to register to vote. It continued to climb, reaching 64% in 2017. This was the highest turnout of younger voters since 1992.

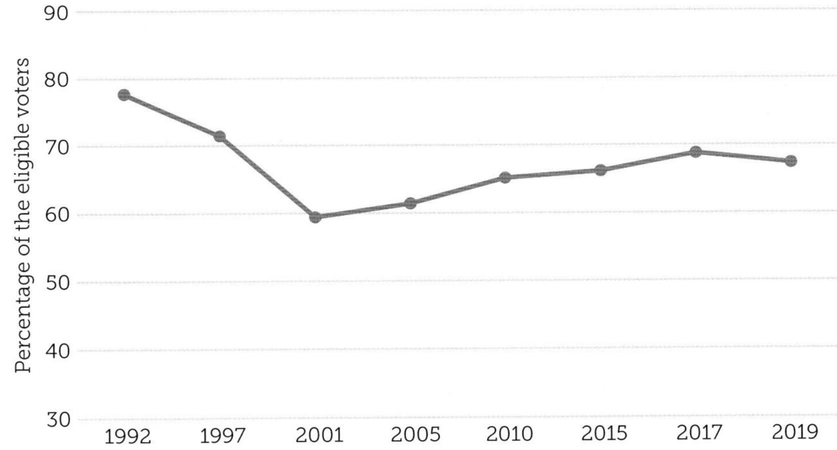

Figure 5.6 Voter turnout in UK general elections

Source of data: Statista, voter turnout in general elections, at www.statista.com/statistics/1050929/voter-turnout-in-the-uk/ accessed 31 January 2020.

hybrid system a system of government in which the president is directly elected, and the prime minister, who heads the cabinet, is chosen by the legislative assembly

The so-called '**hybrid system**' aims to achieve both a stable executive and maximum representation, with an independently-elected president and a prime minister selected by parliament to head the cabinet. The model for this system, also known as the dual executive, is the Fifth French Republic. Apart from Hungary, which has a parliamentary system, the post-communist states of Central and Eastern Europe have adopted the hybrid model. The theory is that the nationally-elected president can foster national unity, playing the role of head of state, while the prime minister plays more of a party-political role, maintaining support for the government in parliament. In practice, these systems may not run as smoothly as envisaged if the two executives are of different parties or, as is almost inevitable, each sees the other as a rival. In new democracies such as Poland and the Czech Republic, where politics tends to focus on personalities, the role of president can be seen as a strong political platform.

MINI CASE STUDY

The rule of law at risk in Poland

Among the EU's fundamental principles are adherence to the rule of law and an independent judiciary. Poland's ruling Law and Justice Party, which took over the reins of government in 2015, has introduced sweeping changes in the country's democratic institutions, causing alarm bells to ring in the EU. The rightwing nationalist party has said that it aims to clean up the corruption of the existing system, that had not been modernized since the fall of communism. However, the reforms it has introduced have had the effect of removing the independence of the judiciary, one of the pillars of the rule of law.

The government has passed laws that give it powers of appointment over the constitutional court, the national judiciary council (which oversees judicial appointments) and the supreme court. A result has been that dozens of judges were effectively removed from office. A new law set the retirement age for the supreme court at 65. This meant that 27 of the 74 judges were to be removed through early retirement. In combination with a law expanding the supreme court to 120 judges, the effect was to allow the government to make new appointments of two-thirds of the supreme court judges. Another new law allowed the government to appoint a new head of the supreme court. This measure led to street protests throughout Poland as people feared for the future of its democracy.

In further judicial reforms, the government intends to introduce a 'disciplinary' chamber and an extraordinary appeal chamber that would allow cases from the last 20 years to be re-opened, and to be heard again by judges appointed by the government. In addition, there is a reform taking place that allows members of the public selected by the politicians to sit alongside judges on the supreme court. The cumulative effect of these reforms gives the government effective political control over the judiciary.

The European Commission launched hearings against Poland for its alleged failure to abide by democratic principles, as required in the EU treaty. This was followed by action in the European Court of Justice (ECJ), which would freeze the changes so that the ECJ could rule on whether Poland complied with EU law. In October 2018, the ECJ ordered Poland to suspend its reforms of the supreme court.

In a show of dissent with the direction the country is taking, young people in Poland take to the streets to protest.

Questions

- Poland's rightwing government feels that its democratic mandate gives it the authority to make the changes in the name of the people. Do you agree or disagree, and why?
- What are the risks to the EU arising from Poland's judicial reforms?

Find out more

See a background article by Steve Crawshaw, 'The rule of law is under assault in Poland', 11 March 2016, in *The Guardian*.

Elections as participation

Free and fair elections are a key element in political participation in a democracy. Voters elect the president if there is one, the legislators, and even judges (in individual US states). They also vote in referendums and other forms of direct democracy. Every voter should have confidence in the fairness, meaningfulness and transparency of the election process: my vote and my voice should matter. Unfortunately, this is not the case around the globe, and even in established systems, there is widespread disillusionment with the electoral process. As we have noted above, the power of big businesses over candidates and policies detract from democratic values. But voters in US presidential elections might also feel their votes do not count, because the constitution gives the electoral college the final say in the election of the president.

proportional representation principle underlying systems of electoral representation in which seats are allocated in proportion to the votes obtained by each candidate or party

two-party system political system in which there are two major political parties, alternating between government and opposition depending on the outcome of elections

multi-party system system in which many political parties participate, representing a wide spectrum of views

Legislators have lawmaking authority in any democratic system. Electoral systems for legislative representatives vary from country to country. It can be the traditional first-past-the-post system or one of the more recent **proportional representation** systems (PR), which allocate seats in proportion to the votes obtained. The first-past-the-post system has predominated in the US and UK, although elections for devolved assemblies in Scotland and Wales are based on PR. The US and UK have a **two-party system**, whereby two mainstream political parties are politically dominant. A **multi-party system**, where there are numerous parties representing a variety of views and interests, is more likely to adopt PR. Most European countries (and also the European Parliament) have opted for PR. Outcomes in PR systems represent a broader political spectrum, giving small parties a greater prospect of winning seats than a first-past-the-post system, where they may win sizeable voter support but fail to win many seats.

PR systems are considered to be friendlier to women candidates. Women worldwide held 23.9% of seats in national legislatures in 2018, up from 18.7% in 2010. There are wide disparities among countries. Figure 5.7 shows the percentages as of 1 January 2019. Cuba comes top with 53% women legislators. Scandinavian countries have relatively large percentages of women parliamentarians. In these countries, governments have introduced policies aimed at increasing the number of women candidates.

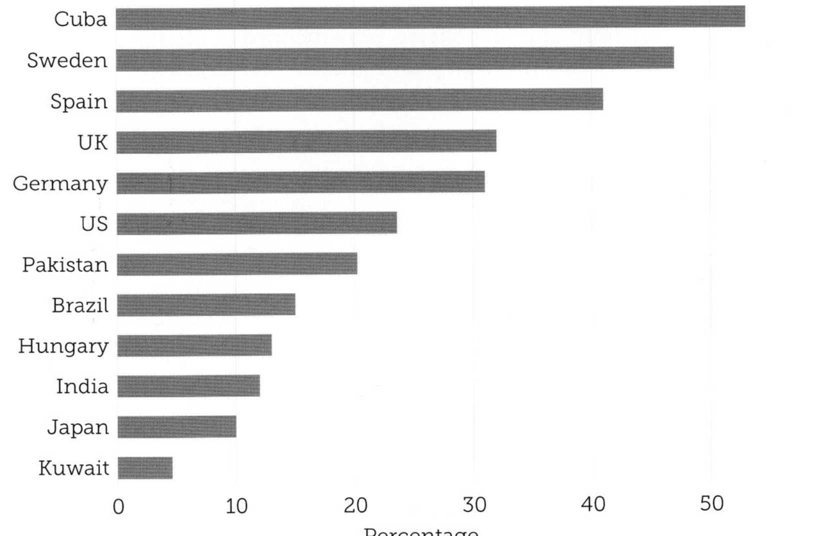

Figure 5.7 Women in national legislatures in selected countries (lower or single house), 2019

Source of data: from Inter-Parliamentary Union, Women in national parliaments, as of 1 January 2019, at https://data.ipu.org, accessed 12 April 2019.

A drawback of proportional representation is that in a multi-party system, if many parties secure seats, it may be difficult to form a government, and political instability could result. In these circumstances, the largest party usually secures support from one or more smaller parties to form a **coalition government**, which is made up of two or more parties. This arrangement can lead to tensions in the tasks of legislating and forming policies. Aware of its power to bring down the government, a minor party in a coalition may demand a 'price' for its co-operation in terms of key policies, to keep it on board. It could be argued that coalition government is more representative of electoral support, and hence more democratic, but a major disadvantage is its potential instability.

coalition government government composed of two or more parties, usually arising in situations where no single party has obtained a majority of seats in legislative elections

Citizens do not vote only for legislators and other officeholders. The **referendum** is an example of direct democracy, and is used to complement the legislative function carried out by the assembly. In a referendum, voters are invited to approve or reject a question on a particular issue. In some states (such as Italy) it is a constitutional requirement; in others (such as the UK) it is optional. Some examples of the varied uses of the referendum are:

referendum a type of direct democracy in which electors cast a vote on a particular issue

- Devolution in Scotland and Wales, 1997
- Decision to join the UN by the Swiss in 2002, following earlier rejection in 1986
- The end of apartheid in South Africa, 1992
- The decision not to join the eurozone by Denmark (2000) and Sweden (2002)
- The decision of voters in Scotland to remain in the UK in 2014
- Vote in the UK in 2016 to leave the EU

The advantage of the referendum is that it acts as a check on elected governments, giving citizens an opportunity to express a view on an issue of the day. A drawback, however, is that citizens are typically asked to make a yes/no decision although the issues are complex. Moreover, ordinary citizens are not necessarily well informed of the ramifications of proposed changes. This was particularly highlighted in the context of Britain's vote to leave the EU, discussed in detail later in this chapter.

Where the referendum is specifically included in a state's constitution, it is usually subject to conditions such as a threshold of voter turnout and a threshold for a majority to succeed. This is the case in Italy, where the referendum is used regularly, and referendums often fail for these reasons. However, one in 2016, a constitutional referendum designed to streamline the legislative process, was decisively rejected, following a high turnout. Anti-establishment voters, especially those protesting over immigration policies, were inclined to use the occasion to protest against the government. The result was an indication of the rise of populist and nationalist politicians.

The president versus the prime minister

Any business prefers an environment in which there is a clear political agenda, followed up by effective governmental institutions that implement the policies set out by the government. Which system of government is more likely to govern in this way: a presidential or parliamentary system?

A presidential system might seem to exert stronger leadership. But in practice, systems with strong executive presidents often unsettle businesses. Why?

Political life in practice

Where do policies and proposed legislation come from? How do democracies differ from authoritarian regimes? And what is the role of business in these processes? These are the questions addressed in this section. Policies and new laws usually emerge in the context of groups, both formal and informal, that participate in political

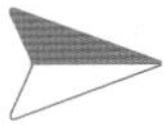

activities within a country. Political parties are the most high profile of these groups, and they are active in both democratic and authoritarian systems. But other types of political grouping are also active, as are interest groups. Organized groups also include business interests. Businesses are highly sensitive to political decision-making processes, and play active roles. Conflicting interests and agendas thus make up the multi-faceted scene of politics in practice.

Political parties and related groups

political party organization of people with similar political beliefs, which aims to put forward candidates for office and influence government policies

Political parties are a feature of political life in many kinds of political system, whether democratic or undemocratic. A **political party** is usually a voluntary organization whose members come together to promote their own political outlook and put forward candidates for elected office. These functions are central to the institutions of representative democracies. Political parties form the link between voters and legislative assemblies. In democratic states, they are essential to the pluralism which characterizes civil society. In authoritarian and semi-authoritarian states, political parties help to cement the ideology of the leadership, and mobilize public support. We look at democratic systems first.

In a pluralist society, parties perform several functions:

1 They provide candidates for public office, who rely on their organizational machinery and funding to get elected. The independent candidate faces an uphill battle, and needs to be very rich.
2 They provide a policy platform, on which voters can decide whom to support. Many voters traditionally are party loyalists, not bothered about who the individual candidate is.
3 When in office, they provide an agenda for government, against which performance can be judged.

Parties vary in their political agendas and in their views of society. Some embrace strong ideological positions, such as communist parties and populist parties. Others are religious in origin, such as Muslim parties and Christian parties. Parties may also emerge from interest groups, such as the Green Party, which concentrates on ecological issues. Most of the narrowly-based parties have little hope of gaining a majority of legislative seats and forming a government; instead, they seek publicity and political influence for their views. They are more likely to win seats in multi-party systems with proportional representation. In two-party systems, such as the US and UK, the trend has been towards the 'catch-all' party, with weaker ideological underpinning. The Brexit referendum, however, led to a more polarized and ideological political scene, in which the two main parties showed signs of splintering. A shift towards a multi-party system could be taking place. Political parties depend on funding largely from supporters, among whom wealthy donors are prominent. Corporate donors are also active. Although many states attempt to regulate funding, for example, by capping election spending, such rules are difficult to enforce, especially in the era of social media. Election spending is a fertile area for corruption, in which politicians and wealthy donors can become enmeshed.

Political parties are usually described in terms of 'left', 'right' and 'centre', with the modern catch-all parties falling somewhere near the centre. These categories are largely based on approaches to economic issues. The Labour Party in Britain is a party of the left, long positioning itself within socialist policies, and it has long had ties with trade unions. Parties on the left generally support high public spending on social services, protection of workers, and trade union rights; they tend to oppose the privatization of public services. The Democratic Party in the US falls broadly within this tradition. Parties on the right, known almost universally as 'conservatives', generally wish to see a minimum of government intervention in business, reduced public spending, and low taxes. They favour more privatization of the

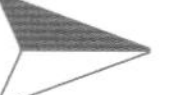

economy, reducing the size of government bureaucracy. The Conservatives in the UK and the Republicans in the US fall into this broad category.

Nationalist and populist political outlooks do not neatly fit the left–right criteria, as we have noted: they rest on cultural and social identities as well as economic concerns. Many nationalist parties are separatist, wishing to form an independent nation-state. There are three separatist Catalan parties in Spain that, together, have exerted destabilizing pressures on the central government, and have also caused uncertainty among Catalan businesses. In Italy, where there is a long history of populism, the Lega Nord, is a northern separatist party. It rebranded itself as simply the 'Lega' in the 2018 elections, and gained support from across Italy, largely because of its anti-immigration stance.

Populism has led to emotionally charged and divisive politics. The populist leader promises to throw out existing party elites and restore the values of the 'people'. Populists have gained support in numerous countries, often winning supporters away from the moderate right and centre-right parties that support multiculturalism. President Trump in the US is such a leader, running for president as a Republican. Anti-immigration measures were among his early priorities, issuing a travel ban that targeted Muslim-majority countries and imposing a harsher regime to prosecute illegal immigrants along the border with Mexico.

In Germany, the extreme right, anti-immigrant AfD (Alternative for Germany) gained an unprecedented 12.6% in the general election of 2017. This result left the dominant centre-right party of the current Chancellor, Angela Merkel of the CDU (Christian Democratic Union) in a weakened position. It was not until four months after the election that she was able to form a coalition government, which was an unstable alliance with the leftwing Social Democrats. A strong factor in the rise of the right was opposition to Mrs Merkel's policy of welcoming migrants in large numbers.

In pluralist societies, numerous other groups exist to promote political agendas reflecting members of the group. Many of these are grassroots organizations, often focused on particular local issues. But they can also be entities established or funded by wealthy businesspeople who seek to influence political decision-making towards their own values and goals. These groups can be 'think tanks', appearing to be quasi-academic, but in fact ideologically inspired. They can be political action committees, as in the US, where they promote particular causes and are active campaigners during elections. Also in the US, they are often created as not-for-profit foundations that are allowed to channel money from wealthy donors to political causes.

A US Supreme Court in a judgment in 2010 known as the 'Citizens United' judgment, held (by a majority of 5 to 4) that a company has a right to free speech analogous to that of the individual citizen. Individuals and companies can thus give unlimited amounts of money to their favoured political causes. The majority of the Supreme Court justices took the view that corporate money did not jeopardize democracy, to the dismay of the dissenting judges, who feared for the democratic principle that 'democracy is founded on an equal access to the public sphere' (Hacker and Pierson, 2010: 293).

The power of business elites has been the main factor in growing economic inequality, and this power now extends into the political sphere, resulting in widening political inequality. The hallmark of democracy, the right of all to democratic participation, seems to have been transformed into a kind of shallow participation. The formalities of participation have persisted, but democratic accountability has arguably been eroded (Wolin, 2008). Wolin argued that the concentration of economic power and political power has thus undermined the democratic institutions enshrined in the US Constitution. Since Wolin put forward these warnings, the influence of business elites has grown. And the rise of populism has seen Mr Trump take a more authoritarian interpretation of the role of the president.

Authoritarian states are typically one-party systems, where parties not approved by the leadership are banned. In China, the Communist Party is the dominant

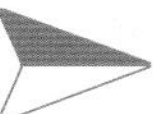

institutional force, in effect capturing the state. The state's institutions, while appearing to be autonomous, are in practice controlled by the party. Russia is a more complex example. Here there was a democratic transition and privatization of the economy, resulting in economic power concentrated in the hands of powerful oligarchs that controlled key industries. Russia under Vladimir Putin, who has been in control since 2000, has taken on the aggressive nationalist and authoritarian style of government that characterized the former Soviet Union. The oligarchs have been tamed by Putin, and the state has reasserted control over Gazprom, the gas giant. Russia's annexation of parts of Ukraine, which became independent after the fall of the USSR, has indicated a resurgence of Russia's expansionist ambitions, and arguably rekindled cold-war attitudes. The dominant United Russia party is firmly in control, and other political organizations, as well as NGOs, have little freedom. With little press freedom and precarious freedom of association, elections fall short of being free and fair.

Business engagement in political processes

Companies, business interest groups, charitable foundations and think tanks: we have already seen the many organizational ways in which businesses can take part in political decision-making. But what are their aims? Businesses are highly sensitive to the political climate in every country where they are active or have active affiliates. They seek stability and certainty in both policy and governmental processes that affect their activities. Governmental organizations can be envisaged as important stakeholders. Positive stakeholder dialogue can contribute to business success in any location, as well as building relations with communities. However, the line between improving relations with governmental bodies and engaging in excessive influence, bribery and other corrupt activities can sometimes be blurred. Businesses routinely lobby governments to promote policies that favour their activities, including tax reductions and reductions in regulation. **Lobbying** is a broad term that covers the activities of business and other groups that seek to influence people in political decision-making offices. In the US, lobbying legislators in Washington, DC, is a multibillion dollar industry. Lobbying is also big business in the UK, other European capitals and the EU. The risk of bribery and corruption is high: legislators can be offered money and other benefits by business interests for promoting an issue, voting a particular way on an issue, or hiring particular individuals. Lobbying is regulated in most of these jurisdictions, in that lobbyists are required to register and maintain transparency in their activities. However, much lobbying is carried on outside these regulatory structures by people not strictly classified as lobbyists. Thus, lobbying activities can be highly influential in accessing politicians while taking place underneath the radar of the regulatory mechanisms.

• **lobbying** political activities of businesses and other groups that seek to influence policies, laws and the decisions made by public officeholders

In the UK, business lobbying has tended to focus on Parliament, but lobbying of the devolved legislative bodies in Scotland, Northern Ireland and Wales, as well as government ministries, is also widespread. Lobbying in the UK has become big business, estimated to be worth £2 billion a year (Transparency International UK, 2015). Most of this activity is associated with legitimate democratic activities of providing information and accessing the views of stakeholder parties. However, various lobbying scandals in the UK have brought to light the darker aspects of how decision-making is being influenced for promoting particular interests. Examples include MPs accepting money to lobby on behalf of a particular cause and officials taking jobs with companies that had been within their remit when they were in public office. It might seem incongruous, but MPs are allowed to have conflicts of interest so long as these are declared, apparently legitimating the practice of accepting benefits from a lobbyist. Political parties in the UK are allowed to accept

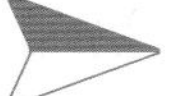

donations without limit, and wealthy donors are typically rewarded with appointment to the House of Lords. Research by Transparency International has found that 76% of UK respondents think that wealthy individuals use their influence on the government to serve their own interests and that there should be stricter rules in place in this respect (Transparency International UK, 2016). Just 100 donors accounted for 95% of the donations to both the 'leave' and 'remain' campaigns in the UK's EU referendum, and over half of these donors were significant donors to political parties.

Lobbying of governments and elected representatives by business interests is often depicted as two sided: on the one hand, politicians who must focus on the public interest and on the other hand, businesses that promote self-interested agendas. In fact, recent years have seen an increasingly active 'revolving door' between politicians and lobbyists. The politician is likely to see a lucrative lobbying role as a logical career step after serving in public office. A political career is more-than-ever entwined with a business one. The revolving door between business and politics in liberal democratic systems poses risks that the interests of ordinary citizens are being squeezed out.

Focus on the European Union

Regional groupings of states have grown in numbers in the post-war period. Most of these are trading alliances, but the most advanced, the EU, represents much deeper economic, social and political integration. It is featured here because its political system has become integral to the national political systems of member states. This process has not been without controversy. Originally comprising a group of six states (Germany, France, Belgium, Luxembourg, the Netherlands, and Italy) under the Treaty of Rome in 1957, the European Community as it then was, envisaged a 'pooling' of national sovereignty. When Britain joined in 1973, the possibility of the erosion of parliamentary sovereignty was a major issue, and it has remained so, particularly among 'eurosceptics'. Despite misgivings about national sovereignty, perceived economic benefits made the EU popular, reaching a total of 28 members (see Chapter 4). However, the EU has faced challenges from national governments and the rise in nationalist populist parties.

EU institutions: democratic reforms

The EU's main institutions are the Council, which was envisaged as holding the main lawmaking authority, the Commission, through which much legislation originated, and the Parliament, which acted mainly as a check on the other two bodies. The judicial function is in the authority of the European Court of Justice, which oversees adherence to EU laws and gives authoritative interpretation of their provisions (see further discussion in Chapter 6). The enlargement debate has raised questions about the effectiveness and democratic credentials of these structures, perceived as unwieldy, over-bureaucratic, and lacking in democratic accountability. A proposed new constitution for the enlarged EU was put forward in 2004, but rejected in referendums in two countries (France and the Netherlands). A revised document was put forward as the Lisbon Treaty. A key aspect of the Lisbon Treaty, which took effect in December 2009, was to enhance the powers of the European Parliament.

The highest lawmaking authority in the EU is the Council of Ministers, renamed the Council of the European Union in 1993. Members are ministers in their own states. Under the Lisbon Treaty, a new president of the European Council was appointed. He was intended to replace the previous arrangement of a six-month rotating presidency among member states, but in fact, the rotating presidency

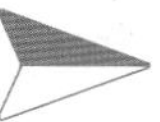

continued. Originally, unanimity among council members was required for a proposal to proceed, but this requirement has been relaxed in some key areas (for example, agriculture, the environment and transport) by 'qualified majority voting' (QMV). A safeguard for small countries is the provision that a vote is carried if it is supported by at least 55% of member states representing 65% of the overall population of the EU. National veto is still retained on issues of tax, defence, foreign policy and financing the EU budget. A new office of high representative for foreign affairs has been created, to oversee the diplomatic service. The aim of creating the new foreign affairs post was to raise the EU's foreign relations profile.

The European Commission is composed of one commissioner from each member state. The Commission is headed by a President. The Directorates-General of the Commission are the heart of the EU's civil service, responsible for its day-to-day running. Importantly, in addition, the Commission takes the lead in proposing legislation, and thus enjoys considerable political power from its 'agenda-setting' initiatives, such as the Single Market and Monetary Union. The 2004 constitutional plan provided for a reduction in the number of commissioners to 18 from 2014 onwards. There were objections to this streamlining of the Commission, and the proposed reduction in size of the Commission was shelved.

The European Parliament is composed of members from each state roughly in proportion to the state's population. The EU Parliament has grown in size from 78 to 736 members. Although Members of the European Parliament (MEPs) have been directly elected by EU citizens since 1979, the parliament does not play the pivotal role which is customary in national systems. The Treaty of Rome gave parliament little direct say in legislation, but with later treaties, it gained greater influence, with an increase from 15 to 38 areas in which has 'co-decision-making' powers with the Council (amounting to two-thirds of all EU legislation). These reforms have come in response to criticism that EU institutions lack sufficient democratic accountability and that they are bureaucratic and inefficient. The new constitutional treaty also provides for increased scrutiny of proposed legislation by national parliaments.

The European Parliament has not as yet resonated with voters to the same extent that national parliaments do. However, due to the enhanced powers contained in the treaty revisions, the parliament has gained in voice and confidence. As Figure 5.8 shows, voter turnout declined with each successive election up to 2014, reaching a low of 42.61% that year. This trend was reversed in 2019, when a rise in participation seemed to indicate a renewed interest in the European Parliament. The EU's PR voting system has facilitated multiple parties, reflecting a wide range of perspectives. The increased turnout owed much to the rise of populist and eurosceptic parties in

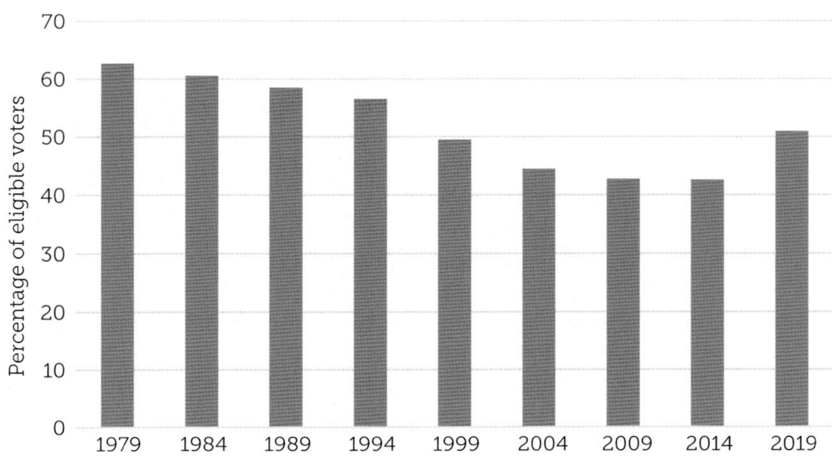

Figure 5.8 Voter turnout in European Parliament elections

Source: Politico, European elections voter turnout, at www.politico.eu, accessed 20 June 2019.

many member states. These parties have become a high-profile presence in national politics, and their members have gone on to stand for office as Members of the European Parliament (MEPs). The newly-formed Brexit Party in the UK gained 29 seats in the European Parliament in 2019, even though it wished to leave the EU.

Britain's path towards exiting the EU

The referendum is a means of directly engaging the public in political decisions. It can perform only an advisory role, or it can be binding, in that the government is compelled to act in accordance with the result. The referendum is commonly included in written constitutions in democratic states, in some cases as part of the process of altering the constitution itself. For such important changes, the constitution might provide safeguards such as a threshold that must be attained in order to adopt the referendum's proposed change. For example, there could be a requirement that the turnout must reach a particular percentage (as in Italy, where the threshold is 50% + 1), or that the proposal must be approved by a 'super-majority' such as 60% of those voting. There could also be a provision that the proposal must be approved by 40% of the total electorate.

In the UK, a referendum on whether the country should remain in the EU was held in 1975. The electorate voted to do so, with a percentage of 67.2% voting to remain. Over forty years later, the Brexit referendum of 2016 was authorized by an act of Parliament, the European Union Referendum Act of 2015. That statute specified that the referendum would be non-binding. None of the thresholds outlined above applied. In the referendum of June, 2016, the British electorate voted in favour of exiting the EU, known as 'Brexit'. In a turnout of 70% of the electorate, 51.9% voted to leave, and 48.1% voted to remain in the EU. The campaign had been bitter, notably galvanized by the 'leave' campaign's anti-immigration message couched in populist nationalist rhetoric. Surveys showed anti-immigration was the decisive issue with voters. The polling organization, Ipsos Mori, found that 55% of voters felt that government should have total control over immigration, even if it meant withdrawing from the EU, while 33% felt that it was important for Britain to remain in the EU, even though this meant that the government did not have total control over immigration (Ipsos Mori, 2016). The leave campaign pressed objections to 'rule from Brussels', highlighting what they saw as excessive regulation from the EU, the supremacy of EU law over UK law and the undermining of British sovereignty. Their message of 'taking back control' seemed to chime with voters, but victory in the referendum turned out to be the start of a very tortuous and complex process with unprecedented complications for government, businesses and ordinary people.

The government of prime minister David Cameron fell following the referendum, and Theresa May took over as the prime minister. She called a general election in 2017, in which the Conservatives emerged as the largest party, but without an absolute majority in the House of Commons. The fragility of a minority government made it difficult for her to govern effectively, amidst splits forming in her own party. As noted earlier in this chapter, the Conservatives reached an agreement with the Northern Irish party, the Democratic Unionist Party (DUP), to support the government in Parliament.

In March 2017, Mrs May triggered the exit process by delivering a letter to the European Council president, which announced Britain's intention to withdraw from the EU. There would be a withdrawal agreement negotiated with the EU, followed by a two-year transition period. A settling of accounts with the EU would have to be negotiated initially, involving a payment of funds by the UK to cover continuing EU liabilities. UK officials negotiated a withdrawal agreement with counterparts in the European Commission, but the UK Parliament rejected this

agreement three times. The exit date was meant to be 29 March 2019, but that date had to be delayed due to the lack of parliamentary approval of the withdrawal agreement. A 'no-deal' or 'hard' Brexit looked likely. This would entail implementing WTO tariffs on all UK-EU trade, entailing severe congestion at UK ports. Ports would have to be geared up to impose the necessary border controls, necessitating considerable extra infrastructure. Delays would inevitably result. Continuing supplies of essentials such as food and medicine would be under threat, not to mention goods essential to supply chains. Having failed to secure support for her withdrawal agreement, Mrs May stepped down as the party's leader and prime minister. The Conservative Party elected Boris Johnson as their new leader, and he became prime minister. A fresh general election was called in December, 2019. The Conservatives campaigned on a promise to 'get Brexit done'. They won a substantial majority of 80 seats. A revised withdrawal agreement was passed, setting the exit date as 31 January 2020.

The main issues in the Brexit debate are outlined below:

- Rights of EU citizens in the UK and UK citizens residing in EU countries – Freedom of movement for people to live and work in other EU countries has been integral to the single market. EU citizens in the UK are employed in large numbers in many sectors, from low-paid jobs in catering to highly-skilled positions in hospitals. The organizations that employ these workers urge that they be allowed to continue to live and work in the UK, but immigration status has been a sensitive issue in the Brexit debate, and the government has been reluctant to concede the single-market position of continued free movement of EU citizens. It has proposed a new registration system for these citizens.
- Trade relations between Britain and the EU – The single market has seen British businesses become highly integrated with European partners in importing and exporting goods freely across borders. Manufacturers and retailers have urged the government that if tariff barriers were to be re-introduced quickly, their businesses would be in jeopardy. Arrangements for a transition period were needed, to avoid the 'cliff-edge' effect of a 'hard' Brexit. Staunch Brexiters were firmly against staying in the customs union, even during a transition period, wishing to see Britain begin as soon as possible to negotiate free trade deals with other countries, such as the US. This approach is based more on nationalist leanings than on the practicalities of negotiating trade agreements, notably the fact that inequality of bargaining power usually results in a poor deal for the weaker country (see Chapter 7). A customs union with the EU would allow Britain to trade freely with EU member states, and it would be constrained to charge the same tariffs as EU countries when trading with non-EU countries. This solution is recommended by some as a 'soft' Brexit, and could even extend beyond a two-year period. In the longer term, the UK could possibly follow Norway's example of joining EFTA (the European Free Trade Area, discussed in Chapter 7). EFTA has joined the EEA (European Economic Area), allowing it to participate in the single market within the EU, while not becoming part of the EU customs union. Norway pays steep fees for its trading relations with the EU, and is bound by EU trade law. However, as a non-EU member, it has no say in EU laws and policies.
- The large body of EU law that applies in the UK – EU law has been highly influential in a number of areas: strengthening consumer rights (for example, in buying goods on credit), workers' rights, employment protection and even the rights of people who buy package holidays that go wrong. The UK government has been determined to end the supremacy of EU law in the country. A 'great repeal bill' was introduced in Parliament, aiming to incorporate the whole of EU

law into UK law as an initial step. The government would then decide over time which laws to keep, which to change and which to remove completely. All the decisions on individual laws, however, were intended to be taken by the executive, with scant scrutiny by Parliament. Parliamentary sovereignty has been a cornerstone of the British constitution, and on constitutional grounds there is cause for alarm at this apparent enhancement of unchecked executive power. But the size of the body of law would make it virtually impossible to scrutinize every provision in a reasonable timeframe.

- A second referendum – In the 2016 referendum, the citizen could choose only 'leave' or 'remain'. But what would a withdrawal deal contain, and how would it affect the economy? There were calls for a second referendum – possibly one on a withdrawal deal. Despite its sizeable majority in the 2019 election, the Conservative Party, with its strong 'leave' policy, won less than half of the popular vote (43.6%), and Brexit uncertainty remained.

Demonstrations in favour of a second referendum were an indication of the deep divisions that Brexit has unleashed in the UK.

The economic climate following the Brexit referendum revealed that many British businesses would be weakened outside the EU, experiencing staffing problems, rising costs of imports and the difficulties of making up for the loss of EU markets. London's large – and highly globalized – financial services sector, which has amassed a large volume of euro-dominated business, would be directly affected. Soon after the referendum, banks, insurance companies and other financial services companies were looking towards shifting operations from London to capitals such as Dublin and Amsterdam after Brexit. For the financially troubled airline company, Monarch Airlines, uncertainty over whether British airlines would be able to continue to fly in EU airspace deterred a possible rescue by another company. Monarch collapsed in 2017, leaving over 100,000 people stranded in holiday destinations. The government was compelled to mount a massive repatriation of Monarch customers – its largest peacetime repatriation to date. Business leaders consistently emphasize that they need, above all, a stable and predictable regulatory environment. Instead,

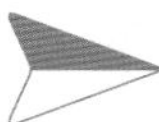

they have seen continuing uncertainties of the protracted Brexit process. In 2019, Honda announced that it would be closing down its car manufacturing in Swindon. It assured the public that this move was not related to Brexit uncertainty, but to uncertainty in the car market generally. However, Brexit would have contributed to the general uncertainty in the minds of Honda executives and other carmakers in the UK.

Brexit and beyond

This is a lecture by Sir Ivan Rogers, entitled 'Where did Brexit come from, and where is it going to take the UK?' It was delivered on 23 January 2019, at the UCL European Institute. Sir Ivan Rogers is the former UK permanent representative to the EU.

Video link: Brexit and beyond

www.youtube.com/watch?v=-PxpHNXIKnY&t=

Global politics

On the international stage, every sovereign state theoretically enjoys equal status with all others. But in practice, international politics revolves around power, both economic and military: the most powerful states in any historical period tend to be the richest and those with the most substantial military establishments. The weight of a country's military helps to ensure that it can assert its will over others, by force if need be. On the other hand, it is increasingly recognized by governments that states no longer have the means to deliver national security and material wellbeing on their own. By co-operating with other states, a government can boost its country's material wellbeing, for example, through trade, and also reach defence agreements with other countries for their mutual security. In this section we look first at some of the institutions which aim to channel sovereign states towards peaceful and prosperous co-existence. We then discuss the changing power relations which help to determine how these institutions function in practice.

International institutions

Interdependence and co-operation have generated numerous alliances and international organizations, dating mainly from the period following the Second World War. The main legally established institutions are governmental, but **non-governmental organizations** (NGOs) have gained in political influence and become part of the international institutional process in some areas of global concern. These include human rights (for example, Amnesty International, at www.amnesty.org) and the environment (for example, Greenpeace, at www.greenpeace.org). UN agencies feature regularly in this book, for the research they carry out and global issues they deal with at international level. Founded in 1945, the UN has grown from 51 member states to 193 states today. It acquired 26 new members in the period 1990–95, mainly the post-communist states of the former Soviet Union. The latest state to join the UN was South Sudan in 2011. The authority of the UN's institutions derive from inter-governmental co-operation. They do not constitute a world government, but they do indicate the extent to which sovereign states are committed to abide by international conventions. Its Secretary-General, while having no executive powers that state leaders possess, commands considerable respect in the international community, and exemplifies the UN's aim of achieving peaceful negotiated settlement of conflicts between states. See Figure 5.9 for a summary of some of the main provisions of the UN Charter.

non-governmental organization (NGO) voluntary organization formed by private individuals for a particular shared purpose, often humanitarian

In the General Assembly, all member states have one vote. The General Assembly thus recognizes the preponderance of developing countries among the total number of UN member states. Because all member states have a say, a resolution of the General Assembly carries considerable persuasive force. However, in terms of authority, the Security Council is the paramount decision-making body. The Security Council consists of 15 members, each with one vote. Five of these are permanent members, with the right of veto over its decisions. These are the major post-war powers – the US, UK, France, China and Russia (formerly the Soviet Union). The other ten member states are elected by the General Assembly for a term of two years. The use of the veto – and threat to use the veto – has hampered the Security Council's effectiveness. When one of the veto-wielding states is possibly acting in breach of the UN Charter, for example, by invading another country, the Security Council is the key institution that can exert authority, but would be unable to act because of the likely veto. A recent development in international law has been the expanded role of the International Criminal Court in prosecuting state leaders for crimes of aggression. The main veto-wielding powers are unlikely to be affected by this new law (discussed in the next chapter), but its aims reflect growing disquiet over illegal state actions in the broad international community.

International Labour Organization (ILO) UN organization that sets international labour standards

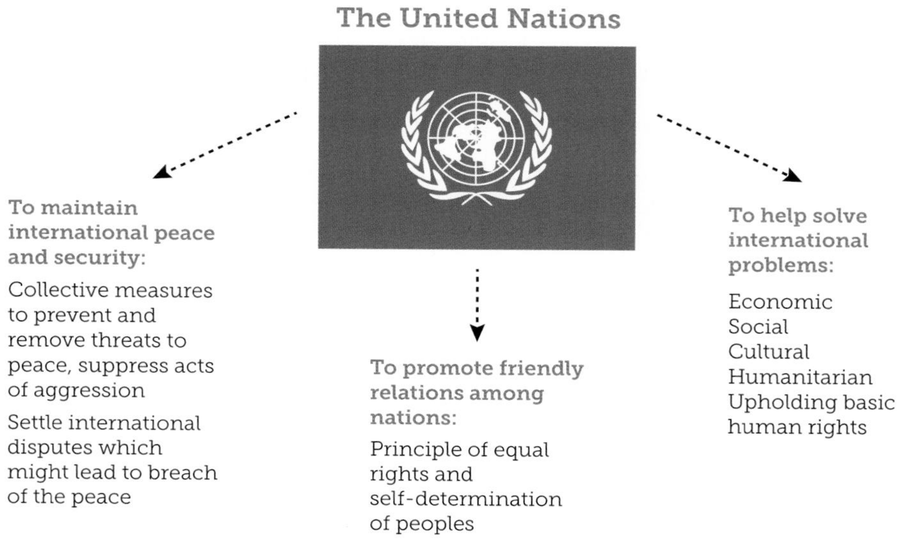

The UN has provided a forum for international debate, and expanded its social and economic activities through its many agencies and affiliated bodies. The **International Labour Organization (ILO)** (www.ilo.org), which actually pre-dates the UN, has set standards for health and safety, workers' rights, and child labour. Its conventions have been ratified by dozens of states, accepting responsibility for implementing them in national law. Similarly, the human rights covenants have been ratified by over 140 states (see Chapter 6). The acceptance by states of the principle that these conventions impose on them a 'higher' duty to comply is an indication of a shift away from the pure theory of state sovereignty.

The United Nations

To maintain international peace and security:

Collective measures to prevent and remove threats to peace, suppress acts of aggression

Settle international disputes which might lead to breach of the peace

To promote friendly relations among nations:

Principle of equal rights and self-determination of peoples

To help solve international problems:

Economic
Social
Cultural
Humanitarian
Upholding basic human rights

Figure 5.9 Main provisions of the UN Charter

Source of text: The UN Charter, at www.un.org

At its founding in 1945, the UN was envisaged as an overarching body that would ensure world peace, but it was a peace dominated by sovereign states, notably the major powers which emerged victorious in the Second World War (Mazower, 2010). This world picture was reflected in the composition of the Security Council, which had three western members (the US, UK and France) out of the five with permanent

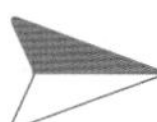

seats. At that time, the UN had only 45 member states in total. The crumbling of empires, both political and economic, which occurred in the following years, creating dozens of new sovereign states, could hardly have been foreseen. These developments have transformed the world. The sovereign state is no longer the preserve of a minority of world powers, but claimed by countries large and small, located all over the globe. The bulk of the UN's current membership is made up of developing countries, representing an incredible shift. Many would argue that this broad base gives the UN a greater mandate to take action, for example, by intervening in situations of human rights abuses. On the other hand, its enshrining of the principle of sovereignty has led it down the path of persuasion and diplomacy, which in many situations appears to be ineffectual. States often reach for unilateral action in preference to UN frameworks. The UN remains active in many spheres, notably peacekeeping and humanitarian aid, but in global politics, it now looks more like a debating forum: although it retains moral authority in theory, in practice it is unable to follow through with actions. One of its enduring accomplishments, which should not be underestimated, however, is its work in negotiating treaties (discussed in the next chapter). The role of facilitator in areas such as climate change is a worthy one, although many would see this role as second best to the political role envisaged by its founders.

The shifting balance of power in global politics

realpolitik view of international relations based on power politics

superpower a state that is able to impose its power over other countries

Global politics can be characterized as power relations between states, often referred to as **realpolitik**, a state of affairs in which each state asserts its own interests and strives for ascendency over states perceived as threats. Historically, the strongest states, economically and militarily, have expanded their reach, acquiring territory through empires and growing rich through distorted trade relations with subservient peoples. Imperial expansion can have numerous dimensions: economic, territorial, cultural and political. Empires rise and fall. The UK, France, Spain and Portugal are among many former imperial powers whose territories are now independent states. Legacies, such as the language of the imperial power, remain, and there is often a lingering sense of injustice associated with the destruction of local cultures. In today's world, the idea of imperialism thus bears a negative moral taint, but states are still concerned with expansionist aspirations. The historical role of imperial powers has given way to today's 'superpowers'. The **superpower** is a state that is able to impose its power over other countries, which nowadays is likely to be mainly in the economic sphere rather than through colonial conquests backed by military might.

In the cold-war period, the two strongest powers, the US and Soviet Union, took on the mantle of superpowers. The US, seeing itself as the champion of freedom and democracy, was driven by ideological abhorrence to the Soviet communist system, which was depicted as an embodiment of evil. China, also a large communist state, was perceived as a lesser threat, mainly because in this period it was still a relatively poor developing country and also lacked the military prowess of the Soviet Union. In these years, the US adopted an all-encompassing anti-communist mission, going so far as propping up dictators in Latin America and elsewhere, who were felt to be bulwarks against the spread of communism. The US was at the centre of the group of advanced economies known as the **Group of Seven**, or **G7**, dating from 1976. The seven members were the US, Canada, the UK, France, Germany, Italy and Japan. While their economies varied from free-market models to more state-centred models, their governments were all grounded in democratic institutions and safeguards of individual freedoms.

Group of Seven (G7) grouping of 7 advanced economies (US, Canada, UK, France, Germany, Italy and Japan)

The collapse of the Soviet Union left the US as the one remaining superpower. Russia joined the G7 in 1998, creating the G8. Russia's annexation of Crimea, along with its support for pro-Russian groups in Ukraine, led to its membership being

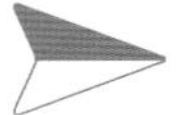

suspended in 2014. Since then, the G7 has met without Russia. However, in 2018, President Trump argued that Russia should resume active membership, and that sanctions against Russia should be dropped. Other G7 members did not concur.

G20 grouping of 20 developed, developing and emerging economies, brought together by the IMF in 1999, which meets regularly, focusing mainly on financial stability

In 1999, a grouping of countries known as the **G20** was launched by the IMF, bringing together a more diverse range of countries than the G7, in terms of both economic systems and political systems. Members of the G20 include the G7 members, but also the EU, Argentina, Brazil, Mexico, China, India, Australia, Indonesia, Russia, South Korea, South Africa, Saudi Arabia and Turkey. The G20 thus represents a number of key emerging countries that are taking on greater prominence in the global economy. The IMF envisaged the G20 as focusing mainly on global financial stability, and it has been active as a forum for policy-making reforms in the aftermath of the 2008 financial crisis. The grouping has no permanent institutional framework or authority to bind member states. On the other hand, because it represents key global economies, its policy initiatives are influential in global politics. The G20 countries participated in the drawing up of the OECD's revised principles of good corporate governance, discussed in Chapter 1.

Since opening up to market forces, China has played a vital role in economic globalization, with growing inward FDI helping to enrich American companies such as Apple. In outward FDI, China has also been building up investments in the US, revitalizing companies and employing thousands of American workers. Economic ties have thus proliferated through trade and investment. While both countries benefit from these ties, it would be a mistake to assume that political divides are melting away. China's military and political leaders control not just political institutions, but large swathes of business activity. The Chinese leadership sits atop a political, military and business hierarchy that has seen the rise of a wealthy elite. Their political ideology is the antithesis of democratic values and individual freedoms – values that would threaten the existing elites.

China has significantly increased military spending, and has taken steps to impose its territorial ambitions on both real and artificial islands in the resource-rich South China Sea, where much smaller countries (notably the Philippines, Vietnam and Malaysia) have long made territorial claims. The Belt and Road Initiative, discussed in Chapter 4, is seen as part of this strategy. The US is also active in these contested waters, from its three bases on Guam, about a three-hour flight from the Philippines. Tensions rise with nationalist moves and demonstrations of power towards other states perceived as threats. Russia has justified its annexation of territory in the Crimea peninsula in nationalist terms, again raising the vision of its ambitions over former Soviet countries that remain in its sphere of influence. Russia has also cultivated closer ties with Saudi Arabia, signalling a shift in Saudi strategy away from its traditional ties to the US. Russia and Saudi Arabia, both large oil producers, have increased their influence in the Middle East. It is notable that the country examples cited here – China, Russia and Saudi Arabia – are focusing their strategies on increased military power. Do these expansionist moves suggest a renewed impetus of realpolitik in international relations?

The rise of nationalism and populism has played a part in the resurgence of realpolitik, squeezing out liberal notions of pluralism and mutual respect among nations. Mr Trump's world-view has been more akin to a deal-making approach, rather than one based on principles. In the post-war era, the US has arguably had a moral advantage in its championing of the values of individual freedoms and democracy, but this mantle has worn thin. US democracy as represented by meaningful participative institutions has given way to control by economic elites. In the post-war era, the UN has been the leading international institution upholding notions of co-operative international relations and mutual respect for sovereign rights of states. But the UN relies on states adhering to this principled approach.

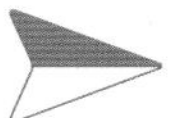

In the absence of such an approach, there has emerged the more adversarial climate of politics as power relations, unchecked by legal and moral constraints. In global politics today, the US, China and Russia have all engaged in more aggressive and confrontational foreign policies.

The way I see it ...

On political leadership in Africa, 'Insufficient care was taken to ensure that Africa's economic growth was inclusive, equitable and job-creating, particularly for young people...Better governance is the only sustainable solution to our peace and security challenges.'

Mo Ibrahim, mobile communications entrepreneur from Sudan, writing in the *Financial Times*, 6 October 2014.

The Mo Ibrahim Foundation established the Ibrahim Index of African Governance, which has reported annually since 2008. The 2018 report is at mo.ibrahim.foundation/iiag. The findings show only a very modest improvement of under 1% in sustainable economic opportunity since 2008, while GDP has grown 40% over that period. Decline in education indicators in 27 countries was one of the findings.

Looking at the 2018 report, what are the main governance failings highlighted, and what steps can be taken to promote sustainable economic opportunity?

The changing political environment: reaching for sustainability?

Sustainability in governance should ensure that today's institutions are designed to serve the needs of current societies and also those of societies in the future. When today's political leaders have ceased to hold office, these institutions should ensure that other officeholders will take up the tasks, promoting public goods and adhering to an established constitutional framework. Moreover, settled democratic institutions in a state should facilitate co-operating with other states to uphold recognized laws and norms at the international level. To what extent do governance structures in today's world reach these goals?

The 'wave' of democratic transformations that followed the dismemberment of empires, as well as the fall of the apartheid regime in South Africa, has given way to a rise in development models. Many have gone the way of authoritarian leadership and weak institutional structures. Despite democratic forms, many mix elitist political systems with business interests. Political and business elites gain handsomely, while social goals take a back seat. A rather pessimistic view of today's global political powers – existing and aspiring – is that business and political elites are gaining, often in tandem with each other, but these gains are not being translated into better societies or more accountable governance. This disequilibrium is unsustainable: the few reap the benefits, to the exclusion of the many. To be sustainable, a democracy must be 'resilient', developing inclusive institutions that peacefully resolve social conflicts and are able to withstand stresses (International Institute for Democracy, 2017). Where citizens are actively engaged in democratic debate, a society's institutions are more resilient in counterbalancing the power garnered by political and economic elites.

Businesses play crucial roles in societies. In many developing countries, companies take lead roles in negotiating with governments for advantageous terms in FDI and trade, often dealing with authoritarian leaders in situations which give rise to corruption. These activities often cast corporate executives in opportunistic roles that suggest private gain at the expense of public goods. Executives in these circumstances argue that the company's role is economic, and its managers rightly pursue goals of wealth creation for their corporate owners. But there is a fine line between legitimate ties with government and exploiting ties with government for private gain.

In the western countries that have been to the forefront in global political debate in the post-war era, it has been common to view the political environment in terms of external influences on businesses. This view holds that the political system is a given, and that business must adapt to the changing political make-up in a state, abiding by new policies and laws. The business is seen in this scenario as reacting to changes, including risks. This thinking rests on a conceptual view that there is a dichotomy between politics, which is about public goods, and business, which is essentially about private actors. This dichotomy has gradually become blurred as businesses have become more active in the formulation of political policies and more involved in government activities. Businesses now participate in broad processes of governance, involving them in dialogue with a range of governmental and quasi-governmental bodies, as well as civil society organizations. This is a more participatory concept than that of government, which implies distinct roles: governments make policy and businesses apply it. Changes in the US political system have seen the rise of businesses in policy-making through lobbying and the funding of political parties and individual candidates for office. The conflicts of interest become starkly apparent: companies typically press for policies that involve either deregulation of existing rules or restraint in passing new regulations, even when there are clear cases that regulatory tightening is in the public interest. An example is the case for emissions controls to combat climate change. Another has been the weak regulatory moves by governments following the 2008 financial crisis, to reform the out-of-control behaviour of banks that had been allowed to flourish in the pre-crisis environment of minimal regulation. Homeowners who lost their homes and workers who lost their jobs had cause to be bitter when executives of failed banks emerged unscathed.

As we have seen, the populist leader often emerges in this context, voicing the concerns of ordinary people who feel passed over – concerns insufficiently addressed by mainstream parties. Maintaining grassroots democratic participation is essential for the health of democratic institutions. Widespread lack of trust in mainstream political parties and their leaders, often perceived to be corrupt, undermines confidence in officeholders, which in turn could undermine faith in the institutions themselves. The prospect of inclusive and sustainable institutions thereby diminishes. Increasingly involved in governance and public services, businesses are part of this equation. A more engaged role in public policy implies responsibilities on businesses, and also invites critical assessment of their behaviour on grounds of public good. But this is unlikely to happen in an environment where economic power dominates political structures. Where voters feel their vote makes no difference, then democratic participation is reduced to a mechanistic one with no sense of participation. This occurs in authoritarian systems, and it is likely to occur in ostensibly democratic countries where economic elites are in control. Neither of these political environments is sustainable and neither serves societal wellbeing.

Conclusions

The political sphere can be identified with structures and processes by which power and influence are allocated, whether among groups in a state or among states in the global political sphere. But an organizational view of politics is only part of the story: the undercurrents of where power lies in society are also influential. As this chapter

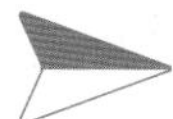

has shown, structures form the framework of political systems, which aim to ensure stability of governance over whole societies. Often set out in written constitutions, political systems should ideally represent an enduring set of institutions that stands above the people in office, and to which they must adhere. All systems change over time, usually incrementally, but sometimes by violent overthrow of an existing regime. Democratic systems are by definition responsive to the citizenry as their source of their legitimacy. When there are grassroots pressures for change, this thinking should be part of the democratic responsiveness of the system, although the voices of ordinary people do not always reach those at the top. Democratic values are closely associated with western political thinking. They have taken root alongside the rise in capitalism, although capitalist development preceded democracy. Individual freedoms are aspects of both developments: freedom of expression and association are linked to economic freedoms. But democracy claims a broader perspective which is ethical and social. Democratic thinking asserts that human dignity matters, whatever the country, and that governmental legitimacy must ultimately rest with the people on ethical grounds, whatever the cultural values of the society.

Democratic values have become enshrined in political systems across the globe, particularly on the dissolution of empires in the last two centuries. But the formal installation of elections and universal suffrage goes only part of the way towards achieving democratic values. Constitutional systems are formal. To work in practice, they must be nurtured through the cultivation of values of civil society, pluralism and responsiveness to societal needs. The leaders that emerge in a political system, however, are more likely to be those who have become adept at cultivating personal power bases within parties and other political groupings. A political outlook, while ideally focused on the good of society, is more often focused on the pursuit of particular interests. Those interests in today's world are likely to be linked with powerful businesses. This can be a positive relationship. Businesses, after all, provide employment, generate wealth and drive development goals. They also provide many public services such as health, education and utilities. But business goals almost invariably clash with the egalitarian goals inherent in democracy.

Businesses have become highly successful at cultivating ties with political leaders, in both democratic and non-democratic systems. Indeed, in some they have become established in the governmental structures. Moreover, business leaders have moved from national political stages to the global stage, as globalization has transformed business relations. A globalized business elite has enjoyed not just greater wealth and an ability to manipulate that wealth globally, but an ascendency over numerous political leaders, who face challenges in distinguishing national interests from those of private-sector companies. In the US, the business elite, largely made up of global companies and wealthy donors, has found allies in politicians who share their corporate values. These clash with the democratic goals of empowering ordinary citizens and building an inclusive society. In authoritarian states, business interests have also found favour, but on terms laid down by leaders. Political risks abound in both environments, whether ostensibly democratic or autocratic. Businesses desire a stable environment, but in taking on quasi-political roles, they inevitably court risks that they will be subject to greater scrutiny, and will be associated with particular political interests that could prove damaging to them in the long term. In engaging with political actors, they are taking on responsibilities that are rooted in social and ethical considerations. The company that takes a 'business as usual' approach to activities with corrupt overtones can find itself out in the cold when the winds turn, as they almost inevitably do. By contrast, the company that focuses on a balance of business and social goals, treating every government as a stakeholder among other stakeholders, is likely to tread a more sustainable path through an increasingly complex global political environment.

CLOSING CASE STUDY

The rise of authoritarian rule in Turkey

Turkey stands at a cultural crossroads between East and West. Many of its inhabitants look more towards Europe, as evidenced by the fact that Turkey applied for EU membership in 1995. But Turkey today is far from leaning towards the values of democracy and freedom that the EU stands for. Its president, Recep Tayyip Erdogan, has become increasingly authoritarian, exerting virtually unchecked power, suppressing dissent and curtailing freedom of expression.

Culturally and politically, Turkey is highly divided. The majority party, the Justice and Development Party (AKP), has a broad base in the Muslim population, and has been the force behind Erdogan's rise. Its business leaders, many of whom are close to the president, have been the main drivers of Turkey's economic growth, which reached a high of 8.8% in 2011, making Turkey a leading emerging economy. Since then, growth has weakened, as export markets for the many consumer products that it produces have stalled. A financial crisis in 2018 was marked by a decline in its stock market and a fall in its currency, the lira, caused partly by high levels of debt, much of it in foreign currencies. At the same time, US President Trump raised tariffs on steel and aluminium imported from Turkey, marking a deterioration in relations with Turkey.

Mr Erdogan's political rise began with the electoral success of the AKP in parliamentary elections in 2002, when he became prime minister, a post he held for three terms, the legal maximum. He was elected president in 2014, winning on a platform that promised to strengthen the office of president. Turkey's constitution, dating back to 1982, had rested on secular values and a parliamentary system, under which the prime minister formed a government and the president was a non-partisan figurehead. Mr Erdogan wished to change the constitution to a presidential system, with greatly enhanced power in the hands of the president. However, a constitutional referendum would reveal the divides in Turkey's polarized politics. The westernized and liberal urban centres, such as Istanbul, differed greatly from the more conservative Muslim population in rural areas. An attempted coup by a group of military personnel was repelled in 2016. Mr Erdogan declared a state of emergency and launched a crackdown against individuals and groups he suspected of having been complicit. Over two hundred people were killed, and many institutions he suspected of disloyalty were purged, including government offices and educational institutions.

The promised constitutional referendum was held in 2017. The new constitution was approved, but by a slim majority of 51.4% in favour, exposing Turkey's political divisions. In the presidential election that followed in 2018, Mr Erdogan won by a majority of 53%, again indicating that his support was not universal. His victory followed a campaign which was criticized by monitors for the government's control of the media and suppression of opposition parties. This election ushered in the new constitution, which hands almost unfettered executive power to the president. The office of prime minister has been

This engineer in Antalya represents the changes that have taken place in Turkey through economic development, offering greater opportunities in highly-skilled jobs – for women as well as men.

abolished. The president can enact laws by decree, and parliament cannot overturn them. The president can dismiss parliament. Mr Erdogan's record of suppressing the activities of the opposition parties and other dissidents, as well as curtailing freedom of speech, has been among the major concerns of the country's liberal-minded citizens, who fear more repressive policies. Any prospect that Turkey might continue its application to join the EU would seem to be dead. Certainly, the EU would not welcome the descent of Turkey into an authoritarian state.

Mr Erdogan has combined nationalism with religious conservativism. Both are characteristic of populist leaders. However, Mr Erdogan seems to be above all an authoritarian who relies on nationalism to attempt to unite the country. Surveys of voters in Turkey have shown that they are generally hostile towards the West: 83% had unfavourable views about the US, and 73% had unfavourable views about the EU. As for religion, 80% of respondents said that Islam was central to their identity, and 70% said that Turkey should be a secular state, with freedom of religion for all (Tharoor, 2018). These poll results suggest that nationalism, rather than religion, is the predominant source of Erdogan's support. Most Turks also seemed to be angry about the presence of Syrian refugees in their country. Embroiled in the Syrian crisis, Turkey has received over three million refugees. It is likely that many Turks blame the government for the influx of refugees, especially in an environment of rising unemployment. This is probably one of the causes of Mr Erdogan's falling short of the large majority he might have expected in the 2018 election.

He looked forward to standing for a third term under the new constitution, which would see him in power until 2028. However, his handling of the continuing financial crisis could lead to political dissent that might destabilize his authoritarian rule. Local elections in 2019 were a test for Mr Erdogan's popularity, even though his name did not appear on any ballot papers. In the event, the key election for mayor of Istanbul was narrowly won by the opposition candidate, Ekrem Imamoglu, of the Republican People's Party. A rerun of the vote was ordered, in which he won a resounding victory. This was a significant setback for Mr Erdogan.

Questions for discussion

- How has democracy lost ground in Turkey?
- To what extent has Turkey turned its back on possible EU membership?
- How is the rule of law being jeopardized in Turkey?
- How does the new constitution affect Turkey's business environment?

Further reading

See the article by Peter S. Goodman, 'The West hoped for democracy in Turkey. Erdogan had other ideas', in the *New York Times*, 18 August 2018.

Multiple choice questions

Visit www.macmillanihe.com/morrison-gbe-5e to take a quick self-test quiz on what you have read in this chapter.

Review questions

1. What are the defining characteristics of the nation-state? How is globalization threatening state sovereignty?
2. Give some examples of internal political risk for businesses.
3. What are the main external threats to states that present political risk in today's world?
4. What are the characteristics of a constitution, and why is it felt to be stable in the long term?

5. What are the differences between authoritarian states and democratic ones? Why is the line between them becoming blurred?
6. Why is populism becoming important as a political force, and what are the consequences for democracy?
7. What are the risks where electoral outcomes can be influenced by the richest in society?
8. What is proportional representation in electoral arrangements, and does it make outcomes more democratic?
9. How do presidential systems compare with parliamentary systems of government? The hybrid system is said to combine the best of both worlds, but does it?
10. What is the role of political parties in democratic systems, and in authoritarian ones?
11. What are the roles of businesses in lobbying?
12. Looking at the main institutions of the European Union, how democratic are they?
13. In what ways have Brexit processes affected the business environment?
14. What institutional mechanisms exist at international level, and what are their limitations?
15. Is China becoming a global 'superpower', and, if so, what impact will it have on global business?

✓ Assignments

1. Assess the ways in which the executive branch of government is becoming more powerful in comparison with the legislature. Choose at least two countries as examples. What are the risks to democracy when the executive expands and upsets the constitutional separation of powers?

2. What is the role of businesses in lobbying to achieve their goals in government and law? Assess how lobbying can undermine democratic institutions and how it can be regulated.

Further reading

Bale, T. (2017) *European Politics: A comparative introduction*, 4th edition (London: Red Globe Press).

Baylis, J., and Smith, S. (eds) (2016) *The Globalization of World Politics* 7th edition (Oxford: Oxford University Press).

Deaton, A. (2013) *The Great Escape: Health, wealth and the origins of inequality* (Princeton: Princeton University Press).

Goldin, I. (2012) *Globalization for Development: Meeting new challenges* (Oxford: Oxford University Press).

Heywood, A. (2017) *Political Ideologies: An Introduction*, 6th edition (London: Red Globe Press).

Hague, R., and Harrop, M. (2016) *Comparative Government and Politics: An introduction*, 10th edition (London: Red Globe Press).

Held, D., and McGrew, A. (2007) *Globalization/Anti-globalization: Beyond the great divide*, 2nd edition (Cambridge: Polity Press).

Mudde, C. (2017) *On Extremism and Democracy in Europe* (Routledge).

Runciman, D. (2018) *How Democracy Ends* (Profile Books).

References

Boone, J. (2013) 'US drone strikes could be classed as war crimes, says Amnesty International', *The Guardian*, 22 October, at www.theguardian.com

Catte, E. (2019) 'Why Trump country isn't as Republican as you think', *The Guardian*, 22 February.

Gilens, M. and Page, B. (2014) 'Testing theories of American politics: Elites, interest groups and average citizens', *Perspectives on Politics*, 12(3): 564–81.

Hacker, J., and Pierson, P. (2010) *Winner-Take-All Politics* (New York: Simon & Schuster).

Hathaway, O. and Shapiro, S. (2017) 'Making war illegal changed the world, but it's becoming too easy to break the law', *The Guardian*, 17 September.

Hawthorn, J. (1993) 'Sub-Saharan Africa', in Held, D. (ed.) *Prospects for Democracy* (Cambridge: Polity Press), pp. 330–74.

Henshall, N. (1992) *The Myth of Absolutism* (London: Longman Group UK Ltd).

International Institute for Democracy (2017) *The Global State of Democracy*, at www.idea.int

Isenberg, D. (2009) *Private Military Contractors and US Grand Strategy*, Report: PRIO 1/209, International Peace Research Institute, Oslo, at www.prio.no

Ipsos Mori (2016) '4 ways the anti-immigration vote won the referendum vote for Brexit', 7 July, at www.ipsos.com

Jackson, J. (2003) 'Sovereignty-modern: A new approach to an outdated concept', *American Journal of International Law*, 97: 782–802.

Laine, J. (2014) 'Debating civil society: Contested conceptualizations and development trajectories', *International Journal of Not-for-profit Law*, 16(1): 59–77.

Lincoln, A. (1863) Gettysburg Address, transcript, at www.ourdocuments.gov

Linz, J. (1993) 'Perils of presidentialism', in Diamond, L. and Plattner, M.F. (eds) *The Global Resurgence of Democracy* (Baltimore: The Johns Hopkins University Press), pp. 108–26.

Mazower, M. (2010) *No Enchanted Palace: The end of empire and the ideological origins of the United Nations* (Princeton: Princeton University Press).

Mudde, C. (2004) 'The populist zeitgeist', *Government and Opposition*, 39(3): 541–63.

Mudde, C. (2017) 'Populism: An ideational approach', *University of Georgia, Selected works of Cas Mudde*, at https://works.bepress.com/cas_mudde

O'Neill, J. (2001) 'Building better global economic BRICs', Goldman Sachs Global Economics Research Group, Global Paper No. 66, at www.gs.com

Pew Research Center (2017) *Public Trust in Government: 1958–2017*, 3 May, at www.people-press.org

Plattner, M. (2010) 'Populism, pluralism and liberal democracy', *Journal of Democracy*, 21(1): 81–92.

Reuters (2019) 'Brazil: Huge rise in deforestation under Bolsonaro, figures show', *The Guardian*, 3 July.

Sands, P. (2005) *Lawless World* (London: Penguin Books).

SIPRI (Stockholm International Peace Research Institute) (2019) *SIPRI Yearbook 2019*, at www.sipri.org

Strauss, D. (2018) 'Law and the slow-motion emergency', in Sunstein, C. (ed.), *Can it Happen Here? Authoritarianism in America* (New York: HarperCollins), pp. 365–85.

Sunstein, C. (ed.) (2018) *Can it Happen Here? Authoritarianism in America* (New York: HarperCollins).

Tharoor, I. (2018) 'The political trend that's more important than "populism"', *The Washington Post*, 16 February.

Timm, T. (2015) 'The hostages killed by US drones are casualties of an inhumane policy', *The Guardian*, 15 April, at www.theguardian.com

Toksoz, M. (2014) 'Investors must prepare for worst case scenarios', *Financial Times*, 29 September, at www.ft.com.

Transparency International UK (2015) *Lifting the Lid on Lobbying: The hidden exercise of power and influence in the UK*, February, at www.transparency.org

Transparency International UK (2016) *Take Back Control: How big money undermines trust in politics*, October, at www.transparency.org.uk/publications

UNDP (2018) *Human Development Indices, Statistical Update*, at www.hdr.undp.org

UN Policy Working Group (2002) *Report of the Policy Working Group on the United Nations and Terrorism*, Ref A/57/273, at www.un.org/terrorism

US Department of Defense (2012) *US Base Structure Report Fiscal Year 2012 Baseline*, at www.acq.osd.mil

US Department of Defense (2016) *US Base Structure Report Fiscal Year 2015 Baseline*, at www.defense.gov

Westcott, B. (2018) 'Socialism with Chinese characteristics?', CNN, 11 March, at https://edition.cnn.com

Wolin, S. (2008) *Democracy Incorporated* (Princeton: Princeton University Press).

Visit the companion website at www.macmillanihe.com/morrison-gbe-5e for further learning and teaching resources.

© iStockphoto

THE LEGAL ENVIRONMENT

Outline of chapter

This chapter will enable you to

- Understand the interrelationships between national, regional, and international legal frameworks in their impact on the international business environment
- Appreciate the divergence in structures, processes and content between national legal systems
- Identify the ways in which legal frameworks impact on cross-border business activities
- Assess the impacts of international law and international dispute settlement in relation to businesses in differing national contexts
- Appreciate the need for sustainable approaches to ethical and legal obligations in diverse societies

OPENING CASE STUDY

Uber Faces Challenges in Global Markets

Uber, the American ride-hailing company was launched in 2010 as a start-up business in San Francisco. Its founders came up with the idea that anyone with a car could offer a ride to passengers as a one-to-one transaction. Drawing on his technology background, its founder, Travis Kalanick, devised a convenient app that could be downloaded by anyone, allowing the driver to offer rides to customers, whenever and wherever needed. The fares were set by Uber, and the driver would hand over a percentage of the takings to the company. This formula could easily be rolled out in any city in the world. Uber expanded rapidly from operating in 9 cities in 2012 to 311 in 2015; 170 of these are in the US. The company adopted an aggressive approach to regulators, going ahead with expansion plans in cities where there were regulatory obstacles yet to be resolved. Uber has come into conflict with conventional taxi services, run by licensed drivers, which are generally more expensive for the consumer than an Uber ride. Much appreciated by consumers, the ride-hailing business has attracted investors globally. By 2018, Uber was valued at over $72 billion, making it one of the world's most highly-valued private companies. However, a number of competitors have entered the global market, providing stiff competition. One of them, Didi Dache, or Didi for short, is a Chinese company, launched in 2012, that has also attracted considerable investor interest, including that of Apple.

Didi is the dominant ride-hailing business in China, where it has 21 million drivers, in comparison with the 2.6 million licensed taxi drivers. The ride-hailing model has overtaken the conventional taxi in China, and aims to expand rapidly in global markets. Ola in India, also a populous market, is another ambitious competitor. Ola has started operations in the UK, in direct competition with Uber. Ola has emphasized that it is taking a co-operative approach towards local authorities, and is concentrating on safety. Lyft in North America, too, is a competitor. In 2016, Didi bought Uber's China business, in a deal that gave Uber a 17.7% stake in Didi. The acquisition of minority stakes has become common. Didi owns stakes in Lyft and Ola. In Latin America, Didi has acquired a controlling stake in the Brazilian ride-hailing business, 99, which is Uber's biggest rival in Brazil. But, despite their global reach and investor interest, the ride-hailing companies are not very profitable. Uber is loss-making. It has expanded its platform, which now extends to food delivery, scooters and electric bikes. Uber launched its IPO on Wall Street in 2019, but its shares soon slumped in the uncertain business environment.

Uber's business model has faced legal hurdles as it has expanded, and has acquired a reputation for aggressiveness. A contested issue is its classification of drivers as self-employed. In California, Uber drivers have been held by the courts to be workers rather than self-employed people. The courts in most countries look at the degree of control the company exerts over the worker, to determine whether the driver is working for the company or is self-employed. Uber controls the driver's fares and monitors the car's movements, but does not control the driver's hours. If a driver is a worker, Uber would have liabilities under employment law. In 2016, an employment tribunal in London held that two Uber drivers were workers, because of the control Uber exerted over them. They would therefore be entitled to the minimum wage, holiday pay and paid rest breaks. Uber appealed against this decision, and lost in the Court of Appeal late in 2018. It was determined to continue with its case, and appealed to the Supreme Court.

Uber and a number of other companies have tested new technology for the self-driving vehicle. However, Uber suffered a setback when a self-driving car that was travelling at 40 mph hit a pedestrian, its sensor having failed to stop the vehicle. She later died. Investigations showed that

Uber's ride-hailing platform has encountered numerous legal hurdles.

Uber was found to have disabled the car's emergency braking system. After the accident, Uber temporarily suspended its testing of such vehicles, but intended to resume in the future. Uber has had a reputation of combativeness, and this accident has also suggested that it has not paid sufficient heed to safety concerns. Waymo, owned by Alphabet (Google's parent company), seems to have gained more industry confidence in terms of safety and reliability.

In 2017, Uber suffered a blow when the authority, Transport for London, refused to renew its licence to operate in London, on grounds that it was not 'fit and proper' as a company. In particular, the company fell down on public safety and security issues, not reporting serious crime properly and falling down on background checks on drivers. At a court hearing in 2018, Uber was granted a short-term licence for a 15-month probationary period. The judge was sufficiently assured that Uber had undertaken to make the necessary changes and adopt a more responsible attitude towards its legal obligations. Uber's aggressive strategy had encountered setbacks from regulators. As the competitive challenges multiply, all of these companies need skills in negotiating with regulators.

Questions

- What are the regulatory issues that surround the ride-hailing business model?
- Why has Uber become controversial?
- Why is Uber criticized over the arrangements with its drivers?
- Why do investors continue to flock to ride-hailing companies, despite the fact that they have regulatory setbacks and make hardly any profits?

Further reading

For a discussion of Uber's loss of its licence in London, see the article, 'Uber stripped of London licence due to lack of corporate responsibility', by Sarah Butler and Gwyn Topham, in *The Guardian*, 23 September 2017.

Introduction

The legal dimension of international business has become more pertinent as business relations across national borders have expanded. This might seem like a paradox: if businesses are more mobile than ever, then the significance of borders might be expected to diminish. This chapter will explain the ways in which borders do still matter, and also how businesses are now becoming adept at skipping over borders. Historically, the legal environment has been determined by national legal systems. Businesses are traditionally advised that obeying national laws in each location is the overriding guide they must follow. But the legal environment is now much more complicated than this rule-of-thumb suggests. Globalization of markets and production has provided scope for companies to do business in a variety of national legal environments, but in many the rule of law is weak and legal risk is a major factor. Moreover, international law, which invokes higher standards than much national law, is increasingly becoming the benchmark for global businesses. The legal environment can be divided into three interacting spheres, as shown in Figure 6.1: national legal systems; regional lawmaking authorities, of which the European Union is the major example; and international law, sponsored by international bodies such as the United Nations and its agencies. This chapter will explore the ways in which these overlapping spheres of law impact on international business.

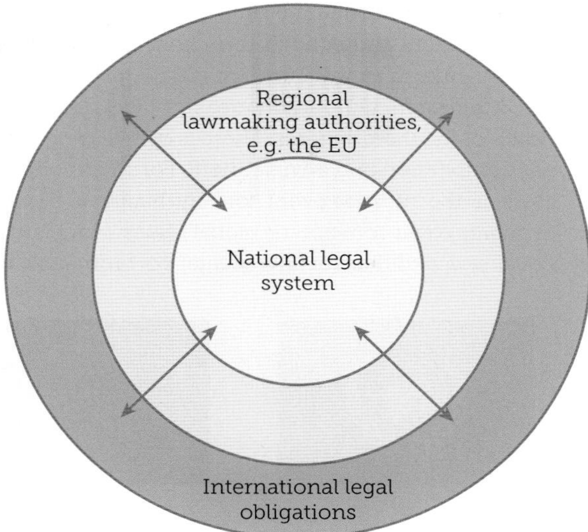

Figure 6.1 **The international legal environment**

For international businesses, national law remains the primary legal backdrop for cross-border transactions. This chapter looks at relevant areas of the law, including contract law, liability for accidents and competition law. Businesses do not just watch on the sidelines as laws are framed and implemented. Increasingly, they take on roles in advising governments and international bodies. They also spend money on lobbying lawmakers around the world. As technological innovation alters business models, lawmakers are called on to respond with regulatory changes. The speed of some developments such as ecommerce has far outpaced the development of the law to cover them. While governments have slowly woken up to the legal implications of advances in technology, they have also realized the limitations of national law in areas such as data protection and privacy, which have become global issues.

All countries appreciate the need for an efficient, modern, impartial legal system, to attract enterprises (both local and overseas investors) and to retain their confidence in its processes. They also see the benefits of harmonization of laws to facilitate international transactions. Governments are aware that relations with businesses, domestic and foreign, offer opportunities to fund investment, provide jobs and promote economic growth. They are also aware that the legal environment plays an important role in ensuring that societal wellbeing is prioritized. Businesses now have extensive ties with governments, and also deepening roles in societies that involve responsibilities to multiple stakeholders. As the last section of this chapter will show, these evolving roles present a blend of legal and ethical considerations much more complex than the traditional view of law as rules that simply have to be obeyed.

Classifying law

law rule or body of rules perceived as binding because it emanates from state authorities with powers of enforcement

Law refers to the rules identified as binding because they emanate from state authorities. Groups within a society, such as sports bodies, create rules for their own participants and members, but the distinguishing feature of law is that it creates obligations for society as a whole. Law touches on almost all aspects of business. While businesspeople are inclined to see legal rules in a negative light, constraining their activities (for example, an application for planning permission), in fact, much law is of an enabling nature (for example, eligibility to apply for public funding). Market-driven economies aim to strike a balance between freedom of enterprise and sufficient regulation to safeguard the public interest. In the post-war era, with an upsurge in welfare-state provisions, the law has extended to areas such as employment protection, consumer protection, and health and safety in the workplace. A more recent concern is data protection of individuals' personal data.

A number of the main areas of legal obligation are shown in Figure 6.2, showing each of the three spheres. There is overlapping jurisdiction in some of these areas, such as competition and environment. For sheer scope of jurisdiction, the national legal system is the most relevant for any business. However, the regional and international spheres cover some of the global issues which are becoming increasingly important for business, and there is now greater co-ordination between the three sets of authorities.

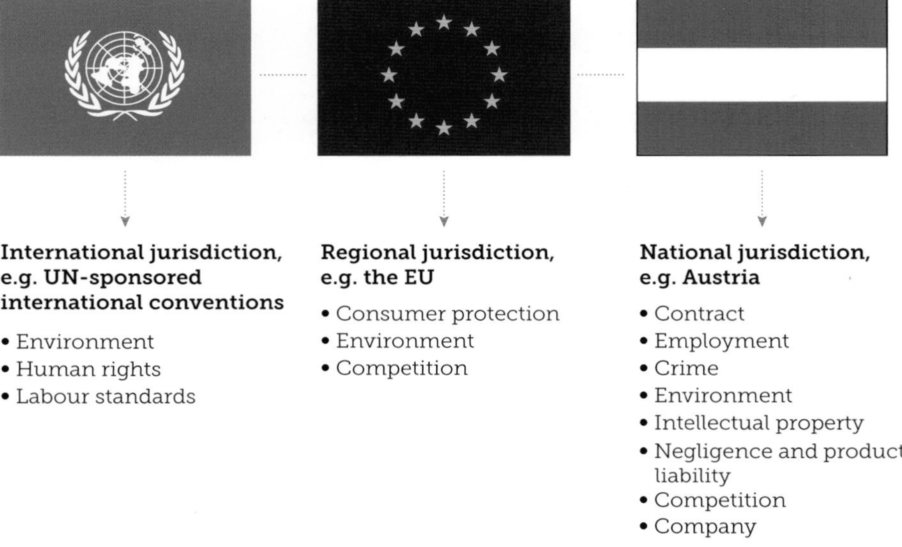

International jurisdiction, e.g. UN-sponsored international conventions

- Environment
- Human rights
- Labour standards

Regional jurisdiction, e.g. the EU

- Consumer protection
- Environment
- Competition

National jurisdiction, e.g. Austria

- Contract
- Employment
- Crime
- Environment
- Intellectual property
- Negligence and product liability
- Competition
- Company

Figure 6.2
Summary of major areas of law affecting business and relevant authorities

public law body of law covering relations between citizens and the state

civil (or private) law law pertaining to relations between private individuals and companies

litigation the use of judicial procedures and the court system to bring claims for damages and other remedies in legal disputes

arbitration the submission of a legal dispute to a named person or organization in accordance with a contractual agreement

Law may be broadly classified into two categories: **public law**, which concerns relations between citizens and the state, and **civil (or private) law**, which concerns relations between individuals (including companies). Tax and social security fall within public law, whereas contract law and employment law are areas of civil law. The state plays a significant, although less direct, role in the civil law. Legislatures enact law regulating employment relations, for example; and the state's courts may be called on to settle disputes between the parties. In a dispute over a contract or an accident at work, the person who has suffered loss or injury (the 'plaintiff') may bring a claim for money compensation ('damages') or a range of other remedies against the 'defendant' in the state's courts. The use of the courts to bring claims for damages and other remedies is referred to as **litigation**. Litigation can be costly and time-consuming. Companies generally prefer to settle disputes 'out of court', saving costs and achieving an agreement more quickly than in judicial proceedings. There are now many mechanisms available which help to facilitate settlements through mediation and negotiation short of full court proceedings. One mechanism is **arbitration** (discussed later in this chapter), whereby the parties agree to allow a third party to step in to settle disputes, which can be included as part of a contract. On the other hand, some companies routinely engage in legal proceedings as an integral part of their global business strategy. Uber, discussed in the opening case study, is an example. Litigation is also commonplace in the high-tech and pharmaceutical sectors, where disputes arise over intellectual property rights.

criminal law laws that designate offences and set out legal procedure for prosecution of those charged with breaches; can be contained in a criminal code

A major body of public law is the **criminal law**, under which certain types of wrongdoing are designated by the state as criminal offences. In these cases, state authorities initiate proceedings, known as a 'prosecution', in the criminal courts, which, on conviction, will lead to a fine or imprisonment of the offender. See Table 6.1 for a breakdown of the distinctions between civil and criminal law. Note that the 'burden of proof' is higher in a criminal case, which means that a greater degree of certainty is required for criminal guilt than for a judgment as to which party succeeds in a civil case.

We tend to think of crime in terms of individual crimes, such as assault and theft. But in business, crimes are often connected with financial transactions, such as fraud, money laundering and false accounting. These are all known as 'white-collar' crimes. Another example is that of 'insider dealing' relating to companies. This is a crime involving a person with inside knowledge of a company using that information to gain personal advantage, thus distorting the market in the company's shares. Financial wrongdoing can also involve defrauding tax authorities. Such crimes have been greatly facilitated by global financial networks and the use of offshore financial centres. The information revealed in large hauls of data from offshore financial centres, in the Panama Papers in 2016 and the Paradise Papers in 2017 were highly illuminating in exposing the extent of offshore finance. While much of this activity is legal, in many cases, the secrecy of these centres is used as a cover for criminal activities.

Table 6.1 Outline of civil law and criminal law

	Criminal law	Civil law
What is it about?	Offences against society	Disputes between private individuals or companies
What is the purpose of the action?	To preserve order in the community by punishing offenders and deterring others	To seek a remedy for the wrong which has been suffered, usually money compensation
Who are the parties?	A prosecutor, usually representing the state, prosecutes a defendant, the accused	A plaintiff sues a defendant
Where is the action heard?	State, regional or local criminal courts	Civil courts, at local, regional or state level
Who has to prove what?	The prosecutor must prove a case against the defendant beyond all reasonable doubt	The plaintiff must establish a case on the balance of probabilities
What form does the decision take?	A defendant may be convicted if found guilty, or acquitted if found not guilty	A defendant may be found liable or not liable
What remedies are handed down by the court?	Imprisonment, fine, probation, community service	Damages (money compensation) to the successful plaintiff is the commonest
What are some common types of legal action?	Offences including theft, assault, drunken driving, criminal damage	Actions for breach of contract; actions in negligence for breach of a duty of care owed to the plaintiff

White collar crime

This video is about the business of white collar crime. It is a documentary published 11 January 2013, by InsideOut Ptv

Video link: White collar crime
https://youtu.be/MEoYxQgYT2w

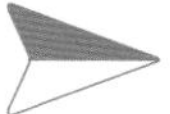

Companies, directors and employees can be guilty of criminal offences, as the mini case study on the *Costa Concordia* disaster shows. Breaches of health and safety law are a common type of corporate crime. In Britain, corporate liability has been extended by a new offence of corporate killing, following unsuccessful prosecutions for manslaughter in relation to ferry and train disasters, including a crash at Paddington, London, in 1999, in which 31 people died. Directors cannot hide behind the facade of the company: they may be personally liable for its crimes. On the other hand, enforcement of the criminal law, which is mainly rooted in national systems, poses major challenges, as many criminal activities have become globalized, and also highly organized.

MINI CASE STUDY

The tragic cruise of the *Costa Concordia*

The Italian cruise ship, *Costa Concordia*, set out on a week-long cruise around the Mediterranean in January 2012, carrying just over 3,000 passengers and 1,000 crew. The captain, Francesco Schettino, ordered the ship to sail close to the island of Giglio on the evening of 13 January, so that local people would have a good view of it, even though this was a deviation from the ship's designated route. The ship went aground on rocks off the coast of Giglio, began to list, and sank within a few hours. Although most of those on board managed to get into lifeboats, 32 died. The captain had left the ship while there were still passengers struggling to escape. He was ordered by the Italian coastguard to return to the ship, but did not do so. Later, the captain was charged with manslaughter and abandoning the ship.

The cruise ship, the Costa Concordia, *sank off the coast of Giglio in Italy.*

In his court trial in Italy in 2014, the captain was found guilty of manslaughter and was sentenced to 16 years in prison. He accepted that he was partly to blame but he felt he had been treated unfairly: he had been singled out for blame, but others were also in the wrong. He also complained about inflammatory media coverage targeted against him. He appealed all the way up to Italy's highest court, where his appeal ultimately failed. He began his prison sentence in 2017. In the firm belief that his trial had been unfair, he launched a complaint in the European Court of Human Rights.

Was the cruise company partly to blame? The cruise company ultimately had oversight over management of the ship, and there were doubts about the safety technology on the ship. The company faced criminal charges, but admitted partial responsibility, and was allowed to pay a fine of one million euros to avoid a trial. Five employees of the company admitted responsibility in connection with the disaster, and were given non-custodial sentences, thus avoiding prosecution proceedings. Victims of the disaster sued Costa Cruises for damages in civil courts. Some sued for damages in the civil courts in Florida, in the US, where Costa has an office. Others sued Costa in Italy, where the company is registered. These civil claims were separate from the criminal proceedings.

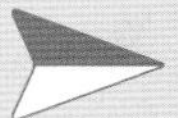

Questions

- In what ways are the civil and criminal proceedings in this case different from each other?
- What does this case reveal about the difficulties in apportioning blame in complex accidents?

Find out more

See the BBC video library on the sinking of the *Costa Concordia*, including, 'Is the design of big cruise ships flawed?', 16 January 2012, at www.bbc.co.uk

Legal risks and responsibilities in international business

For a business, the bulk of the relevant law stems from national lawmaking authorities. Each of the world's sovereign states has its own legal system, which has both lawmaking capacity within its territory ('jurisdiction') and capacity to apply its law to organizations and individuals within its jurisdiction. Legal systems do not exist in a vacuum, but are influenced by the society's social, political and cultural environments. The legal environment, including the content of law and legal processes, are indications of attitudes to law in general, as well as the wider values of a society. It also reflects the historical development of the country's institutions.

legal risk uncertainties surrounding legal liabilities, their implementation in differing legal systems, and the observance of fairness and impartiality in judicial proceedings in differing locations

Legal risk confronts all businesses to some extent, but is more likely to arise where a firm engages in business across national borders. Some of the main areas of risk are shown in Figure 6.3. The degree of risk depends on the extent and nature of the firm's involvement in the foreign location. A firm's involvement in every location entails commensurate responsibilities: the greater its involvement in society, the greater its range of obligations – along with the legal consequences that flow from breaches of those obligations. In each of the areas highlighted, possible legal consequences are shown, involving the foreign firm as either the plaintiff or defendant. In some cases, the consequences involve criminal prosecutions and in some, civil proceedings. In some situations, both types of legal action can arise. Where there is breach of environmental laws, there could be fines for breaches and also claims for damages, as the figure shows.

Contracts are often the first area in which the firm encounters a foreign legal system. If disputes arise with suppliers or customers, then foreign courts could be involved. The MNE which manufactures in a foreign location incurs several types of legal liability. Its operations are affected by local environmental and employment laws, and its products are subject to the law on product liability in each country. For a global company, the impacts can be widely ramified. In 2015, Toyota, Nissan and Honda were compelled to recall an estimated 6.5 million cars due to faulty airbags. Although the airbags were made by a supplier to these car companies, the three carmakers are nonetheless liable to customers for the faults.

Regulatory frameworks apply to many aspects of business. Environmental protection is one area of law that is now prioritized in many countries, and is likely to be strengthened in future by governments acting in the public interest. Other areas of regulation are health and safety at work, employee rights, advertising, financial services, data protection and corporate governance. When the law is strengthened, a company is compelled to comply. This could entail considerable rethinking of how the company conducts its business. The prospect of regulation of social media giants is an example. Social media such as Facebook, Twitter and YouTube are coming under the spotlight for policy issues such as privacy terms. They are criticized for allowing their platforms to be used for a number of questionable practices, such as spreading 'fake' content, misusing personal data, and issuing hate speech.

The misuse of personal data has been associated with the targeting of voters in elections. Governments are contemplating regulatory reforms in the public interest. New regulation of hate speech on the social media has been introduced in Germany. The social media are global in reach, but these companies bear responsibilities in national legal frameworks.

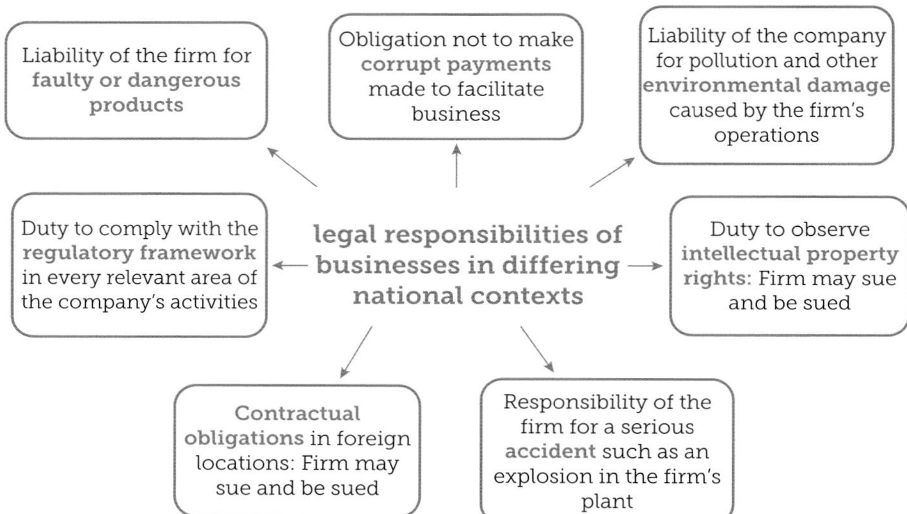

Figure 6.3 **Key legal responsibilities of businesses**

A firm's patents and trademarks, which are areas of intellectual property law, can be difficult to enforce in some locations, even leading companies to exit particular markets. The food company, Danone, is an example of a company which engaged in a long legal battle with a Chinese partner, Wahaha, in a soft drinks joint venture, and eventually decided to sell out its 51% stake. It accused Wahaha of running parallel businesses which infringed its trademarks. Had Danone taken a 60% stake, giving it greater control, it might have been able to prevent the activities which led to legal action.

Businesses are frequently involved in making payments to local officials to facilitate their activities. In many countries where the rule of law is weak, such payments can verge on corruption, but this situation is often accepted locally as normal practice, even though in breach of the country's laws. The foreign business can easily be caught up in this environment, and find that it is targeted for breaches of the law. China is an example. Although functioning in an authoritarian environment, China has adapted its legal system since the 1980s, to accommodate business transactions, including contract law and intellectual property law. A new competition law is based on the EU model. However, despite western forms, the workings of the legal system lack the transparency and independent judiciary that would be expected in western contexts. In 2014, the Chinese subsidiary of global pharmaceutical company, GSK, was found by a Chinese court to have engaged in bribing doctors and hospitals. GSK was fined a sum equivalent to nearly $500 million, but, more significant than the large fine was the prosecution of GSK's country head of operations, and four other company executives, all Chinese nationals. These GSK executives were tried in secret and faced potential prison sentences of four years. All were found guilty and were given suspended sentences; the country manager, who is British, was deported. Although GSK could feel relieved that its employees were not imprisoned, being embroiled in opaque legal proceedings in a country that is known for

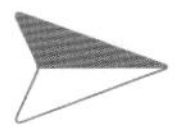

corruption was a warning to the company that it must assess its management systems in light of legal risks and ethical principles (Pratley, 2014).

The authoritative World Justice Project (WJP) surveys the strength of the rule of law in 126 countries. In its annual publication of the results, it reported that in 2019, there had been significant declines in the rule of law around the world for the second successive year. It found that 64% of the countries surveyed had deteriorated towards autocratic rule in the preceding year (see Figure 6.4). Of these, Poland showed the sharpest decline, but other countries that had declined significantly were Serbia, Egypt, the Philippines, China, Hungary and Turkey. The WJP criteria take into account the checks on government power, criminal justice, open government, and fundamental rights (World Justice Project, 2019). The report pointed to the rise in autocratic rule, with authoritarian leaders consolidating their power. It also highlighted declines in an independent judiciary, declines in freedom of the press and the weakness of legislatures to check autocratic rule. The deterioration in the rule of law is taking place almost by stealth, cloaked in apparent legality: laws are being enacted that authorize the weakening of the rule of law. Such changes have the forms of legality, while the effect is to weaken the institutions that should check abuse of power and autocratic government. On the positive side, the report also highlighted notable improvements in the rule of law in Argentina and Estonia.

A selection of diverse countries is given in Figure 6.4. Denmark stands out as the highest example of the rule of law, and this standing has been consistent over a long period. The US has a somewhat lower ranking than other advanced economies listed. The use of a secret court, the Foreign Intelligence Surveillance Court (FISA Court), which is outside the public court system, to authorize the bulk collection of data on members of the public, can be criticized as undermining the rule of law. India and Russia are emerging economies with much lower rankings. India has a democratic political system, and its legal system inherited elements of its British colonial past, including an independent judiciary, but its modest ranking suggests significant corruption. Its ranking is beneath Brazil, which has been shaken by corruption scandals that have resulted in the impeachment of the president (see the case study in Chapter 5). Congo and Venezuela, both suffering from failures of governance, are near the bottom of this list. Venezuela's hardline socialist government has become increasingly authoritarian and plunged the country into economic collapse.

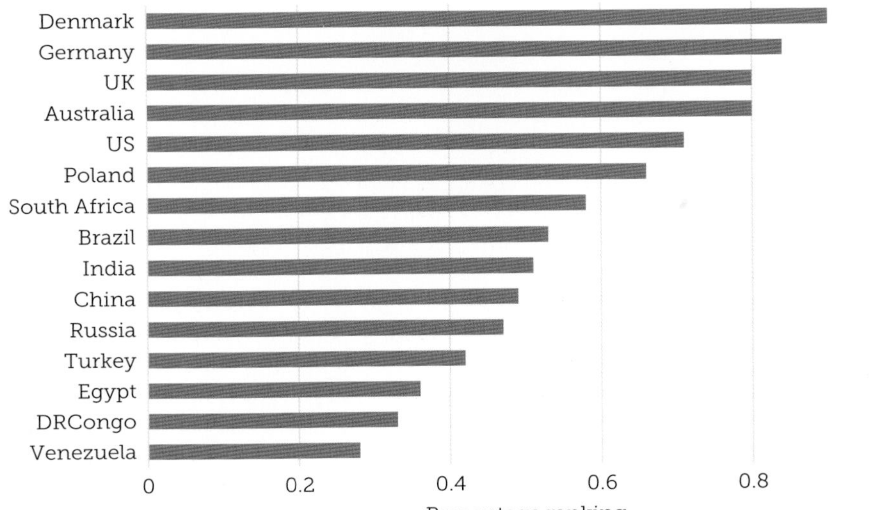

Figure 6.4 The rule of law rankings of selected countries

Source of data: World Justice Project (2019) WJP Rule of Law Index 2019 pp. 6–7, at https://worldjusticeproject.org, accessed 23 September 2019.

Why does the rule of law matter for businesses?

Emerging economies attract global businesses because of their market potential. But these economies tend to provide weaker protections for the rule of law and give greater weight to personal relations in commercial activities. What are the likely repercussions for businesses in locations where the rule of law is weak?

What would you recommend foreign businesses to do in handling the legal risks in these situations?

National legal systems: diversity and interactions

legislation laws enacted by lawmaking processes set out in national constitutions; also known as statute law

judicial system system of courts, usually divided between civil courts and criminal courts

civil law tradition legal system based on comprehensive legal codes which form the basic law

common law tradition legal system based chiefly on accumulated case law in decided judgments, through a system of binding precedents

The pre-eminence of national legal systems derives from the theory of the sovereign state. Every legal system may be divided into two main sets of functional institutions. These are legislation (lawmaking) and adjudication (the settlement of cases). **Legislation**, or statute law, is enacted by the authorized bodies in the state, often under a constitutional framework. In a democracy, the elected legislature is a key lawmaking body. Much lawmaking follows the social and political agendas of elected governments. Legislators can get it wrong, of course. In 1920, the US passed a constitutional amendment prohibiting the manufacture, sale and transport of alcoholic beverages. It proved to be unpopular and virtually impossible to enforce, and was overturned by a later constitutional amendment in 1933.

The system of courts, or **judicial system**, interprets and applies the law in particular cases. The extent to which judges shape legal development is a matter of differing opinions. As will be seen below, 'case law' (judge-made law) is more important in some countries than in others. A general rule is that legal systems attempt to draw a line between lawmaking and judicial functions. But tension inevitably arises between the judicial institutions and the lawmaking branches, which are the executive and legislative. Court systems are designed to prevent the intrusion of political and personal considerations, and judges should be seen to be fair and impartial. The judiciary often finds itself influencing policy, although, in theory, judges are meant simply to apply the law, rather than make it. If judges become 'politicized', this is seen as eroding their independence. On the other hand, justices of the US Supreme Court are openly categorized as 'conservative' judges, associated with Republican Party values, or 'liberal' judges, closer to Democratic Party values in their thinking. It is generally accepted that presidents seek to appoint justices to the Supreme Court who have similar values to themselves, thus ensuring a perpetuation of their political vision in the judicial sphere long after they have left office. Antonin Scalia, a Supreme Court judge who had been appointed by Republican president Ronald Reagan in 1986, died in 2016, leaving a significant legacy in numerous spheres, including the controversial Citizens United judgment (discussed in Chapter 5) which gave the green light to unlimited corporate financing of political campaigns. President Trump nominated a conservative to replace Justice Scalia, and soon afterwards, made a second nomination of a conservative-leaning judge, to replace a judge who was retiring. Both had to be approved by the Senate, where Republicans held a majority. These two appointments would go some way to perpetuate the legacy of Justice Scalia in Supreme Court judgments for many years to come.

The world's legal systems can be classified in terms of legal traditions or legal families. The two major western historical traditions are the civil law tradition and the common law tradition. The **civil law** tradition, prevalent in continental Europe, is founded on a comprehensive legal code, whereas the **common law** tradition,

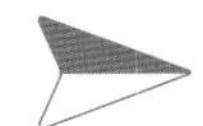

English in origin, emphasizes case law. Both have been adopted in a variety of non-western contexts, as part of modernization processes (see Table 6.2). Newly independent states have tended to adopt the legal tradition of their former colonial power. For this reason, a lawyer from Ghana will find it much easier to understand a lawyer from Kenya or England, than one from the Ivory Coast just next door, which falls within French colonial influence (Zweigert and Kötz, 1998).

Table 6.2 Selected civil law and common law countries

Civil law	Common law
Argentina	Australia
Brazil	Bangladesh
Chile	Canada
China	Ghana
Egypt	India
France	Israel
Germany	Jamaica
Greece	Kenya
Indonesia	Malaysia
Iran	Nigeria
Italy	Singapore
Japan	England
Mexico	United States
Sweden	Zambia

Civil law tradition

The civil law tradition is by far the older of the two, originating in the ancient Roman *ius civile*, which in the sixth century was codified in the Justinian Code. Civil law relies on a legal code for the basic groundwork of the system, on which further lawmaking is built. The legal code is a comprehensive, systematic setting out of the basic law for a country. The modern models of codified law are the French Civil Code of 1804, known as the Napoleonic Code, and the German Civil Code of 1896. Codified law is in fact divided into a number of different codes, depending on the subject matter. The civil code, which contains the body of private law (that is, between citizens), is complemented, for example, by a Commercial Code and a Criminal Code. These codes have demonstrated their adaptability by providing models for numerous other countries in Europe, Latin America, Africa, Asia and the Middle East (see Table 6.2). In the UK, Scotland falls within the civil law tradition. Japan's choice of the civil law model coincided with the country's initial industrialization and modernization policies in the late nineteenth century.

The attraction of the civil law model lies in the supremacy of the single authoritative source of the law. The principles and concepts contained in the codes form the basis of legal reasoning. Although the accumulated decisions of judges are useful as guidelines, they are not in themselves a source of law. This is the major distinction between the civil law and common law systems, shown in Table 6.3. The distinction has been described as one between different legal styles. The urge to regulate and systematize has dominated continental legal thinking, whereas English lawyers have tended to improvise, not making a decision until they have to, on the view that 'we'll cross that bridge when we come to it' (Zweigert and Kötz, 1998: 70).

Table 6.3 Outline of civil law and common law traditions

	Civil law tradition	Common law tradition
Sources of the law	Comprehensive legal codes	Judge-made law and statutes
Role of case law	Guidance, but not binding	System of binding precedent
Legal style	Systematized application of principles	Pragmatic and piecemeal

Common law tradition

The **common law system** originated in England some 900 years ago – long before Parliament had become the supreme lawmaking authority. Common law is essentially judge-made law, known as case law. In deciding a particular dispute, the judge creates a precedent to be followed in similar cases in the future. The body of law builds up through the accumulation of precedents in decided cases. The system has both flexibility and rigidities in practice. Precedents may be applied more loosely or more strictly in later cases, lending flexibility. However, as the court system is hierarchical, the decisions of higher courts form precedents which must be followed by lower courts. Faced with what seems to be a bad precedent, the judge in a lower court has little choice but to follow it. The growth in statute law, in the form of Acts of Parliament, mainly in the last hundred years, has come about mainly in response to the complexities of economic and social changes. Modern judges spend a great deal of their time interpreting and applying statute law. The growing importance of statute law (also referred to as enacted law) suggests a convergence with the civil law tradition, although, when it comes down to interpreting the law in particular factual situations – which is what matters to litigants – the judge still holds a good deal of power.

Common law systems have been transplanted to countries as diverse as the US and India. Like all legal systems, the tradition has been adapted to the local environment. The US, with its division between federal and 50 state jurisdictions, has evolved a particularly complex system, with overlapping jurisdictions that can be confusing to outsiders (and even insiders). Each state constitutes a system within a system – Louisiana even has remnants of French codified law from its own colonial past. The individual states have made efforts to achieve consistency in the law in key areas that affect business, notably through the Uniform Commercial Code, which has been adopted by all the states (although only partially in Louisiana). The American Law Institute has spearheaded the efforts to bring about consistency by producing its Restatements of the law in areas such as contract, tort and product liability. These restatements resemble codified law in all but name, but they do not have the status of a statute as they are not passed by Congress. Their aim is to clarify the law and they act as guidance to lawyers and judges. In matters that raise issues of constitutionality, federal courts, and ultimately the US Supreme Court, are the ultimate authorities.

Non-western legal systems

The growth in commercial law has reached almost all countries, aware that economic development depends on a sound legal framework and an efficient and accessible court system. As has been seen, the groundwork for modern legal systems in much of the world was the legacy of colonial regimes. Legal traditions in many countries which are based on customary law, pre-date western systems, and continue to form an important part of the overall legal environment. In many countries, therefore, we now find a mixture of pre-modern customs, colonial forms, and

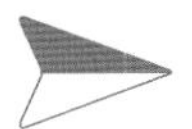

newer codes designed to keep up to date with business needs. The study of evolving legal systems in developing countries reveals much about the relationship between law and social change.

Shari'a the authoritative source of Islamic law

Non-western legal traditions include Islamic, Chinese and Hindu law. Of these, Islamic law, called the ***Shari'a*** (or God's rules), is perhaps the most highly developed. Islamic law can have a direct impact on the way business is conducted in Muslim countries, such as Saudi Arabia and Sudan. Because the *Shari'a* prohibits 'unearned profits', the charging of interest is forbidden. Financing through banks can still be arranged, by devising alternative legal forms to cover transactions, such as profit-sharing and loss-sharing by a lending bank. Islamic countries have introduced codes for the secular regulation of activities like the formation and enforcement of contracts, and foreign investment. Accordingly, most now have secular tribunals for these areas.

Both western and non-western legal traditions have evolved and adapted to different cultural contexts, in response to two related forces. *First*, there has been a perceived need to modernize national legal structures as societies have become more complex, and legal relations, including consumer and employment contracts, have become more common. Most of this development has come through legislation. In the UK, the Consumer Rights Act 2015, which covers the sale of goods, digital content and services, consolidated a number of existing statutes. *Secondly*, the growth of global markets has led to increasing international efforts to achieve uniformity and standardization of laws across national borders. Much of this latter effort has come through multilateral international conventions. These are signed and then ratified by national authorities, ultimately taking on a status similar to the domestic law of the state. In particular, international conventions have played an important role in bringing common legal frameworks for international trade in goods (as will be discussed below). Within the European Union harmonization has gone further, putting in place supranational legal structures for both lawmaking and adjudication.

How do legal systems rate with businesses?

Businesses engage with a country's legal system in numerous contexts. Government permissions, contractual agreements and liabilities for accidents are some of them.

Which of the types of national legal system described here is most likely to be accessible, fair and efficient, from a business perspective?

Legal framework of the European Union

supranational legal institutions above those of domestic law; characterizes EU law

For each member state, the EU is a growing source of law, which has become intertwined with national law. The foundation treaty, the Treaty of Rome of 1957 and later treaties have created **supranational** institutions, that is, institutions above those of domestic law. Under the Maastricht Treaty of 1992, three pillars were designated: the European Communities, the Common Foreign and Security Policy, and the Police and Judicial Co-operation in Criminal Matters. The first of these was supranational, and the other two represented inter-governmental co-operation. The law of the EU was technically referred to as EC law, as it fell under the first pillar. With the Treaty of Lisbon of 2009, the three-pillar system has been abolished, subsuming the second and third pillars. The EU itself now has legal personality: the EU can make treaties in its own name, and its law is 'EU law'.

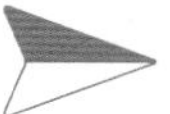

EU lawmaking now extends to a wide range of areas, although not as yet taxation and defence. The legislative function is divided between the Commission, the Council and the European Parliament, through the co-decision procedure (see Chapter 5). EU law falls into two main types. 'Regulations' are directly applicable throughout the EU, becoming incorporated automatically into the law of each member state. They create individual rights and obligations which governments must recognize. 'Directives' require member states to implement their provisions, usually within a given period of time, such as two years. In some cases, the directive may have direct effect, allowing individuals to enforce rights directly, if the member state does not implement the law in the required time limit. For businesses, competition law is an area with growing implications for MNEs (see later section). In competition law, high-profile cases have involved the Commission taking legal action against a company in the European Court of Justice.

European Court of Justice (ECJ) highest court for interpreting EU law

The judicial function centres on the **European Court of Justice (ECJ)** (https://curia.europa.eu/jcms/jcms). It is the sole interpreter of EU law, and can override national legislation in cases of conflict. Although national supreme courts have ultimate authority in domestic matters, in issues involving EU institutions and EU law, the ECJ is the ultimate authority. Much of the impetus behind the UK's referendum on withdrawing from the EU was driven by the wish to be independent of the ECJ's jurisdiction (see Chapter 5). The ECJ interprets the treaties and other legislation. It is modelled on courts in the civil law tradition, in that it is not bound by its previous decisions, but its case law has in fact shown consistency. The ECJ is now divided into sections which hear cases at first instance and those which hear cases in an appellate capacity, that is, on appeal.

Cross-border business transactions

Laws covering trade between businesses in different countries have existed since the medieval period, when the *law merchant* was born of customary rules used by the merchants of the period. These rules, relating to sale of goods and the settlement of disputes, were gradually incorporated into national bodies of law, codified in the case of the civil law countries, and part of the common law in common law countries. In England, the law became enacted in the Sale of Goods Act 1894 (now superseded by the Consumer Rights Act 2015), and in the US the Uniform Commercial Code (1951) harmonized the law between the 50 states. Impetus to achieve international harmonization has come from a number of initiatives.

International codification: facilitating cross-border business

Set up in 1966, the UN Commission on International Trade Law (UNCITRAL) (www.uncitral.org) attempted to devise a framework to satisfy the needs of businesses in trading nations of all continents. The result was the Convention on Contracts for the International Sale of Goods (CISG) of 1980 (the Vienna Convention), which came into force in 1988. The CISG does not apply automatically to international sales. The convention must be ratified by individual states, becoming incorporated in their domestic law. The number of countries which have ratified the convention (83 by 2014) continues to rise, accounting for the bulk of the world's trade. Among major trading nations, the US, Germany, France, China, Brazil and Japan have ratified. Notable among those which have not yet ratified are India, South Africa and the UK. The convention applies to contracts falling within its scope that are concluded by firms in countries which have ratified, or to contracts whose performance is carried out in a country which has ratified. For transactions between firms in non-ratifying countries, the rules of private international law apply (discussed below).

The CISG makes a major contribution in harmonizing rules to do with the formation of contracts for the sale of goods, obligations of the parties, and remedies. It attempts to bridge the gap between civil and common law jurisdictions on questions such as the 'meeting of minds' between the parties over the existence of an agreement, and its particular terms. These are the key areas in which disputes arise, and the CISG attempts to compromise between countries which require certainty and those which allow greater flexibility. For example, the requirement that a contract must be in writing is traditional in the common law countries (although of diminishing importance), whereas civil law countries tend to have no writing requirement. The CISG allows ratifying countries the option, in keeping with their own national law. China, for example, has preserved its writing requirement.

The International Institute for the Unification of Private International Law (UNIDROIT) has complemented the CISG, and approached the need for unification from a different perspective. The UNIDROIT Principles of International Commercial Contracts, first published in 1994, offer general rules for international contracts, and are broadly similar to the CISG, but of wider application. They have been revised in 2004 and in 2010, and are subject to continuing attention from the legal specialists who have sought to make them as relevant as possible to trends in international transactions. The Principles are not confined to the sale of goods; nor are they confined to 'one-off' sales. Much recent legal attention has been devoted to adapting the Principles to long-term contracts and 'relational' contracts (discussed below), whereby parties are involved in ongoing relations over a potentially long period of time. Some examples are service contracts, construction contracts, distributorships, outsourcing, franchising and licensing. In these long-term contracts, relational trust is an important element, and terms may allow for renegotiation and adaptation as circumstances change (Bonell, 2014). The UNIDROIT Principles have therefore adapted to the more complex contractual landscape of globalized businesses. Moreover, as they are not embodied in any binding international convention, they can be incorporated into contracts by firms from any country, not just those that have ratified the CISG. It has been suggested that they come closest to 'the emerging international consensus' on the rules of international trade (Moens and Gillies, 1998: 81). Because the Principles do not themselves have any force of law, they can be adopted and modified as needed, and have even provided models for legislators as diverse as Mexico, Québec and The Netherlands. In particular, they have facilitated the growing trade between Australia and its Asian neighbours.

Cultural factors: why they matter in a globalized world

Negotiation of international contracts usually involves use of a foreign language for at least one of the parties. Apart from problems of translating technical terms, the cultural context of negotiations varies considerably. High-context and low-context languages will have different styles of negotiation. Attention to detailed terms and confrontational bargaining are far more significant in the Anglo-American context than in Asian contexts, for example. The formally agreed contract may be in one language, with an unofficial translation in another, which clarifies the terms. Alternatively, the contract may have two official versions in two different languages. An inescapable difficulty is possible misunderstandings in the translation process. Interpretation of terms, even between speakers of the same language, can differ from country to country. Hence, it should be remembered that while the contract creates legal obligations, these are not necessarily interpreted in exactly the same way by all parties, and, in case of dispute, an arbitrator or judge faces an unenviable task of finding out what the parties intended in a particular situation.

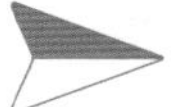

The role of the contract itself is viewed differently in different cultures. In individualistic cultures the detailed formal contract governs business relationships, whereas in the more group-oriented societies, such as Japan and South East Asia, business relies more on informal, personalized relationships. **Relational contracting**, as the latter is known, is rooted in societies where personal ties built on trust, often over a number of years, matter more than formal written documents. In these societies, the preferred method of settling disputes is out of court, rather than through litigation. In China, this cultural approach is known as ***guanxi***, which simply means 'relationships'. In more individualist societies, **arm's length contracting** (in which the agreement is paramount) is more the norm. With the growing numbers of joint ventures and expanding markets across cultural boundaries, an understanding of cultural sensitivities is essential in cross-border contracts. Continuing contractual relations in long-term contracts, as noted above, are now common in global business, and parties that have traditionally relied on formal agreements are becoming more involved in relational contracting. While written contracts are now part of the modern legal systems that have been adopted in non-western societies, the underlying cultural environment is still influential in their negotiation and interpretation. It goes without saying that a 'meeting of minds' over both the terms and the working relationship that flows from the agreement is good insurance against a breakdown which could lead to the courts.

relational contracting business dealings in which personal relations between the parties are more important than formal written agreements

guanxi personal relations which establish the trust and mutual obligations necessary for business in China

arm's length contracting business dealings between people who interact only for the purpose of doing business with each other

tort in common law countries, branch of law which concerns obligations not to cause harm to others in society

negligence breach of a duty to take reasonable care which causes injury or other harm to another; actionable in civil courts

product liability liability of a producer of a defective product to consumers harmed by the product; can extend to suppliers

Negligence and product liability: holding businesses to account

Whereas obligations under contracts are defined by the particular agreement, obligations in **tort** arise from a range of broadly defined obligations owed by those in society to fellow citizens generally. The plaintiff may suffer personal injury or damage to property in an accident caused by the activities of the defendant. If the plaintiff's reputation has been damaged by something the defendant has said publicly, the claim is in libel. There are many different areas of tort law, but the areas which are of greatest relevance to business are negligence and product liability. In a **negligence** claim, the defendant is alleged to have failed to take reasonable care and so caused the plaintiff's injuries or loss. Negligence can cover injury from defective products, and it can also cover situations where there is a service provided, such as professional services. **Product liability** claims impose a duty which is much nearer to 'strict' liability, in which the defendant (usually the producer) is made liable for defective products that cause harm to consumers. The development of tort law in these areas parallels the growth of modern consumer society. Factory-produced goods, mass transport, advanced pharmaceutical products, medical procedures, and industrialized food production all carry risks of accidents and injury, sometimes on a wide scale. All industrialized countries have in place laws protecting consumers and other victims in these cases. In the EU, product liability laws were harmonized by a directive in 1985, which has been incorporated into national law (in the UK, by the Consumer Protection Act 1987). The directive, which includes a 'development risks defence', providing an escape route for producers who have achieved an industry-standard level of product testing, is perceived to be less consumer-friendly than US law.

In the US, tort litigation, particularly product liability, has developed into a booming industry. While product liability laws vary from state to state, the legal climate has facilitated litigation in three key ways: (1) the use of the 'class' action, whereby a group of plaintiffs may come together to bring legal proceedings; (2) the award by courts of 'punitive' damages (intended to punish the defendant for the wrongdoing) to plaintiffs, in addition to compensatory damages. Huge sums have been awarded by American juries as punitive damages (although often reduced on appeal, and punitive damages are capped in some states); and (3) the 'contingency' fee system

 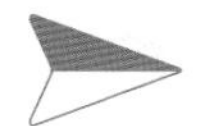

for lawyers' fees, also known as the 'no-win-no-fee' system, whereby the legal fees are an agreed percentage of the damages. With this prior arrangement, the potential plaintiff without huge resources can bring a claim.

In Bhopal, India, in 1984, a chemical disaster resulted in the deaths of 8,000 people in the immediate aftermath, and injuries to several hundred thousand others, including long-term health problems. The victims attempted to sue the parent company, Union Carbide, in New York, arguing that negligence in the design of the plant caused the accident, in which a massive escape of poisonous gases occurred. Their claim failed, as much of the design and engineering that went into the plant was carried out by local engineers in India. The plaintiffs then sought damages in India. A settlement was reached with the Indian government, which took over the case, but where payments were made, they were inadequate, and many victims received no compensation. Meanwhile, contamination remains a blight on the area, over three decades later. Criminal cases against those held responsible were also a story of too little, too late, from the point of view of victims. Seven former employees of Union Carbide, all Indian, were found guilty of criminal negligence in 2010, some 26 years after the explosion. They were given prison sentences of two years each, the maximum possible for criminal negligence, as the original charges of culpable homicide had been reduced by a previous court. There was a public outcry at these light sentences, but they were upheld by India's Supreme Court.

In light of the Bhopal disaster and the legacy of protracted civil and criminal cases, the Indian government was concerned about the legal implications of purchasing equipment for nuclear power generation from foreign suppliers, who would be deterred by legal uncertainties following Bhopal. A new law on civil liability for nuclear damage was enacted in 2010, raising the possibility that the supplier of nuclear reactors and parts would incur liability for nuclear accidents. The US expressed concerns about possible liability, as one of its companies, General Electric (GE), is a major global supplier in the nuclear industry. A clarification agreement between India and the US was reached, reiterating the principle usually accepted as the international norm, which is that the operator bears all the liability and the suppliers bear none. However, this agreement between governments on the interpretation of the new law might well fail to provide the assurance that companies such as GE seek before selling equipment in India.

A GE Mark 1 model of reactor was involved in the Fukushima nuclear disaster in Japan in 2011, in which a major earthquake and tsunami caused meltdown in the six Fukushima reactors. Radiation was released over a large area, affecting hundreds of thousands of people. Blame fell on the power company that operated the plant. It was unable to pay the huge sums involved in dealing with the damage, and the Japanese government was compelled to make up the shortfall. There was arguably negligence in the operation of the plant, and three former executives of the power company were charged with professional negligence, a criminal offence, in 2016 (see Chapter 10). Were there problems with the GE Mark 1 reactor? Dating from the 1960s, the Mark 1 was known to have safety weaknesses, but GE faced no liability (Zeller, 2011). Critics of this situation point out that the nuclear industry is allowed to escape liability for the damage caused by its products, whereas companies in other sectors are made to pay under laws of product liability (Naidoo, 2013). The British oil company, BP, faced huge liabilities for lack of oilrig safety over the Deepwater Horizon oil spill in the Gulf of Mexico in 2010, in which 11 people lost their lives. By 2014, the sum had reached about $58 billion, and was still potentially rising. The payments included $27 billion on cleanup, $13 billion in damages and $18 billion in fines. If global suppliers in the nuclear industry were to incur liability for damage caused by their faulty products, they would arguably devote greater attention to improving safety in their designs.

When a consumer suffers harm as a result of a product defect, a manufacturing company can find itself on the end of product liability claims, where the damage may be multiplied, depending on the number of consumers affected. The large corporation which manufactures for global markets may face claims from millions of consumers worldwide. The **product recall** is a means of limiting the damage. It is recognized by the global companies as part of their legal obligations and is also important in maintaining their reputations. Still, there are many companies that sell unsafe and substandard products globally. These companies calculate that the risks of being caught are low. And, even if caught up in legal proceedings, their legal teams are likely to find ways to avert liability and contest claims.

product recall withdrawal of a product from the marketplace due to defects which might cause harm to consumers

The EU has operated the Rapid Alert System on product safety since 2003, which applies to dangerous products with the exception of food. Figure 6.5 shows a recent rise in the number of notifications of dangerous products. There have been improvements in the mechanisms for detecting risky products and tracing where they have come from. In 2017, the largest category of unsafe products was toys, followed by motor vehicles, clothing, childcare articles and electrical appliances. The main risks arising from unsafe toys are choking from small parts that become detached and injury from chemicals, such as plastic softeners and dyes. An issue in the EU has been the proliferation of consumer goods manufactured in low-cost locations where quality standards are weak or not enforced. In 2014, 64% of unsafe products notified originated in China. In 2017, that percentage was 55%. Most of the dangerous products are purchased on online platforms and marketplaces, often bought by consumers directly from third countries. Enforcing EU safety standards is difficult in these situations. The EU Commission issued a recommendation to online marketplaces in 2018, in an initiative to prevent the spread of dangerous products.

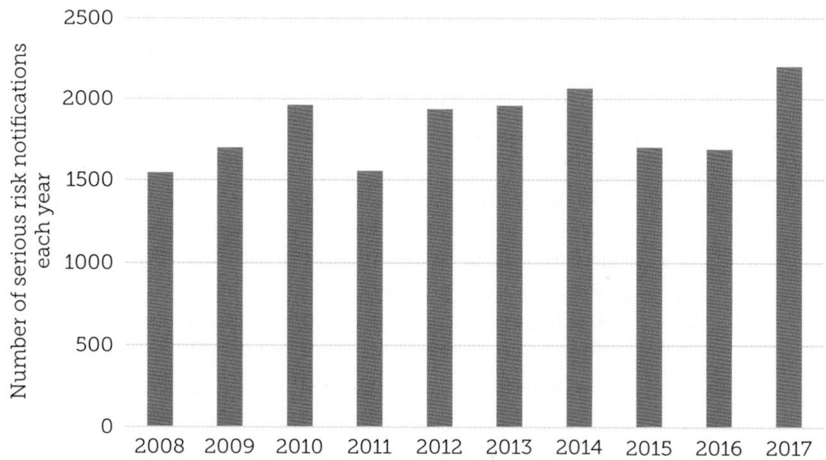

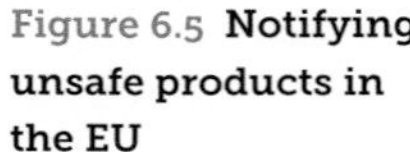

Figure 6.5 Notifying unsafe products in the EU

Source of data: European Commission (2018) Rapid Alert System for Dangerous Products, 2017 Annual Report, at https://ec.europa.eu/consumers/consumer_safety

How effectively does law promote business competition?

Where companies compete fairly and are not allowed to manipulate markets, it is assumed that consumers will benefit in terms of price, value for money and innovation. Competition thus promotes rising standards of living. Most governments would probably prefer that markets remain fair and competitive, but history has shown that unfair practices, such as price-fixing, can occur, either between

companies which are ostensibly competitors or where one firm has a dominant market position. The monopolist has almost complete control of the market, making it nearly impossible for newcomers to get a foothold. Governments can step in to regulate uncompetitive behaviour in these situations. This body of law is known as 'antitrust' law in the US. Here, it dates back to the Sherman Act of 1890, in an era when the large business empires that dominated the end of the nineteenth century had become seemingly invincible. They relied on holding companies, cartels and trusts. All are legal devices constructed to extend corporate ownership over a multiplicity of companies.

MINI CASE STUDY

Breaking up the AT&T monopoly

The US has a long history of contests between monopolist companies and regulators. The American telephone giant, AT&T (American Telephone and Telegraph), also known as the Bell System, was pursued by the government in 1907 for antitrust practices. The dispute was eventually settled in 1913, when Bell agreed to sell off its Western Union telegraph arm and to refrain from buying up companies in local markets. The smaller companies benefited from the settlement, as did Bell, which had avoided becoming nationalized. Regulators again came calling in 1949, concerned over Bell's ownership of Western Electrics, its manufacturing arm, which had a fledgling computer business. In 1956, Bell again agreed a settlement – one that let it retain the telephone business and Western Electrics. But as part of the deal, it had to let go its computer patents – inventions that were to revolutionize the technological landscape in years to come.

In the following years, the company's telephone business went from strength to strength, reaching 90% of US homes by 1969. Known as 'Ma Bell', it was again targeted by antitrust authorities, and in 1982, a landmark agreement was reached to break it up. Ma Bell was compelled to give up its regional operating companies, 'baby Bells', which became independent companies, able to develop and innovate, unshackled from their parent company. These companies thrived, and one of them, Southwestern Bell, eventually took over the parent company, becoming the new AT&T.

Much of Silicon Valley's technological innovation can be traced back to the various break-up measures that were imposed on the old AT&T. IBM, also considered a monopolist, was in the lens of antitrust authorities in 1982, but the lawsuit was dropped, as IBM was seen as an innovative monopolist, in contrast to AT&T. The new AT&T launched a takeover of media giant, Time Warner, in 2018, aiming to create a combined telephone and media empire. The Justice Department was against the merger, possibly influenced by the president's strained relations with these media giants. Arguing against the merger in court, the Justice Department cited the adverse effect the merger would have on consumers, as well as the detrimental effect on innovation. However, the Justice Department lost its appeal, as the federal Appeals Court approved the merger early in 2019. This was a significant boost for AT&T, in creating the new media empire it had envisaged with Time Warner.

Questions

- What did AT&T get right – or wrong – in 1956 and 1982?
- What are the lessons for today's technology companies from AT&T's relations with regulators?

Find out more

See the article, 'Is it time to break up tech giants such as Facebook?' by Larry Elliott, 25 March 2018, in *The Guardian*.

Under the Sherman Act, the US Justice Department can break up monopolies that are not operating in the public interest, and it has done so in some high-profile cases. One of the most famous is the break-up of the telephone monopoly of AT&T in 1982, as the mini case study shows. Its efforts to break up Microsoft in the late 1990s, however, ran into a changing political environment, in which attitudes towards big business had softened. The court held against breaking up Microsoft, but found the company had engaged in anti-competitive behaviour, which it was ordered to stop. The court's judgment was delivered in 2001, the year when Republican president George W. Bush took office. Could the tide change again? In 2019, the US Federal Trade Commission (FTC), which has oversight of consumer protection, announced a fine of $5 billion imposed on Facebook for violations of privacy (see the closing case study). Shortly afterwards, the Justice Department announced an anti-trust investigation into the technology giants for anti-competitive behaviour that could harm consumers. The companies were not named, but would probably include Amazon, Facebook, Apple and Alphabet (the parent of Google). The fact that the Justice Department is commonly viewed as susceptible of swaying to the political winds of the day might have been behind this move. The technology giants are unlikely to face break-up, but could be required to make changes to their businesses (see the further discussion in Chapter 9).

competition law area of law which concerns rules against abuse of a dominant market position and unfair trading practices by one or more firms

cartel group of firms that come together, often informally, to restrict trade or engage in anti-competitive behaviour

Competition law can be divided into distinct areas, each targeting different types of anti-competitive activity:

- Prohibition on agreements which amount to restrictive practices, such as a price-fixing agreement. This prohibition is aimed at **cartels**, that is, groups of firms which come together, often informally, to restrict trade or engage in anti-competitive behaviour.
- Oversight of mergers, to prevent the creation of a monopoly in a particular market.
- In cases where a firm already has a dominant market position, prohibition of behaviour that constitutes abuse of a dominant position in that market.

In every country that has competition law, the government sets up specialist agencies to handle competition matters, including investigation and enforcement of the law. There are wide variations in the size and approach of these bodies. Agencies in some countries consist of only a handful of people on a very limited budget, making it difficult to carry out extensive investigations. In others, competition authorities have greater resources and an ability to take on large MNEs such as Microsoft, which themselves are able to spend large sums on defending anti-competitive cases brought against them. The relevant authority in the UK is the Competition and Markets Authority (CMA) (www.gov.uk/government/organisations/competition-and-markets-authority). Its remit covers all the areas of competition law listed above, taking the approach that its activities are aimed at benefiting consumers. It does not just deal with companies. Although it does not handle individual cases from consumers, it does receive complaints from members of the public on competition matters and poor business practices, which affect consumers generally.

The vigour with which cartels and monopolists are pursued differs from country to country, and over time. Although legislation tends to be worded in a similar way in every jurisdiction, interpretation can vary: a merger could be viewed as compliant in one country, whereas in another, one of the firms might be asked by the authorities to divest itself of some parts of its operations. Historically, competition law has developed in market economies. US and European national competition authorities are examples, as is the EU. The EU has widened its perspective, taking in cases involving state aid to companies, which violates EU competition law.

For international managers, competition law can be an important determinant of strategy. If a firm wishes to take over another in a country where it already has a sizeable market share, the takeover would look attractive from the firm's point of view, but the country's competition authorities might take a dim view. Moreover, it might be many months before the firms are given the decision of the government agency. When the decision does come, it might state conditions which must be met before the merger can go ahead. A competition authority's jurisdiction is ostensibly its own territory, but decisions can compel a firm to divest activities in another country. Although this extra-territorial aspect might seem strange, it is being actively used by Chinese competition authorities.

In the era of globalization, companies are often involved in mergers and acquisition activity that straddles multiple countries. While there is no global competition agency, there is now considerable co-operation among national and EU competition authorities. The European Commission co-operates with competition authorities in over 80 jurisdictions, including regional free trade groupings (http://ec.europa.eu/competition). There now exists an International Competition Network (ICN) that brings together representatives of competition authorities in 132 member states. The ICN as a forum for competition issues can be invaluable, aiding in the understanding of stakeholder perspectives, including governments, businesses and consumers. All the ICN's participants share the same goals of promoting procedural fairness, impartiality, transparency and co-operation (Vestager, 2015). The ICN's annual conference in New Delhi in 2018 was attended by 500 participants from 73 countries. Co-operation among them can help to ensure consistency and fairness in the legal hurdles that are associated with mergers and acquisitions. These developments can benefit companies planning mergers, helping to resolve the complexities and introducing a global – rather than simply national – perspective.

International law framing the business environment

While most of the law that impacts on business is national in origin, the growing body of law at international level is now becoming more important for businesses and for their stakeholders. We look first at the distinctive characteristics of international law, and then we look at the supranational courts that function under the authority of the UN.

The scope of international law

international law body of rules recognized by the international community as governing relations between sovereign states

International law covers the body of rules recognized by the international community as governing relations between sovereign states. It is also referred to as 'public international law', to distinguish it from the rules of private international law discussed in the next section. The world's sovereign states, while recognizing international law, have not (as yet) created a supranational legal system with enforcement mechanisms mirroring those at national level. The functions of lawmaking and dispute settlement, therefore, rely on the co-operation of states and the willingness of state authorities to submit to international law as a matter of obligation. Since the Second World War there has been an accelerated growth in international law, coinciding with processes of globalization. The vibrancy of international law depends on states recognizing that, in the long run, national interests are interdependent. International law has been a means of facilitating cross-border activities of MNEs, and, on the other hand, it has been seen as a tool of international co-operation for mitigating some of the negative impacts that have accompanied globalization. These functions can be seen in Figure 6.6, which shows key areas in which international law affects businesses.

International law: treaties and other multilateral agreements

The natural environment
- Climate change measures
- Emissions controls
- Responsibilities for pollution
- Disaster relief

Trade liberalization
- Multilateral trade agreements
- WTO dispute resolution
- Control of unfair trade practices

Human rights
- Right to life; freedom from torture and slavery
- Due process of law
- Non-discrimination on ethnic, sex and other grounds
- Prohibition of child labour

Global security
- Multilateral resolution of cross-border disputes
- Sanctions against aggressor states
- Terrorism
- Regional peacekeeping
- Weapons control

Figure 6.6 **Areas in which international law affects business**

International businesses have benefited from trade liberalization through international agreements, as Figure 6.6 shows. This has facilitated the growth of global supply chains and has formed the backbone of globalization. But international law also focuses on obligations that fall on companies as well as states. In the areas of environmental protection, global security and human rights, international law now impacts on companies. In these areas, international law often sets higher standards than national law in many countries, guided by ethical principles, as in human rights law (see discussion in Chapter 11). It thus imposes obligations on states to bring national law up to international standards. Most international law comes about through treaties and conventions, and most of these are the result of initiatives by UN-affiliated bodies. **Treaties** may be **multilateral**, involving many countries, or **bilateral**, between two countries. An extradition treaty is an example of a bilateral treaty, requiring states to co-operate on the handing over of persons accused of crimes. Major multilateral treaties may take years in the drafting stages, and do not become law until ratified by a given number of individual states specified in the treaty itself. When the requisite number of states have ratified, the treaty comes into force. Additional states may ratify indefinitely, lending extra authoritative weight to the treaty. When a state ratifies, it is obliged to bring national laws into conformity with the treaty provisions. However, states are sometimes slow to respond and slow to enforce international law, especially if national interest seems to conflict. It is in these circumstances that the effectiveness of international law is tested.

treaties instruments of international law

multilateral treaty international agreement binding many countries

bilateral treaty agreement between two countries, often for reciprocal trade terms

International courts and their growing impacts

International Court of Justice (ICJ) UN-sponsored international court which hears legal cases relating to disputes between member states

The **International Court of Justice (ICJ)** (www.icj-cij.org/) is the pre-eminent international court. Based in The Hague in The Netherlands, the ICJ is a UN body, whose authority derives from its governing Statute, attached to the UN Charter. While the ICJ's prestige is acknowledged, its effectiveness is limited by the restrictions to its jurisdiction. The major one is that it hears only disputes between sovereign states. A non-state organization cannot apply to it, although cases can – and often do – involve the activities of individuals and companies. The Hague is also home to the

 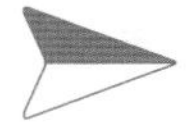

International Criminal Court court established under the auspices of the UN and the International Court of Justice, which hears cases involving crimes against humanity, war crimes and crimes of aggression

International Criminal Court (ICC) which was established by the Rome Statute in 1998, a time when reports of the genocide in Rwanda were causing alarm about the weaknesses of international responses. At its inception, the ICC's statute authorized it to prosecute leaders responsible for three categories of crime: crimes against humanity, genocide and war crimes. As a supranational court, its prosecutors would launch prosecutions in situations where national authorities have failed to act. This presents a formidable set of challenges. The ICC has no police powers itself, and must rely on the co-operation of national legal authorities, in, for example, arresting those who it has charged with crimes. There are now 124 state parties, newer members including Bangladesh, Chile, the Philippines and Tunisia. The US, Russia, China and India have not ratified the treaty, but the US government was a signatory. Although the ICC faces challenges in attaining its goals, it can be encouraged by the fact that the membership of 124 countries indicates an acknowledgement of international legal obligations in the area of human rights.

A fourth crime has now been added to the Rome Statute. It is the crime of aggression, to cover the many situations in which wars of aggression are launched against other states, in breach of the UN's Charter. It is contained in an amendment to the Rome Statute that dates from 2010. The precedent for the amendment goes back to the Nuremburg tribunal following the Second World War, which prosecuted Nazi leaders for planning and waging 'a war of aggression' (Weisbord, 2008: 164). As was highlighted in Chapter 5, a worrying trend has been the propensity of states to launch military invasions of other states, even though against the UN Charter, which establishes the role of the Security Council. The new article defines an 'act of aggression' as 'the use of force by a State against the sovereignty, territorial integrity or political independence of another state, or in any other manner inconsistent with the Charter of the UN'. The article specifies that there must be a 'manifest' violation of the UN Charter, indicating that the violation is a serious one. Acts of aggression include invasion, military occupation or sending forces of mercenaries that use armed force against another state. Significantly, the amendment maintains the pre-eminence of the Security Council in deciding whether illegal force has been used. Where it finds illegal force has been used, it will refer the case to the ICC. In cases where the permanent members (China, France, Russia, the US and UK) have held back a referral by use of their veto power, the referral can be made after six months have elapsed. A legal limitation, however, is that, unlike the original three crimes, the crime of aggression cannot be prosecuted against non-State parties. Thus leaders of terrorist groups such as Islamic State would be outside the new crime, but would still fall within the ICC's jurisdiction for other human rights violations.

The amendment was activated in July 2018, becoming the new Article 8 of the ICC Statute. By that date, 35 countries had ratified; the UK was not among them. The article does not apply retrospectively, only to crimes committed from one year following its activation. Thus, leaders responsible for the invasions of Iraq, Syria and Ukraine could not be prosecuted (Bowcott, 2018). The crime of aggression is specifically focused on the responsibility of states' political leaders, targeting a 'person in a position effectively to exercise control over or to direct the political or military action of a state' (van der Vyver, 2010: 16). The perpetrator is in a position of leadership, knowing the circumstances, planning and launching the act of aggression that was in violation of the UN Charter. The political dimension is highlighted because the act in question is essentially an act of state – one for which its leaders can be held accountable in international law. President Bush of the US and Prime Minister Blair of the UK would have been liable to be prosecuted for the invasion of Iraq under the new crime of aggression, had the article been in place in 2003. However, neither country has ratified the new article, and both are permanent members of the Security Council, with the power of veto.

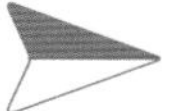

Despite the limitations of the new law, the framework to identify and measure the crime of aggression sends a strong message to the international community, to both the countries that have suffered invasions and to the high officials of those countries that have committed crimes of aggression.

The two major international courts have established a forum in which to bring sovereign states – and, in the case of the ICC, their leaders – to account for breaches of international law, exerting moral as well as legal pressures on states to comply.

The way I see it...

'The ICC is not mission impossible: it is just mission difficult.'

Sang-Hyun Song, ICC President, in an interview with the *Financial Times*, 14 March 2015.

Approaching the twentieth anniversary of its founding statute in 2018, the ICC came under unprecedented fire from the newly appointed US national security advisor, John Bolton. Claiming that the court is illegitimate, he strongly objected to the idea of launching actions against US military for possible war crimes and crimes against humanity in Afghanistan, stating that the US would consider sanctions against the court and prosecution of ICC judges. See the article, Bowcott, O. (2018) 'ICC will continue "undeterred" after US threats', *The Guardian*, 11 September. The article contains a link to the article elaborating on the views of Mr Bolton.

Following this attack by Mr Bolton, the ICC's mission would seem to have become even more difficult. To what extent do you feel these threats from the US will impact on the overall mission of the ICC in human rights around the world?

International dispute settlement

private international law the body of law for determining which national law pertains in cases between individuals and firms in more than one country

Every international business, sooner or later, becomes involved in a dispute with a foreign dimension. The exposure to legal risk is greater for international businesses than domestic ones, mainly because of multiple jurisdictions. Disputes are likely to arise over contractual terms, licence agreements and in the area of tort, in which the firm either alleges wrongdoing or becomes the defendant in a negligence or product liability claim. The area of the law concerned is **private international law**, which determines which national law pertains between individuals and firms in more than one country. Also referred to as 'conflict of laws', private international law seeks to establish rules for deciding which national law to apply to a particular situation. The rules of private international law give guidance on three broad issues: (1) the choice of law governing transactions; (2) the choice of forum, that is, the country in which a case should be heard; and (3) the enforcement of court judgments. The harmonizing of private international law has been an important aim of international conventions. The Rome Convention on the Law Applicable to Contracts 1980 and the Brussels Convention on Jurisdiction and Enforcement of Judgments in Civil and Commercial Matters 1968 have both been incorporated into English law.

In the basic transaction of buying or selling goods, at least one of the contracting firms is likely to find its rights governed by foreign law, thereby adding to the legal risk in a number of ways. First, there is the question of what contract law in the foreign jurisdiction actually stipulates. Then there is the possibility of having to go through the courts in that country to obtain redress. Finally, the firm may face problems of getting a judgment of the foreign court enforced in its own country.

Contracts between firms based in different countries may specify a 'choice of law' to govern their contract. This choice will also normally govern the forum in which any disputes will be heard. Most countries recognize choice-of-law clauses. For EU member states the Rome Convention provides that if the parties have not made a clear choice of law, the contract is governed by the law of the country with which it is most closely connected. In practice, this is likely to be the law of the party who is to carry out performance of the contract. The Brussels Convention provides that jurisdiction depends on whether the defendant is 'domiciled' in the EU (which, for a firm, means that it must have a 'seat' of business there). In employment contracts, the employee can sue where his or her duties are carried out. In consumer contracts, the Brussels Convention (now an EU regulation) gives the consumer the right to sue in local courts. This regulation has profound implications for online traders, who may be liable to be sued in national courts of any EU member state where their business activities are directed. For enforcement of judgments, most states will recognize the judgment of a foreign court if the foreign law and procedure are broadly compatible with their own. Within the EU this recognition is automatic, as it is between states within the CISG.

Litigation is costly, time-consuming, and may bring unwanted publicity if the case is a high-profile one. Added risks in international disputes are the distance, unfamiliarity of the law, and unfamiliar legal cultural environment. While US businesses have become accustomed to a culture of litigation, the costs in damages can be astronomical, and the high cost of liability insurance is a consequence. In contract disputes, the incentives to find other means of dispute resolution are therefore strong. Practising lawyers, far from suggesting litigation in all cases, emphasize the benefits of 'alternative dispute resolution'. Alternatives to litigation are:

- Settlement by the parties 'out of court'
- Mediation, in which the parties agree to bring in a third party, who attempts to settle their differences
- Arbitration, which is the submission of the dispute to a named person or organization in accordance with the agreement.

Arbitration has grown in popularity in recent years. It is usually thought to be cheaper and quicker than litigation, but can still be costly, as both legal fees and arbitrators' fees have to be taken into account. Major arbitration centres in the US and London have seen increases in workload in the last decade. Only about 18% of the cases handled by the London Court of International Arbitration originate with parties from the UK. So strong is its global reach, its caseload involves businesses from every continent. In many cases, legal services at this level of expertise are not available in the parties' home countries. In Asia, the Singapore International Arbitration Centre (SCIA) has seen a remarkable rise in workload, as shown in Figure 6.7. There has recently been a steep rise in the number of new cases: in 2015 there were 271 new cases, and in 2016, there were 343. In comparison to courts, arbitration processes are informal. They also offer flexibility and privacy which court-based litigation does not. On the other hand, the settlement of disputes out of court, often cloaked in secrecy, contributes little to the development of a body of commercial law. Danone's dispute with Wahaha, its joint-venture partner, discussed earlier in this chapter, is one of many cases settled by arbitration.

investor-state dispute settlement (ISDS) provision in a treaty that allows companies from one of the ratifying countries who invest in another ratifying country to bring cases in a tribunal when they feel their businesses have been prejudiced in the host country

A growing area of arbitration is that involving companies suing sovereign states for compensation in cases where a foreign investor feels its economic interests are jeopardized. The legal basis on which it can bring a case is the inclusion of a clause in a treaty between the two countries that incorporates **investor-state dispute settlement (ISDS)**. These treaties are often trade agreements between two or more

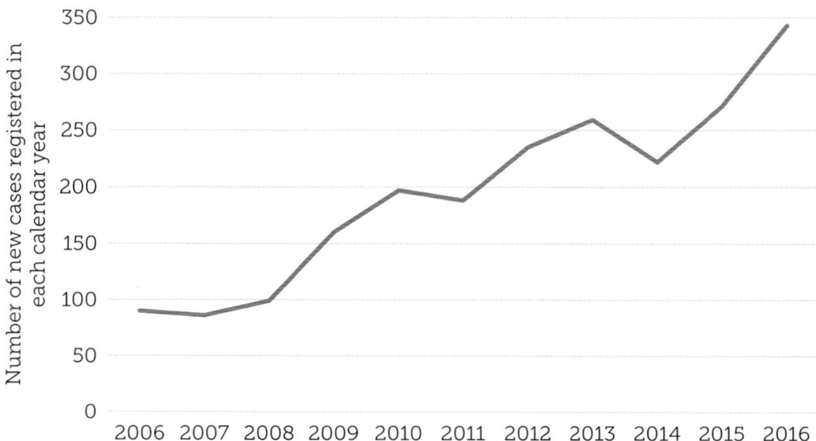

Figure 6.7 Growing number of new cases handled by the Singapore International Arbitration Centre, 2006–2016

Source of data: Singapore International Arbitration Centre, Statistics, at www.siac.org.sg, accessed 5 July 2019.

partners (see discussion in Chapter 7). There are now some 3,000 such treaties in existence. Arbitration tribunals facilitate the resolution of these investor-state disputes, the numbers of which have grown dramatically. The system dates from the 1960s, when there were concerns that foreign companies would be reluctant to invest in developing countries because of the risks involved, including economic and political uncertainties, such as possible nationalization of the investor's assets. The **International Centre for the Settlement of Investor Disputes (ICSID)** (https://icsid.worldbank.org) was set up as a limb of the World Bank Group at a World Bank meeting in Tokyo in 1964. At the time, 21 countries, mainly Latin American, objected that the process would undermine state sovereignty. But the World Bank pressed ahead with the system, feeling it would be necessary to encourage the foreign investment that drives development. The dispute settlement system was little used for three decades, but as Figure 6.8 shows, it became much more popular among investing companies from 2000 onwards. They are probably influenced by the likelihood that their claims will be upheld by the ICSID's tribunals. Of the cases decided, 63% are won either partially or in full by the corporate claimant. Just 12% of claimants have all their claims dismissed, and in 25% of cases the tribunal declines jurisdiction (ICSID, 2018).

International Centre for the Settlement of Investor Disputes (ICSID) tribunal system set up by the World Bank which is tasked with handling investor-state disputes arising under treaties

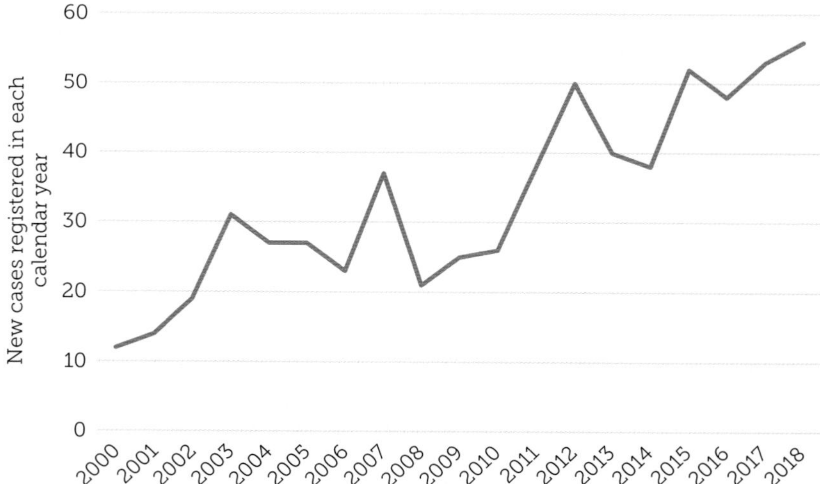

Figure 6.8 Cases registered by the ICSID

Source of data: ICSID (2019) The ICSID Caseload – Statistics (2019-1), Chart 1, p. 7, at https://icsid.worldbank.org, accessed 5 July 2019.

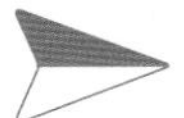

With the rise in the number of cases, the ISDS has given rise to renewed debate. The US government pressed for its inclusion in both the Trans-Pacific Partnership (TPP) and the Transatlantic Trade and Investment Partnership (TTIP), but objections arose among partner countries and also from legislators in the US Congress. In 2017, the US ceased to participate in these agreements, but could renew its participation if it wished. A system that was envisaged as giving legitimate assurances to investors seems to have been transformed into a system that is increasingly weighted towards large multinationals, to the detriment of public interest in the countries where they do business. In some cases, the sums of money being demanded run to billions of dollars.

The system of tribunals and compensation cases now envelops about half the world's countries, both developing and developed. The scope for companies to take cases to tribunals has expanded to include actions for future loss of profits from changes in environmental law, social legislation, employment protection law and other social legislation. For example, foreign investors in some Central and Eastern European countries provided private healthcare in the early years of post-communist independence, but changes in the law later introduced national health services, reducing the role of private medical services. The foreign companies involved sued for compensation amounting to billions of euros. In 2012, Ecuador was ordered by a tribunal to pay $1.8 billion to an American oil company for cancelling an oil exploration contract. This is roughly the equivalent of the country's entire health budget for a year (Provost and Kennard, 2015). There is no appeal process against the decision of the tribunal, and if a state does not pay up, its assets can be seized in any country through local courts.

Reform proposals for ISDS have been put forward by the UN Conference on Trade and Development (UNCTAD), targeting specific areas of concern. The areas of concern are summarized below (UNCTAD, 2013: 110–12):

- **Legitimacy** – The private individuals who sit on ISDS arbitration tribunals are appointed ad hoc. It is questionable whether they should be taking decisions affecting public interests, including development goals of sovereign states.
- **Transparency** – Proceedings can be held entirely in secret. This seems inappropriate where issues of public interest are being decided.
- **'Nationality planning'** – A company can restructure to establish a subsidiary in a country where it can make use of the ISDS to bring a case against a country that it would not otherwise be able to do.
- **Consistency of arbitration decisions** – Arbitration tribunals decide each case individually, and there are inevitably inconsistencies, including divergent interpretations of treaties. This gives little guidance as to how treaties should be interpreted in future.
- **Erroneous decisions** – Where a substantive mistake has occurred, there is no process for putting it right. There is a provision for annulment of a particular decision, but an appeals process would be preferable.
- **Arbitrators' independence and impartiality** – Arbitrators are recommended by the parties. The individuals appointed as arbitrators can serve as lawyers representing parties in future cases. The system, which is very lucrative for specialist lawyers, thus allows them to 'change hats', exerting considerable influence over outcomes.
- **Financial stakes** – The ISDS process has become very expensive. When a state wins against an investor, it is common for the arbitrators to award no costs to be paid by the losing party. The costs of arbitrators and lawyers is, on average, $8 million per case, making these proceedings a significant burden on public finances in the country.

UNCTAD has proposed a number of possible reforms (UNCTAD, 2013: 113–16). Among the main ones are introducing an appeals procedure. A second is requiring documents to be available for public access, to increase transparency. On the investor side, companies could be restricted in their use of corporate restructuring to bring an investor within a treaty. They could also be required to exhaust the national legal system in the country before launching an ISDS claim. A long-term possibility would be a standing international investment court. This would replace ad hoc arbitrators with a court staffed by tenured judges who have no ties with interested parties.

SHINING A LIGHT ON BUSINESS DECISIONS

When companies sue countries...

The traditional view is that any company enters a new market on the basis that it is subject to national law, and that national law might change. Nowadays, because of ISDS provisions, global companies can pursue claims against governments for possible losses from changes in legislation. Some have been criticized for aggressively targeting poor countries that lack the resources to defend such claims. How would a foreign company in a poor country justify launching a legal action in this situation?

What are the legal and ethical considerations that companies should address before pursuing claims for compensation against countries in international tribunals?

The global legal environment: providing the foundations for sustainability?

The rule of law is the cornerstone of a sustainable legal environment. Sustainable governance relies on regulatory frameworks underpinned by the rule of law. Relevant legal authorities in every country should inspire confidence in the frameworks that exist to enforce the laws. Legal institutions and regulators are under obligation to serve the public good and function in transparent and impartial ways. In practice, however, these ideals are far from reality in today's global environment. As we have seen, regulatory frameworks in key areas such as finance, safety standards, labour laws and environmental protection have historically been matters for national law and policies. These diverse frameworks are of limited effect when confronted by the reach of today's globalized companies and holders of wealth. The internet, technology and social media giants, in particular, have greatly increased their reach and power – over governments, businesses and people's lives. Global players have thus become adept at circumventing national legal frameworks, giving themselves maximum latitude to pursue their activities in ways that maximize profits above other considerations, such as societal concerns. But at what cost in terms of goals of sustainable governance?

Global manufacturers have gravitated towards countries like China, where they have encountered few environmental regulations and weak employment protection. But China is now imposing stronger legal obligations on firms, as concerns about societal wellbeing and the need to control corruption rise up the agenda. On the other hand, the Chinese government's actions against corruption are sometimes linked to suppressing political dissent. Where the rule of law is weak, it is often due to the opaque workings of an authoritarian regime that subordinates law enforcement to political considerations. However, corruption exists across the entire political spectrum from democratic to authoritarian governments. Transparency International (www.transparency.org) publishes a Corruption Perceptions Index, in which the least corrupt countries have the highest scores out of 100, and the most corrupt have the lowest. Selected scores are shown in Figure 6.9. In the 2018 results,

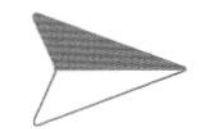

122 out of the 180 in total scored less than 50, including a number of democratic countries. These disappointing scores continue a trend of relatively low scores, despite efforts by many governmental authorities to clean up corruption. All the emerging economies shown in the figure scored less than 50. They include authoritarian and democratic systems.

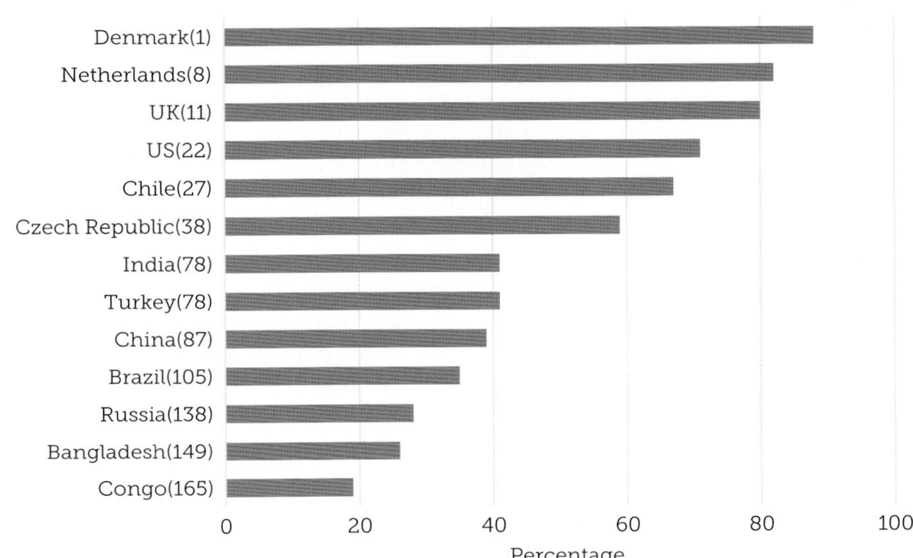

Figure 6.9 **Transparency International's Corruption Perceptions Index: findings for selected countries**

Notes: Country scores are percentages. The rank of each country is shown in brackets after the country name. There are 180 countries overall in the ranking.

Source of data: Transparency International, Corruption Perception Index for 2018, at www.transparency.org/cpi, accessed 22 February 2019.

Where regulators are either weak or influenced by political concerns, corruption is likely to flourish, along with shadowy financial dealings that escape regulatory oversight. In the area of finance, which is one of the most globalized of business activities, companies and wealthy individuals have long turned to offshore financial centres, such as micro-states in the Caribbean. This allows them to structure transactions and locate funds out of the reach of national authorities. The primary attraction of offshore finance is its secrecy. While many clients have a legitimate need for privacy, others seek secrecy and anonymity to hide criminal activity such as money laundering. Globalization has seen a boom in offshore finance: it is estimated that as much as a tenth of global GDP is held offshore (Kitchener, 2017). Offshore centres are often described as 'tax havens', as they facilitate the hiding of money away from the eyes of the tax authorities in the owner's national jurisdiction. While much of this activity is legal in the strict sense, a proportion relies on complex tax-avoidance schemes that are unethical at best and can be illegal if artificial structures are used simply to evade tax. Disclosures of leaked documents from a number of tax havens have recently shone a light on how the very rich are able to bypass national laws to conceal wealth. In 2015, investigative journalists uncovered a trove of some 11.5 million documents, known as the 'Panama Papers', centred on a firm of specialist offshore lawyers based in Panama. Numerous companies and individuals, including leading politicians, were found to have used their legal services, often to set up shell companies for the untraceable channelling of money.

Another large trove of documents was similarly revealed in 2017. Known as the 'Paradise Papers', these detailed similar legal services provided by a large firm of lawyers, headquartered in Bermuda, with a network of international offices, mainly in the Caribbean and other offshore locations. Prominent among these locations are the British overseas territories of the Cayman Islands, Bermuda and the British Virgin Islands. Also benefiting from offshore finance are the British crown dependencies of the Isle of Man and Jersey. Crucially, these jurisdictions are all legally independent of the UK. The clients revealed in these leaked files, as in the Panama Papers, were companies and wealthy individuals, mostly resident in the US.

The effectiveness of offshore finance depends heavily on the expertise of the key firms that act as hubs: most of the clients of these firms probably do not actually understand how their arrangements work. These firms typically transmit through established financial centres. Despite laws against money laundering, London channels billions of dollars from crown dependencies and overseas territories. Some countries, such as Ireland and the Netherlands, offer similar attractions as tax havens. Complicit governments are another element in this picture. The British tax authorities have a record of making agreements with global companies, including banks, that are widely characterized as 'sweetheart' deals. Ireland openly attracts companies that seek to reduce liabilities for tax in the places where they do business. Apple is allowed to route through Ireland all the profits of its iPhone sales throughout Europe, saving it huge sums in tax. These practices have not gone unnoticed. The European Commission, which has greater regulatory reach than a national regulator, has imposed a bill for €13 billion on Apple for the taxes that it estimates the company should have been paying in Ireland (Farrell and McDonald, 2016).

Widespread disclosure of the activities of tax havens helps to reinforce the perception that legal obligations such as tax can be avoided by the rich and powerful. The use of the ISDS process, discussed in the last section, is another aspect of the advantages that the economically powerful company enjoys. These realities reflect the overriding impacts of inequality in societies. In an environment of extreme inequality, there is little prospect of effective rule of law and sustainability in regulatory frameworks. The implications for societies are that much of the legislation that serves public goods can be bypassed, and tax revenues are not as high as they should be. Public spending comes under strain, jeopardizing programmes such as education and healthcare. For their part, governments have considerable legal authority to regulate and to enforce existing regulations, but often lack the will to do so. Widespread media coverage of the role of governments and businesses in tolerating regulatory failings has highlighted the need for transparency, but calls for reform are met by fierce lobbying by businesses. Measures to rein in inequality go hand in hand with the promotion of greater sustainability in legal and regulatory frameworks that ultimately contribute to a more inclusive society.

Conclusions

A system of laws that is legitimately authorized and fairly enforced serves all within the borders of a state, including individual people, civil society groups, businesses and governments. A legal system that enjoys the confidence of those in society is vital to people's sense of security and to a firm's confidence in conducting business activities within the country. In countries where laws go unenforced and corruption is rampant, it is sometimes said that the 'law of the jungle' prevails, implying that the only rule is one of 'might is right'. There is little security in such an environment, and little sense that it is worth planning for the future. Few businesses are attracted to such a location. While businesses often complain about too much regulation, too little regulation – or unpredictable regulatory interference – is also a disincentive. The world's legal systems vary greatly, and governments are increasingly conscious that the legal environment of their country is a factor in attracting businesses, whether in developed countries or developing ones. Governments, especially in developing economies, must look to a range of goals beyond simply presenting a

seemingly attractive package to would-be investors, notably featuring light regulation. Development provides opportunities for investors, but also must serve societal goals. Otherwise, development hopes can turn to disillusionment for many in society.

Opportunities for international expansion and growing financial returns attract businesses to foreign investment. Does the business see a foreign location merely as a source of short-term profits, aiming to move on to a more advantageous location in a few years' time? Some firms might profess not to take this view, but in practice are constantly looking for new locations from a mainly cost-cutting perspective. This is feasible in some cases where there is little capital invested. But the commitment of capital involved in a large FDI project usually suggests that the firm takes a longer view, as do the governments of host countries. Firms cultivate relations with governments, and, in many cases, with civil society groups. Their activities contribute to development, but for businesses in today's world, the focus should be on sustainable development, involving all in society. International law now plays a growing complementary role to national lawmakers, highlighting global issues from a perspective of higher ethical standards, and becoming a beacon guiding both governments and businesses.

CLOSING CASE STUDY

Facebook's business model under scrutiny

From its creation in 2004, Facebook was a success story closely identified with one of its founders, Mark Zuckerberg, a star among the Silicon Valley entrepreneurs. His global ambitions for the social media platform, combined with WhatsApp, Instagram and Messenger, seemed destined to grow inexorably into a social media empire. Facebook's IPO in 2012 opened the way to expand globally. He was able to control the company through a share structure in which the voting system gave him control of the company. He attempted to restructure Facebook in 2017, retaining control even though reducing his shareholding. This was met with a lawsuit from shareholders, claiming the restructuring was unfair to them, and that the board had been in breach of their legal duty in approving it. Zuckerberg withdrew the plan, and investors could claim success. By that time, Zuckerberg had other problems on his mind.

Mr Zuckerberg has long felt that the idea of sharing was central to Facebook. In 2010, he said that privacy was no longer a 'social norm' (Johnson, 2010). The indications were apparent then that Facebook would encounter difficulties with privacy regulators. It was clear then that Facebook's approach to users' data was that they could be used freely to generate revenues: this was its business model. Facebook gave developers of data apps access to data. A complaint to the Irish data protection authority by a law student, Max Schrems, in 2011, stated that Facebook had no control over what developers did with the data, or

Facebook has been at the forefront in the rising popularity of social media, but now faces greater scrutiny in terms of privacy of personal data.

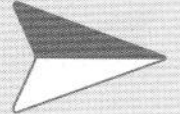

the data of a user's friends, even though they had not given consent. Facebook made changes to the platform in 2015, but data that had been harvested had already been incorporated in the system. By then, the wholesale harvesting of data was difficult to reverse.

In 2018, it was revealed that Cambridge Analytica, a data company that was taken on by the Trump campaign and by the Brexit Leave campaign, had obtained Facebook data on 50 million people, which it used to micro-target voters with political advertisements. That number was later revised upwards to 87 million. Facebook was called to appear before investigative committees of legislators in the UK and the EU, and to give testimony before Congress in the US. The answers by Mr Zuckerberg and other executives contained apologies, but left legislators unconvinced when questions about the core business model were raised. When Mr Zuckerberg was asked by a Congressman whether he was willing to change his business model to protect individual privacy, he replied, 'I'm not sure what that means' (Hern, 2018). The company's share price plummeted 20% in a few days in July 2018. Its number of users was up to 1.42 billion globally, but the number had stalled in the US and fallen in Europe, which are Facebook's biggest advertising markets. Costs were rising, as the company was compelled to deal with security matters, suspending hundreds of apps as a result of the Cambridge Analytica scandal. It was compelled to clamp down on political advertising, the spread of fake news and the spread of hate speech. Facebook apologized for its failure to act responsibly in dealing with third-party developers, and for its inadequate approach to privacy. However, it has become clear that Facebook's micro-targeting of users has been the attraction that it offers advertisers, and this has involved harvesting vast amounts of data. If regulators were to clamp down on these practices with stricter rules, it would be very costly for Facebook. Investors and users have cause to be concerned.

The EU's General Data Protection Regulation (GDPR) took effect in May 2018. It provides for users to opt in, rather than out, of some data sharing. This would impact on Facebook in the EU. Mr Schrems, has already filed four complaints under the GDPR. Companies in breach face fines of 4% of global revenue. For Facebook in 2017, that would have been $1.6 billion. Mr Schrems complained of forced consent: the user had to consent or be denied access to services. In the US, Facebook has already launched products that breach GDPR rules. Facebook has become extraordinarily profitable through a business model based on data harvesting, which it acknowledged was irresponsible. It was a costly path to take, undermining public and investor confidence in the social media giant. Mr Zuckerberg is now seeking to boost the profile of Instagram, which has proved very popular. In part, he is seeking to compensate for the woes of Facebook in public perceptions. Adding to the threats of escalating costs have been moves in a number of countries to force tech companies, which have been adept at tax avoidance arrangements, to pay more in taxes in the country jurisdictions where they operate.

The US regulator, the Federal Trade Commission (FTC) imposed a massive fine of $5 billion on Facebook in 2019, for privacy violations stemming from the Cambridge Analytica scandal. This was by far the largest fine ever imposed by the FTC. However, the FTC did not order the company to make any structural changes. As a result, many feared that Facebook was not likely to make the changes to its behaviour that would safeguard privacy in future (Davies and Rushe, 2019).

Questions

- Why is Facebook's business model now in question?
- In what ways is Zuckerberg to blame for the failures of corporate responsibility?
- What are the risks for the company and its relations with shareholders in the climate of 'tech backlash' that many ordinary people feel?
- What should Facebook be doing to win back confidence?

Further reading

See the article by Hannah Kuchler, 'Facebook in struggle to regain its balance', in *The Guardian*, 7 April 2018.

Multiple choice questions

Visit www.macmillanihe.com/morrison-gbe-5e to take a quick self-test quiz on what you have read in this chapter.

Review questions

1. What is meant by the interlocking spheres of national, regional and international law? Which is the most important in the business environment, and why?
2. What are the differences between civil and criminal law? Give an example of each.
3. What are the legal risks in countries where the rule of law is weak?
4. What are the main functions of a national legal system?
5. How do codified legal systems differ from common law systems?
6. How can non-western and western legal systems be designed to function in the same country?
7. What are the difficulties facing a defendant company in a federal system such as the US?
8. What international conventions exist for harmonization of national commercial law?
9. Distinguish between arm's length contracting and relational contracting. What are the factors to consider for joint ventures across the two cultural approaches?
10. What factors account for the global growth in product liability claims?
11. What are the difficulties for plaintiffs in claims for damages following disasters in which there are multiple possible defendants, including parties in other countries?
12. What are the alternatives to settling legal disputes in court?
13. Why is national competition law inadequate to deal with global takeovers and mergers?
14. What is provided by an investor-state dispute settlement (ISDS) provision in treaties? What criticisms has it incurred?
15. In what ways is the International Criminal Court facing obstacles in exercising its authority under its statute?

✓ Assignments

1. Compare the legal risks that arise for businesses in countries where the rule of law is established with those that arise in countries where the rule of law is weak.
2. In what ways does international law impact on businesses? Discuss both the enabling aspects and those that constrain or impose liabilities.

Further reading

Adams, A. (2018) *Law for Business Students*, 10th edition (Pearson).

August, R., Mayer, D. and Bixby, M. (2012) *International Business Law: Text, Cases and Readings*, 6th edition (Pearson).

Bell, S., McGillivray, D. and Pedersen, O. (2013) *Environmental Law*, 8th edition (Oxford: Oxford University Press).

Elliott, C., Quinn, F., Allbon, E. and Dua Kaur, S. (2018) *The English Legal System*, 19th edition (Pearson).

Harris, D. and Sivakumaran, S. (2015) *Cases and Materials on International Law*, 8th edition (London: Sweet & Maxwell).

MacIntyre, E. (2018) *Essentials of Business Law*, 6th edition (Pearson).

Schaffer, R., Earle, B. and Augusti, F. (2011) *International Business Law and its Environment*, 8th edition (Cengage Learning).

Shaw, M. (2017) *International Law*, 8th edition (Cambridge: Cambridge University Press).

References

Bonell, M. (2014) 'The UNIDROIT Principles of International Commercial Contracts and Long-Term Contracts', Position Paper, October, at www.unidroit.org

Bowcott, O. (2018) 'ICC crime of aggression comes into effect without key signatories', 17 July, *The Guardian*, at www.theguardian.com

Davies, R. and Rushe, D. (2019) 'Facebook to pay $5 bn fine as regulator settles Cambridge Analytica complaint', *The Guardian*, 24 July.

Farrell, S. and McDonald, H. (2016) 'Apple ordered to pay 13 billion euros after EU rules Ireland broke state aid laws', 30 August, *The Guardian*, at www.theguardian.com

Hern, A. (2018) 'What is the fallout from Zuckerberg's sessions in the House?', *The Guardian*, 14 April.

ICSID (2018) *The ICSID Caseload – Statistics (2018-2)*, p. 31, at https://icsid.worldbank.org

Johnson, B. (2010) 'Privacy no longer a social norm, says Facebook founder', *The Guardian*, 11 January.

Kitchener, G. (2017) 'Paradise Papers: are we taming offshore finance?', BBC news, 5 November, at www.bbc.com

Moens, G. and Gillies, P. (1998) *International Trade and Business: Law, Policy and Ethics* (Sydney: Cavendish Publishing).

Naidoo, K. (2013) 'Fukushima disaster: holding the nuclear industry liable', *The Guardian*, 11 March, at www.theguardian.com

Provost, C. and Kennard, M. (2015) 'The obscure legal system that lets corporations sue countries', *The Guardian*, 10 June 2015, at www.theguardian.com

Pratley, N. (2014) 'GSK still has questions to answer over bribery case in China', *The Guardian*, 19 September, at www.theguardian.com

Sands, P. (2007) 'Realm of the possible', *The Guardian*, 8 January, at www.theguardian.com

UNCTAD (2013) *World Investment Report 2013* (Geneva: UN).

Vestager, M. (2015) 'Enforcing competition rules in the global village': speech delivered in New York, 20 April, at https://ec.europa.eu/commission/commissioners/2014-2019/vestager/announcements/enforcing-competition-rules-global-village_en

Van der Vyver, J. D. (2010) 'Prosecuting the crime of aggression in the International Criminal Court', *University of Miami National Security and Armed Conflict Law Review*: Vol. 1 (1-56).

Weisbord, N. (2008) 'Prosecuting aggression', Harvard International Law Journal, Vol 49, No. 1, pp. 161–220.

World Justice Project (2019) *WJP Rule of Law Index 2019*, at https://worldjusticeproject.org

Zeller, T. (2011) 'Experts had long criticized potential weakness in design of stricken reactor', *New York Times*, 15 March, at www.nyt.com

Zweigert, K. and Koltz, H. (1998) *Introduction to Comparative Law*, 3rd edition (Oxford: Clarendon Press).

 **Visit the companion website at** www.macmillanihe.com/morrison-gbe-5e **for further learning and teaching resources.**

PART 3 DRIVERS OF INTERNATIONAL BUSINESS

Chapter 7, *International trade and globalization*, takes us more deeply into the international environment, looking at the ways in which competitive forces, many of them from emerging economies, are shaping the business landscape. We examine the nature and patterns of international trade from a range of perspectives, including nation-states and business organizations. Economic integration, at global and regional levels, has created greater interdependence, but we find that national forces are still powerful influences. The WTO has sought both to liberalize trade and achieve fairness in trade practices among the many differing national perspectives. Preferential trade agreements have become common, both within regions and between countries. However, trade tensions and protectionist policies have increasingly impacted on international business. Growing tension among trading partners represents challenges to the WTO's multilateral system.

In Chapter 8, *Global finance*, we explore a sphere of business activity which has seen rapid growth, but which has also seen increased risks, especially those that led to the global financial crisis of 2008. Equity investment, debt financing and the role of derivatives trading are discussed in the chapter. MNEs have been aided by a liberalization in national financial systems, which has opened opportunities for raising capital in different locations. However, the risks have multiplied with the broadening opportunities. Successive financial crises have pointed to a need for greater regulation, but national governments are keen not to discourage investors. Inter-governmental institutions such as the IMF are concerned that global stability and sound financial institutions are maintained, and they warn that excessive debt can lead to instability.

Chapter 9, *Technology and innovation* focuses on the role of innovation and the impacts of technological innovation in diverse environments. Innovation has long been recognized as key to competitiveness, and with more and more countries building greater innovation capacity, the scope for innovative technology now encompasses a wide range of countries, notably the large emerging economies. Transforming an innovative idea into a successful product requires a range of skills spanning entire organizations. Environmental factors, including the legal protection of intellectual property, are crucial. So too, is the need for a business climate in which entrepreneurs can obtain the resources needed to pursue their new ideas. For developing economies, technology transfer and diffusion of technology are important in catching up with more advanced economies and in promoting sustainable development.

© Getty, BRAND X

INTERNATIONA TRADE AND GLOBALIZATIO

Outline of chapter

This chapter will enable you to

- Appreciate the contributions of theories of international trade to an understanding of the ways in which companies, industries and nations compete in the global environment
- Understand the rationale and mechanisms of national trade policies
- Understand both the achievements and setbacks of the multilateral trading system
- Critically assess the rise of regional, bilateral and plurilateral trade agreements and their roles in facilitating trade relations
- Assess the impacts of trade on societies in developed and developing countries in terms of the essential needs of all in society and sustainability of livelihoods

OPENING CASE STUDY

Huawei's global success dented by US security fears

Huawei's beginnings go back to 1987, when it started making telecoms equipment in Shenzhen, China. The company faced an uphill battle as a private company in a sector dominated by state-owned businesses. As these companies dominated the lucrative urban areas, Huawei opted to find business opportunities in the rural areas, developing infrastructure that could cope with a variety of conditions, such as extreme weather and uncertain power supply. Its innovative solutions were crucial in these markets, and that approach has held the company in good stead as it has grown. Its strategic decisions were inspired largely by its founder, Ren Zhengfei, a former army officer. His guiding belief has been that competitiveness rests on the company's innovation, producing better products that business customers and individual consumers appreciate. He set his sights on global markets, seeing greater opportunities to become established outside China. These include smartphones as well as telecoms infrastructure. In each sector, his aim has been to take a lead through innovation.

Ren's approach has been successful in attracting highly talented researchers and engineers to Huawei. They are aided by the company's focus on R&D, backed by a huge R&D budget of $13 billion to spend. Huawei is a private company that is owned by its employees, who are its shareholders. The company's approach to its workers and its markets has paid off in terms of growth. By 2011, its equipment was connecting a third of the world's mobile phones. When British Telecom (BT) sought to shift from its analogue to a digital network in 2005, it contacted a number of suppliers, but decided on Huawei, as it offered flexibility and showed a willingness to work with BT in adapting to Huawei's needs. That contract, worth £10 billion, proved to be a way into European markets. By 2015, more than half its sales came from markets outside China. It has focused on 5G networks and on sales of smartphones. Sales of Huawei smartphones globally overtook Apple iPhones in 2018, but are still behind Samsung. Huawei has become highly successful in promoting its brand in the highly competitive smartphone market globally.

It is the recognized global leader in 5G technology. However, within the UK, there has been uneasiness about the rise of Huawei because, as a Chinese company, it could come under Chinese government influence. There are fears that the equipment could be used for spying, and that knowledge of the codes could allow networks to be closed down at the behest of the Chinese government. These fears stem largely from US government policy, which has taken a hostile stance against China's companies. The fact that Huawei's founder was formerly an army engineer influenced US authorities to raise national security fears. The US declared Huawei and another Chinese company, ZTE, to be security threats in 2012, curtailing their ability to operate in the US. Huawei emphasizes that it is a private company, not controlled by the Chinese government.

In 2018, Huawei's chief financial officer, Meng Wanzhou, was arrested in Canada at the behest of the US, over allegations that the company violated US sanctions against Iran. Ms Meng is the daughter of Huawei's founder. Huawei has denied that Ms Meng had committed any wrong, and China was quick to respond, condemning the arrest as a provocative action. In a follow-up, US prosecutors filed 23 criminal charges against Huawei. They included alleged theft of trade secrets of a US-owned phone company, T-Mobile, although Huawei has said that the dispute with T-Mobile was settled in 2014. Many of these charges relate to the alleged breach of sanctions imposed on Iran by the US. Sanctions had been in place against Iran because of its nuclear programme, but these were due to end under an accord in 2015 between Iran and other nations. The UN confirmed that Iran had complied with the accord. In 2018, the US under President Trump withdrew from this accord. The US then imposed unilateral

China's progress in building digital networks, exemplified by the city of Shenzhen, owes much to the expertise of Huawei.

sanctions on Iran, with the effect that any company dealing in the Iran market could face prosecution in the US.

Relations between the US and China became more acrimonious in 2018, as new tariffs were announced on both sides. Their implementation was put on hold, pending talks to reach an agreement. As one of the world's largest telecoms companies, and a Chinese national champion, Huawei has again found itself in a vulnerable position. US national security officials have tended to see trade issues in broader terms of political and military power. The coming technological shift to 5G computer and phone networks is crucial to future development. In this respect, Huawei has a competitive edge as a supplier of the new infrastructure, but national security issues remain part of the equation.

Questions

- What are the reasons behind Huawei's success in global markets?
- Why has Huawei encountered national security barriers in the US?
- To what extent can Huawei reduce the impacts of the perceptions that it poses a security threat in some key markets?
- In what ways does Huawei have competitive advantages that can help to overcome the barriers that it has faced in some markets?

Further reading

See the article by Martin Wolf, 'The challenge of one world, two systems', in the *Financial Times*, 29 January 2019.

Introduction

Across the ages, businesses have looked to trade beyond their home country. Growth in international trade has been a major contributor to the rise of the industrialized countries, stretching back to the Industrial Revolution. Indeed, when we look at the flourishing trade between Asia and Europe as far back as the medieval era, we are tempted to think that globalization has been happening for a long time. However, both the volume of trade and the patterns of trade between nations have changed greatly over the years. In the decades following the Second World War, the dominant trading powers were the US, Japan and Europe. From the 1990s and into the twenty-first century, there has been a shift towards Asia. Two major factors can be highlighted: globalization of supply chains by MNEs and the opening up of national economies. Understanding the impacts of these factors on the global trading system, including particular regions and national economies, is key to formulating business strategies in the changing environment.

We begin this chapter with an overview of international trade, highlighting shifts in trading relations now taking place. We look at the major theories which help to explain changing patterns of world trade. We then analyze the divergent views on the issues of free trade and protectionism, which have shaped national perspectives. Trade policies go beyond economic considerations, extending to impacts on societies, including issues such as employment, food security and the use of natural resources. While these have economic dimensions, they also have important social dimensions that governments must take into account. Belief in the benefits of free trade has underpinned agreements to open markets, guided particularly by the World Trade Organization (WTO). We examine the role of the WTO as trade envelops more developing and emerging economies. Each has a range of goals in relation to national needs and priorities. These concerns are increasingly part of the backdrop for companies wishing to create trade links with these newer trading nations.

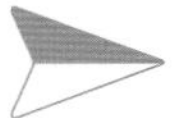

Trends in world trade: impacts of globalization

trade the exchange of something of value, usually goods or services, for a price, usually money

export selling products in a country other than the one in which they were made

import the purchase of goods or services from a supplier in another country

Trade involves the exchange of something of value, usually goods or services, for a price, usually money. **Exports** are products leaving a country, and **imports** are products entering a country. Goods traded are classified as 'primary' and 'secondary' products. Primary goods include natural resources and agricultural produce, while manufactured goods are secondary. The 'tertiary' sector covers services. Historically, thriving trade has aided countries in becoming economically powerful, especially following the transformation of national economies by industrialization. In the eighteenth and nineteenth centuries, Britain imported cotton from India, to be processed and made into clothing in the newly industrialized cities in the north of England. The textile industry transformed the economies of these northern cities, and also brought about changes in society due to the rise in industrial employment. Since the end of the Second World War, trade has grown at a remarkable rate. From 1950 to 2002, the volume of world exports tripled, while production doubled. In the 1990s, world trade grew on average 6.5% annually, while output grew at 2.5% annually. The following decade showed similar growth, but the global financial crisis precipitated sharp declines in both world output and the global volume of trade. Global trade shrank over 10% in 2009, but rebounded the following year.

The value of international trade grew annually at a modest rate of less than 2% from 2011 to 2014 (see Figure 7.1). Then, in 2015, trade suffered a sharp decline of 10% (UNCTAD, 2017). Trade in physical goods (merchandise) was harder hit than trade in services. The volume of merchandise exports amounted to $16 trillion, down from $18.5 trillion in 2014. The slump of 2015 was largely caused by a fall in commodity and energy prices. The price of oil fell from over $100 a barrel in 2014 to roughly $50 a barrel in 2015. Trade in primary products declined 33% in 2015, and trade in energy products declined 37%. Countries particularly affected were those that rely heavily on exports of oil and mining products, many of them developing countries. International trade rebounded in 2017, growing by 4.7%. World merchandise exports rose to $17.73 trillion in value. As the figure shows, both developed and developing countries saw growth in trade.

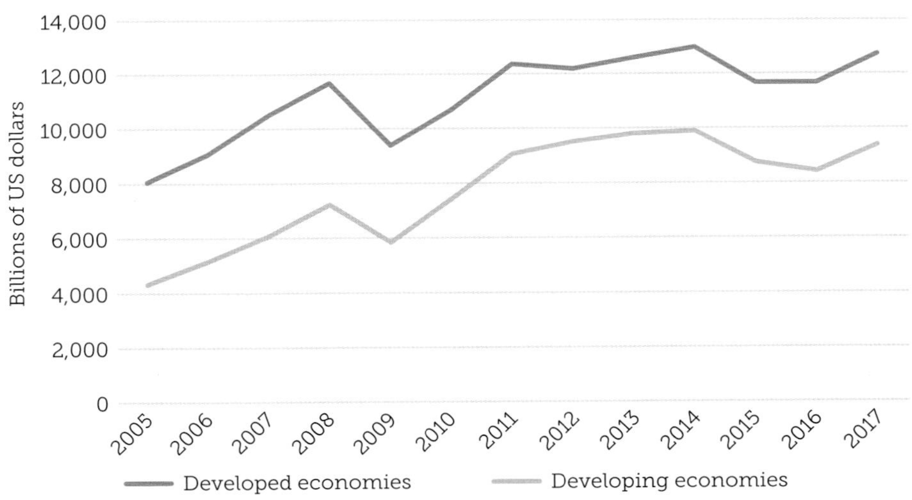

Figure 7.1 Comparison of developed and developing countries' trade

Source of data: UNCTAD statistics, Exports and imports of goods and services, at www.unctad.org, accessed 26 August 2018.

Developed countries have long been the main actors in global trade. Their dominance is now receding, as developing countries become more active traders. Developing countries' share in merchandise exports increased from 33% of the total in 2005 to 43% in 2017 (WTO, 2018). Trade in services is still dominated by developed countries, accounting for two-thirds of the exports of services. The rise of export-oriented manufacturing in developing countries, notably in East Asia, has been driven largely by the global supply chains of the world's MNEs, most of which originate in developed countries. The leading developed countries in trade are traditionally known as the **'triad'** countries of Europe, North America and Japan. Japan was the last of these economies to experience industrialization (in the 1970s and 80s). The triad countries have now experienced shrinking manufacturing sectors and a growing emphasis on high technology and services, while developing economies have experienced growth in manufacturing for export markets.

triad countries advanced economies of North America, the EU and Japan; Australia and New Zealand are also in this category

Figure 7.2 shows the shift that has taken place in world merchandise exports in the post-war period. We see that North America's share of total merchandise exports has fallen from 28.1% to 13.8%. Asia's exports are the mirror opposite, having risen from a global share of 14% in 1948 to 34% in 2017. European countries continue to hold a prominent position, while the exports of African countries, mainly primary goods, have halved. The contrast between Asia and Africa highlights that developing countries represent a mixed picture in terms of trade performance.

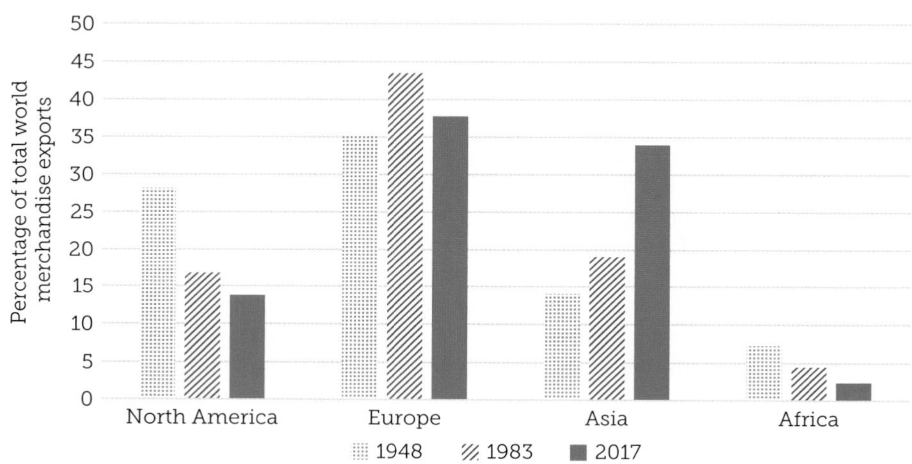

Figure 7.2 Merchandise exports from selected regions, 1948, 1983 and 2017

Source of data: WTO, *World Trade Statistical Review 2018*, Table A4, p. 122, at www.wto.org

Behind the growing integration of developing countries in world trade lie divergent national scenarios. East Asian economies stand out as star performers, whose development has been based on export-oriented manufacturing industries (see Figure 7.3). In a trend similar to that of China, East Asian developing countries are now entering a phase of focusing more on manufacturing for their own markets and importing less. These countries' exports and imports of manufactured goods have declined, partly accounting for the weaker trade performance of developing countries generally. Globally, trade in manufactured goods far exceeds that of natural resources. Many sub-Saharan African and Latin American countries fall into the latter category. Developing countries' exports make up three-quarters of global trade in natural resources. A critical difference between the two groups of developing countries has been the rise of global supply chains.

In today's world, most trade in manufactured goods is determined by production supply chains. These are often referred to as 'global value chains', highlighting the fact that value is added at each stage in the chain (see Chapter 2). Through these supply chains, goods and services are provided in diverse locations, co-ordinated by MNEs. Manufactured goods account for 70% of the total $17.73 trillion in merchandise exports in 2017. The EU was the largest exporter of manufactured goods in 2017, exporting $4.57 trillion-worth of goods. The next two largest exporters of manufactured goods

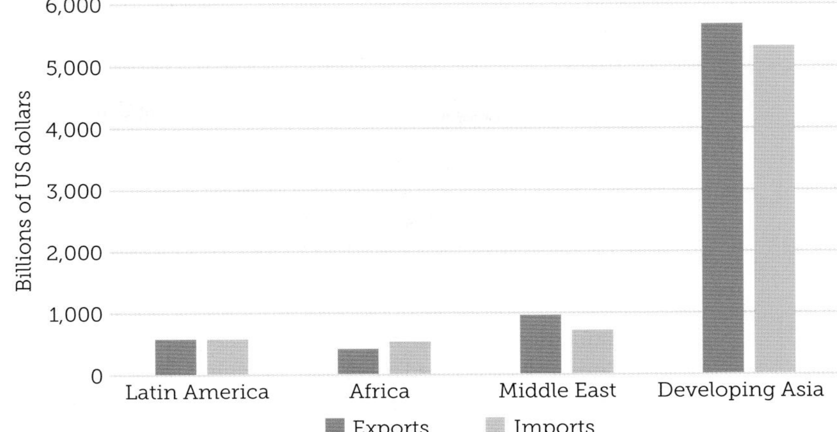

Figure 7.3 **Divergence in the merchandise trade profiles of developing economies, by region (2017)**

Source: WTO, *World Trade Statistical Review 2018*, Tables A58 and A59, pp. 180-82, at www.wto.org

were China ($2.13 trillion) and the US ($1.13). About $7 trillion-worth of manufactured exports are classified as **intermediate goods**, consisting of components which cross national borders more than once before being made into final products. MNE strategies co-ordinate a variety of linked firms, including affiliate companies, licensed or contract manufacturers and arm's-length contractors. A complex product like a car is likely to contain numerous imported components, amounting to 50% of the value of each finished vehicle.

intermediate goods components and parts which cross national borders before being made into final products

Participation in global value chains has benefited those developing countries that have focused on attracting FDI in export industries. Electronics and textiles are examples of industries transformed by global supply chains. Asian emerging economies have been particularly successful in this respect. Differing trade profiles are shown in Figure 7.4. In the figure, Country B is analogous to a developing country such as China that imports intermediate goods, incorporates them into finished products, and exports them to other countries. Destinations typically include countries like Country C, from which it has sourced intermediate goods, including high-value components. Country B thus benefits from the foreign value added to its exports. Country C in the figure is mainly an importer, and is likely to be a developed country like the US. It imports manufactured goods from Country B and also goods from Country A, which are likely to be natural resources and energy. Country A in

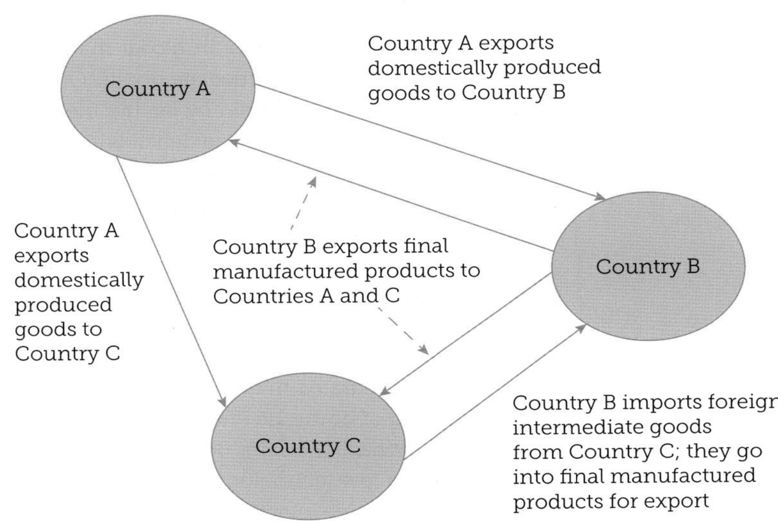

Figure 7.4 **Trade profiles of contrasting countries**

the figure exemplifies developing countries that depend on exports of primary products. These countries, which include many resource-rich African countries, must import manufactured goods, and must also import commodities and energy that they cannot produce. Their position is more precarious than Countries B and C, as they are highly vulnerable to swings in prices in commodity markets, affecting both their revenues from trade and their ability to import goods they require. These countries suffered in the decline in trade that occurred in 2015. For such countries, diversifying their economies into manufacturing would contribute to sustainable growth, but these economies often struggle to convert this advice into practice.

Transition economies, notably the post-communist countries of Central and Eastern Europe, bear similarities to Country B in Figure 7.4. Their manufacturing industries have grown from FDI, increasing their integration into the EU economy. Germany has played a key role in driving this growth, as its large industrial companies have invested heavily in productive assets in these newer EU member states, whose exports are mainly destined for other EU member countries, especially Germany itself. Germany has also remained a major exporter of domestically produced goods, and has retained a large manufacturing sector. Germany's trade is thus more evenly balanced between exports and imports than that of the US, which has a huge trade deficit.

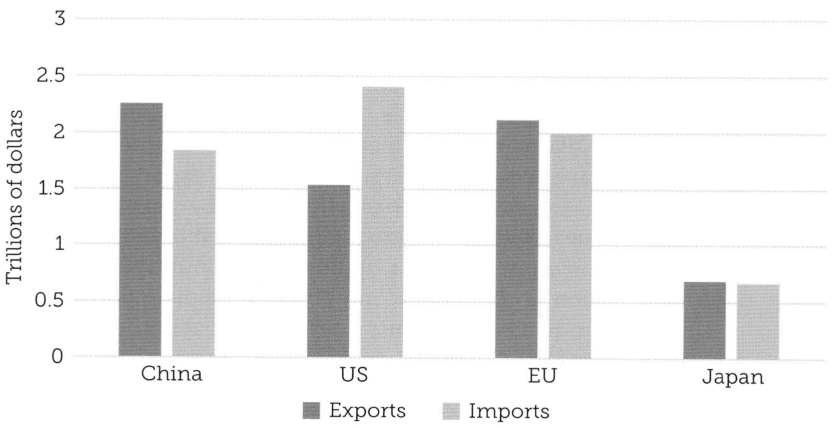

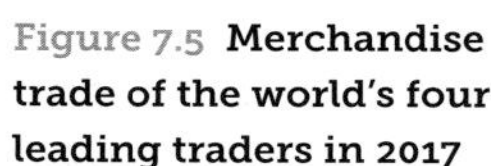
Figure 7.5 Merchandise trade of the world's four leading traders in 2017

Note: For the EU, the trade represented is extra-EU, that is, exports to countries outside the EU and imports from countries outside the EU.

Source of data: WTO, *World Trade Statistical Review 2018*, Table A6, p. 124, at www.wto.org

Figure 7.5 shows the world's leading traders, including the EU as a whole. China is the world's largest exporter of merchandise. Favourable tax treatment of foreign investors, including tax-free export zones, has helped to turn the country into a powerhouse for exports of consumer goods in global markets. About half of China's imports *and* exports are made up of intermediate goods. Of the four leading traders, the US stands out as being the largest importer by far, but the US has the greatest imbalance between exports and imports. The US trade deficit with China in goods has grown from roughly $50 billion in 1998 to over $400 billion in 2018 (see Figure 7.6). Consumer electronics and clothing are among the many goods imported from China. Most of these goods bear the brand names of American companies, often using raw materials shipped from the US.

Value-added trade can contribute greatly to a country's GDP, more so in developing countries than in developed ones. Economic growth per capita flows from a developing country's participation in global value chains. While this is good news on the face of it, there are wider concerns that pose challenges for governments that wish to become more integrated in global value chains. For many, that involvement can lead to the nurturing of domestic enterprises and technological development. This is now occurring in China. For others, dependence on low-tech manufacturing activities can set in, delivering few technological spillovers. In these circumstances, globalization is not contributing to development goals to the extent hoped for. Indeed, globalization

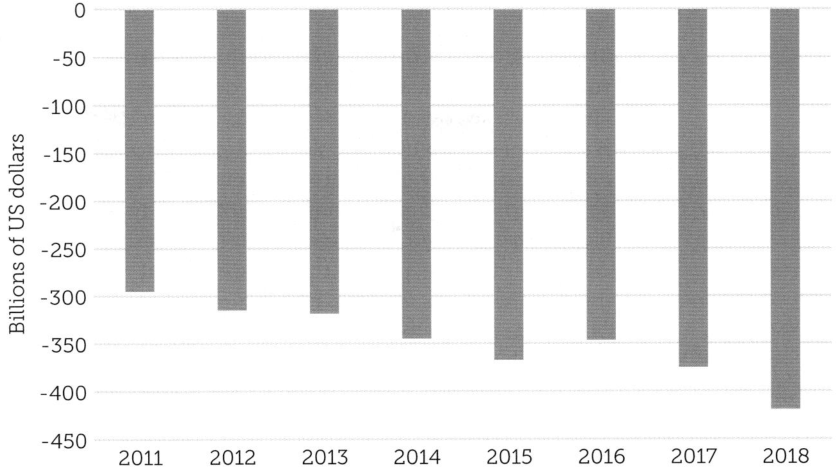

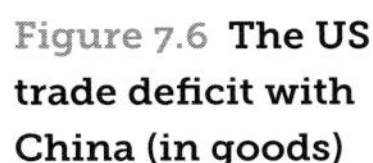

Figure 7.6 The US trade deficit with China (in goods)

Source of data: US Census Bureau, *Trade in goods with China*, at www.census.gov/foreign-trade, accessed 6 July 2019.

poses risks that MNE strategists will shift activities to other locations, adversely affecting the economies of communities where its activities had provided employment. By the same token, the shift of large swathes of manufacturing to developing countries has posed problems for the developed countries now importing goods they once produced domestically. The decline of manufacturing has brought economic hardship throughout much of America's former industrial landscape, with repercussions in communities. Following the collapse of Detroit's motor industry, the city declined rapidly, becoming the largest municipal bankruptcy in US history. MNEs have realized the benefits of scanning the globe to achieve lower-cost production, while consumers rejoice in lower prices on goods, from clothes to trainers. The benefits of globalized production must be weighed against the negative impacts in societies, in both developing and developed economies.

Trade and development

A company in a developing country that seeks to export its products enjoys location advantages in some sectors such as low-cost manufacturing, but there are risks in this strategy over the long term, both for the company and for the country where it operates.

What are those risks? How can developing economies expand trading relations that achieve sustainable economic growth? In what ways does such a strategy benefit the domestic company seeking to export?

Theories of international trade

Theories of trade have emerged with the rise in industrialization, with its potential to expand trade on a large scale. The first major theorist of international trade, Adam Smith, believed that all countries benefit from unrestricted trade. Free trade is said to exist where citizens can export and import without restrictions or barriers imposed by the governments of either the exporting or importing country. In his book, *The Wealth of Nations* (published in 1776), Smith argued in favour of 'the invisible hand' of market forces, as opposed to government intervention. When countries produce the products in which they are the most efficient producers, they are said to have an **absolute advantage** in these products. A country may then sell these goods overseas, and purchase from overseas goods which are produced more efficiently elsewhere. Thus, both countries benefit from trade.

absolute advantage advantage enjoyed by a country which is more efficient at producing a particular product than any other country

The theory of comparative advantage

comparative advantage advantage enjoyed by a country where production of a particular product involves greater relative advantage than would be possible anywhere else

Starting from the principle of absolute advantage, David Ricardo ([1817]1973), writing some 40 years after Adam Smith, developed his theory of **comparative advantage**. His theory contends that, if Country A is an efficient producer of wheat and Country B an efficient producer of clocks, it pays A to purchase clocks from B, even if it could itself produce clocks more efficiently than B. According to Ricardo, if countries specialize in the industries in which they have comparative advantage, all will benefit from trade with each other, consumers in both countries enjoying more wheat and more clocks than they would without trade. According to Ricardo's theory, therefore, trade is not a 'zero-sum' game, i.e. where one side's gain is the other's loss, but a 'positive-sum' game, i.e. one in which all parties benefit.

In reality, most countries do not specialize in ways envisaged by Ricardo's theory. Further, the model does not allow for dynamic changes that trade brings about. Economists base the benefits of free trade on 'dynamic gains' that lead to economic growth. Free trade leads to an increase in a country's stock of resources, in terms of both increased capital from abroad and greater supplies of labour. In addition, efficiency may improve with large-scale production and improved technology. Opening up markets and creating more competition can provide an impetus for domestic companies to become more efficient. Trading patterns are also influenced by historical accident, government policies, and the importance of MNEs in the global economy – all of which have been incorporated into newer trade theories.

Product life cycle theory from the trade perspective

Raymond Vernon's theory of the international product life cycle was introduced in Chapter 2, for its early contribution to our understanding of FDI and the location of production. The theory also helps to explain trade from the perspective of the firm (Wells, 1972). It traces a product's life from its launch in the home market, through to export to other markets, and, finally, to its manufacture in cheaper locations for import into its original home market. The theory observes that, over the cycle, production has moved from the US to other advanced countries, and finally to developing countries, where costs are lower.

This theory of product life cycle rests on a US-centric approach which reflected American manufacturing prowess of the 1950s and 60s, when other industrialized nations were preoccupied with post-war rebuilding of their economies. In the decades that followed, however, FDI and industrial development throughout the world have gradually reshaped the global economy. Globalization has seen a major shift in the manufacturing of mass-market consumer goods to low-cost Asian countries, most notably China, overtaking Vernon's model. In modern supply chains for more complex and high-tech products, a firm may use components from various locations, and choose yet another for assembling the final product. Because of the rapid pace of technological innovation and short product life cycles, a company in industries such as consumer electronics may well introduce a new product simultaneously in a number of markets, wiping out the leads and lags between markets. Globalization of production and markets has been made easier by the lowering of trade barriers between countries, aided by the WTO's multilateral system based on trade liberalization. MNEs have been major beneficiaries, while governments have been more ambivalent in their perspectives. They welcome the inward FDI and the employment opportunities, and they also applaud the ability of their MNEs to grow through global expansion. On the other hand, political leaders are sensitive to the need to nurture and maintain key domestic industries. A result is that trade barriers of various kinds (discussed later in this chapter) are typically imposed to block imports or protect local industries.

Newer trade theories

More recently, theorists have turned their attention to the growing importance of MNEs in international trade, taking into account the globalization of production and trade between affiliated companies (see Chapter 2). Krugman, in his book, *Rethinking International Trade* (1994), emphasized features of the international economy such as increasing returns and imperfect competition. More precisely, he said, 'conventional trade theory views world trade as taking place entirely in goods like wheat; new trade theory see it as being largely in goods like aircraft' (Krugman, 1994: 1). For companies, innovation and economies of scale give what are called **first-mover advantages** to early entrants in a market. This lead increases over time, making it impossible for others to catch up. For firms able to benefit in this way, the increased share in global markets has led to oligopolistic behaviour in some industries, such as the aircraft industry. For countries, there are advantages to be gained from encouraging national firms which enjoy first-mover advantages. There are clear implications here that government intervention can play a role in promoting innovation and entrepreneurship, thereby boosting competitive advantage of nations.

first-mover advantages precept that countries or firms which are first to produce a new product gain an advantage in markets which makes it virtually impossible for others to catch up

Porter's theory of competitive advantage

In his book, *The Competitive Advantage of Nations*, published originally in 1990, Michael Porter developed a theory of national **competitive advantage**. He attempts to find out why some countries are more successful than others. Each nation, he says, has four broad attributes that shape its national competitive environment. Porter envisaged the four attributes as forming the four points of a diamond. Assessing each of these attributes gives a picture of the country's competitive advantage.

competitive advantage theory (devised by Porter) that international competitiveness depends on four major factors: demand conditions, factor conditions, firms' strategy and supporting industries

The first two attributes relate to the national environment. The first, factor conditions, is about the nation's factors of production, such as skilled labour, infrastructure and natural resources. The social and cultural environment is also relevant to this analysis. The second attribute, demand conditions, relates to the nature and depth of home demand for particular goods and services. In emerging economies, the rise of the middle class is a strong indication of rising demand in consumer products and services. The third and fourth attributes relate to the country's firms and industries. The third attribute focuses on related and supporting industries, which contribute to competitive advantage. If the country is home to a host of supporting industries, including innovative entrepreneurial businesses, this is a good sign of growing national competitiveness. The fourth is firm strategy, structure and rivalry. This includes conditions in the nation governing how companies are created, organized, and managed. It also involves the nature of domestic rivalry (Porter, 1998a: 71). Where firms are focused on innovation, sensitive to changing demand, and continually rethinking quality improvements, there are advantages to be reaped in international markets.

Porter stresses that the four determinants are interdependent. Favourable demand conditions, for example, will contribute to competitive advantage only in an environment in which firms are able and willing to respond. Advantage based on only one or two determinants may suffice in natural resource-dependent industries, or those with lower technological input, but to sustain advantage in the modern knowledge-intensive industries, advantages throughout the model are necessary.

Porter adds that there are two additional variables in his theory. They are chance and government. Chance can open up unexpected opportunities in a variety of ways: new inventions, external political developments, and shifts in foreign market

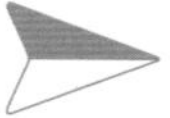

demand. He cites the fall of communism, which resulted in the opening of Central and Eastern Europe, as an example. His categorization of these occurrences as happening as if by chance is perhaps unfortunate, and it would be preferable to see them from the business perspective as simply opportunities. On the other hand, government policies can be highly influential.

Government policies highlighted by Porter include a strong antitrust policy, which encourages domestic rivalry, and investment in education, which generates knowledge resources. Government policies can play a crucial role in building national competitive advantage. Porter stresses that this role, however, is indirect rather than direct (Porter, 1998b: 184–6). Government remains an 'influence' rather than a 'determinant' in his model. However, it is arguable that government policy has had a larger direct role than his model suggests. Governments in market economies have taken on a more directly interventionist role, including ownership stakes in companies, in addition to a regulatory role. This has been particularly noteworthy since the financial crisis of 2007–8. In countries climbing the economic ladder, the role of government has been a key to international success.

Government guidance was critical in Japan's economic development, but was indirect, as Japan's large companies were mostly private sector. By contrast, in the more recent emerging economies, such as China, the state has played an active role in the development model, leading with large state-owned companies. Schemes to attract FDI, business-friendly taxation regimes and the setting up of special economic zones are aspects of government policy that have become common in emerging economies that seek to build competitive advantage. In addition, government policies are instrumental in the development of infrastructure. China and India provide contrasting examples. Transport and other infrastructure have developed rapidly in China, but have progressed slowly in India, largely because of lack of government impetus and complex rights over land. On the other hand, the Indian government has prioritized investment in high-technology education, in order to attract computing and IT services industries, which have driven the country's economic growth.

Porter's theory is useful in demonstrating the interaction between different determinants of national competitive advantage, but it probably underemphasizes world economic integration and the role of production supply chains.

Competitive advantage of nations

Porter's theory of competitive advantage of nations helps to explain why some countries are more successful economically than others. But in today's world, companies are often looking for a location's particular attributes that would create value in supply chains. How do these diverge from Porter's theory?

To what extent do Porter's four determinants continue to be relevant in describing a country's national competitiveness?

National trade policies

mercantilism in international trade, the approach of a country which sees trade mainly as promoting its own economic gains

National economic prosperity for almost all countries is more than ever tied in with international trade. But, as we have seen, all countries are not equal in building prosperity from trade. A stronger country is in a position to gain national economic benefits through trade. This approach, known broadly as **mercantilism**, is associated with imperialism, whereby a strong country is able to dominate and exploit a weaker one. Mercantilist thinking goes back to the sixteenth and seventeenth centuries, an era of powerful state-sponsored companies, such as the Dutch East India Company. These companies spearheaded trading ties around the globe, enriching the traders and enhancing the economic power of their governments. The prevailing view was that

national wealth was closely equated with trade. Achieving dominance over the seas and over the lucrative trade routes equated to economic ascendency over other countries.

Richer countries are in a stronger position than poorer countries to use trade to foster national goals, such as food security, or benefit particular industries, such as the car industry. Governments face innumerable political and social, as well as economic, pressures to intervene in trade. **Protectionism** is the deliberate policy of favouring home producers, for example, by subsidizing home producers or imposing import tariffs. Politically, protectionism is associated with nationalism, including protection of domestic employment, hostility towards immigrants and rejection of foreign ownership of domestic firms. Protectionism fosters an isolationist and aggressive foreign policy rather than a policy of co-operative international relations whereby ties with other countries are mutually beneficial. Protectionism is thus likely to lead to retaliation by trading partners, as happened in the 1930s in the US, with the highly protectionist Tariff Act, known as the Smoot-Hawley Act after the two senators who sponsored the law. The Tariff Act, passed in the era of the Great Depression, raised tariffs on some 20,000 imported goods. While aimed at protecting American jobs, it was arguably counterproductive, causing US exports and imports to fall dramatically. It thus exacerbated the devastation of the Great Depression and slowed the recovery process (Eichengreen and Irwin, 2009).

protectionism government trade policy of favouring home producers and discouraging imports

Figure 7.7 summarizes the pros and cons of free trade which are discussed in this section. The term 'free trade' is misleading. There has never been 'free' trade in the sense of no cross-border barriers at all. 'Trade liberalization' is therefore more accurate, to indicate measures *towards* free trade, which involve reducing border controls and reducing governments' scope for curtailing imports. Trade liberalization has been an important contributor to globalization, facilitating cross-border movements of goods. As we saw earlier in this chapter, benefits of greater integration in global supply chains come mixed with risks of negative impacts that are of concern to national decision makers. In this section, we look first at national priorities and then at policy tools for promoting them.

The free trade debate

In favour of free trade:	In favour of Protectionism:
• Free trade benefits all countries. • A country risks falling behind if it is isolated from global markets. • Costs of protecting industries can be high, and tend to go to uncompetitive industries.	• Protection of national industries promotes independence and security. • It protects domestic employment. • It supports national industries, allowing them to compete globally, and adding to national wealth.

Figure 7.7 **The pros and cons of free trade**

Government perspectives on trade

Governments are perceived as ultimately responsible for the safety and wellbeing of those within its borders, including individual citizens, groups of people, industries and companies. Governments are expected to be guided by 'national interest' in designing trade policy. But policies designed to please some of these groups can conflict with the interests of others. Governments are thus faced with a balancing act. We highlight below four major policy areas in which trade policy is shaped by national interests:

Promoting industrialization

Industrialization may be promoted by restricting the flow of imported products, thereby encouraging domestic manufacturing. We have seen that industrialization in many countries, such as Japan and the later industrializing countries of South

East Asia, has been guided by government, through industrial policy. These countries have made rapid transitions from mainly agricultural to industrial economies. The 'infant industries' argument holds that developing countries should protect infant industries in which they have potential comparative advantage until they are strong enough to survive when protections are removed. Japan is an example of both successful infant industry support and industrial policy (Gilpin, 2000). For Singapore and other Asian economies, foreign direct investors provided the impetus of development. Industrialization may focus on **import substitution**, that is, producing goods for domestic consumption which otherwise would have been imported. India is an example. Domestic industries nurtured through protective measures in this way do not always become competitive in world markets. Export-led development, by contrast, focuses on growth in export-oriented goods. Industrialization in China has taken this route.

import substitution approach to economic development which favours producing goods for domestic consumption that otherwise would have been imported

Protecting employment

By restricting imports, governments aim to safeguard domestic jobs. However, the situation is seldom as simple as this. Many US manufacturing jobs have been transferred to lower-paid overseas workers. Work in lower-skilled jobs, as in the textile industry, is particularly vulnerable to being lost to low-cost imports. Propping up uncompetitive domestic industries is costly and leads to declining competitiveness in the long term.

Workers in industrialized countries who are displaced by global competitive forces are usually those without the skills to benefit from the newer job opportunities. Whole regions can suffer decline as a result. Payments to displaced workers fall on the public purse and can provide a safety net, but in the long term, governments must look at the education and training needs of the economy to enhance competitive advantage. Nonetheless, protectionist pressures are very strong, and special interests' regional strongholds are often effective in mobilizing political support. In the US, the presidential campaign of Mr Trump was targeted at Americans in numerous 'rustbelt' areas, where manufacturing jobs had disappeared. However strong the protectionist urge is, these derelict industrial sites cannot realistically be brought back to their former glory. The campaign rhetoric based on nostalgia and emotional appeal struck a chord with voters in these areas, but, in practice, there was little hope of turning the clock back.

Protecting consumers

Conventional wisdom holds that consumers benefit from free trade in that competition in markets brings down prices and increases choice. Consumers can choose between imported and locally produced goods in a variety of sectors, from clothing to vehicles. Agriculture and consumer electronics have become global industries. The industrialization and globalization of the food chain have resulted in agricultural produce and livestock being transported hundreds – even thousands – of miles to markets. In theory, the consumer benefits from the availability of many products that would not be available locally. But an outcome is that any health and safety concerns, such as contamination from BSE in beef, can have wide ramifications.

Governments have at their disposal a variety of regulatory measures in respect of consumer products such as food and medicines, whether produced at home or abroad. However, levels of regulation and quality controls differ from country to country. Governments that take a stance against **genetically-modified organisms (GMOs)**, for example, are often accused of using safety as a barrier to keep out legitimate goods. American pharmaceutical companies and agribusiness companies are active in lobbying, pressing their cases to the US government to seek greater access to foreign markets. Their interests are often reflected in US trade policy.

genetically-modified organisms (GMOs) plants and animals that have been altered genetically in ways that do not occur in nature

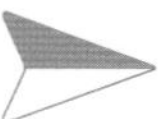

Promoting strategic interests

Strategic interests cover a number of considerations. It is often thought that the strategic sensitivity of defence industries dictates that domestic suppliers are preferable to foreign ones, and thus should be protected. The strategic necessity argument can be extended to a great number of products. It was used to provide federal funding for the semiconductor industry in the US in the 1990s, as semiconductors are crucial to defence systems. Food production is one of the most heavily protected industries, because of the strategic importance of safeguarding food supply and also agricultural employment. On this reasoning, subsidies and import restrictions have long benefited Japanese farmers, while Japanese consumers have paid well above world prices for their food. These barriers are only slowly coming down. Sharp rises in global prices of basic commodities, such as wheat and rice, in 2008, caused shortages around the world, leading to food riots in some countries. As a result, food security has become a greater preoccupation of governments.

Strategic industries are also a target of policymakers. Strategic trade policy holds that governments can assist their own firms in particular industries to gain competitive advantage. This theory mainly applies to oligopolistic industries such as the aerospace industry, in which the US helped Boeing (www.boeing.com) by providing it with lucrative defence contracts, while European governments helped Airbus (www.airbus.com) through subsidies. Both sides have accused each other of breaching WTO rules restricting state aid, resulting in a long-running legal action under the WTO's dispute settlement procedure.

Trade policies may be linked to foreign policy objectives, as was clearly demonstrated during the cold war, when trade followed political and military alliances. Government overseas aid packages to developing countries may be tied to trade. Trade policies are often based on historical relationships between countries, such as those between the former colonial powers of Europe and their former colonies. This resulted in another long-running dispute between the EU and US. The so-called 'banana dispute' had its roots in the preferential treatment that former colonies in the Caribbean received, which were found to contravene WTO rules.

Protecting national culture

For governments, maintaining national culture and identity is an important aspect of social stability. This covers cultural products such as literature, film and music. The growth of the internet and global media has led to fears of cultural globalization, prompting some national authorities to limit foreign content and foreign ownership in these sectors. Internet censorship, which has become highly elaborate in some countries, such as China, is based in some measure on the perception by the government that the free flow of content from abroad can undermine national cultural and social values.

Tools of governmental trade policy

Government policies affect trade in numerous ways, both directly and indirectly. Of direct impact is the manipulation of exchange rates. Devaluing a country's currency will have the immediate effect of making exports cheaper and imports more expensive (see Chapter 8). However, governments now have less scope for manipulating exchange rates in increasingly interlinked currency markets. Similarly, most governments are now party to multilateral, regional and bilateral trading arrangements which curtail their ability to control trade. We will therefore look at government policy options in the context of changing global and regional contexts. The traditional tools for controlling trade are tariffs, quotas, subsidies, and other non-tariff barriers to trade.

tariff a tax imposed by governments on imported goods and services

The classic tool of trade policy is the **tariff**, or duty payable on goods traded. Tariffs are usually imposed on imported goods, but they can also be imposed on exports.

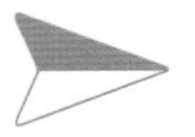

When we think of protectionism, we think naturally of tariff barriers. The tariff raises the price of an imported product, thereby benefiting domestic producers of the same product. Japanese whisky producers have been protected in this way by huge import duties levied on foreign whisky. The sums collected also swell government coffers. The main losers are the consumers, who pay higher prices for the imported product. While tariffs on manufactured goods have diminished dramatically, thanks to the multilateral GATT (discussed later), tariffs on agricultural products are still common.

import quota a barrier to trade which consists of limiting the quantity of an imported product that can legally enter a country

The **import quota** limits the quantity of an imported product that can legally enter a country. Licences may be issued annually to a limited number of firms, each of which must stay within the amounts specified in its import licence. Limits are set so as to allow only a portion of the market to foreign goods, thus protecting the market share of domestic producers. Restricting supply in this way is likely to result in higher prices for consumers. Import quotas are sometimes evaded by companies shipping goods via other countries with quota to spare when their home country's quota is used up. An exporting firm may ultimately set up production in a country to avoid the imposition of quotas.

voluntary export restraint (VER) tool of government trade policy by which trading partners wishing to export into a country are encouraged to limit their exports, or risk the imposition of quotas or tariffs

local content requirements trade policy that requires foreign investors to use local component suppliers in, for example, manufacturing

An alternative to the import quota is the **voluntary export restraint (VER)**, which shifts the onus onto the exporting country to limit its exports, or possibly risk the imposition of quotas or tariffs. A leading example of the VER has been Japanese car exports to the US. In the 1980s, when the Japanese motor industry was growing apace and making rapid inroads in the American market, the US government persuaded Japan to agree to a VER. To sidestep these restrictions, Japanese manufacturers set up local operations in the US through FDI. Governments can introduce **local content requirements**, to insure that local component suppliers gain. Japanese motor manufacturers have responded by locating associated Japanese component manufacturers near to assembly plants in overseas locations, thus facilitating just-in-time operations while maintaining high local content.

non-tariff barriers national legal requirements, such as health and safety standards, that act to prevent the imports from other countries that are not in conformity

Local content requirements can be viewed as a type of **non-tariff barrier** to trade, also referred to as an 'administrative' barrier. Such barriers serve as indirect means of keeping out imports. As we noted earlier, rules regarding product safety and public health are also sometimes viewed as similarly deterrent. American agribusiness giant, Monsanto, along with the US government, extols the safety of food products containing GMOs. Research carried out by Pew Research Center found that while 88% of scientists considered GMOs safe, 57% of ordinary American consumers disagreed, considering GMOs unsafe (Funk and Rainie, 2015). Polls have consistently shown that over 90% of Americans desire GMO labelling. Ballot propositions on GMO labelling in some states have been defeated, largely due to the multi-million-dollar anti-labelling campaigns run by the large food businesses. One trade association was fined $18 million for violations of political campaign finance laws – the largest ever campaign finance penalty in the US. A federal statute on GMO labelling was passed in 2016, shortly before the end of Mr Obama's presidency. Two years later, that law was still not implemented.

As of 2018, 64 countries required GMO labelling, including all member countries of the EU, Japan, Brazil and Russia. Monsanto and other agribusiness companies have targeted African countries as lucrative new markets, where they are pressing the virtues of GMOs in obtaining higher crop yields in harsh conditions (see the mini case study on Monsanto in Chapter 8). However, the control exerted by the agribusiness company over smallholders engaged in GMO farming raises concerns that farmers and farming will become subordinated to corporate goals rather than national development priorities. African governments are in a relatively weak position to resist the strong overtures of the agribusiness industry and their US government backers.

subsidies payments from public funds to support domestic producers; there are also export subsidies to home producers to bolster a country's exports

Government **subsidies** can also amount to non-tariff barriers. These are payments and other financial help from public funds to support domestic producers.

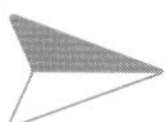

The way I see it ...

'...the mandatory labelling of GM foods does not provide consumers with meaningful information. Mandatory labelling can actually be misleading to consumers who interpret foods produced, either in whole or in part, from or with biotechnology, as unsafe.'

Cargill's views, in 'Does Cargill support mandatory labelling legislation for foods containing GM ingredients?', at www.cargill.com, accessed 27 July 2015.

As of 2018, detailed guidelines under the new federal labelling law had still not been agreed: labels could be words, pictures or a bar code to be scanned by smartphone. Consumers might well be more confused than ever. The term 'GMO' might not appear on the label, and 'bioengineered' might not appear either: just 'BE', which would not be familiar to all consumers. Some foods would be exempt from GMO labelling if they are basic ingredients such as sugar or cooking oils – almost all of which contain GMOs.

See the article by Levitin and Slavin, 'Food giants back US consumers in battle for meaningful food labelling', Ethical Corporation, 3 September 2018, at www.ethicalcorp.com

Socially responsible food producers are urging greater transparency in labelling in the industry, in order to inform and win over consumers. How do you feel the food industry can regain the confidence of consumers?

Governments often justify subsidies to domestic producers as a strategic need to ensure livelihoods of farmers who provide basic domestic food supplies. This can be distinguished from the argument used to justify programmes to boost farmers' incomes for the purpose of enabling them to export cheaply. The latter line of reasoning is that the extra funds, which are export subsidies, will boost the local producers' competitive position in global markets. Export subsidies are against WTO rules as they distort markets. Some types of state funding fall into a more nebulous, 'grey' area. For example, R&D grants, viewed as legitimate, help local producers indirectly. Funds to promote green technology are similarly viewed as legitimate. There are other types of state aid, including loans at preferential rates and tax concessions.

Advocates of trade liberalization criticize subsidies on several grounds. They argue that subsidies work against a 'level playing field' for trade, as unsubsidized firms face unfair competition. When rich developed countries pay local producers subsidies, producers in poor developing countries that trade in the same product markets are disadvantaged. The impact on markets is likely to be a downward movement of prices.

The EU has provided substantial subsidies for farmers since 1962, creating considerable trade friction with other nations. The extent of EU support diminished in the 1990s, but agriculture continues to be a highly politically sensitive sector. The EU's spending on agriculture is determined by the Common Agricultural Policy (CAP), which comes under the broad heading of 'sustainable growth'. There are two 'pillars': direct payments to farmers and subsidies for rural development. Together, they amount to over €408 billlion, or 38% of the EU budget for the period 2014–20.

Cotton is one of the world's most widely grown and traded agricultural products. Most of the world's cotton is grown in developing countries, but it is the US that has the greatest impacts in world markets. The world's third largest producer (behind China and Brazil), the US is by far the largest exporter of cotton, accounting for about one-third of global cotton exports, as shown in Figure 7.8. Moreover, in 2019, US cotton production grew by nearly 20%. About 75% of its crop is exported, its main destination being China's large textile manufacturing sector.

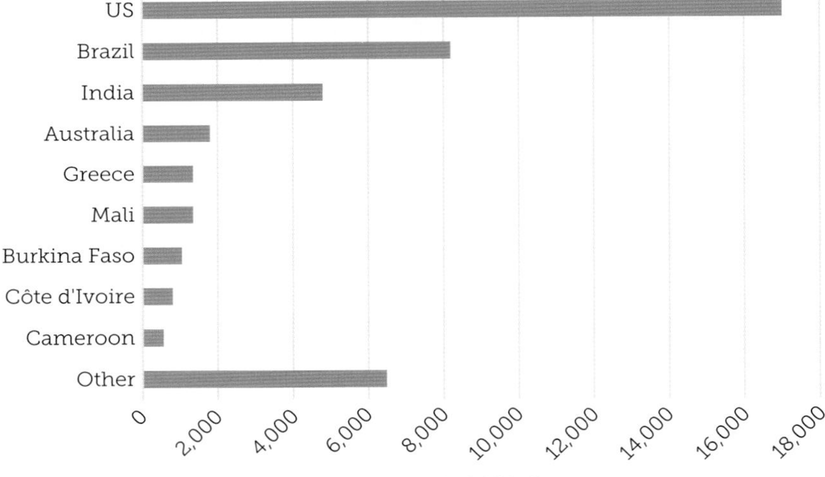

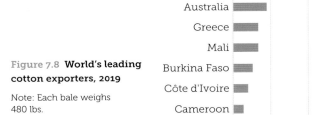

Figure 7.8 **World's leading cotton exporters, 2019**

Note: Each bale weighs 480 lbs.

Source: US Department of Agriculture (Foreign Agricultural Service) *Cotton: World Markets and Trade*, Table 02, p. 9, June 2019, at www.fas.usda.gov/data

Both China and the US heavily subsidize their cotton growers. China's crop mainly supplies local factories, whereas most of the US crop is traded in world markets. US export subsidies, mostly in the form of insurance payouts that violate WTO rules, help to keep global prices low. Brazil used the WTO's dispute resolution procedure (discussed below), successfully bringing a case against US subsidies. In 2005, the WTO ordered the US to stop its subsidy programme and export guarantee programme. In 2009, the US lost its appeal against this decision, and the WTO granted Brazil the right to impose retaliatory measures, in recognition of the unfairness suffered by Brazilian cotton producers. But instead of changing the non-compliant subsidy regime, the US has offered money compensation of several hundred million dollars to Brazilian farmers, and Brazil agreed. Two such deals have been approved by the WTO, the latest in 2014. Although settled between the two parties, bilateral

This cotton farmer in Mali, like others in the poor, cotton-growing countries of Africa, is in a weak position in relation to the large agribusinesses that dominate world cotton markets.

 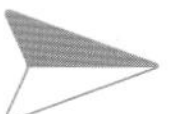

settlements such as these do not resolve the overall unfairness from the perspective of other developing countries that depend on cotton exports. In four poor West African countries alone (Benin, Burkina Faso, Chad and Mali), 10 million people depend on revenues from cotton (Pelc, 2014). These countries cannot afford the costs of bringing WTO legal actions. Nor do they have influence in the corridors of power in Washington, D.C. By contrast, farming in both the US and Brazil is dominated by large agribusinesses that have considerable influence on political leaders. US agribusinesses and insurance companies that handle the payout schemes have been highly effective in lobbying politicians to perpetuate subsidies from public funds, despite their illegality by WTO rules (Pelc, 2014). Farmers in Africa would have hoped for an outcome from the WTO that focused on justice for all stakeholder countries involved in cotton trading.

Liberalizing trade at the international level: progress and setbacks

The Brazilian cotton farmers' deals with US authorities resolved trade disputes between the two countries only in the short term. Continuing subsidies to US cotton growers will probably prompt Brazil to launch new claims for redress. Meanwhile, the distortions in global markets remain. This unsatisfactory situation highlights the need for multilateral agreements to promote fairness in world trade for member countries – large and small, rich and poor. The WTO's predecessor framework dates from the immediate aftermath of the Second World War. The preceding era, scarred by the Great Depression of the 1930s, had seen protectionism and a decline in world trade. Indeed, it was in that period that the US government began its farm subsidy programmes, to support farming communities in hardship. Under the **Bretton Woods agreement** reached at a conference of the allied nations in 1944, exchange rate stability would be achieved by pegging every currency to gold or the US dollar (see Chapter 8). It also envisaged **multilateral** treaties as a means of dismantling barriers to trade. Negotiators laid plans for an international trade organization (ITO) to bring down tariff barriers, but the plan was met with little enthusiasm from nations, still reluctant to endorse free trade. Instead, a more modest set of proposals for a weaker institutional framework was formulated, in the **General Agreement on Tariffs and Trade (GATT)**.

Bretton Woods agreement agreement between the allied nations in the aftermath of the Second World War, which was intended to bring about exchange rate stability and foster multilateral agreements to dismantle trade barriers

multilateral treaty international agreement binding many countries

General Agreement on Tariffs and Trade (GATT) series of multilateral agreements on reducing trade barriers

Under the GATT, successive rounds of negotiations have brought about global trade liberalization, leading to the establishment in 1995 of the WTO, reminiscent of the stronger body envisaged in early days after the War. As of 2018, the WTO had 164 members, most – but not all of them – nation-states. The most recent state to join was Afghanistan in 2016. The EU is a member in its own right, as it is a customs territory with capacity over trade policy. EU member states are also members. In addition, the WTO includes 23 observer governments. Building on the GATT, the WTO now oversees a global framework for multilateral agreements.

GATT principles

The GATT provided the principles and foundation for the development of a global trading system, which were carried forward into the WTO. Perhaps the most important of these is non-discrimination, or the **most-favoured-nation** principle (MFN). There are two aspects to this principle:

1. Favourable tariff treatment negotiated with one country will be extended to similar goods from all countries;
2. Under the principle of 'national treatment', imported goods are treated for all purposes in the same way as domestic goods of the same type.

most-favoured nation (MFN) principle GATT principle by which the most favourable tariff treatment negotiated with one country is extended to similar goods from all countries

MFN status is negotiated between countries, and while it is the norm among trading partners, there are exceptions. Because of its poor human rights record, China was granted only temporary MFN status from 1980 onwards, which was renewed annually. Unconditional MFN status came in 2000, paving the way for China's WTO membership. After years of negotiation, Russia joined the WTO only in 2012, becoming the last of the BRIC countries to join.

Other GATT principles include reciprocity, requiring tariff reductions by one country to be matched by its trading partners; and transparency, ensuring that the underlying aims of all trade measures are clear. The principle of fairness allows a country which has suffered from unfair trading practices by a trading partner to take protectionist measures against that country. Defining fair practice is at the heart of many trade disputes, as countries naturally have differing perspectives on what is and is not fair. An example is **dumping**, or the sale of goods abroad at below the price charged for comparable goods in the producing country. The GATT **anti-dumping** agreement of 1994 allows anti-dumping duties to be imposed on the exporting country by the importing country, in order to protect local producers from unfair competition. The country which makes allegations of dumping against another can ask the WTO to investigate the matter. The WTO receives hundreds of anti-dumping complaints every year. Member countries sometimes bypass the WTO mechanism and take unilateral action against countries they allege are engaging in dumping and other activities that they deem are unfair. The US has been active in this respect, as discussed below.

dumping the sale of goods abroad at below the price charged for comparable goods in the producing country

anti-dumping agreement WTO rules which allow anti-dumping duties to be imposed on the exporting country by the importing country, in order to protect local producers from unfair competition

The Uruguay Round, culminating in the GATT 1994, laid the groundwork for future trade liberalization, while allowing countries to take limited steps to safeguard national industries. It resulted in worldwide tariff reductions of about 40% on manufactured goods. Less spectacularly, it made strides in the more difficult areas of reducing trade barriers in agricultural products and textiles. It also initiated agreements on intellectual property rights and services, both crucial areas in growing world trade. The agreement on **Trade-Related Aspects of Intellectual Property Rights (TRIPS)** was a landmark agreement designed to provide a framework by which developing countries would implement stronger IP laws while also having the right to issue a 'compulsory licence' to use medicines under patent. The compulsory licence would be appropriate when the society's public health is at risk, and the country is unable to afford the prices charged by the global pharmaceutical companies. Finally, the GATT 1994 created the WTO as its successor institution.

Trade-Related Aspects of Intellectual Property Rights (TRIPS) multilateral agreement on the protection of intellectual property, which aims to bring national legal regimes into harmony

WTO and the regulation of world trade

Whereas in 1947 the GATT created only a weak institutional framework, the WTO, which came into being in 1995, was designed on firmer legal footing, with a stronger rule-governed orientation. This approach is reflected in its organizational structure. A Ministerial Conference, consisting of trade ministers of all member states, is the main policy-making body, which meets every two years. Under the **Dispute Settlement Understanding (DSU)**, the WTO oversees a dispute settlement procedure for specific trade disputes between countries. This new legal procedure for resolving disputes marked a departure from the GATT procedure, which had no power of enforcement.

Dispute Settlement Understanding (DSU) WTO framework for the settlement of trade disputes between member states

The WTO procedure aims to resolve trade disputes through impartial panels before they escalate into damaging trade wars in which countries take unilateral action against each other. A country which feels it has suffered because of another's breach of trading rules may apply to the WTO, which appoints an impartial panel for hearing the case within a specified timetable. A country found to be in breach of trade rules by a panel may appeal to the Appellate Body. If it is again found to be in the wrong, the WTO may authorize the country whose trade has suffered as a result, to impose retaliatory trade sanctions.

 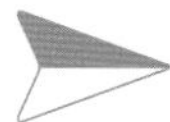

For the WTO's procedure to succeed, countries must adhere to its decisions, even when they disagree with them. All countries enjoy a recognized right to safeguard national interests, but this principle, as well as interpretation of WTO rules themselves, is subject to considerable latitude in interpretation. If countries impose unilateral sanctions, bypassing the WTO, then WTO procedures, and the authority that underlies them, could be eroded. The US law known as Section 301 is such a provision. Originally enacted in the Trade Act 1974, it was strengthened in 1988 to 'Special 301'. It authorizes the US Trade Representative (USTR), on the advice of the US International Trade Commission (the ITC) to identify policies or practices of countries that are considered unreasonable in their interpretation of WTO rules and that restrict US trade. A country singled out is placed on a 'watch list' or a 'priority watch list', leading to the possible imposition of unilateral sanctions by the US. A country could lose access to the entire US market, not merely that of the offending product.

The legislation has been criticized for its aggressive unilateral approach, which flies in the face of WTO rules. A country could be in compliance with all multilateral and bilateral agreements to which it is bound, but nonetheless be targeted with US sanctions. Monitoring by the USTR has focused on intellectual property (IP) rights, relevant to medicines under pharmaceutical patents and copyright material. The TRIPS agreement specifies that parties are obliged to use the WTO's dispute settlement procedure in case of disputes, and unilateral sanctions such as the Special 301 procedures are prohibited (Flynn, 2010). Indeed, it is arguable that the watch lists themselves are in breach of WTO rules, notably the GATT's most-favoured nation principle. However, the US has continued to use Special 301 procedures, and indeed, the number of actions increased following the TRIPS agreement. India, which has a thriving generic medicine sector, has repeatedly been targeted, although it is in breach of no treaties. The aggressive US stance stems in large part from the power of the country's large pharmaceutical companies, who feel threatened by generic producers (see Chapter 9). However, the US has also targeted China under Section 301, for alleged theft of intellectual property from US businesses that operate in China.

In a far-reaching complaint to the WTO by Canada against the US, launched late in 2017, the Canadian trade authorities detailed a long catalogue of anti-dumping and anti-subsidy actions imposed on countries by the US. The Canadian complaints were submitted under the DSU and made an initial request for consultation. The complaint document details 200 cases over two decades involving not just Canada, but numerous other countries, including European countries, Brazil, China and India (Kassam, 2018). The cases are highly diverse, ranging from steel imports from China, pasta from Italy and timber from Canada. In these submissions, Canada alleges that the US, in administering its system for levying anti-dumping and anti-subsidy duties on trading partners, is in breach of WTO rules, often retaining sums of money in excess of what would be consistent with WTO recommendations. It also complains that the process administered by the US ITC under the US Tariff Act of 1930 is one of 'institutional bias' against the other country (WTO, 2017).

Concerns over US protectionism were reinforced in 2018, when, in moves designed to further the 'America First' trade policy, the US announced a series of new tariffs on imports from China, notably steel and aluminium. The US president defended these moves on grounds of national security – grounds which would normally be used in times of emergency, such as war. Instead, the US president pointed to alleged breaches of American intellectual property rights by Chinese firms that have business relations with American ones. In retaliation, the Chinese government announced tariff rises targeted at a wide range of products imported from the US. Among them were numerous agricultural products, which have become important for American exporters and have enjoyed support of US government trade policy. These moves marked the onset of a possibly damaging trade war between the US and China.

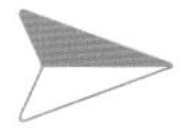

MINI CASE STUDY

Trade in soya beans causes friction

Dalian, a port in Northeast China, pictured on the cover of this book, has become a focal point in the trade wars between the US and China. The *Peak Pegasus*, a cargo ship carrying 70,000 tonnes of American soya beans, set sail from Seattle, Washington on 8 June 2018, for a month's voyage to China. As it was approaching the harbour at Dalian, the Chinese government announced new tariffs of 25% on its cargo. These were in response to tariffs announced on Chinese goods exported to the US. The new tariffs would add $6 million to the cost the importer would have to pay for the ship's cargo. The deal fell through, and the ship was left circling aimlessly outside the harbour. Each day that went by cost the owners $12,500. After a month of idling, the *Peak Pegasus* eventually docked in Dalian, the owners of the cargo having negotiated a deal with the Chinese buyers.

In the space of two decades, China has become the world's biggest importer of soya beans, used mainly in animal feed for its pork industry. This demand is driven by the rise in meat consumption by China's growing middle class: meat consumption has more than doubled, from 20kg per person to 50kg since the late 1980s. Soya beans are the preferred protein-rich source of feed for livestock, but domestic production would run out after only six weeks. The US farming industry has tapped into this demand, exporting soya beans worth $12 billion in 2017, which is about 60% of US soya bean exports.

By November 2018, imports of soya beans from the US to China had fallen to zero. Instead, China shifted to importing soya beans from Brazil, which also has a large agribusiness sector. In November, imports from Brazil amounted to 5.07 million tonnes, up 80% from the same month in 2017. In December, as Brazilian supplies were beginning to diminish, China resumed buying US soya beans, after a truce was agreed with the US, but tariffs were still in place. Meanwhile, China has been exploring ways of altering its feed to pigs, to reduce the amount of soya beans needed (see the recommended article below). Chinese experts feel that increasing imports from Brazil and adjusting the soya bean content of animal feed will free them from reliance on US farms.

Chinese leaders are well aware that US soya bean farmers are concentrated in rural regions that have been loyal supporters of President Trump. In July 2018, the US government allocated a package of $12 billion for payments to US farmers of soya beans, as well as wheat, corn, cotton and other crops. In 2019, an even larger payment of $16 billion was allocated in subsidies to US farmers. For over two decades, US farmers had made significant investments in shifting their focus to soya beans for the Chinese market, only to find it had evaporated overnight. The US has strong reasons to urge the Chinese to reduce their tariffs on American agricultural imports.

Will these American soya beans find a market? Farmers in the Midwest of the country face an uncertain future.

Questions

- Looking at all the parties in this case, who are the winners, if any, and who are the losers? Explain your reasons.
- Are US farmers likely to turn against the US president as a result of his trade policies?

Find out more

See the article published by Reuters, 'Inside China's strategy in the soybean trade war', by Josephine Mason, Halie Gu and Karl Plume, 27 December 2018, at https://uk.reuters.com

The US has pursued an aggressive trade strategy under President Trump, taking a hostile approach to all trading partners of the US in his narrowly focused view of US interests. It has threatened to withdraw the US from the WTO, seemingly unwilling to recognize the many benefits to the US that have flowed from WTO membership. President Trump has also pursued a policy of blocking all new appointments to the WTO's dispute settlement appellate body, with the result that vacancies have not been filled. Ultimately, a shortage of staff would prevent the WTO body from functioning. The settlement of disputes is a vital function of the WTO, and its ceasing to carry out its duties would greatly undermine the WTO trading system. In addition, the trade war between the two economic superpowers undermines the WTO's authority, with damaging impacts on world trade and, ultimately, on the global economy.

The WTO's multilateral system was designed to offer a level playing field for all, developed and developing countries. However, we have seen how the multilateral system is threatened in a number of ways. The example of the Brazil cotton settlement, noted earlier, is one. The unilateral imposition of sanctions by the US is another. Then there is the growing use of the investor-state dispute settlement process (the ISDS), discussed in Chapter 6. There, we noted concerns over the legitimacy, transparency, consistency and impartiality of these arbitration processes. The US has pressed for the ISDS process to be included in two proposed plurilateral treaties – the Trans-Pacific Partnership (TPP) and the Transatlantic Trade and Investment Partnership (TTIP). The US withdrew from both sets of negotiations in 2017, but seemed to be open to re-entering at a later date. Countries in the Pacific grouping have maintained a revised TPP is possible and are pressing ahead. Both TPP and European negotiations have raised criticisms of the ISDS process, and would look to revise this and other aspects of future plurilateral agreements.

Multilateralism in crisis

The WTO has made a dramatic impact in focusing international attention on issues of world trade, and it has also sparked considerable controversy. Since its creation in 1995, issues of globalization and the rise of developing nations have come to the fore, involving the WTO in wider debates. Its meetings have been targeted by demonstrations, from anti-capitalist protesters to environmental activists. In addition, NGOs have been instrumental in vocalizing environmental and human rights issues. Within multilateral negotiations themselves, national interests have remained divergent. Developing and emerging countries seek the opening of markets in rich countries, while rich countries wish to export more easily to markets in the developing world. Both developed and developing countries fear that the removal of barriers will open their economies to damaging competition, which could jeopardize local industries; hence, all are reluctant to make concessions.

An ambitious round of multilateral trade negotiations commenced in Doha, Qatar, in 2001, known as the Doha round. Negotiations continued at several ministerial conferences which followed, but the major policy areas which had been carried forward from the Uruguay round generated sharp divergences of perspectives, mainly between developed and developing countries. It was intended that the new Doha agreement would be in place by the end of 2008, but negotiations faltered once again, and the deteriorating global economic situation at the time seemed to dampen national leaders' appetites for further multilateral talks. Areas in which agreement was sought included agriculture, rules for trade in services, and access to patented drugs. Other issues were labour standards, environmental protection, and competition policy. Doha was described as a 'development' round, focusing on issues central to developing countries. These countries have been firm in their view that progress must be made by rich countries in reducing farm subsidies and tariffs. However, it became clear that the interests of the large emerging economies, such as Brazil, diverged from those of the smaller and poorer developing countries, as we saw in Brazil's dispute with the US on cotton subsidies.

International trade tensions

This is a lecture by Professor Ralph Ossa of the University of Zurich, Geneva. It is in the WTO Dialogues series, and is entitled, 'Trade talks and trade wars: How high are the gains and the costs?' The lecture took place in Geneva, 14 June 2017. Professor Ossa talks about trade tensions and multilateralism.

Video link: International trade tensions
www.youtube.com/watch?v=EIw7Xglp8KA

The appointment of a Brazilian, Roberto Azevêdo, as director-general of the WTO, in 2013, seemed to seal the growing voice of developing countries in global trade policies. However, the hoped-for conclusion of the Doha round, in December 2013 in Bali, rapidly turned into disappointment. The Bali meeting focused on a Trade Facilitation Agreement (TFA), designed to cut the red tape required of businesses when sending goods across national borders, including goods in transit, which are crucial to global supply chains. The TFA was particularly championed by the US, mindful of the globalization strategies of America's large multinationals. The TFA had wide support, but was blocked by objections from India, which refused to agree unless the US dropped objections to India's system of subsidies and price support for farmers. In November 2014, India and the US struck a temporary accord. India and other developing countries that have similar food security concerns, had hoped that the WTO's ministerial meeting in Buenos Aires in 2017 would lead to a permanent resolution of this issue among all the parties. However, the US rejected any discussion along these lines.

The India–US conflict had highlighted the difficulties that had troubled the Doha round for over a decade. The WTO has focused on trade liberalization as the primary goal, assuming it to be beneficial to all countries. This assumption underlies its approach to both trade negotiations and dispute settlement. However, as the Doha round foundered, it became clear that countries have divergent interests economically, and that broad issues such as societal goals and environmental concerns should also be taken into account.

The liberalizing of trade in services has been an aspiration of multilateral talks, but the Doha round made no progress. An initiative from the US has seen the coming together of 23 parties representing 50 countries, including the US and EU, in negotiations for a Trade in Services Agreement (TiSA). This would cover services like financial services, e-commerce and health, aiming to reduce regulatory restrictions and to dismantle barriers for companies that provide cross-border services, such as healthcare. It would also apply to the industrial sector, including mining services such as fracking. Talks among the parties have been held in secret since 2013, and information has become available only through leaks. It has emerged that a draft agreement provides for 'technological neutrality', which is equivalent to a level playing field (Inman, 2015). The implication is that fracking companies or others in fossil-fuel extraction would be able to bring a case to a tribunal under the ISDS process if a government subsidizes renewable energy investment. The TiSA would thus seem to be a blow against efforts to combat climate change. The TiSA would also provide that once a service such as healthcare function is privatized, the government would be barred from taking it back under public control. These measures would imply a weakening of governmental powers over policies to act in the public interest. Although the TiSA talks appeared to have been stalled in 2017, the parties have remained optimistic that further talks and an eventual agreement are possible.

Regional, bilateral and plurilateral trade agreements

bilateral treaty agreement between two countries, often for reciprocal trade terms

free trade agreement (FTA) trade agreement between countries which aims to liberalize trade between them; can be bilateral or multilateral

regional trade agreement (RTA) free trade agreement among a number of countries in the same broad geographic region

plurilateral trade agreement trade agreement among a number of countries in different regions that come together deliberately for the purpose of liberalizing trade and investment among them; separate from the WTO's multilateral system

Running in parallel with the WTO's activities, countries have long been active in making their own agreements with trading partners, both within their own geographical regions and beyond. It is common to make a distinction between a **bilateral** agreement, between just two countries, often just called a **free trade agreement (FTA)**, and a **regional trade agreement (RTA)** among a number of countries in the same broad geographic region. However, from the WTO's perspective, both types of agreement, which lie outside the multilateral system, are treated broadly as regional trade agreements. The RTA is often referred to as a 'preferential trade agreement' (PTA), reflecting the fact that its terms give preference to goods and services from countries which are parties to the particular agreement. The number of RTAs (including bilateral agreements) notified to the WTO grew strongly in the decade to 2016, the cumulative total of RTAs in force reaching 445 that year. Growth slowed in 2016, the total rising to 455 that year, with no further notifications in 2017. RTA member countries are highly likely to also be WTO members, creating overlapping ties, as shown in Figure 7.9. What is more, the prospect of new **plurilateral trade agreements**, between many countries, such as the proposed Trade in Services Agreement (TiSA), Trans-Pacific Partnership (TPP) and Transatlantic Trade and Investment Partnership (TTIP), would constitute further overlapping obligations. The overlap is particularly evident in dispute resolution, as shown in the figure. In any dispute, there could be three or more routes available, which could be pursued simultaneously. They include the national legal systems of member countries, ISDS and the WTO's dispute settlement system.

Categories of regional trade agreement

Countries look naturally to trade with their neighbours. Not only does regional trade make sense in terms of costs, firms are likely to have greater familiarity with firms and industries in their own region than with those oceans away. RTAs are designed to bring down trade barriers among their member states, thus opening up regional markets for national producers. A group of countries which have joined in an RTA

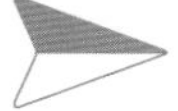

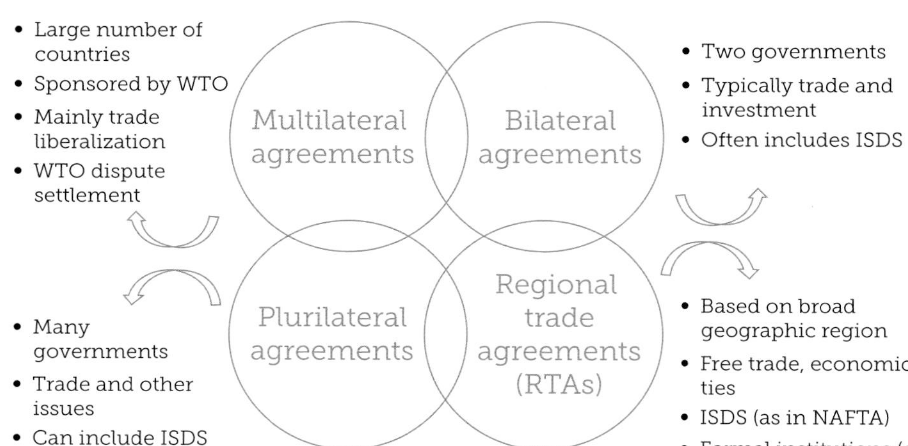

Figure 7.9 **Overlapping spheres of trade agreements among countries**

are sometimes referred to as a **free trade area or bloc**. The RTA can cover a range of issues besides trade, including investment, intellectual property protection and environmental protection. Political considerations can play a key role, as economic integration is inseparable from the political power balance within any region, and regional trading blocs are influential in global politics. We begin by looking at the categories of regional groupings, expanded from the one originally devised by Bela Balassa in *The Theory of Economic Integration* (Balassa, 1962). They can be categorized accordingly:

- **Free trade area** – Member states agree to remove trade barriers among themselves, but keep their separate national barriers against trade with non-member states.
- **Customs union** – Member states remove all trade barriers among themselves and adopt a common set of external barriers.
- **Common market** – Member states enjoy free movement of goods, labour and capital.
- **Economic Union** – Member states unify all their economic policies, including monetary, fiscal and welfare policies.
- **Political Union** – Member states transfer sovereignty to the regional political and lawmaking institutions, creating a new 'superstate'.

Most of the world's nations belong to at least one regional grouping, the vast majority of which fall into the first two categories – free trade area and customs union (see Table 7.1.) The categories can be seen as successive steps towards deepening economic integration. Only the EU has reached the stage of economic union. Political union is still some way off, but reforms in 2009 have enhanced the role of the European Parliament, discussed in Chapter 6. Free trade areas are now in place in all the world's regions, although with less regional economic integration than in Europe.

Regional trade groupings

The world's large geographic regions differ in the extent to which regional neighbours trade with each other. RTAs are intended to foster intra-regional trade. In Europe and in North America, intra-regional trade has shown strong growth as a result of the opening of borders to trade among member countries, as shown in

Table 7.1 Regional trade groupings

Region	Group	Current members	Date of formation	Type of agreement
South America	MERCOSUR (Southern Common Market)	Argentina, Brazil, Paraguay, Venezuela	1991	Common market
South America	Andean Community	Bolivia, Colombia, Ecuador, Peru	1989	Customs union
Asia-Pacific	APEC (Asia Pacific Economic Co-operation)	Australia, Brunei, Canada, Indonesia, Japan, South Korea, Malaysia, New Zealand, Philippines, Singapore, Thailand, US, China, Hong Kong, Taiwan, Mexico, Papua New Guinea, Chile, Peru, Russia, Vietnam	1989	Co-operation group
South East Asia	ASEAN (Association of Southeast Asian Nations)	Indonesia, Malaysia, Philippines, Singapore, Thailand, Brunei, Cambodia, Laos, Myanmar (Burma), Vietnam	1967	Free trade area
Caribbean	CARICOM (Caribbean Community)	Antiqua, Bahamas, Barbados, Belize, Dominica, Grenada, Guyana, Haiti, Jamaica, Monserrat, St. Lucia, St Kitts and Nevis, Trinidad & Tobago	1973	Common market
Europe	EFTA (European Free Trade Area)	Iceland, Switzerland, Norway, Liechtenstein	1960	Free trade area
Europe	EU (European Union)	Austria, Belgium, Denmark, France, Finland, Germany, Greece, Ireland, Italy, Luxembourg, the Netherlands, Portugal, Spain, Sweden, UK, Czech Republic, Poland, Hungary, Slovenia, Slovakia, Estonia, Lithuania, Latvia, Cyprus, Malta, Romania, Bulgaria, Croatia	1957	Economic union, moving towards political union
North America	NAFTA (North American Free Trade Agreement)	Canada, Mexico, US	1994	Free trade area
Africa	ECOWAS (Economic Community of West African States)	Benin, Burkina Faso, Côte d'Ivoire, Gambia, Ghana, Guinea, Guinea Bissau, Liberia, Mali, Niger, Nigeria, Senegal, Sierra Leone, Togo, Cape Verde	1975	Customs union
Africa	COMESA (Common Market for Eastern and Southern Africa)	Comoros, Djibouti, Eritrea, Ethiopia, Somalia, Egypt, Libya, Sudan, Tunisia, Madagascar, Mauritius, Seychelles, Burundi, Kenya, Malawi, Rwanda, Uganda, Swaziland, Zambia, Zimbabwe, DR Congo	1994	Free trade area
Africa	SADC (Southern African Development Community)	Angola, Botswana, Comoros, DR Congo, Lesotho, Madagascar, Malawi, Mauritius, Mozambique, Namibia, Seychelles, South Africa, Swaziland, Tanzania, Zambia, Zimbabwe	1980	Co-operation group

European Union (EU) regional grouping of European countries which evolved from trade agreements to deeper economic integration

Figure 7.10. Europe is the region with the largest intra-regional trade flows, facilitated by the **European Union (EU)** (https://europa.eu/european-union). The second most integrated region in terms of trade is North America. Here, intra-regional trade has been dominated by the large US market for goods from Mexico and Canada. Regional trade is also significant in Asia, home to the manufacturing powerhouses of China, Japan and South Korea. In developing Asian countries, intra-regional trade is also thriving, although the causes are more to do with industrial development focused on low-cost locations that benefit from globalization of supply chains. We begin with Europe.

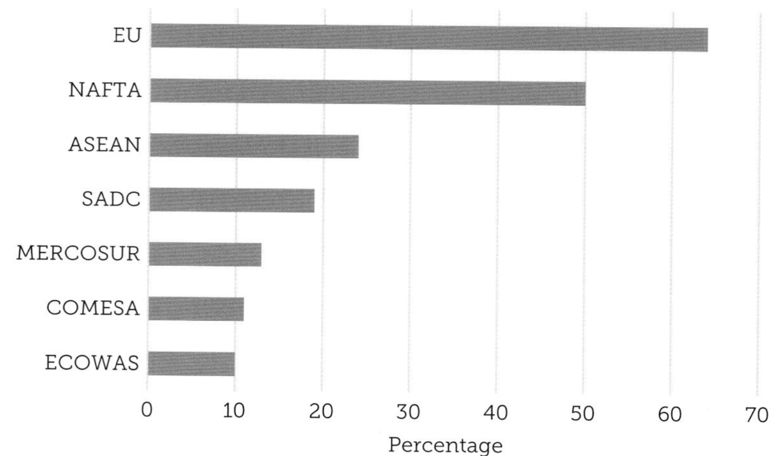

Figure 7.10 Intra-regional trade: the percentage of members' exports destined for other members

Source of data: WTO, *World Trade Statistical Review 2018*, p. 74, at www.wto.org

Europe

European countries trade mainly with each other. In the EU, the Single European Act of 1987 aimed to dismantle internal barriers and establish a single market by 1992. There would be free movement of goods, services, people and capital. Businesses would be able to move seamlessly from one member country to another, without bureaucratic frontier procedures. Product standards would be recognized between member states. Financial services would be liberalized, so that firms such as banks and insurance companies could compete across national borders. The value of intra-EU trade in goods grew from nearly €2,000 billion in 2002 to over €3,000 billion in 2016 (Eurostat database). The enlargement of the EU in 2004 led to export-oriented FDI in the new member states of Central and Eastern Europe, where lower costs were an attraction for investors. For example, Poland grew from being a net importer to a net exporter of goods to other EU member states, as shown in Figure 7.11.

There is considerable variety in the trade profiles of EU member states, as shown in Figure 7.11. Germany has consistently maintained a trade surplus with EU member states, although its trade balance in goods has weakened slightly since 2003. Meanwhile, France has seen an increase in its trade deficit with other EU countries. In 2015, the year before the Brexit referendum, the UK had the largest trade deficit by far of any EU member state. For the UK, leaving the EU would involve the risk that the huge amount of imports entering the country would revert to being subject to varying levels of WTO tariffs, together with the bureaucratic border checks that pertain outside the single market.

From its inception, the EU has been subject to continuing debate on principles of sovereignty and national identity. These have become political issues both in member states and in states outside the EU that have trading ties with EU member states.

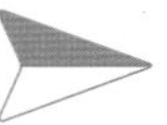

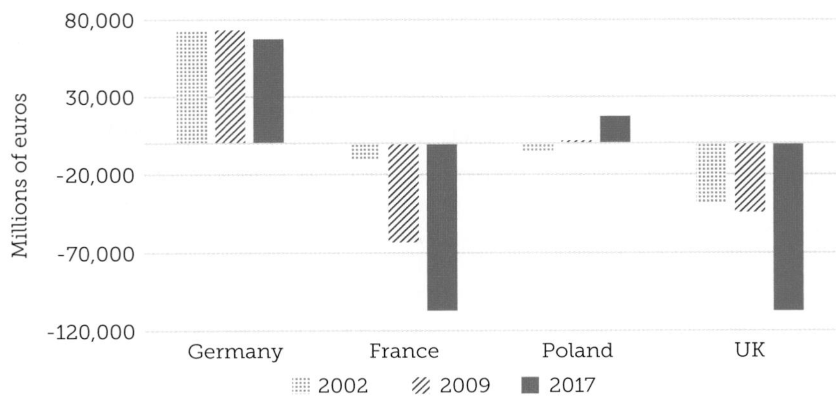

Figure 7.11 Merchandise trade balance among selected EU member states

Source of data: Eurostat database, Intra-EU trade in goods – recent trends, Table 2, at https://ec.europa.eu/eurostat, accessed 2 March 2019.

As Table 7.1 shows, Europe has long had a free trade area co-existing with the EU. The **European Free Trade Area** (EFTA) was formed in 1960 by countries not signed up to the Treaty of Rome. They were Austria, Denmark, Norway, Portugal, Sweden, Switzerland and the UK. They were later joined by Iceland and Finland. As most of these countries joined the EU, EFTA has four remaining members (Iceland, Switzerland, Norway and Liechtenstein), as shown in the table. With the exception of Switzerland, EFTA members have become a part of a wider **European Economic Area** (EEA), which is a single market with the EU.

European Free Trade Area (EFTA) grouping formed in 1960 by countries not signed up to the Treaty of Rome (which created what is now the EU)

European Economic Area (EEA) grouping of EFTA and the EU, forming a single market

Andean Community South American free trade area

MERCOSUR South American common market

North American Free Trade Agreement (NAFTA) free trade area comprising the US, Canada and Mexico

The Americas

In the Americas, the Andean Pact, later changed to the **Andean Community** (www.comunidadandina.org) is the oldest of the regional trade groupings. Political instability in the 1970s set back plans to establish a customs union. With the upsurge in global commodities markets that occurred in the 1980s, South American countries saw economic gains from commodity exports. The two largest traders, Brazil and Argentina, joined forces in 1988 to form a grouping which became **MERCOSUR** (www.mercosur.int/en/) with the addition of Paraguay and Uruguay. These countries are all associate members of the Andean Community. Similarly, Andean Community member countries are associate members of Mercosur. Venezuela, one of the continent's largest trading nations, and also an oil exporter, applied to join Mercosur in 2006, and is now a full member.

The **North American Free Trade Agreement (NAFTA)**, which came into effect in 1994, comprises the US, Canada and Mexico. While NAFTA did not envisage the degree of economic integration of the EU, its provisions and future developments raise similar issues, including political concerns and the question of sovereignty. Market access provisions were the main substance of NAFTA, by which the parties agreed to eliminate tariffs on most manufactured goods over a 10-year period. NAFTA's investment rules allow investors from any of the three countries to be treated in the same way as domestic investors. These rules apply to both FDI and portfolio investment. For settling disputes, NAFTA introduced the investor-state dispute settlement (ISDS) (discussed in Chapter 6), which, it was thought, was needed to protect US and Canadian investors in Mexico. Over time, the dozens of cases launched, mainly by US corporations, have frequently targeted Canada, which has been compelled to pay out large sums in compensation.

Unlike the EU, NAFTA operates no common external trade policy. Also in contrast to the EU, it has no formal institutions. At its inception, NAFTA aimed to increase exports between partners, who already traded heavily with each other, and to create

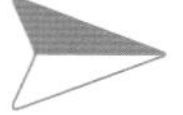

jobs in all three countries. Mexico's economy has become transformed in the ensuing years. Nearly 80% of Mexico's exports go to the US. Its exports to the US have multiplied six-fold since 1994, totalling $346 billion in 2018. And its imports from the US have multiplied five-fold, amounting to $265 billion in 2018 (US Census Bureau, 2019). While Mexico has benefited from export-oriented manufacturing jobs, its agriculture has suffered decline, unable to compete against the imports from highly subsidized American farmers. Mexico lost some 1.9 million jobs as a result of food imports from its northern neighbour. Mexico's economy has become highly dependent on trade relations with the US as a result of NAFTA.

The staunchly protectionist President Trump has said that NAFTA is a poor deal for the US. Both Canada and Mexico have cause to be concerned that the millions of jobs that NAFTA has facilitated could be in jeopardy. Mr Trump has pointed to the large number of motor vehicles being made in Mexico and imported into the US. Re-negotiation of NAFTA among the three countries was envisaged in 2018, but Mr Trump reached a bilateral deal with Mexico, excluding Canadian participation. This left the Canadian government in a perilous situation of being frozen out of a trade agreement with its largest trading partner. Three-quarters of its exports are sent to the US, and 2.5 million Canadian jobs are dependent on trade with the US. Without a new NAFTA, Canadian-made vehicles would face tariffs at the US border.

A tentative deal between the US and Mexico was reached, and Canada was later included, in an agreement late in 2018. The new NAFTA was named the **United States-Mexico-Canada Free Trade Agreement (USMCA)**. The new NAFTA would provide that 75% of a vehicle would have to be produced in the country to qualify it for tariff-free status. This represents a rise from 62.5% in NAFTA. It also provides that at least 30% (ultimately rising to 40%) of a vehicle would need to be made by workers earning $16 or more an hour – a provision intended to discourage the shift of manufacturing to lower-cost Mexico, where wages are one-third this level.

US-Mexico-Canada Free Trade Agreement (USMCA) North American free trade agreement that is the successor to NAFTA

NAFTA had contained two dispute resolution processes. One was the use of panels to resolve disputes over anti-dumping and duties, between the countries. The other was the ISDS dispute procedure. The new agreement retained the first of these, but the ISDS, which was objected to by Canada, was removed for Canada, and reduced in scope for Mexico. This means that the large US oil companies would be able to complain should Mexico renationalize its oil industry. The US wished the new agreement to be of short duration, whereas the other partners desired a longer agreement. They reached a compromise. The agreement would be for 16 years; it will be reviewed after six years, and could then be extended for another 16 years. Despite this apparent progress, getting the new trade agreement enacted in law looked problematic. By January 2019, Mexico had a new socialist president, Mr López Obrador, and in the US, the Democrats had become the majority party in the House of Representatives.

MINI CASE STUDY

Canadian motor industry fears for jobs

Windsor, Ontario, in Canada, is just across the river from Detroit, Michigan, and the car industry on both sides has been vital to the livelihoods of citizens. The Fiat Chrysler (FCA) factory in Windsor has 6,400 employees. It produces 1,500 vans a day, the vast majority of which are exported to the US. Under the NAFTA, there were no duties to pay, as the free trade deal facilitated cross-border trade. On any day, 200 to 300 trucks carry FCA engines from the US to Windsor, for assembly, while roughly the same number of trucks travel the other direction, taking Ford engines to Michigan, to be assembled into pick-up trucks.

Being so close to the US border, this motor town has had bad times as well as good times. After the 9/11 terrorist attacks, it suffered from stricter border controls. During the global financial crisis, unemployment in the town rose to 15%, but as the recovery gained momentum, it diminished to 5.5%. FCA felt encouraged to build a new minivan factory, under the guidance of the company's late CEO, Sergio Marchinonne, who was a graduate of the local university.

The US president's threat to impose tariffs on cars made in Canada introduced fresh worries for Windsor's economy. Mr Trump was vocal in his criticisms of NAFTA as being bad for the US. However, in truth, workers on both sides of the border would be at risk without NAFTA. Michigan would be one of the states the hardest hit in the US if there were to be no successor to NAFTA.

The agreement reached in the USMCA was beneficial to Canadian car workers, who are all paid more than the threshold rate of $16 per hour. Canada had had other concerns, however. Should the US decide to tax vehicles imported into the US, there is a provision of 'accommodation' to protect Canada. Although unclear, this accommodation could mean that Canada might be exempted from any new vehicle tariffs if it agrees to limit its exports to the US. Canada agreed to give US farmers access to its large dairy market. Canadian negotiators remained concerned that the US tariffs on steel and aluminium remained in place, the US having refused to lift them.

Workers in Canada's auto industry were relieved that a deal to replace NAFTA was struck, but the provisions about possible tariffs on cars remain vague, and the deal faces a rocky road in being ratified in all three countries.

Questions

- Why have supply chains across the US–Canada border benefited those on both sides?
- How satisfactory is the new NAFTA for Canada's car workers?

Find out more

See the article, 'US, Canada and Mexico just reached a sweeping new NAFTA deal. Here's what's in it', by Heather Long, in *The Washington Post*, 1 October 2018.

Asia

Association of Southeast Asian Nations (ASEAN) co-operation agreement of South East Asian countries

Regional Comprehensive Economic Partnership (RECEP) regional free trade area encompassing ASEAN members and partner countries

Asia Pacific Economic Co-operation Group (Apec) co-operation agreement of countries bordering on the Pacific

Asia's economies vary from the small city state of Singapore to the industrial giants, China and Japan. Despite some cultural affinities among the many Asian countries, they are diverse in their economies and political systems. The **Association of South East Asian Nations (ASEAN)** (https://asean.org) brings together ten South East Asian countries (see Table 7.1). Even among these economies, there is considerable diversity and differing levels of economic development. Singapore has developed as an FDI-oriented market economy with rather autocratic political rule, while Vietnam is a poorer country, whose communist leadership is keen to foster economic growth and market reforms. For these countries, links in global supply chains are key to development. There is a proposal for a new regional free trade agreement, known as the **Regional Comprehensive Economic Partnership (RCEP)**, which would create a large regional free trade area. Negotiations have been ongoing since 2012. They involve the ten ASEAN members and the six countries with which they have existing FTAs, which are Australia, China, India, Japan, the Republic of South Korea and New Zealand. RECEP would cover almost 30% of global GDP and roughly a quarter of world exports. The agreement would include goods, services, investment, intellectual property and e-commerce. It would also include a dispute resolution procedure. RECEP can be viewed as a rival trade deal to the US-proposed Trans-Pacific Partnership (TPP), which has been in abeyance since Mr Trump became US president.

The **Asia Pacific Economic Co-operation Group (Apec)** (https://apec.org) is the other large regional grouping, although it lacks the coherence of most free trade areas. It is hardly regional, as its members, all bordering the Pacific, are located on three different continents. As yet, it does not function as a free trade area, and its large size, encompassing more than half of the world's economic output, makes it rather different from regional groupings. Its members attend regular summits, at which bilateral agreements are negotiated. A proposed Free Trade Area of the Asia-Pacific (FTAAP) was endorsed in 2014. The FTAAP is being supported by China, and would present an alternative agreement to the proposed Trans-Pacific Partnership.

Africa

Economic Community of West African States (ECOWAS) organization for co-operation among West African states

East African Community (EAC) common market of East African countries

Common Market for Eastern and Southern Africa (COMESA) common market of Eastern and Southern African countries

Southern African Development Community (SADC) inter-governmental organization for countries of Southern Africa

African countries, many of which are rich in oil and other natural resources, are becoming increasingly important in world trade. Co-operative agreements focusing on regional trade, in the western, southern and eastern regions, have not as yet led to deepening regional integration (see Figure 7.10). Poverty and poor governance have combined with internal instability in many countries, which has spilt over into regional conflicts. These have all been factors in slowing the economic development that Africans had hoped for as post-colonial independent states. One of the oldest African groupings at the institutional level is the **Economic Community of West African States (ECOWAS)** (www.ecowas.int), which has a Commission, Parliament and Court of Justice. The Commission's specialized agencies focus on development projects in areas such as health and sport. The **East African Community (EAC)** (www.eac.int), which started as a free trade area, became a customs union and is now being transformed into a common market. A number of regional co-operative agreements have been entered into, often with overlapping membership. Among these are the **COMESA Common Market for Eastern and Southern Africa (COMESA)** (www.comesa.int) and the **Southern African Development Community (SADC)** (www.dirco.gov.za). These inter-governmental organizations, together with the EAC, came together to form a free trade area in 2008. In 2016, the EU entered an Economic Partnership Agreement with a group of SADC countries (Angola, Botswana, Lesotho, Mozambique, Namibia, South Africa and Eswatini, which was formerly known as Swaziland). This agreement gives better terms of access to the EU for the SADC countries and better access for the EU to SADC markets.

Plurilateral agreements: the way forward?

Trans-Pacific Partnership (TPP) trade and investment agreement among countries bordering the Pacific

A plurilateral agreement can potentially cover a number of states, and is not limited to those in a particular region. An example discussed earlier is the Trade in Services Agreement, on hold as of 2018. The US has been the lead party in the talks to establish plurilateral agreements to date, but President Trump withdrew from negotiations involving these multi-sided agreements. Talks to create the **Trans-Pacific Partnership (TPP)** go back to 2010. They involved 11 countries at that time: Australia, Brunei, Canada, Chile, Malaysia, Mexico, New Zealand, Peru, Singapore, the US and Vietnam. Japan joined the talks in 2013. These countries overlap with the two Asian regional groupings and with NAFTA. Negotiations were classified as secret. US corporations were involved, but not members of Congress. The officially secret status of the talks raised suspicions among members of Congress and civil society organizations. While trade issues, such as reducing barriers to imports, were involved, it became clear that priority was being given to enhanced protection for IP rights, which would mainly benefit the large US companies in the pharmaceutical, software and entertainment sectors. These extra protections would exceed those in existing trade agreements, and have been a cause of concern for the smaller countries, especially over access to medicines. Also adding to their fears was the inclusion of a clause providing for the ISDS mechanism. Many bilateral negotiations have taken place under the broad TPP umbrella. Talks between the US and Japan over trade barriers in food and motor vehicles continued into 2015. It appeared that the TPP was finally agreed and signed in October 2015, but US president Trump withdrew the US

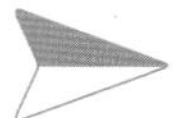

from the agreement. The other participating countries wished to press ahead nonetheless, and set about revising the agreement, to reflect their own priorities, rather than those of the US. This new agreement is the Comprehensive and Progressive Agreement for the Trans-Pacific Partnership (CPTPP), agreed in Chile in March 2018.

The CPTPP would limit the use of the ISDS procedure. It would also shorten the duration of IP rights, including patents on medicines and copyright on written material. The IP provisions, in particular, diverge significantly from those pressed by the US, which included technological protection of satellite and cable signals, and safe harbours for internet service providers. The US could join the agreement, but it would need to negotiate terms on the basis of the revised version.

Transatlantic Trade and Investment Partnership (TTIP) proposed trade and investment agreement between the EU and the US

The **Transatlantic Trade and Investment Partnership (TTIP)**, also driven by the US at the outset, has been more ambitious in its scope, talks having begun in 2013. Trade in goods and services are only one aspect of the talks. Another is known as 'regulatory co-operation', including non-tariff barriers to trade in respect of both goods and services (EU Commission, 2015). The EU has strict regulatory regimes in a number of areas, including employment rights, labour rights, human health and the environment. In all these areas, US laws are less stringent, and there has been a fear that the US position would prevail, weakening much EU protective legislation and undermining the social priorities of many member governments. There have been fears among EU countries that any deal would allow imports of food containing GMOs and hormone-treated beef. Other issues in this category are environmental rules and rules on animal health and welfare. In the area of services, health services and education are areas in which the US would see opportunities for its companies to make inroads in EU countries as public services become increasingly privatized. The secrecy of the negotiations has added to public concerns, notably voiced by members of the European Parliament. They have also objected to the inclusion of the investor-state dispute settlement (ISDS). The possible dilution of much regulatory legislation, combined with advantages to investors from the ISDS, suggest that the US position is based on facilitating the expansion of its large corporations. For many in the EU, opposition to the TTIP has rested on the view that facilitating the ascendancy of American corporate interests risks undermining democracy. Under President Trump, TTIP talks have been suspended. The US stance has given an indication to the UK government that similar positions would be taken in any talks with the UK on a post-Brexit trade agreement with the US. Mr Trump's hostility to NAFTA and to the WTO are also indicators that his administration would take an uncompromisingly US-centric approach to future bilateral trade agreements.

Globalization and world trade: sustainable strategies?

Changing patterns in world trade have accompanied the global shift in manufacturing towards Asia. China stands out as the leading new trading power, and other developing countries are following its example of attracting export-oriented manufacturing. In China, economic growth has rested on rapid industrialization and urbanization, which has seen rising GDP per capita, but also high levels of pollution and increased risks to health. Economic data look flattering, but daily life for millions of workers has not matched the expectations of continuing improvement that China's market transformation had promised. The rise of Asia as a trading power has been associated, above all, with global supply chains. Political leaders in China take credit for their development model that embraced globalization in manufacturing industries, but they must also shoulder the main responsibility for dealing with the social challenges of improving wellbeing in a society where people now aspire to a better quality of life, not just in economic terms, but in terms of meeting human needs. This is, of course, a goal of sustainable development in the broad sense. It has proved more elusive to attain than China's economic goals and growing role in world trade. Can trade and sustainability be conceived as going hand in hand?

A challenge for both companies and governments is to meet human needs and sustain development goals in the context of growing corporate power in supply chains in which global companies are in a position to dictate their own terms – terms that are likely to be profit-oriented above all. Developed regions of the world, including the US and UK, have mourned the loss of manufacturing jobs, while global companies based in these countries have profited hugely from outsourced production to Asia and other developing regions. The global brands that have driven the rise in trade in intermediate goods have benefited from the location advantages of low-cost labour, weak employment protection laws, and numerous policies instituted by governments to smooth the flow of cross-border trade. Global trading companies in commodities and mining have benefited from surging Chinese demand for resources, raw materials and energy. With that growth now slowing, new challenges of sustainability and public expectations are becoming more urgent, for governments and for businesses.

China is the main supplier of the consumer goods that Americans rely on every day, from appliances, TVs and iPhones to clothing and toys. Indeed, China's export successes in meeting American demand has led to the huge trade deficit between China and the US. In the process, of course, American industries have declined, unable to compete with Chinese imports. Donald Trump's populist message of restoring America's greatness had particular appeal in the 'rustbelt' states that had suffered most from loss of jobs. In office, Mr Trump increased tariffs on numerous Chinese imports. But how could raising tariffs on products such as Chinese washing machines and solar panels be an answer to the deep-seated economic and social problems associated with de-industrialization? It is impossible to turn the clock back to America's historical golden age of the 1950s and 60s.

Globalization has benefited the rising powers in Asia. And the impetus from the 1990s onwards has come from US-based global companies that have co-ordinated global supply chains. However, Chinese companies now challenge their established western counterparts, evidenced by their strategic expansion both at home and in outward foreign investment. The US reaction has been to start a trade war which is damaging to businesses in the US, as well as in China. Instead of this protectionist approach, the US in the current environment would be better advised to grasp the need for sustainable trade policies. This means refocusing on co-operative trading relations with partners, rather than on fuelling trade wars with them. It also requires a rethinking of national goals in accord with principles of sustainability and societal wellbeing, rather than on narrowly focused images of a bygone era.

Resources are often seen as a 'curse' in developing countries, with rewards flowing to corporate and sectoral interests rather than towards providing public goods. In the best scenarios, countries manage resource wealth responsibly, looking to share wealth with all in society. Trade can, and should, follow sustainable development goals. But this is an ideal, rather than reality, requiring governments to focus on public goods rather than political self-interest. And it also requires the large companies, that are essential to the dynamics of world trade, to shift from a focus on profit maximization towards social goals and human needs. Most MNEs nowadays speak of sustainability and CSR as part of their global outlook, but how far does this go? Large trading and mining companies typically include CSR projects such as education and training in their investment projects in developing countries. However beneficial, these projects are ultimately in the hands of corporate providers, who, if business conditions deteriorate, exit the country, setting back development goals. CSR conceived as an adjunct to business goals is inherently at risk in a context of global corporate strategy if the MNE is constantly looking for new locations that offer better rewards for its owners.

The resource curse and developing countries

To what extent does responsibility lie with large foreign investors when the resource curse strikes developing countries?

Conclusions

A country with no trade at all would be a distinctly dismal place to live. No country is self-sufficient in the many areas that make up what we would consider essential to minimal living standards, including food, natural resources, manufacturing capacity and energy. The closed economy would inevitably be poor, probably relying on subsistence agriculture, with little scope for human development. But it does not follow from this depressing picture that free trade is unqualifiedly good.

In the nineteenth century, trade was controlled by imperial powers that extracted riches from the natural resource wealth of colonial territories, whose leaders had no say over these one-sided arrangements. However, the inequalities of trade did not die with the break-up of empires. Those in the driving seat nowadays are global companies from the large trading nations, presiding over complex supply chains, through which they are able to extract value. They are usually aided by the trade policies of the governments in their home countries, and by compliant co-operation in partner countries, keen to attract investment. Among the latter are developing countries in Africa. The smallholder in Africa is likely to be tied into a deal with a large foreign agribusiness company that exerts decisive control over not only production, but all processing and transport. Increasingly, through the global strategies of MNEs, foreign investment has been the facilitator of trade, aided by governments of both investing and host countries.

Trade liberalization, sponsored by the WTO and its predecessor, the GATT, aspired to bring the benefits of trade to all countries and all peoples. Multilateral agreements would remove barriers to trade, allowing access to markets for all on equal terms, enshrined in the most-favoured nation principle. However, in reality, trade is dominated by the rich and powerful, be they countries or companies. The WTO recognizes, at least in theory, the equal voice of each of its 164 members. Through its regulatory structures, including the dispute settlement process, it aspires to ensure that global markets retain a level playing field. However, the ambitious Doha round of multilateral negotiations, ostensibly focusing on development goals, failed to resolve differences between developed and developing countries. Governments of emerging economies, Brazil and India, both growing in influence, reminded the world that national social priorities must be accommodated. The US under President Trump made clear that its America First policy would dominate its trade relations.

National decision-makers and regulators exercise legal authority over trade policies within their borders – a reality acknowledged by the WTO. Governments see trade policies as an aspect of national security, employing protectionist measures as they deem necessary, despite commitment to WTO principles. The WTO, for its part, has tended to focus on markets in the product traded rather than on *how* the product is produced. Hence, issues such as environmental practices and food safety tend to be treated simply as barriers to trade. This approach is considered a shortcoming by many people concerned with broader societal issues, but is widely supported by the global companies, who view national regulations generally as unjustifiable barriers to trade. National priorities, such as food subsidies to the poor, are also viewed as crucial in developing countries, although seen as trade-distorting by the WTO.

The failure of Doha can be depicted as failing the needs of developing countries. The WTO's attempts to maintain a multilateral consensus have given way to a more fragmented trading environment. Although the US has asserted a more nationalist trade policy, it is now challenged by new trading superpowers, notably China, in the continuing dynamic of global inequalities that characterize world trade.

CLOSING CASE STUDY

High stakes in Glencore's trading activities

Glencore, the global mining and trading company, has an eventful history of seizing opportunities in places where the risks are high, but so are the potential rewards. Its roots go back to 1974. Originally, the company was Marc Rich & Co, a private company founded by Marc Rich, known as the 'godfather' of modern commodity trading. Traditionally, the large trading firms are closely run and secretive. Rich was controversial, in that he traded with regimes such as the apartheid regime in South Africa, Libya during its military dictatorship, and Iran, in breach of a US embargo. Pursued by the US Justice Department, he was indicted in 1983, on 65 criminal counts for tax evasion, racketeering and trading with an enemy country. He was on the FBI's wanted list and became a fugitive from US justice, fleeing to Switzerland, where he carried on the business. Ivan Glasenberg, another trader, joined the firm in 1984. In 1994, Glasenberg and other senior traders led a buyout of the business from Rich, who from then onwards played no role in the firm. In 2001, Rich was pardoned by President Clinton. The firm remained based in Switzerland, and was renamed Glencore. Glasenberg became its CEO in 2002. He is known as a competitive, round-the-clock trader who always plays to win.

The presence of this UN peacekeeper in the Democratic Republic of Congo should help to bring stability in areas where Glencore faces ongoing insecurity in its copper and cobalt mining.

Opportunities opened up with the growth in commodities trading in the 2000s, bringing unprecedented profits to the world's large trading companies, in many cases outshining the financial performance of the Wall Street banks such as Goldman Sachs. The trading companies were operating in volatile environments, often in developing countries where governance was problematic, political risks were high and much business took place through shadowy individual go-betweens. Such dealings can be tinged with corruption, as well as money laundering. They can be targeted by regulators, as Rich had learnt. After 37 years as a private company, Glencore went public in 2011, listing in London. The London debut promised to make the six traders at its heart all billionaires. As a PLC, Glencore, valued at £39 billion, would attract greater scrutiny by regulators henceforth, and would be subjected to greater public disclosure requirements.

The commodities boom had lifted mining companies as well as traders, and Glencore eyed the miner, Xstrata, as a takeover target. The takeover of Xstrata would cost $30 billion, but by the time it was completed, in 2013, the slowdown in global demand for commodities was already evident. Xstrata, moreover, had borrowed heavily to fund investment projects aimed at boosting mine production, and was saddled with debt of $15 billion, which Glencore inherited. Glencore

had envisaged that trading activities would be consistent performers financially, compensating for the fluctuations in fortune that affect mining operations. After the takeover, however, the company found itself heavily dependent on mining, and also carrying a worrying level of debt. The timing of the Xstrata takeover was unfortunate, and critics have said that Mr Glasenberg and his fellow traders probably made a strategic mistake in purchasing Xstrata (Hume, Wilson and Sheppard, 2015). However, Glencore's business model had evolved to encompass both mining and trading.

In recent years, Mr Glasenberg has been involved in a number of deals that have attracted notice from US regulators. One was a deal in 2016 with the Qatar Investment Authority to buy a 20% stake in Rosneft, the Russian oil company under sanctions over Russia's incursions in Ukraine. However, Glencore's activities in the Democratic Republic of Congo (DRC) have attracted greater attention. These activities involve ties with an Israeli businessman, Dan Gertler, who is on a US sanctions list for corrupt mining deals in the DRC. The DRC's vast mineral resources are a source of immense potential wealth, but the country is beset by weak governance, and rival armed groups contest control of different areas of the country, endangering the lives and livelihoods of ordinary people. A health crisis caused by the ebola virus has been worsened by the conflicts. Humanitarian groups are struggling to control the spread of disease in the conflict zones.

Glencore operates copper and cobalt mining in the DRC, which contains half the world's reserves of cobalt, a resource necessary for the production of electric car batteries. In addition to Glencore's difficulties in operating in this insecure environment, its dealings with Mr Gertler have attracted the attention of the US Treasury and also the Department of Justice, which started investigations into bribery and corruption. Such investigations could run for years, and would blight Glencore's share price for the duration. The potential crimes fall under money-laundering statutes and the Foreign Corrupt Practices Act (FCPA). Some of the relevant evidence emerged from revelations in the Paradise Papers in 2017. These were the result of research by investigative journalists, and shone a light on offshore financial dealings (see Chapter 6). The Serious Fraud Office in London is also investigating the company. How will these investigations affect the company's business model? It is possible that Glencore will withdraw from its risky trading activities, and concentrate more on its mining businesses. However, mining activities, especially in conflict zones, are themselves highly risky. For Glencore, the risk-taking inclination of its owners, especially Mr Glasenberg, is part of its culture.

Questions

- What does the history of Glencore reveal about the rise in commodity trading as a globalized activity?
- How does mining as a global activity differ from commodity trading?
- Why is Glencore particularly in the firing line in terms of scrutiny by regulators?
- Should global traders be subject to international, rather than national, regulation? Explain.

Further reading

See the article, 'Trouble in the Congo: the misadventures of Glencore', by Franz Wild, Vernon Silver and William Clowes, in *Bloomberg Businessweek*, 16 November 2018.

Multiple choice questions

Visit www.macmillanihe.com/morrison-gbe-5e to take a quick self-test quiz on what you have read in this chapter.

Review questions

1. How relevant is the theory of comparative advantage to modern trade patterns?
2. What are the main contributions of Porter's theory of competitive advantage?
3. What is meant by strategic trade policy?
4. Outline the motivations underlying government trade policy.
5. Summarize the arguments for and against free trade.
6. What are the main tools of government trade policy?
7. Define the GATT principles of most-favoured nation and national treatment.
8. In what ways does the WTO represent a step on from GATT?
9. What did the Doha round of multilateral talks accomplish?
10. Identify the main groupings that represent distinctive interests in multilateral trade talks.
11. What is the Trade in Services Agreement, and why is it significant?
12. Why have regional trade groupings become popular, and in what ways, if any, do they undermine multilateral trade liberalization efforts?
13. How has the presidency of Mr Trump in the US, with his protectionist policies, affected the future of multilateral and plurilateral agreements?
14. How has the NAFTA been revised, and who are the winners and losers in the new NAFTA agreement.
15. Why do developing countries have ambivalent feelings about trade liberalization?

Assignments

1. Assess the contrasting perspectives and interests of developed countries, the large emerging economies and the weaker developing countries with respect to global trade liberalization.
2. Assess the likelihood that a potentially damaging trade war could erupt between the US and China.

Further reading

Baldwin, R., and Wyplosz, C. (2015) *The Economics of European Integration*, 5th edition (McGraw-Hill).

Beckett, S. (2015) *Empire of Cotton: A global history* (Vintage).

Feenstra, R. and Taylor, A. (2017) *International Trade*, 4th edition (Worth Publishers).

Gilpin, R. (2001) *Global Political Economy: Understanding the international economic order* (Princeton: Princeton University Press.)

Goldin, I. and Reinert, K. (2012) *Globalization for Development: Meeting new challenges* (Oxford: Oxford University Press).

Gallagher, K. (2014) *The Clash of Globalizations: Essays on the political economy of trade and development policy* (Anthem Press).

Kassam, A. (2018) 'Trump-Trudeau love-in threatened as Canada attacks US over trade', *The Guardian*, 13 January, at www.theguardian.com

Krugman, P., Obstfeld, M. and Melitz, M. (2018) *International Trade: Theory and policy*, 11th edition (Pearson).

Oatley, T. (2018) *International Political Economy*, 6th edition (Routledge).

Ravenhill, J. (ed.) (2016) *Global Political Economy*, 5th edition (Oxford: Oxford University Press).

References

Balassa, B. (1962) *The Theory of Economic Integration* (London: Allen & Unwin).

Eichengreen, B. and Irwin, D. (2009) 'The protectionist temptation: Lessons from the Great Depression for today', Centre for Economic Policy Research (CEPR), 17 March, Vox CEPR Policy Portal, at https://voxeu.org

EU Commission (2015) TTIP: Basics, benefits, concerns, at www.ec.europa.eu/trade/policy, accessed 24 July 2015.

Flynn, S. (2010) 'Special 301 of the Trade Act of 1974 and global access to medicine', *Journal of Generic Medicines*, Vol. 7, 451–72.

Funk, C. and Rainie, L. (2015) 'Public and scientists' views on science and society', Pew Research Center, 29 January, at www.pewinternet.org

Gilpin, R. (2000) *The Challenge of Global Capitalism: The world economy in the 21st century* (Princeton: Princeton University Press).

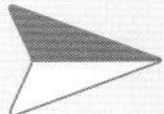

Hume, N., Wilson, J. and Sheppard, D. (2015) 'Glencore scrambles to halt downward spiral', *Financial Times*, 3 October.

Inman, P. (2015) 'Secret talks could weaken climate targets set in Paris, warn campaigners', *The Guardian*, 3 December, at www.theguardian.com

Kassam, A. (2018) 'Trump-Trudeau love-in threatened as Canada attacks US over trade', *The Guardian*, 13 January, at www.theguardian.com

Krugman, P. (1994) *Rethinking International Trade* (Cambridge, MA: MIT Press).

Pelc, K. (2014) 'Why the deal to pay Brazil $300 million just to keep subsidies is bad for the WTO, poor countries, and US taxpayers', *The Washington Post*, 12 October 2014, email 14 July.

Porter, M. (1998a) *The Competitive Advantage of Nations* (London: Palgrave Macmillan).

Porter, M. (1998b) *On Competition* (Boston, MA: Harvard Business Review Publishing).

Ricardo, D. ([1817] 1973) *Principles of Economy and Taxation* (London: Dent).

Smith, A. ([1776] 1950) *An inquiry into the Nature and Causes of the Wealth of Nations* (London: Methuen).

US Census Bureau (2019) Foreign trade data, at www.census.gov/foreign-trade, accessed 6 July 2019.

UNCTAD (2017) *Key statistics and trends in international trade 2016* (Geneva: UN).

Wells, L.T. (ed.) (1972) *The Product Life Cycle and International Trade* (Boston, MA: Harvard Business School Press).

WTO (2017) United States: Certain system trade remedies measures, Requests for consultations by Canada, submitted under the DSU on 20 December 2017, at https://docs.wto.org

WTO (2018) *World Trade Statistical Review 2018*, at www.wto.org

Visit the companion website at www.macmillanihe.com/morrison-gbe-5e **for further learning and teaching resources.**

© Getty, Towfiqu Photography

GLOBAL FINANCE

Outline of chapter

This chapter will enable you to

- Gain an overview of the elements that make up the international financial system, including the extent and implications of financial globalization
- Analyze the ways in which shifting patterns of global finance have impacted in diverse economic environments, including developed, industrializing and developing countries
- Understand the diverse causes of financial crises and roles played by reforms and regulation
- Grasp the trends in cross-border markets for corporate control, and implications for stakeholders
- Appreciate the current challenges for global finance in building more sustainable and socially responsible businesses

OPENING CASE STUDY

The rise and fall of Carillion

Carillion was a UK PLC formed in 1999, but its origins are much older. It was formed by the breakup of the construction company, Tarmac, which was over a hundred years old. Carillion listed on the London Stock Exchange (LSE), and grew rapidly, acquiring other businesses and expanding into a number of different sectors beyond its original construction business. It acquired a rail maintenance company, and it expanded into support services. Although a private-sector company, most of its activities derived from contracts for work in the public sector. Its activities became highly diverse. It was involved in the construction of hospitals and the high-speed train line, HS2. It had contracts to maintain fifty prisons, run meal services in 900 schools, and carry out catering and cleaning in many NHS hospitals. It also became a multinational company, acquiring a number of Canadian businesses. By 2016, it had 43,000 employees, 19,000 of whom were in the UK. A year later, the company was in financial difficulty. How did such a large provider of public services apparently get into dire trouble so rapidly? Its activities, one supposed, were scrutinized by the government authorities awarding the contracts, as well as by the company's accountants.

Carillion's finances deteriorated in 2017, causing it to issue a series of profit warnings. Even before the profit warnings, there were signs of trouble ahead, as hedge funds and other investors 'shorted' its shares – selling them with a view to buying them back later for less. Revenues were disappointing, causing liquidity worries. The construction work on two hospitals had encountered difficulties, leading to delays and cost overruns. In one of them, asbestos was found on the site, and cracks had appeared in the concrete beams. The company was heavily indebted, and there was a worrying deficit of £600 million in the pension fund. And yet, the company continued to take on new business. The HS2 contract was taken on after a profit warning. It also continued to pay bonuses to the directors, which were approved by the board's remuneration committee despite the financial peril of the business. Carillion collapsed in January 2018, under debts of £1.5 billion, following the refusal by the British government to bail out the company.

There were severe repercussions from the collapse of such a large construction company and provider of public services. In addition to the Carillion employees who lost their jobs, many other workers were affected. Thousands of suppliers and subcontractors were left unpaid. Work on a major hospital was halted. Relevant government bodies had the immediate problem of ensuring that public services were continued in the schools, prisons and hospitals affected. The company held 420 public-sector contracts at the time of its collapse, amounting to £1.7 billion. The firm had £2.6 billion in pension liabilities. The pension reserve fund that is sponsored by the industry as a whole would have to step in as a lifeline.

The collapse of Carillion led to enquiries by parliamentary select committees, during which the underlying reasons became clearer. Failures in corporate governance stood out. The board, including non-executive directors, failed to deal with the urgent financial issues, such as funding of the pension scheme, and, instead, bowed to the calls from directors for increased remuneration. Carillion paid dividends to its shareholders every year. One of the select committees concluded the directors had shown 'recklessness, hubris and greed' (Inman, 2018). The company's auditors painted too optimistic a picture of the company's finances, approving the accounts despite the excessive debt burden. The people that should have taken prudent oversight of corporate finances had fallen down on the job. The mechanisms for accountability to shareholders had thus failed. The share price fell precipitously, from 192p before the first profit warning, to 14p before trading in the shares ceased.

When Carillion collapsed, the jobs of thousands of workers like this hospital cleaner were suddenly put at risk.

© Getty Images

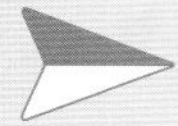

Where were the government departments that had awarded the contracts, and the regulators that should have spotted financial misconduct? Government departments seemed to be partly to blame in continuing to invite Carillion to bid for contracts, even as it was nearing bankruptcy. The regulator, the Financial Conduct Authority, launched an inquiry in 2018, looking at the possibility of insider dealing before the first profit warning. Insider dealing occurs when directors use their insider knowledge to trade in the company's shares, making personal gains, but causing unfair market distortion. On a broader level, the collapse of Carillion was a result of an irresponsible corporate culture, abetted by a government outsourcing model that showed too little oversight over the contracts it awarded to private-sector companies.

Questions

- What were the reasons for Carillion running into financial troubles?
- Carillion's directors were heavily criticized for extracting money from the company, damaging the many thousands of workers and contractors who lost out in the liquidation of the company. What does this say about the corporate culture?
- What lessons could be learned from Carillion's collapse?
- What could the regulators have done differently, to avoid Carillion's collapse?

Further reading

See the article by Dave Rogers, 'Carillion analysis: the fall of a titan', in *Building*, 18 January 2018, at www.building.co.uk

Introduction

Finance is among the most globalized of all international business activities, largely thanks to technological advances. With globalization, many more firms, including SMEs, are internationally active, in a diverse range of countries. Many of these are in developing regions that are becoming integrated in global financial networks. Growing trade and overseas investment have led to the growth of global capital markets and global financial institutions. This expansion has been made possible, first and foremost, by the opening of national economies to financial flows. National financial systems have become more deeply enmeshed than ever before in global financial networks. For companies, governments and individuals, opportunities for accessing financial markets have expanded. However, these opportunities have also given rise to risks, as the recurrence of financial crises around the globe is evidence.

Global financial markets are now 24-hours-a-day, fast-moving and complex processes, whose operations are on a scale which dwarf many national governments. This chapter will attempt to demystify these processes as they impact on businesses – and societies. A major aim is to explain in relatively simple terms how international financial institutions interact with businesses, investors and national financial systems. As will be seen, sharply differing perspectives have emerged between enterprises, consumers and governments. The growth of international financial institutions, raising broad questions of stability and control in financial markets, has drawn both praise and criticism. From the business point of view, there are huge benefits from integrated markets, which have been particularly evident in emerging markets, but there are also risks of instability and vulnerability to financial shocks. MNEs have been major drivers of financial globalization. Shifting patterns of corporate control, now evident on a global scale, have revealed the differing perspectives of corporate management, shareholders, lenders, consumers and governments. With globalization has come greater awareness of the interactions between markets.

 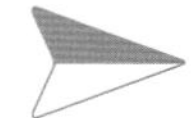

Evolution of the international monetary system

The foundations of the international monetary system have formed the backdrop of global finance. International institutions aim to provide stability and guidance to the governments of sovereign states. However, national interests and perspectives vary, and stability ultimately rests on co-operation between governments and international institutions. In order to understand the challenges currently confronting international financial institutions, we will look briefly at how the international institutions have evolved. Currencies are generally controlled by national central banks, and, in the case of the EU, the European Central Bank (ECB). But central banks cannot always ensure exchange rate stability against other currencies. Currencies are linked in global financial networks, which have become more integrated as trade and FDI have grown.

The gold standard

gold standard the setting of exchange rates based on the value of gold

The rise in trade and financial flows from the late nineteenth century onwards led to growing internationalization of finance. To facilitate these movements, the world's major trading nations adopted a global **gold standard** system, which lasted from the 1870s to 1914, a period in which Britain was the strongest trading nation. Under the gold standard, all currencies were 'pegged' to gold, which removed the uncertainty of transactions involving different currencies. For each currency, a conversion rate into gold ensured stability. The system required countries to convert their currency into gold on demand, and did not restrict international gold flows. Governments willingly endorsed the system even though, in theory, it reduced their control over their own economic policy. In practice, governments did not always play by the 'rules of the game,' and there was more national monetary autonomy than supposed (Eichengreen, 1996: 28).

Significantly, national interest rates, while they showed some convergence, were largely influenced by domestic conditions. The gold standard period nonetheless represented the emergence of a global financial order. The maintenance of the gold standard depended on central banks' continuing commitment to external convertibility. This system broke down with World War I, when governments used precious metal to purchase military supplies, and restricted movements in the gold market, thus causing currencies to float. The system collapsed despite efforts to resurrect it in the inter-war period, during which government priorities had shifted from exchange-rate stability to domestic economic concerns. Moreover, the domination, or hegemony, that Britain had exerted over capital markets had declined. American commercial and financial power had grown, but this did not lead to its taking on a similar role in the international system (Eichengreen, 1996: 92).

Bretton Woods agreement agreement between the allied nations in the aftermath of the Second World War, which was intended to bring about exchange rate stability and foster multilateral agreements to dismantle trade barriers

International Monetary Fund agency of the UN which oversees the international monetary and financial systems

World Bank organization established in the aftermath of the Second World War to fund development projects and broader development programmes

The Bretton Woods institutions

The **Bretton Woods agreement**, dating from the close of the Second World War, created a broad institutional order to restore financial stability. The GATT, which was the forerunner of the WTO, dates from this agreement (see Chapter 7). The two major financial institutions created were the **International Monetary Fund** (IMF) (www.imf.org) and the International Bank of Reconstruction and Development, better known as the **World Bank** (www.worldbank.org). We will look first at the institutions, which have endured, and, in the next section, the agreement itself, which did not. The IMF aimed to maintain global financial stability, by helping out countries with balance-of-payments difficulties and providing assistance to heavily indebted poor countries. The IMF is now more known for its loans to countries suffering from financial crisis. The World Bank was intended from the outset to be more development-oriented,

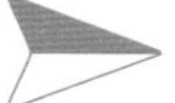

beginning with post-war reconstruction. Money would be channelled through governments towards specific development projects. As the organization has evolved, however, it has shifted towards the financing of broad programmes.

The membership of both financial organizations has grown to 188 countries, the majority of them developing economies. While the WTO was established on the basis of one-country-one-vote, the voting structures of the World Bank and IMF are more like corporations. They allocate voting rights that reflect the share ownership stakes of member countries. This system greatly favours the US and other advanced economies. The US holds 16.74% of the voting rights in the IMF. The UK's voting rights amount to 4.92%, and China's, 3.81%. As voting on important issues requires an 85% majority, the US can singlehandedly block any measure it does not favour. Both organizations are based in Washington, D.C., which has given its name to their broad outlook: the **Washington consensus**. The IMF, in particular, has been criticized for imposing conditions on recipient countries that are dictated by American thinking on free markets and minimal government. The Washington consensus was originally conceived by economist, John Williamson, who focused on countries of Latin America. He set out ten principles that represented the Washington consensus. These are set out in Figure 8.1.

Washington consensus market-oriented outlook adopted by the World Bank and IMF

Figure 8.1 **The Washington consensus in John Williamson's original formulation**

Source: Inspired by Williamson, J. (2004) 'A short history of the Washington Consensus', Paper given at the conference, 'From the Washington Consensus to a new global governance', Fundación CIDOB, Barcelona, 24–25 September, pp. 3–4, at www.piie.com/publications/papers/williamson0904-2.pdf

10 Property rights	1 Fiscal discipline – reduce large deficits	2 Reordering public spending priorities towards 'pro-growth' and 'pro-poor'
9 Deregulation	**The Washington consensus: 10 principles**	3 Tax reform
8 Privatization		4 Liberalizing interest rates
7 Liberalization of inward FDI	6 Trade liberalization	5 A competitive exchange rate

The ten principles can be seen as an approach to economic development generally. It is striking that these principles as presented by Williamson are balanced between market reforms and considerations of public goods (Williamson, 2004). Fiscal discipline involves reducing budget deficits and trade deficits, which can lead to high inflation and cause the most harm to the poor in society. Taking a 'strictly neutral' view of how big the public sector should be, he says the priorities for public spending should be pro-social investments, including education, health and infrastructure (Williamson, 2004: 2). While Williamson emphasizes deregulation, he explains that this relates primarily to entry and exit barriers, not regulations that, for example, protect public health and safety or the environment. The inclusion of property rights refers to reforms needed in the large informal sector in many developing countries, to help poor people to become part of the mainstream economy, as advocated by the Peruvian reformer, Hernando de Soto (see Clift, 2003). While many of the ten principles are plainly market-oriented, it is clear that market reforms are intended to be moderated by social needs. However, as interpreted by the Bretton Woods institutions, the Washington consensus was translated into a rather doctrinaire, one-size-fits-all set of market reforms. They came in for particularly sharp criticism during the Asian financial crisis, discussed later.

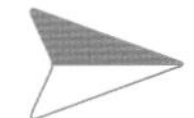

The Washington consensus: diverse conceptions of capitalism

Are Williamson's ten principles 'pro-business' in the sense of free-market capitalism, or closer to a model of capitalism slanted towards social responsibility?

If the IMF had applied a more nuanced interpretation of Williamson's principles, would the progress of economic development in the countries it has aided have been towards more sustainable business models?

The Bretton Woods legacy

In the immediate aftermath of the War, the IMF sought to restore a stable foreign exchange framework, but could not turn the clock back by re-introducing the gold standard, given the huge development goals. The US was the dominant economy in the world. It had been spared the devastation of war, and was by far the world's richest economy. It owned 60% of the world's gold. Under the Bretton Woods agreement, currencies were pegged to the dollar, with the dollar fixed in terms of gold at $35 an ounce. This was an 'adjustable peg'. A country could alter its currency only if it was in 'fundamental disequilibrium', which was not fully defined. Controls were permitted, to limit private financial flows. The agreement aimed to liberalize world trade, but also took into account governments' wishes to maintain systems of social protection and other domestic objectives. This meant that governments had considerable autonomy to pursue domestic economic policies.

In the post-war period, the priority for many economies, including those in Europe and Japan, was getting industries back on their feet. The US embarked on a huge aid programme, the Marshall Plan, that aimed to fund redevelopment in Western Europe, notably West Germany (as it then was). The period 1945–73 is sometimes referred to as the 'golden age of capitalism', characterized by healthy economic growth, relatively full employment and financial stability (Glyn et al., 1992). In the world as a whole, output of manufactured goods quadrupled from the early 1950s to the early 1970s. Exports of manufactured goods rose, mainly from developed countries to other developed countries. Corporate gains were impressive, enabling companies to invest in future expansion. But alongside corporate profitability, there was a bigger picture of social and political contexts. Employees saw rising wages, feeding through into rising consumption. Employee protection and labour rights were consolidated in this era, including rights of collective bargaining and the minimum wage. Governments played active roles in many areas, including the expansion of welfare-state measures. Spectacular economic growth in Japan, at rates around 8% in the 1960s and 1970s, rested in large part on guidance from the Japanese state (Ito, 1996). State-owned enterprises in a number of European countries (including France, Norway and Austria) contributed to high growth. In the UK, where more free-market thinking had hitherto prevailed, the post-war Labour government created the National Health Service (NHS). In the US, government funding flowed into key strategic industries, including aircraft and pharmaceuticals. For many developing countries, this period was marked by optimism, with the birth of new independent states following the departure of colonial rulers. These countries, too, enjoyed steady growth. The US did not see economic growth on the scale experienced in Western Europe and Japan. And its growing imports and balance-of-payments deficit became contributors to global financial instability.

Even in the 1960s and 70s the Bretton Woods system was coming under strain. Three factors can be highlighted. First, the US in the 1960s was gripped by inflation and a mounting trade deficit, fuelled by increasing imports, largely from the growing economies of Europe. Secondly, there arose the 'Euromarkets', which were systems for taking foreign currency deposits, such as dollar deposits in European banks

(Kapstein, 1994: 32). The source of the dollars could be individual investors, central banks or firms. From the 1950s, a Eurocurrency market grew, as funds flowed into European banks, and European economies were growing. European banks were able to expand their Eurocurrency business, unrestrained by national regulations and capital controls. Thirdly, the 'oil shock' of 1973 saw a sudden quadrupling of the price of oil. This was brought about through the price co-ordination of member countries in OPEC (the Organization of the Petroleum Exporting Countries) (www.opec.org), who were able to control the supply and price of oil. These oil-rich countries, which accumulated large sums from higher oil prices, invested in international money markets, swelling the funds of international banks. Large sums flowed from the oil-importing countries to the oil-exporting countries, many of them developing countries, thus contributing to the expansion of global financial flows. The effects of a booming Eurocurrency market, combined with US inflation and a growing trade deficit, led to speculative activities against the US dollar, the linchpin currency of Bretton Woods. In 1971, President Nixon announced that the dollar would no longer be convertible to gold, heralding the collapse of the Bretton Woods system, with its system of fixed exchange rates. This brought about extreme volatility in exchange rates.

Instilling stability in the exchange rate system

Post-Bretton Woods, the IMF was concerned to curb volatility, opting for a policy of greater exchange rate flexibility. This recognizes several means by which governments and central banks can determine exchange rates, ranging from a fixed rate to a free-floating currency. The key free-floating currencies are recognized by the IMF as reserve currencies for the purposes of their 'Special Drawing Rights' (SDR). These have been the US dollar, the Japanese yen, the UK pound and the euro. The Chinese currency, the yuan, was added to this basket of currencies by the IMF in 2015.

Many countries adopt a middle position between market valuation and a fixed rate, known as the 'managed float' of the currency. This allows the currency to fluctuate within a band. Another option is the **'pegged' exchange rate**. It has the benefit of a peg to a 'harder' currency, usually the US dollar or euro. The peg is intended to act as a stabilizing factor. It is often seen as an advantageous policy by governments of developing and transitional economies, as it attracts foreign investors. The currency peg helps to facilitate economic growth, but when an economic downturn occurs, the policy can have a deleterious effect on the currency, leading to pressure to devalue. In currency markets, as in financial markets generally, confidence is a crucial element. When a national economy appears to be in trouble, the currency comes under pressure, but when a whole economy is in trouble, the government bailout is likely to be beyond the means of a country's national reserves. Sound policies can help to prevent a crisis arising, but with the opening of national financial systems, risks can arise from external as well as internal vulnerabilities.

'pegged' exchange rate exchange rate which links the value of a currency to that of another, usually stronger, currency

If a country's currency is perceived to be undervalued, its exporters enjoy an advantage in global markets. China's currency, the yuan, has been pegged to the dollar, but its economy has slowed, wages have risen, corporate debts have grown (see next section), and its exports are struggling to compete with those of other Asian emerging economies. These factors combined with a strong dollar brought the currency under pressure in 2015. China dipped into its huge foreign currency reserves to prop up the currency. There followed a policy shift, in which the dollar peg was effectively dismantled and replaced with a mechanism that was more market-oriented to a mix of currencies. The result was akin to a *de facto* devaluation, seeing the currency fall some 3% in a few days. As a policy measure, the currency devaluation is a boost for the country's exports, but critics would say it is a

manoeuvre to undercut competitors, which could lead to 'currency wars'. It would also lead to even more anti-dumping actions against Chinese goods in the WTO (see Chapter 7). An alternative explanation for the devaluation was that China was becoming more market-friendly, seeking the status of reserve currency from the IMF, which it would consider only if a currency is close to a free-floating one. These policies proved successful from this point of view, with the recognition of the yuan as a reserve currency late in 2015.

Governments desire exchange rate stability, and they share this broad goal with the IMF. But the IMF sees markets as the best long-term means of ensuring stability. Pegged and manipulated currencies have a poor record of precipitating financial crisis when the peg comes under pressure, and governmental efforts to prop up their currencies from accumulated foreign currency reserves usually fail. A conundrum for governments is that they wish their economies to be attractive to foreign investors, but they also wish their currency to be shielded from destabilizing shocks that occur in global financial markets.

International capital flows

debt financing raising capital by borrowing

equity financing raising capital by issuing shares

Access to capital is essential for every business. Firms may turn to banks and other institutions for loans, raising capital by **debt financing**. Or they may raise capital through share offerings, known as **equity financing**. In practice, companies rely on a combination of equity and debt financing, which are discussed in this section. Capital markets handle flows of capital, including equity investments (portfolio investment) and also bonds, which are loan instruments. Students of international business might expect that the biggest and most influential players in equity and debt markets are the large MNEs, but this would be only partially true in today's world. Some of the largest players are governments, which are active in many global markets, and some of the more influential players have been the world's private investment funds, which act as catalysts in both debt and equity markets. This section sheds light on the interactions among these diverse players.

Equity markets

initial public offering (IPO) first offering by a company of its shares to the public on a stock exchange; also known as a 'flotation'

When a company is publicly 'floated', it is listed on a stock exchange, and its shares are offered through an **initial public offering** (IPO) (discussed in Chapter 1). Founders of private-sector companies typically take the decision when to 'go public' and list their company, inviting the public to subscribe for shares in the new PLC. These companies, such as Google or Microsoft, it will be recalled, are still private-sector companies. The 'public' aspect refers to the offer of shares to the general public. When governments wish to privatize an organization in the public sector, such as the post office, for example, they typically create a PLC, listing the company on a stock exchange and offering a portion of the shares to the public (often retaining a large stake in state hands). The government-controlled PLC is not uncommon in many countries, especially those that tend towards a more statist model of capitalism. The share offerings that attract media attention are often those of companies such as Alibaba of China, where a charismatic founder seeks a greater presence on the global stage.

stock exchanges regulated markets in which shares in public companies and other securities are traded

Shares in listed companies are traded on the world's **stock exchanges**. A rise in the value of a company's traded shares is an indication of market sentiment towards the company, and also towards the sector and the general economic environment. When the investment climate is buoyant, shares can trade at many times their nominal value, but when sentiment declines, corporate values can decline sharply. This is what happened to the Royal Bank of Scotland (RBS). It grew spectacularly in the decade leading up to the financial crisis, its shares trading at £60 in 2007, but their value had plunged to £3 by 2009.

Since then, stock markets have shown impressive rises in value, and this optimism has encouraged increased numbers of IPOs. Total IPO activity in 2017 amounted to $338.4 billion globally, and the number of IPOs that year was 1,974, making it the most active year for IPOs since 2007 (EY, 2017). The number and size of IPOs is a good indication of the investment climate. When share prices are rising generally, a company is confident that its IPO will find subscribers, and its value will rise in subsequent trading. Choosing a stock market is also an important decision, and a stock market's volume of IPOs indicates global confidence in its investment prospects. Nonetheless, market volatility leads many companies to be cautious. Each year, hundreds of IPOs either contemplated or already in the pipeline are postponed, indicating a nervousness to take the plunge. In 2017, Asian exchanges accounted for more than half the number of IPOs and just over half their overall value, as shown in Figure 8.2.

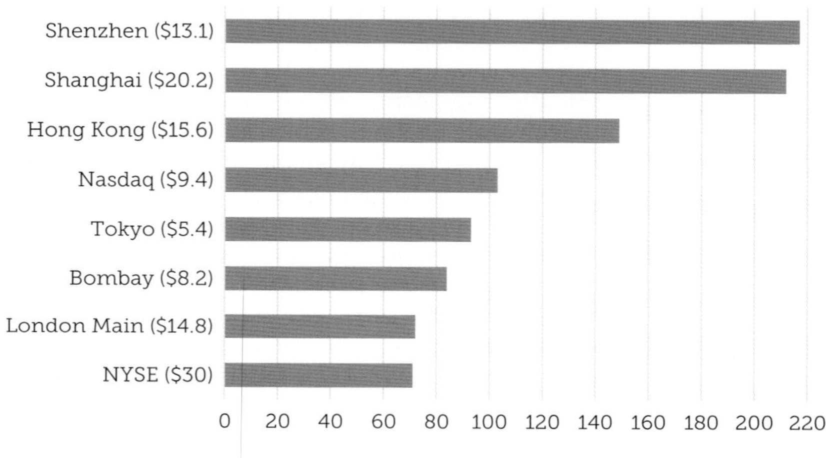

Figure 8.2 **Number of IPOs on leading stock exchanges, 2017**

Note: Value of IPOs of each exchange appears in brackets, stated in billions of US dollars.

Source of data: Ernst & Young Global Limited (2017) EY Global Trends 2017, at www.ey.com, accessed 23 September 2019.

The main US exchanges, the New York Stock Exchange (NYSE) (www.nyse.com) and the Nasdaq (National Association of Securities Dealers Automated Quotations system) (www.nasdaq.com), remain powerful in global equity markets, attracting more cross-border listings than exchanges in other regions of the world. Foreign companies make up 24% of listings on US exchanges. The NYSE traces its history back to 1790, making it by far the older of the two. The Nasdaq, founded in 1971, trades mainly in technology and other 'new economy' stocks. Technology stocks have seen considerable fluctuation in value. In the year following the crash in dot-com stocks of 2000, shares traded on the Nasdaq lost half their value in what was known as the 'dotcom crash'. Since then, they have shown stellar growth, notably in the decade following the financial crash of 2008. Much of the post-crash growth in share prices of US-listed technology stocks is attributable to the success of companies such as Facebook, Apple, Alphabet (Google's parent company) and Amazon. Apple became the first trillion-dollar company in 2018, and Amazon is not far behind. Even so, share prices can fall as well as rise, engendering an air of nervousness over long-term values. Facebook's share value suffered a loss of $120 billion in a single day in 2018, due to concerns over the leakage of users' data. This was the largest one-day loss of value ever recorded for a single company in US history. Inevitably, there were doubts over how long these giant technology and communication services companies could continue their strong growth.

Asia is home to some of the exchanges with the strongest growth. The Hong Kong, Shanghai and Shenzhen exchanges have benefited from the effects of Chinese growth. However, these exchanges are also volatile. While Hong Kong, with its long tradition of attracting Chinese companies, is well established, the younger mainland Chinese exchanges, Shanghai and Shenzhen, are more prone to swings in value. Most of the shareholders in listed Chinese companies are small investors. These small retail investors, numbering over 90 million people, hold 80% of listed shares. The low interest rates paid to savers in China's regulated banking sector have had the effect of sending private investors to look for greater returns on stock markets. Many of these investors do not simply invest their savings: they turned to borrowing to fund investment. But risks abound in equity markets, especially when investors are also indebted, and it is a concern of the Chinese government that millions of small investors are taking risks that impact on household finances.

The trend in capital markets generally in the developed economies has been in the opposite direction. Individual investors are investing less in specific companies, and opting instead for investment funds and other vehicles that spread risks. In these markets, there has been a growth in institutional investors like pension funds and other investment funds. These institutional investors deal in huge share transactions, and often have substantial holdings in key companies. They value stability as well as financial returns from their investments, targeting companies that are considered well-governed and transparent. Also important in equity markets are the sovereign wealth funds that operate under the control of state authorities. These investors, too, look for stability and good returns. But many investors, particularly some types of investment fund, take an altogether different view of equity markets, looking for short-term gains that can be rapidly reinvested in other equities. This type of investor has come to the fore in recent years, facilitated by advances in the technology that drives trading platforms.

From the mid-2000s some of the major stock exchanges saw rapid growth in 'high frequency trading', whereby large numbers of trades take place in fractions of a second, programmed by algorithms. The software decides when, what and where to buy and sell, without any human intervention. Each trade is designed to generate a profit from the tiniest movement in prices; although each trade is small in itself in terms of value, the volume of trades is immense. In New York, where the practice grew rapidly, regulators considered banning it in 2014, but they rejected such a ban, and high-frequency trading has become established. The traders themselves argue that they are in fact improving the efficiency of the exchanges for all users, not just themselves. Nonetheless, the risks of system overload that can cause systems to crash are a concern for the exchanges, as any breakdown in trading systems can cause losses to participants and damage to the reputation of an exchange for dependability.

Public companies and their investors depend on the smooth running and prudent administration of stock markets. Stock exchanges are subject to national regulation, and differ in their rules for corporate listing and for trading of shares. Regulatory systems aim to maintain confidence in their fairness, integrity and transparency. Just as there are different national approaches to regulatory issues in general, financial regulation differs from country to country. Many exchanges are themselves listed companies, and compete with other exchanges to attract listings. If the listing rules of a particular exchange are more generous in respect of insider-dominated companies, that exchange is likely to attract such companies. However, public companies that are controlled by insiders, with only a small portion of free-floating shares, are not in keeping with the values of transparency and fairness that stock exchanges aim to uphold.

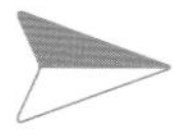

Securities and Exchange Commission (SEC) US stock market regulator

The US regulator, the **Securities and Exchange Commission (SEC)** (www.sec.gov) was founded in 1934, in the reforms that followed the stock market crash of 1929. The SEC's role includes protecting investors, maintaining fair and efficient markets and also serving the companies that come to the market to raise capital. In the UK, the regulation of financial services was reformed by Financial Services and Markets Act 2000, which set up the Financial Services Authority (FSA), under the oversight of the Bank of England. Its philosophy of light-touch regulation, rather than direct oversight, reflected the free-market thinking that has contributed to the UK's rise in attractiveness for financial services. However, the financial crisis of 2008 dealt a blow to the UK's reputation as a financial centre, when regulatory failures were seen as partly to blame for banking collapses that ensued (discussed later in this chapter). The banking crisis, which saw the Royal Bank of Scotland (RBS) effectively nationalized, with 79% of its shares owned by the UK Treasury, led to a rethinking of the UK's financial services regulatory framework generally. The FSA was replaced by new regulatory frameworks, including the Financial Conduct Authority (FCA), to oversee financial market behaviour. The Bank of England took over direct supervision of the banking system, and the Prudential Regulation Authority (PRA), part of the Bank of England, took over the oversight of financial services firms.

Global equity markets

Share ownership and corporate IPOs are no longer predominantly national phenomena. As they become increasingly globalized, what are the new opportunities, and threats, for companies contemplating listing on a stock exchange?

Debt financing

People, companies and governments borrow money to pay for assets and services that they need. They must pay off their debt, of course, and also pay interest on loans. But if the interest payments are manageable, borrowing can be a good way of financing big expenditures. Exchange risk often comes into the equation: if the money owed to a creditor is in US dollars, for example, and the debtor is relying on income in local currency to make payments, then the debtor is at risk when the local currency falls in value against the dollar. In a period of just five months between October 2014 and February 2015, the dollar appreciated 14% in nominal terms against a range of foreign currencies, causing consternation for anyone holding dollar-denominated debt (IMF, 2015: 42). When credit is easy and interest rates are low, the temptations to borrow seem irresistible. But how much debt is too much? This is a question often posed for governments and companies, as well as for individuals.

leverage extent to which a company relies on debt financing

Levels of debt are carefully monitored in all economies. The main categories are government debt, corporate debt of non-financial companies, and household debt. The extent of debt is usually expressed as a percentage of GDP: the debt-to-GDP ratio. Debt is often referred to as **leverage**. Where the debt burden is high, the indebted economic entity is said to be highly 'leveraged'. This need not always be a worrying indicator, if servicing the debt is manageable. But there are inherent risks in taking on large debts, as repayment difficulties can lead to financial disaster. Despite the fact that the global financial crisis of 2008 followed boom years of cheap credit, global debt since the crisis has actually increased, rather than decreased. Recession and slow recovery led to further borrowing to stimulate economic activity. A result has been that all the world's major economies have seen an increase in borrowing. For national economies, increasing debt can damage prospects of

growth. This is especially relevant where the debt is linked to global financial markets and exposed to exchange rate risk.

bond a loan instrument which promises to pay a specific sum of money on a fixed date, and to pay interest at stated intervals

eurobond a bond denominated in a currency other than the one of the country in which it is issued

Loans are a class of asset, and can be traded. Debt financing has given rise to an international bond market which facilitates trade in a variety of loan instruments. A **bond** is a loan instrument which promises to pay a specific sum of money on a fixed date, and to pay interest at stated intervals. Bonds are marketable securities that can be issued in different currencies. An 'external bond' is one issued by a borrower in a capital market outside the borrower's own country. The external bond may be a foreign bond, which is denominated in the currency of the country in which it is issued. **Eurobonds**, by contrast, are denominated in currencies other than those of the countries in which they are issued. Dollar-denominated bonds issued outside the US are examples of eurobonds. Their attraction has been that they escape official regulation. Global bonds are the most flexible of bonds, as they may be sold inside as well as outside the country in whose currency they are denominated. Dollar global bonds are regulated by the SEC in the US. The World Bank is the leading issuer of global bonds. Governments have also raised money in this way, with the practice recently spreading to governments of developing countries.

Government debt, or 'sovereign debt', has grown to huge proportions in some countries, as we noted in Chapter 4. Many governments rely heavily on borrowing, feeling confident that economic growth would be stimulated, and that the debt burden would be manageable. However, the recession following the 2008 financial crisis put extra strain on governments, leading to increased borrowing. This was largely attributable to a combination of decreasing revenues from taxes and increasing social payments, including unemployment benefits and housing benefits. It is also the case that ageing populations, especially in the advanced OECD countries require increasing funds to pay for pensions and healthcare. Government debt varies greatly from country to country, and the most indebted are not always, as one might expect, the ones that have the most expansive social welfare systems.

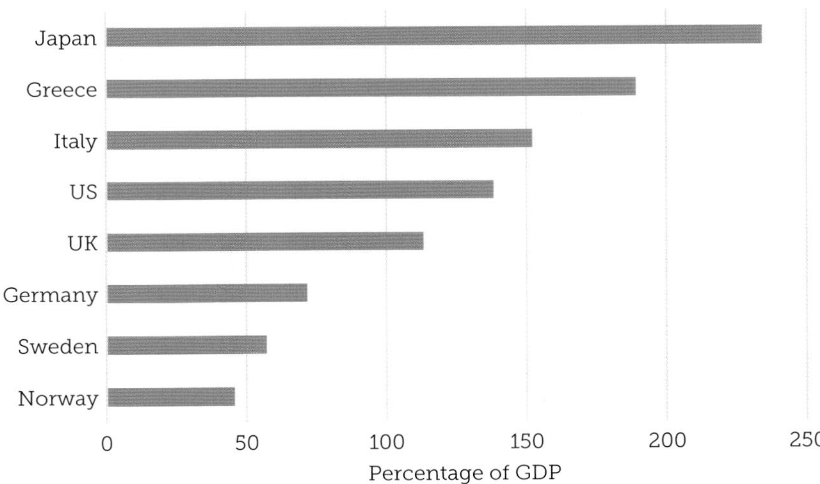

Figure 8.3 **Government debt as a percentage of GDP in selected OECD countries, 2018**

Source of data: OECD, OECD data: General government debt, at https://data.oecd.org, accessed 7 July 2019.

Looking at Figure 8.3, Norway and Sweden, countries among the highest in human development ranking, have relatively low government debt. These Scandinavian countries have relatively balanced economies, with adequate revenues to fund social programmes. Recall Figure 4.9, which showed that Denmark's tax revenues amount to nearly 50% of GDP. Tax revenues in the US are much lower, and US government debt, in terms of percentage of GDP, is nearly double that of Sweden.

The worrying examples in Figure 8.3 are Italy, Greece and Japan. Italy struggles to collect tax revenues, and struggles to fund generous social programmes and a generous pension system. Greece was on the verge of sovereign default for several years, and has survived on a lifeline of loans from the IMF and EU. But what about Japan, which looks in worse shape? Japan's huge government debt has mounted over two decades of deflation and a stagnating economy, combined with the burdens of an ageing population. However, Japan is a rich country, with growth potential, and is not perceived as likely to default, despite the massive government debt. Another factor is that Japanese people, like Asians generally, are frugal and have not accumulated huge household debts.

Emerging economies' appetite for debt to propel growth has been striking, especially among corporate leaders. Debt has grown faster than GDP in all major emerging markets. Figure 8.4 shows the growth in debt in the non-financial sector (both corporate and household debt) in emerging markets. Debt rose from 110% of GDP in 2007 to nearly 177% in 2018. This growth mainly reflected the rising debt burdens of private-sector companies. In 2017, the IMF expressed concern over the risks to global financial stability (IMF, 2017). In most emerging markets, bank loans are a major source of funding for companies. High levels of corporate debt present risks to the banks, which can jeopardize the stability of the financial system and set back progress on development goals. Economic growth in many emerging economies is dependent on sectors such as commodities (for example, Brazil) and energy (for example, Russia). These sectors are subject to price volatility in global markets, which, in turn, can adversely affect domestic companies' capacity to repay debt. The IMF warned in 2017 that a major risk to growth in emerging markets is the uncertainty surrounding political policies – especially the risk of protectionism – in the advanced economies (IMF, 2017).

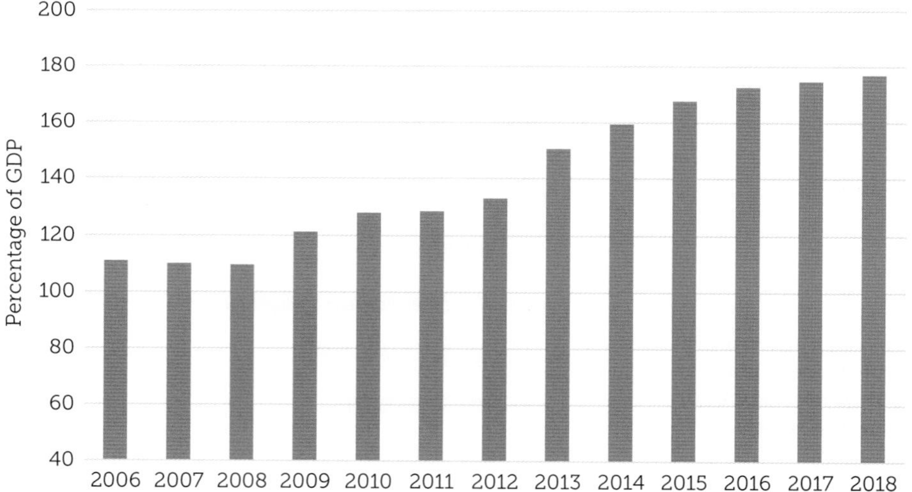

Figure 8.4 **The rise of private-sector debt as a percentage of GDP in emerging market economies**

Source of data: BIS (Bank for International Settlements), BIS total credit statistics, Total credit to the non-financial sector, Table F1.1, updated by BIS 4 June 2019, at www.bis.org/statistics, accessed 23 September 2019.

Among emerging markets, China stands out for its high levels of corporate debt. China's level of government debt, at 40% of GDP, is not unduly high; nor is its level of household debt. But the debt burden of its non-financial companies reached a worrying 'bubble' level of 200% in 2017 (Orlik et al., 2018). By 2018, it had risen to 254% (BIS, 2019). The IMF has estimated that the impact of losses in Chinese banks' corporate loan portfolio could be as high as 7% of GDP. Much of this debt is owed not to official banks, but to financial institutions in the 'shadow' banking sector. Chinese companies and banks have also taken advantage of near-zero interest rates available

in the US since the financial crisis. In China, construction and real estate are sectors in which debt has dramatically accumulated, resulting in firms being highly leveraged. China's political leaders have tightened credit, but face a balancing act in wishing to maintain strong growth. The Chinese economy, it advises, is in urgent need of restructuring its corporate entities, closing the ones that are failing and downsizing where appropriate. Reforming corporate governance is also needed as an essential element of sustainable growth.

MINI CASE STUDY

Funding Circle, the peer-to-peer lender

Funding Circle is a young company, formed in 2010 by three friends in the dark days following the financial crisis. Samir Desai, James Meekings, and Andrew Mullinger saw the difficulties small businesses were having in accessing loans. The banks had been battered in the financial crisis, and were not interested in lending to small businesses, yet businesses were desperate for funds to get back on their feet. The three founders came up with the idea of allowing businesses to borrow from ordinary investors, known as peer-to-peer lending, or P2P. Since 2010, they have lent more than $5 billion to 50,000 small businesses in the UK, US, Germany and the Netherlands. This money has come from 80,000 investors, both individuals and firms.

The type of business that seeks out Funding Circle is one that it is in need of capital quickly and has been turned down by a traditional bank. The firm is able to borrow up to £1 million. Funding Circle matches up these businesses with investors through innovative technology using data analytics. The company itself has been fortunate in obtaining the backing of venture capitalists who have been keen to invest in promising start-ups. One is Heartland, the investment fund owned by Anders Holch Povlsen, the Danish businessman who is the main shareholder in Asos, the online retailer.

Funding Circle decided to launch an IPO on the London Stock Exchange in 2018. The flotation valued the company at £1.5 billion. The first day of trading turned into a disappointment: the shares fell some 25%, and the company had a market value of £1.25 billion. The founders had been optimistic about a successful IPO for their growing innovative business in the financial technology sector, but the market was more cautious. It was a new company that did not have a strong record of earnings, and investors were therefore wary. It had made losses as it built up the business, but could be happy with revenue growth up 55% to £142 million in 2018. It still looked to have a bright future, and it was confident that its business of focusing on SMEs was a worthy enterprise. The average loan is £75,000, and the average business is one employing eight people. It was thought that the economic uncertainty surrounding Brexit would not affect these small companies, and that opportunities for peer-to-peer lending would still flourish. By mid-2019, however, Funding Circle was finding that demands for loans from small businesses were decreasing. It seemed that Brexit uncertainties were impacting on its business. The optimism of its IPO of the previous year began to look like a distant memory.

Questions

- Why is peer-to-peer lending on the rise?
- What does the disappointing debut of Funding Circle on the LSE tell us about the stock exchange?

Find out more

See the article by Eugenia Omarini (2018) 'Peer-to-peer lending: Business model analysis and the platform dilemma', *International Journal of Finance, Economy and Trade*, 2(3): 31–41.

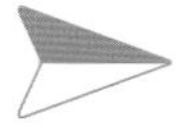

Global financial risks and their consequences

A number of financial risks have been highlighted in this chapter. They include volatile stock prices, foreign exchange risk, and excessive reliance on debt financing, especially when coupled with exchange risk. All companies that engage in cross-border activities are subject to some of these risks, including both non-financial and financial firms. But globalization has greatly ramified the sources of risks and the extent of the damage when market volatility undermines financial planning. Financial experts have become highly innovative in seeking new opportunities for gains, but these come with greater risks. The aura of gambling has thus crept into finance. With the possible risks extending to whole sectors, whole economies and societies, the potential for disasters has risen markedly. In this section, we look at the sources of risk, the broader consequences that lead to financial crises, and the possible ways in which global finance can be reformed.

How globalization has increased risks

Interconnectedness, liberalization and deepening integration of markets have become hallmarks of globalization, as we have seen in sectors such as manufacturing. The global company typically seeks to have its product manufactured in a place that offers location advantages. For societies in the host country, this can be a mixed blessing: jobs are on offer, but the employer could pull out if conditions become adverse. In finance, we see an analogous pattern. Liberalization and deregulation have contributed to encouraging cross-border finance. Opportunities for investment are rapidly multiplying, investors often taking advantage of factors affecting different locations, such as currency fluctuations and interest rates. Capital flows benefit individual countries, but investors can exit if internal fundamentals deteriorate. A financial crisis can develop relatively quickly. The consequences of a generalized exit by investors, known as a 'flight of capital', are far more serious for an economy than the exit of a global brand's manufacturing operations.

International business is traditionally built on trade in goods. An exporter or importer is directly affected by foreign exchange rates. To protect it from adverse currency fluctuations, it may turn to trading in currency markets. The currency **futures contract** allows a business to buy or sell a specific amount of foreign currency at a designated price in the future. They are therefore said to have a **hedge** against future fluctuations which can adversely affect their business. An example is the airline company that hedges future purchases of jet fuel for its fleet of planes. The company might also find the **option** a useful tool in hedging against currency risk: the option gives the firm the right, rather than an obligation, to purchase the currency in the future at a specific exchange rate. Some airline companies have taken advantage of low fuel prices by negotiating option contracts well into the future. Futures contracts and options are types of derivatives. For most non-financial MNEs, dealings on the currency markets are incidental to their main business. They see finance as a function that serves their main productive activities.

futures contract contract to carry out a particular transaction on a designated date in the future

hedge a financial tool or arrangement which insures a firm against adverse currency movements in its international financial activities

option contractual device used to allow a person or company the right to purchase something of value at a future date

Banks traditionally shared this view of financial activities. Historically, they existed to serve customers, including individuals, companies and governments. Contrast this view of finance with one that sees finance as a business in its own right. The growth in global financial markets has come about largely as a result of this shift in the way finance is viewed. Finance is no longer a means to an end: it *is* the end. Finance thus became a significant sector in its own right – one that grew rapidly. As we have seen in the case of exchanges, technological innovation has played a big role. It is paradoxical that risks have multiplied partly due to innovative financial products that purport to offer new ways to spread risk. Banks once focused on traditional banking activities, but saw tempting opportunities for growth and

globalization through these newer activities in global finance. They thus transformed themselves into 'universal banks', covering both retail operations and capital investment units. The latter more risky operations were formerly required to be conducted via separate entities in the US, under the Glass-Stegall Act of 1933, passed following the Great Depression. That law was repealed in 1999, allowing the universal bank to flourish – and become highly globalized.

Central to these more ambitious activities has been the rise of new players such as hedge funds, whose businesses rest largely on the more risky types of investment. Derivatives trading brings together both of these trends.

derivative financial instrument whose value is dependent on another asset class such as stock

Financial instruments broadly classified as **derivatives** have become a large market in their own right. Since 1998, primary securities have remained stable, at about double world GDP. But derivatives, amounting to two-and-a-half times world GDP in 1998, were twelve times world GDP by 2007 (Blundell-Wignall, 2011: 2). The value of any derivative depends on the value of some underlying asset, such as cash or property. Derivatives have facilitated growth in the securitization of debt, that is, the packaging of debt as securities which can be traded. There are many classes of securitized debt. The basic form is an 'asset-backed security' (ABS). The security lies in the repayment of the loans, which is a future event subject to risk that the original debtors will default. There are many types of ABS. They can be mortgage-backed securities, either residential or commercial. As it is difficult to assess the value of derivatives, debt instruments thus came to be 'structured', packaging a range of assets, some higher risk than others. This was deemed to be a relatively safe strategy. The likelihood was that if there was a fall in the value of one, the remainder would suffice as security. It was not thought likely that all could fall, but that is what happened when the housing market in the US collapsed in 2007.

hedge fund investment fund managed by an individual or firm which is active in securities markets

Among the main players in derivatives markets are investment funds known as **hedge funds**. They are considered short-term investors. They specialize in speculative strategies that generate short-term profits rather than long-term growth. They occasionally take stakes in companies they deem to be underperforming, with a view to shaking up the existing management to boost growth. This type of activity must be distinguished from the hedging which non-financial companies engage in on a daily basis in the course of business. Hedge funds are active in futures markets, where their speculative skills are to the fore. For example, we would expect the market in crude oil to be about the price of oil in physical cargos, but in fact, the main forces in the crude oil market are the funds that trade in futures, speculating on a rise or fall in demand that would push prices up or down.

Hedge funds are also investors in sovereign debt, many specializing in purchasing government bonds for a fraction of their face value on secondary markets. The owners of these so-called 'junk' bonds bet on their ability to pursue claims for their full face value, through the courts, if need be. Funds that specialize in 'distressed' securities are usually called 'vulture funds' because of their aggressive strategies targeting poor indebted countries. They are the object of criticism on ethical grounds from both governments and corporate leaders, especially when they move, vulture-like, on weak targets, be they governments or companies. Argentina was pursued for over a decade by 'hold-out' creditors who purchased Argentinian bonds at the time of its sovereign default in 2001.

The funds have engaged in forum-shopping among legal jurisdictions, choosing the best location for launching legal action. In 2010, the UK passed legislation, in the form of the UK Debt Relief (Developing Countries) Act, to limit the scope of vulture funds to pursue such claims in its courts. Many funds then shifted their claims to the offshore jurisdiction of Jersey, a Channel Island legally independent of UK law. In 2012, Jersey's legislature voted to bring the island into line with UK law on debt relief, its government having been disquieted by the use of its courts for this type of

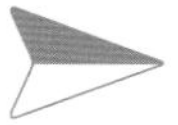

litigation (Neate, 2012). Globally, there still remain alternative legal routes open to the hedge funds to pursue such claims. This type of litigation, while strictly legal, is generally perceived as unethical. Hedge funds have fully exploited the opportunities presented by global financial markets. However, the aggressive legal strategies of the funds have been associated with negative consequences that can result in enduring damage in poor countries.

Rising corporate debt in emerging economies

Borrowing to invest became highly inviting to corporate leaders, keen to take advantage of global opportunities, and seeing little risk lurking in growing markets. But the risks of accumulating excessive debt can weigh heavily. How has globalization increased financial risk for MNEs?

When financial crisis strikes whole nations

Individual people can go bankrupt, unable to pay their debts. Companies can default, failing to pay their creditors, and go into liquidation. National financial systems have in place legal frameworks that allow possible debt restructuring, and failing these attempts, an orderly way of winding up the company, ensuring that creditors are fairly dealt with. In the financial crisis of 2008, some companies, such as Lehman Brothers in the US, collapsed, while others in difficulties were bailed out with public money. These included those deemed to be 'too big to fail'. Most of these companies, including both financial and non-financial firms, had indulged heavily in derivatives trading. While regulators were highly critical of these companies' high-risk strategies, they nonetheless took the view that rescue plans for these major companies were integral to restoring order and confidence in financial markets. When a whole country is on the brink of crisis, national regulators and central banks are not able to mount a rescue. In these circumstances, it usually falls to the IMF to organize the loans needed to alleviate the situation, but IMF terms inevitably include harsh remedies and austerity measures. We look at examples from three continents, beginning with the Asian financial crisis that struck in 1997.

Currency crises and IMF responses

The Asian financial crisis spread from Thailand to South Korea, Malaysia and Indonesia. In each case, there are specifically national factors involved, but there are also issues of 'contagion', whereby the woes of one country spread to others in the region. In all these countries, policies of liberalization and deregulation in the 1990s led to inflows of capital, as investors were attracted to high rates of interest, and trusted that governments would not allow their banks to fail. Net capital inflows more than doubled between 1994 and 1996 in the four countries (Singh, 1998). The investment boom, however, was largely financed by borrowed money, much of the borrowing in US dollars.

The crisis originated in Thailand. Thai financial institutions had engaged in imprudent lending on local property development, and found themselves at risk of defaulting on dollar-denominated debt to international financial institutions. The Thai government attempted to defend the currency, the *baht*, by increasing interest rates and buying baht with its own foreign currency reserves, but this effort exhausted the reserves of the central bank. Under increasing pressure, the baht was floated in 1997, and immediately dropped 20% in value.

A swift deterioration in confidence followed, causing investors to flee. Banks and businesses found the burden of dollar debts increasingly crippling. The

banking crisis was thus directly related to the currency crisis, the combined effect of which was to send the economy into meltdown (Krugman, 1999). Contagion spread to other Asian economies. Large sums by way of credits were made available by the IMF to South Korea and Indonesia, to support the currency and meet external debts. IMF conditions to strengthen fiscal and monetary stability were imposed, in the hope that confidence in capital and foreign exchange markets would be restored.

In its Asian rescue packages, the IMF has been criticized for exacerbating the problems, rather than curing them. In particular, its one-size-fits-all market-oriented solutions, administered as shock therapy, have been criticized as not taking into account national conditions that vary from country to country. In giving assistance, it imposed strict monetary and fiscal conditions on recipient countries. This approach was held up as exemplifying the Washington consensus, but in fact, as we have seen, was motivated more directly by purely market values. This criticism is expressed by Joseph Stiglitz, former chief economist at the World Bank, who has pointed out that the IMF programme in Indonesia helped to cause a recession. Rocketing unemployment and economic hardship in ethnically divided Indonesia contributed to social and political strife, causing the government to fall (Stiglitz, 2000).

Since the crisis, the Asian economies have enjoyed a revival in economic growth, largely driven by China. In response to continuing US dominance in the structures of the IMF and World Bank, China launched the **Asian Infrastructure Investment Bank** (AIIB) (https://aiib.org), envisaging an Asia-focused institution that would be similar to the World Bank, but with China as the main shareholder and India as the second-largest. The AIIB's signing ceremony went ahead in 2015, with an initial 50 member states signing up, including Germany, the UK, Australia and South Korea. By 2019, the AIIB's membership had grown to a total of 97 member states, 71 regional and 26 non-regional. There are also prospective members, including Brazil, Argentina and South Africa. The US has objected to the AIIB from its inception and has no intention of joining. Japan, another non-member, is considering becoming a member.

Asian Infrastructure Investment Bank (AIIB) development bank launched by China, providing funding on a similar basis to the World Bank

The Asian crisis also impacted on Russia, where the 1990s did not bring the economic growth and prosperity that had been hoped for at the fall of the Soviet Union. The IMF was active in Russia in the 1990s, encouraging liberalizing reforms and the growth of the private market economy, which accounted for 70% of Russia's GDP by 1998. But Russia's prosperity depended on natural resources and commodities. When the Asian crisis struck and demand for oil fell, the Russian economy was threatened. The currency, the rouble, was subject to a 'floating peg' with the US dollar, which meant that it had to be maintained within a band of value. When the rouble came under pressure, the central bank intervened, using foreign currency reserves to buy roubles and thus try to sustain the peg. The IMF stepped in with loans, but with confidence in the currency draining away, the peg had to be abandoned in 1998. When the rouble was allowed to float, it lost two-thirds of its value against the dollar. The financial crisis soon translated into a political crisis, with the fall of the government. Stepping into the role of rescuing Russia from the financial crisis was Vladimir Putin, elected president in 2000. He took a more statist approach to the economy in contrast to the market reforms sponsored by the IMF, and he also pursued a more nationalist and expansive political agenda. A resurgence in the price of oil and other resources helped the Russian economy to recover, although, two decades later, it remains highly dependent on resource wealth. In that period, Mr Putin has consolidated his hold on power over both the political system and the economy.

Financial collapse rooted in excessive sovereign debt

Argentina, another resource-rich country, enjoyed strong economic growth in the 1990s, but Argentina's government had imprudently accumulated unsustainable levels of sovereign debt, leading to default in 2001. A number of hedge funds purchased Argentine debt in the form of 'junk' bonds, gambling on their ability to obtain full payment. Argentina became embroiled in legal battles with creditors, despite two deals in which the vast majority of creditors accepted a debt restructuring compromise deal. It has become apparent that the terms agreed with bondholders could have been designed more tightly, to restrict the ability of a small minority to hold up a collective agreement. The country's leftwing government persistently refused to pay the 'holdout' creditors, but elections in 2015 ushered in a new centre-right government. The new president, Mauricio Macri, aimed to bring in liberal, market-friendly economic reforms, in contrast to the subsidies and nationalized companies that had characterized the previous government. He negotiated a settlement with the relevant hedge funds in 2016. The huge payout required was costly, and aroused considerable domestic criticism (see the closing case study).

Argentina's financial crises

'Peso Pressure: Argentina faces another financial crisis'. This is a documentary produced by France 24 English, 6 September 2018.

Video link: Argentina's financial crises
https://youtu.be/YT3IxleOCB8

Greece is the last stop on this tour of economies that have suffered from financial crisis. Greece is a eurozone country, propped up by both the European Central Bank and EU Commission, which formulated rescue packages to restructure its sovereign debt of nearly €300 billion, following the 2008 financial crisis. The Greek government had been spending beyond its means for many years, accumulating dangerous levels of debt since before it joined the euro in 2001. When the cost of borrowing rose following the 2008 financial crisis, the government was no longer able to pay off its loans. The terms of its bailout featured a package of austerity measures including drastic spending cuts and tax rises. These spelt hardship for ordinary people, already suffering from high unemployment, and led to violent protests and political unrest, leading to the collapse of the government in 2014. In the elections that followed, the radical leftwing party, Syriza, campaigned successfully on an anti-austerity platform, taking the lead in a coalition government in 2015. However, Syriza leaders, too, were compelled to commit to anti-austerity measures. By 2018, Greece came to the end of its bailout programmes, but for Greek society, the hardship was far from over, with unemployment still high at 19%, but lower than its peak of 27% in 2013. Particularly worrying has been youth unemployment, which reached 58% that year, but was still 25% in 2017. Between 2008 and 2016, 4% of the population emigrated to other countries, many of them young people. The exodus led many to focus on the 'lost generation' of young Greeks with little prospect of fulfilling employment (Molloy, 2018). Disillusion in Greece contributed to dwindling support for Syriza, which was defeated in snap elections in 2019. The winning party was the centre-right party, the New Democracy party, whose leader, Kyriakos Mitsotakis, a former banker, promised liberal economic reforms.

How can he make ends meet? The hardship suffered by this pensioner in Athens is indicative of the effects of the financial crisis that were felt by millions of ordinary people.

© Getty, Thanasis Zovoilis

The IMF was criticized for the harsh terms of its bailout packages in both Argentina and Greece. In both countries, much of the thrust of public opinion was against the IMF as well as against the political leadership of the country. When a whole country is on the brink of default, there is no international framework equivalent to national bankruptcy law, although there have been calls for such a system to be considered (Stiglitz, 2015). In these cases, decision-makers in government are usually at least partly to blame, like imprudent managers in a business. But, often, external shocks are a crucial factor for national economies, especially in light of globalized markets. The risks inherent in global markets were major factors in the global financial crisis of 2008, to which we now turn.

The way I see it...

On Greek debt as an investment opportunity, 'One of the reasons it's so attractive is everyone thinks it's as mysterious and dangerous as being in *Game of Thrones* or something'.

Hans Humes, founder of Greylock Capital Management LLC, a hedge fund, in an interview with Bloomberg news, 10 June 2015.

Hans Humes is an experienced hedge fund manager with an appetite for risk and nerves of steel, investing in sovereign debt that most investors avoid. Having endured the turbulence of Argentine and Greek debt restructuring, he continues to look for opportunities in the debt of countries in financial distress. He has recently invested in distressed bonds of Venezuela. Venezuela is in the throes of political and economic turmoil, with high inflation, a collapsing currency and shortages of basic products. See Thomas, L. (2017) 'Venezuelan debt now has the vultures circling', *The New York Times*, 14 November.

The hedge fund sees opportunities where others fear to tread, but how can an opportunity based on the distress of a sovereign state be considered a legitimate investment?

The global financial crisis of 2008

The decade preceding 2008 seemed like a golden age for financial markets. Easy credit, high returns and stable markets provided ideal conditions for continuing growth – or so it seemed. However, two aspects of the boom in finance posed potential threats. First, there were the risks underlying derivatives trading, which included the securitization of debt. Banks, unshackled from traditional banking models, became skilled at repackaging their loans into bonds which could be sold on, thus removing them from the balance sheet. Banks took to funding lending through inter-bank borrowing. Banks were able to use short-term debt to fund further lending, thus enabling them to lend far more than would have been possible under traditional rules of capital adequacy, which required banks to have a substantial asset base. This type of trading was outside regulated exchanges, generating large sums of money for participants, which included not just banks, but firms in non-financial sectors that were drawn by the possibilities of greater profits from financial activities. Secondly, the appetite for risk that gripped the firms involved, and, in particular, the decision-makers within those firms, seemed to know no bounds. The idea that 'greed is good' implied that self-interested financial gain was the only goal to aim for, by whatever means that seemed likely to yield the most money. This approach led to excessive risk-taking.

The origins of the crisis go back to the boom in the US housing market from the early 2000s. Government policies encouraged home ownership, making it easier for people to obtain mortgages, which in turn led to a housing boom. But much of the growth in mortgage lending was in 'sub-prime' mortgages. These were loans to people who in earlier eras would have had little hope of obtaining a mortgage. These mortgages carried a high risk of non-payment, but as long as property prices continued rising, the risk seemed negligible. The market peaked in 2006, but risks lurked beneath the surface. The new sub-prime borrowers were vulnerable to interest rate rises and falling property values. For lenders such as banks, there is always a risk that borrowers will default, but default rates would normally be manageable, and traditionally, the property itself is 'concrete' security. With sub-prime debt, these assumptions became problematic. To alleviate the risks, sub-prime mortgages were repackaged with higher value assets and sold on as securitized debt. However, as noted above, valuing derivatives is not a science. When cracks appeared in the housing market, and defaults started to rise, the underlying riskiness of securitized mortgage debt became apparent. The housing boom collapsed, and uncertainty rapidly spread through financial markets, affecting the many financial institutions that had built businesses around derivatives trading.

There followed falls in equities, as confidence in corporate finances was rapidly fading. Lending abruptly stopped, with devastating repercussions for activities in the wider economy. Banks were caught in a 'credit crunch', as their access to short-term lending, on which they had come to depend, was cut off. Their asset bases, which in earlier times would have held them in good stead, looked inadequate. Moreover, banks and other financial institutions had built up global operations, often intertwined with each other. When losses mounted, it became clear that these banks were overstretched and overexposed in high-risk markets.

The aftermath of 2008: responses by national authorities

The US and UK, both with large financial sectors, saw the most immediate impacts of the crisis, and also relatively quick policy decisions from their central banks, the US Federal Reserve and the Bank of England. Also affected were smaller countries that had opened their borders to global finance – and its attendant risks. These

included Ireland and Iceland, both of which suffered financial crises. The banking systems in both countries were rescued through nationalizing the banks.

The UK government and Bank of England stepped in to rescue two major UK banks on the verge of collapse: Royal Bank of Scotland (RBS) and Halifax Bank of Scotland (HBOS). RBS had expanded rapidly through global acquisitions, acquiring 280 subsidiaries in 38 countries. Its shares were over £55 in April 2007, and fell to under £3 by April 2009. Its CEO was compelled to step down, and the bulk of the shares were transferred to the UK government in the years 2008 and 2009, with a view to selling them back to private investors in the future. The company is now a shadow of its former self. Having exited 25 countries, it has become more like a national bank. In 2015, nearly 6% of the shares were sold off to private shareholders. In 2018, a further sale of 8%, or 925 million shares, took place, valuing the shares at 271p, considerably below the 502p paid for them by the Treasury ten years before. While the sell-offs are seen as a move in the right direction, the fact that taxpayers lost out suggested that the woes of the banking sector were not as yet resolved. Indeed, in the years following the financial crisis, evidence of further mismanagement and mis-selling of financial products and services revealed an even more widespread slippage in ethical standards than had emerged at the time of the bailouts.

A number of banks in the US and UK were implicated in scandals involving the concerted rigging of the interbank lending rate (Libor) and rigging of foreign exchange rates. Rates were rigged to ensure that the traders would always gain and the clients would lose out. Market rigging is a serious type of anti-competitive practice, subject to prosecution. For these malpractices, five banks (Barclays, JP Morgan Chase, Citicorp, RBS, UBS and Bank of America) received fines totalling $6 billion in the US. In addition, these banks face civil lawsuits from the many investors, including pension funds and institutional investors, who suffered losses as a result of rigged rates. In the UK, banks have faced fines for mis-selling a range of financial products to retail clients, including insurance, structured investment products and pensions. In all these examples, banks have been compelled to compensate the customers who were misled about the nature of the products. These legal actions have targeted the banks themselves, not individuals within them.

Similarly, it has come to light that in the aftermath of the crisis, the Global Restructuring Group (GRG) of the RBS, systematically mistreated thousands of customers from 2008 to 2013. Most of these customers were small businesses that owed the bank money on existing loans and were struggling to recover from the effects of the crisis. The FCA commissioned a report, published in 2018, which revealed that the GRG had intentionally exploited these customers, deliberately worsening their situation, despite a professed aim of aiding their financial recovery. The report stressed that accountability for these wrongs should fall to those at the top, but it was up to the FCA to investigate and take action against the individual executives. The GRG scandal again pointed to the fact that the culture of the banks themselves was a root cause. However, it was also revealed that a government agency, the Asset Protection Agency, which is in the Treasury, had influenced the disastrous treatment of RBS customers, even when RBS officials had objected (Verity, 2019). Following the financial crisis, there was widespread anger that those responsible were not punished. There would again be condemnation of regulatory authorities if RBS and GRG executives were to escape punishment. The FCA published the results of its investigation in 2019, and refrained from blaming any individuals for the wrongs committed in the GRG scandal. This failure to apportion blame was interpreted by critics as a 'whitewash' (Makortoff, 2019).

A report on banking culture in the UK, published in 2014, revealed that an 'aggressive sales culture' had taken over from the traditional banking focus of serving clients' needs. This had been a major factor in the spate of bank failures (Spicer et al., 2014: 9). This aggressive culture was dictated from the top by the more recently appointed banking executives whose focus was capital markets – the trading activities that have been likened to the 'casino' side of the business, which was the most profitable. Greed and bad practices had become so engrained that it would take years to bring about the culture change needed to restore to banks a sense of ethical principles and social purpose. Regulation has a role to play, but regulation alone cannot bring about the cultural transformation that is required. The Financial Services (Banking Reform) Act of 2013 (UK legislation, at www.legislation.gov.uk) has gone some way to address the regulatory issues, although the implementation of the different elements of this legislation has taken place over a period of several years.

Under the 2013 legislation, retail banking would be 'ring-fenced', to make certain that the banking activities that serve ordinary customers and small businesses are separated from the investment activities that left the banks overexposed to risks. This structural change, which is to be effected by 2019, is more modest than a full-scale separation of these activities into separate entities. In respect of senior managers, there is a new criminal offence of taking decisions that are so far beneath what would be expected of a reasonable person in that position that they caused a bank to fail. In effect, this provision criminalizes reckless management of a bank, and on conviction, the manager could face seven years in prison. This provision came into force in 2016.

In addition to the legislative reforms, an independent Banking Standards Board (BSB) (www.bankingstandardsboard.org.uk) was set up through an initiative within the banking sector itself, designed to monitor banking standards in practice, with an aim of improving the culture of banking. Membership of the BSB is voluntary, and fifteen UK banks, including some of the largest, have chosen to join. The BSB monitors member banks; it is not a regulator and has no statutory powers. The BSB reports annually on its findings which are published in annual reports. In its report of 2018, findings on employee perceptions regarding accountability present a mixed picture. The BSB found that just 65% of banking employees surveyed believed that their senior leaders take responsibility, especially when things go wrong. Although this is a slight improvement on the previous report's results, it is a disappointingly low percentage in a sector that is under scrutiny over just this issue. When asked whether they see people in their organization avoid responsibility when things go wrong, 35% agreed that they did (BSB, 2018).

The legacy of the UK's light regulatory approach is likely to persist into the future, despite the stronger oversight envisaged by legislators. Culture change derives in large part from the tone set by the senior executives, but must also engage employees, who are the crucial intermediaries in interacting with clients. The direction provided by the board of directors is central to bringing about culture change. Boards focused on maximizing shareholder value are associated with prioritizing short-term profits. In the decade leading up to the financial crisis, boards were highly unlikely to complain about corporate strategy and policies when members saw impressive growth in profits. As the Spicer report found, many in banking say that shareholder demands can act as a barrier to culture change in banking (Spicer et al., 2014: 70). However, it became clear that the profits-above-all model failed, and many shareholders now accept that a more sustainable banking model is better, serving a range of stakeholders. The regulatory reforms, especially the increased liability of senior managers, reinforce this culture change. The Spicer report found that the light-touch regulation that had characterized the more liberal market economies had proved insufficient to curb the market excesses.

How to bring about changes in business culture

The culture of banking sector was partly to blame for the financial crisis of 2008, but there is little evidence of changes in culture from one of aggressive profit-seeking to one of greater accountability to stakeholders and commitment to high ethical standards. Is greater mandatory regulation needed, and why?

The role of monetary policy following the crisis

quantitative easing monetary policy of creating money to purchase assets, mainly government bonds, with the aim of stimulating the economy

In 2008, the US and UK governments focused on the broader issues of monetary policy in a deteriorating economic environment. In co-ordinated policies, the monetary authorities launched a series of measures designed to stimulate economic growth. Interest rates were reduced to levels under 1%, to provide stimulus. This would be good news for borrowers, but not for savers, thereby encouraging households to spend rather than save. The unconventional policy of **quantitative easing** (QE) was introduced in both countries. In the UK, the Bank of England effectively created money electronically. Although this is often referred to as 'printing' money, no new notes are put into circulation. The money created was used to purchase assets, mostly government bonds, but also some corporate bonds, from private financial institutions such as banks and insurance companies. They could then use the money to lend to businesses or buy equities. The aim was to inject money into the financial system that would help to stimulate the economy. One of the results was a rise in equity markets. These measures were intended to be temporary: QE would come to an end when growth resumed in earnest, and the Bank of England would then raise interest rates. This process has been slower than anticipated, but interest rates have been raised gradually in the US – a process that would have repercussions around the world.

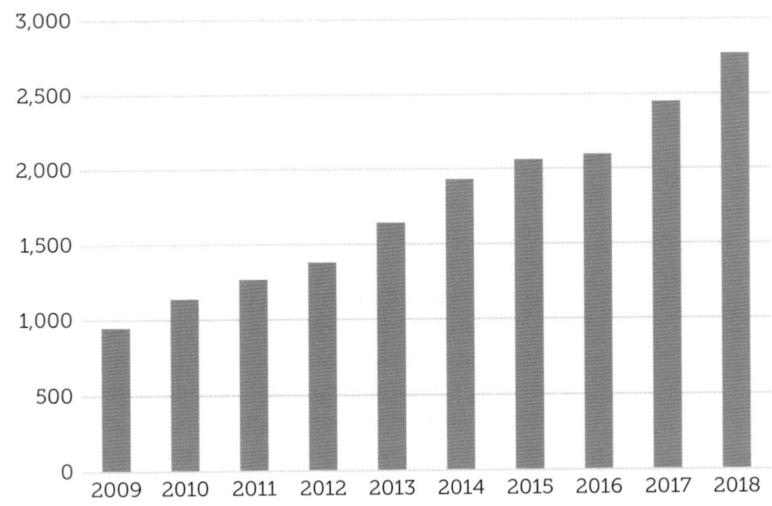

Figure 8.5 **The S&P 500 index: average closing price over ten years**

Source of data: Macro Trends, 10-year daily data, at www.macrotrends.com, accessed 20 October 2018.

The US Federal Reserve tightened monetary policy by raising interest rates very slightly in 2015. Emerging economies had cause to worry about this rise, depending on the proportion of their debt that was denominated in dollars. Unsustainable debt – whether by governments, businesses or individuals – is one of the recurring elements in financial crises. In this respect, the financial crisis that struck the advanced economies in 2007–8 was similar to the crises that have struck emerging economies (Reinhart and Rogoff, 2013). As a monetary policy designed to stimulate

US recovery, QE had injected huge sums of new money into the economy – amounting to over $4 trillion. US central bankers perhaps underestimated the global impacts of this glut of money. Investors unhappy with the low returns from government bonds piled into equities, sending stock markets soaring, as shown in Figure 8.5. The Standard & Poor's 500 Index (S&P 500) features the 500 prominent companies listed on the NYSE and Nasdaq. It is recognized as an authoritative indicator of US stock markets. As the figure shows, an impressive surge in US equities has characterized this post-crisis period.

And the abundance of cheap money encouraged firms and households to take on debt. These trends were global in their effects. At the same time, concerns for national finances were growing, in a context of rising levels of national debt and increased calls on public spending. QE policies saw benefits flowing mainly to investors and businesses. It was hoped that economic recovery would generate new jobs and increase incomes. In reality, employment lagged behind while stock markets soared. Were there clouds on the horizon? Slowing growth in China, combined with high levels of corporate debt, have become a concern.

Markets for corporate control

The globalization of financial flows has facilitated MNEs in their expansion strategies. Cross-border acquisitions and mergers, known generally as 'M&A' activities, forge ahead when markets are buoyant, but can slow down markedly when markets are weak. In this section we look at mergers and acquisitions from a financial perspective, and the impacts of the financial environment on current trends.

Mergers

merger coming together of two or more companies to form a new company

horizontal integration merger or acquisition between two or more companies in the same industry

A **merger** occurs where two or more companies agree to come together to form a new company. For example, GlaxoSmithKline (www.gsk.com) was formed by a merger between Glaxo and SmithKlineBeecham, the latter of which was a product of earlier mergers. Mergers are a feature of consolidation in an industry which has become globalized. Mergers can also be referred to as **horizontal integration**, because the merger takes place between companies in the same industry. There have been waves of consolidation in the pharmaceuticals and chemicals sector, for example, in the late 1990s. In research-intensive sectors, a main rationale for consolidation is the increasing returns to scale in R&D. There are other reasons at work, too. Pharmaceuticals enjoy a lucrative global market. A merged company is in a stronger position in large national markets, having, for example, greater resources for marketing than the two firms would be able to access independently.

If mergers bring together two large players in a market, there are implications for competition policies in the countries where their businesses are carried out. Competition authorities can take an aggressive approach towards a proposed merger if they feel there is a possibility that the combined company will be in a dominant position from which it can act anti-competitively. Competition issues are now a major concern in global M&A strategies. In 2014, Holcim of Switzerland and Lafarge of France, two cement giants, proposed to merge, creating the world's largest cement maker, with a presence in 80 countries. The merger would facilitate cost-cutting efficiencies in the context of a shrinking global demand for building materials. The merger went ahead in 2015, creating a combined company, Lafarge-Holcim, but it involved the selling off of assets in numerous locations, to satisfy competition authorities in the different countries involved. Since then, globalized manufacturers of building materials have attracted attention on ethical grounds. The Mexican company, Cemex, which is one of the world's largest cement companies, announced it would not help to build the wall on the US border with Mexico, in

order to fulfill President Trump's promise of a wall to keep out migrants crossing into the US. It would, however, be willing to provide materials. The same issue arose for LafargeHolcim, which agreed to provide cement for building the wall, but incurred criticism from the French government for doing so.

Acquisitions

A favoured growth strategy of MNEs is the acquisition of a business (see Chapter 2). Acquisitions help to build market share quickly in new markets (discussed in the closing case study). The acquirer often benefits from the strengths of an existing business, shortening the timescale in which the profits from the acquisition start to flow.

In the case of an **acquisition**, or takeover, one company takes over another, often turning the target company into a subsidiary. The predator must pay for the firm it buys, which usually means raising money. How to finance the acquisition is a major concern, which can influence whether the purchase goes through at all. The acquirer can raise fresh capital through a rights issue, involving issuing more shares, to finance the acquisition. Alternatively, it can finance the deal through debt, issuing bonds or seeking loans from banks. The **leveraged buy-out** (LBO), financed through debt, is a favoured strategy of private equity groups. The **private equity fund**, which usually lasts for a fixed term of several years, invests on behalf of wealthy investors. Like hedge funds, private equity groups look for relatively short-term gains. Their strategies include buy-out activities, often buying companies which are then saddled with large debt burdens. Private equity groups would be looking to purchase productive assets cheaply in the event of sell-offs resulting from the Holcim-Lafarge merger.

acquisition investment in which an investor purchases an existing company

leveraged buy-out acquisition of a company's equity by a firm or group of individuals, financed by borrowing

private equity fund investment fund managed on behalf of wealthy investors, which is active in equity markets

Financing a takeover depends in part on the size and status of the target company. If the target company is a private company rather than a public one, the acquirer need only buy out the owners. If the target company is a public one, however, the shareholders become involved. The acquirer will make an offer to the board, which it will put to the shareholders. If the board rejects the offer, the bid becomes 'hostile'. A hostile bidder must win over the owners of the majority of shares in order to succeed. In countries where the norm in corporate governance is to adopt a 'one share, one vote' policy, this can be relatively straightforward, assuming the shareholders find the offer appealing. The UK is such an environment. Shareholders are sometimes offered a combination of cash and shares in the acquiring company. In countries where companies operate weighted voting systems (in which a few dominant shareholders control most of the votes), there is an inbuilt barrier to takeovers. This situation prevails in many continental European countries. By contrast, the takeover of Cadbury of the UK by Kraft of the US in 2009 was facilitated by the ease with which it was possible to accumulate shareholder support in the UK. In 2012, Cadbury was spun off into a new company, Mondelèz, bringing together numerous snack brands (www.mondelezinternational.com). Kraft was itself merged with Heinz in 2015 (www.kraftheinzcompany.com), in a takeover by Brazilian private equity investors and the famous US investor, Warren Buffet. In 2018, the Brazilian investors sold off most of their stake, raising doubts over the long-term prospects for the company, following years of weak financial performance.

Prospects for growth in technology and media industries have led to large takeover deals, as company strategists seek to meet competitive challenges, such as the rise in online and streaming services. Netflix has grown rapidly, posing challenges for traditional broadcasters. AT&T, the US telecommunications giant, has branched out from its traditional telephone business to satellite and cable TV businesses (see the mini case study in Chapter 6). In 2018, it mounted an audacious takeover bid for Time Warner, the media company which owns numerous content providers, including CNN, HBO (maker of *Game of Thrones*), and Warner Brothers

vertical integration acquisition of firms involved in successive stages of a production process

conglomerate large, diversified company in which there is no single identifiable core business

films (maker of *Harry Potter*). This takeover was one of **vertical integration**, whereby a company takes over another that makes products which do not compete with it, but have a strategic fit in successive stages of production (see Chapter 2). This merger, valued at $85 billion, would create a **conglomerate** encompassing telephone, internet, television and entertainment businesses. The US Justice Department launched a lawsuit against the merger on grounds that it would create too dominant a company. The court disagreed, and the deal was approved in the first instance. The Justice Department then appealed against the ruling, and lost again. This approval was taken as a green light to other large US companies that are contemplating a merger.

MINI CASE STUDY

Bayer takes over Monsanto: What are the implications?

Monsanto, the American agribusiness company, is best known for its business in genetically modified organisms (GMOs) used in seeds for crops, together with the Roundup products. Both have been controversial from the environmental perspective. Roundup glyphosate herbicide is gradually being banned in the EU. GMOs and Roundup products are widely used in the US and many areas of the world, but highly restricted in Europe, where they are associated with 'Frankenstein' crops. Apparently undeterred, the German chemical and pharmaceutical giant, Bayer, launched a takeover bid for Monsanto in 2016, worth $66 billion. The price was considered high, indicating that Bayer was prepared to pay more than the company's market value. Bayer already makes products for farms, so there was an element of horizontal integration in the deal. But Bayer is also an important company in healthcare products. Its most famous product is Bayer aspirin, which dates back to 1898. The purchase of Monsanto would make Bayer one of the world's largest seeds and pesticides companies. There has been considerable consolidation in the agribusiness sector, and a number of mergers have taken place, as companies have sought to cut costs and gain efficiencies.

Pesticide risks were among the uncertainties that Bayer had to consider in its takeover of Monsanto.

© Getty Images/EyeEm

The takeover raised competition issues, and needed to be cleared by competition authorities in up to 30 jurisdictions. It was cleared in Brazil, and, after two years of consideration in the US, the Justice Department cleared the deal in 2018, but only after Bayer agreed to sell off much of its US business in vegetable seeds and herbicides to the chemical company, BASF.

The takeover contributes to the concentration of global agribusiness, and boosts the agricultural business of Bayer, but the Monsanto purchase is controversial. Farmers and environmentalists have long highlighted the detriment to biodiversity caused by GMOs. Farmers who use GMO seeds are locked into a technological pathway dependent on the range of Monsanto products, including pesticides and herbicides. For them, the choice of products is likely to be reduced and the range will be streamlined. Moreover, prices are likely to rise. Monsanto faces ongoing class-action lawsuits from

farmers in the US over damage caused by the company's products. There are also US lawsuits brought on behalf of farm labourers for human rights abuse. The payment of any damages under these lawsuits would fall on Bayer. Moreover, such cases can take many years proceeding through the legal system. In a landmark case decided in California, Monsanto was held liable to pay damages to a farmer suffering from cancer (Levin, 2019). Another financial concern is the huge debt that Bayer has incurred in the acquisition of Monsanto.

The name Monsanto will disappear, and Bayer will hope that the notoriety it has evoked will fade away. However, hostility to the type of agrochemical business it represents continues to raise ethical issues. The EU has had in place policies that promote sustainability in farming. Bayer's acquisition of Monsanto could come back to haunt it.

Questions

- Why has Bayer acquired Monsanto?
- Who benefits from the acquisition of Monsanto?

Find out more

See the paper by Ioannis Lianos with Dmitri Katalevsky, 'Merger activity in the factors of production segments of the food value chain: A critical assessment of the Bayer/Monsanto merger', Centre for Law, Economics and Society, Faculty of Law, University College London, CLES Policy Paper series, 2017/1.

Trends in cross-border mergers and acquisitions

Historically, there have been periods of heightened merger activity generally, resulting in the rise of large conglomerates, as happened in the 1960s in the US and Europe. From the 1980s onwards, waves of privatizations in former state-owned industries, such as telecommunications and utilities, have accounted for much acquisition activity, attracting foreign investors, usually global companies keen to expand into new markets.

Rapid growth in emerging markets drove much M&A activity in the early years following 2000. Among the more active acquirers were Indian companies, such as Tata, which acquired British car manufacturers, Jaguar and Land Rover, purchasing the brands from Ford Motor Co. of the US in 2008. The Indian steel magnate, Lakshmi Mittal, achieved one of the more ambitious takeovers of the decade by purchasing European steelmaker, Arcelor, to create ArcelorMittal, now the world's largest steel company. Mexican cement maker, Cemex, has pursued a successful acquisition strategy, becoming a global force in the industry. It became the world's third largest building materials company, behind Holcim (first) and Lafarge (second) with the acquisition of Rinker Group of Australia in 2007. Cemex has purchased some of the cement works that Holcim and Lafarge are being forced to sell. Chinese companies have focused more on acquisitions in the developing regions, pursuing resource-seeking strategies. Figure 8.6 compares the value of M&A activity before and after the financial crisis. As the figure shows, M&A activity fell dramatically following the financial crisis, and has remained lower than pre-crisis levels. Worldwide totals for M&A for 2017 were 33% less than in the same period in 2007. Trends that stand out are the decline in advanced economies as targets of M&A deals, and the rise of emerging economies as favoured targets. In particular, China has strengthened as a destination of mergers and acquisitions. US total M&A deals fell in value 40% and China's total grew nearly 600%.

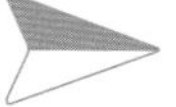

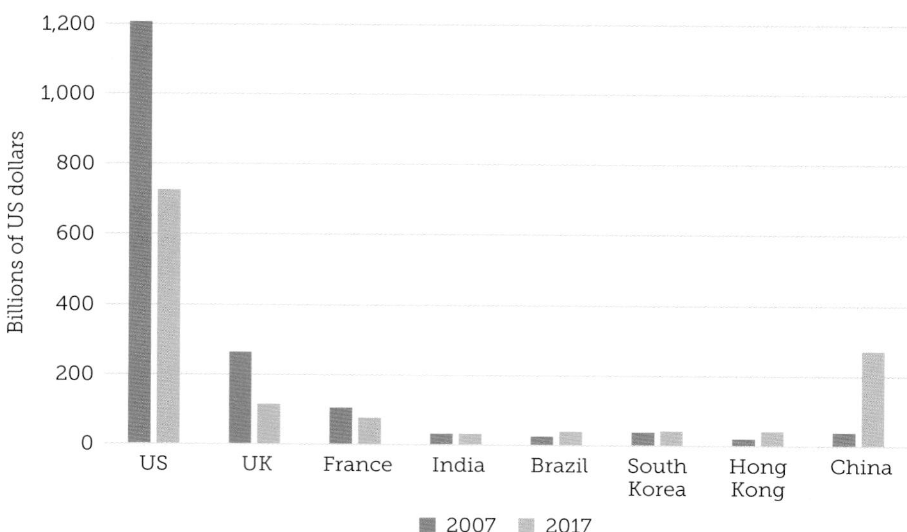

Figure 8.6 Value of M&A deals in selected target economies, 2007 and 2017

Note: Data cover the period 1 January to 9 August in 2007 and 2017.

Source of data: Thomson Reuters, Thomson Reuters M&A (Mergers and Acquisitions) database, *M&A today: A pre-financial crisis comparison*, at www.refinitiv.com, accessed 21 October 2018.

A recent trend has been for large, highly diversified conglomerates to slim down to what is conceived to be their core business. This involves selling off, known as 'divesting', the non-core businesses. The urge to sell weakly performing businesses can arise at any time, but is particularly associated with periods of economic downturn. In extreme cases, companies have felt forced to raise money by selling businesses even though they would have liked to keep them. In other cases, corporate executives conclude that it is best to reduce the number of brands on which to focus. From 2014, P&G (Procter & Gamble) (www.pg.com), the world's largest consumer goods company, has embarked on this strategy, aiming to sell 100 brands in all. In 2015, it sold 43 beauty brands, including Clairol, which it had purchased in 2001, when the company's thoughts were more on expansion. The beauty brands were sold to Coty, the cosmetics company, for $12.5 billion, effectively doubling the size of Coty's existing business. In the years following the financial crisis, competitiveness has been a challenge in the context of the multiplicity of brands that P&G had acquired. It has retained key brands, Pantene and Head & Shoulders, considered to be core brands in the company's hair and skincare portfolio. P&G has also sold the Duracell battery business, and other brands ranging from coffee to soap. For P&G, as for other large companies, re-focusing on core brands aims to restore competitiveness.

Global finance: towards sustainability in global financial markets?

The bedrock of classical economic thinking has been the assumption that a free market, made up of individuals and firms pursuing self-interested goals, is inherently stable. This article of faith has been dislodged by market failures that have led to financial crises. 'Self-regulation' is the seemingly contradictory term often used in connection with market economies, suggesting that if governments refrain from mandatory regulation, markets will function more smoothly, and economic prosperity will be unleashed for the benefit of all. The implication is that the players themselves will behave in responsible ways. But, as we have seen, the financial sector has shown little sense of long-term responsibility for the consequences of their activities on stakeholders. The challenges for firms and

governments are to allow an enterprise culture to flourish, but in an environment in which the emphasis is on sustainability. This entails a sense of broad responsibilities to stakeholders, including employees, customers and whole communities.

Finance as a business has long attracted the exuberant trader, but it has also had a long history of highly responsible and socially focused corporate ownership. Most of the banks highlighted in this chapter have distinguished histories of serving communities, in eras when bankers were respected members of society. Those times have given way to the image of the adrenalin-fuelled trader on the floor of the stock exchange. The evidence of illegal and unethical practices is testimony to the need for change in the culture of financial services generally – not just banking. Regulatory reforms are now under way at national level, but reforms do not take place in a vacuum. A long period of consultation preceded the Banking Reform Act in the UK, and there will be an even longer wait for implementation. The ring-fencing provisions are coming into force over a decade after the banking meltdown. Moreover, these ring-fencing provisions are themselves a compromise: banks are not being required to restructure radically.

Financial services touch every member of society, either directly or indirectly: people need funds for housing, trustworthy banks for their household finances, pensions they can rely on, and many other financial services. The backlash against greedy bankers was widespread in 2008, when executives responsible for bank failures were paid generous rewards while ordinary employees lost their jobs. The new criminal offence of causing a bank to fail is largely in response to this situation. But culture change is as important as regulatory reform – and more difficult to bring about. The bigger challenge for firms and governments is to shift towards a more sustainable and stakeholder-focused business model. In theory, this should be uncontroversial, as the excesses of high-risk strategies had disastrous consequences that saw banking empires crumble. However, the culture of finance in the boom period of the last two decades has tended towards the casino mentality, as trading activities became the big money spinners. The gambler persists in believing with every bet, this could be the big one that could win the jackpot.

Conclusions

Finance is essential to the functioning of whole economies, businesses, governments and households. Without well-managed financial systems, businesses would be fearful of investing, governments would be reluctant to embark on large projects and householders would face uncertainty in how to support families and cope with old age. Stability is perhaps the one feature most prized in the financial environment. But stability has become more elusive as finance has become globalized. Finance was once seen through the lenses of national financial systems, overlaid with co-ordination at international level to maintain exchange rate stability, as in the era of the gold standard. The era of globalization has brought about dramatic changes in the way financial activities take place and in the kinds of transactions involved. While opening up new opportunities, global financial markets have also generated new risks. Innovation and computer technology have been instrumental, facilitating the growth of large financial sectors in countries such as the US and UK. At the same time, some of the most dramatic growth in financial markets has come in emerging markets, now increasingly involved in global capital flows. Global financial markets allow businesses everywhere to aspire to cross-border investing and borrowing. But the stability of these markets has raised questions for all participants. In particular, responsibilities have fallen on international businesses and governments.

Stability at the national level is almost impossible to attain unless there is a stable framework at the international level. The IMF and World Bank date from the late 1940s. The creators of these institutions could not have envisaged the challenges posed by the scale and complexity of today's global financial markets. Nor could they have envisaged the global roles now played by emerging economies, notably China. The creation of an Asian development bank (the AIIB), along the lines of the World Bank, is an indication that international institutions need to recognize these shifts in power. The IMF has been instrumental in co-ordinating the rescue packages of heavily indebted countries, and, despite its shortcomings, it remains the only inter-governmental institution fulfilling this role globally. However, rescue packages are put in place when financial systems have already failed, with the huge damage suffered by societies in the ensuing economic recession. Despite the abundant signs that financial globalization has spun out of control, there is no global regulatory framework analogous to the role played by national regulators. Taming markets to serve the goals of all stakeholders is perhaps not 'mission impossible', but very difficult.

CLOSING CASE STUDY

Argentina on the edge of financial crisis – again

As an emerging market, Argentina in the 1990s enjoyed economic growth, but much of the development was funded by over-indulgence in borrowing in international capital markets. The country accumulated sovereign debt liabilities on a colossal scale, issuing over a hundred types of bonds in numerous currencies and in numerous jurisdictions. Many were issued to institutional investors, and many were issued to private investors, including ordinary Argentinians. The IMF became involved, attempting to structure rescue packages, but these had little success. Unable to meet repayments, Argentina defaulted on nearly $100 billion in sovereign debt in 2001, and the currency was devalued.

Agreements with 93% of the bondholders were achieved in 2005 and 2010, by which they would receive about 30% of the face value, in a restructuring 'haircut'. This could have led to a resolution of the country's debt problems. However, a number of 'holdout' creditors, amounting to about 7% of the total, were outside these agreements. These holdout creditors were hedge funds, led by NML Capital (owned by Elliott Management), which had bought Argentine bonds following the country's financial crisis. These creditors, referred to as 'vulture' funds, mounted numerous legal battles for full payment. These battles extended over the following 12 years, but the holdouts were confident in the strength of their legal case. They obtained numerous awards of damages in the US civil courts, although these were not paid by Argentina's government.

For the owner of this organic market in Argentina, hopes for the future of his business depend on the government continuing to pursue sound economic and financial policies.

For millions of Argentinians, the consequences were disastrous: their savings were wiped out, poverty levels soared, and unemployment was in the range of 20%. The crisis was both economic and social. It also became political. For twelve years, from 2003 to 2015, the country was ruled by presidents from the leftist populist Peronist party, which is descended from the post-Second World War era of extreme nationalism. Under the presidency of the late Nestor Kirchner, from 2003 to 2007, and then under Cristina Fernandez de Kirchner, from 2007 to 2015, Argentina's public finances were in a precarious state, while the demands from bondholders to be repaid dragged on.

The political tide turned with the election in 2015 of a new centre-right president, Mauricio Macri, who promised to settle with the holdout creditors and to restore confidence in the economy. An agreement with four leading holdout hedge funds was reached, worth a total of $4.65 billion. The price was high, but the country could then access international capital markets. Still, he faced an uphill task in the changing global financial climate. The US dollar was strong, and rising US interest rates were in the pipeline, spelling difficulties for emerging markets. Argentina's currency, the peso, was falling perilously, and inflation was climbing. The country was in recession. The agriculture sector had been hard hit in 2018 by the worst drought in decades, while the cost of energy imports was rising. The beleaguered Argentine population was still suffering from 20% unemployment, and one-third of the population was in poverty. In 2018, Mr Macri went back to the IMF to request standby funding of $50 billion, which was soon raised to $56 billion.

The president's strategy of returning to the IMF had the immediate effect of sending people onto the streets to protest. Many Argentinians remained convinced that the IMF was the ultimate cause of their woes in 2001, which many felt left them in a situation similar to being a 'colony'. Years of austerity measures were blamed on the IMF. With a presidential election looming in late 2019, Mr Macri needed, first of all, to stabilize the currency. The backing from the IMF would help in the eyes of global investors. The IMF has appreciated that a gradual approach to reducing the budget deficit is called for. While reducing public spending is unpopular, especially in an election year, he was concerned that he must maintain the confidence of investors by reducing the budget deficit. Investors, for their part, were likely to be worried that if he cannot promote economic recovery, the voters would turn again to a populist government.

While former president, Cristina Fernandez de Kirchner, remained popular among the Peronist supporters, many saw Mr Macri as the best hope for responsible financial governance. When the election took place in October 2019, the Peronist candidate, Mr Fernández, won 48% of the votes, to Mr Macri's 40%. The victory saw the return of Ms Fernández de Kirchner as Vice President. Argentinians have hoped for a new stability and a better future, but the economic woes that had taken their toll on society ultimately led to the political downfall of Mr Macri.

Questions for discussion

- To what extent did Argentina's government mismanage its sovereign debt?
- What has been Mr Macri's policy in attempting to steer an economic recovery?
- What has been the role of the IMF in its most recent intervention in Argentina?
- Why are international investors crucial in Argentina's recovery?

Further reading

See the article by John Paul Rathbone, 'Argentina's fickle fortunes turn sour once again', 12 May 2018, in the *Financial Times*.

Multiple choice questions

Visit www.macmillanihe.com/morrison-gbe-5e to take a quick self-test quiz on what you have read in this chapter.

Review questions

1. How have capital markets become globalized, and what are the implications for listed companies?
2. How can a company benefit from the issuing of bonds, and how do bondholders differ from shareholders?
3. Explain the benefits that were enjoyed under the gold standard system.
4. What were the aims of the Bretton Woods agreement? What were the reasons behind its collapse in the 1970s?
5. What is the 'Washington consensus', and how has it been criticized?
6. Explain the differences between fixed, floating and pegged exchange rates.
7. Summarize the initial aims of the Bretton Woods institutions – the IMF and World Bank. How have their roles evolved since their formation?
8. What are the problems faced by countries issuing sovereign bonds that can lead to national financial crisis?
9. What is the role of hedge funds in global finance?
10. What lessons could be learned from the Asian financial crisis of 1997–98?
11. How did global banking strategies contribute to the collapse of banks that had to be bailed out following the 2008 financial crisis?
12. What regulatory failings contributed to the financial crisis?
13. How did governments respond to the financial crisis?
14. How have banks become sounder since the 2008 financial crisis?
15. Mergers and acquisitions have become increasingly important in the markets for corporate control. What are the driving forces behind them?

Assignments

1. Globalizing capital markets have provided investment opportunities for investors, but these flows of capital have been a source of instability, particularly in countries with vulnerable financial systems. Discuss the extent to which this is an accurate statement, with reference to countries that have experienced sovereign debt crises.
2. Assess the extent to which financial reform has attempted to stabilize national and global financial markets following the global financial crisis, together with the weaknesses in regulatory frameworks that still pose risks of future crises.

Further reading

Cable, V. (2016) *After the Storm: The world economy and Britain's economic future* (Atlantic Books).

Eichengreen, B. (2008) *Globalizing Capital: A history of the international monetary system*, 2nd edition (Princeton: Princeton University Press).

Eichengreen, B. (2015) *Hall of Mirrors: The Great Depression, the great recession, and the uses – and misuses – of history* (Oxford: Oxford University Press).

Kay, J. (2015) *Other People's Money: Masters of the universe or servants of the people?* (Profile Books).

Krugman, P. (2008) *The Return of Depression Economics and the Crisis of 2008* (Harmondsworth: Allen Lane).

Krugman, P. (2013) *End this Depression Now!* (W.W. Norton).

Martin, I. (2014) *Making it Happen: Fred Goodwin, RBS, and the men who blew up the British economy* (Simon & Schuster).

Tooze, A. (2018) *Crashed: How a decade of financial crises changed the world* (Allen Lane).

Turner, A. (2015) *Between Debt and the Devil: Money, credit and fixing global finance* (Princeton: Princeton University Press).

Zestos, G. (2015) *The Global Financial Crisis: From US subprime mortgages to European sovereign debt* (Routledge).

References

BIS (Bank for International Settlements) (2019) BIS total credit statistics, at www.bis.org/statistics

Blundell-Wignall, A. (2011) 'Solving the financial and sovereign debt crisis in Europe', *OECD Journal: Financial Market Trends*, Issue 2: 1–23.

BSB (2018) *BSB Annual Review 2017/2018*, at www.bankingstandardsboard.org.uk

Clift, J. (2003) 'Hearing the dogs bark', *Finance and Development*, December, pp. 8–11 at https://imf.org

Eichengreen, B. (1996) *Globalizing Capital: A history of the international monetary system* (Princeton: Princeton University Press).

EY (2017) Ernst & Young Global Limited, EY Global Trends 2017, at www.ey.com

Glyn, A., Hughes, A., Lipietz, A. and Singh, A. (1992) 'The rise and fall of the Golden Age', in Maglin, S. and Schor, J. (eds) *The Golden Age of Capitalism: Reinterpreting the postwar experience* (Oxford: Clarendon Press), pp. 39–125.

IMF (2015) *Global Financial Stability Report*, April (Washington, DC: IMF).

IMF (2017) *Global Financial Stability Report: Getting the policy mix right*, April, at www.imf.org

Inman, P. (2018) 'FCA investigates allegations of insider trading at Carillion', *The Guardian*, 28 June.

Ito, T. (1996) 'Japan and the Asian economies: A "miracle" in transition', *Brookings Papers on Economic Activity*, Vol. 2: 205-72, at www.brookings.edu

Kapstein, E.B. (1994) *Governing the Global Economy: International finance and the state* (Cambridge, MA: Harvard University Press).

Krugman, P. (1999) *The Return of Depression Economics* (Harmondsworth: Penguin).

Levin, S. (2019) 'Monsanto found liable for California man's cancer and ordered to pay $80 million in damages', *The Guardian*, 27 March.

Makortoff, K. (2019) 'FCA report into RBS called a complete 'whitewash' by critics', *The Guardian*, 13 June.

Molloy, D. (2018) 'End of Greek bailout offers little hope to young', BBC news, 19 August, at www.bbc.co.uk

Neate, R. (2012) 'Jersey puts stop to vulture funds circling its courts', *The Guardian*, 20 November.

Orlik, T., Chen, F., Wan, Q. and Jimenez, J. (2018) 'Sizing up China's debt bubble: Bloomberg Economics', Markets Magazine, 8 February, Bloomberg, at www.bloomberg.com

Reinhart, C. and Rogoff, K. (2013) 'Financial and sovereign debt crises: Some lessons learned and those forgotten', IMF Working Paper, WP13/266, at www.imf.org

Singh, A. (1998) '"Asian capitalism" and the financial crisis', Centre for Economic Policy Analysis Working Paper Series III, No. WP10 (August, 1998), https://mpra.ub.uni-muenchen.de/24937

Spicer, A., Gond, J., Patel, K., Lindley, D., Fleming, P., Mosonyi, S., Benoit, C. and Parker, S. (2014) A report on the culture of British retail banking, New City Agenda and Cass Business School (City University London) at www.newcityagenda.co.uk

Stiglitz, J. (2000) 'The insider', *New Republic*, 222(16/17): 56–60.

Stiglitz, J. (2015) 'Sovereign debt needs international supervision', *The Guardian*, 16 June.

Verity, A. (2019) 'Treasury agency had role in controversial RBS unit GRG', the BBC, 29 January, at www.bbc.co.uk/news

Williamson, J. (2004) 'A short history of the Washington Consensus', Paper given at the conference, 'From the Washington Consensus to a new global governance', Fundación CIDOB, Barcelona, 24–25 September, at www.piie.com/publications/papers/williamson0904-2.pdf

Visit the companion website at www.macmillanihe.com/morrison-gbe-5e **for further learning and teaching resources.**

TECHNOLOGY AND INNOVATION

Chapter outline

This chapter will enable you to

- Appreciate the role of technological change in economic progress
- Gain an insight into the ways in which innovation is generated and diffused in different societies
- Understand the interactions between national systems of innovation and the diffusion of technology
- Assess the roles of governments and business in promoting and exploiting technological innovation
- Appreciate the dynamic links between technological innovation and sustainable development

OPENING CASE STUDY

Automation: opportunities and threats

Much of the history of technological innovation has been in machines that can do tasks traditionally done by human beings. In the nineteenth century, there were instances of people breaking up machines in the textile factories. The protesters, known as the 'Luddites', could not be allowed to hold up technological progress. The name stuck, as did the feeling of helplessness and hostility directed towards machines that displace workers.

Technological advances have been at the heart of economic development. Automation includes artificial intelligence (AI) and robotics. It is because of these advances that productivity is increased, leading to economic growth. These benefits save money for owners. They can invest in technology, which involves capital outlay, but over the long term, they employ fewer people. Examples are the self-driving car and the algorithms that can answer customer service queries. But there are also new jobs being created by new technology. And the people hired are likely to be better skilled and making better salaries than those in the manual jobs that disappeared. Their work is also likely to involve greater responsibility. Hence, one of the basic messages of automation is that of changes in the nature of work. The new jobs require greater education and skills, and are likely to be both more satisfying and more rewarding. But who are the winners and losers?

A study in 2018 in the UK found that in northern formerly industrial areas, one in four jobs is vulnerable to automation, as jobs are replaced by machines (Partington, 2018). Some of these jobs are in warehouse work, retail sales, customer services and back-office administration. Warehouses that fill orders for online retailers are among the types of work likely to become more automated, as are food preparation services. In more affluent parts of the country, jobs are less likely to disappear due to automation. Also, new jobs made possible by technological advances are likely to be more plentiful in the more affluent areas than in the areas where work is mainly low skilled and low paid. In poorer areas, workers are most vulnerable to displacement from automation. A risk, therefore, is that automation is fuelling inequality.

Research across 46 countries indicates that, on average, 15% of jobs could potentially be affected by automation, but there are large variations between countries (McKinsey, 2017). Advanced economies are more likely to be affected than developing ones. In some developing countries, the impact would be slight, but in advanced economies, one-third of work activities could be affected by 2030. The workers affected are likely to be those in low-paid, low-skilled jobs. The implications are that 3% to 14% of the global workforce would need to change occupation. This amounts to between 75 million and 375 million workers. In addition, all workers, including those in jobs that continue to exist, will need to change the way they carry out their tasks. Some of that adaptation requires greater educational and skills development. For the workers affected, there are challenges for the individuals themselves, for governments and for businesses. The ILO is concerned that more than half the global workforce is not entitled to social protection, in the form of unemployment benefits, when jobs disappear. It is also concerned that gender inequality will be exacerbated by the trends towards automation.

Notions of education and skills are being constantly revised to reflect technological changes. This includes addressing the fact that new skills are needed by people in midcareer. The ILO has called on governments to address the issues of retraining and a universal entitlement to lifelong learning. When we think about the introduction of the personal computer, it should be recalled that it has created millions of jobs in the long term, in many different sectors, from call centres to travel agents. The electronic spreadsheet made manual bookkeeping skills obsolete, but the new spreadsheets were cheaper

The automated system that operates in this warehouse is typical of the changes taking plac as machines replace workers in numerous types of employment.

and fast, and facilitated the creation of more jobs as new uses for them evolved.

Historically, changes in the nature of work have taken place over a long period. In the US, the shift from predominantly agricultural to industrial took place over a long period: agriculture was 60% of overall work in 1850, and less than 5% by 1970. Manufacturing employment was 26% of the US workforce in 1960, but less than 10% now. Today's technological shifts are taking place rapidly, and across many sectors of the economy simultaneously.

Questions

- Which jobs are vulnerable to automation?
- What are the impacts of advancing automation in an advanced economy?
- What are the challenges facing governments in dealing with the disappearance of jobs due to automation?

Further reading

See the report by McKinsey Global Institute, 'Jobs lost, jobs gained: Workforce transitions in a time of automation', December 2017, at www.mckinsey.com/featured-insights/future-of-work/jobs-lost-jobs-gained

Introduction

A new medicine, a smartphone, a cleaner fuel — technological innovation holds out the prospect of changes that will improve lives and benefit the environment. Businesses are at the heart of these processes, making technology a key driving force in the world economy. Technological innovation and the capacity to sustain a technological lead are crucial to success in the competitive environment, for both companies and countries. No longer the preserve of engineering and design departments, technology now penetrates every aspect of business, linking R&D, design, production and distribution, in global networks. In particular, advances in computing, telecommunications and transport have resulted in dramatic improvements in all sectors, from car manufacturing to vaccines to fight diseases. Technological changes have impacted on the ways in which organizations operate, both internally and, increasingly, in interdependent global networks. They have also transformed the daily lives of people around the world, as illustrated by the huge rise in internet and mobile phone use globally in the last decade. In 2000, there were about 400 million internet users in the world, mostly in developed countries. That number has risen dramatically, as shown in Figure 9.1. By 2017, there were 3.5 billion people using the internet globally. The steepest rise has been among people in developing countries, and especially among young people. Whereas just 40% of the population overall in developing countries are using the internet, 67% of those between 15 and 24 do so (ITU, 2018). This dramatic rise in internet use has been facilitated largely by the growth in mobile broadband, which is more affordable than fixed broadband. While internet use still lags behind that of developed countries, where 94% of young people use the internet, its rapid expansion among the young is dramatically transforming the social and economic environment. By comparison, those in the least developed countries (LDCs), concentrated in Africa and the Asia Pacific regions, are lagging behind. Only 30% of young people in these countries are online, and this is significantly higher than the 17.5% of the population of these countries as a whole that access the internet. For these poor countries, the falling price of mobile broadband offers the best prospect of further expansion of internet use and the achievement of development goals.

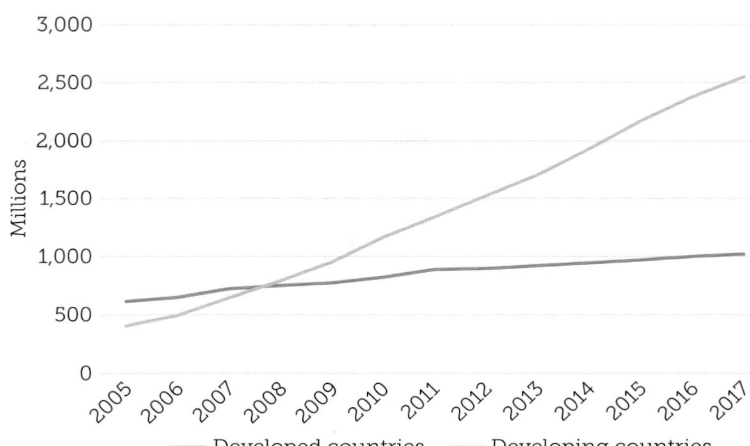

Figure 9.1 **Number of individuals using the internet**

Source of data: ITU, ICT Facts and Figures, Key ICT Indicators: Individuals using the internet, at www.itu.int, accessed 29 October 2018.

'Cutting edge' technology can be an important source of competitive advantage for businesses. There is hardly a company that would not welcome the competitive edge that developing its own new technology can deliver. However, the relationships between knowledge, technological innovation and markets are now recognized to be more complex than was once thought. The growth of international markets has focused attention on differences between national systems of innovation, as well as differences in organizational structures that can promote or inhibit innovation. Social, cultural and political factors in national environments can influence the creation and adoption of technological know-how. Globalization processes have raised these questions particularly in relation to technology transfer and knowledge transfer. Thus, while organizations see the need for a strong focus on technological innovation, they are becoming increasingly aware that technology must be viewed in the context of the wider business environment. In particular, the regulatory environment in many countries impacts on MNE strategies, reminding us that, even in this most globalized of areas, national forces remain potent. For countries, technology is directly relevant to development goals, and governments are keenly aware of the need to nurture education and technological innovation as part of their development agenda. Their hopes are that benefits will flow both to the domestic economy and society. This chapter aims to explain the broad processes of technological innovation and diffusion in the context of national environments, and to assess the changes that result in national economies and societies.

technology methodical application of scientific knowledge for practical purposes

invention product or process which can be described as 'new' in that it makes a significant qualitative leap forward from the state of existing knowledge

Concepts and processes

We begin by defining the basic terms which are used in this chapter. **Technology** can be defined as the methodical application of scientific knowledge to practical purposes. It is a concept at the intersection of learning and doing. Throughout history there have been talented, imaginative individuals, able to assimilate scientific knowledge and transform its principles into practical inventions. An **invention** is a product or process which can be described as 'new', in that it makes a significant qualitative leap forward from the state of existing knowledge. Inventions come under the broad heading of **innovation**. Innovation is a broad term, including improvements which are less radical but offer commercial benefits. The OECD defines innovation as 'the implementation of a new or significantly improved

innovation wide range of activities which seek new and improved products and services, or new ways of carrying out an organization's activities

product (good or service), or process, a new marketing method, or a new organizational method in business practices, workplace organization or external relations' (OECD, 2010: 1). It can be 'new to the firm, new to the market or new to the world' (OECD, 2010: 1). An innovation can be new to the firm, although having been adopted by other firms already. Similarly, it can be new to a particular market, although it already exists in other markets. If an innovation is new to the world, it has not been done before by any firms or in any markets. If a particular innovation proves successful, it is soon taken up by other firms and in other countries, and has the capacity to transform markets. While such transformation is seen as generally beneficial, a salutary lesson to bear in mind is that innovations in financial markets were largely responsible for the boom in global finance that led to the devastating crash of late 2008 (see Chapter 8). Innovations unlock opportunities for improvements, but they also entail risks. Key to harnessing their benefits is the responsible management of the development of new technologies, their applications and the rewards that flow from them.

research and development (R&D) seeking new knowledge and applications which can lead to new and improved products or processes

Research and development (R&D) is a function that covers the broad range of innovations, not just inventions. Larger firms typically have an R&D budget and employ specialist R&D staff. Governments in many countries help to fund R&D, often in conjunction with specific industrial sectors. While many inventions, including patented ones, are never commercially produced, innovations, by definition, are economically valuable. Technical innovation has thus been described as the matching of new technology to a market, or 'the first commercial application or production of a new process or product' (Freeman and Soete, 1997: 201). Inventions can be legally protected by a patent, which gives the inventor (or more often, a company) 'ownership' of its rights of exploitation. An innovation may be a less dramatic step forward, for example, an improvement that speeds up an industrial process. While not patentable, it is nonetheless significant in that it can lead to scale economies.

Scientific knowledge plays a crucial role in the genesis of technical innovation. But it is only the start of the process. As Figure 9.2 depicts, there are many steps along the way from turning a scientific discovery into a workable invention that can be commercially exploited. Figure 9.2, although highly simplified, shows the flow of ideas from science to applied research, and then to development for commercial

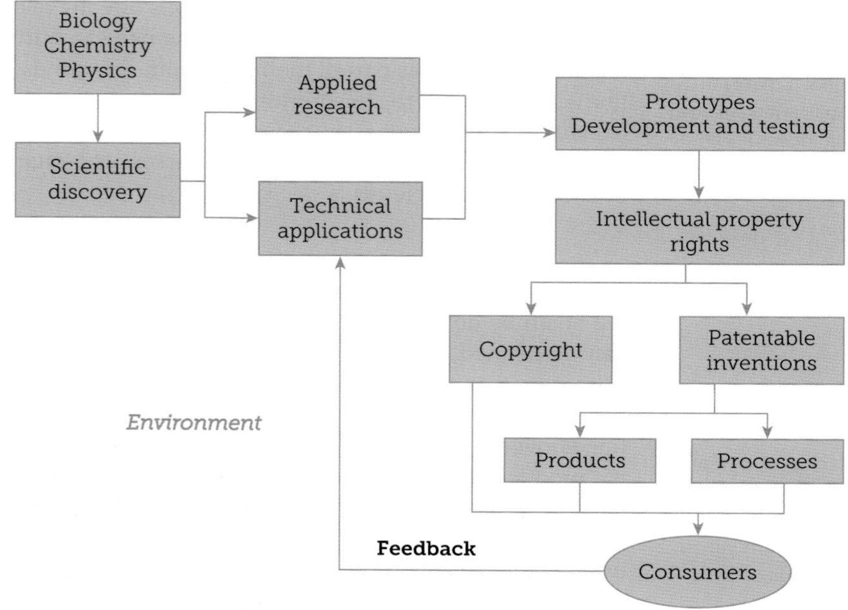

Figure 9.2 **The innovation process for intellectual property**

application. Note that consumer feedback is integrated into the process, helping to generate improved products and further innovation. The successful innovator is not simply a person with a flair for coming up with a great idea. The innovator has a mixture of qualities, including knowledge and awareness of commercial opportunities – and perseverance. The process that appears in Figure 9.2 can take years to unfold, with missteps along the way. National and corporate environments can facilitate the bringing of innovative ideas to commercial fruition (Tellis et al., 2009).

Historians puzzle over two key questions in relation to technology. First, why do science and invention flourish in particular societies during certain eras, but not in others? And secondly, why are some societies with high levels of learning, scientific knowledge, and creative inventors, still not able to convert learning into invention, or invention into technological advancement at the level of society? David Landes points to two examples. Islam, in its golden age, 750–1100, 'produced the world's greatest scientists, yet a flourishing science contributed nothing to the slow advance of technology in Islam' (Landes, 1998). More remarkable were the Chinese, with a long list of inventions, including the wheelbarrow, compass, paper, printing, gunpowder and porcelain. In the twelfth century, the Chinese were using a water-driven machine for spinning hemp, anticipating English spinning machines by some 500 years. Yet such technical progress made little impact on the Chinese economy. The Chinese, it seems, had the scientific knowledge to produce the steam engine, but for some reason that still baffles historians, failed to do it. Summarizing the debate, Landes points to China's lack of 'a free market and institutionalized property rights' as key factors that discouraged initiative (Landes, 1998: 56).

We generally assume that in societies where learning is valued, a high level of science education will lay the foundations for people with technological talent to flourish. Their skills will feed into the country's industries, fostering economic prosperity. However, the relative importance of 'demand-pull' and 'science-push' is debated. Both forces play a role in technological innovation. An emphasis on demand-pull factors, as in product life cycle theory, has been criticized as one-sided. How, it might be asked, can consumers judge a revolutionary new product of which they have no knowledge (Freeman and Soete, 1997: 200)? Many of the early inventors, with their scientific backgrounds, had little idea of the economic potential of their innovations, or of the many possible applications of their technology. Science-push was clearly important among the early inventors and entrepreneurs, who formed new companies in order to exploit their inventions. However, there were instances where demand predominated, and these certainly became more prevalent when innovation became 'routinized' within large firms. Whereas large firms with huge R&D expenditure account for the bulk of innovations, radical innovations often come from small firms. This is particularly the case in the rapidly growing digital sphere, in which the small start-ups are gaining competitive ground.

MINI CASE STUDY

Continuous innovation at Lego

The Danish toy company, Lego, is most famous for its colourful building-block toys. It is also well known for its focus on innovation, which has guided it towards change throughout its history. Innovation at Lego has been broadly conceived, ranging from the toys, the materials, diversification into other products, and theme parks. Not all have been successful, but the company has kept faith with its belief that innovation is at the heart of its culture. Lego has been owned and run as a family business from the outset. When the company was set up in the 1930s, Lego blocks were made of

Children all over the world enjoy building-block toys. A shift from oil-based plastic to sustainable materials is becoming possible through research.

wood. After the Second World War, the owner acquired a plastic injection moulding machine, and he shifted to plastic. The plastic bricks became popular, and Lego expanded into numerous markets. Its toys now sell in 130 countries.

Lego's success, however, inevitably led to competition from firms able to produce similar toys at cheaper prices. For Lego, the challenge was to tap into its innovative capacities to come up with new and better ideas that would excite consumers. It now makes a variety of play materials using new technology. Its latest challenge is to shift to sustainable materials.

The company now aims to shift away from oil-based plastics to more sustainable materials. The new materials can be recycled or plant-based, but they have to be compatible with each other and with the traditional Lego products. The company has invested in a centre for sustainable materials, with the aim of achieving sustainability targets by 2030. Plant-based plastics involve lower emissions, and are being gradually introduced. Plant-based polyethylene is already being substituted for oil-based polyethylene in a number of pieces, but this is only a first step. The greater challenge is to eliminate ABS (acrylonitrile-butadiene-styrene), which is used for the classic bricks. Even when scientists have found a suitable substitute material, the further challenge is to produce it on a scale that can be used in large manufacturing operations. Despite competition from low-cost rivals, Lego saw its profits grow by 4% in 2018. Profits grew at double that rate in the Chinese market, where families were particularly taken by the educational and skill-development dimensions of the company's toys. Lego keeps its ultimate goals of innovation in sustainable materials to the forefront.

Questions

- How has Lego managed to compete effectively in global markets?
- Sum up Lego's approach to innovation.

Find out more

For Lego's background, see the article, 'Innovation almost bankrupted LEGO – until it rebuilt with a better blueprint', Knowledge@Wharton, 18 July 2012, at https://knowledge.wharton.upenn.edu/

Technological innovation and economic change

Technological innovations bring about changes in economies that affect all in a society – some more immediately and directly, others more indirectly. While changes are usually seen as progress towards a better life, as in the case of new medicines, the beneficiaries of changes are not evenly spread. All change involves winners and losers, as this section will show. When new technology replaces the old, financial gains flow to owners of the new technology, giving them the means to seek future innovations

 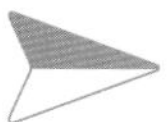

that will sustain their technological lead. Meanwhile, competitors are likely to emerge, posing challenges in terms of products and markets. Ground-breaking innovations can result in changes throughout an economy and improvements in wellbeing throughout society. Throughout history, technological innovations have transformed economic activities, bringing new sources of wealth and better means of satisfying societal needs. The importance of 'improvements in machines' was recognized by Adam Smith at the outset of his *Wealth of Nations*. The twentieth-century theorist, Joseph Schumpeter, introduced probably the most influential theory of technological innovation in his analysis of creative destruction.

Creative destruction: the key to economic growth and wellbeing?

creative destruction process by which new technologies and ways of doing things replace the old, bringing about changes in economic structures

Schumpeter held that the concept of **creative destruction** lies at the heart of capitalism. Creative destruction is associated with processes by which new products, new methods of production, and new forms of organization emerge continuously, 'revolutionizing economic structure, *from within*' (Schumpeter, 1942: 83 [Schumpeter's emphasis]). Stressing this point, he said that this is the 'essential fact' about capitalism (Schumpeter, 1942: 83). Technological innovations give rise to new businesses and new sectors which replace the old, allowing capitalist economies to evolve continuously. Businesses in old sectors dwindle as resources are ploughed into the new sectors and new processes. Schumpeter held that these processes are the engine of economic growth, which is necessary to improve standards of living. The entrepreneur is crucial to these processes, and so, too, is the environment: people with new ideas need the freedom and resources to pursue them.

The key actors in the Industrial Revolution were both talented inventors and entrepreneurs, who often went into production, making (and improving) their own inventions. The cotton-spinning industry, for example, was transformed by the inventions of Arkwright, Hargreaves and Crompton in the late eighteenth century. Richard Arkwright, for one, embodied important qualities as inventor and entrepreneur, protecting and exploiting his patents, with a partner, Jedediah Strutt, providing needed capital for further investment. Large-scale machine production dramatically increased output and brought down the prices of many basic goods, which came within the reach of workers in the new industries. These workers benefited from the steady income of salaried work, which gradually replaced the more precarious traditional work in agriculture and related activities. These were described by Schumpeter as a qualitative change in the nature of work. By contrast, creative destruction negatively affects workers with older skills, and it can blight geographic locations whose economic activity depends on older technology. The effects can be widely ramified. During the Industrial Revolution, the owners of the new industrial enterprises gained in wealth and economic power, posing a threat to existing elites whose wealth and power were based on land ownership. The changes thus unleashed challenges to holders of political power, leading ultimately to democratic reforms. Aristocratic elites lost not just their economic dominance, but also their political power (Acemoglu and Robinson, 2013).

Schumpeter focused especially on the organizational environment of innovation. Writing in 1942, he saw a shift in technical innovation from the individual inventor to the professional R&D researchers within large firms. Large organizations often grow by buying out smaller competing firms, thus leading to market dominance in a sector. The large firm had greater resources to commit to R&D than the individual entrepreneur, thus, in theory, promoting cutting-edge research that will benefit society. But its control over products, supply and prices are not necessarily in the consumer's interest. The large organization is able to price its products so as to reap the financial benefits of its near-monopoly hold on the market. Theoretically, in capitalist markets, competition ensures that firms are always being challenged by creative destruction. But where there is a dominant firm, competitive pressures are greatly reduced. Should we be worried that dominant firms distort markets and do not necessarily serve consumers' interests?

It is questionable whether the large dominant organization is better than small entrepreneurs at promoting economic growth and improvements in quality of life for all in society. Academic researchers have found that large firms with monopolistic advantages have not consistently proved to be the most successful at producing technological advances (Diamond, 2006). Schumpeter held that the large firm will tend towards monopolistic practices. It will become less efficient, less innovative, and more bureaucratic. The large firm often retains its dominance not so much through continuing innovation as through practices that stifle competitors.

Innovation can encompass not just technical, but also marketing and organizational innovations. A company such as Uber is often considered the epitome of creative destruction, as its business model is based on 'digital disruption', challenging traditional taxi businesses with its ride-hailing technology – also challenging the regulatory framework which governs them (Birkinshaw, 2017). While these innovations are welcomed by consumers, Uber's treatment of drivers has raised serious questions in a number of countries on issues of worker status in the gig economy. The taxi transport sector is highly competitive in most markets, and also highly regulated. Uber's founder was undeterred by restrictions in some cities and countries, challenging regulators from the outset (see the case study in Chapter 6). The example of Uber and similar businesses seems to show that disruptive innovations can face numerous hurdles in many markets, but can eventually be integrated into reformed regulatory frameworks, thereby bringing about benefits for consumers.

Technological advances take place at increasingly shorter intervals and product life cycles shorten, making it more difficult for incumbent companies (that is, existing leaders in a sector) to maintain market leadership. Start-up firms in high-tech industries are capable of growing quickly, often supported by venture capital. The 'unicorn' has become a popular term for the most successful of these firms. The unicorn is a private start-up company that has a valuation of $1 billion. These are the firms that are likely to produce the disruptive innovations that challenge the dominant firms. A dominant firm such as Apple is astute in launching innovations in the form of new models and features, but, technologically, these do not constitute creative destruction. Apple did not invent the smartphone. Technological innovations such as the touchscreen were already known. Apple's iPhone is seen as revolutionizing the smartphone – creating, designing and marketing a product to appeal to customers in a variety of markets globally (see the closing case study). It also excelled in its manufacturing model based on outsourced labour in China. It has been highly successful in these respects, growing profits and building its brand.

Competitive markets would naturally see companies on the rise while others are declining. But these American technology giants are dominant market players. As such, they have records of being pursued by regulators for abuses of their dominant market position, notably in the EU, but less in the US, where their power bases are located. US regulators launched antitrust lawsuits against Microsoft in 1998, but the pursuit of antitrust actions slowed in the 2000s under President Bush (see Chapter 6). The Web's inventor, Sir Tim Berners-Lee, is concerned that these companies have acquired too much 'financial and cultural power', and it would be better if they were broken up (Falconbridge and Sandle, 2018). Will market newcomers be able to topple them, or could antitrust actions be launched against them? Compulsory break-up would be unlikely in the current business-friendly legal and political environment of the US, but public opinion could be changing. As we have noted in Chapter 4, the US economy is dominated by big businesses and wealthy owners, who constitute a

powerful elite that enjoys considerable financial control over elections and political policies. The US economy has shown relatively strong growth in the years following the financial crisis, but the rewards have gone mainly to those at the top. The recovery has been marked by a continuing rise in inequality, weak wage growth, more losses in manufacturing jobs, and little improvement in quality of life for low- and middle-income groups in society. Economic growth that is not inclusive stands little chance of being sustainable, posing challenges for political as well as business leaders. This point is now recognized around the world, and especially in countries that are lower down the ladder of economic development.

Technology and economic development

Technological innovation has long been recognized as key to economic development, but the processes involved are more complex than might appear (Lall, 1992). Although development is a broader concept than economic growth, the two are closely related. The technological advances described in the last section took place in developed countries, involving qualitative changes in societies. There is a 'technology gap' between the developed economies and the developing ones, spurring the latter to 'catch up'. This is sometimes depicted in theory as a matter of convergence, but in practice, the process is uneven, combining periods of convergence and divergence. It might seem that this is just a question of the developing country simply replacing old technology with new (Fagerberg and Verspagen, 2002). However, while at firm level, a foreign investor in a developing country might well build a new factory with the latest technology, this need not contribute directly to achieving development goals: the investor is above all looking for cheap labour, and could well move on to another country. Technological changes take place continually in all industries, with considerable variation among industries. Firm-level factors and national environmental factors come into play. Moreover, technology does not stand still. It is constantly changing, so catching up is not simply a matter of bridging the gap in a simplistic way. Development is about qualitative changes in economies and societies (Fagerberg and Verspagen, 2002). The ways in which technology drives these processes are both direct and indirect. Firms in developing countries can draw on technology from both foreign and local firms. They are subject to both internal and external factors, public and private, as they evolve firm-level technology strategies (Lall, 1992). The process is incremental, dependent on a number of factors, including social systems, institutions and government interventions. Non-economic as well as economic factors play a part. This means that technological catch-up is more challenging than might appear, as it involves institutional contributors as well as technological capabilities.

Foreign direct investment (FDI) has brought about the globalization of production, but the diffusion of technology does not necessarily follow. Technology transfer from FDI has brought benefits in some national environments, but absorption depends on numerous factors, including technological and scientific capabilities in the host country. Industrialization driven by FDI can boost economic growth, as the experience of China shows. China's development model was based on FDI investment in mass manufacturing for export markets. The political leadership has faced greater challenges in fostering goals of nurturing domestic technological innovation, which would contribute to more sustainable development. While technological innovation is recognized as a driver of economic growth, its contribution to development goals is more elusive. As we will see, governments look to technological innovation to contribute to improvements in society, including more and better jobs and higher living standards. These broader aims do not flow automatically, but depend on a range of national and firm-level contexts.

Technology catch-up: the elusive target

What are the disadvantages faced by developing countries in technological catch-up with advanced countries? In your view, have these disadvantages to some extent been alleviated in the digital era and with the rapid pace of globalization?

National systems of innovation

First Britain, then the US, and later, Japan and Germany, have all been able to achieve high levels of technological innovation coupled with economic growth. It has long been recognized that the national environment is important in stimulating or inhibiting innovation. Writing in 1841, Friedrich List in his *National System of Political Economy*, addressed ways in which Germany could catch up with England. Significantly, he emphasized the importance of social and cultural factors, and also government policy, for example, in the protection of infant industries and the setting up of technical training institutes (Archibugi and Michie, 1997). Indeed, List anticipated many of the aspects of the national environment which were later to be grouped together under the term 'national system of innovation'. There is a considerable body of literature on national systems, their different approaches to innovation and how they interact (see Tellis et al., 2009).

innovation system the structures and institutions by which a country's innovation activities are encouraged and facilitated, both directly and indirectly

A national **innovation system** is broadly defined as the structures and institutions by which a country's innovation activities are encouraged and facilitated, both directly and indirectly. The term 'system' might imply that these institutions and policies are co-ordinated, when in fact levels of co-ordination vary between countries. The word 'network' has been used to describe the relevant linkages between companies, disciplines and institutions (Patel and Pavitt, 2000). Summing up these threads, Mowery and Oxley define a national innovation system as 'the network of public and private institutions within an economy that fund and perform R&D, translate the results of R&D into commercial innovations and effect the diffusion of new technologies' (Mowery and Oxley, 1997: 154).

A national innovation system consists of both institutions and interactions. Educational and government inputs are institutional in nature, while collaboration, scientific research and technology networking are more interactive. In practice, these dimensions are mutually reinforcing; for example, research institutions facilitate collaborations between education and industry.

Key aspects of a national innovation system

Five key aspects of a national innovation system can be highlighted (Archibugi and Michie, 1997):

Education and training

Achieving high rates of participation in education at all levels, from primary through to higher education, helps to promote economic growth, but there is no simple correlation. Educational attainment is one of the main ways in which citizens are able to acquire higher-skilled employment that offers more scope for personal development and satisfaction than the lower-skilled jobs that largely characterize developing economies. Governments of developing economies are also keen to see investment in education, whether public or private-sector funded, in order to raise the level of technology and innovative capacity in the country. In general, public spending on education in developed countries is much higher than in developing countries. In Denmark and Norway, spending on education is over 7% of GDP. These percentages are consistent with the high levels of social spending that are associ-

ated with Scandinavian countries. Other advanced economies tend to spend closer to 5% of GDP on education, but commitment to funding of education differs over time. Public spending priorities are continuously reviewed and spending on education is likely to decline in periods when public spending is cut back. In the US and UK, the share of national wealth spent on education has decreased since 2010, in the aftermath of the financial crisis. Education spending in the UK was 5.75% of GDP in 2010, but by 2018, had declined by 1.5% to 4.27%.

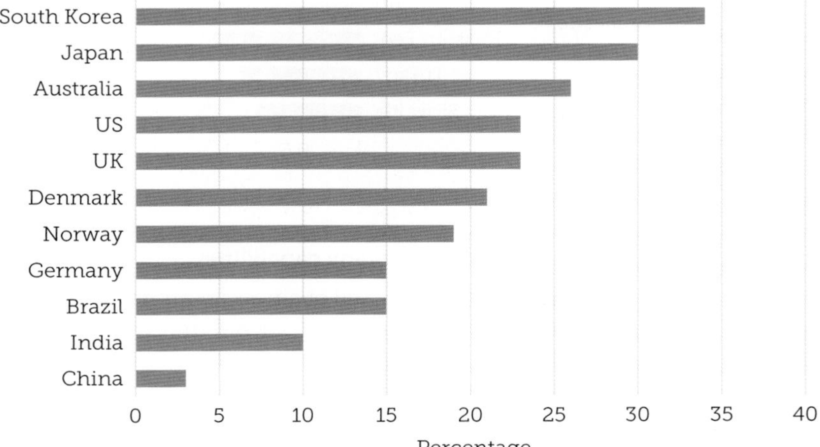

Figure 9.3 **Percentage of people aged 25 to 64 who have bachelor degrees or the equivalent**

Source of data: OECD, Education at a Glance 2018, OECD Indicators, Table A1.1, at www.oecd.org, accessed 9 November 2018.

Spending on education includes every level from pre-primary education through to secondary and tertiary education. Higher education is especially relevant for enhancing domestic technological capacity and promoting innovation. China and India are rapidly expanding their education systems, especially university education. China now has nearly 3,000 colleges and universities, which represents a rise of nearly a thousand since 2006. Figure 9.3 shows the percentage of people in the age group 25 to 64 who have a bachelor degree or its equivalent as their highest level of attainment. As the figure shows, South Korea and Japan have excelled. In South Korea particularly, this reflects the importance of education in national cultural values. South Korea has one of the world's most highly educated populations. Furthermore, its education system is strong in science and technology, reflecting the country's view that they are key to competitive advantage.

China is now attempting to catch up. Its political leaders have taken note of the examples of South Korea and Japan, both of which successfully linked greater educational participation with development goals. Only about 3% of Chinese people have degrees. Similarly, in India, which has sought to promote higher education in technological specialisms, only 10% of the population have degrees. Both countries are increasing capacity in their colleges and universities. In 2008, 28.6% of Chinese people aged 18 to 22 were in higher education. This had risen to 51% by 2017 (UNESCO, 2018). Chinese and Indian students have also sought qualifications from universities in the US, where science and technology are among their favoured subjects. Students from China and India constituted over half of the million international students in the US in 2015. Over 360,000 of these students were Chinese – a total that had grown from just 60,000 in 2000. But since 2017, there has been a decline in applicants from overseas, possibly indicating a concern that they might no longer receive as warm a welcome in the US, given a perceived rise in anti-immigration sentiment.

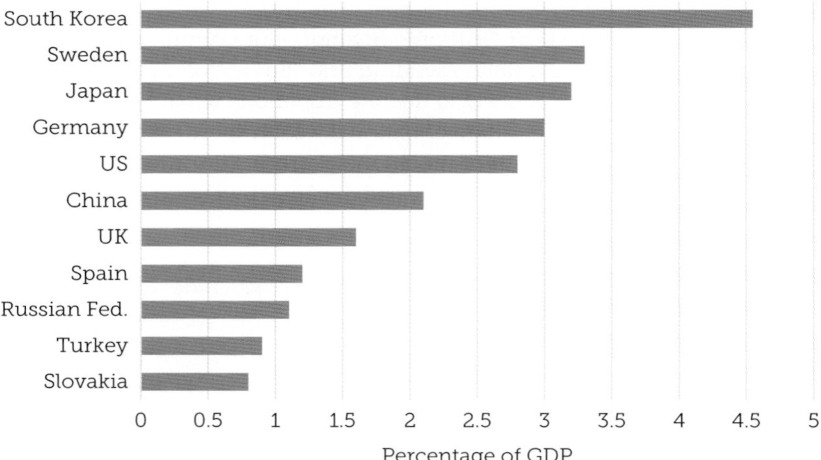

Figure 9.4 **Gross domestic expenditure on R&D as a percentage of GDP, 2017**

Source of data: OECD.stat, Main Science and Technology Indicators, at https://stats.oecd.org, accessed 13 July 2019.

Science and technology capabilities

National authorities and business enterprises take decisions on what types of R&D to fund and how to meet the expenditure. The bulk of funding for R&D is provided by businesses rather than governments. In general, about 10% of R&D funding on average is provided by governments. Expenditure on R&D can be expressed as a percentage of GDP, providing an indication of the country's technological ambitions. These are shown in Figure 9.4. South Korea stands out for spending 4.5%, while Sweden and Japan are also impressive, devoting 3.3% of GDP to R&D. The percentages for the US (2.8%) and China (2.12%), which are much larger economies, are rather lower. However, in terms of actual expenditure, these countries are the largest spenders by far, as shown in Figure 9.5. The US has long been in this pre-eminent position, but is now challenged by China, which has rapidly increased its R&D spending. In 2001, China spent just $50 billion on R&D. This had risen to over $250 billion by 2012, and in 2017, its spending on R&D reached $495 billion. China's spending now greatly exceeds that of Japan, South Korea and Germany.

Competition between China and the US is increasingly shaping the future of the technological landscape. China's rise has coincided with its leaders' ambitions for global prominence in other spheres, including political and military power. As an

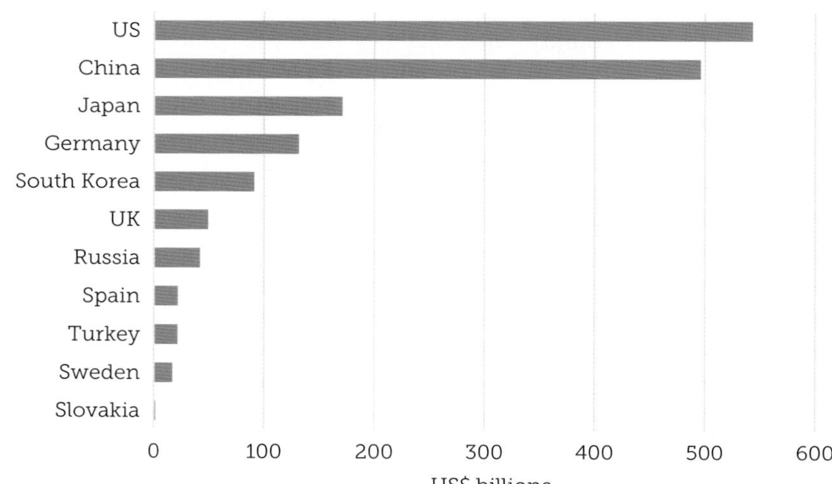

Figure 9.5 **Gross domestic expenditure on R&D, 2017**

Source of data: OECD.stat, Main Science and Technology Indicators, at https://stats.oecd.org, accessed 13 July 2019.

indication of its progress, China is marching ahead in investment in 5G wireless technology, which opens the door to a wide range of technological connectivity (see case study on Huawei in Chapter 7). These advances extend beyond smartphones to a world of machines and devices that can be reached by network effects. The potential economic benefits from this expansion of 5G connectivity would bestow significant competitive advantage over other countries. In this respect, China has taken a great leap forward in building communications infrastructure, representing huge capital investment. It is estimated that its leading company in the sector, China Tower, added 460 sites per day to its network in 2017. By comparison, the US tower companies added fewer sites in the previous three years than China Tower added in three months (Deloitte, 2018). US technology companies would have cause to be concerned that, despite the country's continued leadership in R&D spending, they are not as yet matching this level of investment.

Industrial structure

Large-scale business investment in R&D is borne mainly by a country's large firms, as they have more resources and greater ability to shoulder risks than smaller firms. Of course, simply spending a lot of money on R&D does not ensure successful innovation. Interfirm rivalry and competition in home markets can lead to 'imitative' increases in R&D in particular product fields (Patel and Pavitt, 1994). Small firms can play a role, as has been the case in high-technology areas. The small start-up is flexible and less bureaucratic than the large established firm, providing a fertile environment for innovation. Smaller, younger companies tend to grow more quickly, and can spur technological change. Where industrial structures have been dominated by large firms, as in the EU, the promotion of R&D-intensive SMEs can help to revitalize innovation and improve competitiveness. In the EU, large firms (that is, firms with 250 or more employees) are the source of about four-fifths of business R&D expenditure. SMEs (firms with 10 to 249 employees) represent only one-fifth of R&D expenditure (European Commission, 2018: 11). The EU's Innovation Scoreboard of 2018 has reported that innovation performance is gradually improving in the EU. Notably, improvements in an innovation-friendly environment have helped to encourage start-ups. Improvements in broadband penetration in EU countries have been a factor, as has the rise in venture capital for funding SMEs. The EU budget for 2021–2027 includes a commitment of €100 billion for innovation investment, via its programme, Horizon Europe.

Science and technology strengths and weaknesses

Countries where manufacturing is a large share of GDP are more likely to have a strong focus on innovation, as are countries with strengths in high-technology activities. Countries differ in their areas of specialization and in the intensity of R&D activities. Electrical machinery is the top field for patent applications from China, Japan and South Korea. For US applications, the top field is computer technology; for German applications, it is transport. In the EU, 85% of R&D expenditure is in medium–high- and high-tech sectors. Where a country pursues a particular technological strength in an area of growing global importance, it stands to gain competitive advantage. Japan's intense investment in R&D in the fast-growing consumer electronics industry in the 1970s and 80s is an example. Japanese electronics firms overtook both European and US firms in taking out patents, both at home and in the US (Freeman, 1997). Many of Japan's technology SMEs remain global leaders in specialized areas of technology. India has targeted computing and high-tech research as areas of competitive advantage, and its government has fostered the growth in educational institutions which excel in these areas.

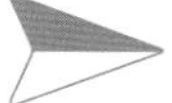

Much of a country's R&D spending goes on the salaries of researchers and support staff. The number of active researchers in a country generally reflects its overall spending on R&D. This can be measured as 'researchers per million inhabitants', an indicator of the density of research activity. A selection of countries is shown in Figure 9.6. The leading countries are South Korea, Sweden and Japan. There are some anomalies. The number of active researchers in employment in China still lags behind leading developed economies. However, as with R&D spending overall, China appears in a different light when we look at overall numbers. Its total of 1.69 million researchers are more numerous than those of any other country, including the US, which is home to 1.38 million overall. Japan is the third largest in absolute terms, with 0.67 million (UNESCO, 2018).

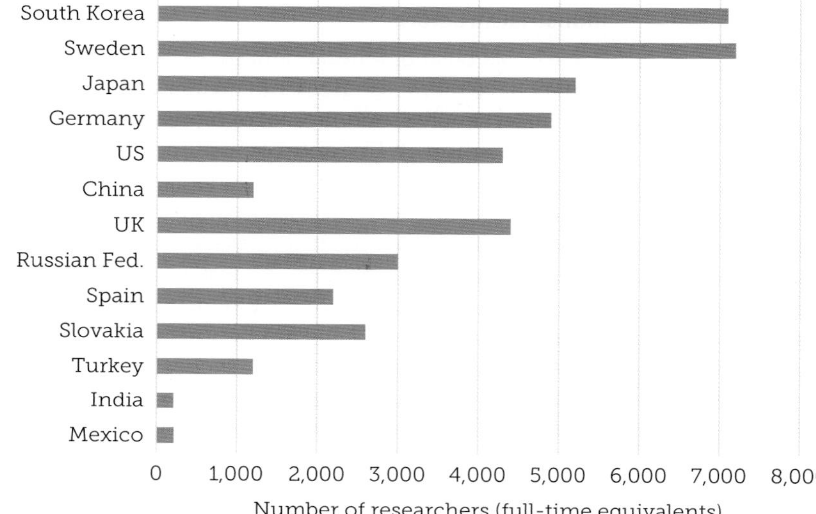

Figure 9.6 **Researchers per million inhabitants**

Source of data: UNESCO Institute of Statistics (2018), R&D data release, 28 June, at http://data.uis.unesco.org, accessed 8 November 2018.

Interactions within the innovation system

Interactions, whether formal co-ordination or informal networking, contribute to innovation activities within a country, and to their diffusion. Government guidance can be crucial in stimulating some industries to innovate – and discouraging others. The co-ordinating role of Japan's Ministry of International Trade and Industry is often cited for its importance in the country's economic development. Strong state guidance in the Soviet Union, by contrast, was much less successful. There, separate research institutes for each industry sector had only weak links with each other. The Soviet system's concentration of R&D expenditure on military and space projects, coupled with the rigid command economy, left little scope for civilian innovation links to develop (Freeman, 1997). A more recent trend globally has been growing interaction between academic researchers and firms, as scientific research is playing a more important role in the development of many new technologies, such as life sciences.

National innovation systems in context

There is no one model of innovation system that can be said to be superior in generating and diffusing technological innovation. While it is clear that technological change through innovation is linked to economic growth, countries display a good deal of diversity in their national innovation systems. Simple quantitative comparisons

of R&D expenditure tell only a partial story. Social, cultural and historical differences have an influence on the ways in which learning, scientific curiosity, and entrepreneurial flair are allowed to flourish in national environments. Government initiatives can be influential. Huge investment in industrial R&D in Germany and Japan in the post-war period was crucial in efforts towards economic catch-up.

The ability to assimilate and imitate innovations from elsewhere as the basis of further local innovative developments has been a particular feature of Asian economic development. This process of technology transfer (introduced in Chapter 2) holds out to all nations the possibility of benefiting from innovation. In theory, a country can benefit from the technology of foreign investors through technology transfer. However, technical change has proceeded unevenly among countries and among individual companies. Adaptation of technology and use in local environments is still dependent on diverse national systems. Why are certain countries and certain firms innovative when others are not? Tellis et al. (2009) highlight four factors:

- An educated and skilled workforce, especially in science and technology, at national and firm levels
- The availability of capital and financial resources generally, within firms and within the country; includes banks, stock markets and private investors
- The role of government and the national innovation system; includes protection of intellectual property and encouragement of collaboration between academic researchers and industry
- The role of culture, including national culture and corporate culture in particular firms

Of the four factors, Tellis et al. see convergence between developed and developing countries in the first three: skilled workers, capital and government policies. These developments are attributable largely to globalization. They include research links in integrated supply chains, global financial markets and the tendency for governments to use policies such as R&D tax incentives to gain national competitive advantage. Culture remains more rooted in national environments, and is a crucial factor in how a country's innovation system functions in practice. For example, relevant aspects of corporate culture that foster innovation include a willingness to take risks and to sacrifice profits flowing from established products in order to develop new ones. Also important is the empowerment of creative individuals within firms. This is more of a challenge in large companies. It is not difficult to see why policy-makers stress the fostering of SMEs as a route towards enhancing a country's innovative capacity.

How can business culture foster innovation?

What aspects of culture foster innovation? In which countries at present do you feel there is the best cultural environment for encouraging innovation, and why?

Patents and other intellectual property (IP) rights

Patents are often referred to as a type of 'industrial' property, and patent activity is an indicator of levels of innovation. We should be cautious, though, not to read too much into patent statistics, as many innovations, such as informal and incremental improvements, fall outside patent activity. That said, patent statistics are an often-cited barometer of innovative activities.

Protection of property which exists in inventions and other products of human intellect has been the subject of heated policy debates from the days of the Industrial Revolution through to the present. Many would argue that technology should be freely available for anyone anywhere to use. Governments in industrialized countries, on the other hand, have legal frameworks for protecting intellectual property, in the belief that only by doing so will the incentive be provided for people to devote time and resources to innovation. Emerging economies are now following this example, with legal frameworks for the protection of IP.

From research and design through to testing, a new product can take many years before it reaches consumers. Companies, it is felt, would be unwilling to commit resources in the absence of a system for granting exclusive rights over the product for a reasonable period of time. It is acknowledged that limited monopolies are created, restricting competition, but is this a price that must be paid to ensure technical progress continues? Many in developing countries argue that they are effectively frozen out by these policies because of the concentration of intellectual property ownership in the industrialized countries. It is also the case that IP rights in developing countries tend to be weakly enforced, deterring innovators from seeking patents in the first place. In this section, we look at the nature of IP rights and how they come into being.

What is a patentable invention?

patentable invention a new product or process which can be applied industrially

The **patentable invention** is a new product or process which can be applied industrially. These basic requirements are similar across most countries, with some variations. In Europe, the main source of law is the European Patent Convention 1973 (EPC), which member states have incorporated into national law. (This has been adopted by EU states, plus Switzerland, Monaco and Liechtenstein.) A European Patent Office was set up under the convention. In the UK, the relevant law is the Patents Act 1977. US patent law requires that the invention be 'useful', rather than 'industrially applicable', as required by the EPC. The requirement that the invention must be an industrial product or process rules out discoveries, scientific theories, and mathematical methods, as they relate to knowledge and have no technical effect. Mere ideas or suggestions are also excluded, as a complete description of the invention must be submitted with the patent application. Moreover, the invention must not have been disclosed prior to the patent application: once disclosed, it becomes 'prior art' and can no longer be said to be new.

Many inventions are not entirely new products, but improvements on existing ones. The threshold for a 'new' product differs from country to country. Where the threshold is low, it is possible for a pharmaceutical company to obtain a new patent on a medicine that is, in effect, a continuation of the previous patent. An example would be changing the dosage to one-a-week from one-a-day. Known as 'evergreening', this can be a means of effectively extending the life of a patented medicine (see the closing case study in Chapter 11). While we tend to think of only the most formal inventions as patentable, in fact the scope of potentially patentable inventions is expanding all the time, extending to software, micro-organisms, and business methods.

Computer software and business methods are both patentable in the US, but only to a limited extent in Europe. In Europe a software-based invention is patentable if it has a 'technical effect'. This means that a new programme which affects how the computer operates is patentable, whereas a computer game is not. The game, like most software, is protected by copyright. The expansion of software patents has been a trend in the US since they were recognized as patentable by the Supreme Court in 1981. In the US, a 'way of doing business' is patentable. Amazon, the online retailer, was able to patent its 'one-click' shopping method in 1999. Since then, there

has been a growth in business methods patents in the US, mainly in areas where new technology changes processes. However, in 2014, a judgment of the Supreme Court imposed a stricter interpretation of the law, disallowing a patent that simply used a computer for updating records (Preston, 2014). In a unanimous decision, the justices held that to be eligible for a patent, the process would need to involve a more substantial role for the computer. The many business process patents that have been granted on a rather looser interpretation of the law in the last two decades are not invalidated, but following this decision, future business methods patent applications will probably face a stricter test for eligibility.

MINI CASE STUDY

AbbVie and the pipeline for pharmaceutical patents

AbbVie was formed as a spin-off by US pharmaceutical company, Abbott Laboratories, in 2012. At that time, Abbott's best-selling drug, Humira, was approaching the end of its patent life. The drug is particularly effective for sufferers from rheumatoid arthritis. Abbott feared that the diminishing sales of Humira would make a sizeable dent in their profits, and there were not enough new drugs in the pipeline to compensate. The expiry of the Humira patent was sure to unleash a wave of generic manufacturers, who would copy the drug and sell it for much less than AbbVie. But six years on, events have turned out to be more favourable to AbbVie than had been expected. AbbVie has been able to apply for continuation patents in the US, which have prolonged their patent protection.

Humira's European patent ran out in 2018, and sales were expected to fall by about a quarter by 2019. Generic makers such as Mylan and Sandoz launched generic versions, at prices between 10% and 80% less than AbbVie's Humira. Sales outside the US would therefore fall, but many patients will still prefer the original, as generic copies are not exact replicas. Generic drugs are biosimilars, and in these cases, they might not take away much market share from the original patented drug, even though the latter is much more expensive. In the US, the patent on Humira will not expire until 2023. And there, the price of Humira has risen substantially since the company was floated off. Revenues have risen substantially, and they continue to rise. One dose of Humira at $3,000 costs three times what it did ten years ago. Healthcare funders, whether national health services or private, look carefully at costs, and AbbVie's prices look steep.

AbbVie's shares lost a fifth of their value in 2018, even though the sales of Humira were stable. Going forward, a lawsuit in California could be damaging, as it alleges the company paid medical practitioners to favour their products when prescribing, and other malpractices. AbbVie's medicines in the pipeline show promise, with five medicines in the area of immune disease treatment showing good prospects. One of these is a treatment for Crohn's disease, which could prove to be helpful for many

Patients trust the doctor to provide the best professional advice, but what about the power of the pharmaceutical companies in healthcare provision?

sufferers. Shareholders therefore have reason to be relatively happy that AbbVie will continue to gain from its new drugs, but they remain fretful about the ultimate fall in sales of Humira.

Questions

- Why do generic manufacturers pose a threat to AbbVie?
- How is AbbVie confronting the issues of declining sales of Humira?

Find out more

See the article, 'Humira biosimilars launch in Europe, testing AbbVie', by Ned Pagliarulo, 19 October 2018, in BioPharma Dive, at www.biopharmadive.com. This article provides insight into the divergent patent practices in the US and EU.

Patent rights in practice

patent type of intellectual property which gives its owner an exclusive right for a limited period to exploit the invention, to license others to use it, and to stop all unauthorized exploitation of the invention

The **patent** gives its owner an exclusive right for a limited period, to exploit the invention, to license others to use it, and to stop all unauthorized exploitation of the invention. Eighty per cent of patentholders are companies, not the actual inventors. The duration of a patent in the UK is four years, renewable up to 20 years. Renewal fees become steeper over time, and most inventions have been superseded by new technology long before the 20 years have expired. In the US, the normal duration is 20 years at the outset, with 'maintenance' fees payable at intervals. Any patentholder of a commercially valuable patent faces the prospect of legal challenges to the patent, sometimes by companies that exist simply for this purpose. Defending legal challenges is expensive, but probably outweighed by the earnings potential of the patent. When the patent on a drug has expired, 'generic' manufacturers are able to compete, but there are still profits to be made for the patentholder, as the original brand has a marketing advantage, especially in markets where counterfeit drugs are a problem. Being able to license the technology to other manufacturers entitles the patentholder to collect royalty fees agreed with the licensee. Much foreign direct investment relies on the licensing of technology. A patent may be sold outright ('assigned') to someone else, who is then entitled to exploit it commercially. In common with other IP rights, 'exhaustion of rights' applies to patents. Under this principle, once the patentholder has consented to the marketing of the product in specific countries, they cannot prevent 'parallel imports', that is, importation of the product from another country, usually a lower-cost one. A consequence is that the owner of a patent for a product which is sold in a number of countries might find it difficult to maintain price differentials between them.

For an inventor, the process of applying for a patent can be complicated, long and expensive. The process of patent office 'examination' of a patent application typically takes from two to four years. The help of expert professionals is almost always needed, stacking the odds against the individual inventor-entrepreneur. The simplest route for the inventor is to apply for a patent in his or her home country, but in that case, the patent granted will cover only that country, which most nowadays would find inadequate. There is no such thing as a global patent! For the multinational company with global markets, there are means available to alleviate the need to make separate applications in every country.

European Patent Office (EPO) patent office of the EU

The **European Patent Office** (EPO) (www.epo.org) in Munich was established by the European Patent Convention of 1977. A patent application to the EPO allows the applicant to designate particular countries, typically eight, in which the

patent will be valid. However, the grant is a bundle of individual national patents, each of which must be translated into the national language, and enforced in national courts. The expense of translation into several languages adds considerably to the overall expense, making European patents several times more expensive than US or Japanese patents. For many years, businesses have pressed the European Commission for a simplified system which would allow a single application submitted in one language, making the process much more efficient and cheaper. This 'unitary patent', which would be valid in 26 participating EU member states, is now close to being a reality (the two non-participating states are Croatia and Spain). Regulations governing the unitary patent took effect in 2013, and the final piece of the process will be the establishment of a Unified Patent Court (UPC) under the Unified Patent Court Agreement of 2013. The court is expected to be in place by 2019. The UPC will have jurisdiction over the new unitary patents and the older European patents described above. This new unified legal framework will bring an end to the need to litigate in a multiplicity of different national systems of member states. Henceforth, litigation should be simpler, quicker and less expensive for the parties involved in litigation on validity and infringement of patents.

An alternative route is offered by the Patent Co-operation Treaty (PCT) procedure, which covers over 100 countries. Under the PCT, the applicant makes one application, to a regional office, and the process is divided into an 'international' phase and a 'national' phase. For the applicant with a global market in mind, there are considerable savings to be made in comparison with multiple individual country applications. The process is overseen by the World Intellectual Property Organization (WIPO) (www.wipo.int) in Geneva.

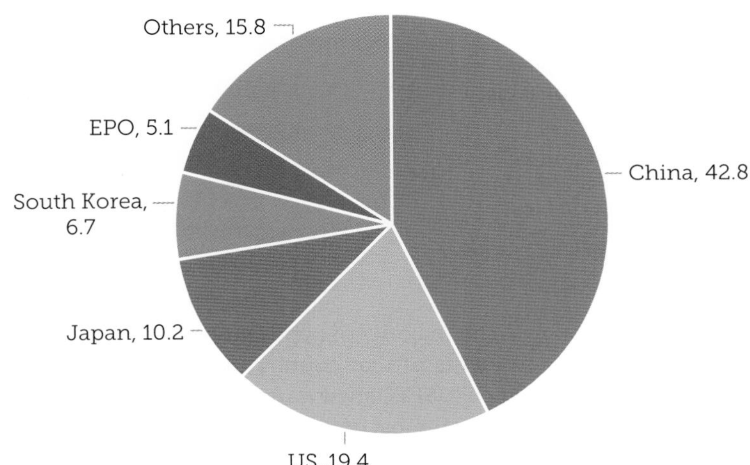

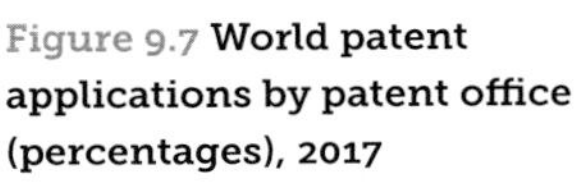

Figure 9.7 World patent applications by patent office (percentages), 2017

Notes: Each patent office's percentage of the world total number of applications = 3,127,900
EPO = European Patent Office

Source: WIPO (World Intellectual Property Organization) (2018) *WIPO IP Facts and Figures 2017*, p. 11, at www.wipo.int, accessed 13 November 2018.

As Figure 9.7 shows, China is now the world leader in patent applications. Its applications amounted to nearly 1.3 million. This is double the number of applications it made in 2012. Asian patent offices received nearly 70% of all patent applications made in the world in 2016. A note of caution in respect to China's recent surge is called for, as increased numbers of applications do not necessarily indicate a substantial rise in the quality of patent activity (Santacreu and Zhu, 2018).

A number of factors help to explain China's rise in patent activity. China subsidizes patent applications, and this funding has a tendency to encourage applicants who might otherwise not have come forward. Most applicants are Chinese residents, and most of their applications are for low-technology patents, known as 'utility models', rather than higher-technological inventions. In addition, China has a large failure rate: only 23.44% of applications are granted, whereas the equivalent percentage in South Korea is 45.5% (Santacreu and Zhu, 2018). Only about 4% of Chinese applicants file applications in other countries, whereas over 40% of US applicants file for patents overseas. The reticence of Chinese innovators partly reflects the fact that China is still in the process of catching up with countries that are globally recognized leaders in innovation. However, China's continued investment in innovation looks set to lead to improvements in the quality as well as the quantity of its IP research.

In comparing innovation levels between countries, it is illuminating to take into account the size of the national economy. In this respect, South Korea outperforms China (see Figure 9.8). Inventors in South Korea filed 9,000 patent applications per unit of GDP ($100 billion), while those in China filed 6,000 per unit of GDP. Asian inventors take the top three places by this measurement, with German and Swiss inventors taking the next two. The US occupies sixth place.

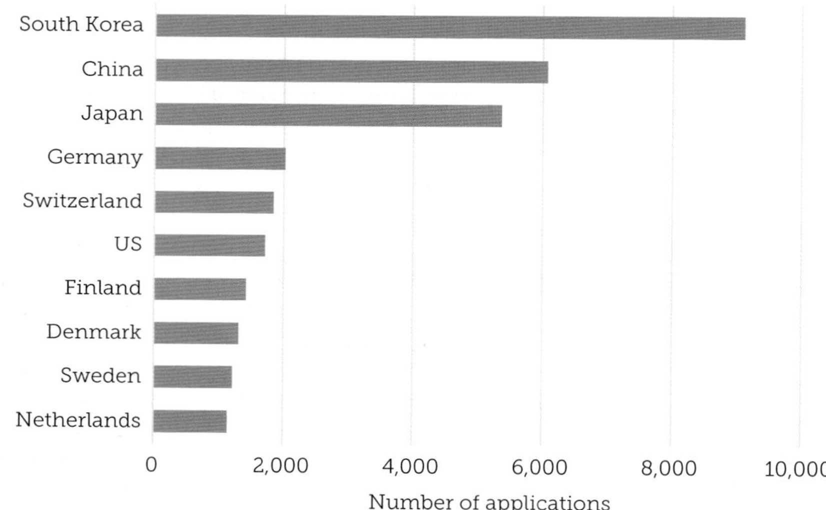

Figure 9.8 **Patent applications per unit of GDP ($100 billion), 2017**

Source of data: WIPO (World Intellectual Property Organization (2018) *IP Facts and Figures 2017*, p. 14, at www.wipo.org

The majority of applications filed in each country's patent office tend to be from residents of that country. An exception is the US. The US Patent and Trademark Office (USPTO) (www.uspto.gov) received 19.4% of the world's patent applications in 2017, and most of these applicants were foreign. The percentage of grants to foreign residents has risen over the years, to about 52.8% in 2015. That year, the actual number of grants to US applicants fell, from about 144,000 to 141,000, while those to foreign applicants rose slightly, to 157,000 (USPTO). This trend reflects the globalization of R&D and innovation activities.

Patent activity should be placed in perspective when looking at overall innovative behaviour. Patented inventions, however excellent, must be commercially viable and meet consumer needs. Capacity to build brands and reputation are as critical as winning products in achieving competitive advantage. Moreover, many innovations, such as new working practices, lie outside the category of patentable inventions.

The way I see it…

'We needed to turn a profit on this drug…The companies before us were just giving it away almost.'

Martin Shkreli, CEO of Turing Pharmaceuticals, in an interview with Bloomberg, September 2015.

The drug in question is Daraprim, a drug used by Aids patients. Turing acquired the rights to Daraprim in 2015, from a company that was charging patients $13.50 per pill. Turing raised the price per pill to $750, although the pill costs just $1 to produce. Martin Shkreli was showered with public condemnation over this 5,000% price rise. Three years on, Daraprim is still selling for $750 a pill, bringing the cost of a prescription to $35,000, which is funded by federal Medicaid for the poorest patients. Mr Shkreli is no longer in charge. He is serving a jail sentence for unrelated convictions for financial fraud at two hedge funds he ran. Turing has changed its name to Vyera. See Mole, B. (2018) 'Drug made famous by Shkreli's 5,000% price hike is still $750 a pill', *Ars Technica*, 4 May, at https://arstechnica.com/

Daraprim is a generic drug that is vital for the few thousand people who need it, but the company faces virtually no competitive pressure and can dictate the price. Patients, insurers and other funders are left to pay – leading to higher insurance premiums.

How would criticism of Shkreli's comments today be any different than in 2015?

The Trade-related Aspects of Intellectual Property (TRIPS) agreement

Trade-related Aspects of Intellectual Property (TRIPS) multilateral international agreement on the protection of intellectual property which aims to bring national legal regimes into harmony

There have been significant efforts to harmonize national laws on intellectual property rights through multilateral agreements. Following the Uruguay Round of GATT, the agreement on **Trade-related Aspects of Intellectual Property (TRIPS)** (www.wto.org/english/tratop_e/trips_e/trips_e.htm) attempted to bring national legal regimes into harmony. Obligations of national treatment (equal treatment for foreign and domestic individuals and companies) and most-favoured-nation treatment (non-discrimination between foreign individuals and companies) apply. These provisions took effect from 1996 for most countries, with transitional periods allowed for developing countries to comply. Most developing countries had a further five years, but the least developed countries had until 2006. TRIPS does not aim to make all countries conform to a single system, but to set certain 'minimum standards', with latitude for national variations. It specifies 20-year protection of patents on both process and products. In the controversial area of plants and animals, TRIPS provides that plant varieties must be patentable, but members may exclude certain types of plants and animal inventions. The TRIPS Council of the WTO monitors national laws for conformity. Disputes under TRIPS are settled through the WTO dispute settlement procedure.

TRIPS has come in for a great deal of criticism from developing countries. Critical areas for developing countries are new drugs to fight diseases and new seeds for crops. Both areas rely on research in biotechnology, or life science technology. In industrial countries, the trend away from publicly funded research to private funding has brought the increasing domination of a few large multinationals in these areas. Many developing countries have become concerned about the grip of large MNEs in areas involving public goods.

Patents: what are the benefits?

Patents are expensive to acquire, maintain and defend when legally challenged. Moreover, challengers are constantly at work, coming up with ways to reproduce the product or process without infringing the patent. Why do companies still believe the benefits outweigh the drawbacks?

Technology diffusion and innovation

technological diffusion processes by which advances in technology spread from one country to another, usually from developed to developing countries

technology transfer process of acquiring technology from another country

Technological diffusion was once thought to be the simple acquisition and adoption by developing countries of the technologies of developed countries, akin to adopting a set of 'blueprints', without any further creative contribution. It is now recognized that this view is oversimplified: the processes of diffusing technology are more dynamic, involving the spread of technical changes and adaptations to specific local conditions. Technological diffusion is likely to be a gradual process rather than an acquisition in the form of an event or transaction. When technology is acquired through a deliberate interaction between countries, it is known as **technology transfer**. The term usually refers to transfers from advanced economies to industrializing economies, but it also covers transfers between industrialized countries. Technology transfer has been crucial to the processes of industrial growth and global integration. It is now recognized that technology transfer is not a simple one-way process, but a more interactive and complex process of diffusion, both direct and indirect. The main means of technology diffusion are shown in Figure 9.9.

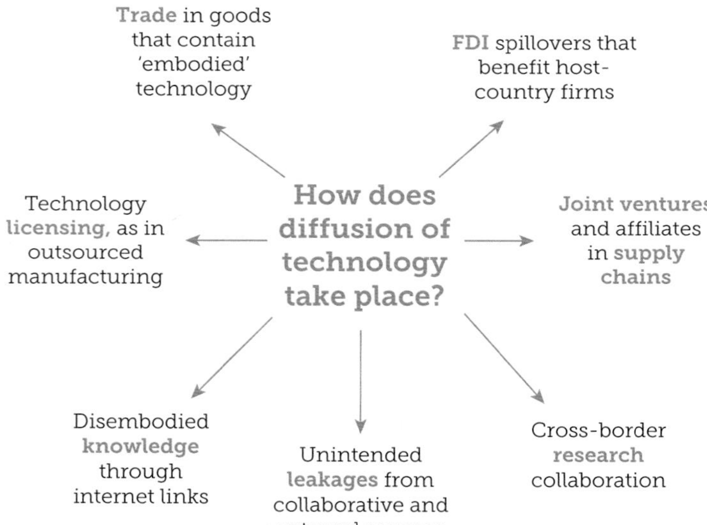

Figure 9.9 **Technology diffusion in different contexts**

FDI has been a major source of technology for developing countries. For the host country, the benefits derive from observing, imitating and applying the technologies, including the management methods. Spillover effects can include linkages developed with domestic suppliers, but to exploit spillover effects requires incentives for local firms to adopt the new technologies. Technological learning, or 'absorptive capacity', is at the heart of these processes. Formal education and training clearly play a part, but much learning is also acquired by doing, as in 'on the job' training. To benefit from technological accumulation, local firms need to

develop skills and know-how to improve the technology acquired from abroad. Interactions with foreign investors can help to ensure that the investor sees the value of continued investment in the location. Where these links are weak, and local innovation capacities are low, the investor is less committed to the location (Lall and Narula, 2004). Japan and Germany are examples of countries that have combined imported technology with development of local technological capabilities. On the other hand, foreign investors are often reluctant to incorporate the latest technology in foreign operations, for fear of 'leakage' of IP. This is particularly the case in countries that have weak IP legal protection, either through weak laws or lax enforcement.

Other sources of technology for developing countries include technology licensing. The owner of a patent may license a foreign manufacturer to produce the product under licence, in return for royalties (see Chapter 2). Many late-industrializing countries have relied significantly on licences for technology, particularly from the US and Japan. South Korea's spending on licences increased tenfold in the period 1982–91 (Mowery and Oxley, 1997). Technology licensing is often combined with FDI. Crucial to China's manufacturing boom in electronic gadgets, such as Apple iPhones, was the influx of FDI from elsewhere in Asia, notably Taiwan. Global car manufacturers have flocked to China, often using joint ventures to manufacture vehicles under licence for the Chinese market.

Much acquisition of technology comes through less deliberate processes. Trade in goods is an example, as shown in Figure 9.9 Sometimes called 'embodied' technology transfer, imported machinery and equipment provides a means to assimilate the technology. By 'reverse engineering', discovering how a product has been made, it is possible to develop and refine the technology further. Japan's post-war industrial development is a good example of the benefits of imported technologies, which were assimilated and complemented by local R&D and engineering capabilities. Japanese firms similarly benefited from licensed technology, building on substantial investments in R&D and engineering (Bell and Pavitt, 1997). However, reverse engineering is not always as successful as the Japanese example. Machines can be reproduced, but this does not mean that local people have mastered the technology that went into making the machine in the first place (Fu et al., 2011).

Globalization has expanded the ways in which technology is acquired, both through formal mechanisms of technology transfer and through more nebulous means such as interactions with supply chain partners. R&D has become internationalized through alliances, allowing partners to share R&D. Less structured is the dissemination of knowledge from a variety of sources via the internet in unintended ways. These processes can provide the impetus for learning, whereby external knowledge becomes part of the innovation process. Much depends on the capacity of indigenous firms to absorb the technology available and to develop domestic innovation capabilities independently. However, indigenous firms in developing countries face challenges of developing innovative capacity that serves the needs of the country, in contrast to technologies that serve the interests of foreign investors in, for example, outsourced manufacturing.

The benefits of technology transfer and knowledge spillovers in any country depend to a great extent on the country's level of income. It is unrealistic to expect poorer countries simply to catch up with richer ones. The types of technology that many developing countries need is in low-skilled and low-tech operations, in which indigenous innovation is probably more relevant than imported technology from advanced economies. Some developing economies become locked into sectors where FDI has been targeted at low-wage production that depends on imported technology. This policy can lead to economic growth, but does not serve the long-term needs of the host country, which are to develop innovative capacity to lift it up to more knowledge-based sectors. Economies dependent on low-wage production are said to be 'path dependent', and local R&D risks being 'crowded out' by imported technology. Building indigenous innovation capacity requires both domestic R&D and the institutional framework at national level that supports indigenous innovation.

Globalization and the diffusion of technology

How have evolving globalized value chains contributed more to the diffusion of technology in developing countries than the older pattern of specific FDI projects combined with technology transfer?

Technological innovation and sustainable development

Technological innovation drives economic progress, with the potential for greater prosperity, individual fulfillment, and a better quality of life for all in society. From the innovations that have shaped industrialized production through to the high-technology breakthroughs in computing and digitalization, the countries that have been at the forefront in enjoying the fruits of these changes have been today's developed economies. But, as we have noted, technology is one of the dimensions of the environment in which globalization has made the greatest strides towards economic integration. Many emerging and developing economies are increasingly participating in the latest technological advances. Innovations in green technology are contributing to combating climate change, and such innovations are taking place in many developing countries. Technological innovations promise inhabitants economic development that will transform their economies from low-level manufacturing and agriculture to high-technology value-added activities. Moreover, this transformation will enhance domestic technological capacity. These countries seek, above all, for technological innovation to be sustainable, contributing to an overall model of sustainable development, including environmental and social dimensions. But to what extent are today's innovators focusing on goals of sustainability?

Technological change is inherently disruptive. At its heart lies creative destruction: the old becomes obsolete and the new takes over. These processes are crucial to economic development, dramatically demonstrated by the Industrial Revolution. When looking back at technological advances, we tend to forget that change produces losers as well as winners, affecting individuals and societies. Industrialization brings the prospect of new jobs and earning capacity for those able to take up the opportunities, but many are left behind – without the skills or in the wrong place. Factory jobs bring in steady wages, but factory environments introduce new environmental risks and social upheaval. As we have seen, governments can promote these developments, but they can also do the opposite – reject them. This is what happened in the early nineteenth century, when the Industrial Revolution was in full swing in Britain. In swathes of Europe under Hapsburg rule, the building of factories and construction of railways were discouraged, as they posed threats to the existing elites (Acemoglu and Robinson, 2013: 226). In these traditional agrarian societies, where peasant workers were tied to landowners, the prospect of individuals being given freedom to take up salaried employment of their choice posed a threat. Change had the capacity to empower people – and still does.

Technology of energy

Economic development and green growth; Bob DiMatteo and Richard Schmalensee. This is a lecture in the series, MIT opencourse ware; 29/3/ 2013

Video link: Technology of energy

https://youtu.be/hVYBgsi0JcM

The digital era has seen an unprecedented growth in the ability of people to communicate, acquire knowledge from open sources and engage in social interactions. This empowerment has been associated with democratization of the internet. But, at the same time, the digital era has seen the rise of dominant high-technology companies that are in a position of power over the tools of their creation – and also power over the billions of users of their technology. Internet tools, smartphones or social media have now grown to exert an unprecedented global reach, beyond the scope of national regulators. Recall that there are 3.5 billion people using the internet, most of them in developing countries. Individual users have cause to be concerned about the misuse of their personal data; the rise of fake news and hate speech on the social media; and the rise of unregulated political advertising that has infiltrated election processes. In particular, Facebook has made numerous promises to rein in the illicit use of its platforms, but such efforts are inherently piecemeal. Ultimately, Facebook is accountable to its shareholders for profits, not to the general public.

Governments, companies and individuals value technological innovation for the undoubted benefits that flow from them. At the everyday level, they help people keep in touch. At the more rarified level, they help solve the world's most difficult problems, such as curing diseases and protecting the environment. But an important technological innovation such as a new medicine will result in an IP monopoly for the corporate owner, whose profits will depend on steep prices that only the richest can afford. Governments everywhere face challenges in ensuring that the development associated with innovation is inclusive, benefiting all in society. For this reason, indigenous innovations in poor countries, such as encouraging entrepreneurs to find cheap and efficient ways of improving agriculture, are more likely to produce sustainable development than attempts to create centres of excellence in high technology. Poor infrastructure and unreliable electricity supply can sometimes frustrate these latter initiatives in any case. Inequalities within countries can be just as potent obstacles to boosting innovation as inequalities between countries. This need not mean that governments in developing countries should refrain from supporting high-technology innovation. Digital technology is a good example of the potential for inclusive innovation: it can aid the poor farmer or the scientific researcher. Businesses are crucial to these developments, not simply for economic opportunities, but because of their responsibilities towards sustainable development.

Conclusions

Technological innovation has the power to transform economies and societies. Companies that do not commit themselves to innovation will soon fall behind their competitors. And countries whose governments are reluctant to grasp the possibilities of innovative technology to fuel economic growth will fall behind. With hindsight, these might seem simple calculations, but all change brings risks that disruption of the old ways will be for the worse, or be perceived by ordinary people as devaluing their lives. Industrialization has been the major driver of economic and social change, the advanced industrialized countries setting the examples that others have followed. For developing countries, this has meant opening their economies to FDI and global MNEs as a route to rapid industrialization, and, with it, rapid economic growth. But as we have seen, a risk has been the proliferation of low-technology operations and the reliance on low-skilled workforces, with little long-term prospect of climbing up the technological ladder. The expansion of supply chains in global production networks is now altering this path-dependent development. Developing countries have greater opportunities to engage in R&D, and there is greater scope for domestic innovation to find a wider stage. However, as we have seen, in issues of the absorption capacity for technological innovation, not all countries are equal.

National innovation systems present a range of divergences, from educational systems to industrial structures. While it has been thought that economic development based on industrialization would lead to convergence, it is now clear that catching up is not as simple as it seemed. The hope of acquiring technology through means such as FDI and technology transfer can prove a reality, but in many cases turns to disappointment. By contrast, a combination of foreign imports and local know-how can lead to innovation that is more in tune with development goals, and also more likely to be sustainable. At the heart of this process is the vital role of entrepreneurs. Entrepreneurial SMEs are rich sources of innovation in any country. An encouraging environment and the availability of funding are essential elements that can help domestic innovation. Governments are now aware of the need to encourage entrepreneurs and to target innovation policies in areas of social importance, such as biotechnology and clean energy. Profits are to be had, but so are benefits in which all can share.

CLOSING CASE STUDY

Apple facing new challenges

In 2018, Apple became the first public company to be worth $1 trillion on the New York Stock Exchange. Other technology stocks have also seen rising market values, all riding the waves of the digital revolution.

Apple is a mature company among American technology giants. Founded in 1976, it is older than most, having been listed in 1980. Its legendary co-founder, Steve Jobs, who died in 2011, had a vision of Apple's potential that has been a key to its success. Jobs worked closely with its design genius, Jony Ive. The iMac, with its innovative design, was launched in 1998. The launch of the iPod and iTunes in 2001 caused a sensation. The iPod was not the first music player, but, together with iTunes, they were a major step forward in the digitalization of music. The iPod had an instant design appeal that won over consumers. Similarly, the iPhone, launched in 2007, with its aesthetic design appeal and many functional features, raised the smartphone to a new level.

As consumers become more price-conscious, premium products must justify their high price tags.

Sales of iPhones reached 1.4 million in the first year, and the market value of Apple reached $106 billion. The launch of every new model has been promoted by Apple as a media event, and has been eagerly awaited by loyal users. This was another of Jobs' innovations. Sales grew continuously until 2016, and then started to fall slightly, partly because users were not replacing their phones as frequently as Apple had predicted. Could Apple have peaked? Has Apple's innovative capacity fallen behind competitors?

In 2017, Apple still sold 216 million iPhones, and the company's market value was $179 billion. Sales of iPhones represent nearly 60% of Apple's revenues. When the company announced in 2018 that it would no longer be disclosing how many iPhones, iPads and Macs it sells, the news was met with scepticism, and the share price went down. It impliedly confirmed that iPhone sales had been falling. Apple's profits have relied on high prices and larger margins than its competitors. Apple raised prices of iPhones in 2018, to maintain revenues, but this policy risks losing potential sales. Meanwhile, competitors have gained market share. By 2018, Apple was third behind South Korea's Samsung and China's Huawei in smartphone sales globally. Alongside Apple, their high-specification smartphones at lower prices look appealing. How will Apple respond to these new challenges?

Apple's main market remains the US. But China has become an important market for Apple, generating 25% of its revenues. China's consumers have been drawn to the features of the iPhone, along with its cachet as an up-market brand. China's middle-class urban consumers are highly brand-conscious, and sensitive to symbols of affluence. But these discerning consumers are now spending more cautiously. Apple must also think about sales in emerging markets where consumers are more price-conscious. Apple's competitors have been shrewd in developing smartphones for these markets, such as India, Turkey and Brazil.

Apple has been gradually increasing its revenues from its sales of services such as Apple Music, iCloud, the App Store and Apple Pay. All of these involve enhancing user experiences and building brand loyalty. They also maintain relations with consumers who make recurring purchases. Apple has tended to focus on its iPhone, and its revenues have reflected this faith in its enduring popularity. Under its CEO, Tim Cook, Apple is now rethinking its focus towards services, building on its strong brand image. He announced a new Apple TV streaming platform in 2019, in a high-profile launch event in California. Apple will face strong competitors such as Netflix in this market.

Brand image can be volatile, and is affected by corporate reputation. Tech companies, such as Facebook and Google, have taken serious knocks to their reputations over user privacy, anti-competitive practices and tax avoidance. Apple's business model rests on manufacturing carried out by millions of migrant workers in China, whose harsh working and living conditions are documented. Apple is also well known for its tax arrangements and offshoring of assets to minimize tax liabilities. Its premium brand image masks an unsustainable business model. Could a new iPhone recapture the magic? The challenges became even greater in 2019, when Jony Ive announced that he was leaving the company to set up his own design consultancy. So great has been his impact, Apple's shares fell following the announcement of his departure.

Questions

- What are the sources of Apple's strengths in innovation?
- What can Apple do to meet the challenges posed by iPhone's competitors?
- To what extent is Apple's business model posing risks for the company?
- What should Apple do to make its business more sustainable?

Further reading

See the article by Rob Davies, 'Apple becomes the first trillion-dollar company', 2 August 2018, in *The Guardian*. There is a link in this article to another, which gives a background look at Apple's record of innovation. It is 'From Macs to iPods and apps: How Apple revolutionised technology', by Alex Hern, 2 August 2018, in *The Guardian*.

Multiple choice questions

Visit www.macmillanihe.com/morrison-gbe-5e to take a quick self-test quiz on what you have read in this chapter.

Review questions

1. Explain science-push and demand-pull in the development of new technology.
2. What is Schumpeter's view of technological innovation and waves of economic development?
3. How should developing countries promote technological innovation in order to generate economic growth?
4. Outline the elements of a national system of innovation. How relevant is the educational and training environment of the country?
5. Which countries have evolved particularly successful national innovation systems, and why?
6. Why are patents crucial to technological lead?
7. What are the conditions which must be satisfied before a patent may be obtained for a process or product?
8. What is a generic medicine, and why are these medicines important in global healthcare?
9. Why is the TRIPS agreement said to be disadvantageous to developing countries?
10. How does FDI contribute to technology transfer?
11. In what ways has globalization impacted on technology transfer?
12. How can it come about that a country is 'stuck' in terms of technology, unable to catch up with more developed countries?
13. What is 'embodied technology', and why is it important for developing countries?
14. Why are some countries falling behind in the global diffusion of technology?
15. How can technological innovation be directed towards sustainable development?

✓ Assignments

1. Assume you are advising a government of a developing economy. Report to the government on: (a) policies designed to bolster national innovative capacities; and (b) policies to gain maximum benefit from technology transfer afforded by its inward investors.
2. Discuss the extent to which digital advances are becoming increasingly dominated by the global tech giants such as Google and Facebook, and what are the implications for sustainable development?

Further reading

Acemoglu, D. and Robinson, A. (2013) *Why Nations Fail: The origins of power, prosperity and poverty* (London: Profile Books).

Afuah, A. (2018) *Business Model Innovation*, 2nd edition (Routledge).

Bently, L., Sherman, B., Gangjee, D. and Johnson, P. (2018) *Intellectual Property Law*, 5th edition (Oxford: Oxford University Press).

Bessant, J. and Tidd, J. (2015) *Innovation and Entrepreneurship*, 3rd edition (John Wiley & Sons).

Goffin, K. and Mitchell, K. (2016) *Innovation Management: Effective strategy and implementation*, 3rd edition (London: Red Globe Press).

Landes, D. (1998) *The Wealth and Poverty of Nations* (London: Abacus).

Tidd, J. and Bessant, J. (2013) *Managing Innovation: Integrating technological, market and organizational change*, 5th edition (London: John Wiley & Sons).

Trott, P., van der Duin, P., Hartmann, D., Scholten, V. and Ortt, R. (2015) *Managing Technology Entrepreneurship and Innovation* (Routledge).

References

Acemoglu, D. and Robinson, A. (2013) *Why Nations Fail: The origins of power, prosperity and poverty* (London: Profile Books).

Archibugi, D. and Michie, J. (1997) 'Technological globalization and national systems of innovation: an introduction', in Archibugi, D. and Michie, J. (eds) *Technology, Globalisation and Economic Performance* (Cambridge: Cambridge University Press), pp. 1–23.

Bell, M. and Pavitt, K. (1997) 'Technological accumulation and industrial growth: contrasts between developed and developing countries', in Archibugi, D. and Michie, J. (eds) *Technology, Globalisation and Economic Performance* (Cambridge: Cambridge University Press), pp. 83–137.

Birkinshaw, J. (2017) 'Uber – a story of destructive creation', *Forbes*, 16 October, at www.forbes.com

Deloitte (2018) '5G: the chance to lead for a decade', Deloitte Development LLC, at www2.deloitte.com

Diamond, A. (2006) 'Schumpeter's creative destruction: A review of the evidence', *The Journal of Private Enterprise*, 22(1): 120–46.

European Commission (2018) *European Innovation Scoreboard: 2018*, at https://ec.europa.eu/growth/industry/innovation

Fagerberg, J. and Verspagen, B. (2002) 'Technology-gaps, innovation-diffusion and transformation: An evolutionary interpretation', *Research Policy*, 31: 1291–304.

Falconbridge, G. and Sandle, P. (2018) 'Father of Web says tech giants may have to be split up', Reuters, 1 November, at https://uk.reuters.com

Freeman, C. (1997) 'The national system of innovation in historical perspective', in Archibugi, D. and Michie, J. (eds) *Technology, Globalisation and Economic Performance* (Cambridge: Cambridge University Press), pp. 23–49.

Freeman, C. and Soete, L. (1997) *The Economics of Industrial Innovation*, 3rd edition (London: Cassell).

Fu, X., Pietrobelli, C. and Soete, L. (2011) 'The role of foreign technology and indigenous innovation in emerging economies: Technological change and catching up', *World Development*, July, 39(7): 1204–12.

ITU (International Telecommunications Union) (2018) *ICT Facts and Figures, Key ICT Indicators: Individuals using the internet*, at www.itu.int

Lall, S. (1992) 'Technological capabilities and industrialization', *World Development*, 20(2): 165–86.

Lall, S. and Narula, R. (2004) 'FDI and its role in economic development: Do we need a new agenda?', *European Journal of Development Research*, 16: 447–64.

Landes, D. (1998) *The Wealth and Poverty of Nations* (London: Little, Brown & Company).

List, F. ([1841]2005) *National System of Political Economy: History*, Vol. 1 (New York: Cosimo Inc.).

McKinsey Global Institute (2017) 'Jobs lost, jobs gained: Workforce transitions in a time of automation', December, at www.mckinsey.com/featured-insights/future-of-work/jobs-lost-jobs-gained

Mowery, D.C. and Oxley, J. (1997) 'Inward technology transfer and competitiveness' in Archibugi, D. and Michie, J. (eds) *Technology, Globalisation and Economic Performance* (Cambridge: Cambridge University Press), pp. 138–71.

OECD (2010) *Ministerial Report on OECD Innovation and Strategy*, May, at www.oecd.org/sti/inno

Partington, R. (2018) 'Automation to take 1 in 3 jobs in UK's northern centres, report finds', *The Guardian*, 29 January.

Patel, P. and Pavitt, K. (1994) 'National innovation systems: why they are important and how they might be measured and compared', *Economics of Innovation and New Technology*, 3(1): 77–95.

Patel, P. and Pavitt, K. (2000) 'National systems of innovation under strain: the internationalization of corporate R&D', in Barrell, R., Mason, G. and O'Mahony, M. (eds) *Productivity, Innovation and Economic Performance* (Cambridge: Cambridge University Press), pp. 217–35.

Preston, R. (2014) 'Supreme Court toughens business process patents test', *Information Week*, 6 June, at www.informationweek.com

Santacreu, A. and Zhu, H. (2018), 'What does China's rise in patents mean? A look at quality vs. quantity', *Economic Synopses*, No. 14, 4 May, Economic Research, Federal Reserve Bank of St. Louis, at https://doi.org/10.20955/es.2018.14

Schumpeter, J.A. ([1942]1975) *Capitalism, Socialism and Democracy* (New York: Harper & Row).

Smith, A. ([1776]1950) *An Inquiry into the Nature and Causes of the Wealth of Nations* (London: Methuen).

Tellis, G., Prabhu, J. and Chandy, R. (2009) 'Radical innovation across nations: the pre-eminence of corporate culture', *Journal of Marketing*, April 73: 3–23.

UNESCO (2018) Education and literacy in China, at www.uis.unesco.org, accessed 10 November 2018.

USPTO (US Patent and Trademark Office) U.S. Patent Statistics Chart (Summary Table), 1963–2015, at www.uspto.gov, accessed 14 November 2018.

Visit the companion website at www.macmillanihe.com/morrison-gbe-5e for further learning and teaching resources.

GLOBAL CHALLENGES AND SUSTAINABILITY

In Chapter 10, *Ecology and climate change*, we take an overview of the impacts on the natural environment caused by human activity, and, in particular industrialization and urbanization. Paramount among these impacts is climate change, a global issue, but one which can have devastating effects in local environments, especially severe in the poorest and most vulnerable countries. Combatting climate change has become the focus of moves to achieve international agreement on limiting harmful emissions. However, achieving consensus has become more difficult in a world in which the developing economies are becoming the largest emitters. Closely intertwined are issues of scarce resources and the pressing need to shift to cleaner energy. Diverse national agendas and political sensitivity towards any measures which might dampen economic growth have affected the environmental policies of both governments and businesses.

Chapter 11 is *Ethics and social responsibility*. Although distinguishing ethical from unethical behaviour might seem straightforward in principle, in practice, large areas of grey can make decision-making difficult. In many cases, a business might be faced with 'lesser evils', neither of which it would happily choose in an ideal world. In this chapter, we look at the foundation principles of ethical decision-making, taking the view that understanding how the definitions of good and bad behaviour have evolved aids in handling the practical situations which can arise. Ethics and CSR have become important elements of strategic decision-making for MNEs, not just because of high-profile corporate scandals. Certainly, CSR is compelling companies to look at their corporate governance and stakeholder responsiveness.

Chapter 12, *Sustainable business: the prospects*, is the concluding chapter. We revisit the six elements of sustainability, explaining how each has been illuminated by the various business and government players that have been highlighted throughout the book. The following section assesses the risks in the global environment from a number of perspectives: economic and financial; social and cultural; rising nationalism and geopolitical tensions; and risks in the natural environment. There follows a section on government and business responsibilities in the areas where sustainable progress is at risk. They include democratic institutions and stakeholder concerns. Finally, there is a discussion of the prospects for a sustainable future.

ECOLOGY AND CLIMATE CHANGE

Outline of chapter

This chapter will enable you to

- Understand the nature and causes of the major environmental challenges, such as climate change and transboundary pollution
- Appreciate interconnections between local, regional and global concerns
- Gain insight into the role of governments and international co-operation in tackling environmental challenges
- Identify at a practical level the initiatives businesses can take in environmental management and sustainable development strategy
- Assess the progress made towards reaching targets for reducing emissions and meeting sustainable development goals

OPENING CASE STUDY

The end for diesel?

Diesel was once hailed as the super fuel. It was fuel-efficient and thought to be cleaner than petrol. For motorists, running costs on diesel engines were lower in the long term, and they emitted less CO_2 than petrol engines. Governments concerned with rising carbon emissions urged consumers to buy diesel cars to help save the planet. The advice was based on the low carbon benefits of diesel, which were crucial to their environmental superiority over petrol. Governments in Europe were all convinced this was sound advice. In 2001, the UK took the step of reducing fuel tax on diesel, encouraging consumers to switch. And switch they did. Sales of diesel cars rose to half of all new-car sales in the UK. A similar story unfolded in other European countries. By contrast, the US did not go down this route. There, petrol was cheaper and plentiful. The shift towards cleaner motoring was directed towards electric vehicles and hybrids.

In 2012, research began to cast doubt on the benefits of diesel. It emerged that, although lower in carbon than petrol, diesel had harmful amounts of nitrogen oxides and dioxides (NOx) and also particulate matter (PM). Nitrogen dioxide (NO_2) in diesel emissions was singled out by the European Environment Agency as being particularly dangerous to health. In 2012, a World Health Organization expert considered that diesel exhaust fumes were a cause of lung cancer (Kelland, 2012).

The carmaker, Volkswagen, promoted 'clean diesel'. This was a message that had helped to grow its sales in Europe, and, to some extent, in the US. In 2015, testing of Volkswagen's fuel emissions data in the US revealed systematic tampering with cars by the company. Volkswagen eventually owned up to having used cheating devices to understate emissions. The repercussions were felt more severely in Europe than in the US, where Volkswagen sold far fewer cars. In Europe, wider problems emerged in the car industry. Claims made by manufacturers in their emissions test results were based on laboratory testing conditions, and were found to diverge widely from real-world performance of diesel cars. Harmful emissions were greater than the manufacturers' claims, and exceeded recommended safety limits.

Governments faced a dilemma. They had encouraged consumers to buy diesel, and then they were compelled to do a U-turn, advising the opposite. Governments were aware of the damaging impact of such contradictory advice on the domestic car industries in their own countries. Especially in the aftermath of the financial crisis, governments would have been loath to take a hard line against consumers who had followed their earlier advice. They were also concerned about the viability of their car manufacturers, who were heavily dependent on diesel sales. By contrast, cities did not shy away from taking a hard line. Paris, Madrid and Berlin were among the cities that brought in schemes to restrict diesel in city centres, with a view to ultimately banning it. In London, in April 2019, an ultra-low emission zone was introduced. London's black cabs, many of which are diesel, have complained about clean-air restrictions. Uber, by contrast, has welcomed them, seeing this as a source of competitive advantage over traditional taxis. London now has in place an incentive scheme for taxi drivers to replace old taxis with electric ones. The bans on diesel in cities are controversial. In some, the latest diesel cars that meet the Euro 6 standards, escape a ban.

Where does it leave diesel? Fiat Chrysler is phasing out the production of diesel cars by 2022. Toyota plans not to introduce any new diesel models. Manufacturers are all investing in electric models. Consumers who live and work in and around cities have become concerned about a ban on diesel inhibiting their ability to go about their lives. Diesel sales are falling, and resale values of diesel cars are falling. Has the pendulum swung too far the other way?

The shift away from diesel is leading ultimately to electric cars.

Not all diesel vehicles are alike. New clean technology has greatly improved diesel engines. And new advanced diesel models are much cleaner. The French government is considering classifying the newest clean diesels in the same category as the cleanest petrol cars. But consumers have become sceptical about diesel test results after the Volkswagen scandal. Now, tests have tightened up, and real road tests are taking place. New diesel cars are less pollutant, but consumers remain unsure, and the new safer diesel cars are more expensive. The cities that have introduced restrictions have focused on ridding their roads of the older, highly pollutant models. The shift away from diesel is pointing ultimately to electric vehicles. The UK has announced a ban on all petrol *and* diesel cars and vans by 2040.

Questions

- Why did diesel fall out of favour so quickly?
- What was the effect of the Volkswagen emissions scandal on the diesel car industry?
- In what ways was the shift in government policy damaging in the perceptions of consumers?
- What impact has been made by the restrictions on diesel in cities?

Further reading

For background on cities banning diesel, see the article by Matt McGrath, 'Four major cities move to ban diesel vehicles by 2025', 2 December 2016, in BBC news, at www.bbc.co.uk/news

Introduction

Challenges posed by the environment are increasingly impacting on societies, governments and businesses. They include global warming, depletion of natural resources and pollution. These, and other, processes are detrimental to human well-being, and they also harm plants and animals, both on the land and in the seas. While it is impossible to bring back species which have become extinct or replace resources which have become exhausted, it is possible to slow down and control harmful processes, and with the aid of research, to find ways of combatting the harmful effects. Whereas environmental issues were once seen as mainly local, they are increasingly perceived in the wider context of regional and global implications. Similarly, because it is about the public interest, the environment was once seen mainly as a matter of government concern, whereas the role of businesses – whether for bad or good – is now attracting more attention. Governments and businesses now co-operate in environmental protection at national, regional and international level. Often, this co-operation includes international organizations, both governmental and non-governmental (NGOs). The role of specialist environmental NGOs has been important in raising awareness of 'green' issues and also in promoting green alternatives to environmentally damaging activities. Greater weight has been given to these efforts by advances in scientific research, which have shed light on trends affecting the planet as a whole and also provided details of the effects of different types of pollution in specific locations.

Much past and present environmental damage stems from the effects of economic development. These processes include industrialization, changes in farming methods, and depletion of natural resources. As has been seen in Chapter 3, industrialization leads to urbanization, as rural dwellers flock to urban areas in search of work in new industries. While these twin processes began two centuries ago in the advanced economies, the centres of today's industrialization are in the developing

world, and the processes are taking place much more quickly than during the first wave of industrialization. Moreover, current environmental changes are occurring in a context of unprecedented population pressures, mainly in the developing world. Protecting the environment, therefore, is crucial to sustainable development, which takes a long-term view of development and its impacts. Sustainable development should be an imperative in the strategic thinking of international managers.

This chapter will first highlight the major environmental challenges, including climate change and transboundary pollution. National regulation and international co-operation are explored, highlighting diverging national interests. The concept of sustainable development is discussed in the section on international frameworks to promote sustainable development. Business responses and shifts in thinking on environmental management are highlighted in the following section. The last section discusses the extent to which governments and businesses are committed to sustainable development goals (SDGs).

Environmental degradation in context

ecology study of the relationship between organisms and their environment

biodiversity the variety of living organisms and species co-existing in the same habitat

environmental degradation environmental change caused mainly by human activity which has detrimental effects on ecological systems

Ecology focuses on the interactions between living organisms and their habitats. Organisms range from plant and animal life to human beings, in a variety of habitats, including urban centres as well as rural areas, forests, waterways and the sea. A change in any of these habitats impacts on the living creatures they support: the variety of living organisms (called **biodiversity**), their distribution and number, are affected by even slight changes in environment. While environmental changes can occur naturally through changes in climate and weather, **environmental degradation** refers specifically to environmental change caused mainly by human activity. The development of agriculture in Europe and North America in the seventeenth and eighteenth centuries is an example, which saw a huge expansion in the area of cultivated land, technological innovations and the emergence of capitalist market relationships in agriculture (Maddison, 2001). Forests were cut down, heathland was cleared, and numerous species of wildlife declined as their habitats were destroyed.

With the Industrial Revolution, the capacity for environmental degradation started to grow dramatically, in both intensity and geographic scope. Factory production relying on power sources such as coal was joined by newer industries, such as synthetic chemicals, which generated a mixture of old and new pollutants. As urban areas grew up around these industries, environmental problems spread, posing threats to health associated with air pollution and poor access to clean water and sanitation. As Maddison points out, although city dwellers in the early period of industrialization enjoyed higher incomes than those in rural areas, their mortality rates were significantly higher, mainly due to the spread of infectious diseases, which took their greatest toll among infants and recent migrants to the urban areas (Maddison, 2001).

As Chapter 3 highlighted, almost all the current population growth is now taking place in the developing world, especially in Africa. In general, these countries' economies are heavily reliant on agriculture, but agriculture can be precarious, and is unlikely to promote sustainable economic growth in today's world. Moreover, the effects of climate change, including extreme weather events and desertification, are taking their toll on agricultural production in the developing world. Meanwhile, there is growing demand for food from the large emerging economies, such as China and India, both of which are food importers. The world now faces stern challenges in growing enough food and managing its distribution.

Although industrial development has brought much-needed employment and income, it has also led to environmental degradation, including resource depletion and pollution. Major causes of environmental degradation are shown in Figure 10.1.

Industrialization ushered in processes that resulted in environmental degradation. Urbanization, consisting of new infrastructure, housing and transport had detrimental impacts on natural ecosystems, destroying natural habitats. Growing prosperity, industrial employment and urban lifestyles also led to increasing demand for the trappings of modern consumer lifestyles and processed food, inevitably involving increased demand for power generation and transport. Growing demand for food has led to deforestation. **Deforestation**, which is the felling of forests for fuel or to use the land for other purposes, has proceeded hand in hand with growth in the world's population. The main cause of deforestation is the demand for land for agriculture and livestock (FAO, 2018). The FAO estimates that the demand for food globally will rise 50% between 2018 and 2050. The greatest pressure on forests will occur in the regions of the world with the fastest-growing populations. These are in sub-Saharan Africa, South East Asia and Latin America. Forests covered 31.6%, of the world's land surface in 1990, but this area is constantly shrinking, and by 2015 was about 30.6%. Latin America has seen some of the most extreme deforestation. About 9% of Latin America's forest area was lost between 1990 and 2010, mostly to clear land for crops and grazing. At that rate, Latin America would be totally without forests in 220 years. Deforestation and the degradation of existing forests present severe threats to biodiversity: many plants and animals are unique to particular areas and become extinct when their ecosystem is disrupted. Deforestation also leads to soil erosion, the capacity of the land to retain water and rising carbon emissions. Forests are, in effect, large stores of carbon, and felling trees releases emissions from stored-up carbon.

deforestation the felling of forests for fuel or to use the land for other purposes

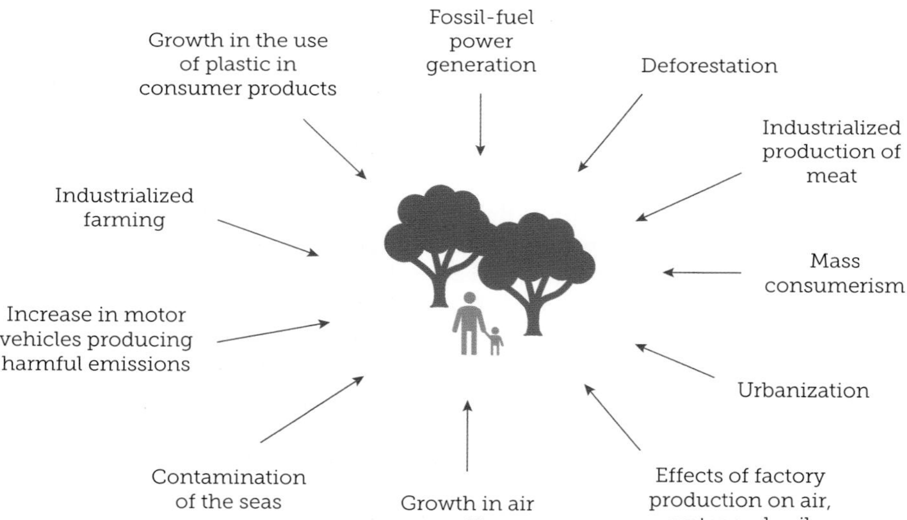

Figure 10.1 Global causes of environmental degradation

'Global commons' refers to the resource domains that are not within the jurisdiction of any one country (UNEP, 2015). They include the high seas, the atmosphere, Antarctica and outer space. These areas are viewed as the common heritage of all humanity. With creeping environmental degradation caused by human activity such as pollution, as is happening in Antarctica, it is now recognized that international co-operation is needed to address the issues of degradation of the global commons. Interconnections between local, regional and global phenomena are increasingly being revealed. For example, air pollution or waste dumped into a river from a single factory may travel long distances, heedless of national boundaries. In

the wider picture, air pollution generated by industrial agglomeration, we now know, depletes the ozone layer of our atmosphere.

Large emerging economies have enjoyed growing prosperity, both from growth in their home countries and in their outward FDI. Their expanding MNEs have become enmeshed in the societies in which they operate, being called upon to take account of their host societies' needs. Governments have tended to view economic development in their home countries as the top priority, and environmental damage, both at home and abroad, as a price worth paying. Now, as emerging economies have become global forces, and as the effects of decades of industrialization become apparent, they face environmental challenges. Action must be taken to safeguard societies – and plan for more sustainable growth in the future. They face environmental pressures from three broad directions:

- From their own societies, where pollution threatens health and welfare
- From societies in other countries where they operate, and where similar health and environmental concerns arise
- From the international community, concerned that the developing countries take greater responsibility for global environmental damage.

The first two of these groups would broadly be recognized as stakeholders, and companies can see the direct links between their activities and social impacts. However, the third, international pressure, is more abstract and rests more on a sense of moral duty. As we will see in the next section, the climate change debate has brought out these differing perspectives.

The global commons are everybody's business

Companies perceive stakeholders typically in terms of interests such as suppliers and consumers. How can a company be persuaded that it should take action to preserve the global commons?

Climate change

climate change any change in the climate over time, whether from natural causes or human activity

global warming global rise in temperatures impacting on all forms of life, caused by the build-up of greenhouse gases in the earth's atmosphere

greenhouse gases (GHGs) mixture of heat-trapping gases, mainly carbon dioxide (CO_2)

Climate change covers any change in the climate over time, whether from natural causes or human activity. Climate experts generally believe that we are now experiencing a slow process of **global warming**, caused by the build-up of heat-trapping gases, or **greenhouse gases** (GHG), in the earth's atmosphere. In particular, carbon dioxide is to blame. Carbon dioxide (CO_2) emissions quadrupled over the second half of the twentieth century, a period of rapid economic growth in Europe, the US and Japan. The burning of fossil fuels, mainly in coal-fired power stations, is responsible for over half of greenhouse gas emissions globally. Energy and transport are the main contributors to rises in emissions. These trends are pronounced in the world's large developing economies, where there is growing demand for the trappings of modern consumer lifestyles, such as cars and air travel. The advent of low-cost air travel has led to a boom in leisure travel, but with the result that aviation is now the fastest-growing source of emissions in the transport sector. CO_2 emissions from international aviation rose 110% between 1990 and 2017, and the rise between 2005 and 2017 was 29%, according to the European Commission Research Centre, cited in Figure 10.2. In 2018, the low-cost airline, Ryanair, became the first non-coal company to enter the top ten largest carbon emitters in the EU, its emissions having risen 50% in the previous five years (Staines, 2019).

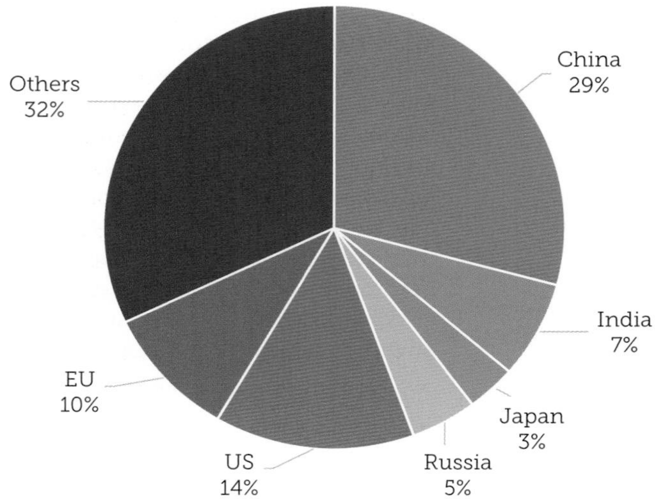

Figure 10.2 Global shares of greenhouse gas emissions by leading countries

Source of data: European Commission Joint Research Centre, Emissions database for global atmospheric research (EDGAR), GHG emissions of all world countries, 2018, at http://edgar.jrc.ec.europa.eu, accessed 14 July 2019.

Shares of greenhouse gas emissions by the countries with the highest levels of emissions are given in Figure 10.2. Emissions are measured in gigatonnes (Gt), a gigatonne being one billion tonnes. Greenhouse gas emissions reached a record high of 37.1 Gt of CO_2-equivalent in 2017. China's share of that total was 10.9 Gt. Coal consumption is responsible for 40% of global emissions, most of this emanating from China, but the US and India have also seen increases in coal consumption. India relies mainly on coal for power generation, and an increase of 7.9% in coal consumption was largely responsible for India's high level of emissions, at 2.5 billion Gt. India's emissions of CO_2 per capita, however, remain low, at 1.8 tonnes of CO_2.

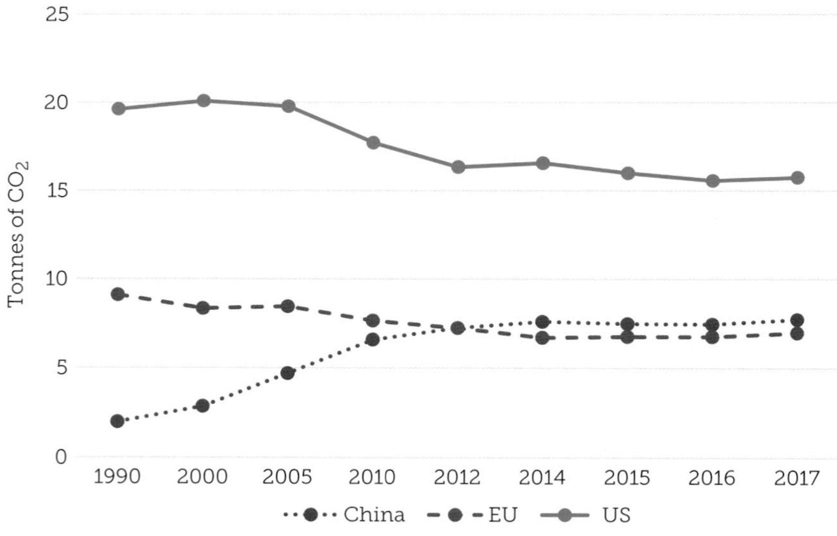

Figure 10.3 Emissions of CO_2 per capita, 1990–2017

Source of data: European Commission Joint Research Centre, Emissions database for global atmospheric research (EDGAR), CO_2 emissions per capita, at http://edgar.jrc.ec.europa.eu, accessed 14 July 2019.

In general, per capita emissions of emerging and developing countries are low, while those in the developed regions of the world are high. Rising emissions are associated with industrialization, as has happened in China. High emissions per capita are characteristic of countries that are oil and gas producers. These include the US, Australia, Canada, and the Gulf states of the Middle East, such as Qatar,

where CO_2 emissions are 38.52 tonnes per capita. The small Gulf states are among the world's richest as well as being the highest per capita contributors to global warming. Their development model has rested on massive construction projects designed to create luxury urban business centres in these naturally inhospitable desert environments. By contrast, in countries where heavy industries have declined or where cleaner energy has been introduced, per capita emissions have fallen. In the EU, greenhouse gas emissions have been falling since 2006. China's emissions per capita overtook those of the EU in 2014, as seen in Figure 10.3. In 2017, the EU per capita emissions of 6.97 tonnes were less than those in China, at 7.72 tonnes, but both were less than half the per capita emissions in the US, which was 15.74 tonnes of CO_2. China has invested heavily in renewable energy, but its economy remains so dependent on coal that it cannot make major changes swiftly, and it remains the world's largest emitter of greenhouse gases.

What is known about climate change?

Theories of climate change have been around for over a hundred years, but only since the 1980s have scientists been able to monitor the changes with precision in a variety of locations. It is impossible to measure directly climate changes which took place before human civilization, but climate scientists are able to study a range of phenomena, such as rock and ancient Antarctic ice, which give them data on the earth's climate history. These studies show them the changes brought about by natural variations in CO_2. They estimate that the last three decades have been successively warmer than any decade since 1850 (IPCC, 2014). These data help them to assess current changes in the atmosphere, oceans, temperatures and rainfall. The UN established the **Intergovernmental Panel on Climate Change** (IPCC) (www.ipcc.ch/) in 1989, which brought together a panel of hundreds of scientists. Its aim was to consolidate the scientific evidence about what changes are occurring, aiding governments and other decision-makers. Their reports, beginning in 1990, have been influential in forming views about the nature and impacts of climate change. The research confirms the connection between increasing levels of CO_2 in the atmosphere and global warming.

Intergovernmental Panel on Climate Change (IPCC) UN body of scientists that brings together evidence of climate change and issues reports of their findings

The scientific data amassed by scientists show that global warming is a reality, and that it is happening because of human activity. In its fifth report, the IPCC found that the evidence of human influence on global warming has strengthened in the years since its fourth report (IPCC, 2014: 5). Factors they highlight include the size of population, the types of economic activity, lifestyle, technology and climate policy.

The rate of increase in CO_2-equivalent emissions (CO_2 and other greenhouse gases) is the key factor in determining the extent of global warming. If there are no further measures to stop emissions growth than those in place now, temperatures by 2100 could have risen by 3.7° to 4.8° C above the levels of 1850–1900. A rise on this scale would have severe impacts on ecology and human welfare. The IPCC estimated that limiting the rise to 2°C above pre-industrial levels would be an attainable target. This would require that emissions generated by human activity be reduced by 40–70% from their 2010 level by 2050, and to be reduced to zero by 2100. The concentration of CO_2 in the atmosphere is expressed as parts per million (ppm). Before the Industrial Revolution CO_2-equivalent concentrations in the atmosphere were 280 ppm. In November 2018, the concentration was 408.54 ppm (CO_2earth, 2018). To keep the rise in temperature to 2°C requires that greenhouse gas emissions must not exceed a concentration of 450 ppm of carbon in the atmosphere. Once released into the atmosphere, carbon dioxide can persist for a century, and there is no current technology to remove it on a large scale. This means that there is very little leeway for further rise, and action needs to be taken urgently to slow the rise in emissions.

There is a good deal of technology for reducing emissions and utilizing clean alternatives in many spheres of activity. However, implementing changes on a large scale involves government action and regulation to compel businesses and individuals to change their behaviour. It also requires co-operation among national authorities. Among the many concerns highlighted by the IPCC is the persistent rise in the burning of fossil fuel for power.

The effects of climate change are complex, as climate is more than just temperature, but includes interactions of temperatures with winds and rainfalls in different locations. Heatwaves, droughts, floods and hurricanes are all associated with climate change. It is estimated that all continents can expect shifts in their climate, and thus their ecology, as a result of global warming. The IPCC says that it is 'very likely' that there will be more heatwaves and fewer spells of extreme cold over most land areas (IPCC, 2014: 10). Severe flooding is likely to occur in some places, and desertification in others. Arid and semi-arid areas in Africa and Asia will have higher temperatures, causing loss of vegetation and depletion of water sources. Because the polar ice caps are melting, sea levels are rising. Island nations and low-lying regions, such as Bangladesh, risk becoming submerged beneath the sea, while the Sahara Desert in Africa is expanding. Subterranean aquifers are becoming depleted and rivers are drying up. Extremes of drought and flood, as well as extreme events such as storms, pose risks to agriculture and lead to insecurity of supplies of food and clean water. Agriculture is already becoming problematic in Australia because of drought, and agriculture in Spain, which supplies many European countries, would also be affected.

It has long been known that climate change poses serious threats to developing countries, mainly in Africa, which have fewer resources to cope with natural disasters or to change existing agricultural systems. It is now becoming apparent that rich countries are also vulnerable to floods, droughts, severe storms and rising sea levels. Although technologies, such as flood defences, exist, costs are high, and hurricanes can wreak havoc in the most advanced economies. The IPCC says that the existing risks and new risks of climate change will impact more heavily on disadvantaged people and communities everywhere, not just in developing countries, but in countries at all levels of development (IPCC, 2014: 13).

In a report in 2018, the IPCC reiterated its warnings to take urgent action, saying that a target of 1.5°C should be attainable (IPCC, 2018). This maximum of 1.5°C would be needed to reduce the risks of droughts, floods, heatwaves and poverty for millions of the world's people. A maximum of 1.5°C would mean that the number of people exposed to water stress would be 50% less than at 2°C. In addition, problems of food scarcity and climate-related poverty would be less severe.

International co-operation to combat climate change

As in other spheres, such as trade, international co-operation relies on individual nations having the will and means to achieve goals which they share. The UN, like the WTO, can bring delegates to the negotiating table, but cannot force them to make an agreement or, if agreement is reached, to stick to it. The first climate change treaty was the Kyoto Protocol, which was signed in 1998 and came into legal force in 2005, despite non-ratification by the US, which was then the world's largest carbon emitter. The Kyoto Protocol contained a framework for international co-operation to deal with the effects of climate change. The treaty specified goals of emissions reductions to be achieved by 2008–12, and laid the foundations for further treaty-making.

The Kyoto Protocol envisaged the world divided into developed and developing nations. Its targets for reduction in emissions were linked to these categories. This approach seemed appropriate at the time. Who in 1998 would have foreseen that China, a developing country, would become the world's largest emitter of green-

house gases? Unfortunately, with hindsight, the treaty sowed the seeds of a rift among nations which has widened since then along political lines, making it difficult to bridge the gap in subsequent negotiations. Developing and emerging countries have pointed to industrialization in developed countries as the main historical cause of today's climate change crisis, and argued that these countries therefore should bear the main responsibility for measures to mitigate the impacts, including contributing financially to developing countries. India is a leading exponent of this argument. Although the world's fourth-largest GHG emitter, it has been reluctant to commit to reductions. Recall from the discussion of country comparisons above that its emissions per capita are very low compared to developed economies. Its government argues that its priorities must be relieving extreme poverty and providing electricity and sanitation for the millions of its inhabitants in need. It holds that for these goals to be realized, economic growth based on industrialization and substantial reliance on coal-fired power stations is essential well into the future. On the other hand, India is committed to being part of the solution to climate change, by expanding the use of renewable energy sources in the long term.

The Kyoto Protocol set 2008–12 as a target date by which developed countries would reduce their combined GHG emissions to 5% below 1990 levels. There were no targets for developing countries. It introduced the principle of emissions trading, in the Clean Development Mechanism, allowing polluting industries simply to buy emission 'credits' from other countries, in order to meet their national targets without actually cutting emissions in their domestic economy. The emissions trading principle now looks inadequate to bring about the reductions needed. But did the Kyoto Protocol succeed in reducing emissions, despite the abstention of the US and the non-inclusion of China? The EU more than succeeded in meeting its target of 8% reduction by 2008–2012. By 2013, GHG emissions had been cut by 18% below 1990 levels (European Commission, 2013). However, globally, emissions continued to rise, as the reductions recorded in the EU were outweighed by the growth in emissions from the US and from emerging economies, mainly China. Moreover, it should be borne in mind that the rise in emissions in China has been driven by demand for imported goods in the EU and other developed countries. This would contribute to the 'carbon footprint' of each of these countries (Clark, 2012). **Carbon footprint** thus gives a more accurate picture of impacts on climate change, as it represents both direct and indirect emissions. Hence, the carbon footprint of a toy includes the manufacturing process and also the process of making the plastics that go into the product (Berners-Lee and Clark, 2010).

carbon footprint the amount of greenhouse gases produced either directly or indirectly by an organization or country

Despite the inevitable conclusion that the Kyoto Protocol failed to achieve its goal of reducing global emissions, there were positive precedents set. It was the first international attempt to set mandatory targets for reducing GHG emissions, and it was also pioneering in its emissions trading scheme. These precedents have been important in follow-up meetings to continue the Kyoto process.

Negotiations to agree a follow-up treaty to the Kyoto Protocol included all the major emitting countries. Meetings in Copenhagen (2009), Durban (2011) and Doha (2012) made only limited progress in laying the groundwork for a new treaty. The Copenhagen meeting agreed the goal of limiting warming to 2°. The Durban conference agreed that both developing and developed countries would be expected to take climate change action. And the Doha conference agreed the principle of funding poor countries for 'loss and damage' due to climate change. When delegates of 195 countries met in Paris in December 2015, there was considerable pressure to reach agreement on all major points.

Prior to the Paris talks, countries were encouraged to put forward their own 'intended nationally determined contributions' (INDCs), which included intended reductions in GHG emissions. Each country's INDC would become its 'nationally determined contribution' (NDC) when it ratifies the accord. By the start of the conference, 186 countries had submitted their INDCs. While this was a step on the way to committing both developed and developing countries, these targets were not legally binding, and, taken in aggregate, would reduce warming to 2.7°C, not 2°C. In an ambitious move at the conference, it was proposed to set the target at 'well below 2°C and endeavour to reach 1.5°C' (Vidal et al., 2015). This was accepted in the final agreement, but only after considerable negotiation. It was felt that give-and-take was the key: each country would see some of its desired goals in the agreement, but not all it wished to see. China, formerly reluctant to accept targets, was now willing to accept them. It was reluctant to accept monitoring, but was persuaded to go along with the consensus in the end. The pledges contained in the INDCs are to be revisited every five years in a 'stocktaking', a review mechanism, the first of which under the agreement will be 2023. The stocktaking, which gives rise to setting stiffer targets, is a means of verification of each country's progress – or lack of it. Stocktaking at designated intervals offers a means of 'naming and shaming' countries that fail to live up to their defined contributions.

In recognition of the concerns of developing countries, especially poor countries that are vulnerable to the impacts of climate change, there was an agreement on assessing loss and damage in financial terms. This also includes preventive measures, but, at the insistence of the US, which was concerned about the legal position of its large corporations, the agreement specifically rules out any liability or compensation. Finally, there were the financial provisions, under which developed countries pledged $100 billion per year towards aiding developing countries to take measures to lessen the impacts of climate change and to make the transition to clean energy.

The financial provisions are set out in the preamble, rather than the body of the agreement, signifying intention to pay, but not legal obligation. The other commitments made by the 195 countries in Paris are intended to be legally binding on each. Representatives of over 170 of these countries came together for formal signing at the UN's headquarters in New York in April 2016, signifying a high level of national commitment. The accord came into effect in international law on 4 November 2016, 30 days after the date when it was ratified by 55 countries representing at least 55% of global greenhouse gas emissions. As of 2018, 184 out of 195 signatory countries have ratified the agreement.

The Paris accord represents an agreement by the signatory countries to be bound to the processes and mechanisms, such as the setting of INDCs, stocktaking and monitoring, in good faith on the basis that all feel obliged to comply themselves; and all expect each other to comply. The commitment of China was a significant step forward. However, political changes in some countries have dealt potential setbacks to meeting the Paris targets. Populist leaders, President Trump in the US and President of Brazil, Jair Bolsonaro, have expressed an intention to withdraw from the agreement. Brazil's president also wishes to withdraw from commitments to halt deforestation of the Amazon, opening it up to a greater extent to agribusiness.

Climate change and the Paris agreement

This is a University of Oxford lecture, featuring Christiana Figueres, speaking on 'What now? Next steps on climate change', 19 November 2018. This public lecture is at the Oxford Martin School, University of Oxford. She is from Costa Rica, and she is the former Executive Secretary of the UN Framework Convention on Climate Change.

Video link: Climate change and the Paris agreement
https://podcasts.ox.ac.uk/what-now-next-steps-climate-change

 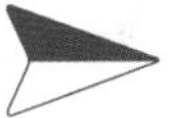

Climate change initiatives and business responses

No business is unaffected by climate change, just as no individual person is unaffected. Some sectors, such as those that use large amounts of energy or water, are more affected than others. But all must focus on issues of energy consumption and the carbon footprint of their products. Ideally, they would take initiatives on grounds of sustainability. But, in practice, they are inclined to wait for regulation to compel them to make changes in the ways they operate. Businesses in every sector have watched astutely the developments of climate change negotiations, knowing the outcomes will imply strategy shifts to more low-carbon alternatives in their operations. But uncertainties can arise following inter-governmental negotiations that have given no clear indications of new regulations or a detailed timeframe for changes.

Environmental regulations at the level of national law are likely to weigh more heavily with businesses than agreements of inter-governmental bodies. There is a long time lag before commitments are translated into law. National law is more immediate in its impact, and national regulators are able to impose legal penalties for breaches. Ideally, businesses would be proactive, but in practice they take more notice of the impacts that affect their profits in the short term. This has been shown in an extensive survey carried out in the run-up to the Paris conference in 2015. In interviews with CEOs of 142 of the world's largest companies, researchers found that only 46% said that a binding agreement in Paris would persuade them to prioritize climate change measures (PwC Global, 2015). In the view of the CEOs interviewed, the main influence on their climate change stance was public opinion, and the second greatest influence was national regulation. Business leaders are clearly sensitive to public opinion, as consumer perceptions of their activities affect sales and profits. The CEOs generally viewed climate change as having negative impacts on their businesses, rather than looking at the opportunities for innovation and sustainable solutions. Those that did embrace climate change initiatives mainly did so on the grounds of improving shareholder value, which represents an essentially economic perspective rather than an ethical one.

Large companies, especially in the energy sector, are among the groups lobbying against climate change measures. In 2015, major companies lobbied against EU measures to promote renewable energy, favouring instead greater use of gas, which is a fossil fuel (Nelson, 2015). The companies included oil giants, BP and Shell; BASF, a chemical company; and the steel producer, ArcelorMittal. These companies co-ordinate their lobby activities through organizations such as trade associations that specialize in lobbying decision-makers. One of these, BusinessEurope, the EU's largest business lobby group, has urged against any further strengthening of climate change commitment. The EU's target has been at least a 40% reduction in emissions by 2030, based on 1990 levels. Following an agreement on renewables and energy-efficiency targets, the EU's climate action commissioner has updated the target for reduction in emissions to 45%. BusinessEurope's stance is against raising the EU's target for reducing emissions, despite the urgent warnings issued by the IPCC (Vaughan, 2018).

The member companies of BusinessEurope all profess to take climate change seriously in their corporate strategy. A group of 25 large investors in many of these same companies (including BP, EDF, Total and P&G) wrote to the CEOs of the companies in which they have stakes, querying their membership of trade associations that pursue anti-climate change lobbying (Fagan-Watson, 2015). For these critical shareholders, the ethical case and the case based on long-term shareholder value are coming together.

Also indicative of shifting views of shareholders is the shift away from fossil fuel investments by investors on ethical grounds. Many investors, including both institutional funds and private investors, have decided to sell their shares, or 'divest', in fossil fuel companies. Among them are Norway's sovereign wealth fund and two large pension funds in California, whose policies are seen as indicative of broad shareholder thinking.

Projects to develop green technology and renewable energy can be costly. Businesses in these sectors often work closely with governments. Government incentives and funding can be crucial in encouraging investment. However, there are also likely to be policy shifts when governments change. In such an environment, companies are disinclined to commit resources, and CEOs are disinclined to take on big projects. Nonetheless, legal obligation is only one reason, albeit a strong one, for undertaking greener strategies. Companies with strong CSR and stakeholder commitments will proceed with their own targets for reducing emissions despite the slowness of governments to bring in legislation. Companies with weak environmental records face issues of stakeholder objections and reputational risk. Moreover, there are many areas of environmental regulation on issues such as pollution which are already subject to international law.

Transboundary pollution and energy strategy

transboundary pollution the transmission of pollutants through the water, soil and air from one national jurisdiction to another

Transboundary pollution refers to the transmission of pollutants through the water, soil and air from one national jurisdiction to another. The transmission may be intentional, as in the transport of hazardous waste, or it may be unintentional, as in an accident at a nuclear power plant.

Industrial enterprises commonly release waste into rivers and produce harmful emissions, such as sulphur dioxide, that are released into the atmosphere. Only in the twentieth century was there a dramatic increase in the capacity for pollution on a large scale, with potential for devastating environmental effects. In addition, industries like nuclear power generation raised the possibilities of catastrophic accident. The cataclysmic event which is usually cited as causing a shift in the environmental paradigm was the meltdown of the nuclear power station at Chernobyl in the former Soviet Union in 1986 (Landes, 1998). The fire, which burned for five days, released more than 50 tonnes of radioactive poison into the atmosphere, affecting Belarus, the Baltic states, and the Scandinavian countries. The disaster, and the inept handling of the aftermath, are cited as factors which contributed to the eventual collapse of the Soviet command economy (Landes, 1998).

acid rain acid from greenhouse gases that falls out of the atmosphere, in the form of rain or wind-blown gases

Less dramatic has been the quiet destruction that acid rain has caused in the environment, becoming visible only when rivers and forests appear to be dying. **Acid rain** is the term used to describe acid which falls out of the atmosphere. It may be wet, in the form of rain, fog and snow, affecting the soil on which plants and animals depend. Or it may be dry, in the form of acidic gases and particles, which may blow onto buildings and trees and into homes. Its main components are sulphur dioxide and nitrogen oxides. It causes trees to gradually wither, buildings to decay and aquatic life to die. Aquatic ecosystems are particularly endangered. The burning of fossil fuels such as coal for electricity is particularly blamed for acid rain. International co-operation for lowering acid rain emissions in Europe and North America has helped to reduce levels, but industrialization in the developing world has spread these problems to more countries.

Coal remains the dominant fuel for power generation. It is responsible for 40% of the world's electricity generation and 30% of the world's carbon emissions from energy consumption. Moreover, coal's share in the fuel mix for power generation has remained relatively unchanged since 1998, despite the progress that has been made in the use of renewable energy sources, and despite the warnings of climate

experts. Many countries have ambitious policies to shift away from coal because of its carbon emissions and other environmental impacts, but in practice, there has been little overall reduction. This is mainly because China and India, the major economies dependent on coal, are making only slow progress in reducing their dependence on it.

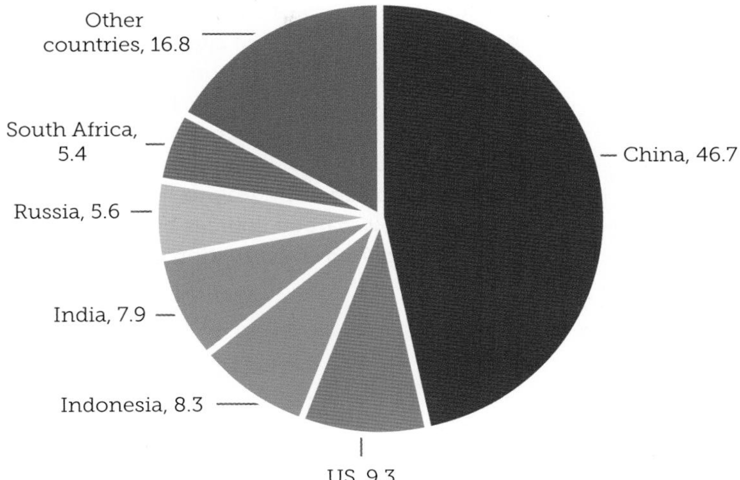

Figure 10.4 Percentage shares of global coal production of major producing countries, 2018

Source of data: Statista, Distribution of coal production by country, 2018, at www.statista.com, accessed 14 July 2019.

Production of coal has grown in response to demand for coal in electricity generation. Global production of coal totalled 3,000 Mt (million metric tonnes) in 1973. By 2018, total production had grown to over 7,300 Mt globally. China and India are large producers of coal for domestic use, and they are also large importers. China relies on coal-burning power stations for 70% of its power, and India's power is 75% dependent on coal. As Figure 10.4 shows, China is by far the world's largest producer of coal. In the 2000s, the demand of its fast-growing economy outstripped supply, leading to a steep rise in imports.

As China's economic growth slowed, the government has sought to re-balance supplies towards domestic production. The government is also seeking to improve standards for cleaner energy production, in order to deal with high levels of pollution, especially the thick smogs that envelop eastern cities. More stringent anti-pollution standards have prompted the building of cleaner power stations in western regions, and also acted as a brake on low-quality imports. India's demand for coal has continued to rise strongly, mainly to extend electricity to the third of India's population of 1.25 billion people who are still without. The government is hoping to meet most of this demand through new coal-fired power stations, but hopes of becoming self-sufficient seem a long way off.

renewable energy energy from natural sources such as wind, sun and water, whereby the sources are naturally replenished

Governments are now focusing on **renewable energy**, such as wind turbines and solar power, offering opportunities for companies in these sectors. Investment in renewables is now one of the major drivers of growth in electricity generation. And much of this investment is in emerging and developing economies. With improving technology and falling costs, wind and solar power are expected to account for nearly half of new investment in global power capacity in the years to 2020. However, government policies and financial commitment are still holding back these developments, especially the continuing reliance on fossil fuels for power generation.

The case for nuclear power generation rests on its low level of emissions, combined with concerns over the depletion of non-renewable energy sources such as coal and oil. Some countries have invested heavily in nuclear capacity, as Figure 10.5 shows. Indeed, France's energy giant, EDF (Electricité de France), is in a strong global position in building nuclear power stations. However, the expansion of nuclear power has brought risks. Risks have emerged with the growth in the nuclear reprocessing and recycling industries, combined with the need for safe treatment and storage of nuclear waste. Further, the safe transport of nuclear waste across land and sea, to reach reprocessing sites, has created new concerns, not just because of the risk of accidents, but also from the fear of terrorist attack. The risks associated with nuclear-related industries have become dispersed geographically as these industries have grown. China has become a major investor in nuclear, but its nuclear capacity in 2008 was only 1% of its overall power generation, and is expected to rise to 8.9% by 2030. India pledged in 2015 to generate 40% of its electricity from renewable and alternative low-carbon sources by 2030. But this goal seemed too optimistic in light of India's growing consumption of coal.

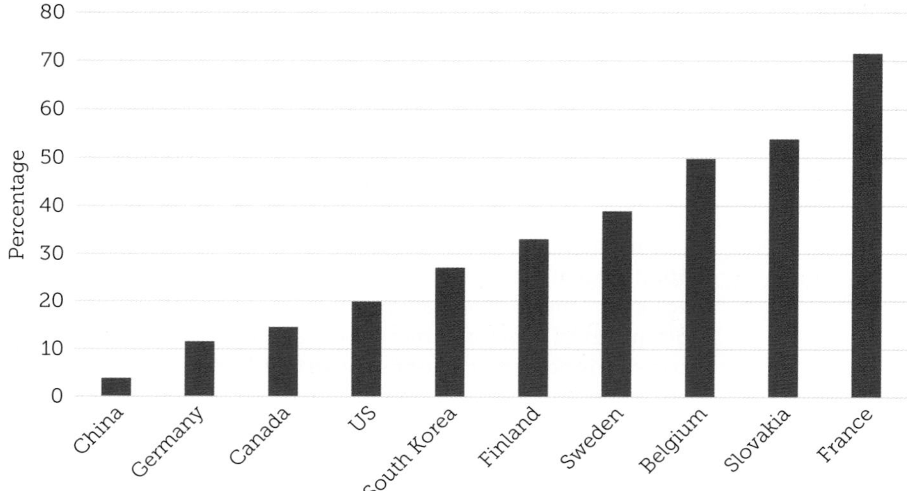

Figure 10.5 Share of nuclear power in electricity generation, 2017

Source of data: World Nuclear Association, Nuclear generation by country, issued April 2018, at www.world-nuclear.org, accessed 14 July 2019.

The Fukushima disaster in Japan in 2011 has had a profound effect on the expansion of nuclear power. An earthquake and subsequent tsunami destroyed the Fukushima nuclear power plant, releasing massive radioactive contamination which rendered an area of 300 square miles of land unfit for human habitation. The overall death toll was 18,000, and over 150,000 surviving victims were displaced. A larger area of 4,500 square miles was affected by long-lived radioactive cesium above Japan's legal limits. Radioactive cesium contaminates the entire ecosystem – water, soil, plants and animals. Decontamination has been unsuccessful. Homes and land can be decontaminated, but water flowing down the hills from melting snow soon contaminates an area again. The catastrophe resulted in the largest-ever radioactive discharge into the ocean. As noted in Chapter 6, the design of the nuclear reactor was considered problematic even at the time of its construction in 1970. Recent research highlights evidence that many mistakes and miscalculations were made by TEPCO (Tokyo Electric and Power Company), the operators of the power plant, who had failed to take account of the risks in areas prone to earthquakes and tsunamis, although these risks were known in other areas of Japan and internationally (Noack, 2015). Public prosecutors twice considered prosecuting TEPCO executives, but felt a

prosecution would stand little chance of succeeding. However, this stance was overturned by an independent judicial panel, made up of 11 ordinary citizens. The panel ruled that three former executives should be prosecuted for criminal negligence. The trial commenced in 2017, and all three pleaded not guilty. The trial became protracted, taking into account a large amount of evidence that seemed inconclusive. As of late 2018, the trial was continuing, and it was beginning to look as if the prosecution of the three individual executives was unlikely to lead to a clear result.

Damage caused by transboundary pollution, whether intentional or unintentional, may be long-lasting, and, in some cases, the full extent of the damage is not apparent for many years. How to apportion responsibility and compel polluters to compensate (insofar as possible) for the harm they cause is complicated by the fact that different legal jurisdictions are involved. Often, the victims are in developing countries, and have meagre resources to launch legal actions, especially if they must resort to litigation in another country. This was seen in the example of the Bhopal explosion, discussed in Chapter 6. Co-operation between governments has led to numerous international regulatory regimes designed to monitor pollution and reduce the risk of accidents.

Is nuclear the answer?

The Fukushima disaster highlighted the risks of nuclear power. Do the benefits of nuclear still outweigh the risks?

International frameworks to promote sustainable development

The harmful effects of transboundary pollution on ecosystems and human well-being may emerge only gradually. By contrast, environmental disasters, such as the Exxon Valdez oil spill off the Alaskan coast in 1989 and the Chernobyl nuclear plant disaster in 1986, have an immediate impact, as well as lasting effects which can continue to harm the environment for many years. Such disasters have dramatically raised public consciousness of the need for co-operation between states. The United Nations Environment Programme (UNEP) dates from 1972. The UN Conference on Environment and Development (UNCED) produced a report in 1987, usually referred to as the Brundtland Report. It introduced the concept of **sustainable development**, which is 'development which meets the needs of present generations without compromising the ability of future generations to meet their own needs' (United Nations, 1987). This concept was at the heart of the Declaration on Environment and Development produced by the Rio Summit of 1992, sometimes referred to as the 'Earth Summit'.

sustainable development view of economic development involving continuing investment for future generations, taking into account the long-term viability of industries, both in terms of human values and environmental protection

The Rio principles

The main principles of the Rio Declaration appear in Table 10.1. The principles apply to a variety of activities and incidents, whether involving state agencies or commercial enterprises. Note that, although the principle of state sovereignty over resources is acknowledged, it is qualified by the principle of sustainable development. The 'polluter-pays' principle is acknowledged, although, when it comes to dispute resolution, the polluting state will seldom consent to international adjudication or arbitration. Principle 5 links sustainable development with poverty reduction. Critics have argued that this principle seems to indicate an underlying assumption of the Declaration that reducing poverty requires economic development, although the historical evidence suggests a more complex relationship than simple cause and effect (Castro, 2004). Poverty includes dimensions other than purely economic ones, especially in the context of sustainable development. Reducing poverty in economic terms can be short-lived, whereas sustainable livelihoods entail the capacity to provide for today's needs in an environmentally sound way that will continue into the future. As the benefits of market-based economic development are not spread evenly in societies, policy-making in relation to resource allocation, as well as social priorities, are factors in reducing poverty (Castro, 2004).

Table 10.1 The Rio Declaration on Environment and Development, 1992

(selected key principles)

Principle 2	States have, in accordance with the UN Charter and the principles of international law, the sovereign right to exploit their own resources pursuant to their own environmental and development policies, and the responsibility to ensure that activities within their jurisdiction or control do not cause damage to the environment of other States or of areas beyond the limits of national jurisdiction.
Principle 3	The right to development must be fulfilled so as to equitably meet developmental and environmental needs of present and future generations.
Principle 5	All States and all people shall cooperate in the essential task of eradicating poverty as an indispensable requirement of sustainable development.
Principle 8	To achieve sustainable development and a higher quality of life for all people, States should reduce and eliminate unsustainable patterns of production and consumption and promote appropriate demographic policies.
Principle 13	States shall develop national law regarding liability and compensation for the victims of pollution and other environmental damage.
Principle 16	...the polluter should, in principle, bear the cost of pollution...
Principle 25	Peace, development and environmental protection are interdependent and indivisible.

Source: UN Environment Programme, *The Rio Declaration* (1992), at www.unep.org

The Rio Summit of 1992 adopted the Convention on Biological Diversity and the Convention on Climate Change. The Biodiversity Convention aimed to protect and sustain biodiversity by a number of measures, including national monitoring of biodiversity, environmental impact assessments and national progress reports from individual countries. It re-enforced the principle of sustainable development. In 1992, the UN also adopted a Convention on the Transboundary Effects of Industrial Accidents, placing an onus on states to take preventive steps and also to respond responsibly when accidents occur. A Convention on Nuclear Safety followed in 1994. While these international instruments focus on state responsibility for implementation of their provisions within their own jurisdictions, it should be noted that states vary in their commitment to prevent and control harmful activities. Developing countries, above all, may lack the resources to regulate environmental protection. Awareness of environmental implications by business enterprises is therefore a crucial factor in the environmental protection landscape. In particular, the responsibility of the large MNEs as important global players is increasingly recognized in environmental issues.

UN sustainable development goals

In 2000, the UN Millennium Summit of world leaders introduced eight Millennium Development Goals (MDGs) aimed at improving wellbeing over the next 15 years. There were eight MDGs, covering the following areas: poverty and hunger, educa-

tion, child mortality, maternal health, disease, the environment and global partnership. Within these areas, specific targets were set, some quite ambitious. Although considerable progress was made over the 15 years, most of the targets were not met. The aim was to halve the number of people living in extreme poverty (on less than $1.25 a day). The number was reduced from 1.9 billion to 836 million in 2015, falling slightly short of the target. Progress towards the target of halving the number of people without access to safe drinking water and improved sanitation was better. The number without safe drinking water was halved, but that still left 663 million people without (Galatsidas and Sheehy, 2015). The target for halving the number of people without improved sanitation was missed by nearly 700 million people.

Sustainable Development Goals (SDGs) UN development goals, superseding the Millennium Development Goals (MDGs), covering environmental, institutional and governance issues

In 2015, the UN launched the **Sustainable Development Goals** (SDGs), an even more ambitious set of goals for the following 15 years. This set of 17 goals is broader in scope, covering institutional and governance issues, as well as the basic goals of improving human wellbeing that were the focus of the MDGs. The SDGs are shown in Figure 10.6.

UN Sustainable Development Goals (SDGs)

1 End extreme poverty (less than $1.90 a day)

2 End hunger; achieve food security and sustainable agriculture

3 Ensure good health and wellbeing

4 Ensure inclusive and quality education

5 Achieve gender equality

6 Ensure safe drinking water and sanitation for all

7 Ensure affordable, clean energy for all

8 Promote decent work and inclusive, sustainable economic growth

9 Promote inclusive and sustainable industrialization, including infrastructure and innovation

10 Reduce inequality within and between countries

11 Make cities safe, inclusive and sustainable

12 Ensure sustainable consumption and production

13 Combat climate change

14 Conserve the oceans and seas

15 Promote sustainable use of land

16 Promote peace, justice and inclusive institutions

17 Strengthen global partnership for SDGs

Figure 10.6 UN Sustainable Development Goals (SDGs) 2015–2030

Note: Updated by the UNDP on 9 April 2019, to adjust the threshold for absolute poverty.

Source: Derived from UNDP (UN Development Programme) (2015) *Sustainable Development Goals Booklet*, 28 September, at www.undp.org

The first six SDGs, like the MDGs, concern poverty, hunger, health and education, but with the more radical aim of wiping out extreme poverty and hunger everywhere. SDGs 7, 13, 14 and 15 directly address issues of climate change and the environment. Included are the need for clean energy that all can afford (SDG 7), sustainable use of the land (SDG15), climate change (SDG13) and conservation of the seas (SDG14). Sustainable consumption, as well as production, is emphasized, reflecting the Rio Declaration (SDG12). These are compatible with sustainable agriculture, which is part of SDG1, forming a comprehensive set of goals relating to ecology and climate change. However, they are very broadly worded, articulating ideals rather than attainable targets. Remaining goals highlight the need for inclusiveness. Look at the numerous aspects of SDGs 8 and 9. These are broadly worded goals related to a development agenda, which raise questions for governments and businesses.

What kind of development is being encouraged, how is it being financed, and who is benefiting? Economic development typically relies on foreign investors, with their capital and technology, which governments of developing countries are keen to attract. But the interests of investors and societies do not automatically coincide. For example, large agribusiness companies like Monsanto base their business on the use of **genetically-modified organisms (GMOs)**, which are plants and animals that have been altered genetically in ways that do not occur in nature. Monsanto presses for the adoption of GM crops in Africa, where drought and flooding can play havoc with traditional agriculture. However, GM crops are linked with damage to biodiversity and ecosystems. In addition, small farmers become tied to the company that provides the seeds and other products needed for GM production – a situation that involves not just being locked in contractually, but, for many, indebtedness caused by the loans they must incur (see the mini case study in Chapter 8). Included in the goal on sustainable economic growth (SDG8) is the issue of debt relief for the many heavily indebted developing countries. Most of the debt of these countries is owed to lenders in rich countries. There has been progress on a scheme of debt relief through the IMF and World Bank, but SDG8 does not envisage any stronger mechanism (Jones, 2015).

genetically-modified organisms (GMOs) plants and animals that have been altered genetically in ways that do not occur in nature

Industrialization and infrastructure projects, highlighted in SDG9, often serve mainly the interests of investors rather than all in society. As we saw in Chapter 9, governments play key roles in promoting domestic innovation that can contribute to sustainable development. SDGs 10, 11 and 16 specifically address the role of institutions and governance. SDG11 refers to the growth of sprawling urban areas of mostly poor inhabitants in much of the developing world. Problems of health, clean water, employment, education and clean affordable energy are all associated with slums, setting back the prospects of improving human wellbeing. Indeed, these poor living and working conditions pose some of the greatest obstacles to achieving most of the other SDGs in this list. They also represent threats to social cohesion. SDGs 11 and 16 recognize the problems of huge disparities between the rich and poor, not just in terms of income, but in institutions that perpetuate inequality.

Are the new SDGs achievable, or simply a wish list? Like the MDGs before them, progress in achieving some of the goals, such as piped water, can be measured. But others relate to more fundamental aspects of economies and political systems. Governments of any hue, whether democratic or authoritarian, can promote universal education, but where power rests with political and business elites, often with corrupt links, the weak are likely to come off worst. This throws into doubt the hopes of achieving the more radical of these SDGs. The poor, whether in rural communities or precarious urban dwellings, remain most vulnerable to being exposed to environmental degradation and the ravages of climate change. Although the goals are perhaps too optimistic, the new SDGs do serve to draw attention to the importance of politics and institutions in achieving inclusive development.

SDGs: too ambitious?

Which of the SDGs are most crucial for achieving sustainable livelihoods among the world's poorest inhabitants? What should businesses be doing to achieve them?

Managing environmental impacts

Land, water and air are the components of the physical environment which have been affected by industrial processes associated with economic development. Managers have become accustomed to dealing with local pollution problems arising from their operations, entailing interaction with local community authorities. However, wider

issues such as climate change and biodiversity, while nonetheless real, seem remote, complex, and not susceptible to the usual means of resolution. What is more, scientific evidence is not always clear-cut, and regulatory regimes differ in their monitoring and enforcement. NGOs such as Greenpeace and other 'green' groups have raised public awareness of environmental issues and climate change. As we have seen, the views of consumers and shareholders tend to influence corporate executives more than the more abstract arguments based on ethical principles.

Sustainable development in the business context

Businesses are becoming more conscious of the need for new, cleaner technologies, partly because of growing social and ethical considerations, and also because of international instruments that are gradually becoming part of national law. But how does a broad principle like sustainable development translate into a business strategy? The following statement from the International Institute for Sustainable Development (IISD) provides some indication:

> For the business enterprise, sustainable development means adopting business strategies and activities that meet the needs of the enterprise and its stakeholders today while protecting, sustaining and enhancing the human and natural resources that will be needed in the future. (IISD, 1992)

In terms of strategy, the statement is still rather general, but it does highlight the duty to stakeholders, and also the duty to both human and environmental resources. The IISD has revisited this definition in light of Sen's concept of development as freedom of individual choice or capabilities (Sen, 1999). Development in this wider sense would reflect the perspective of human development articulated by Castro (cited above). This would apply not just in developing countries, but in any country where there are wide disparities in income and life opportunities between the rich and the poor. Where a business is party to environmental degradation, it can be impeding sustainable development in this wider sense. For example, eroding a resource such as a river on which a community depends will impair livelihoods and impact on future generations.

Companies are encouraged to take a broader view of their 'environmental footprint', looking at all phases of their operations, from production processes to the nature of the products they sell, to assess whether they can be made more environmentally friendly. Consumers have been a source of pressure, creating new demand, for example, for products which are recyclable. Environmental protection and economic efficiency, once seen as posing a dilemma of choice, could be seen as merging together. Protecting the environment should be at the heart of sustainable business strategy, viewed as value-enhancing, rather than as a constraint on business. Environmental issues are closely linked with social responsibility, and many businesses now publish sustainability reports on a regular basis.

MINI CASE STUDY

Oil companies and reforestation strategies: how sustainable are they?

The business of oil companies is essentially activities associated with fossil fuels. And, although they are the major contributor to CO_2 emissions, fossil fuels are still in demand and will be for a long time to come. Many investors, notably pension funds, are taking a critical view of companies' carbon footprints. Boards are therefore facing pressures to respond with positive proposals for climate action. In the case of oil companies, this is particularly challenging. Some are now turning to the idea of 'carbon offsets', that is, investing in activities such as forestry, that will mitigate the effects of their core activities of exploring and drilling for oil and gas. Is this just cynical 'greenwash', or does it genuinely contribute to climate change action?

Norway's large oil company, Equinor (formerly Statoil) has announced plans to invest in forestry, aiming for investments amounting to one million tonnes of CO_2, which would equal the size of its footprint in its US and Brazilian operations. Other companies that have introduced carbon offsets as a way to preserve their core business model are BP, Total and Shell. Climate experts criticize this approach, saying that carbon offsets do not actually mitigate climate change. While protecting tropical forests and reforestation is essential to responding to climate change, the environmentalists' message to oil companies is that they need to change their business models to reduce their emissions. This would involve changing their operations and, in addition, investing in renewables. They would need to define targets for reducing emissions, and to monitor performance regularly.

A drawback of companies' aims to direct corporate investment in reforestation is that companies are not well placed to carry out such plans on their own. Regulatory changes are often needed at the national level, and these need not be forthcoming or suitable for private-sector businesses. Even with an authorized scheme in place, the costs can be very high, and there is no guarantee that in 20 or 30 years the trees will still be there.

Under pressure from institutional investors, Royal Dutch Shell announced in 2018 its intention to link long-term executive pay with progress towards energy transition, involving reductions in carbon emissions. These investors support the aim of reducing emissions to levels that would limit global warming to well below 2°C. In 2017, the company had announced a broad ambition of halving its carbon emissions by 2050, with an interim step of a 20% reduction by 2035, but there were no shorter-term targets spelt out. The 2018 proposal is intended to be more detailed, with shorter-term targets of three or five years. There would be specific net carbon footprint targets, and the company would publish annual updates on its progress. This proposal is subject to approval by the shareholders at the AGM in 2020, but the strengthened proposal linking executive pay and energy transition would seem to be in keeping with the wishes of these long-term investors.

Discussion questions

- How effective are carbon offsets in combatting climate change?
- Shell is breaking new ground with its proposal outlined in the case study. Should other companies follow their lead, and why?

Find out more

See the article by Adam Vaughan, 'Shell boss says mass reforestation needed to limit temperature rises to 1.5C', in *The Guardian*, 9 October 2018.

Environmental management in practice

environmental management assessing environmental impacts and devising suitable strategies across a company's total operations

Environmental management, assessing environmental impact and devising suitable strategies, is now seen as central to companies' operations, especially in the industries which are by nature more pollutant. These include chemicals, mining, pulp and paper, iron and steel, and refineries. For the large MNEs that use subcontracting and licensing arrangements, there is a question of how much control can be exerted on subcontractors in terms of environmental management. This question is often posed for MNEs operating in developing countries with weaker environmental protection laws.

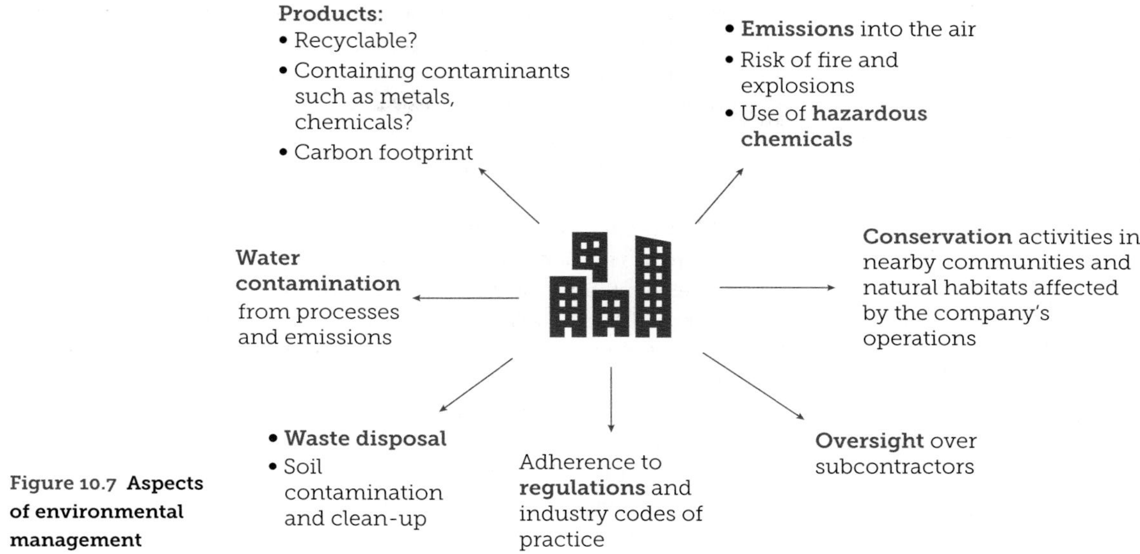

Figure 10.7 Aspects of environmental management

Research and increased awareness of the damaging effects of climate change have impressed on businesses the need to look at the green implications of their operations, and especially their levels of emissions. One consideration is that reductions are likely to be legally required in the future, and it is preferable to get a head start. Another is that companies are in a position to take the lead in positive action to alleviate potentially harmful global warming, especially in industries that have high levels of emissions. Figure 10.7 shows the areas of environmental management in both processes and products. Industrial processes impact on the air, water and land, in the immediate vicinity of operations and often further afield. Emissions of gases, particulate matter and chemicals can cause damaging air pollution. There are also risks of fires and explosions, which are high in some industries, especially in the energy sector.

The oil company, BP, has faced liabilities in the US for many billions of dollars following an oil spill at a rig in the Gulf of Mexico (see Chapter 6). These huge bills for damages, fines and clean-up activities that were incurred in the US are exceptional. Most companies that operate in sensitive environments are unlikely to face the years of litigation and punitive damages claims that BP faced. Contamination of water from industrial processes can affect all types of waterways, both surface and underground. Much of this contamination is hard to detect, and it can be difficult to prove who is responsible. In many cases, a fine payable under local law is the only penalty. But the effects can be long-lasting. Where water is becoming scarce, industrial use can be controversial, as whole communities can experience water shortages. Adapting processes to use less water, as well as reducing waste water, has become a priority in industries which are heavy users of water.

Soil contamination and degradation are more localized than emissions into the atmosphere, but can have long-lasting impacts on the land, affecting its use for human habitation and other uses such as agriculture. Waste disposal can be costly for firms, and in developing countries where environmental controls are weak, firms are more likely to be lax about how waste is disposed of than in more regulated environments. Ecuador is an example, where serious environmental degradation was caused by Texaco's operations between 1964 and 1992. Because environmental restoration requirements agreed by the company with the Ecuadorian government were minimal, there was little inhabitants could do to make the company clean up and restore sites when they left the country in 1992. Enduring contamination was impairing human health, leading to cancers and other illnesses. Legal claims to obtain redress have been staunchly resisted by Chevron, the company that now owns Texaco. Ecuadorian villagers initiated legal proceedings against Texaco in the US courts in 1993, which culminated in a judgment against the Ecuadorians in 2002, on the grounds that Ecuador would have been the appropriate forum. In 2003, the Ecuadorian villagers launched a class action in Ecuador against Texaco, which was by then part of Chevron. The decision of the Ecuadorian judge in 2011 was that Chevron should pay $8.6 billion in damages and clean-up costs, increasing to $18 billion if Chevron did not issue an apology. Chevron did not accept this ruling, and filed legal actions in the US against Ecuador's lawyers, alleging conspiracy to extort billions of dollars from the company.

In 2012, the Ecuadorian villagers initiated action in Canada to enforce the Ecuadorian judgment against Chevron's assets in Canada, and in September 2013, the Canadian Supreme Court decided that Canada would have jurisdiction in the case. This seemed to be a step forward for the Ecuadorian villagers, and the case was heard in Ontario. However, the Ontario Court of Appeal ruled in 2018 that the Ecuadorians had no case under Canadian law. The court expressed sympathy with their plight and their efforts to obtain justice. The disappointed Ecuadorians then appealed to Canada's Supreme Court. The Ecuadorian villagers still have had no payment from the company, and Chevron acknowledges no liability for the contamination.

Meanwhile, concurrently with the court actions, Chevron had used the investor-state dispute settlement process (ISDS) to bring cases against Ecuador, claiming Ecuador had violated a US–Ecuador bilateral investment treaty (see Chapters 6 and 7). Arbitration panels have ruled in favour of Chevron, stating that Ecuador should suspend enforcement of its court's order against Chevron. In a further case heard by an international arbitration tribunal in The Hague in 2018, the arbitration panel held that the decision by Ecuador's court in 2011 was tainted by fraud and corruption. Chevron would thus be entitled to damages, to be decided by a later hearing of the tribunal. Ecuador is appealing against this decision. Of course, an arbitration tribunal is not a court of law, and cannot invalidate a judgment of a country's courts. The tribunal decisions have favoured Chevron consistently.

Surface disturbance, as well as waste disposal, is a factor in mining. Much of the world's coal reserves do not lie in deep mines but near the surface, in opencast mines. Extracting this coal despoils the land, and the operations can be widespread, affecting the ecology over large areas. Canada's oil sands are an example, where surface mining operations cover an area of 54,000 square miles. These mining operations to extract bitumen, a type of heavy petroleum, use large amounts of water and generate large amounts of GHG emissions. There are serious concerns about environmental damage from these operations. There are also concerns over the risks incurred in the transport of the fuel by rail and road to destinations in Canada and the US.

Cutting pollution, while it can be seen as a cost, is also a business opportunity. Much research is being carried out into changing the nature of consumer products, to make them less pollutant. As Figure 10.7 highlights, recycling is one aspect of greener products. Products which have been designed to be environmentally friendly use fewer metals and chemicals and are easier to recycle. The Global Commission on the Economy and Climate, headed by the former Mexican president, Felipe Calderon, makes the case that investments in cleaner infrastructure, transport and energy are affordable and cost-effective in the long term.

The way I see it...

'The structural and technological changes unfolding in the global economy, combined with multiple opportunities to improve economic efficiency, now make it possible to achieve both better growth and better climate outcomes.'

The Global Commission on the Economy and Climate, in its report, *Better Growth, Better Climate*, 2014, at https://newclimateeconomy.net

In an article published by the Global Commission in 2018, Paul Polman, the former CEO of Unilever, who retired on 1 January 2019, is forthright in stating that better progress could be made. See Polman, P. (2018) 'Commentary: Action needed to tackle climate change', 19 December, at https://newclimateeconomy.net. He highlights actions needed, such as the ending of subsidies for fossil fuels and reducing deforestation (forest-related funding amounts to only 3% of climate mitigation funding).

These are structural changes that need both government and business support. To what extent do these policies look more – or less – likely at present?

triple-bottom-line reporting corporate reporting focusing on social and environmental aspects of the company, in addition to traditional financial information

The extent to which businesses will voluntarily set targets for emissions reductions will affect global progress towards reaching national targets. Environmental reporting, detailing the ways in which a company's operations impact on the environment, has become an element in **'triple-bottom-line' reporting**. In addition to financial reporting, some companies report on social and environmental aspects of their operations, making up the three elements of triple-bottom-line reporting. While the latter two impact reports are voluntary, they are increasingly viewed by shareholders and other stakeholders as indicative of good governance. The International Organization for Standardization (www.iso.org), which produces ISO standards, has developed a certification for standards of environmental management. The initial standards were set out in ISO 14000, updated to ISO 14001:2015. Many MNEs are finding that, in the new context of social responsibility, it is advantageous to take a global approach to their environmental management, wherever the location.

Sustainable consumption

sustainable consumption principle that consumer lifestyle and purchasing decisions should take account of the environmental needs of future generations

When we think of consumers and green issues, we tend to think mainly of recycling waste and buying organic produce. However, green consumerism covers a wide range of lifestyle decisions. Besides shopping for environmentally friendly products and recycling, it covers using less pollutant transport, using complementary medicine, exploring eco-tourism for our holidays, and investing our money in socially responsible funds. In addressing the role of consumers in environmental issues, the UNEP focuses on a broad notion of **sustainable consumption**, which covers the many lifestyle decisions made by consumers which impact on the environment over the long term, whether directly or indirectly. The Oslo Symposium of 1994 provided a broad definition of sustainable consumption as

> 'the use of goods and services that respond to basic needs and bring a better quality of life, while minimizing the use of natural resources, toxic materials and emissions of waste and pollutants over the life cycle, so as not to jeopardize the needs of future generations' (Oslo Roundtable on Sustainable Consumption and Production, 1994).

The Oslo Symposium definition envisages a distinction between patterns of consumption and volumes of consumption. Substituting more efficient and less polluting products will improve environmental quality through changing patterns of consumption. Consumers will more readily adapt to changing patterns of consumption than reducing the volumes of consumption of a product or service. Typical measures that environment-conscious householders invest in are solar energy installations, energy-efficient boilers and lightbulbs, electric vehicles and bicycles.

'Green consumerism' has seen a rise in popularity of environmentally friendly products, often at premium prices. In some instances, such as GM-free products, the reasoning is based on health fears as much as environmental concerns (see Chapter 7 on GM labelling). Sceptics of green consumerism argue that, even if consumers in rich countries change their buying habits, the effects will be limited unless people are persuaded to consume less. The trend in the large emerging economies has been in the opposite direction. Development has tended to be equated with western consumer lifestyles, dependent on cars, cheap air travel and throw-away appliances, all of which have been on the rise in emerging economies. In the five years to 2019, the number of Chinese airlines offering long-haul air travel has more than doubled, to 29. China saw the launch of 30 new long-haul routes added in 2018 alone. Between 2009 and 2018, China's international passenger traffic grew from just under 15 million to nearly 64 million, while domestic passenger traffic grew from 211 million to 548 million in the same period (CAPA Centre for Aviation, 2019). This boom in the Chinese airline industry takes place against a backdrop of highly publicized risks to the climate crisis caused by aviation.

Development, both past and present, tends to mean economic growth, with little heed for environmental consequences. Carmakers are lured to the emerging economies. Here, consumers are keen to acquire cars – and the new mobility they bring. With far fewer cars per inhabitant than the advanced economies, there is much scope for growth in these markets. Sales of passenger cars and trucks reached a record high of 90 million globally in 2017. Nearly 29 million of these sales were in China, the world's largest car market by volume. In 2005, sales of passenger cars in China numbered about 4 million. This figure had more than doubled by 2010, and in 2014, had reached nearly 20 million. Since then, the growth in sales has slowed, largely because of the slowing rate of economic growth. However, other factors have been the government's policies of cracking down on corruption and measures taken in large cities to rein in car ownership, to deal with traffic congestion and air pollution.

For businesses, especially manufacturing firms, the notion of defining sustainable consumption as reduced consumption meets with little appeal. Similarly, for governments, reduced consumption is not likely to find favour. Reduced consumer spending tends to pose headaches, as highlighted in Chapter 4: reduced output is linked to decreases in employment, falling tax revenues and weak economic growth. Governments, however, are in a position to promote changes in consumer behaviour and changes in manufacturers' approaches, towards more sustainable consumption.

Sustainable consumption – every day?

As consumers, we depend on a variety of industrialized products, from ready meals in packets to drinks in cans. Businesses are inclined to say that they continue to produce these products because these are what consumers want. To what extent would you be able and willing to give up these everyday products?

The impacts of climate change: sustainability in the balance

The imperative for governments and businesses to act on the impacts of climate change has become urgent. Industrial production, extraction and exploitation of resources are environmental issues for all countries, whatever their stage of economic development. Developed economies, while their economies have long been more focused on services than manufacturing, continue to have high levels of carbon emissions, due in large part to consumer lifestyles. Emerging economies, where western consumer lifestyles are now spreading rapidly among the growing middle classes, are the sources of the biggest rises in carbon emissions. Urbanization in developing countries, where infrastructure is struggling to catch up, is causing problems for maintaining clean air, access to clean water and sanitation. Sprawling cities are also prone to suffer from food and energy shortages. Whereas these issues were once seen as matters of local concern, we now see them as part of a global picture. Similarly, global attention focuses on areas of the world where population pressures and depletion of natural resources are causing hardship to both humans and other sentient beings such as wildlife.

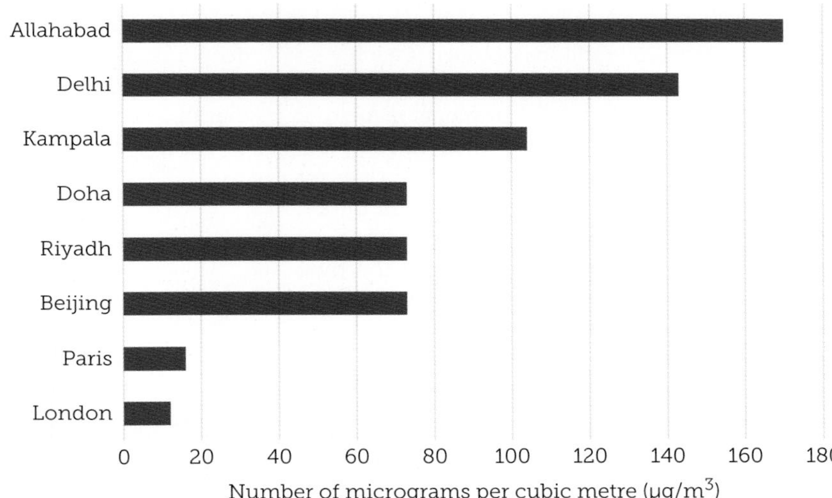

Figure 10.8 Air pollution in selected cities

Note: Annual mean concentration of particulate matter of a diameter of 2.5 microns or less.

Source of data: WHO, Global ambient air quality database, update 2018, at www.who.int, accessed 24 November 2018.

Levels of pollution in the growing cities in developing and emerging countries have overtaken those in the developed countries. Air pollution is measured in terms of particulate matter (PM) per cubic metre. Particles smaller than 2.5 micrometres or microns, known as $PM_{2.5}$, are found in emissions from vehicles, burning waste and metal processing. They present a serious risk to health, especially to people in the cities with the highest concentrations. The WHO reports concentrations of $PM_{2.5}$ in over 2,000 cities worldwide. A selection of these is set out in Figure 10.8. A concentration of under 9 is considered a relatively safe level, and up to 25 is considered moderate. But concentrations over 25 are unhealthy for sensitive people, and concentrations over 40 are unhealthy for everyone. The WHO's data reveal that cities in India are among the world's most pollutant. Beijing's pollution has received much attention, due to its rapid industrialization and urbanization. China has made considerable progress in reducing pollution. Pollution in Beijing has fallen 40% since 2000, while Delhi's has risen. India is now facing severe challenges to human health, the natural environment, and the preservation of historic buildings. The two most pollutant cities shown in Figure 10.8 are in India. Car sales in India have been rising quickly. Sales of passenger vehicles rose over 9% in 2017, amounting to an additional 3.2 million units more than in 2016. From about 50 million cars on India's roads in 2000, the number grew to over 200 million in 2018. This is good news for the car industry in India, but it is a major contributor to pollution. While the new mobility is welcomed by vehicle users, grinding traffic congestion and toxic emissions have been the price. Electric cars have made little progress in India due to the slowness of introducing charging infrastructure.

MINI CASE STUDY

Saving the Taj Mahal

People all over the world would recognize a photo of the Taj Mahal in India's northern city of Agra, whether they have been there or not. One of the seven Wonders of the World, the seventeenth-century Taj Mahal is one of India's most famous buildings, visited by millions of tourists each year and recognized as a world heritage site by UNESCO. Enjoying this level of global esteem, it might be assumed, would guarantee that its preservation and protection would be top priorities for Indian officialdom. But such an assumption would be wrong. Pollution, environmental damage and negligent management of the river Yamuna, have left the building in an unsound state, with crumbling foundations, deterioration of its marble facades and discolouration. The tourist expects to see this jewel of the Mughal era as it is depicted in idealized photos, with shimmering white marble and set in serene gardens.

What the tourist actually sees today is a rapidly deteriorating palace of yellow and green discolouration, with visible signs of damage to the marble facade. Much of the outward damage is being caused by sulphur dioxide (SO_2) and particulate matter that combine with the moisture in the air to produce acid rain that causes the yellowing. Diesel emissions and pollutants from industries in the Agra area are largely to blame, including foundries, chemical plants and refineries. India's northern cities are among the most polluted in the world, and the situation is worsened by climate change. The heavily polluted Yamuna River, on whose banks it sits, is drying up, destabilizing the wooden foundations of the building. Waste accumulates in the river, and insects have bred in the contaminated water, leaving green deposits on the buildings.

Officials at local and federal level have recognized the need to protect the Taj Mahal. And the Supreme Court of India has held that polluting industries in the vicinity should be closed. But saving the historic monument raises an array of deeper issues. To many, local economic activities must take priority. Environmentalists would argue that this is a short-term perspective: cleaning up or closing down pollutant industries is the only

Not the image of the Taj Mahal that tourists would recognize – but one that reflects the current plight of this historic site.

sustainable way forward. Health issues for local residents who are suffering from the high levels of pollution are tied in with the pollution that is devastating the Taj Mahal.

Local officials and political leaders are ambivalent. Built by Emperor Shah Jahan, the Taj Mahal dates from the Mughal era, when northern India was ruled by Islamic emperors. Some of India's Hindu nationalist politicians are against conserving this historic monument, as it represents a period similar to the colonialism of British rule. Others say that this is a false analogy: Mughal rulers were Indian, not colonial powers. What is not in dispute is that the tourists who come to Agra generate large revenues. Most countries would consider a world-renowned tourist attraction to be a huge asset to the economy – and the country's global image. In addition, UNESCO has urged India to take action to conserve the site as one of global cultural heritage. As the debate continues, time is running out to save the Taj Mahal.

Questions

- What should be done to save the Taj Mahal?
- How likely is it that authorities in India will take the necessary steps to save the monument?

Find out more

See the article on the Taj Mahal and other pollution issues in India, 'As the Taj Mahal changes colour, pollution leaves India cities gasping for breath', by Kerean Watts, *Health Issues India*, 8 May 2018, at www.healthissuesindia.com

Challenges and responsibilities for environmental damage and climate change are intertwined with other challenges, such as reducing poverty, improving food security and providing sustainable livelihoods. It is not difficult to see why governments of large emerging countries, such as India, seem ambivalent on responsibilities for the impacts of rising emissions. Improving human wellbeing, however, rests ultimately on sustainable development rather than unfettered industrialization. The Indian government wishes to be part of the solution to climate change, but has been reluctant to recognize that it has become part of the problem. India is seeing sustainable solutions springing up on a local basis, and its government is coming under pressure to take action at the national level to reduce emissions.

The UN has taken a lead in initiatives to report on the scientific findings of climate change, and also to promote co-operation among countries to reduce emissions. The Paris agreement marked an important shift, with governments taking responsibility for defining their own targets, through their nationally determined contributions (NDCs). Accepting responsibility in principle is still a long way from legislating changes in behaviour, such as compulsory limits on emissions. Since the Paris agreement, the UN has become concerned that there is an 'emissions gap', in that governments are moving more slowly in reducing emissions than had been hoped. If countries do no more than meet the targets in their NDCs, the aim of reducing global warming to 1.5°C maximum cannot be achieved. The G20 countries (introduced in Chapter 5), encompassing major emerging economies, are key to climate change action. As of 2018, half the G20 countries were not on target to reduce emissions in keeping with their NDCs.

Figure 10.9 sets out the recommendations made by the UN Environment Programme (UNEP, www.unenvironment.org). The report urges that there is much governments can do in revising targets and reducing emissions. Governments that continue to fund fossil-fuel subsidies should be phasing them out, but many con-

Strengthen national government policies on emissions reductions
- Scale up NDCs
- Reduce transport-related fossil-fuel subsidies
- Raise emissions standards, e.g. for heavy-duty vehicles

Action by non-state and subnational actors
- Networks that co-ordinate climate pledges
- Co-operation of cities, regions and companies, e.g. in industry transition

Climate change action

Use of fiscal policy to promote a low-carbon economy
- Raise tax on fossil fuels
- Subsidize low-emissions alternatives

Accelerate innovation in low-carbon technology
- Public money towards financing innovation and shouldering risk
- Mission-oriented innovation

Figure 10.9 UN recommendations for climate change action

Source: Derived from recommendations in UNEP (2018) *Emissions Gap Report 2018*, United Nations Environment Programme, Nairobi (Kenya), at www.unenvironment.org

tinue to pay these subsidies, including over a third of G20 countries. Reducing transport-related fossil-fuel subsidies is highlighted in the report. Fiscal policy is an area in which it finds much more could be done by way of carbon pricing. Taxes can be imposed on fossil fuels, and also a system of permissions can be used to license the use of fossil fuels. The report highlights the importance of innovation in low-carbon technology. Governments can fund innovation projects, including those that require 'patient' finance over a long time period. They are thus in a position to absorb the risk involved, which private-sector companies are reluctant or unable to afford.

The UNEP highlights that non-state and subnational players are important in climate change action. They include cities, regions, NGOs and private-sector businesses. While businesses have accepted sustainable development as a guiding principle, they have tended to wait for government regulation, rather than to pursue green initiatives on grounds of social responsibility. However, various collaborative initiatives under the UNEP's overall strategy have encouraged and guided businesses to co-operate with each other in projects they would be unable to pursue on their own.

Conclusions

Industrialization, growing urban populations and changing patterns of consumption: these are all aspects of the effects of human activity on the environment. Industrial work and urban living present opportunities to improve human wellbeing through, for example, better housing, clean water and better healthcare. But urbanization that is haphazard and lacking sufficient infrastructure can be detrimental to humans – and the natural environment. Much of the human activity that has led to increasing economic development has also brought a downside of environmental degradation and risks to health and wellbeing – not just for the present generation, but for future generations, too. We now know far more about the impacts of global warming than earlier generations could have known. The case for making changes in behaviour is clear. But where does responsibility lie? To say it lies with everyone on the planet is certainly true, but so abstract that no single person or organization actually feels responsible. Businesses have tended to take the view that environment and climate change measures are for governments to legislate, and in the absence of

regulation, there is no obligation to change behaviour. But even if there is no legal obligation, there is moral obligation for impacts that are clearly known to be detrimental.

International agreements have made headway in urging governments to raise environmental standards, reduce levels of GHG emissions, and slow deforestation, but national governments are ultimately the bodies that determine what regulations will apply. And, as we have seen, businesses look first to national laws as sources of obligation. If governments are slow to regulate, so too are businesses slow to make changes. The company whose activities pollute a river or emit toxic pollution into the atmosphere is often able simply to carry on. There might be no law against it, or, if there is, little likelihood of being caught. In some countries where enforcement systems are in place, the company can simply pay the fines that arise from time to time, considering the fines cheaper than cleaning up its operations. Whole communities and ecosystems can be at risk, with little realistic prospect of legal redress. Pressure on businesses to change their behaviour can seem weak in the absence of strict regulation. However, both governments and corporate leaders are frequently criticized by consumers and other stakeholders on grounds of ethics and social responsibility. These criticisms weigh with businesses, who are part of the communities in which they operate. Cumulatively, the impacts of stakeholder voices, including those of shareholders, are helping to shift the thinking of corporate decision-makers from short-term economic goals to sustainable business practices.

CLOSING CASE STUDY

Plastic waste and what to do about it

Plastic is part of everyday life for just about everybody. Although plastic packaging is now grabbing attention, plastic is about much more than packaging. The commonest types of clothing are largely derived from plastic, in the form of polyester, lycra or other synthetic fibres. Ordinary consumer products, from cars to televisions, contain high proportions of plastic. Then there is packaging. Food in the developed economies is mostly packaged, as are consumer products from appliances to toys. Much clothing, too, comes packaged, having travelled in containers from Asian manufacturers. Plastic's great attraction has been that it is cheap, light, and disposable, making it ideal for things like takeaway food and drinks. Plastic became part of modern consumer lifestyles. It was bound up with the way people now live. Single-use plastic became universal. It is only since about 2015 that takeaway plastic cup and food containers started to alarm people.

Will these plastic bottles be recycled? Much plastic waste that could be recycled finishes up in landfills.

Plastic derives from fossil fuels. It was developed in the nineteenth century, but became widely used in consumer products during and after the Second World War. It had seemingly infinite uses, and was more malleable than natural products such as cotton, glass, cardboard or wood. The large oil and chemical companies oversaw the growth in the plastics industry. These petrochemical companies included Dupont, Dow Chemical, Mobil, Exxon and Monsanto. They facilitated the explosive growth in the use of plastics, and are still the powerhouses in the industry. Consolidation has occurred: Mobil and Exxon merged; Dupont and Dow have merged; and Monsanto has been taken over by Bayer.

The boom in the plastics industry led to a growing problem over plastic waste. Already in the 1960s, concerns about the collection and disposal of waste were issues. The industry in the US successfully pursued a campaign of Keep America Beautiful, putting the onus on consumers to dispose of waste responsibly. Anti-litter campaigns directed at consumers were portrayed as the solution, when, in fact, the problems lay with the industrial establishment that was churning out pollutant plastics. The plastics industry promoted recycling from the early 1970s, but plastic has proved difficult to recycle, and, ultimately, it still finishes up in landfills or the ocean. The world produces over 300 million tonnes of plastic packaging every year. In the US, only 10% of plastic is recycled.

In the 1980s, the incineration of plastic waste was thought to be a solution, even though incinerators were expensive and also highly pollutant, emitting toxic ash, mercury and dioxins. They continued to be used in the US, and many are still in use, rechristened as recycling processors. The chemical industry has encouraged 'plastic-to-fuel' recycling, whereby consumers bag up plastic waste for collection. The waste is then melted to produce fossil fuels to burn. Most of the world's largest plastics producers are the giant oil and gas companies. As long as they continue to extract fossil fuels, the plastics industry will thrive. A number of companies have come together to form the Plastic Waste Alliance, aimed at combatting plastic waste. Most of these are in fact large producers of plastic themselves. One of its members, Shell, is building a multi-billion dollar plant in Pennsylvania, that will use shale gas to produce 1.6 million tonnes of polyethylene a year. This is the commonest type of plastic. It is cheaper, lighter and more versatile than substitutes. Exxon Mobil is building a similar plant in Texas. These projects are proceeding despite the incontrovertible evidence against plastics.

Scientific research showed in the 1990s that waste in the oceans was made up mostly of non-biodegradable plastic. Plastic waste was washing up on beaches, and the amount was growing. It was found that plastic waste was forming large heaps in calmer waters. Fish and birds were taking in particles of plastic. These alarming stories were gradually becoming known to a wider public. From the mid-2000s onwards, plastic started to be seen not just as litter, but as a dangerous pollutant. In 2010, scientists warned about microbeads, the tiny grains of plastic that are used pervasively in cosmetics, shower gel and cleaning products. Tiny fibres of synthetic fabrics used in clothes are shed every time the item of clothing is washed. These particles, too, enter public drainage systems, and have been found in fish. Plastic has become a pollution problem that is daunting to reverse, in ways similar to the challenges of climate change.

The US and other advanced economies have regularly shipped tonnes of plastic waste to other countries, often developing countries that are poorly equipped to receive it, causing widespread contamination and risks to health. Turning villages in poor countries into dumpsites has been one of the many tragic aspects of the explosion in plastic waste. A breakthrough UN convention aimed at stopping these shipments was agreed by 187 countries, meeting in Basel in Switzerland in 2019 (Holden, 2019). The US was not one of the signatories. In January 2019, China, which had been receiving cargos of plastic waste from the US, decided to stop such imports. As a result, the US increased shipments to poor developing countries. In addition, a number of American cities have increased the burning of waste. The challenge is not just disposal, but reducing the use of plastic in the first place. However, reducing our dependence on plastic implies changing patterns of consumption towards more sustainable living. The anti-plastic agenda requires commitment by businesses and governments, as well as consumers.

Questions

- Describe the different aspects of the environmental damage caused by plastics.
- What are the best ways of dealing with plastic waste?
- Where does responsibility lie for reducing plastic use?
- In what ways are the large oil and gas companies part of the problem, rather than part of the solution?

Further reading

See 'Plastic waste and recycling in the EU: Facts and figures', at www.europarl.europa.eu/news/en/headlines/society/20181212STO21610/plastic-waste-and-recycling-in-the-eu-facts-and-figures

Multiple choice questions

Visit www.macmillanihe.com/morrison-gbe-5e to take a quick self-test quiz on what you have read in this chapter.

Review questions

1. In what ways do industrialization and urbanization impact on the environment?
2. What does environmental degradation refer to, and what are its effects?
3. What are the causes of climate change, and what are the effects of global warming?
4. What were the aims of the Kyoto Protocol, and why was the treaty significant in terms of progress towards international co-operation?
5. In the years following the Kyoto Protocol, how have developed and developing countries diverged on climate change issues?
6. What did the Paris conference of 2015 accomplish?
7. Why has transboundary pollution become a global concern? Give some examples of transboundary pollution, and examine ways of dealing with it through collaboration between countries.
8. What are the benefits of nuclear energy, and why is it controversial?
9. Define 'sustainable development'. How does it differ from plain economic development?
10. What are the implications of sustainable development for business strategists?
11. What are the sustainable development goals?
12. What is meant by environmental management?
13. How can environmental reporting contribute to sustainable business strategies?
14. What is meant by 'sustainable consumption', and how can consumer habits be changed?
15. What are the factors that have led to a heightened sense of urgency over climate change targets?

✓ Assignments

1. Assess the commitments agreed in the Paris accord of 2015, and the actions that have been taken by signatories to meet them in subsequent years.
2. To what extent is sustainable development a realistic proposition for developing countries?

Further reading

Bell, S. and McGillivray, D. and Peterson, O. (2017) *Environmental Law*, 9th edition (Oxford: Oxford University Press).

Blewitt, J. (2017) *Understanding Sustainable Development*, 3rd edition (London: Routledge).

Dessler, A. (2015) *Introduction to Modern Climate Change* (Cambridge: Cambridge University Press).

Flannery, T. (2015) *Atmosphere of Hope: Solutions to the climate crisis* (Penguin).

Klein, N. (2015) *This Changes Everything: Capitalism vs the climate* (Penguin).

Landes, D. (1998) *The Wealth and Poverty of Nations* (London: Little, Brown & Company).

Middleton, M. (2013) *The Global Casino: An introduction to environmental issues*, 5th edition (Routledge).

Sachs, J. (2015) *The Age of Sustainable Development* (Columbia University Press).

Stern, N. (2016) *Why Are We Waiting? The logic, urgency and promise of tackling climate change*, Lionel Robbins Lectures (Cambridge, MA: MIT Press).

References

Berners-Lee, M. and Clark, D. (2010) 'What is a carbon footprint?', *The Guardian*, 4 June, at www.theguardian.com.

CAPA Centre for Aviation (2019) 'Chinese airlines: Rapid international growth impacts foreign airlines', 19 March, at https://centreforaviation.com/analysis/reports

Castro, C. (2004) 'Sustainable development: mainstream and critical perspectives', *Organization & Environment* 17(2): 195–225.

Clark, D. (2012) 'Has the Kyoto Protocol made any difference to carbon emissions?', *The Guardian*, 26 November, at www.theguardian.com.

CO_2earth (2018) Earth's CO_2 home page, at www.co2.org, accessed 18 November 2018.

European Commission (2013) 'EU over-achieved first Kyoto emissions target, on track to meet 2020 objective', at www.ec.europa.eu, accessed 22 September 2015.

Fagan-Watson, B. (2015) 'BP, EDF and Procter & Gamble face pressure over climate change lobbying', *The Guardian*, 10 September, at www.theguardian.com

FAO (Food and Agriculture Organization of the UN) (2018) *The State of the World's Forests*, at www.fao.org

Galatsidas, A. and Sheehy, F. (2015) 'What have the millennium development goals achieved?', *The Guardian*, 6 July, at www.theguardian.com.

Holden, E. (2019) 'Nearly all countries agree to stem flow of plastic waste into poor countries', *The Guardian*, 11 May.

IISD (International Institute for Sustainable Development) (1992) 'Business strategies for sustainable development', at www.iisd.org

IPCC (Intergovernmental Panel on Climate Change) (2014) *Climate Change 2014: Synthesis Report* (Geneva: IPCC).

IPCC (Intergovernmental Panel on Climate Change) (2018) *Special Report on Global Warming of 1.5 degrees C*, October, at www.ipcc.ch

Jones, T. (2015) 'Sustainable development goals promise little respite for indebted poor countries', *The Guardian*, 23 September, at www.theguardian.com.

Kelland, K. (2012) 'Diesel exhaust fumes cause lung cancer, WHO says', Reuters, 12 June, at https://uk.reuters.com

Landes, D. (1998) *The Wealth and Poverty of Nations* (London: Little, Brown & Company).

Maddison, A. (2001) *The World Economy: A millennial perspective* (Paris: OECD).

Nelson, A. (2015) 'BP lobbied against EU support for clean energy to favour gas, documents reveal', *The Guardian*, 20 August, at www.theguardian.com

Noack, R. (2015) 'The nuclear disaster at Fukushima didn't have to happen', *The Washington Post*, 22 September, at www.washingtonpost.com

Oslo Roundtable on Sustainable Consumption and Production (1994) 'Defining sustainable consumption', The imperative of sustainable production and consumption, Oslo Symposium, Norway, January 1994, at enb.iisd.org/consume/oslo004.html

PwC Global (2015) *CEO Pulse on Climate Change*, report at www.pwc.com

Sen, A. (1999) *Development as Freedom* (New York: Anchor Books).

Staines, M. (2019) 'New data ranks Ryanair among worst polluters in the EU', *Newstalk*, 2 April, at www.newstalk.com

UNEP (United Nations Environment Programme) (2015) *International Environment and the Global Commons*, at www.unep.org, accessed 20 September 2015.

UNEP (United Nations Environment Programme) (2018) *Emissions Gap Report 2018*, Nairobi (Kenya), at www.unenvironment.org

United Nations (1987) *Report of the World Commission on Environment and Development: Our Common Future (the Brundtland Report)*, at www.un-documents.net

Vaughan, A. (2018) 'Tech companies unclear over stance on potential new EU climate targets', *The Guardian*, 19 September, at www.theguardian.com

Vidal, J., Goldenberg, S. and Taylor, L. (2015) 'How the historic Paris deal over climate change was finally agreed', *The Guardian*, 13 December, at www.theguardian.com

 **Visit the companion website at www.macmillanihe.com/morrison-gbe-5e for further learning and teaching resources.**

© Getty, Mick Ryan

ETHICS AND SOCIAL RESPONSIBILITY

Outline of chapter

Introduction

Philosophical foundations of ethics
- Ethical principles and theories
- Human rights in ethics and law

Ethics in business contexts
- How do ethical principles apply to business?
- Work relationships: obligations and rights
- Workers in the gig economy
- Human rights and the workplace
  - *Wages: do they provide a decent living?*
  - *Migrant workers and forced labour*
  - *Workers' rights to organize*

Social responsibility of the firm
- Theories of corporate social responsibility (CSR)
- CSR in practice
- Reaching for international standards

CSR and corporate governance

The social enterprise

Ethics and CSR: the sustainable business

Conclusions

This chapter will enable you to

- Gain an overview of the foundations of ethical principles and how they are applied in business contexts
- Understand the legal and ethical dimensions of human rights, and how they affect corporate decision-making
- Examine the elements of corporate social responsibility in theory and practice
- Appreciate the impacts of CSR and stakeholder concerns on corporate governance
- Critically assess the extent to which governments and businesses contribute to a sustainable business environment

OPENING CASE STUDY

The textile industry in the UK

The textile industry flourished in the UK in the industrial age. Leicester was one of its thriving centres. The Corah factory employed 6,000 people in its heyday. But like most of post-industrial Britain, the industry declined in the 1970s and 1980s when garment manufacturing shifted to cheaper locations, mainly in Asia. Leicester's garment industry did not disappear totally, however. In a reduced and fragmented form, it continued to function, supplying large retailers on a small scale when they needed top-up orders. Now Leicester's garment manufacturers are enjoying a resurgence as part of today's fast-fashion scene. Online brands are using Leicester suppliers as their preference for fast, cheap fashion. Although this might seem like healthy economic regeneration, in fact it has become a micro-economy of unsafe factories and exploited labour. How has this been allowed to happen openly, despite regulations that should compel these factories to follow employment laws and health and safety laws?

Garment manufacturing in Leicester was an industry that refused to close down when other industrial jobs were disappearing. Fashion retailers sourced supplies from low-cost countries, notably China, India, and Bangladesh, whose low wages were their chief attraction. Working conditions, safety concerns and human rights have remained issues for these outsourcing arrangements in 'sweatshop' locations. Many retailers have responded by supporting ethical trading principles. As in other types of manufacturing, however, such initiatives are difficult to enforce, mainly because of the price pressures on suppliers, the extensive use of subcontractors and the weak enforcement of regulations.

Having an enjoyable day out and taking selfies: these are the consumers that fast fashion retailers particularly target.

But while these problems seem difficult to overcome in developing countries, they would not be so insurmountable in a developed country, one would think. However, Leicester's resurgence from its industrial past tells a different story.

In today's fast fashion, speed is everything. The online retailer wishes to offer customers the look that they saw their favourite celebrities wearing the previous day on Instagram. In this market, the look of the moment can be fleeting, and the online retailer must respond instantly. Research suggests that among young women in the UK, one in three considers an item of clothing worn once or twice as 'old' (McKinsey and Co., 2019). Brands such as Boohoo and Missguided have become experts at satisfying this market, flourishing in the years since the financial crisis. Both these brands source at least half their clothes in the UK. They turn to garment factories in Leicester for the fastest supply, in a trend towards 'reshoring' manufacturing. These factories are a shadow of Leicester's past. These are small, pop-up operations, often set up in old disused factories. A single abandoned factory can have ten small-scale garment factories operating inside, although this is not apparent from the exterior of the building. Health and safety are problematic in these buildings. The average size of the factory is 10 employees, mostly made up of migrant workers, and their average wage is well under the statutory minimum wage, at £3.50 to £4.00. Employers tend to understate workers' hours to conceal their underpayment. Evasion of employment law, safety laws and tax laws are rife in these operations. The ephemeral nature of some of these businesses poses challenges for authorities. Often the company contracted to a retailer uses undisclosed subcontractors to fill orders quickly. And companies are likely to disappear and re-form under different names. Authorities are aware of what is happening in this industry, but these businesses continue to exist in an environment that is only sparsely regulated. Employment law, health and safety law and taxation are subject to selective inspections. There should be health and safety inspections after serious injury, but of 136 workplace injuries in the industry in 2017, only 5 were inspected.

Many retailers, although not Boohoo, have signed up to the Ethical Trading Initiative, but improvement in conditions relies on enforcement, which is patchy. Ethical manufacturers who pay the minimum wage and operate under sound safety regimes do exist in the Leicester garment industry, but they find it impossible to compete with those who do not. It would be impossible for a supplier paying the minimum wage to stay in business when a dress retails for £6. Boohoo has a reputation for aggressively low prices, and has been questioned on just this point by the House of Commons Environmental Audit Committee. Its CEO's response was that it is about customer demand for low prices (BBC, 2018). Boohoo says it is part of an Ethical Trade Audit, that works to promote ethical working conditions. However, supply is often subcontracted out without the retailer's knowledge or permission. Boohoo has been highly successful, with revenues of $500 million in 2018, and pre-tax profits up 40%. It was listed in London in 2014, and its market value has doubled to £2.3 billion since then. Boohoo's co-founder is now a billionaire.

A few key retailers have acquired a commanding position over suppliers who set up cheaply and use a pool of low-cost workers. Both the retailers and the suppliers are responsible, and a solution that addresses these conditions would involve both sides co-operating. Leicester's factories are known as dark factories, reflecting not just the dangerous working conditions and poorly-lit old factories. They are dark in the sense of a nineteenth-century picture of exploitation that is considered an affront to human dignity. It is also illegal in today's more regulated business environment. However, competitiveness for the ultra-fast-fashion retailer has revived the business model of sweated labour.

Questions

- Why has the garment industry in the UK become successful in fast fashion?
- What are unsatisfactory aspects of the Leicester garment industry, in terms of safety and employment practices?
- How should the garment industry be reformed, in respect of working conditions and wages?
- What is your answer to the fast-fashion retailer who says that this business model is simply about consumer demand?

Further reading

See the article by Tamsin Blanchard, 'Did you know sweatshops exist in the UK?' in *Vogue*, 23 August, 2017, at www.vogue.co.uk

Introduction

At the start of this book, we posed some basic questions: 'what does the business exist to do?' and 'how should it go about achieving its goals?' We highlighted an obvious economic goal, to make money for the owners, but also suggested that businesses have a broader role in society. It is this broader role which is the focus of this chapter. It will be argued here that the business plays a multi-dimensional role in society, whether the firm's managers intend it to do so or not. This broader role can be seen through the eyes of stakeholder groups, such as customers and employees, and it can be viewed in even broader terms, such as the firm's role in respect of climate change. Although the planet is not a stakeholder in the traditional sense, we tend nowadays to see the business organization as having responsibilities and duties to take positive action to combat climate change. Where do these duties come from, and how should businesses respond to this range of duties, both to stakeholders and wider global concerns? Does this imply that the traditional economic goals are somehow less worthy? Many businesspeople would argue that social goals are for governments, and that the firm is best sticking to enterprise goals, such as selling goods and services.

This chapter clarifies these different threads of thinking on the role of business in society. We begin by looking at how ethics influences both individual and group behaviour, and how ethical considerations permeate business activities. We discuss different perspectives of corporate social responsibility (CSR), assessing both the 'business case' and the ethical underpinning for companies in global business operations. We look at the role of the social enterprise as an example of unequivocal commitment to social goals. For most businesses, CSR considerations are more peripheral. However, a shift in public expectations of businesses is taking place. In recent years, business ethics have come under the spotlight in a variety of situations, including corporate wrongdoing, such as tax evasion, and individual wrongdoing, such as bribery. What companies aim to achieve and how they go about it are coming more and more into the limelight, focusing on issues of corporate governance, executive rewards and political activities. In a final section, we look at the growing interactions between governments and businesses in both funding and carrying out social aims.

Philosophical foundations of ethics

ethics the study of basic concepts of good and bad, right and wrong, which relate to all people as human beings

morality standards of behaviour considered right and wrong

Ethics focuses on systems of values by which judgments of right and wrong behaviour are made. Value systems are often termed standards of **morality**. As we found in Chapter 3, cultures involve value systems which dictate what is right and wrong within that culture. As businesses soon find when they become internationalized, values in one society may clash with those in another society. Google, for example, by complying with Chinese internet censorship, has been accused of acting unethically. This accusation was more pointed as the company has as its motto, 'Don't be evil'. This was a case of local law conflicting with ethical principles. The company could argue that acting morally in any location involves obeying the law, but accusations of unethical behaviour imply that there is some higher set of rules which should apply to individuals, companies and even governments.

Ethical principles and theories

utilitarianism philosophical thinking based on the individualist view of human nature that each person has wants and needs which are pursued in a self-interested way

consequentialist principle utilitarian principle that the test of the rightness or wrongness of an action depends on the results which flow from it

A source of ethical principles that has deep historical roots is the notion of respect for the individual human being. It is the foundation of theories of human rights (discussed in the next section), and also the foundation of economic and political theories that have been introduced in earlier chapters of this book. We must go back to differing perspectives which emerged in the eighteenth-century Enlightenment. The individualist view that each person has wants and needs that are pursued in a self-interested way is at the heart of **utilitarianism**, which has been highly influential, especially in English-speaking parts of the world. Based roughly on the ideas of Jeremy Bentham, utilitarianism focuses on the aggregate of individual goods. What is good overall is that which promotes the 'greatest happiness of the greatest number'. Sometimes referred to as the **consequentialist principle**, the test of the rightness or wrongness of an action depends on the results which flow from it (Quinton, 1989). The utilitarian favours minimal government interference in society, as the individual requires the maximum amount of liberty, defined as the absence of external constraints, to pursue his/her own goals. This view of human nature was taken up by the classical economists, notably Adam Smith, and has continued to underpin the thinking of economists. Free markets are assumed to be the best way to maximize the overall prosperity of a society, by facilitating as many individuals as possible in fulfilling their desires (Plamenatz, 1958: 173).

We would now criticize this view of the individual in society on a number of grounds. First, it does not seem to take into account that different cultures have different views of the individual human being. Secondly, it takes a narrow view of what human beings desire in life, focusing exclusively on rational acquisitiveness. We look at each of these criticisms in turn.

ethical relativism approach to ethics which holds that principles are not absolute but dependent on values that differ from culture to culture

contextualism in ethical thinking, the principle that ideas of right and wrong stem from specific cultural environments

First, we now realize that different cultures have different value systems. This view, sometimes referred to as **ethical relativism**, holds that principles are not absolute, but dependent on circumstances. Ethical relativism is perhaps a misleading term, as within a culture, right and wrong are clearly delineated. A more accurate term would be ethical **contextualism**, implying that ideas of right and wrong are real, but vary according to the particular belief system. That belief system can be a national culture, the culture of a distinctive people, or, as is often the case, a religion.

In many national environments, acting morally is associated with membership of a nation or state. In ancient Greece, being a citizen involved the capability of acting morally: slaves, not being citizens, were viewed as outside the *polis*, or community, and thus incapable of attaining virtue. It is common among religious believers to hold that their religion alone is the path to a righteous life, looking down on non-believers. Similarly, some state ideologies, such as extreme nationalism and communism, see themselves as the determinants of a society's values. Adopting a moralistic tone, communist political leaders are prone to extol the superiority of their social perspective over the hedonist, individualist values of western cultures, viewed as decadent. Still, individualist values are permeating countries such as China, as market forces become established, giving rise to conflict between materialistic outlooks and the nationalistic ideology of the communist leadership. More broadly, nationalist populists, who are on the rise in many countries, are intolerant of other belief systems and other groups such as ethnic minorities.

Secondly, utilitarianism reduces human motivation to the appetitive element, underestimating the complexities of people's sense of social values which influence their perceptions of right and wrong. Beliefs and feelings which people hold stem in large part from their interactions in society:

> It is as social creatures that men acquire the standards and preferences out of which they build up for themselves images, however, vague, however inarticulate, however changing, of what they are and would like to be, of how they live and would like to live. These are the images that give them a sense of position and of purpose in the world. (Plamenatz, 1958: 176)

We now appreciate the importance of community as a dimension of the individual's values and beliefs. European continental thinkers, notably Rousseau and Hegel, have long recognized the ethical dimension of the community. Contrasting views of liberty illustrate different concepts of the individual in society. Liberty in the negative sense, identified above in connection with the utilitarians, is about people having space to pursue their own personal goals. Liberty in the positive sense is about people being self-directed, each being one's own master: 'I wish to be somebody, not nobody' (Berlin, 1958: 16). As Isaiah Berlin points out in the essay, 'Two concepts of liberty', the two views of liberty would seem to be just two sides of the same coin. But historically, they have developed very differently. The theorists who emphasize self-realization have been accused of underestimating the dignity of the individual. They espouse a sense of community in which individual wills meld into a general will which is always right, even though individuals might not see it. This view of liberty is sometimes accused of opening the way for tyrants, and is at the base of much ideology that is reached for by authoritarian regimes to cloak themselves in legitimacy. Opposition to political tyrants has long rallied to the calls for freedoms of speech and association, famously articulated by one of the most notable of the utilitarians, John Stuart Mill, in his essay, *On Liberty* (1859).

Mill parted ways with the utilitarians' rather dogmatic view of human nature as based on the pursuit of material self-interest. He evolved a more nuanced 'new' utilitarianism, which retained the need for freedoms based on liberty in the negative sense with an ethical notion on individual self-development and self-determination (Halliday, 1976).

Do there exist ethical principles which aim to be universal, above national cultures and not dependent on religious values? Establishing how they arise and defining them has long been a concern of philosophers. They like to strip away religious, ideological, traditional and other sources of values, asking whether there is simply a 'human' basis for ethics. Immanuel Kant came closest to this approach with his postulate that 'every rational being exists as end in himself, not merely as means for arbitrary use by this or that will' (Kant, 1785: 105). This notion of respect for every human being postulates human dignity as the guiding principle for behaviour. This principle is sometimes referred to as the **categorical imperative**. It holds that pure egoistic action, with regard only for oneself is unethical, and that one ought to behave in a way that takes the needs and wants of others into account. This ethical principle is aimed particularly at the personal morality of the individual, but how does it translate to organizations, governments and whole societies?

categorical imperative ethical principle put forward by Kant that respect for every human being should be the guiding principle for behaviour

Ethical behaviour can be conceived in a variety of ways, including obligations, duties, responsibilities, rights and justice. A person has an overall responsibility to act ethically, which imposes particular obligations, such as the duty not to harm other people. An individual also has human rights, such as the right to life. There are many dimensions to human wellbeing, as this book has highlighted. Some of the main ones are food and shelter, education, health and a safe environment. In many societies, even these minimal requirements of a human existence are precarious. We would probably say that governments owe duties towards all the population, including ethnic and religious minorities, in respect of all these dimensions of human wellbeing. However, governments tend to be responsive to those in society that represent the dominant culture, the main economic interests and the dominant political groups. The recognition and enforcement of human rights are thus at risk. This is true not just in authoritarian systems, but also in democratic ones.

The persuasiveness of utilitarian thinking

Businesspeople would probably find utilitarian thinking chimes with their own: enterprise values and maximum freedom to pursue business goals. But this market approach is oriented to economic goals only, and short-term considerations.

Over the longer term, what other ethical principles would the business be advised to adopt on issues such as climate change?

Human rights in ethics and law

Human rights have become an important area of ethics, for both governments and businesses, involving a wide range of ethical principles, from freedom of speech to access to education. Here, we clarify how this rather 'umbrella' concept has evolved. **Human rights** may be defined as basic, universal rights of all individuals, wherever they are, which transcend social and cultural differences. The notion of human rights recognizes the inherent value of the human being. Most people, whatever their cultural background, would agree that slavery, torture and murder are wrong. The right to life is a basic human right, but the notion of human rights has been extended over the years to encompass many other rights, including spheres such as culture and extending to rights of groups as well as individuals.

human rights basic, universal rights enjoyed by all individuals, wherever they are, which transcend social and cultural differences

The origins of modern thinking on human rights lie in the eighteenth-century theorists of individual rights, such as Locke, who spoke of 'natural rights', rather than human rights. Locke saw natural rights as basic freedoms in the negative sense, focusing on life, liberty and property. These reflect western values of individualism, and are the underpinning of capitalist economic thinking. To these values were added rights of free speech and assembly, which we would consider civil and political rights. Locke's thinking was fundamental to modern democratic theory, in that people, he maintained, should have a right to overthrow tyrannical governments that violate individual freedoms. He was arguing, in other words, that despite what the law of the land says, a government trampling on natural rights is acting unjustly. The US Declaration of Independence spoke of 'inalienable rights' in 1776, and the French declaration of the 'rights of man' dates from 1789. These iconic statements have become touchstones for democracy campaigners around the world. They articulated the idea that law and justice are different: the law of the land can, and should, be judged by higher moral principles. It follows that, for the individual or organization, obedience to the law is only one kind of obligation – one that is subordinate to adhering to ethical principles.

Universal Declaration of Human Rights (UDHR) UN foundation declaration setting out human rights

The first general enunciation of human rights came in the **Universal Declaration of Human Rights (UDHR)**, adopted by the UN General Assembly in 1948. A perennial dilemma in the area of human rights is that statements enunciating the principles are of limited benefit to the many victims of human rights abuse unless the principles are transformed into law that is enforceable. As we have seen in Chapter 6, international law in the form of treaties is enforceable in practice if sovereign states legislate accordingly. The UDHR did not have the legal authority of a convention or treaty, but it did provide a comprehensive view of human rights that builds on the earlier concepts of natural rights. It has grown in importance for this reason, and is now recognized as part of international law, giving it considerable authority globally. The UDHR reflected the divergent economic and political systems in the post-war world: the delegates from western countries and those from socialist and communist states. From the western tradition, the UDHR includes the fundamental freedoms of expression, assembly and religion. It also recognizes the basic right to life, including freedom from torture and forced labour. Finally, in this category, it recognizes civil rights, including freedom from arbitrary arrest, equality before the law, and the right to due process of law. From socialist countries, the UDHR articulates a group of rights known as social and economic rights, sometimes called 'second-generation' rights that are more in the vein of positive liberty. These include rights to adequate living standards, employment, health and cultural participation. The social and economic rights are more about qualitative issues of human wellbeing.

International Covenant on Civil and Political Rights (ICCPR) UN convention on human rights, covering civil and political rights, recognized in international law

International Covenant on Economic, Social and Cultural Rights (ICESCR) UN convention on human rights, covering economic, social and cultural rights, recognized in international law

The two rather different groups of rights took more concrete form with the adoption of two conventions in the 1960s: the **International Covenant on Civil and Political Rights (ICCPR)** and the **International Covenant on Economic, Social and Cultural Rights (ICESCR)** (see Figure 11.1). The two covenants and the UDHR are sometimes referred to as the International Bill of Rights. Article 1 in both covenants is identical, setting out the broad context of human rights. This is its first clause:

> All peoples have the right of self-determination. By virtue of that right they freely determine their political status and freely pursue their economic, social and cultural development.

The notions of self-determination and development in Article 1 echo a view of human dignity as self-fulfillment, in the tradition of positive freedom. But it is important to note the emphasis on the free choice and free pursuit of one's goals in the second sentence, emphasizing the importance of freedom from impediments in that pursuit – which originates in the tradition of negative freedom.

Universal Declaration of Human Rights (UDHR)

International Covenant on Civil and Political Rights (ICCPR)	International Covenant on Economic, Social and Cultural Rights (ICESCR)
• Right to life • Prohibition of torture, and cruel, inhuman or degrading treatment • Prohibition of slavery and forced labour • Prohibition of arbitrary arrest or detention • Freedom of movement, assembly, and association • Freedom of expression and religion • Right to privacy (family, home and correspondence) • All persons are equal before the law • Prohibition of discrimination on grounds of race, sex, religion, political opinion, etc.	• Right to work • Right to a fair wage that provides a decent living for the person and family • Equal pay for work of equal value • Right to paid holidays • Right to form trade unions that can function freely • Right to strike, in accordance with law • Adequate standard of living– freedom from hunger • Right to health • Right to education • Right to take part in cultural life

Figure 11.1 Human rights law: the international bill of rights

Source: United Nations, Human rights, at www.un.org, accessed 5 December 2018.

The two covenants can be seen as complementary: negative freedoms complemented by positive rights to fulfil personal goals. The ICCPR makes clear that not all rights are 'absolute'. Some are. The right not to be tortured is one: torture is never justified. However, freedom of assembly, freedom of expression and right to privacy are all qualified, in that they can be curtailed in the public interest and for security. But such encroachment must be done in accordance with law. The rights spelt out in the ICESCR commit states to establishing laws and institutions that promote rights listed in Figure 11.1, including the right to work, health, education and housing. As part of international law, the two covenants commit ratifying states to implement them, bringing national laws up to these international standards. For example, ratifying the ICESCR would entail a government establishing the right in law to form independent trade unions. Despite the fact that a majority of the world's states have ratified both covenants, there are notable exceptions. China has ratified the ICESCR, but not the ICCPR, while the US has done the reverse, objecting to the idea of social and economic rights. The US does have laws recognizing many of the rights in the ICESCR, but some are only weakly established in practice. The right to join a trade union exists in law in the US, going back to the era of the New Deal legislation which bolstered labour rights following the Great Depression of the early 1930s. However, the growth in union membership that followed has now gone into reverse (see discussion later in this chapter on workers' rights to organize).

Endorsing human rights goals in principle does not readily translate into practice. It is often the case that human rights, even when passed into national law, are curtailed in the broadly framed interests of national security. In addition, corporate actors are often able to sidestep the law in practice. An example is child labour, tolerated in many developing countries, despite laws to the contrary. As defined by the ILO, **child labour** is work that is mentally, physically, socially or morally damaging to children, and interferes with their schooling (IPEC). Child labour in its harshest forms is in breach of the ILO convention on child labour, but much work carried out by children is not considered harsh, and national norms differ. Large MNEs which have affiliated manufacturers in many countries have been criticized for failing to take a stronger stand against practices such as using young people in their teens as interns. Such criticisms have become increasingly voiced in today's globalized environment. There is now a means available for individuals and groups that are

child labour work that is mentally, physically, socially or morally damaging to children, and interferes with their schooling

victims of breaches of economic, social and cultural rights to seek justice from the UN when their governments fail to enforce these obligations. This is through a new Optional Protocol to the ICESCR, which became part of international law in 2013 (www.ohchr.org). As of December 2018, 24 state parties had ratified this optional protocol, and a further 25 had signed it. The new protocol is an important milestone in the legal recognition of economic, social and cultural rights globally, and in furthering access to justice for victims of human rights abuse.

The way I see it...

'The only way you're going to end inequality is to give workers enough bargaining power that they can get a bigger share of the wealth and the value they produce.'

Richard Trumka, president of the AFL-CIO union federation in the US, in an interview in 2014, in Jopson, B., and Harding, R., 'US trade unionism views inequality as main fight', *Financial Times*, 1 July.

Mr Trumka saw union membership as a key to reducing inequality. Union membership among workers was slightly up in 2017, notably among private-sector workers. Perhaps encouraged by teachers' strikes for better pay, 8,000 Marriott hotel workers in eight US cities came out on strike for a living wage and safer conditions of work. See Philip, D. (2018) '"One job should be enough": Marriott hotel workers' strike hits eight cities', *The Guardian*, 26 October. This was a strike organized by their union, Unite Here. Their demands were mostly met in the agreement eventually reached with their employers.

To what extent do you think the Marriott workers' strikes are just a one-off event or an indication that the tide might be turning towards growing union membership and better pay for low-paid workers?

As human rights are essentially universal, would it not be logical to establish an international court to adjudicate in cases of alleged abuse? In fact, the authors of the UDHR proposed such a court, with access for states, organizations such as companies, and individuals. The idea was eventually rejected, mainly because of objections on the grounds that such a court would violate state sovereignty. There are some legal routes at international level, however. The International Criminal Court hears cases of crimes against humanity, war crimes and genocide. And in Europe, there is an established court, the **European Court of Human Rights** (www.echr.coe.int), which hears cases arising under the **European Convention on Human Rights** (ECHR), which came into effect in 1953. The ECHR mainly focuses on civil and political rights as set out in the first of the UN covenants in Figure 11.1. Of the rights spelt out in the ICESCR, the ECHR includes the right to join a trade union and the right to education. The latter right is expressed in negative terms, however. It is a right not to be excluded from the educational system as it exists in the country.

European Court of Human Rights international court that hears cases arising under the European Convention on Human Rights

European Convention on Human Rights (ECHR) convention on human rights adopted by members of the Council of Europe

The countries within the ambit of the ECHR are members of the Council of Europe (not to be confused with the EU institution of a similar name). The Council of Europe comprises 47 member states altogether. It includes many countries, from Azerbaijan to Switzerland, which are not members of the EU. The court, which sits in Strasbourg in France, has seen a huge growth in its workload in recent years. The European Court of Justice, the highest court of the EU, also hears human rights cases, arising under the EU Charter of Fundamental Rights, which overrides national legislation in member states.

European countries are thus covered by several human rights legal instruments. There are statements of rights contained in national constitutions; national legislation on many issues; and the UN and European treaties at international level. The ECHR is incorporated in the national law of member states of the Council of Europe. The ECHR became part of UK law through the Human Rights Act 1998. However, this law has been criticized by some leading politicians in the Conservative Party, who have objected to the jurisdiction of the European Court of Human Rights, which they have argued undermines UK sovereignty. Some leading Conservatives have supported the repeal of the Human Rights Act and the substitution of a British Bill of Rights. Lawyers and politicians concerned about civil rights safeguards have urged that the Human Rights Act remains a valuable guarantee of the basic freedoms which underpin the country's values (Smith, 2015). Repealing it would seem to be a worrying step in the wrong direction.

The withdrawal of the UK from the EU would not automatically repeal the Human Rights Act. However, it would remove the UK from the EU Charter of Fundamental Rights. This in itself would weaken human rights protections in the UK. The Charter, while similar to the rights contained in the ECHR, covers some areas of human rights that are not spelt out in the ECHR. They include: the right of human dignity, a free-standing right of non-discrimination, protection of personal data, recognition of a child's best interests, the rights of the elderly, the right to healthcare and a right to collective bargaining in labour relations. In cases where there is a conflict between a basic right contained in the Charter and an Act of Parliament, the Act of Parliament would prevail if the UK were no longer an EU member state.

Ethics in business contexts

Ethical principles apply to a wide range of actors, from individuals to organizations and governments. The person who steals is unethical, and so is the owner of a business who fails to pay the firm's workers their wages. Both acts are wrong, but it is not uncommon for businesses to engage in the latter practice, calculating that delays and underpayment of wages are wrongs that they can get away with, as there is little the worker can do. Much of this section focuses on issues of accountability: the business has obligations to people who work for it, and to customers who buy its products. Both are stakeholders, as are owners and investors who are its shareholders. Stakeholders are not all equal: companies in liberal market economies prioritize shareholder value above all else. Workers and customers are owed legal and ethical obligations, but profits come first, and firms are adept at circumventing obligations in order to reduce costs. A conundrum for businesses is that ethical lapses and accusations of legal wrongdoing can lead to reputational damage, which in turn can be damaging for the business. This is especially true in today's world of social media awareness. Firms that try to cover up ethical failings can find matters are made worse by their cover-up efforts. Being ethical is, at the end of the day, good for business, but this message is slow to take root in many business contexts. We look at a wide range of business relations in this section, highlighting the relevant ethical principles.

How do ethical principles apply to business?

Ethical principles arise in relation to both *what* the firm aims to do and *how* it goes about its activities. Many firms are successfully engaged in businesses such as gambling, manufacturing tobacco products and making alcoholic drinks, all of which can become addictive, and could be considered unethical. These areas, like many types of activity which involve ethical principles, are the subject of laws in most countries. The firm that abides by the regulations regarding gambling, for

example, is engaged in an activity for which there is clearly consumer demand, and, as long as it abides by the regulations, is acting legally. Most companies that make addictive products, such as alcoholic beverage companies, are highly aware of the ethical dimension of their activities, and present themselves as promoting responsible drinking among consumers. In most countries, there are restrictions on selling alcoholic drinks to children, but inevitably some traders are prepared to do so, aware they are probably not going to be caught.

Most of the focus of ethics in business is on how the firm operates. Is it honest and fair in relation to stakeholders such as employees, customers, business partners and the wider community? Some of the major areas are set out in Figure 11.2. Major considerations are transparency and honesty in communications. Is it truthful in its advertising messages, and does it particularly target children? Note that the aspects of ethics highlighted in the figure often overlap with law. For example, there are laws on truthfulness in advertising. Many companies would say that if they abide by the law, that should be the extent of their obligation. But compliance with legal regulation is not as straightforward as it might seem. Many companies are careful to comply with the letter of the law while failing to comply with the spirit or intention of the law. This approach is generally considered unethical.

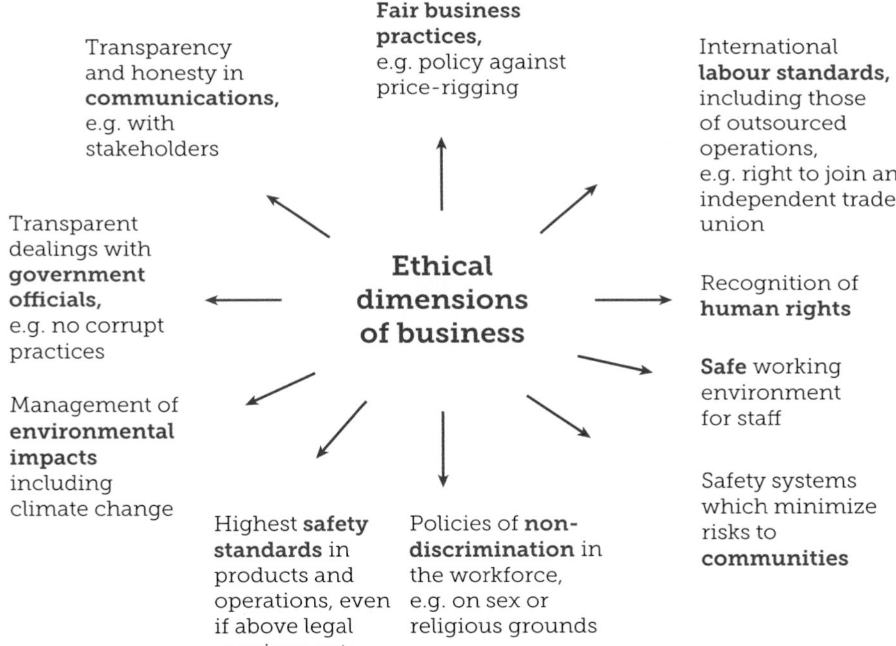

Figure 11.2 Ethical dimensions of business

Legal compliance can be a grey area in many contexts, including advertising, taxation, liability for accidents, and environmental management. Some companies, well aware of the law on advertising, draft messages which rely on half-truths and suggestions: they might well mislead the consumer, but the firm can argue that it abided by the law in the strict sense. In fact, in matters of advertising, truthful but misleading statements are often found to be in breach of the rules. In America, Volkswagen's advertised figures for its diesel cars' fuel economy and low emissions were found to be far too low, as the cars' engines were rigged to understate the results. Moreover, official tests of vehicles typically tolerate the use of techniques that reduce levels of emissions below those that would obtain in ordinary road use. This was standard in the industry, and was misleading, but has been tolerated. Reforms in testing have introduced tests that more accurately reflect real conditions (see the case study in Chapter 9).

In another example, companies can go to great lengths, usually with the help of professional tax consultants, to devise methods of reducing their liabilities to tax. They can claim to be complying with the law, but their sidestepping devices could be seen as unethical. Moreover, pure tax evasion schemes are in breach of the law in many countries. Tax authorities in Europe, including the EU and national governments, have become more active in pursuing large MNEs for tax on operations that take place within their jurisdictions. Apple's subsidiaries set up in Ireland channel 65% of its worldwide income. By agreement with the Irish government, Apple has paid tax at a rate of less than 2%, while Ireland's official corporation tax rate of 12% is itself well below international standards. Ireland's tax deals with Apple and other MNEs have been targeted by the EU. In 2017, the Irish Treasury was compelled by the EU Commission to collect back taxes of €13 billion from Apple. Ireland had been unwilling to collect this tax, wishing to preserve the favourable tax treatment that it affords multinationals.

Manufacturing and extracting industries are sectors where the risk of accidents is high, and where potential damage could be extensive. In all its operations, the business is obliged to observe the duty of **reasonable care**, which is the test for negligence. This can be interpreted in many ways, and in common law countries, there is a great deal of case law on what is meant by reasonable care. The firm is not expected to make operations 100% safe, which is impossible, but it is expected to take precautions which a reasonable person aware of the risks would take. There is a good deal of scope for differing interpretations of how safe an operation must be so as not to expose the employer to an accusation of negligence. Unfortunately, these issues are normally resolved after an accident has occurred, often in court proceedings. It is scant consolation for the victim or the victim's family that the employer was found to be negligent. Sometimes, safety devices would have incurred only small extra expenditures, but firms bent on cost-cutting would balk at the extra expense. By contrast, the firm with a strong ethical policy would take the view that the expense is justified, even if it eats into profits.

reasonable care test used in law to determine whether a person has acted negligently

Environmental management is an area that also involves ethical and legal duties. Usually, duties are owed to a person or group, as in the examples just cited. But in the case of the environment, the reasoning is less clear. As Figure 11.2 shows, firms owe a duty to protect the environment from harm that affects workers and local communities. But the principle of sustainability (discussed in Chapter 10) goes further, resting on what can be termed **inter-generational justice.** This means that firms owe moral obligations to later generations, as *their* standards of living could be at risk if *we* do not take steps to reduce emissions. There is a potential conflict between the needs and wants of today's inhabitants and those of future inhabitants, involving firms in calculations of a possible trade-off between them. As we saw in Chapter 10, firms prioritize legal duties, but the law often lags behind the measures that a strong commitment to sustainability would recommend.

inter-generational justice concept which underlies the principle of sustainability, implying that moral obligations are owed to future generations

Some of the main ethical dimensions of business featured in Figure 11.2 concern the workforce, and a number feature in UN human rights law. Specific areas of human rights that are relevant to the workplace and workers include terms of employment, health and safety, personal treatment, and the rights of workers to organize in trade unions and bargain collectively. National law covers these aspects of employment, but in many cases, national law and enforcement fall short of international legal and ethical standards.

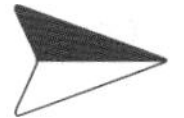

MINI CASE STUDY

The close ties between gambling and football in the UK

Once associated mainly with horse racing, gambling has now become increasingly involved in football. Betting companies traditionally operated mainly out of betting shops, but the advent of online betting in about 2000 greatly expanded their potential market – and their profitability. Football became a primary focus, with 'in-play' betting on live games, accessible through smartphone apps. Betting companies pay for sponsorship and advertising, heavily targeting football. In 2018, nine out of the twenty Premier League clubs had a gambling company as their main shirt sponsor. And 17 out of the 24 Championship clubs did so as well. SkyBet is the sponsor of the Football League and its three divisions. SkyBet is advertised during Sky's live TV coverage. Betting companies are often based offshore, and many are based in Asian countries. Those companies sponsor billboards around pitches during matches, aiming to reach their large Asian audiences. Research has shown that gambling logos and advertising were on the screen for 71% to 89% of the screen time of *Match of the Day* programmes (Conn, 2019).

For online betting companies, football has proved particularly lucrative. Bet 365, which specializes in 'in-play' betting during live matches, has been highly successful. However, the risk is that football fans who watch the matches can become dependent on betting, seeing it as an essential part of watching the match. This can lead to gambling addiction, and is highlighted as a particular problem for many young men. Gambling companies are skilful at marketing to this age group, with offers such as 'free' bets. When the person is signed up to betting accounts and apps, frequent prompts and offers are persuasive encouragements to gamble – and keep gambling. Direct marketing targets gamblers with texts, emails and messages through the social media. A trade association, the Remote Gambling Association, has announced voluntary moves to stop advertisements during live football matches. The ban would apply to all sports except horse racing, and would take effect in the 2019–2020 season. This move reflects the approach of self-regulation that has been adopted in the online betting industry. But should regulation be stricter, to protect vulnerable young people from addiction to gambling? The industry has maintained that its approach is one of 'responsible gambling', placing the onus on the individual to self-exclude (Ford, 2019). However, the marketing is likely to make this difficult.

Gambling companies have become pervasive in football. Bet 365, whose owners formerly operated traditional betting shops, now makes most of its money from in-play betting. It is now the largest online gambling company. It has 35 million customers, and took in over £52 billion in bets in 2018. Its billionaire CEO, Denise Coates, has been highly successful in developing specialist online betting software. She collected a salary of £265 million in 2018, making her the world's most highly paid CEO. Bet 365 is a private company, registered offshore in Gibraltar. The Coates family has contributed much to the economy of its home town, Stoke-on-Trent, which is in a deprived area of the Midlands in England. But there remains the doubtful ethics of building a business empire on an addictive

Betting during live football matches has been highly lucrative for betting companies, but there is a risk that the football fan will be tempted to gamble excessively.

habit – one that is causing particular problems of addiction among young people. The Remote Gambling Association is chaired by Ms Coates' brother, who, along with his sister, must be concerned about the possibility of stricter regulation through legislation.

Questions

- Why has football become so dependent for its finances on betting companies?
- What should be done, in your view, to reduce the risks of problem gambling?

Find out more

Richard Conway, 'Gambling firms agree whistle-to-whistle television sport advertising ban', BBC, 6 December 2018, at www.bbc.co.uk

Work relationships: Obligations and rights

People available for work would ideally be able to choose freely the job they wish to do, and should be able to agree terms with an employer, which become elements in the contract of employment. Each would abide by the terms, and any disputes would be settled amicably. That is what most workers would like ideally, but in practice, people seeking employment may have little choice of the job, the location or the terms. The balance of power in the work relationship is tipped towards the business or other organization seeking workers. There is a wide variety of work arrangements in every national economy, from those that afford the worker considerable independence to those that afford the worker next-to-no independence.

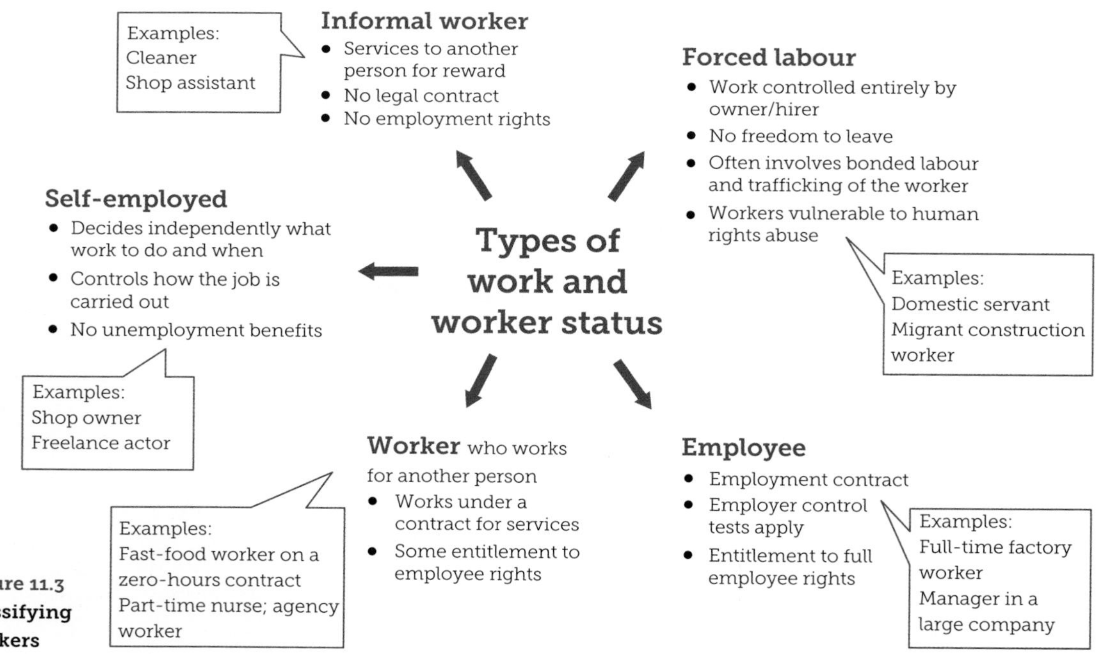

Figure 11.3 Classifying workers

The main types of worker status are set out in Figure 11.3, with a brief indication of the conditions and some examples of the typical work involved. There are significant variables in some key respects. One is the degree of independence, which can be envisaged on a continuum, from complete independence, characterized by the self-employed, to the opposite extreme of forced labour. Another respect in which types of work differ is in the employment protection afforded to the worker by law, often in the form of employer obligations, such as minimum wage laws. In general,

workers classified as employees enjoy greater security of employment and greater legal protections than those that are not, such as the various categories of worker that appear in the figure. Globally, workers in these other categories greatly outnumber those with formal employment contracts.

In many countries, especially in developing regions of the world, work is a matter of an informal arrangement between the parties, often family members. Work within a family enterprise might not be paid, and these workers are vulnerable to exploitation. Where there are no family ties, there is an understanding that the worker will be paid for the work available. Beyond that, there is little obligation towards the worker, and probably little in the way of training. Should there be an accident or injury, the worker would be in a weak position to make a legal claim for compensation against the person who provided the job. This situation is highly insecure and disadvantageous for workers, and it can lead to hardship and mistreatment. Workers often aspire to move from jobs in the informal economy to employment contracts where both parties sign up to contractual obligations specifying the work and the pay. An employment contract along these lines offers greater security to the worker, and it helps the business owner acquire a pool of continuing workers that can be relied on.

Where there is regular work and both sides have obligations, there is a contract for services. Where the work is casual or subject to a **zero-hours contract**, the worker is not guaranteed a minimum number of hours of work, and is paid only for the hours worked. In many sectors, such as fast food, the zero-hours contract has become the norm. While the zero-hours contract gives the employer the flexibility of being able to call on workers as and when they are needed, it is often the case that the worker is not offered enough hours to secure a steady income that will support a family. Neither is the worker likely to receive sick pay or holiday pay.

zero-hours contract employment arrangement whereby the worker is available for work but paid only for the hours worked, and the employer has no commitment to provide work

In 2015, there were an estimated two million workers in Britain on zero-hours contracts. They included public-sector workers as well as those in jobs like fast-food outlets. The number fell to 1.7 million in 2016, but surged again in 2017, to 1.8 million (ONS, 2018). This amounted to 6% of all employment in the UK. Many of these workers would prefer steady full-time work, but have no choice. Some companies, such as McDonald's, have offered existing workers an option to change to fixed employment contracts, but for many of these, the hours on offer are still too few to provide an adequate income.

The traditional factory worker in a car manufacturing plant had a contract of employment in the strict sense. A person is an employee if his or her work is under the ultimate control of the employer, including the nature of the work to be done, the hours of work and the location. The company as employer set out the terms, covering duties, terms and entitlements including paid holidays and pension. This detailed contract of employment is in writing, and terms are interpreted according to the document. There are often other 'perks' of being an employee, such as healthcare and childcare facilities. For the employer, a workforce consisting of full-time employees entails considerable costs and liabilities. It is also inflexible, in that the employee is entitled to be paid even if there is no work, as, for example, when the production line is not functioning.

It is not difficult to see why companies are attracted to arrangements that entail fewer full-time permanent staff and more casual workers. In many organizations, there is a core workforce of permanent staff who have traditional contracts of employment. The company supplements these staff members with other workers under service contracts. Agency work and subcontracting also fall within this latter category. Agency workers are hired by an employment agency to work for particular businesses as needed. These workers are not employees of any of the businesses where they work. In some cases, they are actually employees of the agency, although the name 'employment agency' suggests otherwise. The subcontractor is hired by a firm to carry out work as agreed, for an agreed reward, but is not an employee of the firm. These arrangements can create a two-tier workforce. The full-time employees work alongside the other workers, effectively doing the same jobs and working on the same projects, but in legal terms, they have very different status. But for workers on service contracts, there is greater insecurity, less pay and fewer employment rights. These workers are likely to feel aggrieved and claim that the company where they work is treating them in an unethical and discriminatory manner.

Google is an example of a company with a two-tier workforce, in which Google employees work alongside other workers on service contracts. Many of these workers are in jobs such as security and catering, but many are highly skilled software engineers involved in the company's core activities. As of 2018, almost half of Google's workforce of 170,000 consisted of these latter workers, who were not classified as Google employees. Google calls these workers 'temps, vendors and contractors' (Wong, 2018). But are they employees in reality, and should they therefore be treated on the same terms? Converting them to employee status would be very expensive. Google's parent company, Alphabet, is well aware that this large workforce poses a risk in terms of potential legal obligations and costs if they were challenged in the courts. Google could be found to be a joint employer of these workers: employees of both Google and the firm that has technically employed them. In the 1990s, Microsoft grappled with a similar situation, classifying many workers as 'permatemps', who were not treated as if they were Microsoft employees. There were eight to ten thousand of these workers – far fewer than their counterparts at Google. These workers launched a class action lawsuit, winning a payout of $97 million from Microsoft in 2000 (Wong, 2018). A number of Google's workers held a walkout in November 2018, signalling that they are not averse to taking action to assert what they feel are their legitimate rights.

The flexible workforce

The business enterprise wishes to have a flexible workforce of committed workers, but practices such as the routine use of temporary workers and workers on zero-hours contracts can lead to complaints from these workers that their treatment is unethical and unlawful in some cases. What risks to the business arise in situations where a large segment of the workforce complains of discrimination in this respect?

Workers in the gig economy

In a number of sectors, workers are classified as self-employed but in reality, their jobs are more akin to working for another person. In some, such as delivery, courier and taxi services, the work is carried out by people who are labelled 'self-employed', but whose work falls somewhere between self-employed status and worker status. This work falls within the broad category of the gig economy (defined in Chapter 1), where the worker is treated as a freelancer. However, this classification is controversial. Uber's business model is based on its ride-hailing technology, in which the driver is classified as self-employed. Uber allocates the rides and determines the remuneration that the driver receives, taking a commission. Uber drivers complain of the excessive hours they feel compelled to work, the control over them exerted by the company, and the fact that they are penalized for turning down work. Uber, like Google, employs a core workforce of skilled computing engineers. But the vast majority of the people who work under the Uber banner are classified as self-employed. A number of these workers have questioned the legality of this arrangement in the courts, arguing that their self-employed status is false.

The status of the worker is determined not by the label used by the parties, but by the realities of the relationship, revolving around the extent of control exerted by the company. Legal cases in a number of countries have found that, although the driver

can decide what hours to work, the company's control over the rides and remuneration makes the driver more akin to a worker in law. The implications are that the company owes legal obligations towards the worker, such as payment of the minimum wage, social charges and duties of health and safety. Avoiding this status is of utmost importance in Uber's corporate strategy, as its business model relies on the self-employed status of drivers. Companies such as Uber and Deliveroo have become embroiled in extensive litigation over these issues.

MINI CASE STUDY

The status of workers in the gig economy

People who work in the gig economy, such as delivery drivers and Uber drivers, are usually classified as self-employed, but this classification is controversial. Following cases brought by individuals who question this status, some clarification of the law is now impacting on these businesses. Pimlico Plumbers is a domestic maintenance firm in London, which customers can turn to 24 hours a day for plumbing repairs and installations. The work is carried out by Pimlico's 380 staff. Gary Smith, one of these engineers, worked for the firm for six years, but had a heart attack and asked for reduced hours because of his ill health. Pimlico refused this request, and the firm ultimately repossessed the van it had provided for him. Mr Smith commenced legal proceedings for unfair dismissal, claiming he was an employee. He had been given no sick pay and had no entitlement to holiday pay. He claimed he had these rights under the Employment Rights Act. The case was to become an important milestone in deciding the legal status of people who work in the gig economy.

The court decided Mr Smith was a 'worker', rather than an 'employee'. His status was that of a 'limb-b' worker. The limb-b worker is not entitled to compensation for unfair dismissal or to sick pay, but is entitled to the minimum wage and holiday pay. As a limb-b worker, Mr Smith was not in business on his own account: he was working within the business of the firm, Pimlico Plumbers.

Pimlico Plumbers' colourful CEO had been robust in his defence of his business model, claiming that the firm's 380 tradesmen were all self-employed. At the same time, he conveyed to customers that these were Pimlico Plumbers' workers. Mr Smith had been required to work hours determined by the firm, but could reject work or hire a substitute. The ability to hire a substitute had been seen as a crucial test for self-employment. It is a feature of similar arrangements used by Deliveroo and Uber to assert the gig-economy status of their drivers. In the case of Mr Smith, the Supreme Court said that it would look behind the term, to the actual relationship. If that relationship is one of personal service, then some substitution is possible for a person who is essentially a worker.

Some months after the decision in the Pimlico Plumbers case, there was a settlement of a separate case with Deliveroo, the takeaway delivery firm. In that case, 50 of their couriers won a large sum in compensation. The riders had been classified as self-employed. The settlement recognized their rights to the minimum wage and paid

A worker or a self-employed person? The work carried out by people like this Deliveroo delivery person is likely to be insecure in the gig economy.

© Getty, Dan Kitwood / Staff

holidays. The companies involved in these cases tend to view the judicial decisions as pertaining only to individual complainants, rather than to the business models. Hence, other workers would need to take action themselves, even though their positions are similar.

Questions

- What clarification is now taking place in employment law for workers in the gig economy?
- How should the business models of companies such as Deliveroo and Pimlico Plumbers be changed?

Find out more

The fog surrounding gig economy workers is being slowly clarified, as shown in the article, 'Workplace reforms will protect gig economy workers', at www.bbc.co.uk, 17 December 2018. There are helpful links in this article.

Human rights and the workplace

Human rights cover all aspects of work, including health and safety, pay, personal treatment, rights not to be discriminated against and rights to organize. Labour rights are sometimes treated as separate from human rights, but labour rights are themselves human rights, and are important in the implementation of other human rights in the workplace. We look first at workers' pay.

Wages: do they provide a decent living?

The UN's Covenant on Economic, Social and Cultural Rights speaks of a fair wage that provides a decent living for a person and his/her family. This is usually referred to as a 'living wage'. It is often referred to as a basic right by workers in low-pay environments, including fast-food outlets and retailing. The living wage as a concept is vague. It depends on the cost of living, which varies from country to country, and from region to region within a country. Many countries set a minimum wage per hour as a legal requirement. It was introduced in the UK in 1999. The minimum wage is usually less than what would be considered a living wage. The worker is unlikely to be able to support a family on the minimum wage, especially if the work offered is not full-time. The national living wage was introduced in the UK in 2016. For a person aged 25 or over, this is the national minimum wage, which was £7.83 per hour in 2018, and rose to £8.21 in April 2019. For workers between 16 and 24, there are three minimum-wage bands beneath this level, all of which are increased together.

The hourly wage is only one aspect of a worker's pay and conditions. The number of hours worked is also crucial, as the worker on a minimum wage is at risk of not being able to support a family if the hours of work are too few. For many workers on zero-hours contracts, casual work, or work in the gig economy, the pay often falls short of what a full-time employee would earn at the minimum wage. Research by the Trades Union Congress (TUC, at www.tuc.org.uk) has shown that real wages (that is, allowing for the effects of inflation) in 2018 were £24 per week less than in 2008 (Tily, 2018). While wages were finally rising in 2018, they had still not reached pre-financial crisis levels. The TUC attributed this weakness in wage growth to austerity measures, insecure work and the decline in collective bargaining, highlighting the role of trade unions in achieving better conditions.

In the US, the federal minimum wage is $7.25 per hour, a rate that was set in 2009. Wage stagnation among lower-income groups has been a major factor in widening inequality in the US. The failure to raise the federal minimum wage has resulted in many individual states stepping in: 29 have set a minimum wage above this level,

and many employers pay above this level as their own minimum wage. However, a living wage is a different matter. Pay for work in some of the commonest jobs does not constitute a living wage. Figure 11.4 compares wages in a variety of occupations in the US. Fast-food workers feature at the bottom of the figure. Along with the retail cashier, the hotel receptionist and the dishwasher, they fall beneath the poverty line for a family of four, which is $25,900. The building cleaner makes $27,960 annually. This is several thousand dollars more than most of these other low-paid workers, although the cleaner's job arguably involves less skill and judgment than the receptionist or cashier. Protests and strikes among low-paid workers in fast food and retailing have taken place across the US, targeting in particular large employers such as Walmart and McDonald's. A full-time worker earning the federal minimum wage would earn $15,080 in a year – well below the poverty line for a family of four.

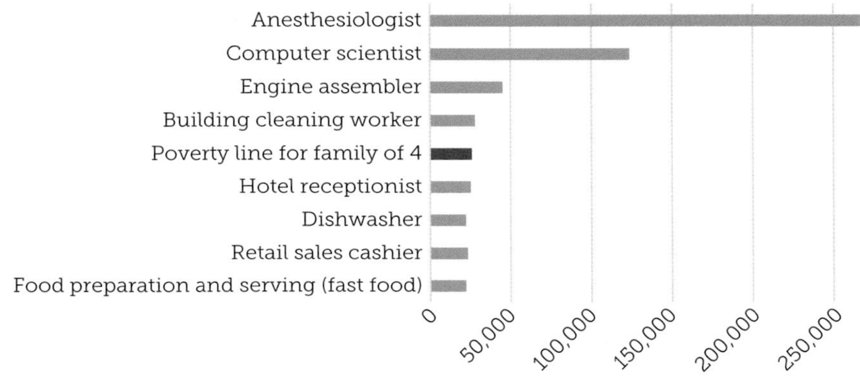

Figure 11.4 What is the job worth? Comparative wages in the US

Sources: US Government Bureau of Labor Statistics (2018) Occupational Employment Statistics, May, at https://data.bls.gov, accessed 16 July 2019; US Census, Poverty thresholds for 2018, at www.census.gov, accessed 16 September 2019.

The most highly paid worker in this figure is the anesthesiologist, whose earnings of $267,020 are more than double those of the computer scientist and 12 times the wage of the hotel receptionist. What is more, the anesthesiologist who specializes in pain management can expect compensation of double this already-large sum. The huge rewards that flow to doctors and other healthcare professionals are an aspect of the very high costs of US healthcare (see Figure 4.12). A factor is the power of the American Medical Association (AMA) over the structures and governance of all key aspects of the medical profession, including not just the pay of doctors, but medical education accreditation, health insurance, and the pharmaceutical industry. The AMA is an active lobbyist, with considerable power in political corridors to influence policies that will profit its members. The AMA has long opposed the idea of a national health service, although there would seem to be a strong ethical case for one, given that the 43 million people who fall beneath the poverty line are at risk of being priced out of healthcare.

Migrant workers and forced labour

In all countries, there are people working in exploitative environments where they are locked into low-paid work that subjects them to inhumane treatment. Among them are migrant workers living in unsafe conditions far from their homes. Migrant labour is common in many sectors, notably manufacturing, construction and mining. The rich Middle Eastern Gulf states depend on migrant workers from countries such as Nepal and India, to construct skyscrapers, football stadiums and hotels such as those built for the FIFA world cup in Qatar in 2022. Migrant workers are often recruited in poor rural areas to work in industries in other regions of their own country. The migrant workers in the textile factories of Bangladesh fall into this category. Others are recruited in poor areas of developing countries, to be transported, often illegally, to other countries where they carry out low-skilled manual work. Their transport and employment are arranged by agencies that work for business owners. There have long been legitimate licensed agencies that serve what has become a global market in labour, hiring workers for foreign employment, providing the necessary documentation. However, there also exist many unlicensed agencies that traffic people illegally and have links with other businesses that control migrants in their destination, often through brutal and repressive means, tantamount to slavery.

forced labour work that people are compelled to do against their will

Forced labour is work that people are forced or compelled to do against their will, and face punishment if they refuse (Anti-Slavery International, 2019). Forced labour is a central feature of modern slavery and is recognized in the ILO's Forced Labour Convention (see Table 11.1). While forced labour is often viewed as an issue in developing and emerging countries, the phenomenon also occurs in developed economies. Exploitative and abusive work conditions have been found to exist in 17 sectors of the British economy. They include domestic work, nail bars, car washes, agriculture, textile manufacturing, warehousing, and construction. These workers are mainly from overseas, having been trafficked from Romania, Albania, Vietnam, Nigeria and other countries. There are tens of thousands of people working in conditions of forced labour in the UK. The numbers are difficult to know, but in 2017, 5,000 people were referred to authorities as victims of slavery, 2,000 of whom were children. While slavery was officially abolished in 1833, modern slavery continues to exist. Many people trafficked for forced labour are trapped by debt owed to traffickers for travel and fees.

In extreme cases, migrants pay agents large sums for travel and other fees, leaving them in a position of debt bondage. Their passports are taken away from them, and their earnings go towards paying off their debts. Such workers are vulnerable to human rights abuse, from which they have no apparent escape. Typically, they work excessively long shifts of 12 to 15 hours a day, and they are deprived of rest days. While they are promised decent wages, in reality they receive less than the legal minimum, and have no choice but to accept. Their terms can include false self-employment contracts and zero-hours contracts, which help to conceal the number of hours worked. In addition, they suffer from dangerous working and living conditions in premises controlled by their employers.

In the UK, there is a National Referral Mechanism to help the victims of human trafficking and modern slavery. This system was set up under the European Convention on Action against Trafficking in Human Beings. Those who engage in trafficking and slavery are committing crimes that can be prosecuted in UK law, the most recent of which is the Modern Slavery Act 2015, which sets out slavery offences and establishes an Anti-slavery Commissioner. In addition, under the 2016 Immigration Act, abusive labour conditions in all sectors can be investigated by the Gangmasters and Labour Abuse Authority. However, investigating and prosecuting slavery and labour abuse is difficult to carry out, and victims, especially undocumented migrants, are often too frightened to come forward. Although a step forward, the Modern Slavery Act is focused more on prosecution than on victim protection, and it has shortcomings. For example, the domestic servant who wishes to leave an abusive employer must first go through the referral process. However, the act introduced a provision that large companies must report annually on how they combat slavery in their global supply chains. This new law is limited in its application, as it applies only to those that make products sold in the UK. Therefore, it does not apply, for example, to human rights abuse on building sites in the Middle

 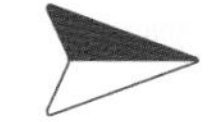

Eastern Gulf states. However, it represents an important step in recognizing the accountability of MNEs that outsource manufacturing in developing countries where abuses of human rights occur.

Factory workers in China's outsourced manufacturing, who are mostly migrant workers from rural regions, are likely to face a plethora of onerous terms: 12-hour working days, excessive overtime, few rest days, penalties such as withheld pay for discipline infringements. While China's employment laws provide that overtime should be limited to 36 hours per month, workers in many factories are effectively compelled to work over the legal limit.

The death of a migrant worker in a Pegatron factory, where Apple iPhones are made, was reported in 2015. The worker had died after an 84-hour week (Fullerton and Chen, 2015). Researchers had earlier uncovered numerous human rights violations in other factories in the Apple supply chain, including underage labour, excessive hours, poor living conditions, abuse by management and environmental pollution (BBC, 2013). Apple's supply chain employs over 3 million workers in hundreds of supplier factories, mostly in China. Apple has a Supplier Code of Conduct which aims to uphold high human rights standards. It monitors violations of human rights, including rights of association. In 2017, it assessed 756 suppliers, who employ over 1.3 million workers. However, its monitoring is carried out internally, and is not independently verified. Results are reported selectively, with little specific detail which would allow independent verification. Apple said in its 2018 *Progress Report*, 'Our dedication to treating people in our supply chain with dignity and respect is unwavering' (Apple, 2018: 13). In 2008, Apple introduced a prohibition on bonded labour, under which its monitoring attempts to uncover debt-bonded labour violations, following which the company pays sums of money to employees who have been affected. Since 2008, 35,000 bonded and trafficked people at these factories have received such payments, 1,558 of them in 2017. Apple reports that the number of offending employers involved in these violations is decreasing, but, as with other human rights abuses, serious violations continue to occur, and Apple's selective internal monitoring process is unlikely to uncover all the violations.

These global brand owners expend much energy in extolling their high standards of human rights in their corporate communications aimed at investors and consumers worldwide, but the reality would seem to be very different for outsourced manufacturing. Selective in-house monitoring cannot suffice to uphold human rights in these situations. The root cause of these failures to uphold decent work and living standards is the business model itself, which depends on millions of exploited workers.

Workers' rights to organize

The rights of workers to organize and bargain with management has long been recognized in employment relations, where the balance of power is inherently weighted towards employers and owners of a business. Ideally, amicable relations between the parties are facilitated by a dialogue between workers' representatives and management. Ultimately, good relations facilitate a more committed workforce and more productive business. Labour relations based on respect of workers as stakeholders are also essential to the business on ethical grounds. Most of the world's countries recognize the right of workers to organize in workplace environments. Benchmark international labour standards are set by the **International Labour Organization (ILO)** (www.ilo.org), through conventions that form part of international law. There are 95 of these, among which eight are considered fundamental. These are shown in Table 11.1.

International Labour Organization (ILO) UN organization that sets international labour standards

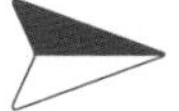

Table 11.1 Fundamental ILO conventions

Convention	Year
Freedom of association and protection of the right to organize convention	1948
Right to organize and collective bargaining convention	1949
Forced labour convention	1930
Abolition of forced labour convention	1950
Minimum age convention	1973
Worst forms of child labour convention	1999
Equal remuneration convention	1951
Discrimination (employment and occupation) convention	1958

Source: ILO, Conventions and Recommendations, at www.ilo.org, accessed 15 December 2018.

Although most of the world's countries have ratified most of these conventions, the one with the fewest ratifications is the first of those listed, that recognizing freedom of association. Bangladesh has ratified this convention, but there are numerous countries that have not. Among them are Brazil, China, India, Iran, South Korea, Malaysia, Morocco, New Zealand, Oman, Qatar, Saudi Arabia, Singapore, Thailand, the UAE, the US and Vietnam. These countries present differing cultural and economic environments. There is a group of mainly Muslim countries, and there are large emerging economies. There are two western market economies: the US and New Zealand. European countries, including all EU member states, have ratified all these fundamental conventions. The US has ratified only two, while Russia has ratified all eight. Companies' legal obligations are dictated by national law predominantly, and those standards are weaker than international standards enshrined in ILO conventions. The US has historically been reluctant to recognize international human rights law, prioritizing the Bill of Rights in its own constitution. This seemingly parochial approach contrasts with the global reach of its large companies. Companies such as Nike and Gap adhere to national labour standards in their outsourced manufacturing in Vietnam and Indonesia, and questions arise about their moral responsibility for human rights breaches. Still, these companies maintain that they take social responsibility seriously.

In most countries, workers have a legal right to join trade unions under national law, but in practice many employers discourage union membership, and workers who join unions can be subjected to disciplinary action and discrimination. In many countries, governments, too, seek to restrict trade union activity in practice, in response to business pressures. Repressive tactics have been used against protesting workers and labour organizers. Where industrial action in the form of strikes is allowed, there are legal frameworks within which the strike must take place. For example, in the UK, a legal strike must be sanctioned by a union vote as required by statute (the Trade Unions and Labour Relations (Consolidation) Act 1992). An **independent trade union** is one unconnected to owners of the business, governmental agencies or political leaders. The independent trade union can play a positive role in industrial relations, helping to create a constructive dialogue between owners and workers. For workers, freedom of association can be crucial to gaining a voice and improving poor working conditions. In the UK, outsourced workers such as cleaners and security staff who work in government departments are typically employed on zero-hours contracts. As members of a trade union, these workers have voted for strike action in some cases, in support of improvements in pay and conditions. They also demand that their contracts be taken back in-house by the government departments where they work. Figure 11.5 shows the intensity of union membership in England, Scotland and Wales.

independent trade union organization of workers unconnected to owners of the business or government

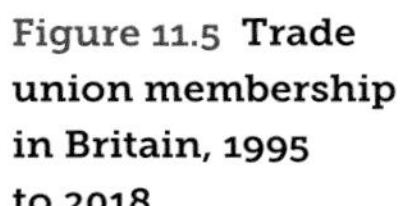

Figure 11.5 Trade union membership in Britain, 1995 to 2018

Source of data: ONS (Office for National Statistics), *Labour Force Survey, Trade Union Statistics 2018*, Table 4.1, Trade union membership by nation, at www.gov.uk/government/statistics/, accessed 16 July 2019.

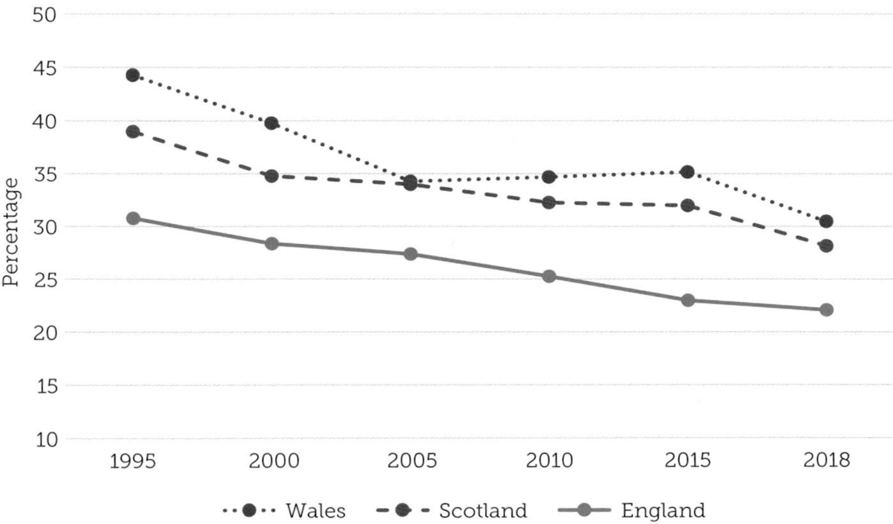

Figure 11.5 shows a decline in trade union membership among workers in the three nations. The decline in Wales is from 44.3% to 30.5% over the period. Historically, Scotland and Wales have had unionized industries such as manufacturing, mining and shipbuilding. Trade union density has been high in these sectors, but these sectors have declined in employment over the period shown in the figure, and trade union membership has declined steeply as a consequence. In the post-industrial landscape, much work has shifted to the service sector and to more insecure types of work, where workers are less likely to be unionized.

During the golden age of US car manufacturing in the 1950s and 1960s, the auto workers union (the United Auto Workers) was a powerful force, achieving highly advantageous conditions for its members. American carmakers saw their fortunes wane as foreign investors such as Toyota and Honda, set up car factories that were more competitive and based on non-unionized labour. In the 1950s, General Motors was America's largest private-sector employer, and its carworkers earned $35 an hour in today's dollars. Now, Walmart is the largest private-sector employer, and its workers earn a fraction of that sum. GM is now a shadow of its former self, and has faced challenges of recovering after a bailout by the government following the financial crisis. Most of GM's workers are now employed outside the US on wages that are much lower than in the 1950s, as are the wages of those GM workers in the US.

Wages in the US and UK have stagnated for many years. Both countries have low trade union membership, and in both, membership has been declining. From a peak of 34.8% in 1954, union membership among all salaried and waged employees in the US had declined to 20.1% in 1983 (Desilver, 2018). The 11.3% of US workers in trade unions is made up largely of public-sector workers. The percentage for the private sector is just 6.7%. American employers are active in keeping out trade unions that seek to organize workers in their organizations, through tactics known as 'union busting'. Such tactics have been effective in curtailing union membership, but have also contributed to a continuing mentality that sees unions and management as inherently hostile in their relations. Industrial action by workers in the US rose sharply in 2018, when a total of 487,000 workers were involved in major work stoppages, the largest number in a single year since 1986 (Bureau of Labor Statistics, 2019). This total was made up mainly of teachers and other public-sector workers, but also included hotel workers (see the feature on 'The way I see it...' in this chapter). Sweden and Denmark, both countries that have high trade union membership, also have high rankings in the UN's human development index (HDI), which takes in income, education and health (see Chapter 2). These countries also have relatively low levels of inequality.

The ILO has long championed co-operative relations between workers' organizations and employers as the best way to ensure both better conditions for workers and a more productive and committed workforce. Where workers are seen as troublemakers, lack of trust and adversarial attitudes take root and are difficult to shift. Attitudes become hardened, and us-and-them attitudes become entrenched. If workers and managers can come together through dialogue, mutual trust is facilitated. Where trade unions are not allowed or discouraged, workers lose a voice in the workplace – a voice that could foster greater trust and understanding between managers and workers. For the employer, dialogue aimed at improving the workplace environment is the best way to ensure a sustainable business that benefits all stakeholders, including those representing social values.

China can boast a high level of trade union membership, but there unions are not independent: they are connected politically to the Communist Party, and are, in effect, under government control. China does not allow freedom of association for workers to join independent trade unions. This is a factor in the continuing problems of excessive hours and poor conditions in China's factories. On the other hand, wage rises have been in the region of 6% or more annually, tracking China's GDP growth. The Chinese manufacturing worker in 2017 made on average $3.60 an hour, up 64% from 2011. Such increases are characteristic of fast-growing emerging economies, but rises on this scale are not always sustainable. Many globalized companies have shifted to lower-cost locations in other countries, and wage rises in China will slow as demand falters in China's export markets, especially if the US imposes tariffs on goods from China.

Social responsibility of the firm

Liberalization policies of national governments have attracted MNEs and drawn countries into global supply chains, often through FDI and outsourcing. An MNE's ties with the various countries involved in supply and production, however, can be tenuous. Some are inclined to see production of their branded products as simply a question of 'supply', denoting a rather neutral involvement, although there could be thousands of workers making a company's products in locations far from its home country. Hence the idea of supplier codes of conduct used by global brands. Other firms recognize a stakeholder relationship with these workers, acknowledging that they are morally responsible in areas of human wellbeing. **Corporate social responsibility** (CSR) refers to the role of the firm in society, which entails obligations to stakeholders in local communities and to the environment. Where the company is active in the place where it is based, and where it has a large number of employees, the concept of CSR seems more appropriate than it does in distant countries where workers making its branded goods are not its employees at all. Japan is an example of the first of these situations. Here, the firm has traditionally been viewed as being part of society and having a social role in addition to its economic activities. For the Japanese employee, the job is more than merely a way of making a living, but a way of life in itself, bound up in the employee's sense of belonging.

corporate social responsibility (CSR) an approach to business which recognizes that the organization has responsibilities in society beyond the economic role, extending to legal, ethical, environmental and philanthropic roles

In individualist western environments, the company has been viewed more narrowly, as performing an essentially economic role. Businesses have tended to feel that, so long as they adhered to existing legal obligations, they are free to focus on 'the bottom line', that is, profits and shareholder value. This simplistic view, which separates social responsibility concerns from business ones is increasingly untenable, for two reasons.

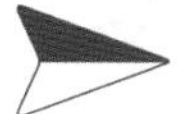

Firstly, while markets have delivered economic results, they have left out of the equation considerations of human and environmental values. The insertion of these concerns in the social market economies is a recognition of market limitations. The human rights and environmental questions posed daily for large corporations, such as oil companies in developing states, also show the inadequacy of viewing business in isolation from the community. No longer can an MNE doing business in a developing country remain disengaged from the live community issues in the places where it operates or sources products. Moreover, as we noted earlier, a minimal policy of obedience to national laws can fall well short of ethical principles.

Secondly, the sheer size of the world's global corporations now dwarfs many national economies. Questions of how they are using this power in socially responsible ways are now being addressed to companies, as well as to governments. Theories of CSR have addressed both the normative and practical aspects of CSR.

Theories of corporate social responsibility (CSR)

Management theorists and corporate strategists for a number of years have been addressing the question of what the role of the company in society should be. While most now agree that its role extends beyond the purely economic dimension, there is much debate on the nature and extent of this expanded social role. There is also a body of theory on social performance and how it can be measured (Wood, 1991). Adding complexity to the discussion is the reality that global companies operate in a number of different societies. Theories which attempt to define the company's responsibility to society are generally grouped together as theories of corporate social responsibility (CSR). These theories typically make reference to stakeholder groups, as well as to society in general. These concepts were introduced in Chapter 1. Here we look at theories of CSR in conjunction with stakeholder theories, which have been the subject of academic debate in recent years (Mitchell et al., 1997).

A 'weak' theory of CSR focuses on philanthropic or charitable contributions and activities, which the firm engages in as an adjunct to its business activities: any costs are weighed against the benefit to be gained in terms of the firm's enhanced reputation as a good corporate citizen. On this view, CSR 'is fine, if you can afford it'. (Freeman, 1984: 40). The setting up of a charitable foundation has become a favoured philanthropic approach, often linked with the concept of corporate citizenship. **Corporate citizenship** visualizes the responsibility of the firm in the community as analogous to that of the individual citizen, entailing obligations to obey the law and pay taxes. As we have seen above, however, these obligations can be interpreted rather loosely. Obeying the law can involve following the letter of the law, but not the spirit of the law. A duty to pay taxes can translate into finding ways *not* to pay the country's taxes. Critics of this approach argue that it is 'skin deep', entailing no rethinking of the firm's strategy and operations in terms of social issues. In theory, a company might be socially responsible in this limited sense, which would include setting up a charitable foundation, while allowing exploitation of the workers who make its products or tolerating damaging environmental impacts.

corporate citizenship concept which visualizes the social responsibility of the firm in the community as analogous to that of the individual citizen, entailing obligations to obey the law and pay taxes

A stronger strategic approach to CSR is found in the work of A.B. Carroll. Carroll has devised a four-dimensional model of CSR (Carroll, 1991), which takes into account economic, legal, ethical and philanthropic dimensions. This model, which can be envisaged as a pyramid, places the economic obligations of the company at the base, recognizing that the business must be economically profitable in order to survive. Above economic activities are legal responsibilities. Legal obligations cover many areas, including employment law, environmental law, health and safety regulations. The law sets minimum standards, which differ from country to country. The firm with a strong CSR policy will aim to go beyond minimum legal standards. Carroll's model sees the need to rise above minimal legal requirements as an aspect of

philanthropy voluntary giving of money or other resources to good causes, often charities

stakeholder theory management theory which focuses on the many different groups and interests that affect the company

primary stakeholders stakeholders directly involved in a firm's business

secondary stakeholders stakeholders indirectly involved in a firm's business

ethical responsibility, along with respect for ethical norms in the society in which the firm operates. The last element is **philanthropy**, such as charitable giving, which, while desirable, is less important than the other three – the icing on the cake. Carroll stresses that the model does not posit an inherent conflict between making profits and being socially responsible: for the manager, all four dimensions of the firm's responsibility should be central to corporate strategy.

While Carroll's model provides an overall framework, analysis of the 'social' component of CSR is provided by **stakeholder theory**. First developed by Edward Freeman, stakeholder theory points to the many different groups and interests that affect the company. Freeman defines them broadly as 'any group or individual which affects or is affected by the achievement of the organization's objectives'. (Freeman, 1984: 46). In this broad category, some groups are clearly more influential than others. Stakeholders may be classified according to the strength of their influence on the company, and how critical they are to the company's operational success at any given time. **Primary stakeholders** are those that have direct impacts on the business. They include shareholders, lenders, employees and customers (see Figure 11.6). In terms of global supply chains, the licensed manufacturer that makes the MNE's branded products would be a primary stakeholder, with whom the MNE has contractual ties. The interests of **secondary stakeholders** have less direct influences on the business. They can be important influences over time, but in the short run, they do not directly affect the firm's performance. As Figure 11.6 shows, they include workers employed by manufacturers in the supply chain. Also included are interests impacted by the company's operations, including communities and the natural environment. However, these interests would come within the ambit of social responsibility.

The multinational enterprise

Primary stakeholders	Secondary stakeholders
• Shareholders in parent company • Employees of parent company • Lenders to the company, e.g. bondholders • Companies contracted to manufacture the MNE's products • Customers and consumers of its products or services	• Workers in supply chains that make the MNE's products • Trade unions representing the above workers • Communities where the MNE's products are made • Governments • NGOs • Communities • The natural environment

Figure 11.6 Primary and secondary stakeholders

Situations in which stakeholder interests conflict with each other pose particular challenges for managers. For example, the decision to outsource an operation to a low-cost location will save money, but cause loss of employment in the company's home country, where most of its shareholders are likely to be located. What do shareholders want? Shareholder value is often assumed to be just short-term profits, but shareholders also have views on long-term prosperity and sustainability. While shareholders would be expected to go along with the management's strategy, this should no longer be assumed. Shareholders can be critical of management on grounds that strategies are not sustainable.

CSR in practice

Many companies subscribe to the weak notion of CSR, equating it with charitable giving and corporate citizenship. On this view, the 'social' element resides in the notion that, once the company has made lots of money, it is in a position to give some of it 'back' to society. This approach rests on a view of CSR as being peripheral, not core to the business. However, many decisions a company takes, such as where to locate production, have both a strategic *and* CSR dimension. Some theorists have combined CSR principles with a framework for applying them in practice. Theories of **corporate social performance** (CSP) reflect this approach, looking at the firm's social responses in differing contexts (Wood, 1991). This approach is akin to stakeholder management, but arguably more slanted towards applications, which would include processes such as monitoring and assessment of the company's stakeholder interactions. Codes of conduct would come into this outlook, as would sustainability reporting. From a managerial perspective, CSP and social responsiveness provide a process-oriented approach to CSR. The CSP approach can be seen as part of the **'business case' for CSR**, involving assessments of relations with various stakeholder groups. Central to this outlook are considerations of corporate reputation.

corporate social performance concept associated with CSR in practice which focuses on responses to stakeholders and broader issues of business in society

business case for CSR argument that business goals will be met more successfully in the longer term through CSR than through a narrow focus on economic goals

The business case for CSR revolves around a number of stakeholder groups, including investors, consumers, employees and the community (McWilliams, 2001). McWilliams argues that, analyzed in terms of costs and benefits, a business case for CSR can be based on a differentiation strategy and can become a source of competitive advantage. Examples of CSR approaches in this context are:

- Products made from sustainable resources, such as recycled materials
- Products made through CSR-related processes, such as organic foods
- Advertising which provides information about CSR attributes, such as dolphin-free tuna labels
- Building brand reputation on CSR attributes.

The business case for CSR based on market considerations treats the choice of CSR attributes as analogous to the other strategic choices a firm makes, in terms of the demand for the attribute and the costs of providing it. This 'instrumental' view of CSR is akin to the weak version of the theory mentioned at the start of this section, in that the CSR case rests on business considerations rather than ethical ones. However, it does highlight the fact that demand exists and that it is coming from numerous stakeholder groups – an indication that social responsibility is one of the criteria guiding consumers and investors in their evaluation of corporate performance.

codes of practice sets of rules which companies voluntarily follow to guide their CSR, ethical and environmental practices

third-party verification the use of outside specialist services or certification to monitor CSR and environmental performance

Many MNEs have in place voluntary **codes of practice** on CSR, ethical principles and environmental policies. These codes of practice contain stated aims which are not always carried through in practice, as we have seen. A way of assuring stakeholders of high corporate standards is **third-party verification**. Certification by specialist monitoring bodies is available across a wide range of industries, from organic produce to tourism. The Roundtable on Sustainable Palm Oil (RSPO) (www.rspo.org) has been an example, aimed at guaranteeing consumers that palm oil is from sustainable sources. It has been only partially successful, as, in practice, it is unable to guarantee sustainable sources.

Fairtrade Foundation a charity that promotes a fair deal for poor agricultural producers in developing countries, licensing producer organizations to use the Fairtrade logo

Another example is the **Fairtrade Foundation** (www.fairtrade.org.uk), which supports principles of sustainable agriculture and a fair return for farmers. Companies that sign up to these principles can use the Fairtrade logo, which signifies to consumers that the product is produced according to fair trade principles. Fairtrade products have become popular with consumers. They include coffee, tea, bananas and chocolate, all of which have been taken up by large food companies and retailers. However, a recent trend has been for large companies to move away from third-party verification such as Fairtrade, and to devise their own schemes in-house. Is this a backward step in the promotion of sustainable agriculture? Corporate schemes lack the element of independent criteria, and a proliferation of differing corporate logos signifying fair trade could be bewildering for consumers. The Fairtrade movement represents a counterweight to the corporate power of large agribusiness companies, emphasizing the need for a fair return for farmers.

Reporting on social and environmental impacts is increasingly seen as part of the MNE's response to CSR concerns. There are different names and formats for this kind of reporting, many of which focus on sustainability as an umbrella category. Many MNEs adopt **environmental, social and governance reporting** (ESG), which covers a range of CSR issues, including human rights and responses to environmental pollution. By ESG reporting, the company aims to disclose information on its CSR performance generally, including how its decision-makers and governance structures are addressing CSR issues. ESG reporting has become widespread, and in many countries ESG reporting for listed companies is now compulsory (Baron, 2014). Among them are France, Norway, India and South Africa; the EU specifies categories of non-financial reporting along ESG lines. Research by KPMG in 2013 showed that, of the world's top 100 companies across 41 countries, 71% reported on ESG, whether this reporting was mandatory or not (KPMG, 2013). More than half of US companies listed on the S&P Index report on ESG, although there is no specific mandatory requirement to do so. Companies are now highly sensitive to reputational issues, and ESG reporting contributes positively to building a reputation for transparency and dialogue with stakeholders. At the same time, companies should be wary of using these reports simply as public relations exercises: stakeholders now expect concrete information on these issues, rather than abstract commitments to principles. On the other hand, presenting data on performance is only part of a CSR approach, and addressing normative issues which are not quantifiable is equally important.

environmental, social and governance reporting (ESG) reporting framework for companies that cover a range of CSR issues, including human rights and responses to environmental pollution

CSR: more than skin deep?

A critical observer might say that, although MNEs are more than ever attuned to CSR issues, this does not imply radical changes in business models – just more professional skill in handling reputational issues. To what extent do you think this a fair assessment, or not?

Reaching for international standards

There are now several sets of international CSR standards designed to guide MNEs in their international operations. Sponsored by inter-governmental organizations which enjoy wide participation by both developing and developed countries, these statements of CSR principles are increasingly recognized as setting the benchmarks in international CSR. We highlight several here, including those from the OECD, the ILO and the UN. These statements focus on broad principles, including human rights, working conditions, employment terms and environmental protection. Here is a brief summary of the main points of each:

OECD Guidelines for Multinational Enterprises – Issued first in 1976, this was among the first statements of principles of CSR. The fifth update of these principles was issued in 2011 (at www.oecd.org/corporate/mne). Participating in the revision were 11 non-OECD countries, mainly developing countries, in addition to the 30 OECD member states. Three areas are now highlighted. First, the responsibility of MNEs over the entire supply chain is highlighted as coming within the firm's sphere of influence, even though the companies are legally independent. Secondly, the

guidelines stress human rights, addressing situations where host-country policies on human rights do not reach international standards, or where the host country has not ratified relevant UN human rights conventions. Thirdly, the guidelines address new environmental issues, including 'green growth' of economies, eco-innovation, biodiversity and sustainability.

International Labour Organization (ILO) Tripartite Declaration of Principles concerning MNEs and Social Policy (MNE Declaration) – The ILO *Declaration* dates from 1977, and its fifth edition was issued in 2017 (ILO, 2017), replacing the fourth edition, which appeared in 2006. The latest edition was revised to take account of the spread of global supply chains, the growing concentration of economic power of MNEs and the changes taking place in the working environment. The ILO's *Declaration* is addressed to governments, MNEs, and employers' and workers' organizations. There are five headings:

1 General principles
    - The primacy of national law and recognition of international conventions, for example, on human rights
    - MNEs' obligations to abide by social and labour law of home and host countries.
2 Employment – addressed to governments and MNEs
    - Promote full, freely chosen employment and decent work
    - Facilitate the transition to formal employment
    - Provide for social protections
    - Prevent and eliminate forced and compulsory labour
    - Prohibit child labour
    - Eliminate discrimination on grounds of race, colour, sex, religion, political opinion, national extraction or social origin.
3 Training
    - MNEs should promote skill formation and lifelong learning.
4 Conditions of work and life
    - Wages, benefits and conditions of work
    - MNEs should take into account the needs of workers and their families
    - Governments and MNEs should maintain highest standards of safety and health
    - Where MNEs provide housing, medical care and food, they should be of a good standard.
5 Industrial relations
    - Workers should have freedom of association and protection against anti-union discrimination in their employment
    - Collective bargaining should be allowed, and there should be consultation with workers' representatives, as provided by national law
    - Where host governments offer FDI incentives, they should not include limitations on workers' freedom of association or right to organize and bargain collectively
    - There should be conciliation mechanisms for settling industrial disputes, involving equal representation of employees and employers
    - Governments and MNEs should have means in place to remedy human rights abuses.

The ILO Declaration speaks directly to MNEs, unlike the UN conventions from which these principles are derived, which address member governments. This latest revision of the *Declaration* focuses on issues that have become urgent in the context of migrant labour and workers that are liable to be exploited and subjected

to human rights abuse. These issues include decent work, forced and compulsory labour, insecure work and the transition from informal to formal work in developing countries. The fifth heading, industrial relations, stresses the importance of freedom of association and collective bargaining in the context of national law. While these rights are typically part of national law, they are only weakly enforced in many countries. The ILO stresses under each of these headings the importance of implementing national law that upholds international human rights and labour standards.

The UN Global Compact – This compact (at www.unglobalcompact.org) between governments, corporations and NGOs lists nine key principles from the Universal Declaration of Human Rights, the core standards of the ILO, and the Rio Declaration. They include support of human rights, the elimination of child labour, free trade unions and the elimination of environmental pollution. These are 'aspirational' rather than binding in their effects. The significance of the initiative is the bringing together of the major players in a single forum for debate about the issues. Nike, Unilever and Royal Dutch Shell were among the corporations that signed the accord, as were Amnesty International and the World Wildlife Fund. By 2018, the number of corporate participants had risen to 9,500 in 160 countries.

International Organization for Standardization (ISO) body which oversees quality and environmental standards recognized across industries

The **International Organization for Standardization** (ISO) www.iso.org oversees quality and environmental standards recognized across industries. Its ISO 9000 is a recognized quality assurance standard, and the more recent ISO 14000 series applies to environmental standards. ISO has now produced ISO 26000, its first guidance on social responsibility, combining principles from the OECD, ILO and UN Global Compact. The guidance it contains is just that – broad guidance. It does not set out standards and certification in the way that other ISO standards do. Neither does it recommend specifically how CSR should be reported. The Global Reporting Initiative (GRI) (www.globalreporting.org) goes back to 1997, and was one of the first organizations to focus on ESG guidelines. These have now evolved into the GRI Sustainability Reporting Standards. Known simply as the GRI Standards, they are relied on by many leading companies around the world. They are recognized as best practice in reporting economic, environmental and social issues.

CSR and corporate governance

In general, corporate boards are accountable to shareholders and other stakeholders through corporate governance mechanisms. However, as we highlighted in Chapter 1, every company is strongly influenced by the national environment of its home country and its own historical legacy. These factors are evident in its corporate culture, including perceptions of its role in society. Views of corporate governance reflect divergence in corporate cultures. Does the company view its primary duty as maximizing shareholder value or achieving wider goals associated with the stakeholder perspective? In countries where liberal market capitalism retains a grip, shareholder value is perceived as paramount, and CSR tends to be marginalized or conceived in terms of enhancing shareholder value. In countries where social market values have dominated, as in Western Europe, the stakeholder perspective is more prevalent. In these countries, especially under the guidance of the EU Commission, liberal reforms have made headway. The EU has been influential in promoting more competitive markets in member states, in reducing state subsidies to businesses and in encouraging the privatization of nationalized industries which have enjoyed monopolies in a number of sectors, such as telecommunications. That said, corporate governance in both the more shareholder-centred tradition and the stakeholder-centred tradition can be criticized on CSR grounds.

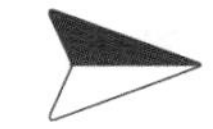

We found in Chapter 1 that even public companies can have ownership structures that concentrate power in the hands of a small group of insiders, often the founder's family and associates. Such power often stems from a dual-class share structure, in which the voting shares are concentrated in the ruling insiders. Ordinary shareholders may have little or no voting power on major issues. Insider control seems to be a phenomenon which crosses national borders. American, European and Asian companies, although divergent in corporate culture, have mechanisms which perpetuate a controlling group of shareholders. This control is typically exerted through appointments of executives and board members.

fiduciary duty duty of trust to act honestly and in the best interests of another; applies to the duty of directors owed to their company

All company directors, whether executive or non-executive, owe a duty to act always in the best interests of the company. This is known as **fiduciary duty**. Fiduciary duty denotes a position of trust. It is owed to the company as a whole, but differing interpretations of the nature of fiduciary duties lead to differing views of corporate governance. In the Anglo-American tradition, the primacy of shareholders over other stakeholders leads directors to think of their duties rather narrowly as maximizing shareholder wealth. Indeed, this principle became the beacon of American capitalism. The spread of market values around the world owes much to the success of American companies. But with the financial crisis of 2008, the assumptions about the stability of markets took a severe battering. Weaknesses in corporate governance are now held to bear much of the responsibility for the persistence of high-risk strategies in many companies, despite the risks to the very shareholder value that the system was meant to uphold. The following are some of the specific weaknesses which emerged:

- Corporate boards tend to go along with the strategic decisions of executive directors, rather than act in an effective monitoring role. Although most boards have independent, non-executive directors, these part-time directors, while legally owing the same fiduciary duties as full-time executives, tend to be compliant with management rather than be seen to 'rock the boat'.
- In corporate governance best practice, the positions of chairman of the board and CEO should be separate, but in reality, the roles are often combined, especially in the US. An effect is to give executive managers greater control over boards.
- Dominant shareholders exert control in many public limited companies, often through dual-share structures. They are in a strong position to influence voting and dictate strategy, leaving 'minority' ordinary shareholders in a weak position. Although there are legal protections for minority shareholders, especially when their interests are at stake, they have little influence on boards, and are usually unable, because of procedural hurdles, to put forward candidates to become directors.
- Committees of corporate boards, such as the remuneration committee and audit committee, tend to be dominated by the insiders who control the company, despite having non-executive members. In theory, payment to managers through stock options and bonuses based on performance, align managers' incentives more closely with owners, encouraging them to be more enterprise-minded. However, in reality, spiralling executive remuneration has come into the spotlight as an example of weak board oversight of managers.

The remuneration of executives, which is referred to as 'compensation' in the US, is typically made up of a number of elements. It includes annual salary, bonuses, incentive payments, and equity-based elements such as shares and share options. All of these elements can simply be considered 'pay'. The equity-based elements, in theory, align the executive's interests with those of shareholders. In practice, executives have been able to use the remuneration arrangements to benefit themselves above all. The steep rise in average executive pay in recent years, rather than serving aims of increasing shareholder value, has allowed executives to extract ever-greater compensation for themselves personally. Executive pay has become the focus of much attention in critical evaluations of corporate governance. In the US, rises in executive pay from 1978 to 2014 (adjusted for inflation) were 997%, which is double the growth in equities in the same period, and contrasts with the 10.9% increase in the pay of the typical worker over that 36-year period (EPI, 2015). Corporate profits and share prices have soared, but the wages of most workers have remained stagnant.

The average pay of the CEO in the top 350 US companies in 2017 was $18.9 million, while that of the typical worker was $54,600 (see Figure 11.7). CEO pay increased 17.6% from 2016, while the typical worker's pay increased just 0.3%. As the figure shows, the gap between CEO pay and that of the typical worker has ballooned since 1965, from a ratio of 20-to-1, to a ratio of 312-to-1 in 2017. The gap has actually narrowed, from a peak of 376-to-1 in 2001. Comparing CEO pay with that of other top earners, top CEOs gained considerably greater rewards, receiving nearly six times more than the rest of those in the top 0.1% of wage earners. Top-paid CEOs tend to say that there is a global market for their skills and talent that justifies these huge pay packages. In reality, their high pay does not reflect better firm performance. What drives these excessive rises has been the virtually unchecked ability of CEOs to get their way in dealing with their acquiescent boards.

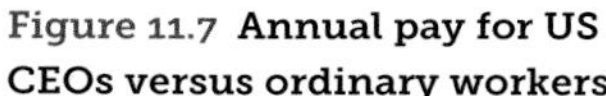
Figure 11.7 Annual pay for US CEOs versus ordinary workers

Notes: CEO pay includes salary, bonuses, long-term incentive payouts and stock options exercised in that year.

The ordinary worker is a private-sector production/non-supervisory worker.

Source of data: Economic Policy Institute (EPI) (2018) 'CEO compensation surged in 2017', report issued 16 August, Table 1, p. 6, at www.epi.org, accessed 23 September 2019.

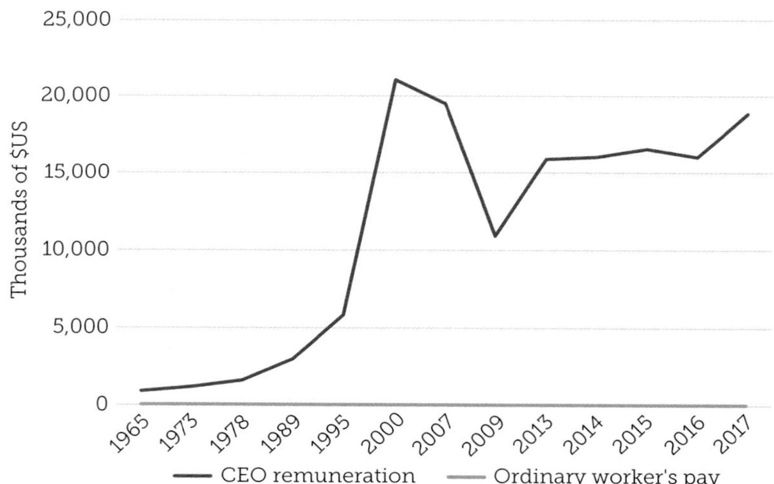

The EPI suggests that policy changes would help to address the imbalance between excessive compensation of CEOs and the stagnant wages of ordinary workers (EPI, 2018). These changes could be implemented with no detriment to economic performance. They are:

- Higher tax rates for the top earners
- Higher corporate tax rates for companies that have high ratios of CEO-to-worker compensation
- A cap on compensation, with taxation on anything above the cap
- Greater use of the 'say-on-pay' by shareholders at the AGM.

The first three of these recommendations are matters of government policy. In practice, both top earners and companies have seen reductions in tax during the Trump administration. The fourth recommendation is a matter of corporate governance. Reforming corporate governance to promote greater accountability has been a much-debated issue, especially in sectors such as banking, which has received large sums of public money in some countries. A key question concerns accountability: to whom is accountability owed: shareholders or all stakeholders? And how is it best achieved? The view that accountability is exclusively to shareholders has been a persistent belief in the US (Reich, 2018). This outlook has rewarded companies and their executives handsomely, but has not led to similar rewards for workers – or created jobs. Economically productive jobs in industrial sectors have dwindled, and inequality has widened.

Corporate governance

This is an interview with Eric Berglof of the European Bank of Reconstruction and Development. It is on corporate governance and the financial crisis, with an emphasis on the European dimension. It took place on 5 November 2010, and it is published by Knowledge@Wharton.

Video link: Corporate governance
https://youtu.be/BS-PY-SmZlw

A focus on stakeholder concerns would help to redress pay imbalances. Stakeholder interests are usually associated with theories of management rather than corporate governance. In continental European countries, employee representatives play a role in governance, but these employee representatives tend to speak for members in the home country. Other stakeholders, including workers in international operations, do not enjoy the same participative role. But stakeholders should be at the heart of corporate governance. This perspective is provided by CSR principles, encompassing all stakeholders, environmental concerns and ethical principles. CSR principles would cause executives to think twice about changing the company's registration to an offshore location for the fiscal benefits such as lower taxes.

Procedural reforms of corporate governance, such as changing voting systems for directors, will go only a limited way in persuading the investing public that companies are being run soundly and sustainably. There have been weak reforms in the US on executive pay, requiring a 'say on pay' in the annual general meeting (AGM), but the vote is not binding. There is now legislation in the EU which requires the capping of executive bonuses at 100% of salary or 200% if shareholders approve. In the UK, following shareholder revolts over excessive executive pay, new regulations in 2018 were intended to introduce greater transparency and accountability in remuneration. The housebuilding company, Persimmon, had paid its CEO £75 million in bonuses, which was rejected by 64% of its shareholders in a non-binding vote. Following the furore, the CEO was compelled to resign. Under the new regulations, companies listed on the London Stock Exchange and employing over 250 people will be compelled to disclose the ratio between their CEO's pay and the median pay of their UK employees each year, beginning in 2019. The company must justify the remuneration package and must also address its accountability to other stakeholders. Persimmon had also failed to pay the living wage to its employees, and was compelled to do so from 2019. The Conservative government undertook to keep an election pledge to introduce employee membership of company boards as part of its reform of corporate governance. Under pressure from business lobbyists, it withdrew this promise in 2018. Employee representation on boards has long been recognized in European countries, and this reform would have been welcome in the UK business environment in which low-paid and insecure working conditions are common. However, the corporate culture of profit maximization has been dominant. A corporate culture of responsiveness, transparency and fairness to stakeholders should be the norm for MNEs. Disappointingly, mandatory regulation might seem to be the only route to shifting focus to a stakeholder perspective.

CSR in the boardroom?

CEOs are imbued with the idea that maximizing profits enhances shareholder value. However, a CSR approach holds that shareholder value would be built more soundly on the wide spectrum of stakeholder interests and ethical principles. What changes would need to be made in corporate governance to refocus on CSR?

The social enterprise

social enterprise an enterprise which lies somewhere between the for-profit and not-for-profit organization, aiming to make money but using it mainly for social causes

The **social enterprise** occupies the area between a for-profits business and a not-for-profits organization. Defined in Chapter 1, the social enterprise seeks to operate as a business and generate profits, but uses the profits for social causes. Its founders, known as social entrepreneurs, are committed to social causes, and see business activity as conducive to that end. The social entrepreneur typically combines a market orientation with entrepreneurial zeal and a commitment to a particular cause. In some cases, the social enterprise operates in an area between mainstream business and government services. These enterprises are active in social welfare sectors, delivering services and providing employment in local communities, often in areas of high unemployment. Housing, education, health and welfare advice for vulnerable groups are some of the sectors in which social enterprises operate in the UK. In many cases, they work alongside local and national government agencies. The social sector is expanding in many countries, as governments struggle to resource welfare needs, for example, care for growing numbers of older people. Social enterprises, which are mainly SMEs, are not a way of outsourcing social services, but offering complementary services, often working with government agencies.

community interest company (CIC) a limited company set up to function as a social enterprise which obeys strict statutory requirements for adhering to social purposes

The social enterprise as an organization can take several forms, from registered charities to ordinary limited companies. There are also different types of charity, ranging from unincorporated associations to incorporated organizations. The UK government has introduced the **community interest company** (CIC) (www.cicregulator.gov.uk) in 2004, which allows the social entrepreneur to form a limited company with strict requirements for adhering to social purposes. The Companies (Audit, Investigations and Community Enterprise) Act of 2004 provides a system of regulation of CICs, which assures the public that assets and profits are used for community purposes.

Social enterprises are popular choices for setting up new businesses. In the UK, the national body for social enterprises is Social Enterprise UK (www.socialenterprise.org.uk), which publishes a report annually. There are over 100,000 social enterprises in the UK, employing 2 million people and contributing over £60 billion to the UK economy (Social Enterprise UK, 2017). Social enterprises compare favourably with mainstream SMEs in terms of generating income and longevity: 47% saw increased turnover in 2017, compared with 34% among mainstream SMEs. In terms of pay, social enterprises in the UK compared favourably with mainstream businesses: 78% report that they pay the living wage to their employees. The ratio between the highest and lowest earners in social enterprises is 2.7 to 1. While we tend to think of social enterprises as mainly local, increasingly, they are branching out globally, especially through trade. And

most of the profits are channelled into social and environmental goals. Social enterprises are also fulfilling needs in emerging economies, some providing simple, affordable solutions adapted to local conditions.

Micro-finance is an example. Micro-finance provides loans and other financial services to the poor, who, because they are perceived as being too high-risk, fall outside the mainstream banking system. Micro-finance has evolved from charitable organizations to social enterprises which are self-financing. Now, mainstream banks are also branching out into micro-finance, demonstrating the potential for business at the 'base of the pyramid'. In developing countries, social enterprises often work alongside NGOs, global charities and government agencies. With strained resources and uncertain funding in the form of aid from donor countries, the governments of developing countries see social enterprises as playing a development role, helping to promote social wellbeing in providing basic services, health and education.

Ethics and CSR: the sustainable business

Work in mines, on construction sites and in textile factories around the world leans heavily on migrant workers. While these types of work rest, in theory, on the free choice of workers, in practice, migrant labour mostly involves one-sided, exploitative relationships that undermine the human dignity of the people who do these jobs, most of whom have no choice. Many migrants travel from rural to urban areas to seek work, but many seek work in foreign lands, facilitated by agents who demand substantial sums of money, often leaving the migrant worker burdened with a large debt to pay off. The worker is trapped in this relationship, in which poor conditions, poor treatment and long hours are inescapable. Human rights groups describe these relationships as forced labour, in breach of international human rights. Vast construction projects depend on vulnerable workers from countries such as Nepal and Bangladesh, whose working and living conditions place them at risk of breaches of their human rights.

Most of the world's countries are parties to the UN's main human rights covenants, but how does this translate into human rights protection? Some countries prioritizing development have been inclined to turn a blind eye to human rights, as highlighted by the ILO's revised *Tripartite Declaration*. But what about companies and businesses in general? They are not covered directly by the covenants. They have moral responsibilities, but not legal obligations under the covenants, except in respect to those aspects of human rights that feature in national law. Hence, UN authorities can target a country, but cannot target a company specifically for breaches. Targeting a country, however, sends a strong persuasive message to governments, which usually have extensive business ties. The UN has endorsed a guideline document on Business and Human Rights, but these guidelines are voluntary, urging businesses to take human rights into consideration, but avoiding holding them liable for breaches of human rights, for example, for abuses that take place in supply chains (Morrison, 2015: 292–3). There is now a mechanism for victims of human rights abuse to complain directly to the UN, leading to UN pressure on governments to enforce human rights law. There is also a requirement in the UK (in the Modern Slavery Act) that MNEs must report annually on how they combat slavery in their supply chains producing goods for the UK market.

MNEs view CSR as a voluntary approach to social responsibility. Companies sponsor numerous CSR projects, such as education and health services, often

filling gaps left by cash-strapped governments. Brand owners took steps to set up fire and safety standards in Bangladesh, following the Rana Plaza disaster, for instance. Should this have been the job of government? (see the mini case study in Chapter 12). The company is not publicly accountable in these situations, and can walk away from the country if the business environment deteriorates. It is ultimately accountable to its shareholders. Indeed, businesses, including those with extensive CSR agendas, are likely to lobby governments for *less* legal regulation. The MNE exists to enhance the wealth of its owners. Should its responsibility involve public accountability? MNEs and their directors can be held accountable in law for disasters that impact on societies, but it is rare. Very few bankers have been prosecuted following the financial crisis. MNEs lobby for the inclusion of the ISDS in trade agreements, allowing them to escape public accountability. Large oil companies could take a lead in sustainable strategies, but their strategies often include lobbying governments to perpetuate subsidies for fossil fuels and to discourage the imposition of a carbon tax.

Governments are rightly criticized for failing to uphold the human rights they have signed up to in the UN covenants. MNEs have no UN covenants to sign, but they nonetheless face the same challenges and responsibilities: to uphold human rights and to accept liabilities for breaches of those rights when their activities are implicated. Just as public opinion criticizes repressive policies of governments, people are coming to criticize the weak adherence to human rights by companies that wield economic power greater than many countries and exert increasing influence over the daily lives of all of us.

Conclusions

No one would doubt that the for-profit company has a role in society, but that role is now seen as multi-faceted. The company's role is sometimes depicted as economic only, free to pursue business aims as it wishes as long as it stays within the relevant law. This simplistic view is challenged by the interactions of companies in the societies where their activities impact. The notion of social responsibility recognizes this dimension, which involves ethical as well as legal obligations. We have seen that MNEs are now treated as responsible for the impacts of their activities throughout supply chains. And these impacts extend to workers and communities as stakeholders. Consumers globally are increasingly concerned about the ethics of supply chains, including the human rights of workers. Western MNEs often include ethics and human rights in their annual reports. They point to their corporate citizenship profiles and hold up their codes of conduct in supply chains, but discrepancies between the rhetoric and the reality continue to emerge.

Despite commitments to CSR, companies are ultimately serving goals of shareholder wealth maximization, which translates into seeking competitive advantage through profits. A shift in corporate culture towards a more balanced stakeholder perspective could well lead to a dip in short-term profits, but the shift to a more sustainable way of doing business would benefit shareholders in the longer term. MNEs from emerging economies, including both state-controlled and private-sector companies, are also facing greater scrutiny on social and environmental issues. Consumers have perhaps been more alert than executives to the multiple dimensions of social wellbeing: they seek improvements in material living standards, but they also think long term about a healthy environment and sustainable livelihoods.

CLOSING CASE STUDY

The Sacklers, Purdue Pharma and the opioid epidemic

A photo of medicine bottles – left by protesters to float in the reflecting pool of the Metropolitan Museum in New York – is one of the images that is now linked to the Sackler family name. Purdue Pharma of Connecticut was acquired by the Sackler family in 1952, and is still owned by some members of the family as a private company. The Sacklers, now the third generation, have built a business empire in the pharmaceutical industry. They are notable for their highly competitive pursuit of market opportunities. The company's most successful product has been its patented painkiller, OxyContin. OxyContin and other opioids have been the major cause of an opioid epidemic in the US. OxyContin is an addictive painkiller, initially intended to give long-lasting pain relief for terminally ill cancer patients, who benefited from its slow-release delivery system. From 1996, however, Purdue shifted its marketing approach, promoting OxyContin as an all-purpose painkiller 'for moderate to severe pain', whatever the cause (Crow, 2018). By then, Richard Sackler, who had joined the family business in 1971, was the company president.

He focused on an aggressive marketing strategy as the key to expanding the business. From 1996 onwards, the marketing strategy targeted doctors, from general practitioners to specialists, with marketing promotions, including free trips to medical conferences. OxyContin was marketed for all manner of common pains, such as arthritis and back pain. The sales of opioids grew enormously. And so did the number of patients who became addicted to it. There was also growth in the abuse of the drug by recreational users. Purdue had been aware of its addictive qualities in 1996. The drug had been approved by the Food and Drug Administration (FDA) although there had been no clinical studies on addiction carried out in connection with the application.

Sackler family members have gained a fortune estimated at $13 billion from their pharmaceutical business. Richard Sackler and other family members have portrayed themselves as mainly philanthropists, particularly in the fields of art and culture. Their name adorns numerous galleries, including the Sackler wing in New York's Metropolitan Museum of Art, the Serpentine Gallery in London, and the Sackler wing of the Louvre in Paris. They value the name recognition gleaned from their philanthropic activities, but distance themselves from Purdue Pharma. They have not accepted that they have been instrumental in causing the opioid crisis. However, their name has come to be increasingly associated with the opioid epidemic, which is estimated to kill 115 people a day in the US. As the public health crisis has escalated, family members are now being targeted. Can the Sacklers escape liability? They have maintained that OxyContin is prescribed and taken on a voluntary basis, as a drug approved by the US Food and Drug Administration. Misuse by doctors, patients and other users, they argue, is not their fault.

However, many lawsuits have been launched for misleading people on the addictive nature of the drug. Family members have consistently settled these civil lawsuits out of court, often

The Sackler wing of the Metropolitan Museum of Art in New York features an ancient Egyptian temple. It presents the philanthropic side of the Sackler family, but the darker side, linked to the opioid crisis, is now attracting the public's attention.

paying out millions of dollars to complainants. In 2007, Purdue Pharma pleaded guilty to a criminal charge of misleading doctors and patients over the risk of addiction, and paid a fine of $600 million. The case had been brought by federal prosecutors. Three executives pleaded guilty to a charge of misbranding, and avoided a jail sentence. Richard Sackler had resigned as president of Purdue in 2003, when federal investigations were taking place. He and other family members also ceased to be executive directors. They stepped down to become non-executive directors, but remain the owners, enjoying the millions of dollars that are generated by the drug each year.

In Massachusetts, the attorney general has launched a case against eight members of the family, who had all served on the board, for overseeing a deceptive scheme to sell opioids. Estimates of the costs of the opioid crisis are enormous, in terms of the burden on public health services such as treatment and rehabilitation. OxyContin has been compared to tobacco – both addictive and both marketed heavily. The Sacklers feel confident they are not to blame. Still, US states are suing the company in the hopes of payouts higher than those that were paid out in the $2 billion settlement with the tobacco industry in 1998. OxyContin sales in the US account for one-third of Purdue's global sales. The company is now marketing it in other markets, anticipating falling sales in the US. These markets include Asia and Latin America. The tobacco companies found this strategy lucrative, especially when their marketing was targeted at less-regulated markets.

In 2018, Richard Sackler was granted a US patent for a drug designed to help addicts to overcome their addiction to opioids. The patent recognizes the opioid crisis and states that the growing demand for anti-addition drugs offers an opportunity for this new drug. It could potentially yield sizeable profits for the family. The mayor of Huntington, West Virginia, a city with one of the highest opioid addiction rates in the US, has expressed outrage that the Sackler family, having made billions from a painkiller that unleashed an epidemic that ruined lives, should now be cashing in again on anti-addiction medicine (McGreal, 2018). He feels compensation through lawsuits is necessary, but he also feels strongly that criminal prosecution and appropriate jail sentences are essential. He makes the general point that paying a fine and carrying on as before has become commonly accepted as part of business, whereas a real prospect of a jail sentence would make more impact in corporate boardrooms. The Sackler philanthropic legacy suffered a setback early in 2019, when the board of trustees of the Tate galleries in Britain decided on ethical grounds that it would accept no further donations from the Sackler family. The Tate has received donations of £4 million from the family, and it intends to retain the Sackler name on the galleries it has sponsored in the past.

Questions

- What are the reasons for Purdue's business success?
- What were the causes of the opioid epidemic?
- Should the Sacklers as individuals be held accountable, and how?
- What steps could be taken to prevent future crises like the opioid epidemic?
- The Sackler name adorns many buildings that are cultural icons. Should their name be removed?

Further reading

For an in-depth background article, see Patrick Radden Keefe, 'The family that built an empire of pain', 30 October 2017, in *The New Yorker*.

Multiple choice questions

Visit www.macmillanihe.com/morrison-gbe-5e to take a quick self-test quiz on what you have read in this chapter.

Review questions

1 In what ways have utilitarian principles influenced ethical thinking, and what are their shortcomings?
2 What is meant by 'ethical relativism', and what is its relevance for international business?
3 Summarize the human rights that are relevant to a workplace environment.
4 In what ways does the gig economy represent a deterioration in workers' rights?
5 How can abuses associated with forced labour be eradicated?
6 Describe Carroll's theory of CSR, and explain the role of stakeholders in Carroll's thinking.
7 What are the weaknesses of corporate codes of practice in relation to CSR?
8 In what ways can the recognition of international guidelines for CSR make companies more responsible in their international operations?
9 What is the role of philanthropy in CSR?
10 Assess the differences between primary and secondary stakeholders.
11 What are the criticisms of the shareholder model of corporate governance, and how can they be remedied?
12 What is the 'business case' for CSR?
13 Why is executive pay perceived as an ethical issue, and what can be done to moderate it?
14 Why is the social enterprise perceived as a way of providing services which governments struggle to fund?
15 How is economic development contrasted with the broader concept of human development?

✓ Assignments

1 Sustainability and social responsibility have become common in corporate rhetoric, but the reality can be ruthless profit-seeking and aggressive lobbying targeted at those in authority, in order to lower standards. Assess the extent to which global companies have actually changed their sustainability strategies, or simply honed their rhetoric, citing examples.

2 This assignment is about the relevance of human rights in work. Focus on a type of work of your choice. Some examples would be factory work assembling gadgets, work in a fast food outlet, work in a warehouse, or making clothes in a textile factory. Assess the ways in which this job is susceptible to breaches of human rights, including labour rights, of workers.

Further reading

Amao, O. (2013) *Corporate Social Responsibility, Human Rights and the Law*, Routledge Research in Corporate Law.

Collier, P. (2008) *The Bottom Billion: Why the poorest countries are failing and what can be done about it* (Oxford: Oxford University Press).

Deaton, A. (2015) *The Great Escape: Health, wealth and the origins of inequality* (Princeton: Princeton University Press).

Dehesa, Guillermo de la (2007) *What Do We Know About Globalization? Issues of poverty and income distribution* (New Jersey: Wiley-Blackwell).

Donnelly, J. (2013) *Universal Human Rights in Theory and Practice*, 2nd edition (Cornell University Press).

Lomborg, B. (ed.) (2009) *Global Crises, Global Solutions: Costs and benefits*, 2nd edition (Cambridge: Cambridge University Press).

Morrison, J. (2015) *Business Ethics* (London: Red Globe Press).

Stiglitz, J. (2017) *Globalization and its Discontents Revisited: Anti-globalization in the Era of Trump* (Penguin).

References

Anti-Slavery International (2019) What is forced labour?, at https://antislavery.org

Apple Inc. (2018) *Supplier Responsibility: 2018 Progress Report*, at www.apple.com

Baron, R. (2014) 'The evolution of corporate reporting for integrated performance', OECD background paper for the 30th Round Table on Sustainable Development, 25 June, Paris, at www.oecd.org

BBC (2013) 'Apple faces new China worker abuse claims', BBC news, 29 July, at www.bbc.com

BBC (2018) 'Fast fashion: how do you justify selling a £3 T-shirt?', 27 November, at www.bbc.co.uk

Berlin, I. (1958) *Two Concepts of Liberty* (Oxford: Oxford University Press).

Bureau of Labor Statistics (2019) Work stoppages data, update 8 February 2019 and annual historical table, at www.bls.gov, accessed 22 March 2019.

Carroll, A.B. (1991) 'The pyramid of corporate social responsibility: toward the moral management of organizational stakeholders', *Business Horizons*, 34: 39–48.

Conn, D. (2019) 'Revealed: the dire consequences of football's relationship with gambling', 10 January, *The Guardian*.

Crow, D. (2018) 'The Sacklers under siege', *Financial Times*, 8 September.

Desilver, D. (2018) 'Most Americans view unions favorably, but few workers belong to one', Pew Research Center, 30 August, at www.pewresearch.org

EPI (Economic Policy Institute) (2015) 'Top CEOs make 300 times more than typical workers', Issue Brief Number 399, 21 June, at www.epi.org

EPI (Economic Policy Institute) (2018) 'CEO compensation surged in 2017', report issued 16 August, at www.epi.org

Ford, J. (2019) 'The bet that failed', FT.com magazine, 20 July, pp. 12–20.

Freeman, R.E. (1984) *Strategic Management: A stakeholder approach* (Boston, MA: Pitman).

Fullerton, J. and Chen, J. (2015) 'Chinese worker, 26, making Apple iPhones died after enduring 12 hour shifts, seven days a week, family claim', The Mail Online, 11 March, www.dailymail.co.uk

Halliday, R.J. (1976) *John Stuart Mill* (London: George Allen & Unwin Ltd).

KPMG (2013) 'Carrots and sticks: Sustainability reporting policies worldwide', at www.kpmg.com and www.globalreporting.org

ILO (2017) *Tripartite Declaration of Principles concerning Multinational Enterprises and Social Policy* (Geneva: ILO).

IPEC (International Programme on the Elimination of Child Labour), What is child labour?, at www.ilo.org, accessed 22 July 2019.

Kant, E. ([1785]1948) *The Moral Law: Groundwork of the metaphysic of morals*, trans. H.J. Paton (New York: Routledge).

McGreal, C. (2018) 'They're drug dealers in Armani suits: executives draw focus amid drug epidemic', *The Guardian*, 30 September.

McKinsey & Co. (2019) *The State of Fashion 2019*, at www.mckinsey.com/industries/retail/our-insights/the-state-of-fashion-2019-a-year-of-awakening, accessed 20 September 2019.

McWilliams, A. (2001) 'Corporate social responsibility: a theory of the firm perspective', *Academy of Management Review*, 26(1): 117–28.

Mill, J.S. ([1859] 1947) *On Liberty*, edited by A. Castell (New York: Appleton-Century-Crofts Inc.).

Mitchell, R.K., Agle, B.R. and Wood, D. (1997) 'Toward a theory of stakeholder identification and salience: defining the principle of who and what really counts', *Academy of Management Review*, 11(4): 853–86.

Morrison, J. (2015) *Business Ethics* (London: Red Globe Press).

ONS (Office for National Statistics) (2018) 'Contracts that do not guarantee a minimum number of hours: April 2018', 23 April, at www.ons.gov.uk, accessed 7 December 2018.

Plamenatz, J. (1958) *The English Utilitarians*, 2nd edition (Oxford: Blackwell).

Quinton, A. (1989) *Utilitarian Ethics* (Chicago: Open Court Publishing).

Reich, R. (2018) 'Trump takes on General Motors (and guess who wins?)' *The Guardian*, 3 December.

Smith, J. (2015) 'Human rights are at risk under our new Conservative Government', *The Independent*, 10 May.

Social Enterprise UK (2017) State of social enterprise report 2017, at www.socialenterprise.org.uk

Tily, G. (2018) '17-year wage squeeze the worst in two hundred years', Trades Union Congress (TUC), 11 May, at www.tuc.org.uk

Wong, J. (2018) 'Revealed: Google's "two-tier" workforce training document', *The Guardian*, 12 December, at www.theguardian.com

Wood, D. (1991) 'Corporate social performance revisited', *Academy of Management Review*, 16(4): 691–718.

Visit the companion website at www.macmillanihe.com/morrison-gbe-5e for further learning and teaching resources.

© Getty

SUSTAINABLE BUSINESS: THE PROSPECTS

Outline of chapter

This chapter will enable you to

- Review the challenges in building sustainability in the global environment
- Identify key areas of global risks confronting managers
- Understand overlapping responsibilities of governments and businesses
- Assess sustainable strategies for global business

OPENING CASE STUDY

Ten years on from the global financial crisis: a sustainable recovery?

Former traders at the failed bank, Lehman Brothers, allegedly planned a reunion party for the autumn of 2018, ten years on from the crisis that shook the global financial system. The collapse of their 150-year-old bank would forever be remembered as the event that triggered the start of the financial meltdown – although the disaster had been long in the making. The meltdown was to be bigger than they could have imagined. It encompassed public and private finance in the globally integrated, dollar-based financial system, and it extended to the eurozone and other countries to the east. The Russian government's relationship with its powerful oligarchs was reconfigured towards greater state control. China's government launched an enormous stimulus programme in response to the crisis, fearing for its exports. Other emerging economies were also affected, to the extent of their exposure to dollar-denominated markets. Ten years on, has there been a rethinking of the risks that brought down markets?

The US has exemplified the liberal market economic model. But risks abounded in the rise of derivatives trading, which was largely unregulated. First, the implosion of the subprime housing market was a warning of the excess of unsound mortgage-backed securities. Banking crises revealed the unmanageable excesses in debt markets, leading to devastating ripple effects in other countries where companies, both financial and non-financial, were involved with dollar investments and liabilities. Governments on both sides of the Atlantic bailed out the banks that were deemed to be posing systemic risk: they were too big to fail. In Britain, in the autumn of 2008, the Royal Bank of Scotland was apparently just hours away from having to switch off its cash machines used by the public. Rescues of the banks propped them up, but the disaster went well beyond the financial sector.

Measures to reform the banking sector have met with scepticism.

Recession followed, bringing hardship to hundreds of millions of people. The mortgage crisis in the US housing market had left millions in distress, without homes or jobs. The recession merged with the continuing post-industrial pain associated with the shift from manufacturing to services. These changes, too, were part of the damaging post-Lehman reality for ordinary people. What was the response of governments to these societal issues?

The level of risk in an out-of-control financial system was the dominant cause of the crisis. Capitalist markets had failed and change was needed, to shore up the financial system, and also to deal with the societal fallout. Looking back to the aftermath of the Great Depression of the 1930s, reforms were radical. The Glass-Steagall Act of 1933 compelled banks to separate out their retail and investment businesses. The Securities and Exchange Commission reformed financial structures. President Roosevelt's New Deal reformed labour rights, provided public works schemes for the unemployed, and established employment rights. These were bold political policies designed to reform the financial system and also introduce social protections for ordinary people. In 2008, there were no such bold visions of society. Governments focused more on supporting the financial sector than reforming it. Bankers responsible for the catastrophe were allowed to walk away, largely escaping censure, to enjoy their gains from the boom times before the crash. By contrast, life went from bad to worse for those who lost their homes in the sub-prime mortgage market collapse. Indeed, American financiers in the foreclosure market prospered from the disaster. Policymakers in the US have done little to reform the law to prevent poor homeowners from losing their homes.

Regulatory reform of the banking sector was widely perceived by an angry public as necessary, but government enthusiasm for reform waned. Reforms were forthcoming in incremental legislative stages. Banks everywhere now face stiffer capital adequacy requirements, and there have been

regulatory reforms of banking conduct. There is now legislation in the UK to hold bankers to account when their banks fail. But the banks were not broken up, as many had thought was necessary. In the US, the Glass-Steagall Act, repealed in 1999, was not brought back to reduce the risks that the global banks courted. Risk management in the UK is now more carefully scrutinized through the reforms that have re-focused on the Bank of England and the Financial Conduct Authority.

In the US, legislative reform in the Dodd-Frank Act has been modest. Retail and investment banking were to be ring-fenced, but the essentials of the financial system remained in place. Indeed, in a contorted rethinking of the causes of the crisis, there has been a shift away from blaming the financial sector to blaming fiscal policy. In this revised scenario, the fault was with out-of-control fiscal policy leading to overblown public spending. Reining in public spending, therefore, has been advocated by those who hold this view. Austerity measures in the UK reflect this thinking, deflecting attention away from financial reform. However, for ordinary people who have suffered from stagnating incomes, unaffordable housing and insecure jobs, austerity measures such as reductions in welfare benefits have resulted in widening inequality, not to mention resentment towards politicians and business elites.

Piecemeal reform of finance has left the market system essentially in place, along with an enduring belief in the virtues of markets – despite the monumental market failure that caused the crisis. Economic and financial concentration remains the predominant characteristic of the global economy. The recovery from the crisis has been weak, and the main beneficiaries have been large MNEs and the top 1% of earners. Roosevelt had believed that shared prosperity was the only way to build a sustainable recovery. This contrasts sharply with the views of US presidents during the ten years since the crisis. Only people in the top 1% saw their incomes grow in the first three years of the recovery. Redistribution of wealth would have been a pathway towards an inclusive recovery, but US policies, including freezing the minimum wage since 2009, have had the opposite effects. Moves towards deregulation and tax breaks for companies and top earners have resulted in redistribution towards those at the top. A result has been disillusion felt by the working and lower-middle classes, among whom support for far-right populists has grown. These disillusioned voters have been motivated by bitterness towards established political elites as well as global capitalism.

The heritage of established western political parties has rested on a belief in liberal democracy: democracy and markets complemented each other. These assumptions have been shaken by the rise of populism, an inherently illiberal way of thinking, witnessed in numerous countries affected by the crisis. A prerequisite for restoring faith in liberal democratic institutions is progressive and inclusive policies, building a sustainable recovery from the financial crisis.

Questions

- What reforms of banking have taken place, and are these reforms sufficient?
- Describe the recovery from the financial crisis. Who are the winners and losers?
- In what ways has the rise of populism been attributed to the fallout from the financial crisis?
- What is the case for introducing stricter regulatory reforms at international level?

Further reading

See the article, 'Voices of the financial crisis', as told to Lilah Raptopoulos, in the *Financial Times*, 15 September 2018. This article features stories told by people of all walks of life who were affected by the crisis.

Introduction

The guiding theme of this book has been framed as a question, 'Towards sustainability?'. To what extent do the different dimensions of the business environment and the key players contribute to sustainability – or undermine it? Today we see a rise in nationalism and populism. The impacts are felt particularly in the political, economic and cultural environments. Goals of peace, co-operation, human rights and democratic values that inspired the UN after the Second World War are under threat. In this chapter, we summarize the diverse answers that this question has elicited, and we reach some conclusions on the way forward. There have been many areas of explanation and discussion in earlier chapters. These will not be repeated here. Key points will be highlighted, making comparisons and drawing out insights. The relevant chapter numbers will be given in brackets. References to case studies will also be given, along with new examples where they add new insight.

We begin with the elements of sustainability, which will be the backbone of this summative discussion. We then bring together an overview of the risks in the global environment. There follows a critical assessment of where responsibilities lie, and how well notions of shared responsibilities and legal obligations deal with issues in practice. What should be changed to bring about a more sustainable business environment? That is the ambitious question discussed in the last section.

What does the business exist to do, and how should it go about realizing its goals? These questions were posed at the start of this book, and the chapters that followed have revealed a wide divergence in outlooks, goals and business methods. Much of this divergence has derived from contrasting business environments – between countries, between industries, between companies and even between corporate leaders with diverging views of business in society. The divergence also reflects differing moral outlooks in terms of cultural leanings and ethical principles. Here we aim to assess the differing business approaches in terms of sustainability. One of the threads that has run through this narrative is that businesses exist in an environment of interaction with numerous stakeholders, including governments, suppliers, workers, consumers, communities and societies in general. The business approach to sustainable goals, therefore, must be one that takes these numerous stakeholders into consideration. By looking at how businesses pursue opportunities and deal with dilemmas, we have been able to assess the ways in which they are meeting the challenges of sustainability – or failing to meet them.

Sustainability: the key elements

A graphic showing the elements of sustainability that appeared in Figure 1.1 at the start of the book has provided the themes for the many illustrations and case studies that have followed. That figure is reproduced as Figure 12.1. Sustainability is multi-faceted. While it has been common to equate sustainability with ecological concerns, it is worth remembering that the concept is much broader. Sustainability is the principle of taking into account the needs of today's inhabitants of the planet in ways which do not constitute a detriment to the ability of future generations to do the same. It is framed in the negative. Turning it into a positive formulation, there are two prongs to the definition. The first is that the needs of people today span numerous dimensions that together make up their lives. The second is that our actions today must be responsible in terms of looking towards the needs of people in future generations.

Six elements of sustainability were listed at the beginning of this book, and appear in Figure 12.1. These elements have been featured in the discussion and case studies that appear throughout the chapters. Here, we bring together some conclusions on how each contributes to a sustainable environment.

Individual and societal wellbeing

Individual and societal wellbeing are inextricably linked. Human wellbeing includes livelihood, housing, health and education. These are part of the UN's concept of human development. Societal wellbeing is broader, encompassing participation and

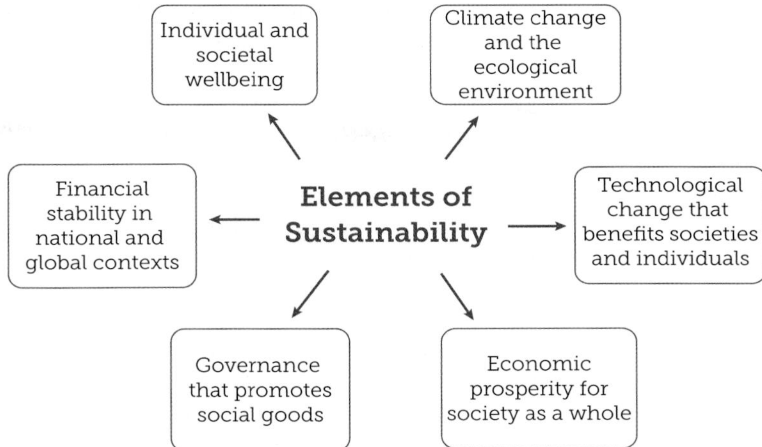

Figure 12.1 Elements of sustainability

engagement in communities and cultural life. It also embraces the notion of self-fulfilment. Everyone wishes to have a life that brings personal fulfilment, a feeling of human dignity and accomplishment. That personal fulfilment is not just for the individual, but as part of a bigger group. A person's personal happiness is linked to that of our family, community or cultural group. The individual's feeling of dignity is linked to the wellbeing of society. Both are encompassed in human rights law, as shown in Figure 11.1. Human rights encompass individual freedoms as well as social and economic rights.

People everywhere desire a conducive environment in which to pursue personal goals, start businesses, strive for educational achievement, express themselves freely, and join with others of similar beliefs and religious faith. People also expect government policies to promote these opportunities for all, not just the privileged and the rich. But there are marked divergences among countries in terms of social goods and social responsibilities. Recall the divergent views of human rights contained in the two foundation covenants noted above. One focuses on negative freedoms, the other on liberty in the positive sense of self-realization. Liberal political thought has traditionally held to the rights of the individual as freedom 'from' interference by the state, to pursue self-interested goals. But in countries where the poor lack opportunities through education, and suffer from inadequate access to healthcare, their 'freedom' has an altogether shallow ring.

The welfare state, now recognized in the more free-market economies as well as the social market economies, is seen as essential in promoting social goods. But the welfare state steps in as a safety net to the market economy, aiming to support market mechanisms. We have seen that decent work and social protections, enunciated by the ILO, are problematic in many contexts (Chapters 3, 4 and 11). The growing number of people in paid work has offered the prospect of individual fulfilment, but much of this work is insecure and in some countries there has been a rise in poverty among people in work. The majority of the world's people enjoy little in the way of basic protections such as sick pay and pension. These weaknesses in social protection are associated with developing countries, but are now occurring in developed countries where the gig economy and casual work have edged ahead of contractual employment. We have seen unsustainably detrimental work environments in a number of situations: textile workers, mining, factory work, construction work and service sector jobs in the gig economy.

Businesses provide jobs, incomes to employees, goods and services that people want, and much else that contributes to wellbeing. They fulfil a vital economic role,

but they are also meeting human needs and influencing how societies function and change. The human and social dimension of business activities confers on them social responsibilities. These can be viewed as CSR, and can also be viewed in an ethical perspective. Companies are justifiably considered to owe obligations of adhering to human rights, not just those recognized in law, but also those recognized as ethical principles. The company that pays wages that do not meet the level of a living wage is operating in an environment where both legal and moral obligations are commonly avoided. Here, both the business and the government share the responsibility.

Similarly, healthcare is a human right, but the prospect of good healthcare for most of the world's people is problematic. Finding cures for diseases and medicines that can alleviate the suffering of people have seen huge advances. This should be good news for sustainability in health provision worldwide. However, profiteering and engrained practices that have affected the protection of intellectual property have had detrimental effects on the access to medicine by all but the richest. The means to improve human wellbeing are more within the grasp of more countries than in earlier generations. Developing countries that have benefited from globalization are examples of these possibilities. However, inequalities have accompanied globalization. Benefits have been enjoyed by those in favoured industries and locations, but do not reach all in society, producing an unsustainable imbalance. This is true of developed as well as developing countries. Governments and businesses both bear responsibility. Governments are entrusted with overriding duties of promoting individual and social wellbeing. To a great extent, this is indirect, by ensuring a stable and secure environment. Governments also act directly to provide basic needs to those living in poverty. Businesses that view their responsibilities as extending to all stakeholders are more likely to pay a living wage. But the norm has been for businesses to prioritize returns to the owners, rather than decent wages for workers. Refocusing on stakeholders would help towards a more sustainable business strategy.

Climate change and the ecological environment

Addressing climate change is one of the main challenges for a sustainability agenda. The consequences of unchecked global warming are catastrophic, in terms of an environment in which human life and the ecological environment are sustainable. This means minimizing emissions, seeking clean technology and minimizing the use of scarce resources or materials that cannot be recycled. These efforts all cost money in the short term, but as has been highlighted, are likely to bring benefits to both the environment and sustainable productive assets in the long term. The impacts of climate change have sometimes seemed remote, and, as has been highlighted in Chapter 10, businesses tend to give these risks low priority. Indeed, the business models of some businesses, such as those in the petrochemical industries, are major causes of climate change. They tend to express the view that it is for governments to legislate, but they lobby actively against climate change measures. The notion of governments making the law and businesses complying with it is one that has been discussed in various contexts in these chapters (another context is taxation). In each, it emerges that the regulatory framework involves both enterprise and government participation. Many businesses support lobby groups that seek to thwart climate change measures proposed by governments, such as subsidies and quotas for renewable energy.

The vested interests of large companies in fossil fuels, agribusiness and chemical industries are among the main obstacles to progress in addressing climate change. They impact directly on food production, one of the most crucial challenges for sustainability globally. The US Midwest is at the heart of America's large-scale farming

sector. Here, the agribusiness companies seek relentlessly to increase production of the major commodity crops, even in a market situation where farmers are producing more than is needed to meet global demand. A key export destination, China, is the subject of a damaging trade dispute with the US (see the mini case study in Chapter 7). Agriculture across much of this vast area of the US is becoming unsustainable from over-farming and excessive use of chemicals. Soil degradation is worsening, and, even with irrigation, crop yields are deteriorating in nutritional value, due to climate change, including rising night-time temperatures and more severe torrential rains in spring and autumn. The use of nitrates and phosphorous contributes to degrading the soil and poisoning the rivers, ultimately polluting the Gulf of Mexico, where fishing is jeopardized by oxygen deprivation. To make farming sustainable would require reducing reliance on chemicals, which would reduce air, soil and water pollution, allowing the soil to regain health. Although farmers individually are aware of the measures that are needed, they are powerless to act against the might of the agribusiness companies that exert oligopolistic control over the agriculture industry (Cullen, 2018). These issues arise in all the countries with significant agricultural sectors. Farmers struggle to make a living in areas threatened by the impacts of climate change, and many give up as a result. The world is facing a crisis in farming at the level of individual farmers, whose businesses need to be reset on more sustainable principles. However, they are up against the agribusiness companies that control the industry.

Moreover, these companies are among the main drivers of the plastics industry, which is continuing to experience unsustainable growth (Chapter 10). Recycling has become an increasingly important issue, and for headway to be made requires government action and often public expenditure. Recycling should be part of a co-ordinated strategy for sustainable solutions to the management of waste. However, dealing with waste often contributes to pollution, through landfill sites or incineration, which causes toxic emissions. These practices are damaging for human health and the environment, and they are taking place in rich countries such as the US, not just in poor developing countries.

Plastics are notoriously resistant to recycling, and the pervasiveness of plastic has become a global issue. Research indicates that microplastics, defined as particles less than 5mm in size, exist just about everywhere, in lakes, rivers and ecosystems. They have become pervasive in the water supply, and are consumed by humans and animals, persisting in their bodies (Carrington, 2019). Reducing the use of plastic should be a priority. Many consumer companies have responded by reducing plastic packaging and plastic straws. Burberry has revealed that it used 200 tonnes of plastic in 2017. It has announced that, by 2025, all the plastic it uses in packaging will be reusable, recyclable or compostable (see the mini case study that follows).

The fossil fuel and chemical giants are at the core of the plastics industry. In conjunction with their shale gas operations, ExxonMobil Chemical and Shell Chemical are investing in new facilities to increase plastic production 40% over the next ten years (Laville, 2019). Fossil fuels, along with plastic, will continue to be in demand (Chapter 10). Fossil fuel companies are major contributors to climate change. They are investing in renewable energy as well as fossil fuels, marking shifts in strategies, but some of these shifts, such as reforestation, are problematic. Reforestation does not reduce emissions; it simply offsets them. The giant energy and agribusiness companies are highly influential in government circles, helping to frame regulations, policies on subsidies and legislation on pollution levels. Laxer pollution regulation has been an obvious result of their influence in government, especially in the US and Brazil, home to some of the largest agribusiness companies. The challenge they face is that their business models depend on rising global consumption of

goods, agricultural products (including meat) and energy, although sustainability as a goal would require *reducing* consumption. It has often been said – rather optimistically – that technological innovation would provide the means to control the impacts of climate change, without requiring radical shifts in lifestyle. While green technology has made enormous strides, as in the case of electric cars, it is a fallacy to assume that technology can solve all climate change and environmental threats. Sustainable solutions point to reducing emissions, reducing reliance on fossil fuels and reducing the use of plastic.

MINI CASE STUDY

Burberry destroys stock to preserve the brand

To the British brand, Burberry, an upmarket image and reputation for quality are important. Although Burberry had a heritage that was built around its British roots and its famous rainwear, it has more recently transformed itself into a fashion label. Its product range has now expanded into fashionable clothes, accessories and perfumes. All have been designed to make the most of its quality image. However, like many upmarket fashion brands, copycat products and counterfeiters are ever present. For Burberry, the characteristic check pattern that is identified closely with the brand has become both a selling point and, unfortunately, a magnet for counterfeiters. Imitations of the check spring up on all types of clothing and accessories. The risk is that they can flood the market and devalue the brand.

The EU stars on the model's shirt complement the Burberry coat, with its signature check lining.

© Getty, Christian Vierig / Contributor

Burberry has burnt large quantities of stock, including clothes, accessories and perfume. The total value of goods destroyed is estimated at £90 million over the last five years, including over £28 million-worth in 2017 alone. The justification for burning these goods is partly to minimize the excess stock, which could find its way to discounters who sell it off cheaply. The company is keen to move the brand upmarket. Any older products sold off cheaply could detract from the new brand image. But how responsible is this extreme tactic of burning the company's own stock?

Burberry has said that it carries out this process responsibly. The energy used in the incineration is captured. And its burning of 10 million bottles of perfume in 2017 has been an unusual step, as the company had to burn old stock, in order to start afresh with Coty, the company that has taken over its perfume business. On the other hand, environmentalists say that these processes are irresponsible. Moreover, Burberry is not the only company that engages in these activities. These practices indicate overproduction in the first place. The answer to overproduction, they say, should be to slow down production, rather than to destroy finished goods, which is wasteful and irresponsible.

Following the adverse publicity, Burberry announced in September 2018, that it would cease to burn unsold goods, and it would stop using real fur in its products. Its CEO has expressed the view that being a luxury company implies being

socially and environmentally responsible (in the article cited below). Burberry is hoping that its revamp of the brand will attract younger consumers, and is experimenting with the idea of monthly launches of new products on Instagram. Is it copying the fast fashion retailers? They have been criticized for fostering throwaway fashion – a label that Burberry should be at pains to avoid.

Questions

- Did Burberry have a good case for incinerating unsold stock, in your view? Explain your reasons.
- Burberry has now recognized the damage that has been caused to its reputation. Has it simply engaged in a PR exercise to repair the damage, or has the company rethought its claim to be a sustainable business? Explain.

Find out more

See the article, 'Burberry stops burning unsold goods and using real fur', the BBC, 6 September 2018, at www.bbc.co.uk. This article has links to other articles focusing on waste in the fashion industry.

Technological change that benefits societies and individuals

New technology can be part of the solution to many of the challenges facing society. One of them is climate change, as noted above. But to be sustainable, new technology must be managed in ways that bring benefits to all in society, rather than riches and power to those who have gained from the first ownership or adoption of the innovation. Much has recently been made of the technological benefits of the knowledge economy. Through digitalization, the knowledge economy and interconnectedness are at the fingertips of everyone, whatever their walk of life. These achievements are praised for their empowerment and democratization, and are indicative of the benefits associated with globalization (Chapter 2). Throughout this book, we have found that the reality is much more ambiguous. The tech companies that dominate social media, search engines and online retailing, profit from vast amounts of users' personal data. This concentration of power over the internet is unsustainable in the long term. As has been seen repeatedly with transformational technology, be it a new drug or a business model, inventors and owners gain a proprietary grip over it that leads to monopolistic power.

The rationale behind regulation – from voluntary or self-regulatory codes of practice through to legal compliance frameworks – has been discussed throughout this book, and notably in Chapter 6. In the EU and UK, there have been concerns that social media moderators are not adequately monitoring and removing offensive and illegal content, such as hate speech. In the UK, there have been suggestions by legislators to make these platforms more directly accountable. For example, the social media company could be subject to a legal duty of care, which would effectively make it liable in law as a publisher of material that appears on the site. Facebook, like other websites, has considered itself a 'platform' only, but, in reality, it is a media outlet. Newspapers are regulated as publishers, and Facebook as a source of news could be covered by a similar regulatory framework. The livestreaming on Facebook of a massacre in New Zealand, in which 50 people lost their lives, served to reinforce the case for greater accountability. Facebook is now coming to accept that regulation is the way forward.

Technological changes have led the way to economic development and improvements in living standards throughout history. New technology brings about changes in an industry, which, initially, give the owners a free hand to exploit. However, as negative impacts emerge, greater regulation inevitably follows. The Industrial Revolution brought about transformation of national economies from mainly rural agricultural livelihoods to urban industrialized societies. These processes involved creative destruction: industries and economies became transformed by new technology, changing organizations and societies in the process. Winners and losers emerged. Entrepreneurial industrialists grew rich. Workers moved from the land to the new industries and to new ways of life. Industrialization opened up the prospect of opportunities and prosperity for all in society, through waged labour. They found mixed fortunes: they earned wages in industrial jobs, but also endured oppressive working conditions that took a heavy toll. Improvements in education and skills opened the opportunities of individual fulfilment for people from poor backgrounds who in previous eras would almost certainly have been destined to be farm labourers or go down the mines in the way their forebears did. Economic development as a result of technological innovation brought empowerment and opportunities. China's development model has seen rapid industrialization and urbanization, and it has now become more urban than rural (Chapter 3).

However, industrialization has been a painful transition wherever it has occurred. The new industrial jobs in Britain entailed harsh conditions, long hours and little in the way of safety provisions. Workers had no right to organize into trade unions until the 1820s. Union activism grew in the 1830s, and labour activism grew into political movements. These ultimately led to political voice. The Trades Union Congress, an umbrella body for the many different trade unions, was formed in 1868, and the Labour Party, the UK's largest leftwing party, was formed in 1893. However, improvements in the lives of working-class people were very slow to materialize, and they were largely driven by trade union and political activism. Urban environments often consisted of poor, crowded housing. Improved affordable housing, preventive medicine, improvements in nutrition and hygiene: these were part of the general reforms following the Second World War. Recall that Britain's National Health Service dates from 1948. It was only gradually that humane living and working environments improved. These improvements now seem to be in jeopardy in much of the developed world, and still beyond the reach of many in the developing world.

In the developed regions of the world, many of the jobs that have been the backbone of the economy, such as jobs in manufacturing, services, food preparation and administration, now face an uncertain future because of automation (Chapter 9). While there are possibilities of new jobs in the digital economy, these new jobs are available only to workers with the appropriate skills. Poorly paid, low-skilled workers are vulnerable. Many of these are workers who have been left behind by globalization, as industrial jobs relocated to low-cost locations in Asian countries, notably China. And in China, too, automation is making headway as advances in technology help to transform industries.

Technology has been crucial to the growth of the gig economy, exemplified by tech start-ups such as Uber and Airbnb. Like the innovators before them, these new businesses represent a change that is disruptive, and they have been controversial (Chapter 6). The worker classified as self-employed is often one whose job is highly controlled by the company that directs his or her activities. But the worker enjoys few of the benefits of employment protection. The companies that utilize this business model have good business reasons for finding it attractive. They are able to avoid paying the social protection charges or employment benefits that they would be obliged to pay for employees. But the position of workers in these occupations is insecure and, in many places, lacks protections such as the right to the minimum wage. Moreover, the gig economy is now a global phenomenon, growing strongly in urban environments everywhere. These jobs offer opportunities to many workers

in economies where formal contractual employment is scarce. In this respect, they are bringing about qualitative improvements. But is this casualized and insecure work sustainable as the backbone of an economy?

In most developing economies, development involves the transition from informal and ephemeral work to more stable formal employment, offering more secure, long-term livelihoods. A business can plan for the future in the knowledge that there is a workforce of experienced employees. This is the opposite of the gig economy. Casualized jobs can justifiably complement the existing workforce, but not replace it. Introducing the concept of the halfway position for workers in the gig economy, to provide a modicum of employment protection, would seem to be a step towards a more sustainable adaptation of the technology-enabled innovations that are changing the nature of work. Such a reform would seem logical for governments to introduce, but many would be ambivalent – wishing to see better security for workers, but fearing that any increase in workers' rights would deter businesses from taking on more workers.

Technological innovation and accountability

Tech giants such as Facebook are facing greater controls over their activities, but their business models are based on an internet that has been something of a 'wild west' environment. What sort of model of the internet is likely to be the most sustainable in the future?

Economic prosperity for society as a whole

Much of the discussion of the national and global environment in this book has focused on the benefits of economic growth and development. Growth in an economy is needed to provide jobs, produce goods and services, and provide for a viable future – for families and societies. Development is broader in scope than growth *per se*. A resource-rich economy can grow rapidly, but if political leaders do not focus on development, the majority of the population will see little benefit from the growth, and have little economic opportunity to partake in the benefits of prosperity. Economists often speak of sustainable growth when they mean continuing economic growth for the foreseeable future. However, sustainable growth is more complicated than mere economic growth. To be sustainable, growth must be inclusive, bringing the opportunity of prosperity to all. Similarly, sustainable development should be the aim of today's developing and emerging economies, resulting in rises up the rankings of the UN's human development index. In many countries, however, wealth is in the hands of the business and political elite, while the country as a whole remains poor, with little hope of participating in economic betterment. Resource-rich countries, as we have noted, are often in this category. As was pointed out by Mo Ibrahim, such economies are not sustainable. The Mo Ibrahim Foundation has found in its index of sustainable development that there has been disappointingly little progress towards sustainable growth (Chapter 5).

Globalization has been the catalyst of impressive economic growth in developing countries. The opening up of economies, through market reforms and openness to FDI, has been a key factor in fostering globalization. No closed economy will become globalized. Opening economies to capitalist incentives and market forces has been vital to globalization – and to growing prosperity. But capitalist markets bring risks of volatility, and must be managed intelligently to remain transparent and competitive. While Adam Smith spoke of the 'invisible hand' (see Chapter 4), he did not assume that capitalist markets were self-regulating. Recurring financial crises remind us that to maintain fair, competitive markets requires policies to curtail market abuse and reduce monopolistic concentration.

Capitalist market economies rest on traditional liberal assumptions of economic freedom and competition. They assume that all people should be allowed to pursue their own self-interested goals, unfettered by constraints on what they want to do and how. While this idea is egalitarian in essence, in reality, capitalist systems tend towards economic concentration and monopolistic practices that have the effect of *reducing* competition. These economies are characterized by rising inequality. Similarly, the market reforms of the world's emerging economies have been accompanied by rising inequality: as they grow richer, they become more unequal. Economists have tended to the view that, for these economies, there comes a point in the development cycle when inequality stops rising and begins to fall (Borghesi and Vercelli, 2003). But this does not happen spontaneously. Enlightened government policies and regulation are key to reducing inequality, for example, by social programmes and minimum wage policies. Governments have introduced laws to curb monopolists and anti-competitive behaviour. Many countries, including China, now have competition laws (Chapter 6). However, in practice, they are often inclined to bow to the pressures of influential large companies. In the US, large agribusiness companies, for example, are in a commanding position. Here, mergers and takeovers are typically allowed by authorities in situations where economic concentration is increased, giving rise to oligopolies.

China has been a success story in raising GDP. It is now the world's second-largest economy, and if adjusted for PPP, it is the largest. GDP per capita is still low at $18,000 at PPP. There has been an impressive reduction in absolute poverty, but the overall picture is uneven, and inequality is high. It is arguable that China's economic growth has not been sustainable, even by the narrow definition used by the economist, simply meaning continued growth. But what about China's development? Has China placed itself on a trajectory of sustainable development?

In pursuing breakneck growth, China has contributed heavily to global emissions, and also to the depletion of vital scarce resources. Quality of life, while better in terms of income, has been set back in terms of air pollution and its resultant health problems. An economy that continues to grow strongly should turn its attention to dealing with the harmful impacts of globalization. But when growth falters, political leaders keep the outdated industries running, to provide jobs, no matter how unsustainable they are. China has experienced a slowdown in growth that has worried its leadership. Exports, which have been vital to China's economy, were falling in early 2019, suggesting that the global economy is experiencing overall slowdown. China's rise has been a warning of the perils of unsustainable growth. On the positive side, China has promoted education and technology development that will pave the way for a more knowledge-based economy, and millions of young people are now seeking these new opportunities. The next phase of development should see the rise of these newer domestic industries, but a slowing economy could jeopardize these prospects. Trade disputes with the US have been unsettling. Hopes that the benefits of growth will trickle down to all in society now look remote.

Also elusive has been the enduring dream held by Americans to be better off and have a better quality of life than earlier generations. Inequality of wealth and stagnating incomes of lower-skilled workers have had the knock-on effects of reducing access to the many benefits that should be within the reach of all in an advanced economy. These include access to healthcare, education, better jobs, decent housing, nutritious food, clean air and safe water. These elements of a good life have long been taken for granted, but they are either declining or becoming unaffordable in many poor areas. An economy in which the means to enjoy a fulfilling, healthy life are concentrated on those at the top is not

sustainable. It is paradoxical that this situation should arise in a democracy – indeed, the world's self-proclaimed leading democracy. Given the power of the vote in free and fair elections, why would citizens not vote for those political leaders who promise to reduce inequality?

Governance that promotes social goods

Sustainable governance implies, as the term suggests, running the affairs of government in ways that ensure social goods for all and a stable institutional framework that will persist into the future, when current political leaders and even parties are superseded by newer generations of leaders. Crucial to good governance is a system of government based on political legitimacy in the eyes of the country's citizens as a whole. It matters that governments view their role as benefiting the whole population – not just the political party that they represent. Also important are the rule of law and transparent institutions that do not allow corruption to get a grip. These basic conditions are the groundwork for sustainable governance. A freely elected democratic government is based on the rule of law, which acts as a buffer to prevent corrupt practices. Where governments are authoritarian, the strong leader claims to represent the will of the people, but its legitimacy is a charade. The dictator rules by executive order. In this situation, personal ties with business leaders are likely to gain in prominence, forming powerful political and business elites. This type of system is unstable and unsustainable. Businesses that cultivate ties with the dictator can find that they evaporate in an instant if a new clique takes control. Most of the world's political systems fall somewhere between these extremes, with legitimacy mechanisms that more or less function, but with levels of corruption that could possibly threaten to destabilize the country's institutions.

Democracies lay strong claims to legitimacy and sustainability because their constitutions have safeguards of free elections, fixed terms of office and mechanisms for making a peaceful handover of the reins of government following elections. Authoritarian systems do not have these safeguards, and factions vie with each other for ascendancy. China's authoritarian system under Communist Party leadership has endured over half a century, anointing a succession of leaders emerging from within the political elite. But this continuity does not bestow institutional stability to the entire political system. The party leaders that dominate government have delivered economic development, but they fear any upsurge in dissent and protest. China has had democracy protesters, but few have been active in the years since the 1989 Tiananmen Square protests. Protests in Hong Kong in 2019 have been more significant and have attracted large numbers of people. While the focus was a proposed new extradition law that would see alleged offenders sent to mainland China for trials, an underlying concern was fear that the rule of law was being eroded. Although the extradition law was put on hold, there were fears for Hong Kong's democratic system, enshrined in the UK's handover of the territory to China in 1997.

Protesters who pose a threat to entrenched autocratic rulers are those such as the young Algerians who flowed into the streets of Algiers in 2019, to protest over their ailing president's intention to stand for a fifth term of office. The regime's response initially was to postpone the election. This would allow breathing space for the ruling clan to put forward a relative of the president to take over. There have also been democracy protests in Russia in 2019, when thousands of people gathered in Moscow to protest that legitimate candidates were being barred from standing in parliamentary elections. These demonstrators were asking for recognition of the basic elements of liberal democracy: voice, fair elections and representative institutions.

A constitutional system that formally guarantees democratic rights does not in itself legitimize a government. A semi-authoritarian regime can overlay an electoral democracy. It has democratic forms, such as regular elections of a president and an elected legislature, but these processes can be captured by political elites that are often linked to the country's largest businesses. Political legitimacy rests on democratic institutions that are supported by the rule of law, freedom of civil-society organizations and an independent judiciary. These are elements that ensure that the system is politically sustainable.

A number of countries that have ostensibly democratic institutions are authoritarian beneath the surface. Among those that have featured here are Turkey (Chapter 5) and Russia (Chapter 3). Democracy has deteriorated in South Africa (Chapter 4), where corrupt business tycoons captured the country's political leaders. Democracy has also deteriorated in India, under the nationalist populist government of Narendra Modi. Poland has seen a sharp decline in the rule of law and an independent judiciary (Chapter 6). In a number of countries, the rise in populist authoritarian leaders has posed a threat for democratic institutions. Turkey has perhaps seen the sharpest shift to authoritarian rule. The US and Brazil are among other countries that have seen the ascendancy of a populist president with little respect for separation of powers or checks and balances. Business elites have been favoured by these populist governments, while social protections and human rights for workers and labour organizations have suffered setbacks. Turkey's authoritarian president has reaped the credit for the country's economic development, but the recent financial crisis and recession could prove politically damaging for him. His party suffered setbacks in local elections in 2019, when voters in 7 out of 12 of the main cities delivered majorities for opposition parties.

In a soundly managed economy, targeted public spending and taxation policies are operated in a fair and transparent way. The Scandinavian countries have been the leaders in this type of social spending, as befits the values inherent in their social market economies. These are market economies, with inbuilt democratic values and social priorities. In Scandinavian countries, the private sector has co-operated with public authorities in health services and education (Chapter 4). Governance is about interaction between government bodies and partners at a variety of levels, including business interests, local authorities and the social and voluntary sectors. In order for processes to function fairly and transparently, these bodies must remain focused on public goods, rather than private interests. Unfortunately, blurring the lines between public interest and private gain is all too common, and can lead to corruption. The use of private-sector outsourcing of public services in the UK has led to numerous scandals. The for-profit delivery of public services, such as health, education and social care, has suffered setbacks, characterized by inadequate oversight by government, weak accountability and private-sector providers that have run into financial difficulties. One large provider of services, Carillion (Chapter 8), collapsed in 2018.

Political leaders are frequently linked to their country's large business interests, as in Brazil (Chapter 5) and Bangladesh (see the mini case study in this chapter). US president Donald Trump is himself a real estate magnate. In these situations, there is a conflict of interest between public goods and private gains. Regulatory mechanisms should serve the public good, but can be influenced by political leaders with vested interests. The result is that societal wellbeing suffers. Both Brazil and Bangladesh have lowly rankings in Transparency International's Corruption Perception Index. Out of 180 countries in total, Brazil lies 105th on a score of 35 out of 100, and Bangladesh lies 149th on a score of 26. Brazil, which has suffered from economic and political instability, has fallen from a rank of 69th in 2015. Other selected rankings appear in Figure 12.2, which replicates Figure 6.9. In places where businesses routinely engage in undeclared payments to officials and others, corruption may become the norm. And in these situations, companies can take false comfort in the fact that others are behaving in the same way. China, which has risen to the

rank of 87th, from 100th in 2015, has sought to reduce corruption. High levels of corruption are a disadvantage in the assessment of a country's competitiveness. Corrupt behaviour is a risky way of doing business, dependent on personal ties rather than contractual terms, and liable to turn sour when there are changes in the people at the top. The US has fallen from 11th place in 2015 to 22nd in 2018, while the UK has risen from 14th in 2015 to 11th in 2018. There is now a significant gap between the Scandinavian countries and the US. The lowest country in this figure is Congo (the Democratic Republic of Congo), featured in the case study on Glencore (Chapter 7). One of the best safeguards against corruption is legitimate political institutions. Congo's weak governance is one of the factors impeding its building sustainable institutions.

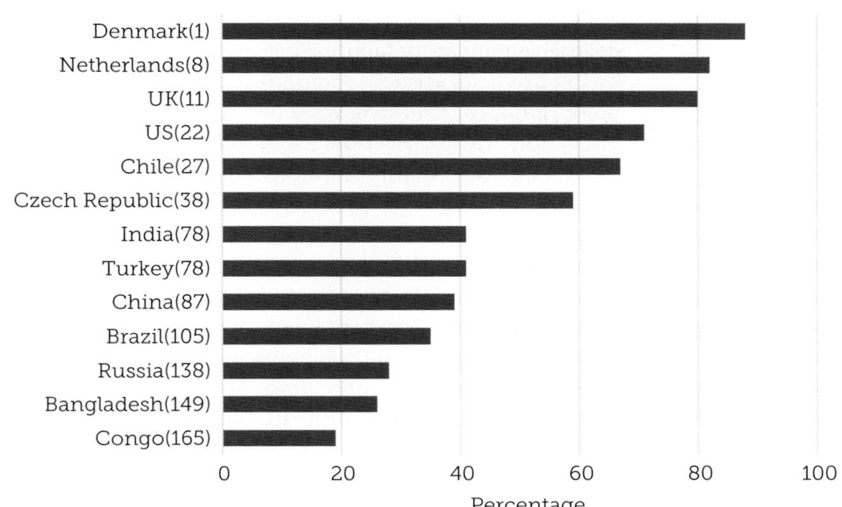

Figure 12.2 Transparency International's Corruption Perception Index: Findings for selected countries

Notes: Country scores are percentages. The rank of each country is shown in brackets after the country name. There are 174 countries overall in the ranking.

Source of data: Transparency International (2018) *Corruption Perception Index for 2018*, at www.transparency.org/cpi2018, accessed 22 February 2019.

Countries with high levels of corruption are often authoritarian or semi-authoritarian political regimes. But corruption is endemic in India, a democratic system, and also one that has been led by a populist, the Hindu nationalist, Rajendra Modi. Robust democratic institutions and an independent judiciary should be able to withstand the threats from ideological extremists, but these assaults threaten democracy and also the perpetuation of sustainable governance.

Political access: how does it matter to businesses?

Wealthy individuals and businesses in the US have been able to pay for access to President Trump at his Florida golf resort, with an eye to doing business deals or influencing policies. These social occasions could be seen as presenting a golden opportunity for gaining presidential favour. However, this is hardly a template for good governance. What detrimental effects are these practices having on governance in the US?

Financial stability in national and global contexts

The opening case study of this chapter focused on restoring sustainability to a shaken financial system following the global financial crisis. Financial markets have a propensity to volatility, calling for regulatory frameworks to maintain stability. But sustainability involves much more than just stability: it requires transparency and fairly governed markets. Banking systems need to be prudently run and overseen by national structures, be they political or independent central bankers. For governments, businesses and households, debt financing is justifiable if the debt is manageable, but excessive debt is not sustainable. Responsible corporate governance, based on stakeholder considerations, should be engrained in the corporate culture of banks and other financial companies. Regulators need to be vigilant, willing to intervene when necessary to protect the system as a whole.

The spread of market economies has highlighted the need for regulation. The purist advocate of free markets is now rare, following the market failures that led to the global financial crisis. And regulation serves not simply to maintain markets, but to promote other public goods, such as consumer safety and environmental protection. The challenges are to design fair regulation and to persuade all players to comply willingly. The global financial crisis is perhaps the most spectacular example of collective regulatory failure. Post-crisis regulation has been slow in coming, resisted by the financial services sector. It soon became apparent that devices to circumvent bonus caps, for example, were being used. A change in culture is hard to introduce, but is nonetheless essential if a regulatory regime is to succeed.

The example of Argentina (Chapter 8) has shown that reforming the financial system goes hand in hand with responsible managing of the national economy, keeping close watch on the plight of those in society who have suffered from years of economic hardship following Argentina's succession of sovereign defaults. Traditional IMF oversight has focused on austerity measures and reducing budget deficits. This position has now been modified to refocus on the social needs of various groups in society, including pensioners and the unemployed. Spending on stimulus measures are possibly more productive for the majority of people in society over the long term. In the years 2015–18, the UK government, in its aims to reduce public spending, introduced austerity measures in social benefits that caused hardship to some of the most vulnerable people in society. Admittedly, public finances looked healthier by 2019, but the price paid was a heavy one, in terms of public lack of trust in politicians to do what is best for all in society.

The IMF has expressed fears that a global slowdown, trade tensions and political instability around the world are dimming the global outlook. This is not to say that another financial crisis is brewing, but the IMF is concerned over the issues of rising inequality and the need for inclusive growth. Booming stock markets have seen excessive profits for the shareholders and executives of large listed companies, but the fruits of the boom have not been shared with ordinary workers. These imbalances are ultimately unsustainable. In its economic outlook in 2019, the IMF highlighted the threats simmering in the global economy, and gave its recommendations on the priorities that policymakers should be adopting. These are summarized in Figure 12.3.

The IMF sees economic slowdown, especially in the advanced economies, as dampening growth. It is concerned that trade tensions should be resolved through multilateral co-operation, rather than through individual countries engaging in the tit-for-tat imposition of tariff increases on each other's goods, as has occurred between the US and China. The Managing Director of the IMF has emphasized that a 'new multilateralism' is needed to resolve not just global trade issues, but to address other shared problems, including reducing corruption and tax evasion, and fighting climate change (IMF, 2019). The IMF has long expressed the view that growth must be inclusive to be sustainable, and this is reflected in the recommendations for policymakers' priorities. It is concerned that economic opportunities are not evenly spread among those who are seeking employment, noting that it is often women and young people who find employment opportunities scarce. It also reminds

Figure 12.3 The IMF's analysis of the world economic outlook

Source of concepts: IMF, *World Economic Outlook Update*, January 2019, at www.imf.org, accessed 24 September 2019.

policymakers that they have responsibilities to look to people whose jobs have been displaced by structural changes in the economy, such as those that have resulted from changes in technology, notably automation. The IMF has also reminded governments that social protections are important in promoting inclusive growth. It notes particularly that in countries dependent on commodity production, too little progress is being made to diversify their economies away from resource industries. Such shifts are necessary for sustainable development, and would help to provide employment opportunities.

Assessing the risks in the global environment

Uncertainties in the global environment cast a shadow over the hopes that many hold in the powers of globalization to bring about prosperity and stability. The positive side of globalization has been in evidence, lifting economies through growth and reducing poverty, but the negative aspects have highlighted risks. Among these are the rising concerns about climate change, especially in the light of rapid economic development. Slowing economic growth in both developing and developed economies, along with rising indebtedness, poses threats to economic and financial stability. Economic growth has often been accompanied by rising inequality. Furthermore, political leadership sometimes reinforces the inequalities rather than setting an agenda for inclusive development. In many countries, poor people have little or no hope of personal betterment. In others, such as China, many now have expectations of continuing improvement in their quality of life. The realities of unemployment, stagnant wages and poor social services can be destabilizing in society, and even divisive. The rise in ethnic and religious tensions in many countries compounds any economic uncertainties. All these dimensions are shown in Figure 12.4. The figure shows four key areas where risks are affecting the global environment.

Economic and financial risks

The global trend towards market economies has been a feature of the era of globalization. More freedom for all to pursue personal goals, everyone would agree, is a good thing. Markets have spread across the world, signalling reforms in formerly closed economies and closed political systems, such as communist states, former military

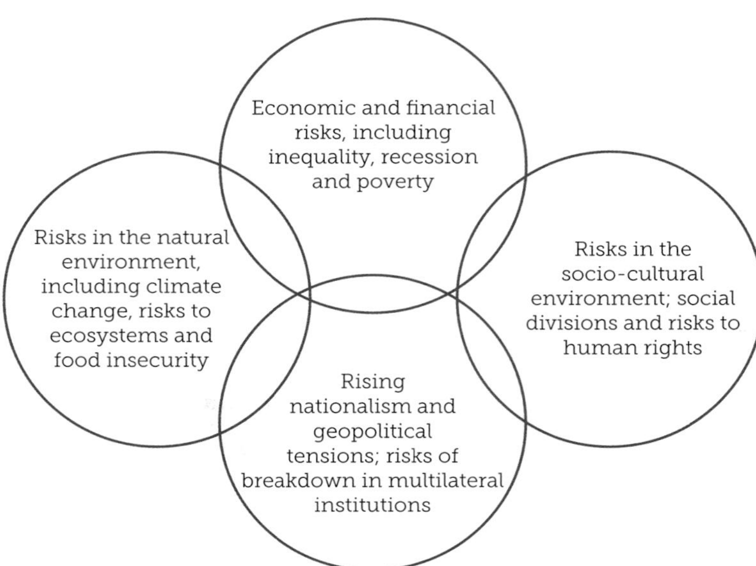

Figure 12.4 Risks in the global environment

dictatorships (such as Myanmar) and theocratic states (such as Iran). Globalization of markets, however, have heightened risks, especially in financial markets. Regulatory reforms following the financial crisis of 2008 have been piecemeal, and worries remain that quantitative easing, rising levels of debt and rising stock markets have increased the risk of a further recession.

Over this same period, there has been a rise in inequality that has occurred in both developed and developing economies. China and the US are prominent examples, but there are many others. This trend has not been universal. Inequality has not increased in the Scandinavian countries or Germany, and it has narrowed in France. These are exceptions. How does inequality become a risk in economies? The free-market capitalist would consider that inequality is inherent in capitalism and is not a problem. And, in the US, surveys of public opinion show that Republicans hold this view, whereas the Democrats tend to see inequality as a problem. Equality of opportunity is an assumption that underpins US thinking on all sides of the political spectrum. It holds that the rich earned their position at the top of the ladder, and those at the bottom, in theory, can climb the ladder as well. The 'American dream' rests on this belief, and goes a long way towards answering the question posed in the section above (on p. 429) on economic prosperity. Improvement for those at the bottom would come with economic growth and rising wages. This assumption held true for the period of post-war growth in the US, but has since worn thin.

Economic growth has now slowed in the emerging economies, and growth is improving only slowly in the developed countries affected by financial crisis. In the post-crisis years, other indicators have not looked very promising. High levels of household, corporate and sovereign debt create burdens verging on the unsustainable. Average wages are rising only modestly, if at all, in many of the countries affected by the financial crisis. But, tellingly, corporate profits, executive remuneration, and the wealth of the richest globally, have soared ever upwards. Inequality has come to be seen from the economic perspective as hindering growth and posing a risk for long-term economic stability.

Two aspects of inequality stand out as undermining economic growth: health and education. A person's position in society and prospects of mobility depend heavily on good health and education. Where money determines access to services,

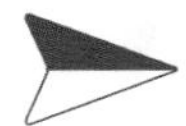

those without the means are likely to suffer poor health, low life expectancy and an inability to pursue a job that offers enrichment in both income and personal fulfilment. This is detrimental not just for the individual, but for the economy as a whole. It means that much potential individual talent and ability to create wealth are not being tapped. A growing middle class that is healthier and better educated than previous generations is linked to economic development. But, while the middle class is enjoying growing prosperity in emerging economies, the situation in developed economies is less promising.

OECD research on its member states has shown that rich households have forged ahead economically, but middle-class households, considered the backbone of the economy, have fallen behind. This is a trend that gives cause for concern in these advanced economies. As the OECD points out, the middle class has been aspirational. People aspire for a better life for their children, with better education and greater economic opportunities. The middle class drives consumer spending, and helps to promote inclusive economic growth. It is a source of entrepreneurial activity, spurring the formation of SMEs. A thriving middle class is also associated with social stability and cohesion. Middle-class citizens are believers in good public services and investment in education. They are considered the bedrock of democratic institutions, upholding beliefs in the rule of law and tolerance of others.

The middle-class family expects a comfortable standard of living, a rewarding job, good housing, access to good education and a lifestyle that is fulfilling. A middle-class household's income is defined as 75% to 200% of the country's median household income. Three decades ago, the aggregate income of these people was four times that of the high-income households in OECD countries. Now, the ratio is less than three (OECD, 2019). The spending of the middle-class household has been squeezed. Inflation has particularly affected house prices, the cost of education and healthcare. Household indebtedness has grown, and so has job insecurity, creating a sense of vulnerability in middle-class homes. Particularly affected have been the millennials (born between 1983 and 2002), whose expectations of going to university and buying a better home than their parents have receded. The middle class today is like 'a boat in rocky waters' (OECD, 2019: 16). Many feel they are slipping down into the lower-income level – indebted, living in rented accommodation and working in short-term employment. They are likely to feel let down by elected politicians. Governments should be responding to these citizens' issues, especially those affecting job security, social protections and poverty. A risk is that their anxieties about their economic situation could incline them to support extremist political movements that would undermine democratic institutions.

Inequality in society can be viewed as an ethical issue, on the grounds that it denies the equal moral worth of every human being. It has also been seen as undermining democracy and political legitimacy, as the few control power in society for their own gains, at the expense of the many (Reich, 2015). For the poor, the system no longer seems to be fair, either economically or politically. Poor health and educational outcomes for a large proportion of society augers ill for an economy, and leads potentially to widening divisions between the haves and the have-nots.

These trends are not inevitable. Where the system has become unfair, governments can devise policies to achieve a fairer distribution of wealth, by spending more on social services and raising taxes on the wealthy. However, where the institutions of government and the judiciary are controlled by the richest, such measures are unlikely.

Inequality and globalization

This is a lecture by the distinguished economist, Thomas Piketty, Professor of the School of Advanced Studies in the Social Sciences (EHESS), Paris School of Economics. It is entitled, 'Rising Inequality and globalization', and was delivered as the Angus Maddison lecture, on 28 May 2018, in the Faculty of Economics and Business, the Growth and Development Centre, in the University of Groningen, the Netherlands.

Video link: Inequality and globalization
https://youtu.be/yvltfEJTFkA

international poverty line line representing extreme poverty, defined as living on less than $1.90 a day

Globalization has contributed to reducing the number of people living in extreme poverty, but progress has been uneven. The **international poverty line (IPL)** defines extreme poverty as living on less than $1.90 per day. This is an updated revision of the older absolute poverty line of less than one dollar per day. In 1990, there were 1.85 billion people in the world living below the IPL. That number had fallen to 736 million by 2015. Most of this progress can be accounted for by China's economic growth. The percentage of people in the world living in extreme poverty was nearly 36% in 1990. In 2010, it was 16% globally, and in 2015 the percentage was 10% (World Bank, 2018). However, progress has not been even. Most countries have reduced extreme poverty, but the number of very poor people in sub-Saharan Africa has increased from 278 million in 1990 to 413 million in 2015. In terms of percentages, most countries have a rate of extreme poverty that is under 13%, but the percentage is 41% in sub-Saharan Africa, as shown in Figure 12.5. Of the world's 28 poorest countries, 27 are here. Among the main factors is economic reliance on extractive industries that do not lead to shared prosperity. These economies remain predominantly rural, and the policies of their governments are not sufficiently focused on inclusive growth and poverty reduction. Other factors are violent conflicts, weak institutions, natural disasters and the ravages of climate change. Climate change impacts are particularly severe in rural areas, where most of the region's very poor inhabitants live. Without progress in improving governance and inclusive growth, poverty is certain to worsen.

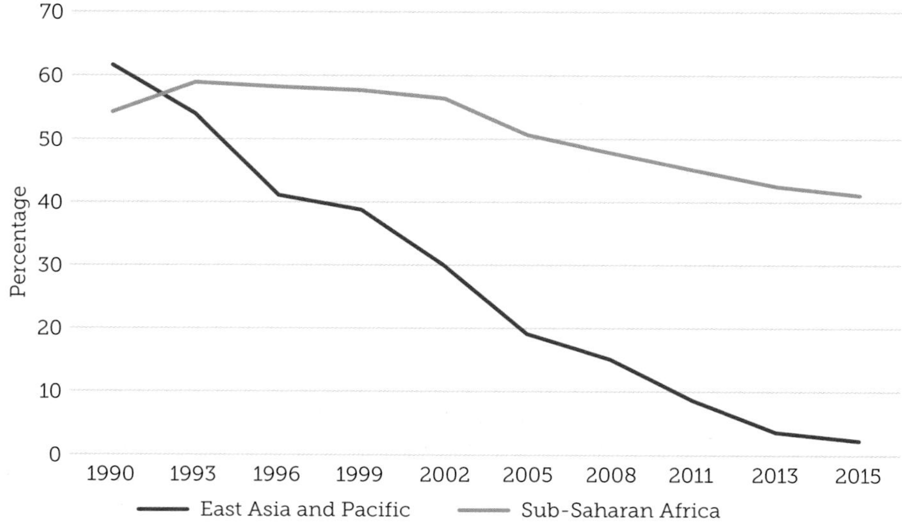

Figure 12.5 Percentage of the population living on less than $1.90 per day: two regions compared

Source of data: World Bank (2018) *Poverty and Shared Prosperity, Piecing together the poverty puzzle*, Table 1A.1(b), *Global and Regional Extreme Poverty, 1990–2015*, p. 42, at https://openknowledge.worldbank.org, accessed 24 September 2019.

The World Bank has added two further poverty lines, to reflect global economic growth. While two decades ago, 60% of the world's population lived in low-income countries, the majority of the world's population now live in middle-income countries. In these countries, people's ideas of what constitutes basic needs for life have been revised upwards, for example, to include a mobile phone. These higher poverty lines are $3.20 a day and $5.50 a day. When we look at the numbers of people beneath these higher poverty lines, the statistics are not so encouraging. A quarter of the world's population lives beneath the poverty line of $3.20 a day, and 46% of the world's people lived on less than $5.50 a day in 2015, a percentage that had fallen from 67% in 1990. Poverty at this level, while not as desperate as the day-to-day struggle to exist on under $1.90 a day, is still a struggle.

Figure 12.6 shows the progress made in the Middle East and North Africa, sub-Saharan Africa, and South Asia. All experienced falls in the percentage of those beneath the $5.50 poverty line between 1990 and 2015. However, these falls were modest, and, because of growing populations, the number of people living in poverty actually increased over this period. These statistics based on the upper poverty lines suggest that, although people everywhere are forming an idea of basic needs based on living standards in middle-income countries, the number of people falling beneath those expectations remains very high. Over 80% of people in South Asia and sub-Saharan Africa still fall beneath the higher poverty line. The focus globally has been on reducing extreme poverty, and, although progress has been impressive overall, a more nuanced picture indicates persistent poverty. Continuing extreme poverty in sub-Saharan Africa is one source of concern. Another is that almost half of the world's population is still struggling with poverty. This is despite the achievements of over two decades of economic growth and globalization.

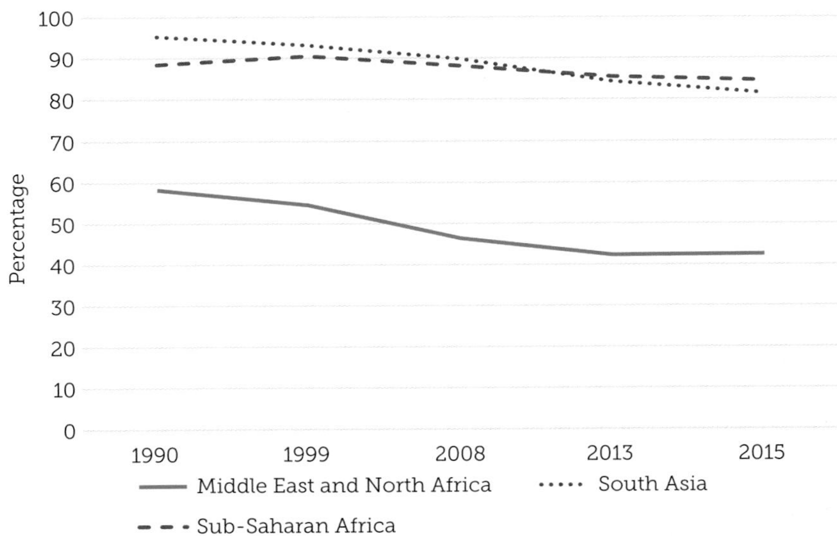

Figure 12.6 Percentage of the population living on less than $5.50 per day: three regions compared

Source of data: World Bank (2018) *Poverty and Shared Prosperity, Piecing together the poverty puzzle*, Table 3.2 (b) Poverty at higher poverty lines, p. 70, at https://openknowledge.worldbank.org, accessed 24 September 2019.

Risks in the socio-cultural environment

A society should provide an environment in which all have a feeling of belonging and a sense of participation. People should be able to participate in civil society organizations, follow the religion of their choice and enjoy a cultural life that brings them fulfilment as individuals and members of society. These are recognized as human rights, with foundations in ethical principles and in international law. Most countries subscribe to the UN's basic human rights conventions (Chapter 6).

These indicate a commitment to uphold them, but the UN's foundation lies in the sovereignty of member states, and they decline to uphold them when they see fit. Both within states and between states, there are risks to societies and cultures, along with risks to human rights, that threaten human and societal wellbeing. Conflicts within countries can erupt into civil wars, and, in reality, many internal conflicts spill over into conflicts between states.

Armed conflict has risen markedly since 2010. The main regions affected have been sub-Saharan Africa, the Middle East and South Asia. These are areas with high levels of poverty, inequality and weak governance, as we found in the last section. Incidents of political violence are on the rise, increasing 11% between 2017 and 2018 (ACLED, 2018). Mostly, the conflicts involve conventional warfare, and state actors are prominent. The most deadly in 2018 was Afghanistan. Together with Syria, Lebanon and Iraq, these four states accounted for over 60% of the world's organized violent conflicts in 2018. And state actors in these countries were responsible for the largest numbers of civilian deaths. But non-state actors, such as terrorist groups, are also influential. The civil war in Syria is an example, taking a heavy toll in civilian deaths and displacements. By early 2019, the terrorist Islamic State that had controlled much of the territory of Syria, had been run off these territorial strongholds, but the menace of these extremist terrorists remained a threat. They are particularly active in the Middle East, Afghanistan and North Africa, where their violent attacks are destructive and destabilizing. They tend to exploit the divisions that are already present in societies.

Within countries, divisions based on wealth, ethnic differences, religious conflicts and gender divides leave the disadvantaged groups behind, often feeling alienated and fearful of oppression from dominant groups. These divisions can be cross-cutting. The poorest are often those in ethnic minorities, such as indigenous people. Broad-based and inclusive economic growth is an important source of stability in societies. Where growth has powered ahead, as in the resource-rich countries discussed in this book, those left behind are disappointed by unfulfilled expectations, leading to tensions within society. Ultimately, these tensions can destabilize the country, as in the Arab spring uprisings that occurred in 2011, and the protests occurring in 2019 in Algeria. Conflicts spring from a number of possible sources. They include factors such as economic stagnation and weak job creation, leading to an increase in the number of young jobless people. Social conflicts can arise from an inflow of migrants, often fleeing conflicts in neighbouring countries. Other causes are disputes over land and the treatment of minorities. Minority groups often feel that they are being excluded from political and economic life. Conflicts can also arise between groups with conflicting political allegiances, often linked to social, religious and ethnic divides. For example, we have seen that there are conflicts between the Hindu nationalists in India and other sections of the population, especially the Muslim population.

The mass displacement of people fleeing violent conflict leads to flows of refugees into other countries, creating humanitarian crises. By 2018, Turkey had received 3.5 million Syrian refugees escaping from civil war. These movements of people are part of a record level of displacement of people globally (Chapter 3). A UN convention of 1951 recognizes the rights of refugees. However, the influx of migrants has become a contentious issue. Some urban areas in Turkey near the Syrian border have more Syrian refugee inhabitants than Turkish residents. Local and civil society organizations attempt to look after their needs, but the Turkish government takes a policy line that the Syrians are temporary residents only. The Turkish public has tended to take a hostile attitude towards the refugees, focusing on the burdens they create on public services. While the Turkish government has taken the view that Turkey has affinities with Syrians in culture and religion, the Turkish public takes the opposite view, one of cultural distance between themselves and Syrians (Kirişci et al., 2018). Although there are provisions for Syrian

refugees to obtain work permits, few have been issued, and Syrians are thus working informally, in situations where they are vulnerable to human rights abuse.

Conflicts include interpersonal violence, gang violence and political violence. Interpersonal violence, often leading to criminal behaviour such as vandalism, tends to occur where the rule of law is weak and social norms tolerate violence. A degree of 'street' violence is often linked to political violence, in countries where social or religious divisions are likely to flare up. In many countries, governance is unstable or distrusted by some groups in society, and in many societies, sections of the population distrust the police. In these situations, it is common for national authorities to impose repressive measures to quell unrest. Repressive policing and arresting large numbers of protesters is usually defended on grounds of national security. In many countries, both democratic and authoritarian, the right of assembly, which is a basic freedom, is curbed by government in the interest of national security. National laws have been strengthened to combat terrorist threats, but such laws can be extended to other types of disorder and unrest. This inflation in the use of national security laws poses risks to the individual freedoms that should exist in civil society.

National security forces, with the benefit of sophisticated technology, are able to engage in mass surveillance, again, ostensibly to fight terrorism. However, such activities risk infringing privacy on a massive scale. The extent of mass surveillance in the US was revealed in detail in 2013, by the whistleblower, Edward Snowden. Much of the activity of national security agencies is in fact carried out with the help of private-sector companies, especially in technology and communications. The companies are themselves under fire for breaches of privacy in their profiting from the gathering of personal data. Facebook allowed other companies to misuse personal data in microtargeted advertising in the UK referendum in 2016 (Chapter 6). Employees in some companies, such as Microsoft, have become concerned that their technology is used by the US government in its border control activities. Surveillance, police-state suppression of freedoms and arbitrary arrests are common in authoritarian regimes, but are considered contrary to basic values in democratic societies. However, especially in the years following the terrorist attacks of 11th September 2001 in New York, human rights have been subordinated to national security in the drafting of anti-terror legislation.

Anti-terror laws can be used in a variety of situations in which public order is involved. In Turkey, the attempted coup in 2016 gave rise to hundreds of arrests for supposed sedition in the interest of national security (Chapter 5). The numbers of demonstrations, riots and protests have been rising in the Middle East, South and South East Asia, where unrest and regional conflicts have grown (ACLED, 2018). While many are political in origin, labour protests can turn into violent confrontations, often in conjunction with strikes. In fact, labour activism and political causes are often linked. Strikes are common occurrences, whether legal or not, and in many industries, especially where there are hostile labour relations, protests are likely. Strikes and protests by garment workers in Bangladesh led to violent clashes with police in 2018, forcing a shutdown of many factories. Workers were angry over low wages and poor conditions, but factory owners took a hard line, sacking hundreds who stopped work (Safi, 2018). A number of union officials were arrested under the country's national security law.

Workplace environments hold some of the greatest risks of human rights abuse (Chapter 6). These risks have multiplied with globalization and outsourced manufacturing in low-cost locations. The so-called 'race to the bottom' in terms of cost-cutting is often linked to excessive hours of work, underpay, disguising of overtime, harsh disciplinary punishments, withheld pay and lack of rest days. Also prevalent in many countries is the use of underage workers, often under headings such as 'interns'. A common thread running through the use of cheap labour in supply chains is that of inequalities of bargaining power, whereby, in extreme cases, workers are subject to forced labour (Chapter 6). Global brand owners hold bargaining power over manufacturers. Manufacturers, in turn, exert control over low-paid workers, in situations where worker voice and organization are minimal or token. Agents who recruit migrant workers from poor countries to work in foreign countries often retain a hold over workers because of indebtedness for recruitment fees and travel. This situation, too, is akin to forced labour or modern slavery. As we have seen, modern slavery can exist just about anywhere – in developed and developing countries alike – and is difficult to uncover and stamp out (Chapter 11). In many cases, legal provisions are in place, but enforcement is weak, especially in a context of the vested interests of businesses.

The risks to individuals and societies in the global environment can stem from government activities and from business activities, whether intentionally or unintentionally. Governments are traditionally held responsible for infringements of human rights, but, even when they commit themselves to international obligations, they are weak enforcers. Companies, too, commit themselves to ethical conduct and social responsibility, but, in reality, engage in numerous activities that risk human rights, often in conjunction with governments.

MINI CASE STUDY

How far has Bangladesh progressed in making its textile industry safe?

How safe are Dhaka's buildings? This is a crucial question facing the many companies whose clothes are made in Bangladesh's factories.

© Getty, Rehman Asad

The textile industry in Bangladesh has been at the forefront of its economic development, helping the country to reach growth of 6.5% in 2018, and contributing $29 billion to the economy. But while poverty reduction and growth have been impressive, development has come at a cost in low human development, high levels of corruption and weak attention to human rights. Low wages have attracted numerous western brands to Bangladesh as a low-cost environment. But unsafe factories and poor working conditions have been a reality for the four million people who work in the industry. Their plight drew world attention in 2013, when the Rana Plaza, a building in Dhaka housing a number of clothing factories, collapsed, killing 1,100 workers.

In the aftermath of the disaster, western brand owners, including Marks & Spencer, Primark and H&M, took initiatives to launch an Accord for Fire and Building Safety, which set up an independent inspection regime for the factories. A second agreement, an Alliance for Bangladesh Worker Safety, including Costco and Walmart, was also put in place. Both were to run for five years initially. The Accord covered 1,690 factories, and the Alliance covered 655. There was also the government agency, which covered 745 factories. Under the

Accord and Alliance, there has been considerable improvement in the safety, identifying and putting right thousands of safety problems. The death toll has fallen from 71 per year to 17 a year in the five years. Still, half the clothing factories in Bangladesh are not covered by any of the three schemes.

In 2018, as the Accord and Alliance were reaching the end of their five-year initiative, the Bangladesh government decided that sufficient progress had been made to terminate the Accord and Alliance. The Alliance signatories agreed to hand over to local partners, but the Accord members said that much still needed to be done in numerous factories. The Bangladesh high court ordered the closure of the Dhaka office out of which the inspections under the Accord operate. The government wished to take over the inspections of the factories that were in the Accord scheme. Experts were doubtful whether the government inspectors could cope with such a huge increase in workload. Their technical capacity had improved, but many experts fear that standards will now deteriorate again. Brands might choose to leave Bangladesh due to the safety risks.

Bangladesh's economic development has been driven by its prime minister, Sheikh Hasina, who was re-elected by a large majority in August 2018. She could well wish to take back control of this aspect of the clothing industry, which has been the country's main source of exports. Some factory owners had complained of the expense in carrying out improvements specified by the Accord inspectors. Factory owners are important politically, and a number are members of parliament. The four million people who work in the garment factories are mainly women, and many are migrants. Their families are dependent on this income. Bangladesh remains a poor country, and political considerations weigh heavily in the industry. The exit of independent safety and fire inspectors is a cause of concern for the hundreds of brands that have their garments manufactured in Bangladesh.

Questions

- In what ways have the Accord and Alliance been a positive influence in improving safety standards in the garment industry in Bangladesh?
- What are the likely outcomes for the industry when the independent inspectors leave?

Find out more

For an article written four years after the Rana Plaza disaster, see Ashley Westerman's article, '4 years after Rana Plaza tragedy, what's changed for Bangladeshi garment workers?', 30 April 2017, in the Parallel series on National Public Radio, at www.npr.org. This article focuses on transparency in supply chain disclosure.

Rising nationalism and geopolitical tensions

The UN's Charter linked peace and stability to self-determination and the adherence to human rights. The decades following the Second World War saw the birth of new nation-states from the break-up of colonial rule around the world. Most of these new states introduced constitutional democracies. A wave of democratic transition states emerged from the break-up of the former Soviet Union in 1991. The world's remaining superpower was the US, economically and militarily dominant, and also the self-proclaimed standard-bearer of democracy. The new nation-states, which included the new democratic South Africa, aspired to consolidate democracy and open their economies to the new global opportunities. Optimism was in the air, and hopes were high, as globalization and economic development would be linked to democratic institutions: they had in common an openness to individual rights and economic opportunities. While China rejected democratic reforms and maintained its authoritarian political system, it nonetheless introduced liberal market reforms that were largely responsible for its spectacular economic growth.

Now, much of the optimism has dissipated. Concerns over the build-up of debt and slowing economic growth have been noted by the IMF, as highlighted above (p. 432). In many countries with democratic institutions, rising inequality, social divisions and hostility to immigration have seen the emergence of populist leaders who reject democratic pluralism and propagate nationalist ideologies. Bitter divisions have emerged within established democracies, as well as the borderline democracies, with intolerance on the rise and risks to civil society organizations. Internationally, political and religious conflicts, as well as trade tensions, have marked a return to a more nationalist and unstable world system.

All the global risks highlighted thus far in this chapter raise issues involving political institutions, and pose challenges for political leaders. Businesses and individuals everywhere look to political leaders to manage economic risks, promote social cohesion and mitigate climate change. These are daunting tasks even in societies that are relatively affluent and homogenous, like the Scandinavian societies that have been highlighted. However, where social and economic divisions have widened, growth has slowed and financial pressures on social protection programmes mount, these tasks become more difficult, causing strains on institutions. In authoritarian political systems, the signs of tension emerge in events such as protests, strikes, detentions, and clampdowns on media that report unrest and criticism of the government. President Xi Jinping has become more authoritarian and has gained a tighter grip on power. Whereas terms of office have been the norm, changes approved by the party would now allow him to be president for life. His 'thought' has become enshrined in the constitution, creating a leadership cult.

Are China's market reforms of the last three decades now at risk under Xi? China is confronting slowing growth, pollution and other issues. Finding suitable jobs for seven million college graduates each year is a challenge. China's new urban middle classes expect improving living standards and health, including reduced pollution. How will continuing disenchantment show itself? They cannot vote out their leadership. Instead of crackdowns, further market reforms would probably be a better recipe for sustainable growth, but these would still be top-down measures, reflecting a political system with inherent instabilities and problematic political legitimacy in the eyes of much of the population.

Now the world's second-largest economy, China is a global power, and has become more assertive in this role. Its increasing attention to building up its military establishment suggests a more nationalist outlook. To some extent, nationalism has long been a unifying force among the many different regions in the country, but this has led to the suppression of minorities and criticisms of China's human rights record. More recently, trade tensions with the US have opened up the underlying differences in ideology between these two superpowers. The US government under the Trump administration introduced a more overtly nationalist America-first approach to foreign policy than his predecessor had pursued. Trade disputes with China resulted, straining relations. There have also been accusations from the US that China has engaged in the theft of intellectual property rights. Also related to business practices, the US believes that the Chinese government supports and influences businesses, including those that are ostensibly private-sector companies. Huawei is an example (Chapter 7).

Mr Trump was elected president on a nationalist and populist agenda, promising to 'make America great again' (Chapter 5). There has been a resurgence in both populist movements and the election of populist leaders around the world. A number have been discussed in this book. They include Turkey (Chapter 5), India (Chapter 4) and Brazil (Chapter 5). These countries are all different economically and culturally, but all have been founded on constitutional systems designed to uphold democratic institutions and the rule of law. As shown in Figure 6.4, the rule of law has deteriorated in all

of these countries, along with the independence of the judiciary. Their governments have shifted towards authoritarianism, posing risks for pluralism and basic freedoms.

Democratic institutions provide the means for the electorate to hold political leaders accountable, at least at the time of elections. As we have seen, democratic systems are not necessarily stable, or, for that matter, very good at pursuing public goods. But they do contain an element of consent of the governed that authoritarian systems lack. Democratic institutions rest on freedoms of speech and association, giving voice to groups in civil society that governments should be listening to. Political parties are no longer necessarily the first choice of those seeking to voice concerns. Indeed, political parties in many places are seen as part of the problem of governance failings. Hierarchical organizations in their own right, parties are often perceived as serving their own interests before the public interest. Corruption and business ties give them a poor reputation, undermining the trust that citizens would ideally hold in democratic institutions. We saw this in the US and Brazil. However, pluralist political systems have the capacity to reform from within, through free and fair elections. These are the 'rules of the game' in a liberal democracy: today's majority party could become tomorrow's opposition party, and vice versa. Both sides accept that democracy is 'the only game in town' (Diamond, 1997: 3). The risks to democracy arise when new movements no longer accept these basic rules, setting out to destroy the democratic system itself.

Immigration is one of the issues that has sparked a rise in rightwing nationalist parties across Europe, which are mainly anti-immigration. Intolerance of minorities – not just immigrants – is characteristic of these parties. Italian senator and human rights advocate, Emma Bonino has said, 'We are really living through an attack on representative democracy, the liberal order, and the constitution...It's all about dictatorship of the majority' (Luce, 2018). Hungary and Poland are strongholds of so-called eurosceptic nationalist parties. Hungary's prime minister, Victor Orban, has been a powerful proponent of these views, becoming increasingly authoritarian, in defiance of the EU's liberal democratic values. In 2018, he won a third term of office in a landslide victory for his Fidesz party, campaigning almost exclusively on a platform of anti-immigration, in defence of traditional white Christian Hungary. Winning a two-thirds majority of the seats in parliament (133 seats out of a total of 199), he was in a position to rewrite the constitution, enhancing executive power even further, and weakening checks and balances. Jobbik, the second-largest party (with 26 seats), is also a rightwing nationalist party. In his years in power, Mr Orban has stifled press freedom and exerted control of the judiciary. He has also consolidated power over the economy, in policies reflecting his expressed admiration for Vladimir Putin of Russia. The EU has taken steps to sanction both Hungary and Poland, but these member states have posed challenges for the EU. These nationalist populist leaders promote their illiberal values, all the while proclaiming that they represent the 'true' democratic will of the people. They are not alone. Anti-immigration, nationalist and eurosceptic parties have gained ground in other EU member states. They include Germany, Austria, the Netherlands, the Czech Republic, France, Italy, and Denmark. These parties are all different, but all tend to mix nationalist, populist and Eurosceptic elements.

The UK's Brexit referendum unleashed similar ideologies. Unlike other EU member states, the UK in 2016 had no members of parliament (MPs) from minority nationalist parties, although there was a strong Eurosceptic wing in the Conservative Party. The referendum of 2016 was 52% in favour of leaving the EU, with 48% voting to remain (Chapter 5). The Conservative government intended to leave the EU by using its executive powers, effectively bypassing Parliament. A legal challenge ensued, culminating in a Supreme Court decision which compelled the government to obtain parliamentary approval for any deal with the EU. In law, the referendum was advisory only, and Parliament is sovereign under the British constitution. With hindsight, the government would have been better advised to seek a consensus on the way forward in the national interest following the referendum, bringing the supporters of 'remain' into the debate. Instead, a stalemate resulted, as Mrs May was unable to obtain parliamentary approval of a deal agreed with the EU. In the years following the referendum, both the main parties, the Conservative Party and the Labour Party, showed signs of splitting, mainly along Brexit lines. At the same time, the new Brexit Party attracted supporters, while voters more sympathetic to the EU gravitated to the Liberal Democrats. These tendencies could mark a shift from a two-party system to a multi-party system in the UK.

Mr Trump's nationalist populism has drawn attention to the pros and cons of populist government. He has promoted a business-friendly environment, emphasizing deregulation and tax reduction for businesses. But as a populist, he is not necessarily the friend of business that he seems: his protectionist, 'America first' policies can damage US businesses that are linked to other companies in global supply chains. He has also been active in expanding the role of the executive branch, having scant respect for the checks and balances of the constitution. He attempted and failed to obtain congressional approval of funding to build a wall along the Mexican border. He then used emergency powers to declare that the influx of immigrants was a national emergency, even though the number had been declining for a considerable time. Both houses of Congress passed legislation to halt the building of the wall, but he used his veto to kill the legislation. The two chambers could have overridden the presidential veto with a two-thirds majority in each house, but this failed. The building of the wall was financed by $2.5 billion diverted from military spending. In 2019, this was approved by the Supreme Court, which by then included the newly appointed justices nominated by Mr Trump. Mr Trump's appointment of dozens of federal judges who hold extreme conservative views will leave an enduring legacy long after he has left office (McCarthy, 2019). This legacy will be greater if he is elected to a second term as president. These views are at odds with the tolerance and open-mindedness that have characterized American democratic values historically, and will be likely to lead to greater polarization in society and a questioning of the independence of the judiciary.

The way I see it ...

'I was elected...to respect the referendum and leave the European Union....we contracted out parliament's sovereignty on the issue of the European Union to the people.'

Liam Fox, British MP and Secretary of State for International Trade, in an interview, reported in *The Guardian*, 25 March 2019.

The cabinet minister expressed the view that, because of the referendum, parliament's views should be bypassed on the issue of Brexit. He said that the government would not treat as 'binding' any indicative votes in parliament that put forward a Brexit deal that was contrary to the government's plan. What are the implications of this view for Britain's parliamentary democracy?

Risks to the natural environment

The Paris accord of 2015 held out hope that an agenda supported by the 195 participating states would deliver the reductions in emissions that would hold global warming to a rise of 2°C, or, more ambitiously, 1.5°C. However, progress depends

crucially on parties sticking to their promises on emissions reductions. It also depends on funds being channelled towards investments in developing countries. The two are linked. Vulnerable developing countries, especially those with low-lying areas and coastal communities, such as Bangladesh, could face the forced migration of millions of people. If temperature rises are kept at 1.5°C, these countries would be able to avoid the worst impact of rising seas. These countries as a group pressed for the more ambitious target at the Paris conference. Also vulnerable are the states most prone to extreme weather events such as drought and flooding. Large swathes of land in Africa that support agriculture are fragile, prone to drought. They face malnutrition, increased incidence of disease and displacement of people from lands that will no longer sustain farming and pastoral livelihoods. The effects of climate change accelerate these extreme conditions. African cities already struggle to cope with growing populations, and a rising influx of people driven from the countryside adds to the challenges of food security, safe housing and healthcare. These are countries that have very low carbon footprints, but pay the price for the rises in emissions in more prosperous regions of the world.

The International Energy Agency reported that greenhouse gas emission rose in 2018, despite the commitments made in the Paris accord. Fossil fuels continue to dominate energy needs, and there was a 2.3% rise in fossil fuel consumption in 2018 (Harvey, 2019). This growth was largely accounted for by the increase in new coal-fired power stations, mainly in Asia. Asia's power stations are mostly young, under 12 years old, and will be generating electricity for three more decades at least. Their emissions have been one of the main contributors, along with vehicle exhaust and industrial emissions, to high levels of fine particulate matter ($PM_{2.5}$) in the air, which have become a leading cause of disease (Health Effects Institute, 2019). Over 90% of the world's population live in areas where air pollution is above the level the WHO considers healthy. There are sharp disparities between developed and developing countries, which have levels of air pollution over four times the level of developed countries. $PM_{2.5}$ is a major cause of respiratory illness and lung disease, as well as strokes and heart disease. India and other countries in South Asia have among the most unhealthy levels of pollution in the world (Chapter 10). China's government has made significant progress in introducing controls over pollution. A comparison of the number of deaths that are attributable to exposure to $PM_{2.5}$ in China and India are shown in Figure 12.7. Both are rising, but the rate has slowed somewhat in China. Asia is not alone in increasing fossil fuel consumption. The US increased gas and oil production 10% in 2018, mainly due to a

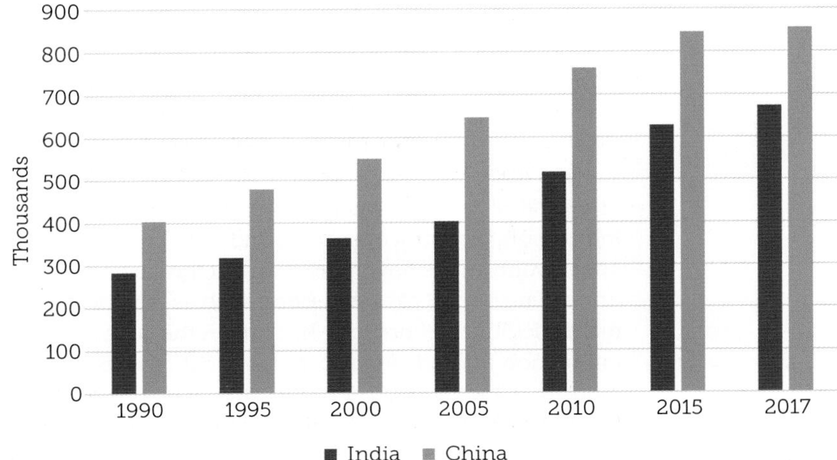

Figure 12.7 Number of deaths attributable to $PM_{2.5}$

Source of data: Health Effects Institute (2019) *State of Global Air: 2019*, at https://stateofglobalair.org, accessed 24 September 2019.

rise in fracking. Canada's rise in CO_2 emissions, also from fossil fuels, has resulted in a rise in temperature more than twice the global average.

While the large energy companies stress their strategies for investing in renewable energy, these are dwarfed by their fossil-fuel businesses. The five largest energy companies listed on stock exchanges are increasing their spending on oil and gas extraction to $115 billion in 2019. Just 3% of that investment is to be spent on low-carbon projects (Laville, 2019). Moreover, these companies spend in the region of $200 million a year on lobbying to block climate change measures. Even when low-carbon investments are announced, they do not always materialize. Chevron constructed two huge – and highly pollutant – natural gas facilities in Australia, which have been producing gas since 2016. As part of the project, it was committed to a carbon capture and storage project, to offset its carbon emissions. However, the storage facility did not come into operation, and there have been questions about the start date under the original contract. The costs of running the offsetting operation would be about A$40 million a year. In frustration in 2019, the Australian government initiated moves to compel the company to begin the carbon storage operations, but there could be legal delays. In the meantime, 8 million tonnes of CO_2 equivalent are produced by the two Chevron gas facilities each year.

The WHO has emphasized the damage to human health caused by pollution, highlighting the toxic pollution caused by deforestation and the burning of peatlands. Climate change is contributing to the rising incidence of disease in these areas. Deforestation is the world's second-largest source of emissions after the burning of fossil fuels, accounting for about 15% of global CO_2 emissions. Yet the tropical forests continue to be destroyed legally. Large agribusiness corporations are the drivers. Globalized markets control the trading of food commodities, and large industrial processors have overseen the globalization of processed foods and other everyday consumer products. Increased demand for palm oil lies behind the clearing of forests for palm plantations, devastating ecosystems, releasing pollution and destroying species. Palm oil is not just in processed foods – it occurs in 50% of the products consumers buy – from breakfast cereal to shampoo. The certification system of the RSPO (the Roundtable for Sustainable Palm Oil) has attracted some large consumer products companies, but, even though founded in 2004, sustainable palm oil accounted for only 19% of the total in 2018. Moreover, RSPO-certified palm oil is not indicated on the brand's label. Palm oil production has doubled in the last decade, and is set to continue increasing, largely due to huge demand in Asian markets, where awareness of sustainability issues is generally low. Indonesia is the world's largest supplier of palm oil, accounting for 55% of global production. Its production has increased rapidly as demand has grown, increasing 230% in two decades. It increased production from 23.6 million to 40.5 million metric tonnes between 2010 and 2018 – a period during which the evidence of the environmental damage of palm oil production was receiving global attention.

Agribusinesses are active in promoting the virtues of technology as an answer to food security globally. However, their operations involve the destruction of biodiversity and damaging social impacts on farming communities and livelihoods. The grip of a handful of agribusiness companies on plant patents is an indication of increasing corporate control over crops and farm livelihoods. Although consumers in developed countries are now more aware of the sustainability issues, these do not have the immediate impact of other issues, such as animal welfare in meat production. In animal agriculture, technology has driven the large meat companies towards increased production and efficiencies, but at what cost to sustainability? The pharmaceutical industry is increasingly active in animal husbandry. The use of antibiotics in animal farming has become widespread, especially in the US, where 70% of medically important antibiotics are sold for use in livestock production. The WHO has expressed

alarm that the drug seen as the miracle cure of the twentieth century is now used in healthy animals, to improve growth. The result is that human resistance to antibiotics has grown, leading to higher mortality from diseases and greater risks to health in routine operations in hospitals. The non-therapeutic use of antibiotics was banned in the EU in 2006, but not in the US. The use of growth hormones in beef, banned in the EU since 1989, is also legal in the US. American consumer fears have led McDonald's to require suppliers to reduce the use of antibiotics in chickens, and also to reduce antibiotics in other meats. These steps have been taken in the US initially, and are being introduced gradually in all the company's markets by 2027.

This section has highlighted global risks, as well as risks in particular regions that exemplify global issues. Risks of extreme weather from climate change, environmental degradation and health risks from the excessive use of chemicals in industrial food production, are having the greatest impacts on those regions of the world where governments and individuals are least able to cope. The devastation caused by cyclone Idai in Mozambique, Malawi and Zimbabwe in 2019 is an example. Wind and torrential rain caused flooding that covered hundreds of square miles, destroying hundreds of villages, along with roads and other infrastructure. Even after several weeks, it was unknown how many people lost their lives. Governments and aid agencies struggled to reach those affected, and, as each day passed, the plight of the victims who managed to make it to shelters became more desperate. Experts say that storms such as this are becoming more common with climate change, including the impacts of rising seas. Environmental risks are not isolated: they are often exacerbated by risks in other areas, such as social divisions, inequality, and poor governance. Mozambique is a resource-rich country, in which business and political insiders benefit, to the detriment of the vast majority of the population, which consists of subsistence farmers. Although formally democratic, the government is classified as authoritarian in the democracy index published by *The Economist* newspaper (EIU, 2018).

Who bears responsibilities for sustainability, and what should they be doing?

The discussion of global risks in this book has emphasized the responsibilities that fall on all players in the global environment. We have highlighted the failures of systems and individuals. To say that a system is to blame is not to exclude the blame that attaches to individuals: they are part of the system. The global financial crisis is an example, showing that corporate strategies were excessively risky, but regulatory failures were also to blame. Here, we draw out some points about decision-making and the behaviour of multiple players. These are the people on whom responsibility falls to build a more sustainable future.

Government responsibilities

Governments have their hands on a great deal of power, including that which is authorized by law and that which comes through economic and political influence. A government represents the sovereignty of the state. It has the capacity to make laws, enforce them, and use coercive powers as it sees fit. It has powers to run a military establishment and conduct foreign relations with other countries, including entering treaty agreements. Although the judicial system is deemed to be independent in most countries, governments in practice exert influence over it. When we take a look back at the risks identified in the last section, we can see that governments are in a strong position to act. They are entrusted with fostering public goods.

Governments have the policy tools to reduce damaging inequality and to ensure that minorities have their human rights safeguarded. They can take steps to encourage entrepreneurs who could provide tomorrow's innovations and jobs. They can introduce measures to maintain fairness in market mechanisms, take action against anti-competitive practices, and impose fair regulatory regimes on businesses. These policies must take account of societal goals and issues of sustainability. For example, channelling money into industries that will provide jobs, but are heavy polluters, is not sustainable. Governments must now recognize the fact that economic growth must take account of a carbon-constrained future environment.

The climate change agreement of 2015 is one example of international co-operation that holds out real prospects for reducing the impacts of climate change. But governments must carry out their intended reductions in emissions. This requires taking actions that many will resist, especially large companies with vested interests in fossil fuels. Canada, mentioned in the last section, is an example. Before the Paris conference, ten global oil and gas companies, including BP, Shell, Total and Statoil, pledged to do more to reduce emissions, but the two American oil giants, Chevron and ExxonMobil did not. This situation was indicative of the difficulties that arise when we expect governments to achieve social and environmental objectives, even when they have the policy tools to hand. These companies, and other American multinationals, also benefit from US trade policy and trade agreements, both bilateral and plurilateral. Incorporating investor-state dispute settlement (ISDS) clauses, these agreements facilitate American companies in overriding environmental and social legislation in countries where they have invested. The US government has thus pursued positive policies to thwart legislation in other countries that attempt to raise standards of sustainability.

Holders of economic power in most countries, notably large businesses, whether in the private sector or state-owned, hold considerable sway over government policies. This is only partly because these companies develop the expertise to lobby effectively. It is mainly attributable to the fact that those holding economic power and those in the corridors of political power overlap to a great extent. Economic elites are the most forceful voices in influencing government policy in the US, as we saw in Chapter 5. A result is that public goods take a back seat to the interests of the country's big businesses. The so-called revolving door between business and politics is a source of corruption. Legislators who design laws at the behest of a large company can expect funding from the company for their next election campaign, and a board seat or consultancy when their term of office ends. Those legislators should be serving the public, but are more likely to serve the interests of those who fund their next political campaign.

Companies commonly portray themselves as simply abiding by the law of the land. This portrayal is disingenuous in many cases, as they actively seek to shape laws and fund friendly politicians' campaigns. Laws that would be unpopular with large companies are unlikely to reach the statute book in the US, and, if they do, could well be challenged through the courts in protracted lawsuits. The Affordable Care Act ('Obamacare') creating a universal health insurance scheme, passed the two houses of Congress late in 2009, when there was a Democratic majority in the lower house, and a majority of just one vote in the Senate, the upper house. By early 2016, it would have stood no chance of passage, and it has been challenged repeatedly in the courts since it was signed by the president in 2010. It has been the subject of two Supreme Court rulings over this period, the latest in 2015, when, by a majority of 6 to 3, the highest court ruled that the subsidies to the poor for health insurance were legal under the constitution. But by 2019, the makeup of the Supreme Court had shifted, following two new appointments by President Trump. Under Mr Trump, funding for the scheme was cut, and he wishes to repeal it in its

1 End extreme poverty (less than $1.90 a day)	**UN Sustainable Development Goals (SDGs)**	12 Ensure sustainable consumption and production
2 End hunger; achieve food security and sustainable agriculture	7 Ensure affordable, clean energy for all	13 Combat climate change
3 Ensure good health and wellbeing	8 Promote decent work and inclusive, sustainable economic growth	14 Conserve the oceans and seas
4 Ensure inclusive and quality education	9 Promote inclusive and sustainable industrialization, including infrastructure and innovation	15 Promote sustainable use of land
5 Achieve gender equality	10 Reduce inequality within and between countries	16 Promote peace, justice and inclusive institutions
6 Ensure safe drinking water and sanitation for all	11 Make cities safe, inclusive and sustainable	17 Strengthen global partnership for SDGs

Figure 12.8 UN Sustainable Development Goals (SDGs) 2015–2030

Source: UNDP (UN Development Programme) (2015) *Sustainable Development Goals Booklet*, 28 September, at www.undp.org, updated by the UNDP 9 April 2019.

entirety. The new members of the Supreme Court would favour his policies, but he would encounter resistance to repealing it in Congress, from the Democratic majority in the House of Representatives.

Looking at the UN's sustainable development goals (SDGs) provides an example of the contrast between expectations of government action and the realities that would seem to nullify those expectations. The SDGs are addressed to governments. There is no mention of what corporations should be committed to do, although all these goals involve business activities. The only reference to companies is in the global partnership mentioned in SDG17. That refers to the UN Global Compact (www.unglobalcompact.org) initiative whereby companies voluntarily sign up to principles of sustainability, anti-corruption and human rights. It involves no compliance obligations or responsibilities that commit corporate leaders. In Chapter 10, we queried whether the SDGs were just a wish list. Governments are in a position to deliver some of them, mostly those that involve public services such as education and health. But what about sustainable agriculture, industrialization and infrastructure? Should not companies bear at least some responsibility for these aspects of development? The assumption underlying the SDGs seems to be that companies essentially pursue profits, not social goals, so companies bear no responsibilities where there is hunger (SDG1) or demeaning work (SDG8). The goal in SDG8 is to 'promote' decent work. But, as we have seen in the mini case study in this chapter, governments are loath to impose high standards of health and safety, for fear of raising costs for companies that might shift production to other, less-regulated, locations. On these assumptions, businesses are grounded in corporate cultures that do not commit them to social and environmental goals. Many would now hold that this situation is unsustainable, and that businesses do have responsibilities, even if the SDGs do not recognize them.

Business responsibilities

A question posed for business at the outset of this book was, 'what does the business exist to do?' It has raised a number of issues beyond the simple aims to make money to carry on producing goods and services. That narrow view of the business is purely economic, and is underpinned by a deeply engrained belief in the validity of self-interested profit-seeking. As this book has shown, however, businesses play roles in societies that go far beyond the economic dimension. Businesses are significant in influencing lifestyles and spending patterns. This role has become ever more powerful with the ubiquitous presence of the internet and social media in our lives. Business policies and activities are key to safe and healthy working conditions, standards of living, air quality, quality of healthcare, food safety, and adherence to human rights. The list could go on. These issues matter to people everywhere, and businesses are as instrumental as governments in determining how high, or low, the prevailing standards are.

A business might take the line that its goal is to maximize wealth for its owners, and it abides by the national laws in place in each country. It would also probably claim that it is thus a good citizen in each. However, this minimalist approach does not translate into the company taking on a sense of responsibility to all the stakeholders in that society. Corporate strategy in the global environment typically includes seeking ways to divert profits to low-tax jurisdictions and doing deals with governments to obtain legal advantages, including tax advantages. For many companies, it also includes denying workers the right to organize, despite labour laws at national and international level. Typically, workers who organize into unions are fired for an unrelated disciplinary reason such as bad timekeeping.

Companies where factory workers make toys for Disney are among those that have been found to be in breach of national laws and also codes of practice that toy manufacturers have established. Researchers for China Labour Watch, an NGO, found in 2018 that workers making Ariel dolls for Disney at a factory in the city of Heyuan were working excessively long hours, being paid beneath the minimum wage and being denied rest days. The workers – mostly women – lived in dormitories near the factory. Researchers found that they were being paid the equivalent of 1p per doll. The Ariel doll sold for £34.99 in retail outlets in the UK. Responding to these findings, a spokesman for Disney said that it subscribed to ethical sourcing principles and to its own code of conduct. He said it would ask the industry trade group to look into the conditions described (Chamberlain, 2018). The impression is that toymakers view these conditions of work as a sourcing issue that can be dealt with through supply-chain intermediaries. They do not – or do not wish to – see the human rights responsibilities that attach to their own company as a matter of international law.

Global brands that source products in developing countries regularly denounce the use of practices such as child labour, but those practices nonetheless continue. To disclaim responsibility in these circumstances is untenable. The companies whose brands appear on the products are responsible, but executives are well aware that they are never likely to be held liable for criminal wrongdoing. And in rare cases when they are, they are usually able to buy their way out of the penalties handed down by courts, simply as a cost of doing business. This was evident in the case study on the Sackler family (Chapter 11). Family members have become cultural philanthropists, distancing themselves from Purdue Pharma, their business empire based on the opioid painkiller, OxyContin. However, as directors, they could be considered liable for the misdeeds of the company.

Four former executives at Barclays Bank, including a former CEO, were prosecuted in the UK for fraud during the financial crisis of 2008, when the bank accepted an investment worth £4 billion from sovereign funds associated with the state of Qatar. The bank had been determined to avoid a bailout by the UK government, and the executives are accused of negotiating hidden fees to Qatar to clinch the investment. The judge in the case criticized the Serious Fraud Office for not adequately pursuing the crucial evidence during its six-year investigation. The former CEO was

acquitted in 2019, and the other three executives were to be retried. Fraud trials are particularly complex, and it is commonly the case that convictions, which must be beyond all reasonable doubt, are difficult to obtain. Very few bank executives have been convicted as a result of wrongdoings that led to the financial crisis, even though these were the people whose strategies brought down their banks. Most of the convictions were in Iceland, not in the financial centres of the US and UK. Convictions in the US have not been handed down to senior executives, but to traders and other agents working in financial services. The crimes targeted have been white collar crimes such as the mis-selling of mortgages, the rigging of interbank lending rates, and the misuse of bailout funds.

Concern about business reputation is one of the means by which a company can be encouraged to engage with social responsibility. Many companies have faced negative publicity for a time, during which they see falls in share values, but share prices soon rebound. In 2018, Facebook weathered a barrage of negative publicity over the misuse of personal data of 87 million users. Its share price fell 4%. It offered apologies and promised to take personal data more seriously (Chapter 6). These responses did not represent a major shift in policy. In just a few months, though, the share price had regained lost ground, user numbers were up and so were profits.

Consumers, workers and the public generally wish to see improved legal and ethical standards of the companies they depend on. Banking and financial services are among the most important, but so too are the tech giants that handle personal data. People feel entitled to adequate safety standards in products and workplaces, an end to tax evasion, and humane treatment of employees. In these respects, they are likely to be disappointed much of the time. These responsibilities are flouted with impunity, sidestepped or observed in name only. If compliance is not enforced by mandatory processes, it is not likely to be observed voluntarily, out of a sense of commitment to social responsibility. This is a sad commentary on business behaviour. It is one which, as we have seen, has become engrained in business culture, despite commitments to sustainability guidelines in their annual reports.

What are the prospects for a sustainable future?

To build a sustainable future requires commitment by all the players that have been highlighted in this chapter. They include businesses large and small, communities, governments, inter-governmental organizations and individuals. Most companies are short term in their focus on profits. In listed companies, executives focus on share price, justifying this preoccupation by the need to constantly deliver shareholder value. Would a long-term approach be closer to one that encompasses social responsibility? Arguably, it would. If businesses were persuaded that long-term sustainable goals are more likely to be profitable, would they alter their fixation with short-term profits? What would shareholders think? It is simplistic to assume that shareholders are interested only in short-term profits. Many are, and many fund investors build business models on this basis. However, shareholders should also be interested in a viable business that can be sustained into the future. If the business is viable, then profits, it is often said, will look after themselves. When Lyft, the ride-hailing company, listed on the Nasdaq in March, 2019, its shares saw a surge in price on the first day of trading, even though the company had never made a profit. IPOs of other young tech companies are in the pipeline, many with high valuations in the multiples of billions. Investors are excited by their potential, but these companies that burst on the scene will not all succeed.

Many investors now look at the links between financial performance and other indicators of viability. Institutional shareholders are now particularly aware of the ethical dimension of investments. Some are divesting shares in fossil fuel industries. This is an ethical decision, but it is also a business-oriented one. The risks associated with fossil fuels are now a major consideration in light of the urgency of climate change. We have seen that these businesses are highly ambivalent: they purport to promote sustainable solutions, but pursue increased investment in fossil fuel extraction, drag their heels on low-carbon projects and lobby actively against climate change measures. The fossil fuel companies and the countries that are subsidizing them, will have to adjust to a carbon-constrained future. A business-as-usual approach to oil extraction is no longer viable. In this instance, ethics and sustainability concerns point towards taking a longer-term approach. The responsibility falls squarely on the companies in these sectors, but this requires shifting to a long-term vision.

Globalization has been a driver of outsourced manufacturing, mainly in developing economies, but in many other countries besides. Poor treatment of workers, as has been shown, is not confined to shady subcontractors, nor to developing countries. Global brands such as Amazon, operating in western environments, are accused of human rights breaches. Numerous sectors in the UK, from garment factories to nail bars, operate in conditions akin to forced labour. It has been thought that the world has progressed beyond Dickensian workshop conditions, but modern methods, though more technologically advanced, are capable of imposing similar harsh conditions on workers. Many other practices, including zero-hours contracts and bogus self-employment, are also human rights violations, but persist nonetheless. The companies that run such businesses typically justify these practices as legitimate, aggressively defending them when challenged by workers in tribunals and courts. For these companies, such as delivery companies and ride-hailing companies, low-cost labour is core to their business models. Is this model sustainable? These are among the companies that are launching high-profile IPOs. The successful IPO can generate millions for founders overnight, but this does not guarantee a viable future. If regulatory changes intervene, as they do in many cities and countries, these companies must adjust radically or exit: this is one of the reasons they have difficulty generating profits.

These gig economy companies would be severely put out if they had to classify workers as employees. Improving conditions and pay, offering sick pay and holiday pay, offering genuine employment contracts for full-time commitment, and becoming liable for compensation for unfair dismissal: these would completely change their business models. These improvements could come about by legislation, compelling compliance, and governments are now being invited to take these steps. Businesses would have to adjust or exit the sector. It is worth remembering that, as we have highlighted in this chapter, decent employment and social protections did not happen automatically. They have been part of the gradual improvement in the nature of work, achieved through trade union representation and political reforms. They are now the benchmarks for governments everywhere, and are enshrined in UN human rights conventions. Individual and societal wellbeing are among the sustainable development goals indicated above. Exploitation of workers, along with rising poverty and inequality, risks setting back these improvements in living standards, especially in a context of weakening trade unions.

Large MNEs have led the way in globalization, aided by governments in, for example, FDI incentives. But, these same MNEs have also come into conflict with governments when socially responsible legislation is introduced. This tug-of-war

between corporate short-term interests and government policies has characterized the relationships between business and governments in most countries. Governments bear responsibility for legislation and regulatory policies that can make a difference to societal wellbeing. They can take initiatives in legislation on employment rights, safety at work, trade union and collective bargaining rights. They can also legislate on rules for more accountable corporate governance, compelling companies to take stakeholder concerns into account. They can tighten laws on offshore tax havens and tax avoidance. They can also legislate and enforce antitrust laws, to curb monopolists. They can introduce laws making social media companies more accountable for their content and their use of personal data. They can introduce strict emission laws to combat climate change. Most of the world's governments have signed up to commitments under the Paris accord. Governments have laws and regulatory policies on all these subjects, some stricter than others. But in liberal market economies such as the US and UK, the bias has been towards enterprise freedoms and against regulation. Laws in a number of these areas are enforced lightly. Voluntary codes are often seen as adequate substitutes. Regulators that are meant to be independent are heavily influenced by industry bodies, and enforcement is limited. Companies, for their part, are able to sidestep much regulation. Public opinion is a factor that can influence them to make changes, and this is becoming more influential.

Excessive greed was one of the aspects of the business culture that helped to bring down global banks in the financial crisis. Greed is not confined to bankers. CEO remuneration in the multiples of millions occurs in many industries, including those that provide public services, such as healthcare and education. Tech company founders have accumulated billions of dollars in wealth, and are now seeking to enhance their legacies as philanthropists (see the case study below). Increasingly, businesses are being subjected to critical public opinion, probing investigative journalism and scrutiny of their overall record in running their companies, along with their links to other companies. Much of what is uncovered reveals an unedifying picture of corporate executives acting unethically, deliberately covering up wrongful behaviour – all the while claiming ever-larger remuneration packages. Businesses, in theory, are accountable to shareholders for the good of the company as a whole, which should take in stakeholder interests. Boards could be required to include other stakeholders as directors. Workers are represented in the dual-board structure in many European jurisdictions, and worker representation has been proposed in the UK, but shelved. The stakeholder approach to boards would go some way towards a stakeholder model of capitalism.

The financial crisis should have been a turning point for building sustainable capitalism. Market economies are traditionally depicted as providing the best of all worlds: individual freedoms and economic growth that will deliver prosperity to all in society. Repeated financial crises have shown this to be false, but financial markets have seen little structural reform since 2008. Economic liberalism re-asserted itself with renewed vigour, aided by quantitative easing, which drove soaring stock markets and soaring executive pay. Dominant companies gain in market strength, undeterred by weak antitrust laws. But the post-crisis years have had widespread negative impacts. Human rights abuse on an industrial scale have continued unabated in manufacturing, while for many in post-industrial economies, there is little hope of a better tomorrow. Low- and middle-income workers have seen stagnating wages, widespread redundancy, under-employment and increased job insecurity. While companies could boast of the benefits of creative destruction, the grassroots view of those in the post-industrial landscape is one of being left behind to find work in low-paid and low-esteem jobs such as fast food. And even these jobs are at risk from automation. Their fears and frustrations did not arise overnight, but were the result of years of feeling overlooked by businesses that ignored stakeholder concerns and politicians that ignored grassroots interests.

The workers who lost jobs and houses in the financial crisis felt a bitterness that has not abated. They have ceased to trust the political establishment that should have responded to the social and economic upheavals of globalization. They have lived through years of stagnant wages during the recession that followed the financial crisis, while there has been a resurgence of the banks that were bailed out by governments. Feelings of voters that their voice does not matter give cause for concern that there is a dwindling faith in democratic institutions. Only 29% of Americans born in the 1980s think that it is 'essential' to live in a democracy, compared to 71% of those born in the 1930s (Mounk, 2018: 106–7). Among those born in the 1980s, 32% feel that a strong leader who does not bother with elections or Congress would be either good or very good (Mounk, 2018: 109).

Enter the populist, who plays on the fears of those who feel their voices are not being heard. The populist condemns the liberal democratic governments that have shaped the post-war era. But the populist's agenda is the antithesis of the values that would promote sustainability, save the planet from the ravages of climate change, and ensure that people everywhere can enjoy a decent way of life. Instead of liberalism, the populist stands for the tyranny of the majority. Believing in an idealized nativist heartland, minority rights would be suppressed. Instead of the rule of law, the strong would be free to impose their will on the weak. Instead of a free press, the media would be turned into a propaganda tool, and all other views would be 'fake news'. Instead of mutually beneficial trade with other countries, the strongman populist sees other countries as enemies in trade wars, in which the strong get their way over the weak. Instead of an international system based on co-operation, the populist view of the world is one of sovereign states seeking gains at the expense of each other.

The gradual decline in democratic institutions has gone hand in hand with the growing power of capitalist markets and their dominant companies. These are the large businesses that have shaped the era of globalization, now epitomized by the tech giants. They have thrived on an aggressive, acquisitive culture, denying the negative impacts of their activities. This was not inevitable, but a result of a warped view of capitalism that somehow became skewed towards the excesses of profit maximization above all other goals. Businesses could have taken a balanced, responsible approach to social purpose as well as pursuing the legitimate interests of their owners. This would have been sustainable, whereas unbridled profit maximization was not. Corporate titans thrived in the liberal market economies that allowed them the free rein they desired, but a result was to undermine the very institutions that allowed them to grow in the first place. These were the liberal democratic institutions that should have safeguarded the public interest, but in fact atrophied under the spread of market powerhouses, especially in the US.

Today's world presents a global business environment in which autocratic governments are on the rise and liberal democracies are under threat. Autocratic rulers are in control in many of the strong emerging economies. Democracies, old and new, are threatened by extremist ideologies in a highly polarized political landscape. What are the alternatives? The surest way to snuff out the appeal of the autocrat or the populist is to support sustainable democratic institutions, in which all views have voice and worth. Pluralism, like individual freedoms, thrives in an open atmosphere – which is the best environment for inspiring an enterprise culture in which business can flourish. Believers in liberal values coupled with social responsibility, both in government and business, still abound, and their message of dialogue, co-operation and human dignity points to the only sustainable way forward.

CLOSING CASE STUDY

Tech billionaires turn philanthropists

Today's tech CEOs control global corporate empires of immense economic power, and also personal wealth of many billions of dollars. Like the tycoons of earlier generations, having accumulated personal fortunes from their business success, their thoughts turn to their legacy. They might wish to 'give back' some of their wealth for charitable causes, to be remembered for making the world a better place. In today's financial environment, they might also be conscious that charitable structures are advantageous vehicles for tax purposes and for investing to enhance their wealth still further. The same attention to managing assets and controlling financial investments that helps them as successful CEOs comes into play in directing philanthropic activities. Thus, Bill Gates, Microsoft's founder, has built a parallel organization, the Bill and Melinda Gates Foundation, which is active in health provision in African developing countries, through its own projects, bypassing governments. It is bringing healthcare and disease prevention that are desperately needed. But this is not publicly accountable through democratic institutions. It is private-sector activity, accountable to its owners alone.

In 2015, Facebook's founder, Mark Zuckerberg, set up the Chan Zuckerberg Initiative with his wife, Priscilla Chan. He explained his aims as 'advancing human potential and promoting equality' (Rhodes and Bloom, 2018). Those ideals now look rather tarnished in light of revelations about Facebook's flagrant breaches of privacy law in pursuit of profits. It emerged that Mr Zuckerberg's initiative was not legally a charity, but a private company. In 2017, it gave $3 million to aid the housing crisis in Silicon Valley, where the concentration of tech companies has led to an astronomical rise in house prices. Those who listened to his idealistic sentiments on equality would justifiably feel they had been misled. Mr Zuckerberg would have learnt that his philanthropic intentions arouse accusations of hypocrisy.

Amazon's CEO, Jeff Bezos, announced in 2018 that he would give $2 billion to a new philanthropic fund for primary schools and housing for the homeless. Although this large sum is intended for social betterment, the announcement fell on a sceptical public. Amazon warehouses are notoriously managed as highly regimented and stressful places to work. Some workers at Amazon's warehouses have resorted to camping in tents next to their workplace, as they cannot afford housing on their low pay. Amazon workers would say he should improve the pay and conditions of his own workers, and allow trade unions to operate. But, of course, his ruthlessness is key to his business success – and his wealth. In Seattle, where Amazon is based, he opposed a local law designed to tackle the area's homelessness crisis.

Amazon paid no federal income tax for the second year running in 2018, despite seeing a doubling of profits from $5.6 billion in 2017 to $11.2 billion in 2018. In fact, it received a rebate of $270 million in 2018. Following a competition among a number of cities, Amazon had planned to build a second headquarters in Long Island City, New York. Cities were unashamedly competing on the lavishness of their tax incentives. The Long Island

The private jet symbolizes the lifestyle of today's billionaire business elites, presiding over empires that span continents. Have they made the world a better place?

location would have been worth nearly $3 billion in state and local subsidies, as well as tax breaks. The company envisaged 25,000 jobs, and the local Democratic establishment approved. There was also support among local residents. But a mixture of opponents, including trade unions and the progressive Democrat, Alexandria Ocasio-Cortez, newly elected to Congress, were opposed, and mounted a campaign against the plan. They feared a rise in house prices and objected particularly to the tax breaks. Hostile questioning of company representatives in a city council meeting focused on Amazon's labour practices globally and on its facial recognition technology that was sold to US Immigration and Customs Enforcement. Amazon decided to pull out of the plan to build in Long Island, rather than to negotiate a way forward.

Today's multibillionaires have been able to build their fortunes not simply because of their entrepreneurial flair, but because the free market economy allows the self-interested accumulation of huge wealth in the hands of the few. For those at the top, what matters most is that this system will be perpetuated by government policies. Specifically, they require a business environment of minimal regulation, few employment rights, weak trade unions and low taxes. They favour low public spending on social programmes, but are happy to accept government money themselves. Policies so tilted towards the owners of wealth and away from the millions beneath them create highly unequal societies. Market economies have thus evolved into market societies, stacked against those at the bottom. For those at the top, concentration of economic power brings political influence in the corridors of government. And their impacts in society are also channelled through educational institutions, political parties, think tanks and charitable foundations. Indeed, many of these, including educational trusts and quasi-research think tanks are legally charitable, not-for-profit organizations.

Problems of poverty, homelessness, inadequate education and poor healthcare are universal. Good governance in any society should ideally seek sustainable and inclusive policies through public accountability. That is the ideal, but in reality, governments are beholden to the powerful elites in society, which means the rich and powerful business interests.

The philanthropist is often drawn to idealistic goals of 'giving back', helping the poor, or funding education. Why not just pay taxes and give to charities? A founder like Mr Zuckerberg wishes his charitable activity to be carried out as he would carry out his business: controlling where the money goes and how the money is spent. His spending on good causes follows the same market orientation as his business activities. Philanthropy thus becomes market oriented. The winners from the inequalities of the system see themselves as the right people to redress the inequalities that they have been largely responsible for creating. In these ways, they extend their sphere of control, penetrating ever more deeply into society.

Questions

- What is the tech billionaire's view of philanthropy?
- Describe the tech CEOs' relationship with government and politicians, as shown in this case study.
- New Yorkers in the area of Long Island City were divided on the building of a new Amazon HQ. Which side would you have been on, and why?
- Look at the question posed in the caption of the photo. Have they made the world a better place?

Further reading

See the article, 'Questioning generosity in the golden age of philanthropy: Towards critical geographies of super-philanthropy', by Iain Hay and Samantha Muller, *Progress in Human Geography*, 2014, Vol. 38(5): 635–53.

Multiple choice questions

Visit www.macmillanihe.com/morrison-gbe-5e to take a quick self-test quiz on what you have read in this chapter.

Review questions

1 What are the aspects of sustainability that relate to individual and societal wellbeing?
2 Why are there fears that the challenges of climate change are not being met?
3 Why does inequality threaten sustainable growth?
4 What are the pros and cons of the gig economy?
5 To what extent can China be criticized as an example of sustainable development?
6 What are the threats to good governance?
7 How does the Corruption Perception Index provide lessons for business?
8 How has the recovery from the global financial crisis caused continuing concern for governments and businesses?
9 Levels of extreme poverty have declined globally, but poverty remains a global problem. Why?
10 Why has rising nationalism around the world posed threats to democracy and political stability?
11 Why are fossil fuel companies at the forefront of concerns over climate change?
12 What should governments be doing to tackle the threats to human rights in the working environments within their countries?
13 To what extent are businesses justified in thinking that any of their ethical shortcomings will soon be forgotten by customers?
14 Why are the sustainable development goals (SDGs) likely to be seen as difficult for governments to deliver?
15 How could businesses commit to relevant SDGs?

✓ Assignments

1 The poorest developing countries face challenges of sustainable development, and yet, they are among the countries that are most threatened by the impacts of climate change. Analyze the ways in which governments and businesses could improve the prospects for inclusive growth and sustainable development in these least-developed countries.

2 Governments bear the main responsibility for regulatory changes that can reduce inequality, tame the large corporations such as tech giants, and improve adherence to human rights. Although politicians and the public would all probably agree that these are laudable goals, governments in most liberal democracies tend to be timid in exerting stricter controls to deal with these issues. What should they be doing under each of these headings, to achieve these goals?

Further reading

Aglietta, M. and G. Bai (2015) *China's Development: Capitalism and Empire* (Rethinking Globalizations) (Routledge).

Collier, P. (2014) *Exodus: Immigration and multiculturalism in the 21st Century* (Penguin).

Deaton, A. (2013) *The Great Escape: Health, wealth and the origins of inequality* (Princeton: Princeton University Press).

Dorling, D. (2015) *Inequality and the 1%* (Verso Books).

Mounk, Y. (2018) *The People vs. Democracy* (Cambridge, MA: Harvard University Press).

Stiglitz, J. (2013) *The Price of Inequality* (London: Penguin).

Tepper, J. (2019) *The Myth of Capitalism* (Hoboken, NJ: Wiley).

Woodward, D. (2015) 'Incrementum ad Adsurdum: Global growth, inequality and poverty eradication in a carbon-constrained world', *World Economic Review*, 4: 43–62.

❒ References

ACLED (Armed Conflict Location and Event Data Project) (2018) ACLED 2018: The year in review, at www.acleddata.com

Borghesi, S. and Vercelli, A. (2003) 'Sustainable globalisation', *Ecological Economics*, 44: 77–89.

Carrington, D. (2019) 'Microplastic pollution revealed absolutely everywhere by new research', *The Guardian*, 7 March.

Chamberlain, G. (2018) 'Revealed: Disney's Ariel doll earns a Chinese worker 1p', *The Guardian*, 6 December.

Cullen, A. (2018) *Storm Lake* (New York: Viking).

Diamond, L. (1997) 'Is the third wave of democratization over?', Working Paper #237, March, Kellogg Institute for International Studies, at https://kellogg.nd.edu

EIU (The Economist Intelligence Unit) (2018) *Democracy Index 2018*, at www.eiu.com

Harvey, F. (2019) 'Global coal use up as greenhouse gas emissions rise', *The Guardian*, 26 March.

Health Effects Institute (2019) *State of Global Air: 2019*, at https://stateofglobalair.org

IMF (2019) World Economic Outlook Update, January 2019, opening remarks by Christine Lagarde, Managing Director, at www.imf.org

Kirişci, K., Brandt, J. and Erdoğan, M. (2018) 'Syrian refugees in Turkey: Beyond the numbers', Brookings Institution, 19 June, at www.brookings.edu

McCarthy, T. (2019) 'Trump's legacy: Conservative judges who will dominate US law for decades', *The Guardian*, 10 March.

Mounk, Y. (2018) *The People vs. Democracy* (Cambridge, MA: Harvard University Press).

Laville, S. (2019) 'Top oil firms spending millions lobbying to block climate change policies, says report', *The Guardian*, 22 March.

Luce, E. (2018) 'The 1930s playbook', *Financial Times*, 23 June.

OECD (2019) *Under Pressure: The squeezed middle class* (Paris: OECD), at https://doi.org

Pew Research Center (2015) 'The American middle class is losing ground', *Social and Demographic Trends*, 9 December, at www.pewsocialtrends.org

Reich, R. (2015) *Saving Capitalism: For the many, not the few* (Knopf Publishing).

Rhodes, C. and Bloom, P. (2018) 'The trouble with charitable billionaires', *The Guardian*, 24 May.

Safi, M. (2018) 'Bangladesh garment factories sack hundreds after pay protest', *The Guardian*, 17 December.

World Bank (2018) *Poverty and Shared Prosperity, Piecing together the poverty puzzle*, at https://openknowledge.worldbank.org

Visit the companion website at www.macmillanihe.com/morrison-gbe-5e for further learning and teaching resources.

GLOSSARY

A

absolute advantage advantage enjoyed by a country which is more efficient at producing a particular product than any other country

acid rain acid from greenhouse gases that falls out of the atmosphere, in the form of rain or wind-blown gases

acquisition investment in which an investor purchases an existing company; a type of FDI if the company is in a foreign location

affiliate company organization connected through ownership stake or other strategic ties to an MNE, often in supply chains

ageing demographic trend characterized by a rising proportion of older people in a population

Andean Community South American free trade area

anti-dumping agreement WTO rules which allow anti-dumping duties to be imposed on the exporting country by the importing country, in order to protect local producers from unfair competition

arbitration the submission of a legal dispute to a named person or organization in accordance with a contractual agreement

arm's length contracting business dealings between people who interact only for the purpose of doing business with each other

artificial intelligence (AI) area of computer science which researches ways in which machines can be developed to work and solve problems like humans

Asian Infrastructure Investment Bank (AIIB) development bank launched by China, providing funding on a similar basis to the World Bank

assimilation of cultures process by which minority cultures become integrated into the mainstream culture of a nation

Association of Southeast Asian Nations (Asean) co-operation agreement of South East Asian countries

Asia Pacific Economic Co-operation Group (Apec) co-operation agreement of economies bordering on the Pacific

asylum right of a person to live in another country, granted on application to authorities in that country, and based on showing a well-founded fear of persecution in the person's home country

authoritarianism rule by a single leader or group of individuals, often sustained by an ideology associated with a one-party state

B

balance of payments total credit and debit transactions between a country's residents (including companies) and those of other countries over a specified period of time

bilateral treaty agreement between two countries, often for reciprocal trade terms

biodiversity the variety of living organisms and species co-existing in the same habitat

board of directors body comprising all the directors of a company, including executive and non-executive, which is accountable to the company's shareholders; can be a single board or a two-tier board

bond a loan instrument which promises to pay a specific sum of money on a fixed date, and to pay interest at stated intervals

born-global firm SME which aims to become global from the outset, often in high-technology sectors

Bretton Woods agreement agreement between allied nations in the aftermath of the Second World War, which was intended to bring about exchange rate stability and foster multilateral agreements to dismantle trade barriers

Brexit name given to the process whereby the UK would exit the EU

BRIC countries collective reference to Brazil, Russia, India and China, as a grouping of emerging economies

Buddhism Asian religion based on the teachings of Buddha

business any type of economic activity in which goods or services (or a combination of the two) are supplied in exchange for some payment, usually money

business case for CSR argument that business goals will be met more successfully in the longer term through CSR than through a narrow focus on economic goals

business model a broad term covering an organization's reasons for existing, its goals and the means it adopts to achieve them

C

capital account in connection with an economy's balance of payments, account based on transactions involving the sale and purchase of assets, such as investment in shares

capitalism economic system based on market principles, entailing an exchange of something of value, such as labour, for something else, typically a 'price' in the form of wages

carbon footprint the amount of greenhouse gases produced either directly or indirectly by an organization or country

cartel group of firms that come together, often informally, to restrict trade or engage in anti-competitive behaviour

caste system social stratification system based on birth, associated with Hinduism

categorical imperative ethical principle put forward by Kant that respect for every human being should be the guiding principle for behaviour

chaebol family-dominated industrial conglomerate characteristic of business organizations in South Korea

checks and balances principle by which the three branches of government (legislative, executive and judicial) share legal authority and accountability

chief executive officer (CEO) a company's senior executive, who oversees its management and is accountable to the board of directors

child labour work that is mentally, physically, socially or morally damaging to children, and interferes with their schooling

Christianity monotheistic religion based on belief in Jesus Christ, whose teachings are in the Bible

civil law tradition legal system based on comprehensive legal codes which form the basic law

civil (or private) law law pertaining to relations between private individuals and companies

civil society sphere of activities in society in which citizens are free to pursue personal interests and form associations freely

climate change any change in the climate over time, whether from natural causes or human activity

coalition government government composed of two or more parties, usually arising in situations where no single party has obtained a majority of seats in legislative elections

codes of practice sets of rules which companies voluntarily follow to guide their CSR, ethical and the environmental practices

co-determination principle of stakeholder participation in corporate governance, usually involving a two-tier board, with employee representation on the supervisory board

common law tradition legal system based chiefly on accumulated case law in decided judgments, through a system of binding precedents

common market regional grouping in which member states enjoy free movement of goods, labour and capital

Common Market for Eastern and Southern Africa (COMESA) common market of Eastern and Southern African countries

community interest company (CIC) a limited company set up to function as a social enterprise, which adheres to strict statutory requirements for adhering to social purposes

company legal form of organization that has a separate legal identity from its owner(s)

comparative advantage advantage enjoyed by a country where production of a particular product involves greater relative advantage than would be possible anywhere else

competitive advantage theory (devised by Porter) that international competitiveness depends on four major factors: demand conditions, factor conditions, firms' strategy and supporting industries

competition law area of law which concerns rules against abuse of a dominant market position and unfair trading practices by one or more firms

Confucianism ancient Chinese ethical and philosophical system based on the teachings of Confucius

conglomerate large, diversified company, in which there is no single identifiable core business

consequentialist principle utilitarian principle that the test of the rightness or wrongness of an action depends on the results which flow from it

constitutionalism set of rules, grounded in a society's shared beliefs, about the source of authority in the state and its institutional forms

consumer price index (CPI) index which tracks the percentage rise or fall in prices, with reference to a particular starting point in time

contextualism in ethical thinking, the principle that ideas of right and wrong stem from specific cultural environments

corporate citizenship concept which visualizes social responsibility of the firm in the community as analogous to that of the individual citizen, entailing obligations to obey the law and pay taxes

corporate governance the highest decision-making structures and processes in the company

corporate social performance (CSP) concept associated with CSR in practice which focuses on responses to stakeholders and broader issues of business in society

corporate social responsibility (CSR) an approach to business which recognizes that the organization has responsibilities in society beyond the economic role, extending to legal, ethical, environmental and social roles

creative destruction process by which new technologies and ways of doing things replace the old, bringing about changes in economic structures

criminal law laws that designate offences and set out legal procedure for prosecution of those charged with breaches; can be contained in a criminal code

cultural convergence diverse cultures gradually becoming more alike through increasing interactions

cultural distance in cross-border business relations, cultural gap between those involved, especially where the parties are from very different cultural environments

cultural divergence differences among cultures, especially those that persist despite globalization

culture a shared way of life of a group of socially interacting people

current account in connection with an economy's balance of payments, account based on trade in goods, services, and profits and interest earned from overseas assets

customs union regional grouping in which member states remove all trade barriers among themselves and adopt a common set of external barriers

D

debt financing raising capital by borrowing

deflation general decline in prices in an economy, associated with recession and falling demand

deforestation the felling of forests for fuel or to use the land for other purposes

democracy system of elected government based on free and fair elections and universal suffrage

demographic change changes in whole populations brought about by rises and falls in the birth rate and death rate, as well as migration

depression situation in which an economy deteriorates significantly, diminishing by one-tenth in size

derivative financial instrument whose value is dependent on another asset class such as stock

developed countries countries whose economies have become industrialized and have reached high income levels

developing countries countries in the process of industrialization and building technological capacity

directors individuals appointed by the company to bear ultimate responsibility for the company's activities; collectively referred to as the board of directors

Dispute Settlement Understanding (DSU) WTO framework for the settlement of trade disputes between member states

dumping the sale of goods abroad at below the price charged for comparable goods in the producing country

E

East African Community (EAC) common market of East African countries

eclectic paradigm theory of FDI by Dunning, based on three sets of advantages: ownership (O), location (L) and internalization (I); also known as the 'OLI' paradigm

ecology study of the relationship between organisms and their environment

Economic and Monetary Union (EMU) EU programme centred on the single currency and an independent central bank that sets monetary policy for eurozone member states

Economic Community of West African States (Ecowas) organization for co-operation among West African states

economic development can refer to any change in a country's overall balance of economic activities, but usually refers to industrialization and resultant changes in society

economic growth a country's increase in national income over time; negative growth occurs where the economy is contracting

economic indicators statistical measures used to analyze a national economy; notable indicators are economic growth and GDP per capita

economic union regional grouping in which member states unify all their economic policies, including monetary, fiscal and welfare policies

emerging economy fast-growing developing country, typically becoming increasingly globalized

employee person who works for another (the employer), usually for wages, and whose work is controlled by the employer

empowerment approach to management that focuses on individual responsibility

entrepreneur person who starts up a business and imbues it with the energy and drive necessary to compete in markets

environmental degradation environmental change caused mainly by human activity which has detrimental effects on ecological systems

environmental management assessing environmental impacts and devising suitable strategies across a company's total operations

environmental, social and governance reporting (ESG) reporting framework for companies that covers a range of CSR issues, including human rights and responses to environmental pollution

equity in corporate finance, the share capital of a company

equity financing raising capital by issuing shares

ethical relativism approach to ethics which holds that principles are not absolute, but dependent on values that differ from culture to culture

ethics the study of basic concepts of good and bad, right and wrong, which relate to all people as human beings

ethnocentrism unquestioning belief that one's own culture and ways of doings things are the best

euro the single currency of the EU

eurobond a bond denominated in a currency other than the one of the country in which it is issued

European Convention on Human Rights (ECHR) convention on human rights adopted by members of the Council of Europe

European Court of Human Rights international court that hears cases arising under the European Convention on Human Rights

European Court of Justice (ECJ) highest court for interpreting EU law

European Economic Area (EEA) grouping of EFTA and the EU, forming a single market

European Free Trade Area (EFTA) grouping formed in 1960 by countries not signed up to the Treaty of Rome (which created what is now the EU)

European Patent Office (EPO) patent office of the EU

European Union (EU) regional grouping of European countries which evolved from trade agreements to deeper economic integration

eurozone member states of the EU which have satisfied the Maastricht criteria and joined the EMU

executive the function of government that administers the laws and policies

executive directors directors who actively manage the company

export selling products in a country other than the one in which they were made

export processing zones (EPZ) geographic areas where goods can be imported and exported duty-free

F

Fairtrade Foundation a charity that promotes a fair deal for poor agricultural producers in developing countries, licensing producer organizations to use the Fairtrade logo

foreign direct investment (FDI) investment in productive assets in a foreign country with a view to exerting control over operations

FDI inflows aggregate value of investments which flow into a country

FDI inward stock the total value of foreign investments that a country has attracted

FDI outflows aggregate value of investments from a country's organizations to overseas destinations

FDI outward stock the total value of foreign investments made by a country's nationals

federal system system of government in which authority is divided between the centre and regional units

fiduciary duty duty of trust to act honestly and in the best interests of another; applies to the duty of directors owed to their company

finance and accounting business function which concerns control over the revenues and outgoings of the business, aiming to balance the books and to generate sufficient profits for the future health of the firm

first-mover advantage precept that countries or firms which are first to produce a new product gain an advantage in markets which makes it virtually impossible for others to catch up

fiscal policy budgetary policies for balancing public spending with taxation and other income in a national economy

forced labour work that people are compelled to do against their will

Fordism approach to an industrial organization based on large factories producing standardized products for mass consumption, named after the automobile magnate, Henry Ford

for-profit organizations businesses that aim to make money

franchise/franchising business agreement by which a business (the franchisee) uses the brand, products and business format of another firm (the franchisor) under licence

free trade agreement (FTA) trade agreement between countries which aims to liberalize trade between them; can be bilateral or multilateral

free trade area regional grouping in which member states agree to remove trade barriers among themselves, but keep their separate national barriers against trade with non-member states

functional areas activities of a business which form part of the overall process of producing and delivering a product for a customer

futures contract contract to carry out a particular transaction on a designated date in the future

G

G20 grouping of 20 developed, developing and emerging economies, brought together by the IMF in 1999, which meets regularly, focusing mainly on financial stability

General Agreement on Tariffs and Trade (GATT) series of multilateral agreements on reducing trade barriers

genetically-modified organisms (GMOs) plants and animals that have been altered genetically in ways that do not occur in nature

gig economy category of work in which the person's working life consists of moving from one job to another, typically working as a self-employed person

Gini index tool used by economists to measure income inequality

globalization processes by which products, people, companies, money and information are able to move quickly around the world

globalization of markets MNEs' ability to serve consumers across the world with their products, taking account of different products for different national markets

globalized production MNEs' ability to locate different stages of production in the most advantageous location; associated with supply chains

global warming global rise in temperatures impacting on all forms of life, caused by the build-up of greenhouse gases in the earth's atmosphere

gold standard the setting of exchange rates based on the value of gold

governance a broader concept than 'government', involving interactions among a range of governmental and

quasi-governmental bodies, as well as civil society organizations

government structures and processes of the state by which laws are made and administered; also refers to the particular office holders at any given time

greenfield investment FDI which focuses on a new building project, such as a factory in a foreign location

greenhouse gases (GHGs) mixture of heat-trapping gases, mainly carbon dioxide (CO_2)

gross domestic product (GDP) the value of the total economic activity produced within a country in a single year, including both domestic and foreign producers

gross national income (GNI) the total income from all the final products and services produced by a national economy within a single year

Group of Seven (G7) grouping of 7 advanced economies (US, Canada, UK, France, Germany, Italy, and Japan)

guanxi personal relations which establish the trust and mutual obligations necessary for business in China

H

hedge a financial tool or arrangement which insures a firm against adverse currency movements in its international financial activities.

hedge fund investment fund managed by an individual or firm which is active in securities markets

high-context culture culture in which communication relies heavily on the behavioural dimension, such as 'body language'

Hinduism polytheistic religion whose followers are concentrated in India

holding company an umbrella company that owns the multiple companies or divisions that make up the business

horizontal integration merger or acquisition between two or more companies in the same industry

Human Development Index (HDI) UN ranking of countries according to three sets of criteria: economic, health (including life expectancy) and education

human resource management (HRM) all aspects of the management of people in the organization, including recruitment, training, and rewarding the workforce

human rights basic, universal rights enjoyed by all individuals, wherever they are, which transcend social and cultural differences

hybrid system a system of government in which the president is directly elected, and the prime minister, who heads the cabinet, is chosen by the legislative assembly

I

ideology all-encompassing system of beliefs and values, or world-view

import the purchase of goods or services from a supplier in another country

import quota a barrier to trade which consists of limiting the quantity of an imported product that can legally enter a country

import substitution approach to economic development which favours producing goods for domestic consumption that otherwise would have been imported

inclusive growth economic growth that brings improved living standards and greater economic security for all in a society

independent trade union organization of workers unconnected to owners of the business or government

industrialization transformation of an economy from mainly agricultural production for domestic consumption to one based on factory production, with potential for export

inequality the difference in wealth or income between the richest and poorest in society

inflation the continuing general rise in prices in an economy

initial public offering (IPO) first offering by a company of its shares to the public on a stock exchange; also known as 'flotation'

innovation wide range of activities which seek new and improved products and services, and new ways of carrying out an organization's activities

innovation system the structures and institutions by which a country's innovation activities are encouraged and facilitated, both directly and indirectly

intangible assets rights over products, such as trademarks and patents, which can be exploited commercially; they can be contrasted with tangible assets.

intellectual property (IP) property in intangible assets, such as patents, copyrights and trademarks, which can be legally protected

interconnectedness improved communications across national borders, facilitated mainly by advances in technology, computing and the internet

interdependence links based on complementarities and co-operation between two or more countries or organizations.

inter-generational justice concept which underlies the principle of sustainability, implying that moral obligations are owed to future generations

Intergovernmental Panel on Climate Change (IPCC) UN body of scientists that brings together evidence of climate change and issues reports of their findings

intermediate goods components and parts which cross national borders before being made into final products

international business business activities that straddle two or more countries.

International Centre for the Settlement of Investor Disputes (ICSID) tribunal system set up by the World Bank which is tasked with handling investor-state disputes arising under treaties

International Covenant on Civil and Political Rights (ICCPR) UN convention on human rights, covering civil and political rights, recognized in international law

International Covenant on Economic, Social and Cultural Rights (ICESCR) UN convention on human rights, covering economic, social and cultural rights, recognized in international law

International Court of Justice (ICJ) UN-sponsored international court which hears legal cases relating to disputes between member states

International Criminal Court (ICC) court established under the auspices of the UN and the International Court of Justice, which hears cases involving crimes against humanity, war crimes and crimes of aggression

International Labour Organization (ILO) UN organization that sets international labour standards

international law body of rules recognized by the international community as governing relations between sovereign states

International Monetary Fund (IMF) agency of the UN which oversees the international monetary and financial systems

International Organization for Standardization (ISO) body which oversees quality and environmental standards recognized across industries

international poverty line line representing extreme poverty, defined as living on less than $1.90 a day

invention product or process which can be described as 'new' in that it makes a significant qualitative leap forward from the state of existing knowledge

investor-state dispute settlement (ISDS) provision in a treaty that allows companies from one of the ratifying countries who invest in another ratifying country to bring cases in a tribunal when they feel their businesses have been prejudiced in the host country

Islam monotheistic religion based on the teachings of the prophet Muhammad, as revealed in the Koran; followers are referred to as Muslims

J

joint venture an agreement between companies to form a new entity to carry out a business purpose, often an FDI project

judicial the function of government that interprets the law and provides checks on the other two branches

judicial system system of courts, usually divided between civil courts and criminal courts

just-in-time (JIT) system which relies on a continuous flow of materials, governed by split-second timing

K

keiretsu grouping of Japanese companies characterized by inter-firm ties and cross-shareholdings

L

law rule or body of rules perceived as binding because it emanates from state authorities with powers of enforcement

lean production approach to mass production that aims to reduce waste and maintain continuous flow; associated with Japanese car company, Toyota

least-developed countries the world's poorest developing countries

legal risk uncertainties surrounding legal liabilities, their implementation in differing legal systems, and the observance of fairness and impartiality in judicial proceedings in differing locations

legislation laws enacted by lawmaking processes set out in national constitutions; also known as statute law

legislative the lawmaking function within government

legislative assembly body of elected representatives within a state, which has lawmaking responsibilities

leverage extent to which a company relies on debt financing

leveraged buy-out (LBO) acquisition of a company's equity by a firm or group of individuals financed by borrowing

liberal market economy capitalist economic system in which supply and demand, as well as prices, are determined by free markets; also known as the free market economy

limited liability principle that the shareholder is liable up to the amount invested in the company

litigation the use of judicial procedures and the court system to bring claims for damages and other remedies in legal disputes

lobbying political activities of businesses and other groups that seek to influence policies, laws and the decisions made by public officeholders

local content requirements trade policy that requires foreign investors to use local component suppliers in, for example, manufacturing

location advantages inherent advantages of a country or region, such as access to transport, access to raw materials and low labour costs

low-context culture culture in which communication is clear and direct, rather than relying on patterns of behaviour

M

macroeconomics the study of national economies

management all the processes of planning, organizing and controlling the firm's business

market mechanisms for exchange of something of value, usually goods or services, for a price, usually money

marketing satisfying the needs and expectations of customers; includes a range of related activities, such as product offering, branding, advertising, pricing, and distribution of goods

mercantilism in international trade, the approach of a country which sees trade mainly as promoting its own economic gains

Mercosur South American common market

merger coming together of two or more companies to form a new company

microeconomics the study of economic activity at the level of individuals and firms

migration movement of people from one place to another, which can be within a country or between countries, with a view to making a new life in the new location

Millennium Development Goals (MDGs) Goals designated by the UN Millennium Summit of 2000, which set targets for improving human wellbeing in developing regions

mixed economy economic system which combines market elements with state controls

modes of internationalization methods by which companies expand internationally

monetary policy economic policies for determining the amount of money in supply, rates of interest and exchange rates

monopoly domination by one firm over the market for particular goods or services, enabling the firm to determine price and supply

morality standards of behaviour considered right and wrong

most-favoured nation principle (MFN) GATT principle by which the most favourable tariff treatment negotiated with one country is extended to similar goods from all countries

multilateral treaty international agreement binding many countries

multinational enterprise (MNE) an organization which acquires ownership (whole or partial) or other contractual ties in other organizations (including companies and unincorporated businesses) outside its home country

multi-party system system in which many political parties participate, representing a wide spectrum of views

N

national budget balance the extent to which public spending exceeds receipts from taxes and other sources

national culture distinctive values, behavioural norms and shared history which distinguish one nation from another

national debt the total debt accumulated by a central government's borrowings over the years

national economy the aggregate of economic activities of governments, businesses and individuals, within the national framework of a nation-state

nationalism belief system that is based on the cultural identity, interests and right of self-determination of a nation or people

nation-state social, administrative and territorial unit into which the world's peoples are divided

negligence breach of a duty to take reasonable care which causes injury or other harm to another; actionable in civil courts

non-executive directors part-time company directors who are independent of the firm's management and owners

non-governmental organization (NGO) voluntary organization formed by private individuals for a particular shared purpose, often humanitarian

non-tariff barriers national legal requirements, such as health and safety standards, that act to prevent the imports from other countries that are not in conformity

North American Free Trade Agreement (NAFTA) free trade area comprising the US, Canada and Mexico

not-for-profit organizations organizations such as charities, which exist for specific good causes in societies

O

offshoring term covering an outsourced activity that can be carried out in a jurisdiction where weak regulation and tax advantages offer attractions

oligopoly domination of an industry by a few very large firms

operations the entire process of producing and delivering a product to a consumer; covers tangible goods and services, and often a combination of both

option contractual device used to allow a person or company the right to purchase something of value at a future date

organizational culture an organization's values, behavioural norms and management style; also known as corporate culture

Organisation for Economic Co-operation and Development (OECD) organization of the world's mainly developed, high-income economies, which supports market economies and democratic institutions

outsourced production as a mode of internationalization, contractual arrangement whereby a company has its branded products produced by another company in a foreign location

outsourcing term covering any activity which an organization considers can be more advantageously carried out by another firm, often in another country

ownership advantages resources specific to a firm, such as patents, which can be exploited for competitive advantage

P

parliamentary system system of government in which voters directly elect members of parliament, from whom a prime minister is chosen

patent type of intellectual property which gives its owner an exclusive right for a limited period to exploit the invention, to license others to use it, and to stop all unauthorized exploitation of the invention

patentable invention a new product or process which can be applied industrially

'pegged' exchange rate exchange rate which links the value of a currency to that of another, usually stronger, currency

PESTLE analysis of a national environment which stands for political, economic, socio-cultural, technological, legal and environmental dimensions

philanthropy voluntary giving of money or other resources to good causes, often charities

planned economy economic system based on total state ownership of the means of production, in which the state controls prices and output

pluralism existence in society of a multiplicity of groups and interests independent of the state

plurilateral trade agreement trade agreement among a number of countries in different regions that come together deliberately for the purpose of liberalizing trade and investment among them; separate from the WTO's multilateral system

political party organization of people with similar political beliefs, which aims to put forward candidates for office and influence government policies

political risk uncertainties associated with the exercise of governmental power within a country, and from external forces

political union regional grouping in which member states transfer sovereignty to the regional political and law-making institutions, creating a new 'superstate'

politics processes by which a social group allocates the exercise of power and authority for the group as a whole

polycentrism openness to other cultures and ways of doing things

populism political ideology or movement based on restoring power to 'the people', as opposed to existing political elites; often based on nationalist values and anti-immigrant rhetoric

portfolio investment buying shares or other securities of a company, with a view to making a financial gain

presidential system system of government in which the head of the executive branch, the president, is elected by the voters, either directly or through an electoral college (as in the US)

primary production agriculture, mining and fishing

primary stakeholders stakeholders directly involved in a firm's business

private equity fund investment fund managed on behalf of wealthy investors, which is active in equity markets

private international law the body of law for determining which national law pertains in cases between individuals and companies in different countries

private limited company company whose shares are not publicly traded on a stock exchange

privatization process of transforming a state-owned enterprise into a public company and selling off a proportion of shares to the public, usually involving the government retaining a controlling stake

product liability liability of a producer of a defective product to consumers harmed by the product; can extend to suppliers

product life cycle theory theory of the evolution of a product in stages, from innovation in its home market to dissemination and production in overseas markets

product recall withdrawal of a product from the marketplace due to defects which might cause harm to consumers

production under licence production of a product by a contractor under an agreement whereby it obtains permission from the company owning the brand, designs, patent or other IP rights

proportional representation principle underlying systems of electoral representation in which seats are allocated in proportion to the votes obtained by each candidate or party

prosperity in an economy, healthy economic growth and rising standards of living

protectionism government trade policy of favouring home producers and discouraging imports

public limited company company which lists on a stock exchange and offers shares to the public

public law body of law covering relations between citizens and the state

'pull' factors factors in a country which attract foreign investors

purchasing power parity (PPP) means of estimating the number of units of the foreign currency which would be needed to buy goods or services equivalent to those that the US dollar would buy in the US

'push' factors factors in a company's home country which persuade it to seek growth potential overseas

Q

quantitative easing (QE) monetary policy of creating money to purchase assets, mainly government bonds, with the aim of stimulating the economy

R

realpolitik view of international relations based on power politics

reasonable care test used in law to determine whether a person has acted negligently

recession two consecutive quarters of negative economic growth in an economy

referendum a type of direct democracy in which electors cast a vote on a particular issue

refugee person forced to move to another country for safety reasons

Regional Comprehensive Economic Partnership (RECEP) regional free trade area encompassing ASEAN members and partner countries

regionalization growing economic links and co-operation within a geographic region, both on the part of businesses and governments

regional trade agreement (RTA) free trade agreement among a number of countries in the same broad geographic region

regulation broad term covering laws and rules relating to a particular type of activity or sector; covers both formal legal requirements and less formal guidance such as codes of practice

relational contracting business dealings in which personal relations between the parties are more important than formal written agreements

religion set of beliefs and moral precepts which guide people in their lives

remittances money sent by migrant workers back to their families in their home location

renewable energy energy from natural sources such as wind, sun and water, whereby the sources are naturally replenished

research and development (R&D) seeking new knowledge and applications which can lead to new and improved products or processes

rule of law principle of supremacy of the law over both governments and citizens, entailing equality before the law and an independent judiciary

S

scientific management theory of management in which each worker's task is strictly defined and is part of a production process that is controlled in minute detail; devised by Frederick Taylor

secondary production industrial production, concentrated in factories

secondary stakeholders stakeholders indirectly involved in a firm's business

Securities and Exchange Commission (SEC) US stock market regulator

self-employed person/sole trader person who is in business on his or her own account

separation of powers the division between legislative, executive and judicial functions, or branches

share in a company, represents ownership of the company to the extent of the amount invested

shareholders legal owners of a company

Shari'a the authoritative source of Islamic law

small-to-medium size enterprise (SME) business ranging from micro-enterprises of just one person to firms with up to 249 employees

social enterprise an enterprise that lies between the for-profit and not-for-profit organization, aiming to make money, but using it for a social cause

socialism economic model which rests on the belief that societal goals rather than private profit should be the basis of the economy

social market economy capitalist market economy with a strong social justice dimension, including substantial welfare state provisions

social protection the set of policies and programmes designed to reduce and prevent poverty and vulnerability through the life cycle

social responsibility the role of the organization in society, with implied duties to communities and the environment

sole trader/self-employed person person who is in business on his or her own account

Southern African Development Community (SADC) inter-governmental organization for countries of Southern Africa

sovereignty the supreme legal authority in the state

sovereign wealth fund entity controlled by a government, which invests state funds and pursues an investment strategy, often active in global financial markets

spillover effects benefits to local firms in host countries from FDI

stakeholder broad category including individuals, groups and even society generally, that exerts influence on the company or who the company is in a position to influence

stakeholder theory management theory which focuses on the many different groups and interests that affect the company

stock exchanges regulated markets in which shares in public companies and other securities are traded

subculture minority culture in a society, often associated with immigrant communities

subsidiary company a company owned wholly or substantially by another company, which is in a position to exert control

subsidies payments from public funds to support domestic industries; there are also export subsidies to home producers to bolster a country's exports

superpower a state that is able to impose its power over other countries

supply chain series of stages involved in producing a product or service, from sourcing through to production, distribution and delivery to the customer, where each stage is co-ordinated to link with other stages in the process

supranational legal institutions above those of domestic law; characterizes EU law

sustainability the principle of taking into account the needs of today's inhabitants of the planet in ways which do not constitute a detriment to the ability of future generations to do the same

sustainable consumption principle that consumer lifestyle and purchasing decisions should take account of the environmental needs of future generations

sustainable development view of economic development involving continuing investment for future generations, taking into account the long-term viability of industries, both in terms of human values and environmental protection

Sustainable Development Goals (SDGs) UN development goals, superseding the Millennium Development Goals (MDGs), covering environmental, institutional and governance issues

T

tangible assets physical property such as machinery and goods

tariff a tax imposed by governments on imported goods and services

technological diffusion processes by which advances in technology spread from one country to another, usually from developed to developing countries

technology methodical application of scientific knowledge to practical purposes

technology transfer process of acquiring technology from another country

terrorism action by an individual or group intended to inflict dramatic and deadly injury on civilians and create an atmosphere of fear, generally for a political or ideological purpose

tertiary sector economic activity that consists of services

third-party verification the use of outside specialist services or certification to monitor CSR and environmental performance

tort in common law countries, branch of law which concerns obligations not to cause harm to others in society

trade the exchange of something of value, usually goods or services, for a price, usually money

Trade-related Aspects of Intellectual Property (TRIPS) multilateral international agreement on the protection of intellectual property which aims to bring national legal regimes into harmony

Transatlantic Trade and Investment Partnership (TTIP) proposed trade and investment agreement between the EU and the US

transboundary pollution the transmission of pollutants through the water, soil and air from one national jurisdiction to another

Trans-Pacific Partnership (TPP) trade and investment agreement among countries bordering the Pacific

transition economies economies of Eastern Europe and the CIS (Commonwealth of Independent States, including Russia) that are making the transition from planned economies to market-based economies

treaties instruments of international law

triad countries advanced economies of North America, the EU and Japan; Australia and New Zealand are also in this category

triple-bottom-line reporting corporate reporting focusing on social and environmental aspects of the company, in addition to traditional financial information

two-party system political system in which there are two major political parties, alternating between government and opposition depending on the outcome of elections

U

unemployment the percentage of people in a country's labour force who are willing to work but are without jobs

UNESCO (United Nations Educational, Scientific and Cultural Organization) UN agency that promotes peace and security through collaboration in these areas, notably in respect of upholding human rights

unitary system system of authority within a state in which all authority radiates out from the centre

United Nations (UN) the world's largest and most authoritative inter-governmental organization

Universal Declaration of Human Rights (UDHR) UN foundation declaration setting out human rights

UN Climate Change Panel (IPCC) UN body which brings together research on climate change and makes recommendations for action by member states

US-Mexico-Canada Free Trade Agreement (USMCA) North American free trade agreement that is the successor to NAFTA

urbanization process of large-scale shift of population from rural areas to cities

utilitarianism philosophical thinking based on the individualist view of human nature that each person has wants and needs which are pursued in a self-interested way

V

value chain concept which identifies the value created at each stage in the production process

vertical integration acquisition of firms involved in successive stages of a production process; strategy of the MNE that consists of acquiring firms in its supply chain

voluntary export restraint (VER) tool of government trade policy by which trading partners wishing to export into a country are encouraged to limit their exports, or risk the imposition of quotas or tariffs

W

Washington consensus market-oriented outlook adopted by the World Bank and IMF

World Bank organization established in the aftermath of the Second World War to fund development projects and broader development programmes

World Trade Organization (WTO) successor to the GATT, set up to regulate world trade and settle trade disputes among member countries

Z

zero-hours contract employment arrangement whereby the worker is available for work but paid only for the hours worked, and the employer has no commitment to provide work

ATLAS

THE WORLD
1 Netherlands
2 Belgium
3 Luxembourg
4 Switzerland
5 Czech Republic
6 Austria
7 Slovenia
8 Croatia
9 Slovakia
10 Hungary
11 Bosnia & Hercegovina
12 Montenegro
13 Serbia
14 Albania
15 North Macedonia
16 Moldova
17 Armenia
18 Azerbaijan
Iceland
Sweden
Finland
Norway
Estonia
Latvia
Lithuania
United Kingdom
Denmark
Rep. of Ireland
Germany
Poland
Belarus
Ukraine
France
Romania
Italy
Bulgaria
Spain
Portugal
Greece
Georgia
Turkey
Russian Federation
Kazakhstan
Mongolia
Uzbekistan
Kyrgyzstan
Turkmenistan
Tajikistan
China
N. Korea
S. Korea
Japan
Morocco
Tunisia
Cyprus
Lebanon
Israel
Syria
Iraq
Iran
Jordan
Kuwait
Qatar
Afghanistan
Pakistan
Nepal
Bhutan
Bangladesh
Thailand
Laos
Cambodia
Vietnam
Algeria
Libya
Egypt
Saudi Arabia
U.A.E.
Oman
India
Western Sahara
Mauritania
Mali
Niger
Chad
Sudan
Eritrea
Yemen
Djibouti
Myanmar (Burma)
Taiwan (Formosa)
Philippines
Senegal
Burkina
Guinea
Côte D'ivoire
Ghana
Nigeria
Cameroon
Central African Rep.
South Sudan
Ethiopia
Somalia
Sri Lanka
Brunei
Malaysia
Singapore
Togo
Benin
Eq. Guinea
Gabon
Congo
Democratic Republic of the Congo (Zaire)
Uganda
Kenya
Rwanda
Burundi
Tanzania
Indonesia
Papua New Guinea
Liberia
Sierra Leone
Guinea-Bissau
The Gambia
Malawi
Angola
Zambia
Mozambique
Madagascar
East Timor
INDIAN OCEAN
Zimbabwe
Namibia
Botswana
Eswatini
Lesotho
Republic of South Africa
Australia

Greenland

Alaska

Canada

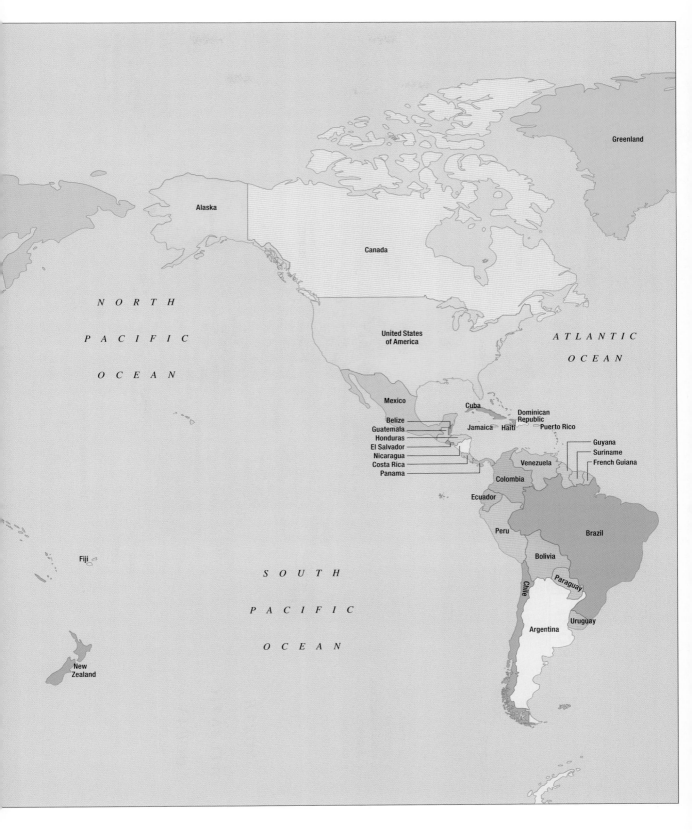

NORTH PACIFIC OCEAN

United States of America

ATLANTIC OCEAN

Mexico

Cuba

Dominican Republic

Belize

Guatemala

Honduras

El Salvador

Nicaragua

Costa Rica

Panama

Jamaica

Haiti

Puerto Rico

Guyana

Suriname

French Guiana

Venezuela

Colombia

Ecuador

Peru

Brazil

Fiji

Bolivia

Paraguay

Chile

SOUTH PACIFIC OCEAN

Uruguay

Argentina

New Zealand

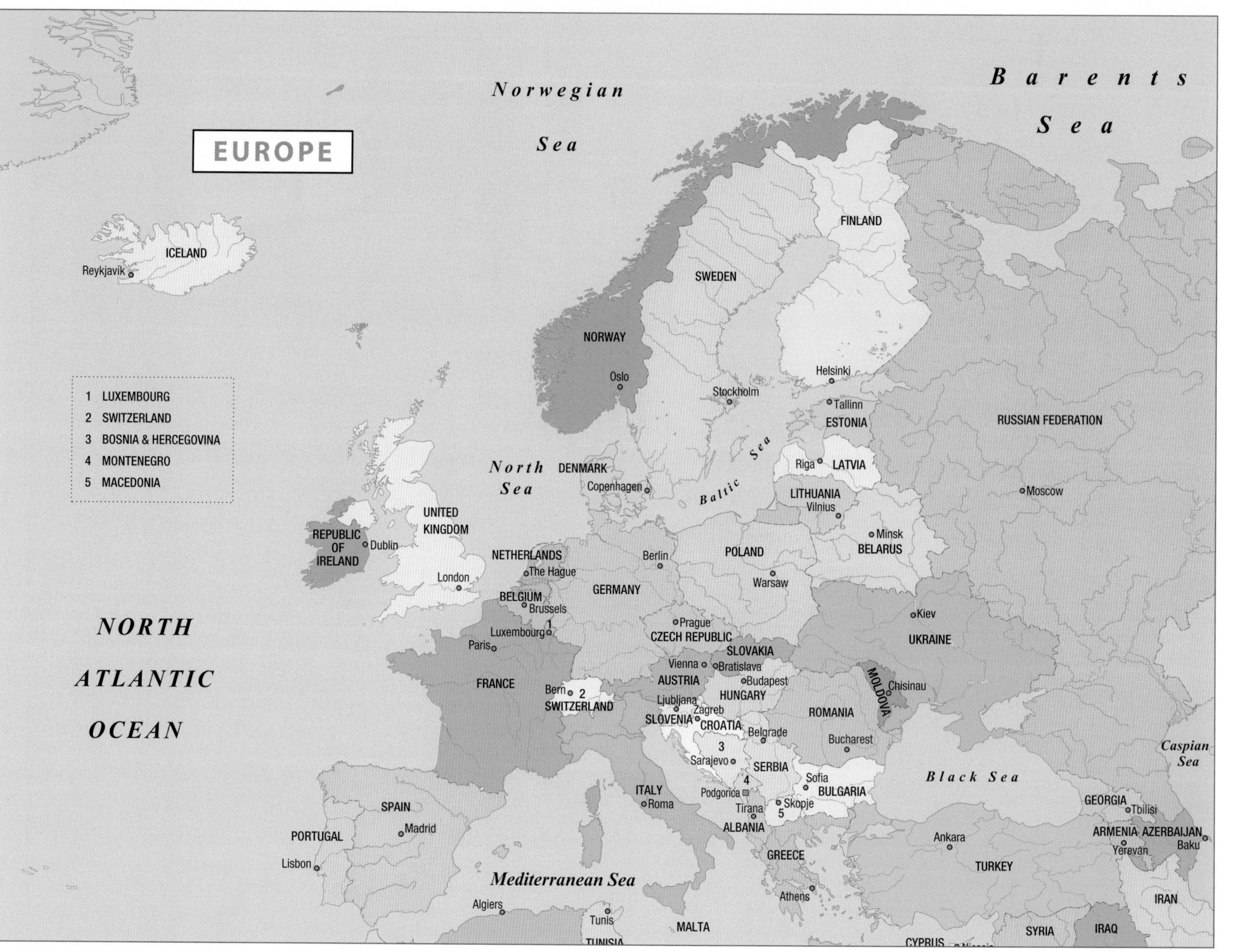
EUROPE
Norwegian Sea
Barents Sea
1 LUXEMBOURG
2 SWITZERLAND
3 BOSNIA & HERCEGOVINA
4 MONTENEGRO
5 MACEDONIA
ICELAND
Reykjavik
NORWAY
Oslo
SWEDEN
Stockholm
FINLAND
Helsinki
Tallinn
ESTONIA
RUSSIAN FEDERATION
Moscow
North Sea
DENMARK
Copenhagen
Baltic Sea
Riga
LATVIA
LITHUANIA
Vilnius
Minsk
BELARUS
REPUBLIC OF IRELAND
Dublin
UNITED KINGDOM
London
NETHERLANDS
The Hague
BELGIUM
Brussels
GERMANY
Berlin
POLAND
Warsaw
Kiev
UKRAINE
NORTH ATLANTIC OCEAN
Luxembourg
1
Paris
Prague
CZECH REPUBLIC
SLOVAKIA
Vienna
Bratislava
AUSTRIA
Budapest
HUNGARY
MOLDOVA
Chisinau
FRANCE
Bern
2
SWITZERLAND
Ljubljana
Zagreb
SLOVENIA
CROATIA
Belgrade
ROMANIA
Bucharest
3
Sarajevo
SERBIA
Caspian Sea
Black Sea
4
Podgorica
Sofia
BULGARIA
ITALY
Roma
SPAIN
Madrid
PORTUGAL
Lisbon
Tirana
Skopje
5
ALBANIA
GREECE
Athens
GEORGIA
Tbilisi
ARMENIA
AZERBAIJAN
Yerevan
Baku
Ankara
TURKEY
Mediterranean Sea
Algiers
Tunis
MALTA
IRAN
SYRIA
IRAQ

MIDDLE EAST

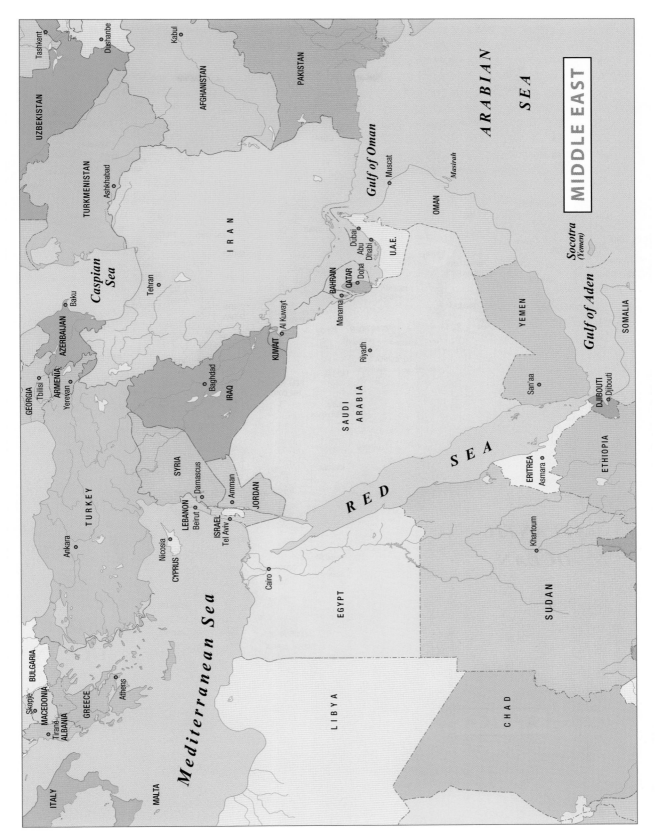

ITALY
MALTA
Mediterranean Sea
ALBANIA
Tirane
MACEDONIA
Skopje
GREECE
Athens
BULGARIA
TURKEY
Ankara
CYPRUS
Nicosia
LEBANON
Beirut
ISRAEL
Tel Aviv
SYRIA
Damascus
Amman
JORDAN
GEORGIA
Tbilisi
ARMENIA
Yerevan
AZERBAIJAN
Baku
Caspian Sea
IRAQ
Baghdad
KUWAIT
Al Kuwayt
IRAN
Tehran
TURKMENISTAN
Ashkhabad
UZBEKISTAN
Tashkent
Dushanbe
AFGHANISTAN
Kabul
PAKISTAN
BAHRAIN
Manama
QATAR
Doha
Abu Dhabi
Dubai
U.A.E.
Gulf of Oman
Muscat
OMAN
Masirah
ARABIAN SEA
SAUDI ARABIA
Riyadh
YEMEN
San'aa
Socotra (Yemen)
Gulf of Aden
SOMALIA
DJIBOUTI
Djibouti
ETHIOPIA
ERITREA
Asmara
RED SEA
EGYPT
Cairo
SUDAN
Khartoum
LIBYA
CHAD

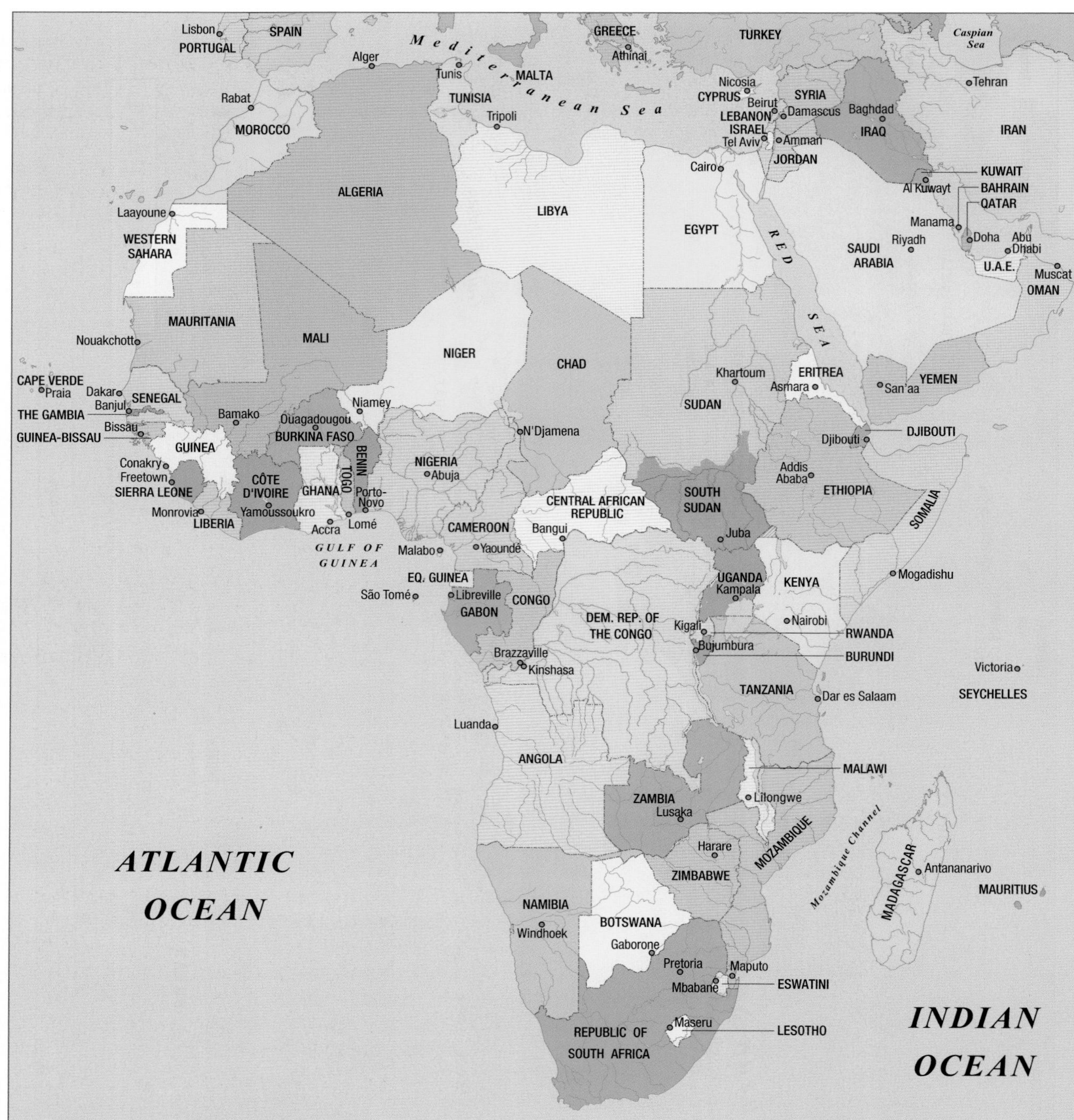
Lisbon
PORTUGAL
SPAIN
Alger
Mediterranean Sea
GREECE
Athinai
TURKEY
Caspian Sea
Tunis
MALTA
TUNISIA
Tripoli
Rabat
MOROCCO
Nicosia
CYPRUS
Beirut
SYRIA
LEBANON
Damascus
Baghdad
ISRAEL
Tel Aviv
Amman
IRAQ
JORDAN
Tehran
IRAN
Cairo
KUWAIT
Al Kuwayt
BAHRAIN
QATAR
ALGERIA
LIBYA
Laayoune
WESTERN SAHARA
EGYPT
Manama
Riyadh
Doha
Abu Dhabi
SAUDI ARABIA
U.A.E.
Muscat
OMAN
RED SEA
MAURITANIA
MALI
NIGER
CHAD
Nouakchott
Khartoum
ERITREA
Asmara
YEMEN
San'aa
CAPE VERDE
Praia
Dakar
SENEGAL
THE GAMBIA
Banjul
Bamako
Niamey
SUDAN
Bissau
GUINEA-BISSAU
Ouagadougou
BURKINA FASO
N'Djamena
DJIBOUTI
Djibouti
GUINEA
BENIN
TOGO
NIGERIA
Abuja
Conakry
Freetown
SIERRA LEONE
CÔTE D'IVOIRE
GHANA
Porto-Novo
Addis Ababa
ETHIOPIA
SOUTH SUDAN
CENTRAL AFRICAN REPUBLIC
SOMALIA
Monrovia
LIBERIA
Yamoussoukro
Accra
Lomé
CAMEROON
Bangui
Juba
GULF OF GUINEA
Malabo
Yaoundé
Mogadishu
EQ. GUINEA
UGANDA
Kampala
KENYA
São Tomé
Libreville
GABON
CONGO
DEM. REP. OF THE CONGO
Kigali
Nairobi
RWANDA
Bujumbura
BURUNDI
Brazzaville
Kinshasa
Victoria
TANZANIA
Dar es Salaam
SEYCHELLES
Luanda
ANGOLA
MALAWI
Lilongwe
ZAMBIA
Lusaka
Mozambique Channel
MOZAMBIQUE
Harare
ATLANTIC OCEAN
ZIMBABWE
MADAGASCAR
Antananarivo
MAURITIUS
NAMIBIA
Windhoek
BOTSWANA
Gaborone
Pretoria
Maputo
Mbabane
ESWATINI
INDIAN OCEAN
Maseru
LESOTHO
REPUBLIC OF SOUTH AFRICA
AFRICA

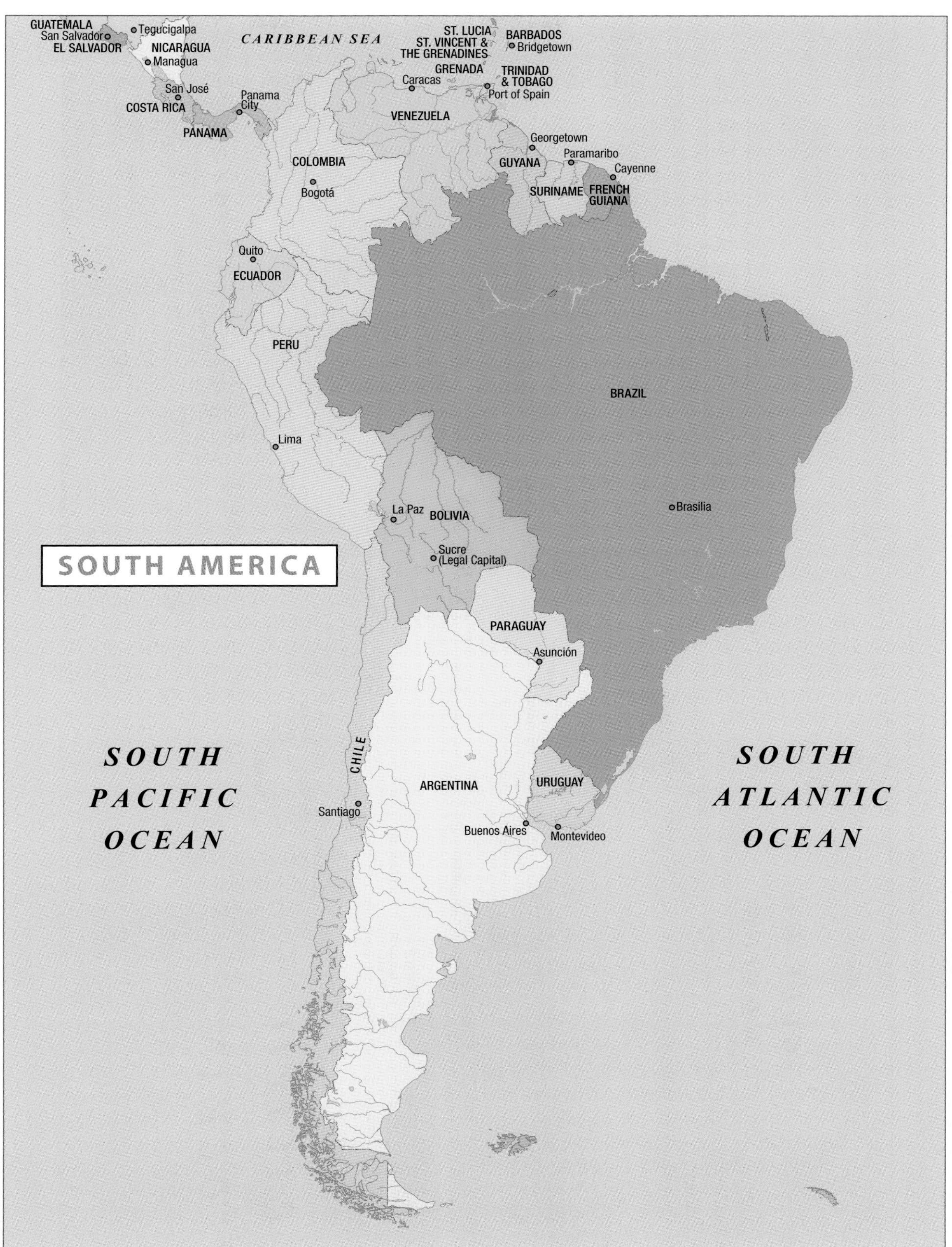
GUATEMALA
San Salvador
EL SALVADOR
Tegucigalpa
NICARAGUA
Managua
San José
COSTA RICA
Panama City
PANAMA
CARIBBEAN SEA
ST. LUCIA
ST. VINCENT & THE GRENADINES
BARBADOS
Bridgetown
GRENADA
TRINIDAD & TOBAGO
Port of Spain
Caracas
VENEZUELA
Georgetown
GUYANA
Paramaribo
SURINAME
Cayenne
FRENCH GUIANA
COLOMBIA
Bogotá
Quito
ECUADOR
PERU
Lima
BRAZIL
Brasilia
La Paz
BOLIVIA
Sucre (Legal Capital)
SOUTH AMERICA
PARAGUAY
Asunción
CHILE
Santiago
ARGENTINA
URUGUAY
Buenos Aires
Montevideo
SOUTH PACIFIC OCEAN
SOUTH ATLANTIC OCEAN

CENTRAL AMERICA

GULF OF MEXICO
CARIBBEAN SEA
PACIFIC OCEAN
MEXICO
Mexico City
GUATEMALA
Guatemala City
BELIZE
Belmopan
EL SALVADOR
San Salvador
HONDURAS
Tegucigalpa
NICARAGUA
Managua
COSTA RICA
San José
PANAMA
Panama City
CUBA
Havana
THE BAHAMAS
Nassau
JAMAICA
Kingston
HAITI
Port-au-Prince
DOMINICAN REPUBLIC
Santo Domingo
PUERTO RICO
San Juan
ST. KITTS AND NEVIS
ANTIGUA & BARBUDA
DOMINICA
ST. LUCIA
ST. VINCENT & THE GRENADINES
GRENADA
BARBADOS
Bridgetown
TRINIDAD & TOBAGO
Port of Spain
VENEZUELA
Caracas
COLOMBIA
Bogotá
GUYANA
Georgetown
SURINAME
Paramaribo
FRENCH GUIANA
Cayenne

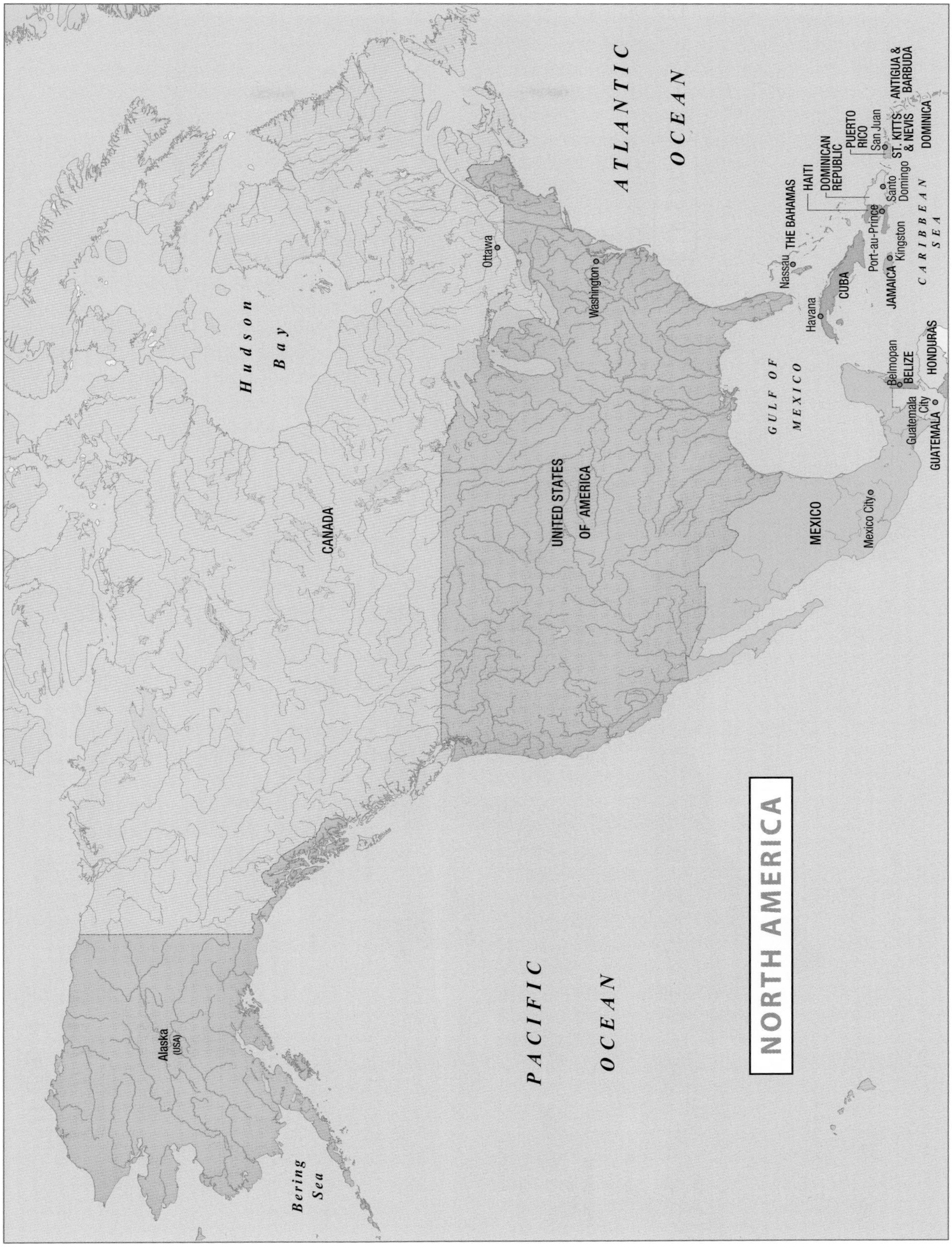

NORTH AMERICA

PACIFIC OCEAN
ATLANTIC OCEAN
Hudson Bay
Bering Sea
GULF OF MEXICO
CARIBBEAN SEA
Alaska (USA)
CANADA
Ottawa
UNITED STATES OF AMERICA
Washington
MEXICO
Mexico City
GUATEMALA
Guatemala City
BELIZE
Belmopan
HONDURAS
CUBA
Havana
THE BAHAMAS
Nassau
JAMAICA
Kingston
HAITI
Port-au-Prince
DOMINICAN REPUBLIC
Santo Domingo
PUERTO RICO
San Juan
ST. KITTS & NEVIS
ANTIGUA & BARBUDA
DOMINICA

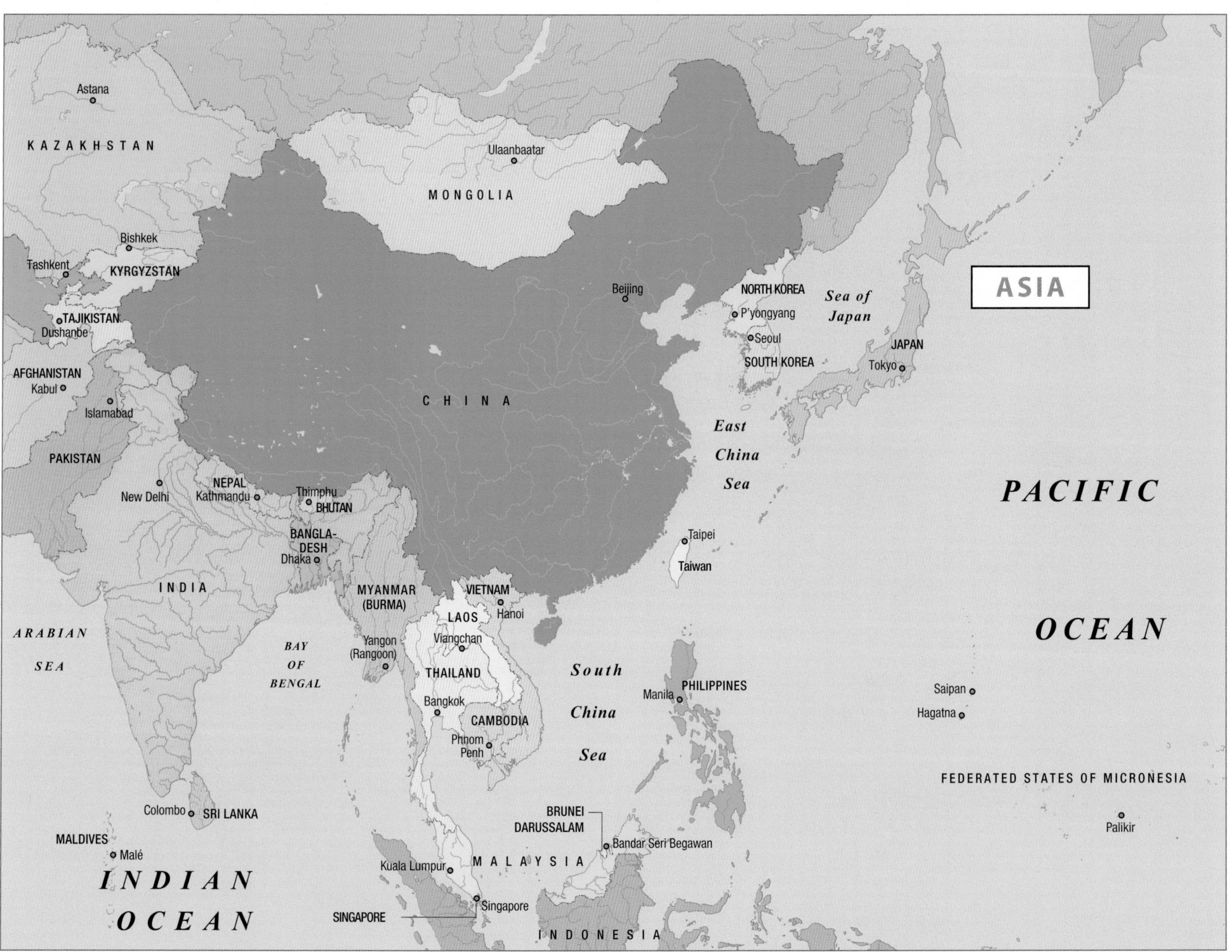
Astana
KAZAKHSTAN
Ulaanbaatar
MONGOLIA
Bishkek
Tashkent
KYRGYZSTAN
TAJIKISTAN
Dushanbe
AFGHANISTAN
Kabul
Islamabad
PAKISTAN
New Delhi
NEPAL
Kathmandu
Thimphu
BHUTAN
BANGLA-
DESH
Dhaka
INDIA
ARABIAN
SEA
BAY
OF
BENGAL
Colombo
SRI LANKA
MALDIVES
Malé
INDIAN
OCEAN
CHINA
Beijing
NORTH KOREA
P'yongyang
Seoul
SOUTH KOREA
Sea of
Japan
JAPAN
Tokyo
ASIA
East
China
Sea
PACIFIC
OCEAN
Taipei
Taiwan
MYANMAR
(BURMA)
Yangon
(Rangoon)
VIETNAM
Hanoi
LAOS
Viangchan
THAILAND
Bangkok
CAMBODIA
Phnom
Penh
South
China
Sea
Manila
PHILIPPINES
Saipan
Hagatna
FEDERATED STATES OF MICRONESIA
Palikir
BRUNEI
DARUSSALAM
Bandar Seri Begawan
Kuala Lumpur
MALAYSIA
Singapore
SINGAPORE
INDONESIA

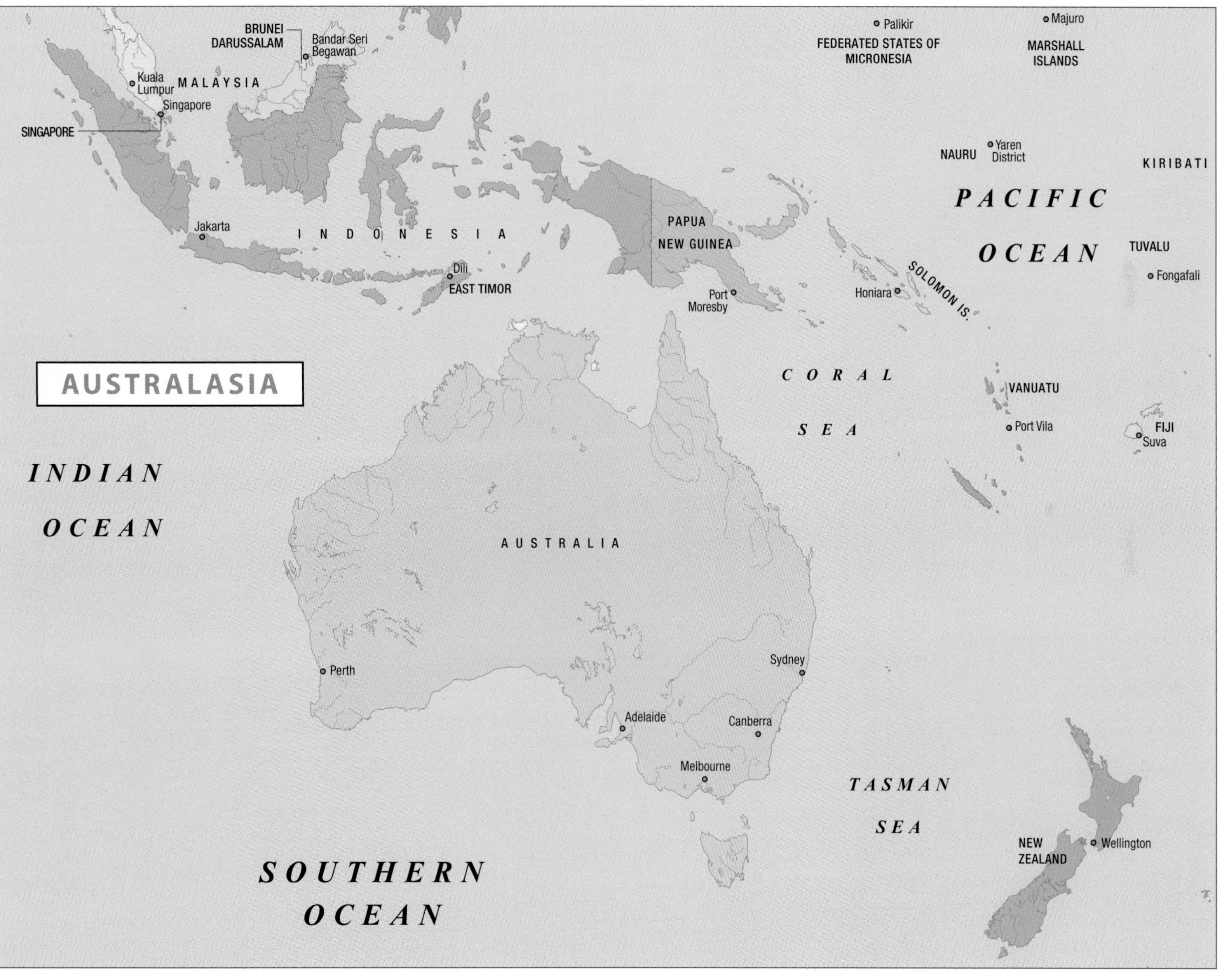
BRUNEI DARUSSALAM
Bandar Seri Begawan
Kuala Lumpur
MALAYSIA
Singapore
SINGAPORE
Jakarta
INDONESIA
Dili
EAST TIMOR
PAPUA NEW GUINEA
Port Moresby
Palikir
FEDERATED STATES OF MICRONESIA
Majuro
MARSHALL ISLANDS
NAURU
Yaren District
KIRIBATI
PACIFIC OCEAN
TUVALU
Fongafali
Honiara
SOLOMON IS.
AUSTRALASIA
CORAL SEA
VANUATU
Port Vila
FIJI
Suva
INDIAN OCEAN
AUSTRALIA
Perth
Sydney
Adelaide
Canberra
Melbourne
TASMAN SEA
NEW ZEALAND
Wellington
SOUTHERN OCEAN

INDEX OF ORGANIZATIONS

INDEX OF PEOPLE

SUBJECT INDEX